# The University of Toledo

## Principles of Macroeconomics
Special Edition

William J. Baumol | Alan S. Blinder

Australia • Brazil • Japan • Korea • Mexico • Singapore • Spain • United Kingdom • United States

**The University of Toledo: Principles of Macroeconomics, Special Edition**

Macroeconomics: Principles and Policy, 13th Edition
William J. Baumol | Alan S. Blinder

© 2015 Cengage Learning. All rights reserved.

ALL RIGHTS RESERVED. No part of this work covered by the copyright herein may be reproduced or distributed in any form or by any means, except as permitted by U.S. copyright law, without the prior written permission of the copyright owner.

For product information and technology assistance, contact us at
**Cengage Learning Customer & Sales Support, 1-800-354-9706**

For permission to use material from this text or product,
submit all requests online at **cengage.com/permissions**
Further permissions questions can be emailed to
**permissionrequest@cengage.com**

This book contains select works from existing Cengage Learning resources and was produced by Cengage Learning Custom Solutions for collegiate use. As such, those adopting and/or contributing to this work are responsible for editorial content accuracy, continuity and completeness.

**Compilation © 2016 Cengage Learning**

ISBN: 9781337035514

Printed in Mexico

**Cengage Learning**
20 Channel Center Street
Boston, MA 02210
USA

Cengage Learning is a leading provider of customized learning solutions with office locations around the globe, including Singapore, the United Kingdom, Australia, Mexico, Brazil, and Japan. Locate your local office at:
**www.international.cengage.com/region.**

Cengage Learning products are represented in Canada by Nelson Education, Ltd.

For your lifelong learning solutions, visit **www.cengage.com/custom.**

Visit our corporate website at **www.cengage.com.**

University of Toledo

# Welcome.

The faculty of the Department of Economics welcome you to our course Econ 1150, PRINCIPLES OF MACROECONOMICS. Over the next few pages we provide you with some general information about our department and this course — as well as some university policies that are important to all students. To begin, the following is a list of full-time faculty members in our department along with their contact information. We also have several other instructors teaching Economics courses each semester. If you need to contact your instructor, and their name is not listed below, please contact the Department Secretary (419.530.2572) and Ms. Stambaugh will have your instructor contact you.

Ajilore, Olugbenga . . . . . . . 419.530.2113 — gbenga.ajilore@utoledo.edu
Amialchuk, Aliaksandr . . . 419.530.4754 — aliaksandr.amialchuk@utoledo.edu
Black, David . . . . . . . . . . . 419.530.4153 — david.black@utoledo.edu
Bland, James . . . . . . . . . . . 419.530.2572 — economics@utoledo.edu
Cook, Larry . . . . . . . . . . . . 419.530.4124 — larry.cook@utoledo.edu
Dowd, Michael . . . . . . . . . . 419.530.2572 — economics@utoledo.edu
Egan, Kevin . . . . . . . . . . . . 419.530.4148 — kevin.egan@utoledo.edu
Keith, Kristen . . . . . . . . . . . 419.530.2801 — kkeith@utoledo.edu
Sapci, Onur . . . . . . . . . . . . 419.530.2572 — economics@utoledo.edu
Smirnov, Oleg . . . . . . . . . . 419.530.6121 — oleg.smirnov@utoledo.edu

Dr. Michael Dowd is the Department Chair and Ms. Regina Stambaugh is the Department Secretary. If you have any difficulties contacting your instructor, please contact Dr. Dowd or Ms. Stambaugh at 419.530.2572.

**Course Description:** *Explaining the level and the growth of economic activity, its fluctuations and ways of achieving greater stability, including the roles of money, banking and international finance.*

Econ 1150 is a General Education course that satisfies one of the two State of Ohio distributive requirements in the social sciences. As a General Education course, it introduces students to two of the University of Toledo's core competency areas: a) Critical Thinking and Integrative Learning and b) Scientific and Quantitative Reasoning. It exposes students to Critical Thinking and Integrative Learning by teaching them to "think like an economist" in terms of tradeoffs, such as the tradeoff involved in society's twin goals of efficiency and equality. It introduces students to Scientific and Quantitative Reasoning by explaining the basics of economic modeling, including the importance and limits of assumptions, the use of graphs to present the underlying theories, and the resulting plausible conclusions.

**Economics Tutoring:** We encourage you to speak with your instructor if you wish to review class material. However, as an additional option, graduate students pursuing a Master's Degree in Economics offer free tutoring services for all students taking Economics courses.

The tutoring schedule will be distributed during the first two weeks of each semester and will be posted on the Department of Economics website (www.utoledo.edu/llss/econ). Or, you may contact the Department Secretary for the tutoring schedule.

**Student Learning Outcomes:**   After completing this course you will be able to:

1. Appropriately use the critical vocabulary of economics;
2. List the assumptions of basic economic models – the Production Possibilities Frontier and Demand and Supply – and be able to discuss outcome changes caused by modeling assumption changes;
3. Critically assess the logical implications from basic economic models;
4. Draw and infer logical conclusions from economic graphs;
5. Derive relational concepts from economic data;
6. Predict the impact of government fiscal and monetary policy – use of deficits, changes in the money supply, etc. – on overall economic performance;
7. Explain and discuss the determinants of economic growth;
8. Discuss the costs and causes of unemployment, and assess policies to ameliorate it;
9. Discuss economic globalization and the inter-connectedness of nations through the importance of international trade;
10. Assess the tradeoff between unemployment and inflation;
11. Reach your own educated conclusions concerning economic policy, acknowledge the limits and assumptions inherent in a given position and the limits and assumptions inherent in others' points of view.

**Student Disability Services:**   This office works directly with students and faculty to provide accommodations for qualified students with disabilities. For information please contact Student Disability Services at 419.386.2189 (VP), 419.530.2612 (TTY), or 419.530.6137 (Fax) – or visit their office in Rocket Hall (room 1820).

**Academic Year Calendar:**   This calendar lists all of the relevant dates for the academic year. This includes, but is not limited to, when classes begin, when they end, fall break, spring break, holidays (i.e., no classes), final exam week, etc. This calendar is available at www.utoledo.edu/offices/provost/calendar.

**University Policies:**   The following items describe some university policies all students should review and fully understand. **Note:** the following policies are revised from time to time, so please be certain that you are familiar with current policy.

Grades and Grading:   Among the issues this policy describes are, but are not limited to, possible letter grades (e.g., A, A-, ... D-, F, W, IN, etc.), or non-letter grades such as no grade (R) or pass/no credit (P or NC). It also describes the procedures for pass/no credit grades, incomplete grades, and progress grades. By reviewing the official ⊔ policy, students will be better informed of their grading options.

Missed Class Policy:   This policy provides for basic protections and reasonable accommodations for ᵾ students who miss class with excused absences. Students are expected to attend every class meeting of courses in which they are registered. Only in specific, unavoidable situations does the University excuse absences from class: (1) personal emergencies, including, but not limited to, illness of the student or of a dependent of the student, or death in the family; (2) religious observances that prevent the student from attending class; (3) participation in University-sponsored activities, approved by the appropriate University authority; (4) government-required activities, such as military assignments, jury duty, or court appearances; and (5) any other absence that the professor approves. Students need to consult official ᵾ policies for complete information on these issues.

Academic Dishonesty:   Among the aims of education are the acquisition of knowledge and development of the skills necessary for success in any profession. Activities inconsistent with these aims will not be permitted, and academic dishonesty will not be tolerated. Students are responsible for knowing what constitutes academic dishonesty. If students are uncertain about what constitutes plagiarism or cheating they should seek the instructor's advice and must consult the university's policy on this matter. A starting point might be to review the *Policy Statement on Academic Dishonesty* (www.utoledo.edu/dl/students/dishonesty.html). However, there are other explicit ᵾ policies you should review to fully understand the relevant issues, rights, responsibilities, and options open to students.

**Student Handbook:**   In this handbook you'll find the policies, procedures and support services that are available to you as a ᵾ student (link located at www.utoledo.edu/studentaffairs). We encourage you to read this handbook carefully. If you find you have questions that occur to you, remember that everyone at The University of Toledo is here to help you, so don't hesitate to ask.

If you have questions on any material in these pages, please do not hesitate in contacting the Economics Department Chair, Dr. Michael Dowd, to discuss your comments, suggestions, or concerns (419.530.2572). The Economics Faculty wish you great success in your PRINCIPLES OF MACROECONOMICS course.

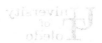

*To our wonderful wives, Hilda Baumol and Madeline Blinder.*

# BRIEF CONTENTS

# TABLE OF CONTENTS

# PREFACE

I t can be argued that, from the point of view of the general welfare, there are two topics of primary importance in economics. One is the analysis of recessions and depressions, with the unemployment and general impoverishment they bring. The second is economic growth and rising productivity, which, in the long run, is the way to reduce poverty in our country and throughout the world.

In earlier editions of this book, before the problems stemming from the recent, terrible worldwide economic crisis claimed the spotlight, the new materials that we added focused more on the growth issue. We discussed, for example, the microeconomic roles of innovation and entrepreneurship, offering far more material on these issues than any other textbook in the field.

Then, for two editions, the biggest changes came in the macroeconomic portions of the book, especially the parts relevant to understanding the financial crisis and the Great Recession of 2007–2009. Those changes remain in this thirteenth edition—including the abandonment, almost unique among principles books, of pretending that there is only one interest rate ("the interest rate"). Instead, we explain and discuss the implications of having many different interest rates, based on differential risk.

As usual, this revision includes literally hundreds of small changes to improve clarity of exposition and especially to update the text material—both for relevant advances in economics and for recent events, particularly the aftermath of the Great Recession—which continues to play out day by day.

## NOTE TO THE STUDENT

May we offer a suggestion for success in your economics course? Unlike some of the other subjects you may be studying, economics is cumulative: Each week's lesson builds on what you have learned prior to that. You will save yourself a lot of frustration—and a lot of work—by keeping up on a week-to-week basis.

To assist you in doing so, we provide a chapter summary, a list of important terms and concepts, a selection of questions to help you review the contents of each chapter, as well as the answers to odd-numbered Test Yourself questions. Making use of these learning aids will help you to master the material in your economics course. For additional assistance, we have prepared student supplements to help in the reinforcement of the concepts in this book and provide opportunities for practice and feedback.

The following list indicates the ancillary materials and learning tools that have been designed specifically to be helpful to you. If you believe any of these resources could benefit you in your course of study, you may want to discuss them with your instructor. Further information on these resources is available at www.cengagebrain.com.

To access additional course materials and companion resources, please visit www.cengagebrain.com. At the CengageBrain.com home page, search for the ISBN of your title (from the back cover of your book) using the search box at the top of the page. This will take you to the product page where free companion resources can be found.

We hope our book is helpful to you in your study of economics and welcome your comments or suggestions for improving student experience with economics. Please write to us in care of Baumol and Blinder, Editor for Economics, Cengage Learning, 5191 Natorp Boulevard, Mason, Ohio, 45040, or through the book's website at www.cengagebrain.com.

## MindTap

MindTap is a personalized teaching experience with relevant assignments that guide students to analyze, apply, and improve thinking, allowing you to measure skills and outcomes with ease.

- Personalized Teaching: Becomes yours with a Learning Path that is built with key student objectives. Control what students see and when they see it. Use it as-is or match to your syllabus exactly—hide, rearrange, add, and create your own content.
- Guide Students: A unique learning path of relevant readings, multimedia, and activities that move students up the learning taxonomy from basic knowledge and comprehension to analysis and application.
- Promote Better Outcomes: Empower instructors and motivate students with analytics and reports that provide a snapshot of class progress, time in course, and engagement and completion rates.

## Aplia

Aplia saves instructors valuable time they would otherwise spend on routine grading while giving students an easy way to stay on top of coursework with regularly scheduled assignments. Currently, Aplia supports college-level courses and has been used by more than 1,000,000 students at over 1,300 institutions. Aplia's economics students use interactive chapter assignments, tutorials, news analyses, and experiments to make economics relevant and engaging. Math and graphing tutorials help students overcome deficiencies in these crucial areas. Economics articles from top news sources challenge students to connect current events to course concepts.

End of Chapter and traditional homework problem sets allow students to work through the economic concepts they have learned in each chapter. Students can choose to "Grade It Now" on a homework problem and will receive instant feedback whether an answer is correct or incorrect. Students can then choose to complete another problem to test themselves on the same concept with randomization. Aplia End of Chapter will also be mobile enabled.

## IN GRATITUDE

Finally, we are pleased to acknowledge our mounting indebtedness to the many people who have generously helped us in our efforts through the history of this book. We often have needed assistance in dealing with some of the many subjects that an introductory textbook must cover. Our friends and colleagues Dean Alderucci, *New York University*; Rebecca Blank, *University of Michigan*; Gregory Chow, *Princeton University*; Avinash Dixit, *Princeton University*; Susan Feiner, *University of Southern Maine*; Claudia Goldin, *Harvard University*; Ronald Grieson, *University of California, Santa Cruz*; Daniel Hamermesh, *University of Texas*; Yuzo Honda, *Osaka University*; Peter Kenen, *Princeton University*; Melvin Krauss, *Stanford University*; Herbert Levine, *University of Pennsylvania*; Burton Malkiel, *Princeton University*; Edwin Mills, *Northwestern University*; Janusz Ordover, *New York University*; David H. Reiley Jr., *University of Arizona*; Uwe Reinhardt, *Princeton University*; Harvey Rosen, *Princeton University*; Joseph Seneca, *Rutgers University*; William Silber, *New York University*; Laura Tyson, *University of California, Berkeley*; Martin Weitzman, *Harvard University*; and Lawrence White, *New York University* have all given generously of their knowledge in particular areas over the course of 13 editions. We have learned much from them and have shamelessly relied on their help.

Economists and students at colleges and universities other than ours offered numerous useful suggestions for improvements, many of which we have been incorporated into this thirteenth edition. We wish to thank the following for their insightful reviews:

Marco Airaudo, *Drexel University*
Rahsan Akbulut, *California State University–Fullerton*
Onur Akmehmet, *Tufts University*
Steven Antler, *Roosevelt University*
Muhammad Anwar, *Framingham State & University of Massachusetts–Lowell*
Mohsen Bahmani-Oskooee, *University of Wisconsin–Milwaukee*
Jeffrey Baird, *The Ohio State University*
Damyana Bakardzhieva, *George Washington University*
James Bang, *Virginia Military Institute*
Nimfa Bemis, *University of Southern California*
Charles Braymen, *Kansas State University*
Morgan Bridge, *Mesa State College*
Raymonda Burgman, *DePauw University*
Scott Carson, *University of Texas–Permian Basin*
Aspi Contractor, *De Anza College*
Jim Couch, *University of North Alabama*
Elizabeth Crowell, *University of Michigan–Dearborn*
Christopher Dabbs, *Wallace Community College Selma*
Norm Dalsted, *Colorado State University*
David Danning, *University of Massachusetts*
Maria Davis, *Indian River State College*
Pierangelo De Pace, *Pomona College*
Juan J. DelaCruz, *Lehman College–CUNY & FIT–SUNY*
Mine Aysen Doyran, *Lehman College–CUNY*
Kevin Egan, *University of Toledo*
Mona El Shazly, *Columbia College*
Mahmoud Elamin, *University of Minnesota*
Layton Franko, *Queens College*
Denise Froning, *Community College of Aurora*
Shailendra Gajanan, *University of Pittsburgh*
Claudia Garcia, *Santa Monica College*
Alex Gialanella, *Iona College*
Dan Giedeman, *Grand Valley State University*
Chris Gingrich, *Eastern Mennonite University*
Tuncer Gocmen, *Shepherd University*
Ann Goldman, *San Francisco State University*
Barbara Good, *Ursuline College*

Lyndon Goodridge, *University of New Hampshire*
Kimberly Goudy, *Central Ohio Technical College*
John Gregor, *Washington & Jefferson College*
Richard Grossman, *Wesleyan University*
Patrycja Grzelonska, *Yeshiva University*
Homan Hajiran, *Wheeling Jesuit University*
William Hart, *Miami University*
Martha Hensley, *University of Kansas*
Peng Huang, *Ripon College*
Amy Ickowitz, *Clark University*
Christos Ioannou, *University of Southampton*
Brian Kench, *The University of Tampa*
Kil-Joong Kim, *Austin Peay State University*
Sharmila King, *University of the Pacific*
Dave Kingsley, *University of Massachusetts–Lowell*
Richard Kramer, *New England College*
Ganesh Krishnan, *Metropolitan State University*
Michael Kuryla, *Broome Community College–SUNY*
Gary Langer, *Roosevelt University*
June Lapidus, *Roosevelt University*
Frederic Lerner, *New York University*
Zhen Li, *Albion College*
Tony Lima, *California State University–East Bay*
Christine Loucks, *Boise State University*
Angelo Luciano, *Columbia College–Chicago*
David Lui, *East Los Angeles College*
Kristina Lybecker, *Colorado College*
Brian Lynch, *Lake Land College*
Leah Marcal, *California State University, Northridge*
Cynthia Mayo, *J. Sargeant Reynolds Community College*
John Mukum Mbaku, *Weber State University*
Erika McGrath, *California State University Monterey Bay*
Alice Melkumian, *Western Illinois University*
Carrie Meyer, *George Mason University*
Ida Mirzaie, *The Ohio State University*
Rashida Mohd Rowther, *Northern Virginia Community College*
Stephen Mullin, *Drexel University*
David Murphy, *Boston College*

Kevin Neuman, *University of Wisconsin–Stevens Point*

Eric Nilsson, *California State University–San Bernardino*

David O'Hara, *Metropolitan State University*

Maria Pia Olivero, *Drexel University*

Martha Olney, *University of California Berkeley*

Wafa Orman, *University of Alabama–Huntsville*

Samir Ouanes, *Metro State University*

Orgul Ozturk, *University of South Carolina*

Mercy Palamuleni, *Kansas State University*

Claudia Parliament, *University of Minnesota*

Peter Pasqualino, *Fulton–Montgomery Community College*

Andrew Pearlman, *Bard College*

Ragan Petrie, *George Mason University*

Barbara Phipps, *University of Kansas*

James Polito, *Marian University*

Jennie Popp, *University of Arkansas*

Gregrory Price, *Morehouse College*

Michael Rabbitt, *Johnson County Community College*

Geetha Rajaram, *Whittier College*

Taghi Ramin, *William Paterson University*

Kolleen Rask, *College of the Holy Cross*

Artatrana Ratha, *St. Cloud State University*

Jim Rathwell, *Tri-County Technical College*

Wendy Rayack, *Wesleyan University*

Michael Roberts, *North Carolina State University*

Malcolm Robinson, *Thomas More College*

Cliff Rochlin, *Loyola Marymount University*

Juliette Roddy, *University of Michigan Dearborn*

Duane Rosa, *West Texas A&M University*

Matthew Rousu, *Susquehanna University*

Neil Sheflin, *Rutgers New Brunswick*

Ian Shepherd, *Abilene Christian University*

Robert Shoffner, *Central Piedmont Community College*

Gary Smith, *Pomona College*

Paul Sommers, *Seattle University*

Blake Sorem, *Pierce College*

Michael Steinberger, *Pomona College*

Josh Stillwagon, *University of New Hampshire*

Carolyn Stumph, *Indiana University–Purdue University Fort Wayne*

Eric Taylor, *Central Piedmont Community College*

Erdal Tekin, *Georgia State University*

Mike Urbancic, *University of California Berkeley*

Kristin Van Gaasbeck, *California State University–Sacramento*

Abu Wahid, *Tennessee State University*

Janice Weaver, *Drake University*

Cathy Whiting, *Willamette University*

Chiou-nan Yeh Yeh, *Alabama State University*

Ali Zadeh, *Susquehanna University*

Madeline Zavodny, *Agnes Scott College*

Xinfu Zhu, *Inver Hills Community College*

Obviously, the book you hold in your hands was not produced by us alone. In revising the thirteenth edition, a special role was played by Baumol's in-office editor, Anne Noyes Saini, who skillfully edited, researched, and refreshed data and information throughout the book. It is probably true that Baumol could not have done it without her.

We also appreciate the contribution of the staff at Cengage Learning, including Michael Worls, Product Manager; Michael Parthenakis, Senior Product Manager; John Carey, Senior Marketing Manager; Jennifer E. Thomas, Product Development Manager; Leah G. Wuchnick, Associate Content Developer; Colleen A. Farmer, Senior Content Project Manager; Sarah Blasco, Media Developer; Michelle Kunkler, Senior Art Director; Jennifer Nonenmacher, Intellectual Property Analyst; and Kevin Kluck, Manufacturing Planner. It was a pleasure to work with them, and we appreciate their understanding of our approaches, our goals, and our idiosyncrasies. We also thank our intelligent and delightful assistants at Princeton University and New York University, Kathleen Hurley and Janeece Roderick Lewis, who struggled successfully with the myriad of tasks involved in completing the manuscript.

And, finally, we must acknowledge—with joy—our continuing debt to our wives, Hilda Baumol and Madeline Blinder. They have now suffered through 13 editions and the inescapable neglect and distraction the preparation of each new edition imposes. Their tolerance and understanding have been no minor contribution to the project.

*William J. Baumol*
*Alan S. Blinder*

# ABOUT THE AUTHORS

## William J. Baumol

William J. Baumol was born in New York City and received his BSS at the College of the City of New York and his Ph.D. at the University of London.

He is the Harold Price Professor of Entrepreneurship Emeritus at New York University, where he taught a course in introductory microeconomics, and the Joseph Douglas Green, 1895, Professor of Economics Emeritus and Senior Economist at Princeton University. He has been a frequent consultant to the management of major firms in a wide variety of industries in the United States and other countries as well as to a number of governmental agencies. In several fields, including the telecommunications and electric utility industries, current regulatory policy is influenced by his explicit recommendations. Among his many contributions to economics are research on the theory of the firm, the contestability of markets, the economics of the arts and other services—the "cost disease of the services" is often referred to as "Baumol's disease"— and economic growth, entrepreneurship, and innovation. In addition to economics, he taught a course in wood sculpture at Princeton for about 20 years and is an accomplished painter (you may view some of his paintings at http://pages.stern.nyu.edu/~wbaumol).

Professor Baumol has been president of the American Economic Association and three other professional societies. He is an elected member of the National Academy of Sciences, created by the U.S. Congress, and of the American Philosophical Society, founded by Benjamin Franklin. He is also on the board of trustees of the National Council on Economic Education and is the recipient of 11 honorary degrees.

Baumol is the author of hundreds of journal and newspaper articles and more than 45 books, including *Global Trade and Conflicting National Interests* (2000); *The Free-Market Innovation Machine* (2002); *Good Capitalism, Bad Capitalism* (2007); *The Microtheory of Innovative Entrepreneurship* (2010); and *The Cost Disease* (2012). His writings have been translated into more than a dozen languages.

## Alan S. Blinder

Alan S. Blinder was born in New York City and attended Princeton University, where one of his teachers was William Baumol. After earning a master's degree at the London School of Economics and a Ph.D. at MIT, Blinder returned to Princeton, where he has taught since 1971, including teaching introductory macroeconomics since 1977. He is currently the Gordon S. Rentschler Memorial Professor of Economics and Public Affairs.

In January 1993, Blinder went to Washington as part of President Bill Clinton's first Council of Economic Advisers. Then, from June 1994 through January 1996, he served as vice chairman of the Federal Reserve Board. He thus played some role in formulating both fiscal and monetary policies, two topics discussed extensively in this book. He has also advised several presidential campaigns and numerous politicians.

Blinder has consulted for a number of the world's largest financial institutions, testified dozens of times before congressional committees, and been involved in several entrepreneurial start-ups. For many years, he has written newspaper and magazine articles on economic policy, including regular columns for the *Boston Globe, BusinessWeek*, and *The New York Times*. Currently, he has a regular monthly column in *The Wall Street Journal*. Blinder also appears frequently on PBS, CNBC, Bloomberg TV, Fox Business, and elsewhere. His recent book on the financial crisis (*After the Music Stopped*, Penguin, 2013) garnered many accolades and was a *New York Times* best-seller.

Blinder has served as president of the Eastern Economic Association and vice president of the American Economic Association, which elected him a Distinguished Fellow in 2011. He has won numerous awards, including the Council for Economic Education's Visionary Award. He is a member of the American Philosophical Society, the American Academy of Arts and Sciences, the American Academy of Political and Social Science, and the Council on Foreign Relations.

Blinder and his wife have two grown sons, two grandsons, and live in Princeton, where he doesn't play tennis as often as he should.

Blinder has served as president of the Eastern Economic Association and vice president of the American Economic Association, which elected him a Distinguished Fellow in 2011. He has won numerous awards, including the Council for Economic Education's Visionary Award. He is a member of the American Philosophical Society, the American Academy of Arts and Sciences, the American Academy of Political and Social Science, and the Council on Foreign Relations.

Blinder and his wife have two grown sons, two grandsons, and live in Princeton, where he doesn't play tennis as often as he should.

# GETTING ACQUAINTED WITH ECONOMICS

Welcome to economics! Some of your fellow students may have warned you that "econ is boring." Don't believe them—or at least, don't believe them too much. It is true that studying economics is hardly pure fun. But a first course in economics can be an eye-opening experience. There is a vast and important world out there—the economic world—and this book is designed to help you understand it.

Have you ever wondered whether jobs will be plentiful or scarce when you graduate, or why a college education becomes more and more expensive? Should the United States trade freely with other nations or protect jobs at home? Why are interest rates so low? How did the U.S. economy manage to stumble so badly after 2007? If any of these questions have piqued your curiosity, read on. You may find economics is more interesting than you had thought!

It is only in later chapters that we will begin to give you the tools you need to begin carrying out your own economic analyses. However, the four chapters of Part 1 listed next will introduce you to both the subject matter of economics and some of the methods that economists use to study their subject.

CHAPTERS

Part

1

# GETTING ACQUAINTED
# WITH ECONOMICS


had thought.

# WHAT IS ECONOMICS?

*Why does public discussion of economic policy so often show the abysmal ignorance of the participants? Why do I so often want to cry at what public figures, the press, and television commentators say about economic affairs?*

ROBERT M. SOLOW, WINNER OF THE 1987 NOBEL PRIZE IN ECONOMICS

Economics is a broad-ranging discipline, both in the questions it asks and the methods it uses to seek answers. Many of the world's most pressing problems are economic in nature. The first part of this chapter is intended to give you some idea of the sorts of issues that economic analysis helps to clarify and the kinds of solutions that economic principles suggest. The second part briefly introduces the tools that economists use—tools you are likely to find useful in your career, personal life, and role as an informed citizen, long after this course is over.

## CONTENTS

## 1-1 IDEAS FOR BEYOND THE FINAL EXAM

Elephants may never forget, but people do. We realize that most students inevitably forget much of what they learn in a course—perhaps with a sense of relief—soon after the final exam. Nevertheless, we hope that you will remember some of the most significant economic ideas and, even more important, the ways of thinking about economic issues that will help you evaluate the economic issues that arise in our economy.

To help you identify some of the most crucial concepts, we have selected seven from the many in this book. Some offer key insights into the workings of the economy, and several bear on important policy issues that appear in newspapers; others point out common misunderstandings that occur among even the most thoughtful lay observers. Most of them indicate that it takes more than just good common sense to analyze economic issues effectively. As the opening quote of this chapter suggests, many learned judges, politicians, and university administrators who failed to understand basic economic principles could have made wiser decisions.

Try this one on for size. If Chinese companies can produce *every* manufactured good more cheaply than American companies can (which, by the way, is not true), must the

United States lose by opening up trade with China? Would all American manufacturing jobs vanish? The perhaps surprising answers are: no. (See Idea 3.)

Ideas for Beyond the Final Exam

Each of the seven *Ideas for Beyond the Final Exam,* many of which are counterintuitive, will be sketched briefly here. More important, each will be discussed in depth when it occurs in the course of the book, where it will be called to your attention by a special icon in the margin. Don't expect to master these ideas fully now, but do notice how some of the ideas arise again and again as we deal with different topics. By the end of the course, you will have a better grasp of when common sense works and when it fails, and you will be able to recognize common fallacies that are all too often offered by public figures, the press, and television commentators.

### 1-1a Idea 1: How Much Does It Really Cost?

Because no one has infinite riches, people are constantly forced to make choices. If you purchase a new computer, you may have to give up that trip you had planned. If a business decides to retool its factories, it may have to postpone its plans for new executive offices. If a government expands its defense program, it may be forced to reduce its outlays on school buildings.

The **opportunity cost** of a decision is the value of the next best alternative that must be given up because of that decision (e.g., working instead of going to school).

Economists say that the true costs of such decisions are not the number of dollars spent on the computer, the new equipment, or the military, but rather *the value of what must be given up in order to acquire the item*—the vacation trip, the new executive offices, and the new schools. These are called **opportunity costs** because they represent the opportunities the individual, firm, or government must forgo to make the desired expenditure. Economists maintain that rational decision making must be based on opportunity costs, not just dollar costs (see Chapter 3 and elsewhere).

The cost of a college education provides a vivid example. How much do you think it *costs* to go to college? Most people are likely to answer by adding together their expenditures on tuition, room and board, books, and the like, and then deducting any scholarship funds they may receive. Suppose that amount comes to $15,000.

Economists keep score differently. They first want to know how much you would be earning if you were not attending college. Suppose that salary is $20,000 per year. This may seem irrelevant, but because you *give up* these earnings by attending college, they must be added to your tuition bill. You have that much less income because of your education. On the other side of the ledger, economists would not count *all* of the university's bill for room and board as part of the costs of your education. They would want to know how much *more* it costs you to live at school rather than at home. Economists would count only these *extra* costs as an educational expense because you would have incurred these costs whether or not you attend college. On balance, college is probably costing you much more than you think. And, as we will see later, taking opportunity cost into account in any personal planning will help you to make more rational decisions.

### 1-1b Idea 2: Attempts to Repeal the Laws of Supply and Demand—The Market Strikes Back

When a commodity is in short supply, its price naturally tends to rise. Sometimes disgruntled consumers badger politicians into "solving" this problem by making the high prices illegal—by imposing a ceiling on the price. Similarly, when supplies are plentiful—say, when fine weather produces extraordinarily abundant crops—prices tend to fall. Falling prices naturally dismay producers, who often succeed in getting legislators to impose price floors.

Such attempts to repeal the laws of supply and demand usually backfire and sometimes produce results virtually the opposite of those intended. Where rent controls are adopted to protect tenants, housing grows scarce because the law makes it unprofitable to build and maintain apartments. When price floors are placed under agricultural products, surpluses pile up because people buy less.

As we will see in Chapter 4 and elsewhere in this book, such consequences of interference with the price mechanism are not accidental. They follow inevitably from the way in which free markets work.

### 1-1c Idea 3: The Surprising Principle of Comparative Advantage

China today produces many products that Americans buy in huge quantities, including toys, textiles, and electronic equipment. American manufacturers often complain about Chinese competition and demand protection from the flood of imports that, in their view, threatens American standards of living. Is this view justified?

Economists think that it is often false. They maintain that both sides normally gain from international trade. But what if the Chinese were able to produce *everything* more cheaply than we can? Wouldn't Americans be thrown out of work and our nation be impoverished?

A remarkable result, called the law of *comparative advantage*, shows that, even in this extreme case, the two nations could still benefit by trading and that each could gain as a result! We will explain this principle first in Chapter 3 and then more fully in Chapter 18. For now, a simple parable will make the reason clear.

Suppose Sally grows up on a farm and is a whiz at plowing, but she is also a successful country singer who earns $4,000 per performance. Should Sally turn down singing engagements to leave time to work in the fields? Of course not. Instead, she should hire Alfie, a much less efficient farmer, to do the plowing for her. Sally may be better at plowing, but she earns so much more by singing that it makes sense for her to specialize in that and leave the farming to Alfie. Although Alfie is a less skilled farmer than Sally, he is an even worse singer.

So Alfie earns his living in the job at which he at least has a *comparative* advantage (his farming is not as inferior as his singing), and both Alfie and Sally gain. The same is true of two countries. Even if one of them is more efficient at everything, both countries can gain by producing the things they do best *comparatively*.

### 1-1d Idea 4: Trade Is a Win–Win Situation

One of the most fundamental ideas of economics is that both parties must expect to gain something in a voluntary exchange. Otherwise, why would they both agree to trade? This principle seems self-evident, yet it is amazing how often it is ignored in practice.

For example, it was widely believed for centuries that in international trade one country's gain from an exchange must be the other country's loss (Chapter 18). Analogously, some people feel instinctively that if Ms. A profits handsomely from a deal with Mr. B, then Mr. B must have been exploited. Laws sometimes prohibit mutually beneficial exchanges between buyers and sellers—as when a loan transaction is banned because the interest rate is "too high," or when a willing worker is condemned to remain unemployed because the wage she is offered is "too low," or when the resale of tickets to sporting events ("ticket scalping") is outlawed even though the buyer is happy to get the ticket that he could not obtain at a lower price (Chapter 4).

In every one of these cases, well-intentioned but misguided reasoning blocks the possible mutual gains that arise from voluntary exchange and thereby interferes with one of the most basic functions of an economic system (see Chapters 3 and 4).

### 1-1e Idea 5: Government Policies Can Limit Economic Fluctuations— But Don't Always Succeed

One of the most persistent and troubling problems of market economies has been their tendency to go through cycles of boom and bust. The booms, as we shall see, often bring inflation, and the busts always raise unemployment. Years ago, economists, businesspeople, and politicians viewed these fluctuations as inevitable: There was nothing the government could or should do about them.

That view is now considered obsolete. As we will learn in Part 2, and especially Part 3, modern governments have an arsenal of weapons that they can and do deploy to try to mitigate fluctuations in their national economies—to limit both inflation and unemployment. Some of these weapons constitute what is called *fiscal policy*: control over taxes and government spending. Others come from *monetary policy*: control over money and interest rates. Both were used on a grand scale to fight the Great Recession of 2007–2009.

But *trying* to tame the business cycle is not the same as *succeeding*. Economic fluctuations remain with us, and one reason is that the government's fiscal and monetary policies sometimes fail—for both political and economic reasons. As we will see in Part 3, policy makers do not always make the right decisions. And even when they do, the economy does not always react as policymakers hope. Furthermore, for reasons we will explain later, the "right" decision is not always clear. To this day, many of the fiscal and monetary policies of 2008 and 2009 remain highly controversial.

### 1-1f Idea 6: The Short-Run Trade-Off between Inflation and Unemployment

The U.S. economy was lucky in the second half of the 1990s. A set of fortuitous events— falling energy prices, tumbling computer prices, a rising dollar, and so on—pushed inflation down even as unemployment fell to its lowest level in almost 30 years. During the 1970s and early 1980s, the United States was not so fortunate. Skyrocketing prices for food and energy sent both inflation and unemployment up to extraordinary heights. In both episodes, then, inflation and unemployment moved in the same direction.

But economists maintain that neither of these two episodes was "normal." When we are experiencing neither unusually good luck (as in the 1990s) nor exceptionally bad luck (as in the 1970s), there is a *trade-off between inflation and unemployment*—meaning that low unemployment normally makes inflation rise and high unemployment normally makes inflation fall. For example, the high unemployment of 2008–2010 pushed the inflation rate down so low that people began worrying about *negative* inflation rates, or *de*flation. We will study the mechanisms underlying this trade-off in Parts 2 and 3, especially in Chapter 17. It poses one of the fundamental dilemmas of national economic policy.

### 1-1g Idea 7: Productivity Growth Is (Almost) Everything in the Long Run

Today in Geneva, Switzerland, workers in a watch factory turn out more than 100 times as many mechanical watches per year as their ancestors did three centuries earlier. The productivity of labor (output per hour of work) in cotton production has probably gone up more than 1,000-fold in 200 years. It is estimated that rising labor productivity has increased the standard of living of a typical American worker approximately sevenfold in the past century (see Chapter 7).

Other economic issues such as unemployment, monopoly, and inequality are important to us all and receive much attention in economics. But in the long run, nothing has as great an effect on our material well-being and the amounts society can afford to spend on hospitals, schools, and social amenities as the rate of growth of productivity—the amount that an average worker can produce in an hour. Chapter 7 points out that what appears to be a small increase in productivity growth can have a huge effect on a country's standard of living over a long period of time because productivity compounds like the interest on savings in a bank. Similarly, a slowdown in productivity growth that persists for a substantial number of years can have a devastating effect on living standards.

### 1-1h Epilogue

These ideas are some of the more fundamental concepts you will find in this book—ideas that we hope you will retain beyond the final exam. There is no need to master them right now, for you will hear much more about each as you progress through the book. By the end of the course, you may be amazed to see how natural, or even obvious, they will seem.

## 1-2  INSIDE THE ECONOMIST'S TOOL KIT

We turn now from the kinds of issues economists deal with to some of the tools they use to grapple with them.

### 1-2a  Economics as a Discipline

Although economics is clearly the most rigorous of the social sciences, it nevertheless looks decidedly more "social" than "scientific" when compared with, say, physics. An economist must be a jack of several trades, borrowing modes of analysis from numerous fields. Mathematical reasoning is often used in economics, but so is historical study. And neither looks quite the same as when practiced by a mathematician or a historian. Statistics play a major role in modern economic inquiry, although economists had to modify standard statistical procedures to fit their kinds of data.

*From The Wall Street Journal—Permission, Cartoon Features Syndicate.*

*"Yes, John, we'd all like to make economics less dismal ..."*

NOTE: The nineteenth-century British writer Thomas Carlyle described economics as the "dismal science," a label that stuck.

### 1-2b  The Need for Abstraction

Some students find economics unduly abstract and "unrealistic." The stylized world envisioned by economic theory seems only a distant cousin to the world they know. There is an old joke about three people—a chemist, a physicist, and an economist—stranded on a desert island with an ample supply of canned food but no tools to open the cans. The chemist thinks that lighting a fire under the cans would burst the cans. The physicist advocates building a catapult with which to smash the cans against some boulders. The economist's suggestion? "Let's assume we have a can opener."

Economic theory *does* make some unrealistic assumptions—you will encounter some of them in this book—but some abstraction from reality is necessary because of the incredible complexity of the economic world, not because economists like to sound absurd.

Compare the chemist's simple task of explaining the interactions of compounds in a chemical reaction with the economist's complex task of explaining the interactions of people in an economy. Are molecules motivated by greed or altruism, by envy or ambition? Do they ever imitate other molecules? Do forecasts about them influence their behavior? People, of course, do all these things and many, many more. It is therefore vastly more difficult to predict human behavior than to predict chemical reactions. If economists tried to keep track of every feature of human behavior, they would never get anywhere. Thus:

> Abstraction from unimportant details is necessary to understand the functioning of anything as complex as the economy.

An analogy will make it clear why economists **abstract** from details. Suppose you have just arrived for the first time in Los Angeles. You are now at the Los Angeles Civic Center—the point marked *A* in Maps 1 and 2, which are alternative maps of part of Los Angeles. You want to drive to the Los Angeles County Museum of Art, point *B* on each map. Which map would be more useful?

Map 1 has complete details of the Los Angeles road system, but this makes it hard to read and hard to use as a way to find the art museum. For this purpose, Map 1 is far too detailed, although for other purposes (e.g., locating a small street in Hollywood) it may be far better than Map 2.

In contrast, Map 2 omits many minor roads—you might say they are *assumed away*—so that the freeways and major arteries stand out more clearly. As a result of this simplification, several routes from the Civic Center to the Los Angeles County Museum of Art emerge. For example, we can take the Hollywood Freeway west to Alvarado Boulevard, go south to Wilshire Boulevard, and then head west again. Although we *might* find a shorter route by poring over the details in Map 1, most strangers to the city would be better off with Map 2. Similarly, economists try to *abstract* from a lot of confusing details while retaining the essentials.

**Abstraction** means ignoring many details so as to focus on the most important elements of a problem.

*Map 1*

**Detailed Road Map of Los Angeles**

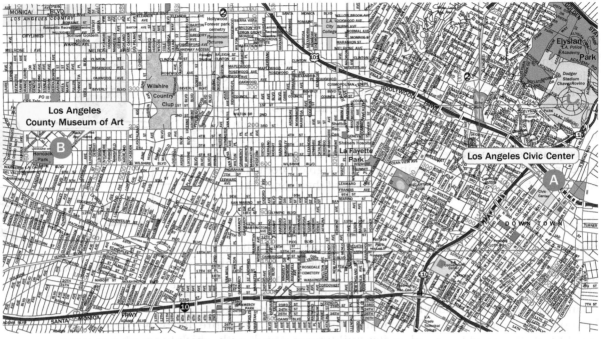

NOTE: Point *A* marks the Los Angeles Civic Center, and point *B* marks the Los Angeles County Museum of Art.

*Map 2*

**Major Los Angeles Arteries and Freeways**

*Map 3*
**Greater Los Angeles Freeways**

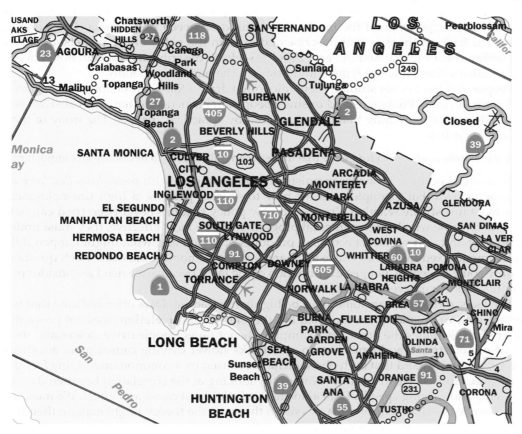

Map 3, however, illustrates that simplification can go too far. It shows little more than the major interstate routes that pass through the greater Los Angeles area and therefore will not help a visitor find the art museum. Of course, this map was never intended to be used as a detailed tourist guide, which brings us to an important point:

> There is no such thing as one "right" degree of abstraction and simplification for all analytic purposes. The proper degree of abstraction depends on the objective of the analysis. A model that is a gross oversimplification for one purpose may be needlessly complicated for another.

Economists are constantly seeking analogies to Map 2 rather than Map 3, walking the thin line between useful generalizations about complex issues and gross distortions of the pertinent facts. For example, suppose you want to learn why some people are fabulously rich whereas others are abjectly poor. People differ in many ways, too many to enumerate, much less to study. The economist must ignore most of these details to focus on the important ones. The color of a person's hair or eyes is probably not important for the problem but, unfortunately, the color of his or her skin probably is because racial discrimination can depress a person's income. Height and weight may not matter, but education probably does. Proceeding in this way, we can pare Map 1 down to the manageable dimensions of Map 2. But there is a danger of going too far, stripping away some of the crucial factors, so that we wind up with Map 3.

## 1-2c  The Role of Economic Theory

Some students find economics "too theoretical." To see why we can't avoid it, let's consider what we mean by a **theory**.

To an economist or natural scientist, the word *theory* means something different from what it means in common speech. In science, a theory is *not* an untested assertion of

A **theory** is a deliberate simplification of relationships used to explain how those relationships work.

alleged fact. The statement that aspirin provides protection against heart attacks is not a theory; it is a *hypothesis*, that is, a reasoned guess, which will prove to be true or false once the right sorts of experiments have been completed. But a theory is different. It is a deliberate simplification (abstraction) of reality that attempts to explain how some relationships work. It is an *explanation* of the mechanism behind observed phenomena. Thus, gravity forms the basis of theories that describe and explain the paths of the planets. Similarly, Keynesian theory (discussed in Parts 2 and 3) seeks to describe and explain how government policies affect unemployment and prices in the national economy.

People who have never studied economics often draw a false distinction between *theory* and *practical policy*. Politicians and businesspeople, in particular, often reject abstract economic theory as something that is best ignored by "practical" people. The irony of these statements is that

> It is precisely the concern for policy that makes economic theory so necessary and important.

To analyze policy options, economists are forced to deal with *possibilities that have not actually occurred*. For example, to learn how to shorten periods of high unemployment, they must investigate whether a proposed new policy that has never been tried can help. Or to determine which environmental programs will be most effective, they must understand how and why a market economy produces pollution and what might happen if the government taxed industrial waste discharges and automobile emissions. Such questions require some *theorizing*, not just examination of the facts, because we need to consider possibilities that have never occurred.

The facts, moreover, can sometimes be highly misleading. Data often indicate that two variables move up and down together. But this statistical **correlation** does not prove that either variable *causes* the other. For example, when it rains, people drive slower and there are also more traffic accidents, but no one thinks slower driving causes more accidents. Rather, we understand that both phenomena are caused by a common underlying factor—more rain. How do we know this? Not just by looking at the correlation between data on accidents and driving speeds. Data alone tell us little about cause and effect. We must use some simple *theory* as part of our analysis. In this case, the theory might explain that drivers are more apt to have accidents on wet roads.

Similarly, we must use theoretical analysis, and not just data alone, to understand *how*, if at all, different government policies will lead to lower unemployment or *how* a tax on emissions will reduce pollution.

> Statistical correlation need not imply causation. Some theory is usually needed to interpret data.

*Two variables are said to be* **correlated** *if they tend to go up or down together. Correlation need not imply causation.*

## 1-2d What Is an Economic Model?

*An* **economic model** *is a simplified, small-scale version of an aspect of the economy. Economic models are often expressed in equations, by graphs, or in words.*

An **economic model** is a representation of a theory or a part of a theory, often used to gain insight into cause and effect. The notion of a "model" is familiar enough to children, and economists—like other researchers—use the term the same way children do.

A child's model airplane looks and operates much like the real thing, but it is smaller and simpler, so it is easier to manipulate and understand. Engineers for Boeing also build models of planes. Although their models are far larger and much more elaborate than a child's toy, they use them for the same purposes: to observe the workings of these aircraft "up close" and to experiment to see how the models behave under different circumstances. ("What happens if I do this?") From these experiments, they make educated guesses as to how the real-life version will perform.

Economists use models for similar purposes. The late A. W. Phillips, famous engineer-turned-economist who discovered the "Phillips curve" (discussed in Chapter 17), was talented enough to construct a working model of the determination of national income in a simple economy by using colored water flowing through pipes. For years this contraption has graced the basement of the London School of Economics. Although we will explain the models with words and diagrams, Phillips's engineering background enabled him to depict the theory with tubes, valves, and pumps.

Because many of the models used in this book are depicted in diagrams, for those of you who need review, we explain the construction and use of various types of graphs in the appendix to this chapter. Don't be put off by seemingly abstract models. Think of them as useful road maps and remember how hard it would be to find your way around Los Angeles without one.

## 1-2e  Reasons for Disagreements: Imperfect Information and Value Judgments

"If all the earth's economists were laid end to end, they could not reach an agreement," the saying goes. Politicians and reporters are fond of pointing out that economists can be found on both sides of many public policy issues. If economics is a science, why do economists so often disagree? After all, astronomers do not debate whether the earth revolves around the sun or vice versa.

This question reflects a misunderstanding of the nature of science. Disputes are normal at the frontier of any science. For example, astronomers once argued vociferously over whether the earth revolves around the sun. Nowadays, they argue about gamma-ray bursts, dark matter, and other esoterica. These arguments go mostly unnoticed by the public because few of us understand what they are talking about. But economics is a *social* science, so its disputes are aired in public and all sorts of people feel competent to join economic debates.

Furthermore, economists actually agree on much more than is commonly supposed. Virtually all economists, regardless of their politics, agree that taxing polluters is one of the best ways to protect the environment, that rent controls can ruin a city (Chapter 4),

*A. W. Phillips built this model in the early 1950s to illustrate Keynesian theory.*

and that free trade among nations is usually preferable to the erection of barriers through tariffs and quotas (see Chapter 18). The list could go on and on. It is probably true that the issues about which economists agree *far* exceed the subjects on which they disagree.

Finally, many disputes among economists are not scientific disputes at all. Sometimes the pertinent facts are simply unknown. For example, the appropriate financial penalty to levy on a polluter depends on quantitative estimates of the harm done by the pollutant; however, good estimates of this damage may not be available. Similarly, although there is wide scientific agreement that the earth is slowly warming, there are disagreements over the costs of global warming. Such disputes make it difficult to agree on a concrete policy proposal.

Another important source of disagreements is that economists, like other people, come in all political stripes: conservative, middle-of-the-road, liberal, radical. Each may have different values, and so each may hold a different view of the "right" solution to a public policy problem—even if they agree on the underlying analysis. Here are two examples:

1. We suggested early in this chapter that policies that lower inflation are likely to raise unemployment. Many economists believe they can measure the amount of unemployment that must be endured to reduce inflation by a given amount. However, they disagree about whether it is worth having, say, three million more people out of work for a year to cut the inflation rate by 1 percent.
2. In designing an income tax, society must decide how much of the burden to put on upper-income taxpayers. Some people believe the rich should pay a disproportionate share of the taxes. Others disagree, believing it is fairer to levy the same income-tax rate on everyone.

Economists cannot answer questions like these any more than nuclear physicists could have determined whether dropping the atomic bomb on Hiroshima was a good idea. The decisions rest on moral judgments that can be made only by the citizenry through its elected officials.

**Although economic science can contribute theoretical and factual knowledge on a particular issue, the final decision on policy questions often rests either on information that is not currently available or on social values and ethical opinions about which people differ, or on both.**

## Summary

1. To help you get the most out of your first course in economics, we have devised a list of seven important ideas that you will want to retain beyond the final exam. Briefly, they are the following:

   a. **Opportunity cost** is the correct measure of cost.

   b. Attempts to fight market forces often backfire.

   c. Nations can gain from trade by exploiting their *comparative advantages*.

   d. Both parties can gain in a voluntary exchange.

   e. Governments have tools that can mitigate cycles of boom and bust, but these tools are imperfect.

   f. In the short run, policy makers face a trade-off between inflation and unemployment. Policies that reduce one normally increase the other.

   g. In the long run, *productivity* is almost the only thing that matters for a society's material well-being.

2. Common sense is not always a reliable guide in explaining economic issues or in making economic decisions.

3. Because of the great complexity of human behavior, economists are forced to **abstract** from many details, to make generalizations that they know are not quite true, and to organize what knowledge they have in terms of some theoretical structure called a "model."

4. **Correlation** need not imply causation.

5. Economists use simplified models to understand the real world and predict its behavior, much as a child uses a model railroad to learn how trains work.

6. Although these **economic models,** if skillfully constructed, can illuminate important economic problems, they rarely can answer the questions that confront policy makers. Value judgments involving such matters as ethics are needed for this purpose, and the economist is no better equipped than anyone else to make them.

## Key Terms

| | | |
|---|---|---|
| abstraction  7 | economic model  10 | theory  9 |
| correlation  10 | opportunity cost  4 | |

## Discussion Questions

1. Think about a way you would construct a model of how your college is governed. Which officers and administrators would you include and exclude from your model if the objective were one of the following:

   a. To explain how decisions on financial aid are made

   b. To explain the quality of the faculty
   Relate this to the map example in the chapter.

2. Relate the process of abstraction to the way you take notes in a lecture. Why do you not try to transcribe every word uttered by the lecturer? Why don't you write down just the title of the lecture and stop there? How do you decide, roughly speaking, on the correct amount of detail?

3. Explain why a government policy maker cannot afford to ignore economic theory.

## Appendix  *Using Graphs: A Review*[1]

As noted in the chapter, economists often explain and analyze models with the help of graphs. Indeed, this book is full of them. But that is not the only reason for studying how graphs work. Most college students will deal with graphs in the future, perhaps frequently.

You will see them in newspapers. If you become a doctor, you will use graphs to keep track of your patients' progress. If you join a business firm, you will use them to check profit or performance at a glance. This appendix introduces some of the techniques of graphic analysis—tools you will use throughout the book and, more important, very likely throughout your working career.

---

[1] Students who have some acquaintance with geometry and feel quite comfortable with graphs can safely skip this appendix.

## Graphs Used in Economic Analysis

Economic graphs are invaluable because they can display a large quantity of data quickly and because they facilitate data interpretation and analysis. They enable the eye to take in important statistical relationships at a glance that would be far less apparent from written descriptions or long lists of numbers.

## Two-Variable Diagrams

Much of the economic analysis found in this and other books requires that we keep track of two **variables** simultaneously.

> A **variable** is something measured by a number; it is used to analyze what happens to other things when the size of that number changes (varies).

For example, in studying how markets operate, we will want to keep one eye on the *price* of a commodity and the other on the *quantity* of that commodity that is bought and sold.

For this reason, economists frequently find it useful to display real or imaginary figures in a two-variable diagram, which simultaneously represents the behavior of two economic variables. The numerical value of one variable is measured along the horizontal line at the bottom of the graph (called the *horizontal axis*), starting from the **origin** (the point labeled "0"), and the numerical value of the other variable is measured up the vertical line on the left side of the graph (called the *vertical axis*), also starting from the origin.

> The "0" point in the lower-left corner of a graph where the axes meet is called the **origin**. Both variables are equal to zero at the origin.

Figures 1(a) and 1(b) are typical graphs of economic analysis. They depict an imaginary *demand curve*, represented by the blue dots in Figure 1(a) and the heavy blue line in Figure 1(b). The graphs show the price of natural gas on their vertical axes and the quantity of gas people want to buy at each price on the horizontal axes. The dots in Figure 1(a) are connected by the continuous blue curve labeled *DD* in Figure 1(b).

Economic diagrams are generally read just as one would read latitudes and longitudes on a map. On the demand curve in Figure 1, the point marked *a* represents a hypothetical combination of price and quantity of natural gas demanded by customers in St. Louis. By drawing a horizontal line leftward from that point to the vertical axis, we learn that at this point the average price for gas in St. Louis is $3 per thousand cubic feet. By dropping a line straight down to the horizontal axis, we find that consumers want 80 billion cubic feet per year at this price, just as the statistics in Table 1 show. The other points on the graph give similar information. For example, point *b* indicates that if natural gas in St. Louis were to cost only $2 per thousand cubic feet, quantity demanded would be higher—it would reach 120 billion cubic feet per year.

Notice that information about price and quantity is *all* we can learn from the diagram. The demand curve will not tell us what kinds of people live in St. Louis, the size of their homes, or the condition of their

*Table 1*

**Quantities of Natural Gas Demanded at Various Prices**

| Price (per thousand cubic feet) | $2 | $3 | $4 | $5 | $6 |
|---|---|---|---|---|---|
| Quantity demanded (billions of cubic feet per year) | 120 | 80 | 56 | 38 | 20 |

*Figure 1*

**A Hypothetical Demand Curve for Natural Gas in St. Louis**

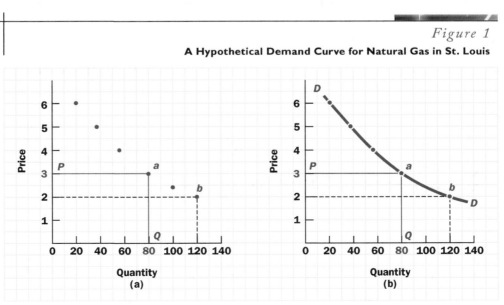

NOTE: Price is in dollars per thousand cubic feet; quantity is in billions of cubic feet per year.

furnaces. It tells us about the quantity demanded at each possible price—no more, no less.

> A diagram abstracts from many details, some of which may be quite interesting, so as to focus on the two variables of primary interest—in this case, the price of natural gas and the amount of gas that is demanded at each price. All of the diagrams used in this book share this basic feature. They cannot tell the reader the "whole story," any more than a map's latitude and longitude figures for a particular city can make someone an authority on that city.

## The Definition and Measurement of Slope

One of the most important features of economic diagrams is the rate at which the line or curve being sketched runs uphill or downhill as we move to the right. The demand curve in Figure 1 clearly slopes downhill (the price falls) as we follow it to the right (i.e., as consumers demand more gas). In such instances, we say that *the curve has a negative slope, or is negatively sloped, because one variable falls as the other one rises.*

> The **slope of a straight line** is the ratio of the vertical change to the corresponding horizontal change as we move to the right along the line between two points on that line, or, as it is often said, the ratio of the "rise" over the "run."

The four panels of Figure 2 show all possible types of slope for a straight-line relationship between two unnamed variables called $Y$ (measured along the vertical axis) and $X$ (measured along the horizontal axis). Figure 2(a) shows a *negative slope*, much like our demand curve in the previous graph. Figure 2(b) shows a *positive slope*, because variable $Y$ rises (we go uphill) as variable $X$ rises (as we move to the right). Figure 2(c) shows a *zero slope*, where the value of $Y$ is the same irrespective of the value of $X$. Figure 2(d) shows an *infinite slope*, meaning that the value of $X$ is the same irrespective of the value of $Y$.

Slope is a numerical concept, not just a qualitative one. The two panels of Figure 3 show two positively sloped straight lines with different slopes. The line in Figure 3(b) is clearly steeper. But by how much? The labels should help you compute the answer. In Figure 3(a) a horizontal movement, $AB$, of 10 units $(13 - 3)$ corresponds to a vertical movement, $BC$, of 1 unit $(9 - 8)$. So the slope is $BC/AB - 1/10$. In Figure 3(b), the same horizontal movement of 10 units corresponds to a vertical movement of 3 units $(11 - 8)$. So the slope is 3/10, which is larger—the rise divided by the run is greater in Figure 3(b).

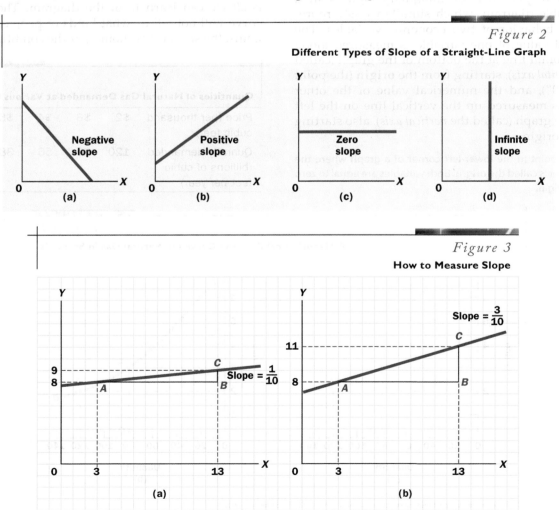

*Figure 2*

**Different Types of Slope of a Straight-Line Graph**

(a) Negative slope  (b) Positive slope  (c) Zero slope  (d) Infinite slope

*Figure 3*

**How to Measure Slope**

(a) Slope $= \frac{1}{10}$  (b) Slope $= \frac{3}{10}$

By definition, the slope of any particular straight line remains the same, no matter where on that line we choose to measure it. That is why we can pick any horizontal distance, *AB,* and the corresponding slope triangle, *ABC,* to measure slope. But this is not true for curved lines.

> Curved lines also have slopes, but the numerical value of the slope differs at every point along the curve as we move from left to right.

The four panels of Figure 4 provide some examples of **slopes of curved lines.** The curve in Figure 4(a) has a negative slope everywhere, and the curve in Figure 4(b) has a positive slope everywhere. But these are not the only possibilities. In Figure 4(c) we encounter a curve that has a positive slope at first but a negative slope later on. Figure 4(d) shows the opposite case: a negative slope followed by a positive slope.

We can measure the slope of a smooth curved line numerically *at any particular point* by drawing a *straight* line that *touches,* but does not *cut,* the curve at the point in question. Such a line is called a **tangent to the curve.**

> The **slope of a curved line** at a particular point is defined as the slope of the straight line that is tangent to the curve at that point.

Figure 5 shows tangents to the blue curve at two points. Line *tt* is tangent at point *T,* and line *rr* is tangent at point *R.* We can measure the slope of the curve at these two points by applying the definition. The calculation for point *T,* then, is the following:

$$\text{Slope at point } T = \text{Slope of line } tt$$
$$= \frac{\text{Distance } BC}{\text{Distance } BA}$$
$$= \frac{(1-5)}{(3-1)} = \frac{-4}{2} = -2$$

A similar calculation yields the slope of the curve at point *R,* which, as we can see from Figure 5, must be

*Figure 5*

**How to Measure Slope at a Point on a Curved Graph**

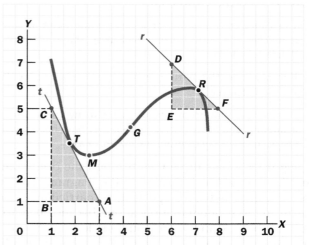

smaller numerically. That is, the tangent line *rr* is less steep than line *tt:*

$$\text{Slope at point } R = \text{Slope of line } rr$$
$$= \frac{(5-7)}{(8-6)} = \frac{-2}{2} = -1$$

**Exercise** Show that the slope of the curve at point *G* is about 1.

What would happen if we tried to apply this graphical technique to the high point in Figure 4(c) or to the low point in Figure 4(d)? Take a ruler and try it. The tangents that you construct should be horizontal, meaning that they should have a slope exactly equal to zero. It is always true that where the slope of a *smooth* curve changes from positive to negative, or vice versa, there will be at least one point whose slope is zero.

Curves shaped like smooth hills, as in Figure 4(c), have a zero slope at their *highest* point. Curves shaped like valleys, as in Figure 4(d), have a zero slope at their *lowest* point.

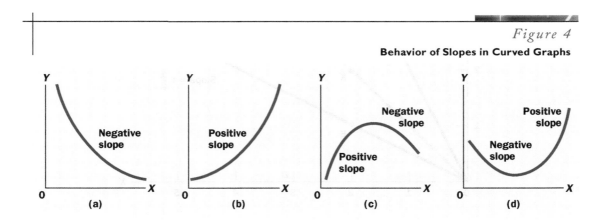

*Figure 4*

**Behavior of Slopes in Curved Graphs**

## Rays through the Origin and 45° Lines

The point at which a straight line cuts the vertical ($Y$) axis is called the **Y-intercept**.

> The **Y-intercept** of a line or a curve is the point at which it touches the vertical axis (the $Y$-axis). The $X$-intercept is defined similarly.

For example, the $Y$-intercept of the line in Figure 3(a) is a bit less than 8.

> Lines whose $Y$-intercept is zero have so many special uses in economics and other disciplines that they have been given a special name: **a ray through the origin, or a ray.**

Figure 6 shows three rays through the origin, and the slope of each is indicated in the diagram. The ray in the center (whose slope is 1) is particularly useful in many economic applications because it marks points where $X$ and $Y$ are equal (as long as $X$ and $Y$ are measured in the same units). For example, at point $A$ we have $X = 3$ and $Y = 3$; at point $B$, $X = 4$ and $Y = 4$. A similar relation holds at any other point on that ray.

How do we know that this is always true for a ray whose slope is 1? If we start from the origin (where both $X$ and $Y$ are zero) and the slope of the ray is 1, we know from the definition of slope that

$$\text{Slope} = \frac{\text{Vertical change}}{\text{Horizontal change}} = 1$$

This implies that the vertical change and the horizontal change are always equal, so the two variables must always remain equal. Any point along that ray (e.g., point $A$) is exactly equal in distance from the horizontal and vertical axes (length $DA$ = length $CA$)— the number on the $X$-axis (the abscissa) will be the same as the number on the $Y$-axis (the ordinate).

> Rays through the origin with a slope of 1 are called **45° lines** because they form an angle of 45° with the horizontal axis. A 45° line marks off points where the variables measured on each axis have equal values.[2]

If a point representing some data is above the 45° line, we know that the value of $Y$ exceeds the value of $X$. Similarly, whenever we find a point below the 45° line, we know that $X$ is larger than $Y$.

---

[2] The definition assumes that both variables are measured in the same units.

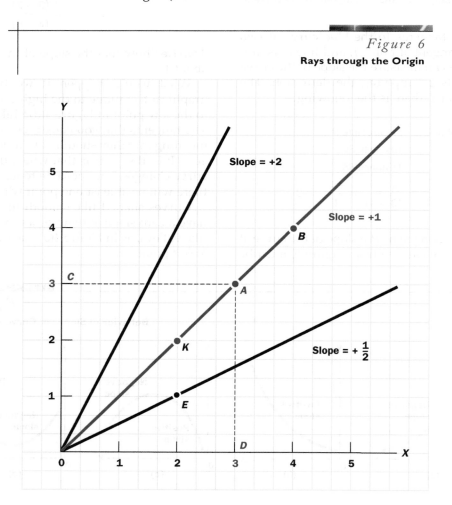

*Figure 6*

**Rays through the Origin**

## Squeezing Three Dimensions into Two: Contour Maps

Sometimes problems involve more than two variables, so two dimensions just are not enough to depict them on a graph. This is unfortunate, because the surface of a sheet of paper is only two-dimensional. When we study a business firm's decision-making process, for example, we may want to keep track simultaneously of three variables: how much labor it employs, how much raw material it imports from foreign countries, and how much output it creates.

Luckily, economists can use a well-known device for collapsing three dimensions into two—a *contour map.* Figure 7 is a contour map of the area just southeast of Eugene, Oregon, including the Eugene Compressor Station. On some of the irregularly shaped "rings" on this map, we find numbers (like 800) indicating the height (in meters) above sea level at that particular spot on the hill. Thus, unlike other maps, which give only latitudes and longitudes, this contour map (also called a topographical map) exhibits *three* pieces of information about each point: latitude, longitude, and altitude.

Figure 8 looks more like the contour maps encountered in economics. It shows how a third variable, called $Z$ (think of it as a firm's output, for example), varies as we change either variable $X$ (think of it as a firm's employment of labor) or variable $Y$ (think of it as the use of imported raw material). Just like the map of the area near Eugene, Oregon, any point on the diagram conveys three pieces of data. At point $A$, we can read off the values of $X$ and $Y$ in the conventional way ($X$ is 30 and $Y$ is 40), and we can also note the value of $Z$ by finding out on which contour line point $A$ falls. (It is on the $Z = 20$ contour.) So point $A$ is able to tell us that 30 hours of labor and 40 yards of cloth produce 20 units of output per day. The contour line that indicates 20 units of output shows the various combinations of labor and cloth a manufacturer can use to produce 20 units of output. Economists call such maps **production indifference maps**.

A **production indifference map** is a graph whose axes show the quantities of two inputs that are used to produce some output. A curve in the graph corresponds to some given quantity of that output, and the different points on that curve show the different quantities of the two inputs that are just enough to produce the given output.

Although most of the analyses presented in this book rely on the simpler two-variable diagrams, contour maps will find their applications.

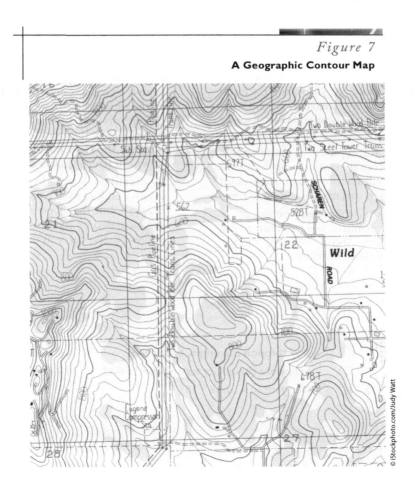

*Figure 7*

**A Geographic Contour Map**

© iStockphoto.com/Judy Watt

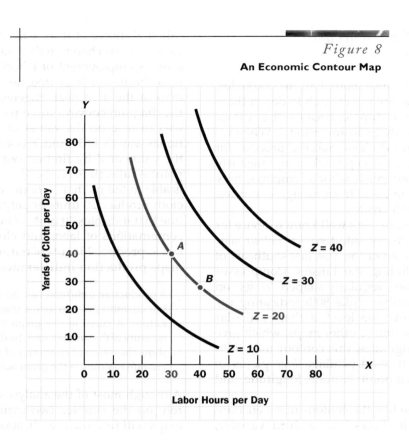

*Figure 8*

**An Economic Contour Map**

## Summary

1. Because graphs are used so often to portray economic models, it is important for students to acquire some understanding of their construction and use. Fortunately, the graphics used in economics are usually not very complex.

2. Most economic models are depicted in two-variable diagrams. We read data from these diagrams just as we read the latitude and longitude on a map: Each point represents the values of two variables at the same time.

3. In some instances, three variables must be shown at once. In these cases, economists use contour maps, which, as the name suggests, show "latitude," "longitude," and "altitude" all at the same time.

4. Often, the most important property of a line or curve drawn on a diagram will be its slope, which is defined as the ratio of the "rise" over the "run," or the vertical change divided by the horizontal change when one moves along the curve. Curves that go uphill as we move to the right have positive slopes; curves that go downhill have negative slopes.

5. By definition, a straight line has the same slope wherever we choose to measure it. The slope of a curved line changes, but the slope at any point on the curve can be calculated by measuring the slope of a straight line tangent to the curve at that point.

## Key Terms

45° line   16

origin (of a graph)   13

production indifference map   17

ray through the origin, or ray   16

slope of a straight (or curved) line   14–15

tangent to a curve   15

variable   13

Y-intercept   16

## Test Yourself

1. Portray the following hypothetical data on a two-variable diagram:

| Academic Year | Total Enrollment | Enrollment in Economics Courses |
|---|---|---|
| 2008–2009 | 3,000 | 300 |
| 2009–2010 | 3,100 | 325 |
| 2010–2011 | 3,200 | 350 |
| 2011–2012 | 3,300 | 375 |
| 2012–2013 | 3,400 | 400 |

Measure the slope of the resulting line, and explain what this number means.

2. From Figure 5, calculate the slope of the curve at point $M$.

3. Colin believes that the number of job offers he will get depends on the number of courses in which his grade is B+ or better. He concludes from observation that the following figures are typical:

| Number of grades of B+ or better | 0 | 1 | 2 | 3 | 4 |
|---|---|---|---|---|---|
| Number of job offers | 1 | 3 | 4 | 5 | 6 |

Put these numbers into a graph like Figure 1(a). Measure and interpret the slopes between adjacent dots.

4. In Figure 6, determine the values of $X$ and $Y$ at point $K$ and at point $E$. What do you conclude about the slopes of the lines on which $K$ and $E$ are located?

5. In Figure 8, interpret the economic meaning of points $A$ and $B$. What do the two points have in common? What is the difference in their economic interpretation?

# THE ECONOMY: MYTH AND REALITY

2

E pluribus unum (Out of many, one)

MOTTO ON U.S. CURRENCY

This chapter introduces you to the U.S. economy and its role in the world. It may seem that no such introduction is necessary, for perhaps you have lived your entire life in the United States. Every time you work at a summer or part-time job, pay your college bills, or buy a slice of pizza, you not only participate in the American economy—but you also observe something about it.

But the casual impressions we acquire in our everyday lives, though sometimes correct, are often misleading. Experience shows that most Americans—not just students—either are unaware of or harbor grave misconceptions about some of the most basic economic facts. One popular myth holds that most of the goods that Americans buy are made in China. Another is that business profits account for a third of the price we pay for a typical good or service. Also, "everyone knows" that the number of federal government jobs has grown rapidly during the past few decades. In fact, none of these things is remotely close to being true.

So, before we begin to develop theories of how the economy works, it is useful to get an accurate picture of what our economy is really like.

## CONTENTS

## 2-1 THE AMERICAN ECONOMY: A THUMBNAIL SKETCH

The U.S. economy is the biggest national economy on earth, for two very different reasons. First, there are a lot of us. The population of the United States is just under 320 million—making it the third most populous nation on earth after China and India. That vast total includes children, retirees, full-time students, institutionalized people, and the unemployed, none of whom produce much output. But as of 2013, the *working population* of the United States numbered almost 144 million. As long as they are reasonably productive, that many people are bound to produce vast amounts of goods and services. And they do.

But population is not the main reason why the U.S. economy is by far the world's biggest. After all, despite having nearly four times the population, India's economy

"And may we continue to be worthy of consuming a disproportionate share of this planet's resources."

Lee Lorenz The New Yorker Collection/The Cartoon Bank

is less than one-quarter of the size of that of the United States. The second reason why the U.S. economy is so large is that we are a very rich country. American workers are among the most productive in the world. In 2013, for instance, our economy produced nearly $53,000 worth of goods and services for every living American—about $116,000 for every *working* American. If each of the 50 states was a separate country, California would be the eighth-largest national economy on earth!

Why are some countries (like the United States) so rich and others (like India) so poor? That is one of the central questions facing economists. It is useful to think of an economic system as a machine that takes **inputs**, such as labor and other things we call **factors of production**, and transforms them into **outputs**, or the things people want to consume. The American economic machine performs this task with extraordinary efficiency, whereas the

**Inputs** or **factors of production** are the labor, machinery, buildings, and natural resources used to make outputs.

**Outputs** are the goods and services that consumers and others want to acquire.

Indian machine runs quite inefficiently (though it is improving rapidly). Learning why this is so is one of the chief reasons to study economics.

Thus, what makes the American economy stronger than all others—at least for now—is our unique combination of prosperity and population. There are other rich countries in the world, like Switzerland, and there are other countries with huge populations, like India. But no nation combines a huge population with high per capita income the way the United States does. China, with an economy two-thirds the size of ours, is the only nation that comes close—although per capita income in

## U.S. Share of World GDP—It's Nice to Be Rich

The approximately 7 billion people of the world produced approximately $87.2 trillion worth of goods and services in 2013. The United States, with only about 4.5 percent of that population, turned out almost 20 percent of total output. As the accompanying graph shows, among the seven largest developed countries of the world, the United States is still the leader in goods and services, with almost $53,000 worth of GDP produced per person (or per capita). These seven major industrial economies (the United States, Japan, Germany, France, Italy, the United Kingdom, and Canada—which account for just over 10 percent of global population) generated almost 40 percent of world output in 2013. But their share has been falling as giant developing nations like China and India grow rapidly.

SOURCES: Central Intelligence Agency, *The World Factbook*, https://www.cia.gov/library/publications/the-world-factbook/rankorder/2004rank.html; https://www.cia.gov/library/publications/the-world-factbook/fields/2119.html#xx; and https://www.cia.gov/library/publications/the-world-factbook/fields/2001.html#xx.
NOTE: Foreign GDPs are converted to U.S. dollars using exchange rates.

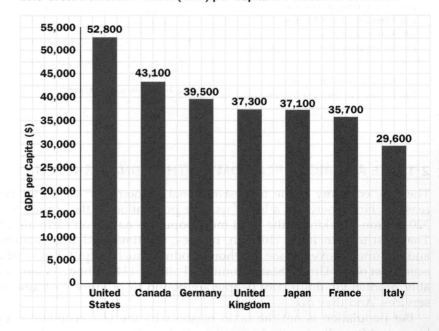

**2013 Gross Domestic Product (GDP) per Capita in 7 Industrial Countries**

GDP per Capita ($)

| Country | GDP per Capita |
|---|---|
| United States | 52,800 |
| Canada | 43,100 |
| Germany | 39,500 |
| United Kingdom | 37,300 |
| Japan | 37,100 |
| France | 35,700 |
| Italy | 29,600 |

China, where the labor force alone is almost triple the size of the entire U.S. population, remains low.

Although the United States is a rich and populous country, the 50 states certainly were not created equal. Population density varies enormously—from a high of about 1,200 people per square mile in crowded New Jersey to a low of just one person per square mile in the wide-open spaces of Alaska. Income variations are much less pronounced, but still, in 2012, the average income for a family of four in Mississippi was only about half that in Maryland.

## 2-1a  A Private-Enterprise Economy

Part of the secret of America's economic success is that free markets and private enterprise have flourished here. These days, private enterprise and capitalism are the rule, not the exception, around the globe. But the United States has taken the idea of free markets—where individuals and businesses voluntarily buy and sell things—further than almost any other country. It remains the "land of opportunity."

Every country has a mixture of public and private ownership of property. Even in the darkest days of communism, Russians owned their own personal possessions. In our country, the post office and the electricity-producing Tennessee Valley Authority are enterprises of the federal government, and many cities and states own and operate mass transit facilities and sports stadiums. But the United States stands out among the world's nations as being one of the most "privatized." Few industrial assets are publicly owned in the United States. Even many city bus companies and almost all utilities (such as electricity, gas, and telephones) are run as private companies in the United States. In Europe, they are often government enterprises, though there is substantial movement toward transfer of government firms to private ownership.

The United States also has one of the most "marketized" economies on earth. The standard measure of the total output of an economy is called **gross domestic product** (GDP), a term that appears frequently in the news. The share of GDP that passes through markets in the United States is enormous. Although government purchases of goods and services amount to about 20 percent of GDP, much of that is purchased from private businesses. Direct government production of goods is extremely rare in our society.

**Gross domestic product (GDP)** is a measure of the size of the economy—the total amount it produces in a year. *Real GDP* adjusts this measure for changes in the purchasing power of money; that is, it corrects for inflation.

## 2-1b  A Relatively "Closed" Economy

All nations trade with one another, and the United States is no exception. As of 2013, our annual exports were nearly $2.3 trillion and our annual imports were more than $2.7 trillion. That's a lot of money, and so is the gap between them. But America's international trade often gets more attention than it deserves. The fact is that we still produce most of what we consume and consume most of what we produce, although the shares of imports and exports have been growing, as Figure 1 shows. In 1959, the average of exports and imports was only about 4 percent of GDP, a tiny fraction of the total. It has since gone up as high as 15.4 percent in 2011, before falling to just under 15 percent in 2013. Although this is no longer negligible, it still means that almost 86 percent of what Americans buy every year is made in the United States.

Among the most severe misconceptions about the U.S. economy is the myth that this country no longer manufactures anything, but imports everything from, say, China. In fact, as of 2013, only about 16 percent of U.S. GDP was imported, with imports from China making up less than one-fifth of all imports.

Economists use the terms *open* and *closed* to indicate how important international trade is to a nation. A common measure of "openness" is the average of exports and imports, expressed as a share of GDP. Thus, the Netherlands is considered an extremely **open economy** because it imports and exports more than two-thirds of its GDP. (See Table 1.) By this criterion, the United States stands out as the most **closed economy** among the advanced, industrial nations. We export and import a smaller share of GDP than all of the other countries listed in the table, including China and Russia.

An economy is called relatively **open** if its exports and imports constitute a large share of its GDP.

An economy is considered relatively **closed** if its exports and imports constitute a small share of GDP.

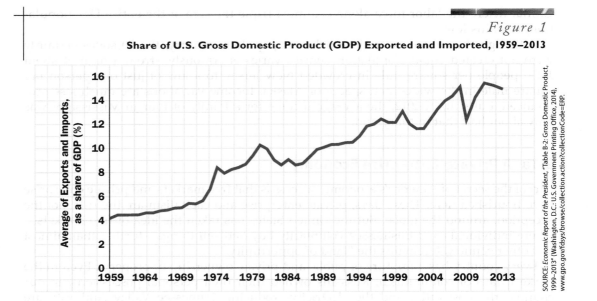

*Figure 1*

**Share of U.S. Gross Domestic Product (GDP) Exported and Imported, 1959–2013**

SOURCE: *Economic Report of the President,* "Table B-2: Gross Domestic Product, 1999–2013" (Washington, D.C.: U.S. Government Printing Office, 2014), www.gpo.gov/fdsys/browse/collection.action?collectionCode=ERP.

*Table 1*

**Openness of Various National Economies, 2013**

| | Openness |
|---|---|
| Netherlands | 77.7% |
| Germany | 42.2 |
| United Kingdom | 33.4 |
| Canada | 30.6 |
| Mexico | 20.1 |
| Russia | 16.7 |
| Japan | 15.5 |
| China | 15.5 |
| **United States** | **14.9** |

NOTE: Openness calculated as the average of imports and exports as a percentage of GDP.

SOURCE: For United States, *Economic Report of the President, 1999–2013* (Washington, D.C.: U.S. Government Printing Office, 2014); for all other countries, Central Intelligence Agency, *The World Factbook,* "Table B-2: Gross Domestic Product, 1999–2013," https://www.cia.gov/library/publications/the-world-factbook.

## 2-1c  A Growing Economy ...

The next salient fact about the U.S. economy is its growth; it gets bigger almost every year (see Figure 2). Gross domestic product in 2013 was more than $15.7 trillion; as noted earlier, that's almost $53,000 per American. Measured in dollars of constant purchasing power,[1] the U.S. GDP was more than five times as large in 2013 as it was in 1960. Of course, there were many more people in America in 2013 than there were then. But even correcting for population growth, America's real GDP *per capita* was four times higher in 2013 than in 1960. That's still not a bad performance: Living standards quadrupled in 50 years.

Looking back further, the purchasing power of the average American increased nearly ninefold over the entire twentieth century! That's a remarkable number. To get an idea of what it means, just think how much poorer your family would become if it started out with an average U.S. income and then, suddenly, eight dollars out of nine were taken away. Most Americans at the end of the nineteenth century could not afford vacations; the men had one good suit of clothing, which they listed in their wills; and they wrote with ink that was kept in inkwells (and that froze every winter).

## 2-1d  But with Bumps along the Growth Path

Although the cumulative growth performance depicted in Figure 2 is impressive, America's economic growth has been quite irregular. We have experienced alternating periods of good and bad times, which are called *economic fluctuations* or sometimes just *business cycles*. In some years—five since 1960, to be exact—GDP actually declined. Such periods of *declining* economic activity are called **recessions**.

A **recession** is a period of time during which the total output of the economy falls.

The bumps along the American economy's historic growth path are barely visible in Figure 2, but they stand out more clearly in Figure 3, which displays the same data in a different way. Here we plot not the *level* of real GDP each year but, rather, its *growth rate*—the percentage change from one year to the next. Now the booms and busts that delight and distress people—and swing elections—stand out clearly. From 1983 to 1984, for example,

---

[1] This concept is called *real* GDP.

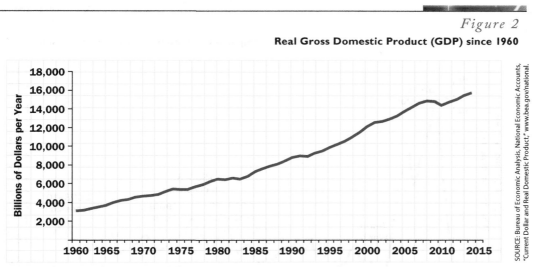

*Figure 2*

**Real Gross Domestic Product (GDP) since 1960**

NOTE: Real (inflation-adjusted) GDP figures are in billions of chained 2009 dollars.

SOURCE: Bureau of Economic Analysis, National Economic Accounts, "Current Dollar and Real Domestic Product." www.bea.gov/national.

real GDP grew by more than 7 percent, which helped ensure Ronald Reagan's landslide reelection. But from 2008 to 2009, real GDP actually dropped sharply, causing all sorts of social distress.

One important consequence of these ups and downs in economic growth is that *unemployment* varies considerably from one year to the next (see Figure 4). During the Great Depression of the 1930s, unemployment ran as high as 25 percent of the workforce, but it fell to barely over 1 percent during World War II. Just within the past few years, the national unemployment rate has been as high as 10.1 percent (in October 2009) and as low as 3.8 percent (in April 2000). In human terms, that 6.3 percentage point difference represents approximately 10 million jobless workers. Understanding why joblessness varies so dramatically, and what we can do about it, is another major reason for studying economics.

*Figure 3*

**The Growth Rate of Real Gross Domestic Product (GDP) in the United States since 1960**

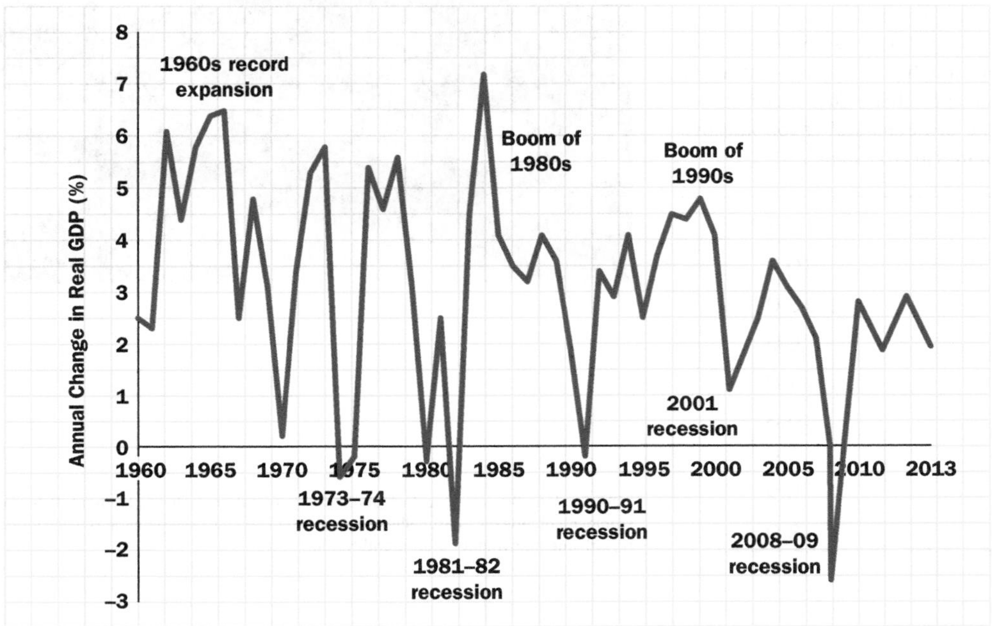

NOTE: Growth rates are for 1959–1960, 1960–1961, and so on.

SOURCE: *Economic Report of the President*, "Table B-4: Growth Rates in Real Gross Domestic Product by Area and Country, 1995–2014" (Washington, D.C.: U.S. Government Printing Office, 2014), www.gpo.gov/fdsys/browse/collection.action?collectionCode=ERP.

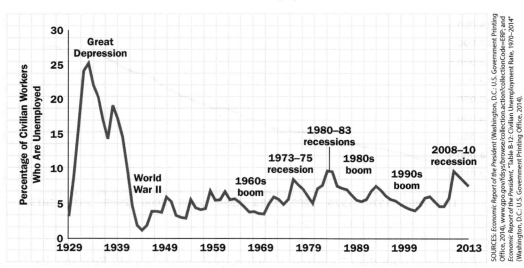

*Figure 4*

**The Unemployment Rate in the United States since 1929**

SOURCES: *Economic Report of the President* (Washington, D.C.: U.S. Government Printing Office, 2014), www.gpo.gov/fdsys/browse/collection.action?collectionCode=ERP; and *Economic Report of the President*, "Table B-12: Civilian Unemployment Rate, 1970–2014" (Washington, D.C.: U.S. Government Printing Office, 2014).

## 2-2  THE INPUTS: LABOR AND CAPITAL

Let's now return to the analogy of an economy as a machine turning inputs into outputs. The most important input is human labor: the men and women who run the machines, work behind the desks, and serve you in stores.

## Unemployment Rates in Europe

For roughly the first quarter-century after World War II, unemployment rates in the industrialized countries of Europe were significantly lower than those in the United States. Then, in the mid-1970s, rates of joblessness in Europe leaped, with double digits becoming common. And they were higher than U.S. unemployment rates in almost every year since—until recently, when the U.S. unemployment rate jumped by 60 percent, from 5.8 percent in 2008 to 9.3 percent in 2009. By 2012, unemployment rates in the United States had fallen back to roughly 8 percent—just about average, when compared with European and other industrialized economies. Put on a comparable basis by the U.S. Bureau of Labor Statistics, unemployment rates in the various countries in 2012 were:

| U.S. | 8.1% |
|---|---|
| Italy | 10.8 |
| France | 10.0 |
| United Kingdom | 8.0 |
| Sweden | 7.9 |
| Canada | 6.3 |
| Germany | 5.5 |
| Australia | 5.2 |
| Japan | 3.9 |

SOURCE: U.S. Bureau of Labor Statistics, "International Unemployment Rates and Employment Indexes, Seasonally Adjusted, 2009–2013," accessed online at www.bls.gov/fls/intl_unemployment_rates_monthly.pdf.

LEON NEAL/Getty Images

## 2-2a  The American Workforce: Who Is in It?

We have already mentioned that as of 2013, about 144 million Americans held jobs. Just over 48 percent of these workers were men; nearly 52 percent were women. This ratio represents a drastic change from two generations ago, when most women worked only at home (see Figure 5). Indeed, the massive entrance of women into the paid labor force was one of the major social transformations of American life during the second half of the twentieth century. In 1960, women accounted for just over 30 percent of the American labor force; as of 2013, women made up more than half of the labor force. As Figure 6 shows, the share of women in the labor forces of other industrial countries has also been growing. The expanding role of women in the labor market has raised many controversial questions—whether they are discriminated against (the evidence suggests that they are), whether the government should compel employers to provide maternity leave, and so on.

In contrast to women, the percentage of teenagers in the workforce has dropped significantly since its peak in the mid-1970s (see Figure 7). Young men and women ages

*Figure 5*

**The Composition of Employment by Sex, 1950 and 2013**

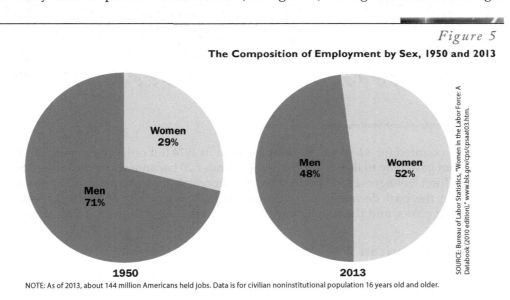

**1950**

Men 71%

Women 29%

**2013**

Men 48%

Women 52%

SOURCE: Bureau of Labor Statistics, "Women in the Labor Force: A Databook (2010 edition)," www.bls.gov/cps/cpsaat03.htm.

NOTE: As of 2013, about 144 million Americans held jobs. Data is for civilian noninstitutional population 16 years old and older.

*Figure 6*

**Working Women as a Percentage of the Labor Force, 1960 versus 2012**

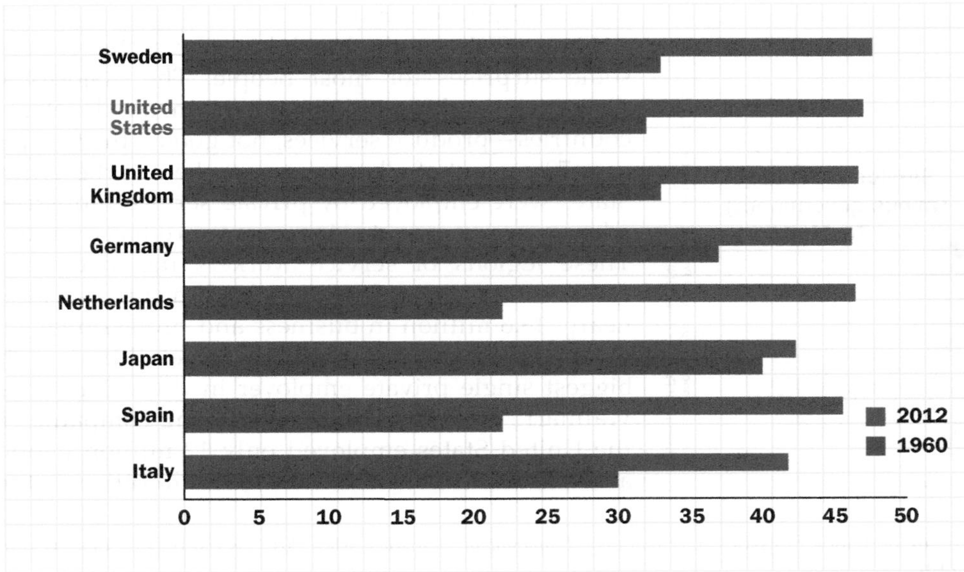

Sweden
United States
United Kingdom
Germany
Netherlands
Japan
Spain
Italy

0   5   10   15   20   25   30   35   40   45   50

■ 2012
■ 1960

SOURCES: "A Survey of Women and Work," *The Economist*, July 18, 1998, p. 4; and Organization for Economic Cooperation and Development, ALFS Summary Tables: Annual Labor Force Statistics, "Civilian Employment: http://stats.oecd.org.

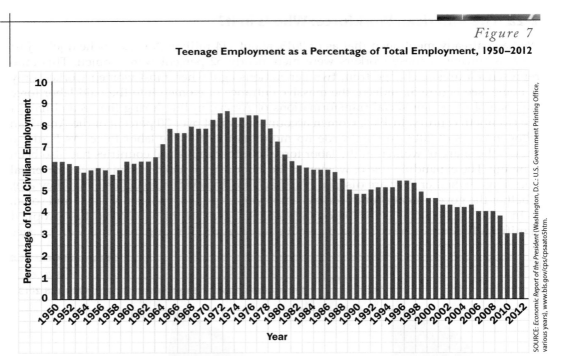

*Figure 7*

**Teenage Employment as a Percentage of Total Employment, 1950–2012**

NOTE: Data is for civilian noninstitutional population 16 to 19 years old.

SOURCE: *Economic Report of the President* (Washington, D.C.: U.S. Government Printing Office, various years), www.bls.gov/cps/cpsaato5htm.

16 to 19 accounted for 8.6 percent of employment in 1974 but only 3 percent in 2013. As the baby boom gave way to the baby bust, people under 20 became scarce resources! Still, just over 4 million teenagers hold jobs in the U.S. economy today—a number that has declined steadily in the past decade. Most teenagers fill low-wage jobs at fast-food restaurants, amusement parks, and the like. Relatively few can be found in the nation's factories.

## 2-2b The American Workforce: What Does It Do?

What do these 144 million working Americans do? The only real answer is: almost anything you can imagine. In May 2013, America had 84,210 architects, 312,340 computer programmers, 580,570 carpenters, almost 2.4 million truck drivers, 592,670 lawyers, roughly 755,210 secretaries, 157,800 kindergarten teachers, 30,890 pediatricians, 67,810 tax preparers, 17,340 physicists, 302,870 fire fighters, and 17,230 economists.[2]

Figure 8 shows the breakdown by sector. It holds some surprises for most people. The majority of American workers—like workers in all developed countries—produce services, not goods. In 2013, just over 70 percent of all non-farm workers in the United States were employed by private service industries, whereas only about 14 percent produced goods. These legions of service workers included about 21.1 million in educational and health services, nearly 18.6 million in business and professional services, and more than 15 million in retail trade. (The biggest single private employer in the country was Walmart.) By contrast, manufacturing companies in the United States employed only 12 million people, and almost a third of those worked in offices rather

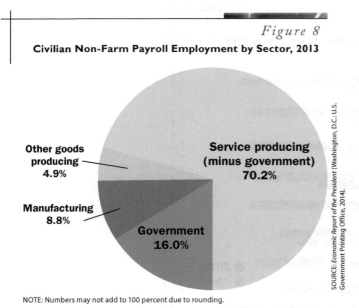

*Figure 8*

**Civilian Non-Farm Payroll Employment by Sector, 2013**

Other goods producing 4.9%

Manufacturing 8.8%

Government 16.0%

Service producing (minus government) 70.2%

SOURCE: *Economic Report of the President* (Washington, D.C.: U.S. Government Printing Office, 2014).

NOTE: Numbers may not add to 100 percent due to rounding.

[2] U.S. Bureau of Labor Statistics, *Occupational Employment Statistics, May 2013*, www.bls.gov/oes/current/oes_stru.htm.

than in the factory. The Homer Simpson image of the typical American worker as a blue-collar worker is really quite misleading.

As of 2013, federal, state, and local governments employed about 22 million people but, contrary to another popular misconception, few of these civil servants work for the *federal* government. Federal *civilian* employment was about 2.8 million—about 10 percent lower than it was in the 1980s. (The armed forces employed about another 1.2 million men and women in uniform.) State and local governments provided almost 19.1 million jobs—or about seven times the number of federal government jobs. In addition to the jobs categorized in Figure 8, approximately 2 million people were working on farms in the United States, and almost 9 million were self-employed.

As Figure 9 shows, *all* industrialized countries have become "service economies" in recent decades. To a considerable degree, this shift to services reflects the arrival of the "Information Age." Activities related to computers, to research, to the transmission of information by teaching and publication, and other information-related activities are providing many of the new jobs. This means that, in the rich economies, workers who moved out of manufacturing jobs into the service sectors have not gone predominantly into low-skill jobs such as dishwashing or housecleaning. Many found employment in service jobs in which education and experience provide a great advantage. At the same time, technological change has made it possible to produce more and more manufactured products using fewer and fewer workers. Such labor-saving innovation in manufacturing has allowed a considerable share of the labor force to move out of goods-producing jobs and into services.

*Figure 9*

**The Growing Share of Service Sector Jobs, 1967 versus 2012**

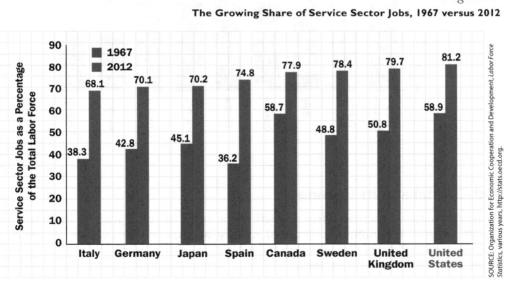

SOURCE: Organization for Economic Cooperation and Development, *Labor Force Statistics*, various years, http://stats.oecd.org.

## 2-2c  The American Workforce: What Does It Earn?

Altogether, these workers' wages accounted for more than 60 percent of the income that the production process generated in 2011. That figures up to an average hourly wage of just over $20 in 2013—plus fringe benefits like health insurance and pensions, which can contribute an additional 30 to 40 percent for some workers. Because the average workweek was about 33 hours long in 2013, a typical weekly paycheck in the United States was almost $680 before taxes (but excluding the value of benefits). That is hardly a princely sum, and most college graduates can expect to earn substantially more.[3] But that pay is typical of average wage rates in a rich country like the United States.

---

[3] As of 2010, high school graduates typically earned just 60 percent of what workers with undergraduate college degrees were earning. Data from Bureau of Labor Statistics, "Labor Force Statistics from the Current Population Survey." Earnings by education, www.bls.gov/emp/ep_chart_001.htm.

Wages throughout northern Europe are similar. Indeed, workers in a number of other industrial countries now receive higher compensation than American workers do—a big change from the situation a few decades ago. According to the U.S. Bureau of Labor Statistics, in 2011 workers in U.S. manufacturing industries made less than those in many European countries (see Figure 10). However, U.S. compensation levels still remain above those in the United Kingdom and many other countries.

*Figure 10*

**Average Hourly Compensation Rates in Manufacturing, 2011**

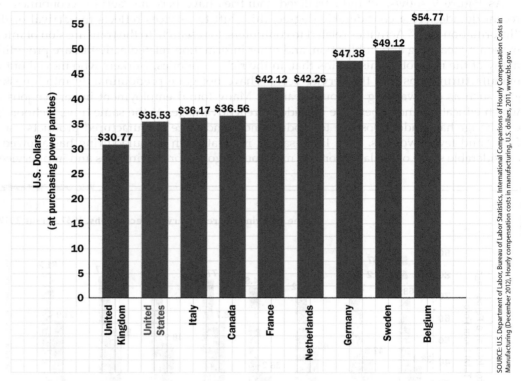

SOURCE: U.S. Department of Labor, Bureau of Labor Statistics, International Comparisons of Hourly Compensation Costs in Manufacturing (December 2012), Hourly compensation costs in manufacturing, U.S. dollars, 2011, www.bls.gov.

## 2-2d  Capital and Its Earnings

The rest of national income (after deducting the small sliver of income that goes to the owners of land and natural resources) mainly accrues to the owners of *capital*—the machines and buildings that make up the nation's industrial plant.

The total market value of these business assets—a tough number to estimate—is believed to be in the neighborhood of $30 trillion. Because that capital earns an average rate of return of about 10 percent before taxes, total earnings of capital—including corporate profits, interest, and all the rest—come to about $3 trillion.

Public opinion polls routinely show that Americans have a distorted view of the level of business profits in our society. The man and woman on the street believe that corporate profits after tax account for about 30 percent of the price of a typical product. (See the box "Public Opinion on Corporate Profits.") The correct number is closer to 8 percent.

## 2-3  THE OUTPUTS: WHAT DOES AMERICA PRODUCE?

What does all this labor and capital produce? Consumer spending accounts for about 70 percent of GDP. And what an amazing variety of goods and services it buys. In 2012, American households spent two-thirds of their budgets on services, with housing commanding the largest share (followed closely by health care). The other 34 percent of American budgets went for goods.

## Public Opinion on Corporate Profits

Years ago, a public opinion poll found that the average American thought that corporate profits *after taxes* amounted to 32 percent of sales for the typical manufacturing company. At the time, the actual profit rate was closer to 4 percent!* Interestingly, when a previous poll asked how much profit was "reasonable," the response was 26 cents on every dollar of sales—more than six times as large as profits actually were.

*This poll was conducted in 1986. Corporate profit rates increased considerably in the 1990s and 2000s.

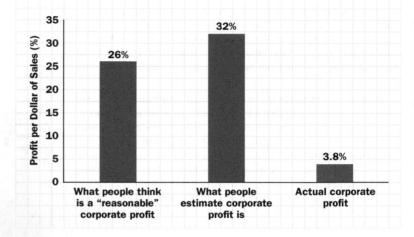

SOURCE: "Public Attitudes toward Corporate Profits," *Public Opinion Index* (Princeton, NJ: Opinion Research Corporation, June 1986).

This leaves about 40 percent of GDP for all *nonconsumption* uses. That includes government services (buying such things as airplanes, guns, and the services of soldiers, teachers, and bureaucrats), business purchases of machinery and industrial structures, and consumer purchases of new houses.

## 2-4 THE CENTRAL ROLE OF BUSINESS FIRMS

Calvin Coolidge once said that "the business of America is business." Although this statement often has been ridiculed, he was largely right. When we peer inside the economic machine that turns inputs into outputs, we see mainly private companies. Astonishingly, in 2011, there were 28.2 million business firms in the United States—about one for every 11 people!

The owners and managers of these businesses hire people, acquire or rent capital goods, and arrange to produce things consumers want to buy. Sound simple? It isn't. In the decade preceding the financial crisis, an average of roughly 10 percent of all businesses failed each year.[4] A few succeed spectacularly. Some do both. Fortunately for the U.S. economy, however, the lure of riches induces hundreds of thousands of people to start new businesses every year—against the odds.

A number of the biggest firms do business all over the world, just as foreign-based *multinational corporations* do business here. Indeed, some people claim that it is now impossible to determine the true "nationality" of a multinational corporation—which may have factories in 10 or more countries, sell its wares all over the world, and have stockholders in dozens of nations. (See the box "Is That an American Company?") Ford, for example, generates more profits abroad than at home, and the Toyota you drive was probably assembled in the United States.

Firms compete with other companies in their *industry*. Most economists believe that this *competition* is the key to industrial efficiency. A sole supplier of a commodity will find it easy to make money, and may, therefore, fail to innovate or control costs. Its management is liable to become relaxed and sloppy. But a company besieged by dozens of competitors

---

[4] This number is the average of the business failure rates for 1997–2007; U.S. Census Bureau, Statistics of U.S. Businesses Annual Data, accessed online at www.census.gov/econ/susb.

## Is That an American Company?

Robert Reich, who was Secretary of Labor in the Clinton administration, argued some years ago that it was already nearly impossible to define the nationality of a multinational company. Although many scholars think Reich exaggerated the point, no one doubts that he had one—nor that the nationalities of corporations have become increasingly blurred since then. He wrote in 1991:

What's the difference between an "American" corporation that makes or buys abroad much of what it sells around the world and a "foreign" corporation that makes or buys in the United States much of what it sells? ... The mind struggles to keep the players straight. In 1990, Canada's Northern Telecom was selling to its American customers telecommunications equipment made by Japan's NTT at NTT's factory in North Carolina.

If you found that one too easy, try this: Beginning in 1991, Japan's Mazda would be producing Ford Probes at Mazda's plant in Flat Rock, Michigan. Some of these cars would be exported to Japan and sold there under Ford's trademark.

A Mazda-designed compact utility vehicle would be built at a Ford plant in Louisville, Kentucky, and then sold at Mazda dealerships in the United States. Nissan, meanwhile, was designing a new light truck at its San Diego, California, design center. The trucks would be assembled at Ford's Ohio truck plant, using panel parts fabricated by Nissan at its Tennessee factory, and then marketed by both Ford and Nissan in the United States and in Japan. Who is Ford? Nissan? Mazda?

Mark Elias/Bloomberg/Getty Images

SOURCE: Robert B. Reich, *The Work of Nations* (New York: Knopf, 1991), pp. 124, 131.

eager to take its business away must constantly seek ways to innovate, to cut costs, and to build a better mousetrap. The rewards for business success can be magnificent. But the punishment for failure is severe.

## 2-5 WHAT'S MISSING FROM THE PICTURE? GOVERNMENT

Thus far, we have the following capsule summary of how the U.S. economy works: More than 28 million private businesses, energized by the profit motive, employ about 144 million workers and about $30 trillion of capital. These firms bring their enormously diverse wares to a bewildering variety of different markets, where they try to sell them to more than 300 million consumers.

It is in *markets*—places where goods and services are bought and sold—that these millions of households and businesses meet to conduct transactions, as depicted in Figure 11. Only a few of these markets are concrete physical locations, such as fish markets or stock exchanges. Most are more abstract "places," where business may be conducted by telephone or the Internet—even if the commodity being traded is a physical object. For example, there are no centralized *physical* marketplaces for buying cars or computers, but there are highly competitive markets for these goods nonetheless.

As Figure 11 suggests, firms use their receipts from selling goods and services in the markets for *outputs* to pay wages to employees and interest and profits to the people who provide capital in the markets for *inputs*. These income flows, in turn, enable consumers to purchase the goods and services that companies produce. This circular flow of money, goods, and factors of production lies at the center of the analysis of how the national economy works. All these activities are linked by a series of interconnected markets, some of which are highly competitive and others of which are less so.

All very well and good. But the story leaves out something important: the role of *government,* which is pervasive even in our decidedly free-market economy. Just what does government do in the U.S. economy—and why?

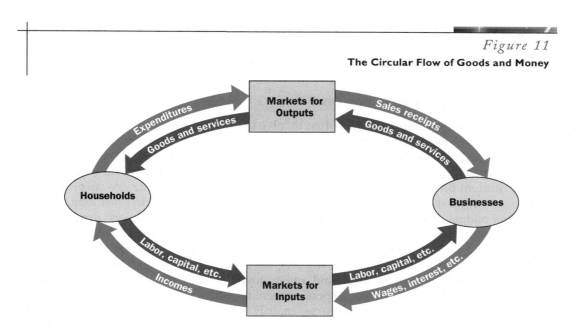

*Figure 11*

**The Circular Flow of Goods and Money**

Although an increasing number of tasks seem to get assigned to the state each year, the traditional role of government in a market economy revolves around five jobs:

- Making and enforcing the laws
- Regulating business
- Providing certain goods and services such as national defense
- Levying taxes to pay for these goods and services
- Redistributing income

Every one of these tasks is steeped in controversy and surrounded by intense political debate. We conclude this chapter with a brief look at each.

## 2-5a  The Government as Referee

For the most part, power is diffused in our economy, and people "play by the rules." But in the scramble for competitive advantage, disputes are bound to arise. Did Company A live up to its contract? Who owns that disputed piece of property? In addition, some unscrupulous businesses are liable to step over the line now and then—as we saw in many cases of fraud that helped bring on the debacle in subprime mortgages in 2007–2009.

Enter the government as rule maker, referee, and arbitrator. Congress and state and local legislatures pass the laws that define the rules of the economic game. The executive branches of all three governmental levels share the responsibility for enforcing them. And the courts interpret the laws and adjudicate disputes.

## 2-5b  The Government as Business Regulator

Nothing is pure in this world of ours. Even in "free-market" economies, governments interfere with the workings of free markets in many ways and for myriad reasons. Some government activities seek to make markets work better. For example, America's *antitrust laws* are used to protect competition against possible encroachment by monopoly. Some regulations seek to promote social objectives that unfettered markets do not foster— environmental regulations are a particularly clear case. But as critics like to point out, some economic regulations have no clear rationale at all.

We mentioned earlier that the American belief in free enterprise runs deep. For this reason, the regulatory role of government is more contentious here than in most other countries. After all, Thomas Jefferson said that government is best that governs least.

Two hundred years later, Presidents Reagan, Bush (both of them), and Clinton all pledged to dismantle inappropriate regulations—and sometimes did. But the financial crisis of 2007–2009 has led to many calls for new and tighter regulations, especially in finance.

### 2-5c  Government Expenditures

The most contentious political issues often involve taxing and spending because those are the government's most prominent roles. Democrats and Republicans, both in the White House and in Congress, have frequently battled fiercely over the federal budget. In 1995 and 1996, such disputes even led to some temporary shutdowns of the federal government. Under President Bill Clinton, the government managed to achieve a sizable surplus in its budget—meaning that tax receipts exceeded expenditures. But it didn't last long. Today the federal budget is deeply in the red, and prospects for getting it balanced are poor.

During fiscal year 2012, the federal government spent more than $3.7 *trillion*—a sum that is literally beyond comprehension. Figure 12 shows where the money went. One-third went for *pensions and income security programs,* which include both social insurance programs (such as Social Security and unemployment compensation) and programs designed to assist the poor. Almost 20 percent went for *national defense.* Another 25 percent was absorbed by *health-care* expenditures, mainly on Medicare and Medicaid. Adding in *interest on the national debt,* these four functions alone accounted for 75 percent of all federal spending. The rest went for a miscellany of other purposes including education, transportation, agriculture, housing, and foreign aid.

Government spending at the state and local levels was about $2.3 trillion. Education claimed the largest share of state and local government budgets (32 percent), with health and public welfare programs a distant second (22 percent). Despite this vast outpouring of public funds, many observers believe that serious social needs remain unmet. Critics claim that our public infrastructure (such as bridges and roads) is only adequate, that our educational system is lacking, that we are not spending enough on homeland defense, and so on.

Although the scale and scope of government activity in the United States is substantial, it is quite moderate when we compare it to other leading economies, as we will see next.

### 2-5d  Taxes in America

Taxes finance this array of goods and services, and sometimes it seems that the tax collector is everywhere. We have income and payroll taxes withheld from our paychecks, sales taxes added to our purchases, and property taxes levied on our homes; we pay gasoline taxes, liquor taxes, and telephone taxes.

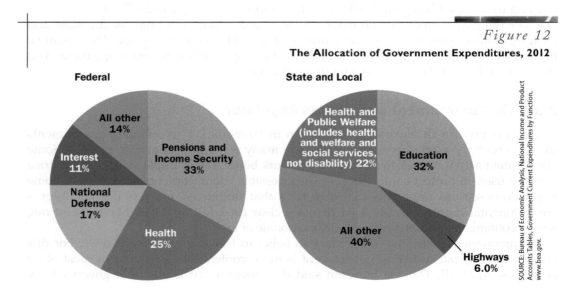

*Figure 12*

**The Allocation of Government Expenditures, 2012**

**Federal**

All other 14%

Interest 11%

National Defense 17%

Pensions and Income Security 33%

Health 25%

**State and Local**

Health and Public Welfare (includes health and welfare and social services, not disability) 22%

Education 32%

All other 40%

Highways 6.0%

SOURCE: Bureau of Economic Analysis, National Income and Product Accounts Tables, Government Current Expenditures by Function, www.bea.gov.

Americans have always felt that taxes are both too many and too high. In the 1980s and 1990s, antitax sentiment became a dominant feature of the U.S. political scene. The old slogan "no taxation without representation" gave way to the new slogan "no new taxes." Yet, by international standards, Americans are among the most lightly taxed people in the world. Figure 13 compares the fraction of income paid in taxes in the United States with those paid by residents of other wealthy nations. The tax share in the United States fell notably during the early years of George W. Bush's presidency, but has since crept up a bit and threatens to go higher.

## Figure 13
### The Tax Burden in Selected Countries, 2012

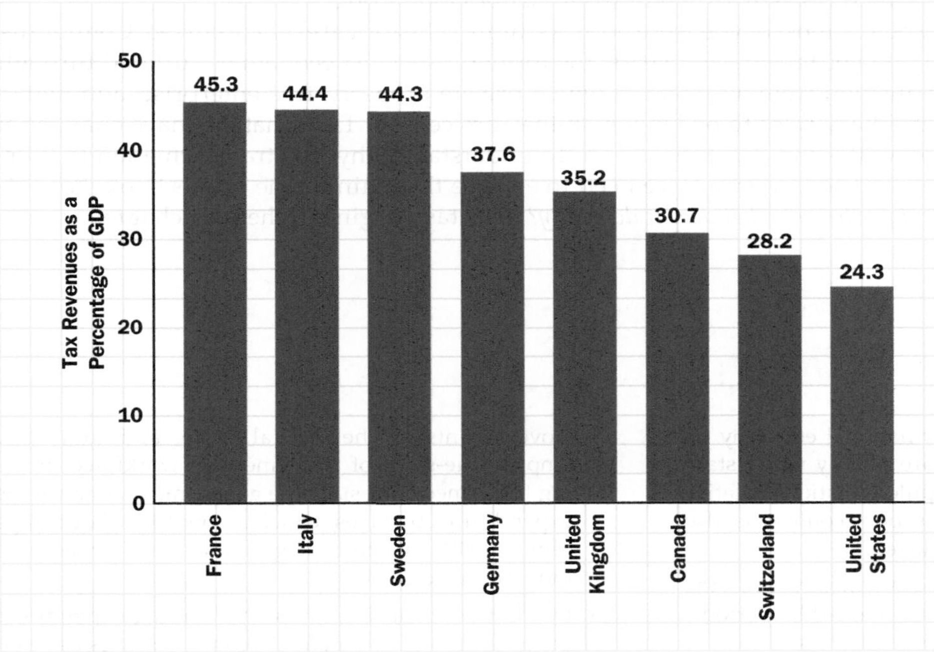

SOURCE: Organization for Economic Cooperation and Development, Revenue Statistics: Comparative Tables, Total Tax Revenue, "Tax Revenue as Percentage of GDP," accessed online at www.stats.oecd.org.

## 2-5e The Government as Redistributor

In a market economy, people earn incomes according to what they have to sell. Unfortunately, many people have nothing to sell but unskilled labor, which commands a paltry price. Others lack even that. Such people fare poorly in unfettered markets. In extreme cases, they are homeless, hungry, and ill. According to popular retellings, Robin Hood transferred money from the rich to the poor. Some think the government should do the same; others disagree.

If poverty amid riches offends your moral sensibilities—a personal judgment that each of us must make for ourselves—two basic remedial approaches are possible. The socialist idea is to force the distribution of income to be more equal by overriding the decisions of the market. "From each according to his ability, to each according to his needs" was Marx's ideal. In practice, things were not quite so noble under socialism in the old Soviet Union, but in Sweden, which borrowed many ideas from socialism when it established its generous social welfare system, incomes are more equally distributed than those in the United States.

The liberal idea is to let free markets determine the distribution of *before-tax* incomes, but then to use the tax system and **transfer payments** to reduce inequality—just as Robin Hood did. This is the rationale for, among other things, **progressive taxation** and antipoverty programs. Americans who support redistribution line up solidly behind the liberal

**Transfer payments** are sums of money that certain individuals receive as outright grants from the government rather than as payments for services rendered.

A tax is **progressive** if the ratio of taxes to income rises as income rises.

approach. But which ways are the best, and how much is enough? No simple answers have emerged from many decades of debate on these highly contentious questions. Lately, as wage disparities have widened, the inequality issue has gained prominence on the national political agenda. It figured prominently in the 2008 presidential campaign, for example.

## 2-6  CONCLUSION: IT'S A MIXED ECONOMY

Ideology notwithstanding, all nations at all times blend public and private ownership of property in some proportions. All rely on markets for some purposes, but all also assign some role to government. Hence, people speak of the ubiquity of **mixed economies**. But mixing is not homogenization; different countries can and do blend the state and market sectors in different ways. Even today, the Russian economy is a far cry from the Italian economy, which is vastly different from that of Hong Kong.

Shortly before most of you were born, a stunning historical event occurred: Communism collapsed all over Europe. For years, the formerly socialist economies suffered through a painful transition from a system in which private property, free enterprise, and markets played subsidiary roles to one in which they are central. These nations have changed the mix, if you will—and dramatically so. To understand why this transformation is at once so difficult and so important, we need to explore the main theme of this book: *What does the market do well, and what does it do poorly?* This task begins in the next chapter.

A **mixed economy** is one with some public influence over the workings of free markets. There may also be some public ownership mixed in with private property.

## Summary

1. The U.S. economy is the biggest national economy on earth, both because Americans are rich by world standards and because we are a populous nation. Relative to most other advanced countries, our economy is also exceptionally "privatized" and closed.

2. The U.S. economy has grown dramatically over the years. But this growth has been interrupted by periodic **recessions**, during which unemployment rises.

3. The United States has a big, diverse workforce whose composition by age and sex has been changing substantially. Relatively few workers these days work in factories or on farms; most work in service industries.

4. Employees take home most of the nation's income. Most of the rest goes, in the forms of interest and profits, to those who provide the capital.

5. Governments at the federal, state, and local levels employ one-sixth of the American workforce (including the armed forces). These governments finance their expenditures by taxes, which account for about 24 percent of GDP. This percentage is one of the lowest in the industrialized world.

6. In addition to raising taxes and making expenditures, the government in a market economy serves as referee and enforcer of the rules, regulates business in a variety of ways, and redistributes income through taxes and **transfer payments**. For all these reasons, we say that we have a **mixed economy**, which blends private and public elements.

## Key Terms

| | | |
|---|---|---|
| closed economy   23 | mixed economy   36 | progressive tax   35 |
| factors of production, or inputs   22 | open economy   23 | recession   24 |
| gross domestic product (GDP)   23 | outputs   22 | transfer payments   35 |

## Discussion Questions

1. Which is the biggest national economy on earth? Why has it remained bigger than other countries with much larger labor forces or those with higher per capita incomes?

2. What is meant by a "factor of production"? Have you ever sold any on a market?

3. Why do you think per capita income in Connecticut is nearly double that in New Mexico?

4. Roughly speaking, what fraction of U.S. labor works in factories? In service businesses? In government?

5. Most American businesses are small, but most of the output is produced by large businesses. That sounds paradoxical. How can it be true?

6. What is the role of government in a mixed economy?

# THE FUNDAMENTAL ECONOMIC PROBLEM: SCARCITY AND CHOICE

# 3

*Our necessities are few but our wants are endless.*

INSCRIPTION ON A FORTUNE COOKIE

Understanding what the market system does well and what it does badly is this book's central task. To address this complex issue, we must first answer a simpler one: What do economists expect the market to accomplish?

The most common answer is that the market resolves what is often called *the* fundamental economic problem: how best to manage the resources of society, doing as well as possible with them, despite their scarcity. All decisions are constrained by the scarcity of available resources. A dreamer may envision a world free of want, in which everyone, even in Africa and Central America, drives a BMW and eats caviar, but the earth lacks the resources needed to make that dream come true. Because resources are scarce, all economic decisions involve *trade-offs*. Should you use that $5 bill to buy pizza or a new writing pad for econ class? Should General Motors invest more money in improving assembly lines or in research? A well-functioning market system facilitates and guides such decisions, assigning each hour of labor and each kilowatt-hour of electricity to the task where, it is hoped, the input will best serve the public.

This chapter shows how economists analyze choices like these. The same basic principles, founded on the concept of *opportunity cost*, apply to the decisions made by business firms, governments, and society as a whole. Many of the most basic ideas of economics, such as *efficiency, division of labor, comparative advantage, exchange,* and *the role of markets* appear here for the first time.

## CONTENTS

| Issue | *What to Do about the Budget Deficit?* |

Thanks to a combination of strong economic growth in the late 1990s and the deficit-reducing policies of the Clinton administration, the federal budget deficit melted away like the springtime snow and actually turned into a budget *surplus* for a few fiscal years (1998 through 2001). For a while, the need to make agonizing *choices* seemed to disappear—or so it seemed. But it was an illusion.

Even during that brief era of budget surpluses, hard choices still had to be made. The U.S. government could not afford *everything*. Then, as the stock market collapsed, the economy slowed, and President George W. Bush pushed large tax cuts through Congress, the budget surpluses quickly turned back into deficits again.

Then the Great Recession of 2007–2009 struck, and the federal budget went even more deeply into the red. Tax revenues fell as the economy sagged, and then the Obama administration pushed through a major fiscal "stimulus" bill in 2009—which both cut taxes and raised spending. By 2010, the size of the fiscal deficit was scaring politicians, who started debating which spending programs should be cut and which, if any, of the Bush tax cuts should be repealed. These debates continue to this day.

Yes, even a government with an annual budget of almost $3.5 *trillion* was forced to set priorities and make hard choices.

The lesson is simple: Even when resources are quite generous, they are never unlimited. So everyone must still make tough choices. An *optimal* decision is one that chooses the most desirable alternative *among the possibilities permitted by the available resources,* which are always scarce in this sense.

© Hisham Ibrahim/Photodisc/Getty Images

## 3-1  SCARCITY, CHOICE, AND OPPORTUNITY COST

**Resources** are the instruments provided by nature or by people that are used to create goods and services. Natural resources include minerals, soil, water, and air. Labor is a scarce resource, partly because of time limitations (the day has only 24 hours) and partly because the number of skilled workers is limited. Factories and machines are resources made by people. These three types of resources are often referred to as *land, labor,* and *capital.* They are also called *inputs* or *factors of production.*

One of the basic themes of economics is scarcity—the fact that **resources** are always limited. Even Philip II, of Spanish Armada fame and ruler of one of the greatest empires in history, had to cope with frequent rebellions in his armies when he could not meet their payrolls or even get them basic provisions. He is reported to have undergone bankruptcy an astonishing eight times during his reign. In more recent years, the U.S. government has been agonizing over difficult budget decisions even though it spends more than $2 *trillion* annually.

But the scarcity of *physical resources* is more fundamental than the scarcity of funds. Fuel supplies, for example, are not limitless, and some environmentalists claim that we should now be making some hard choices—such as keeping our homes cooler in winter and warmer in summer and saving gas by living closer to our jobs. Although energy may be the most widely discussed scarcity, the general principle applies to all of the earth's resources—iron, copper, uranium, and so on. Even goods produced by human effort are in limited supply because they require fuel, labor, and other scarce resources as inputs. We can manufacture more cars, but the increased use of labor, steel, and fuel in auto production will mean that we must cutback on something else, perhaps the production of refrigerators. This all adds up to the following fundamental principle of economics, which we will encounter again and again in this text:

> **Virtually all resources are *scarce,* meaning that people have less of them than they would like. Therefore, choices must be made among a *limited* set of possibilities, in full recognition of the inescapable fact that a decision to have more of one thing means that people will have less of something else.**

In fact, one popular definition of economics is the study of how best to use *limited* means to pursue *unlimited* ends. Although this definition, like any short statement, cannot possibly cover the sweep of the entire discipline, it does convey the flavor of the economist's stock in trade.

To illustrate the true cost of an item, consider the decision to produce additional cars and, therefore, to produce fewer refrigerators. Although the production of a car may cost $15,000 per vehicle, for example, *its real cost to society is the refrigerators that society must forgo to get an additional car.* If the labor, steel, and energy needed to manufacture a car would be sufficient to make 30 refrigerators instead of the car, the **opportunity cost** of a car is 30 refrigerators. The principle of opportunity cost is so important that we will spend most of this chapter elaborating on it in various ways.

> The **opportunity cost** of any decision is the value of the next best alternative that the decision forces the decision maker to forgo.

**HOW MUCH DOES IT REALLY COST?**    The Principle of Opportunity-Cost Economics examines the options available to households, businesses, governments, and entire societies, given the limited resources at their command. It studies the logic of how people can make optimal decisions from among competing alternatives. One overriding principle governs this logic—a principle we introduced in Chapter 1 as one of the *Ideas for Beyond the Final Exam*: With limited resources, a decision to have *more* of one thing is simultaneously a decision to have *less* of something else. Hence, the relevant *cost* of any decision is its *opportunity cost*—the value of the next best alternative that is given up. Optimal decision making must be based on opportunity-cost calculations.

Ideas for Beyond the Final Exam

## 3-1a Opportunity Cost and Money Cost

Because we live in a market economy where (almost) everything has its price, students often wonder about the connection or difference between an item's *opportunity cost* and its *market price.* This statement seems to divorce the two concepts: The true opportunity cost of a car is not its market price but the value to its potential purchaser of the other things (like refrigerators) that could have been made or purchased instead.

But isn't the opportunity cost of a car related to its money cost? The normal answer is yes. The two costs are usually closely tied to one another because of the way in which a market economy sets prices. Steel, for example, is used to manufacture both automobiles and refrigerators. If consumers value items that can be made with steel (such as refrigerators) highly, then economists would say that the *opportunity cost* of making a car is high. But, under these circumstances, strong demand for this highly valued resource will bid up its market price. In this way, a well-functioning price system will assign a high price to steel, which will make the *money cost* of manufacturing a car high as well. In summary:

> If the market functions well, goods that have high opportunity costs will also have high money costs. In turn, goods that have low opportunity costs will also have low money costs.

Nevertheless, it would be a mistake to treat opportunity costs and explicit monetary costs as identical. For one thing, sometimes the market does not function well and hence assigns prices that do not accurately reflect opportunity costs. Moreover, some valuable items may not bear explicit price tags at all. We encountered one such example in Chapter 1, where we noted that the opportunity cost of a college education may differ sharply from its explicit money cost. Why? Because one important item is typically omitted from the money–cost calculation: the *market value of your time*; that is, the wages you could earn by working instead of attending college. Because you give up these potential wages, which can amount to $15,000 per year or more in order to acquire an education, they must be counted as a major part of the opportunity cost of going to college.

Other common examples where money costs and opportunity costs diverge are goods and services that are given away "free." For example, some early settlers of the American West destroyed natural amenities such as forests and buffalo herds, which had no market price, leaving later generations to pay the opportunity costs in terms of lost resources. Similarly, you incur no explicit

*"O.K. who can put a price on love? Jim?"*

Jack Ziegler/The New Yorker Collection/The Cartoon Bank

monetary cost to acquire an item that is given away for free. However, if you must wait in line to get the "free" commodity, you incur an opportunity cost equal to the value of the next best use of your time.

### 3-1b *Optimal* Choice: Not Just *Any* Choice

How do people and firms make decisions? There are many ways, some of them based on hunches with little forethought; some are even based on superstition or the advice of a fortune teller. Often, when the required information is scarce and the necessary research and calculations are costly and difficult, the decision maker will settle on the first possibility that he can "live with"—a choice that promises to yield results that are not too bad and that seem fairly safe. The decision maker may be willing to choose this course even though he recognizes that there might be other options that are better but are unknown to him. This way of deciding is called *satisficing*.

In this book, we will assume that decision makers seek to do better than mere satisficing. Rather, we will assume that they seek to reach decisions that are optimal—decisions that do better in achieving the decision makers' goals than any other possible choice. We will assume that the required information is available to the decision makers, and we will study the procedures that enable them to determine the optimal choices.

An **optimal decision** is one that best serves the objectives of the decision maker, whatever those objectives may be. It is selected by explicit or implicit comparison with the possible alternative choices. The term *optimal* does not mean that we, the observers or analysts, approve or disapprove of the objective itself.

> An **optimal decision** for individual X is one that is selected *after implicit or explicit comparison of the consequences of each of the possible choices* and that is shown by analysis to be the one that most effectively promotes the goals of person X.

We will study optimal decision making by various parties—consumers, producers, and sellers—in a variety of situations. The methods of analysis for determining what choice is optimal in each case will be remarkably similar. So, if you understand one of them, you will already be well on your way to understanding them all. A technique called *marginal analysis* will be used for this purpose. But one fundamental idea underlies any method used for optimal decision making: *To determine whether a possible decision is or is not optimal, its consequences must be compared with those of each of the other possible choices.*

## 3-2  SCARCITY AND CHOICE FOR A SINGLE FIRM

The **outputs** of a firm or an economy are the goods and services it produces.

The **inputs** used by a firm or an economy are the labor, raw materials, electricity, and other resources it uses to produce its outputs.

The nature of opportunity cost is perhaps clearest in the case of a single business firm that produces two **outputs** from a fixed supply of **inputs**. Given current technology and the limited resources at its disposal, the more of one good the firm produces, the less of the other it will be able to make. Unless managers explicitly weigh the desirability of each product against the other, they are unlikely to make rational production decisions.

Consider the example of Jones, a farmer whose available supplies of land, machinery, labor, and fertilizer are capable of producing the various combinations of soybeans and wheat listed in Table 1. Obviously, devoting more resources to soybean production means that Jones will produce less wheat. Table 1 indicates, for example, that if Jones grows only soybeans, the harvest will be 40,000 bushels. But if he reduces his soybean production to 30,000 bushels, he can also grow 38,000 bushels of wheat. Thus, *the opportunity cost of obtaining 38,000 bushels of wheat is 10,000 fewer bushels of soybeans.* Put another way, the opportunity cost of 10,000 more bushels of soybeans is 38,000 bushels of wheat. The other numbers in Table 1 have similar interpretations.

The situation becomes a little more complicated when the objective of the farmer is to earn as large a *money profit* as possible, rather than maximizing quantity of wheat or soybeans. Suppose producing 38,000 bushels of wheat requires Jones to give up 10,000, bushels of soybeans and $4,000 is the profit he would earn if he chose the wheat output,

| Table 1 | | |
|---|---|---|
| **Production Possibilities Open to a Farmer** | | |
| Bushels of Soybeans | Bushels of Wheat | Label in Figure 1 |
| 40,000 | 0 | A |
| 30,000 | 38,000 | B |
| 20,000 | 52,000 | C |
| 10,000 | 60,000 | D |
| 0 | 65,000 | E |

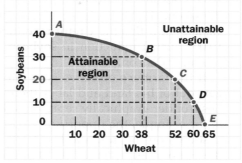

Figure 1

**Production Possibilities Frontier for Production by a Single Farmer**

NOTE: Quantities are in thousands of bushels per year.

whereas $1,200 is the profit offered by the soybean option (that would have to be given up if wheat specialization were decided upon). Then the opportunity cost that our farmer would incur is not the 10,000 bushels of soybeans, but the $1,200 in profits that substitution of soybean production would offer.

### 3-2a  The Production Possibilities Frontier

Figure 1 presents this same information graphically. Point *A* indicates that one of the options available to the farmer is to produce 40,000 bushels of soybeans and 0 wheat. Thus, point *A* corresponds to the first line of Table 1, point *B* to the second line, and so on. Curves similar to *AE* appear frequently in this book; they are called **production possibilities frontiers**. Any point *on or inside* the production possibilities frontier is attainable because it does not entail larger outputs than currently available resources permit. Points *outside* the frontier, representing very large quantities of output, are figments of the imagination given current circumstances because they cannot be achieved with the available resources and technology.

A **production possibilities frontier** shows the different combinations of various goods, any one of which a producer can turn out, given the available resources and existing technology.

Because resources are limited, the production possibilities frontier always slopes downward to the right. The farmer can *increase* wheat production (move to the right in Figure 1) only by devoting more land and labor to growing wheat, but this choice simultaneously *reduces* soybean production (the curve must move downward) because less land and labor remain available for growing soybeans.

Notice that, in addition to having a negative slope, our production possibilities frontier *AE* has another characteristic: It is "bowed outward." What does this curvature mean? In short, as larger and larger quantities of resources are transferred from the production of one output to the production of another, the additions to the second product decline.

Suppose farmer Jones initially produces only soybeans, using even land that is comparatively most productive in wheat cultivation (point *A*). Now he decides to switch some land from soybean production into wheat production. Which part of the land will he switch? If Jones is sensible, he will use the part that, because of its chemical content, direction in relation to sunlight, and so on, is relatively most productive in growing wheat. As he shifts to point *B*, soybean production falls from 40,000 bushels to 30,000 bushels as wheat production rises from 0 to 38,000 bushels. A sacrifice of only 10,000 bushels of soybeans "buys" 38,000 bushels of wheat.

Imagine now that our farmer wants to produce still more wheat. Figure 1 tells us that the sacrifice of an additional 10,000 bushels of soybeans (from 30,000 bushels to 20,000 bushels) will yield only 14,000 more bushels of wheat (see point *C*). Why? The main reason is that *inputs tend to be specialized*. As we noted at point *A*, the farmer was using resources for soybean production that were relatively more productive in growing wheat. Consequently, their relative productivity in soybean production was low. When these resources are switched to wheat production, the yield is high.

This trend cannot continue forever, of course. As more wheat is produced, the farmer must utilize land and machinery with a greater productivity advantage in growing soybeans and a smaller productivity advantage in growing wheat. This is why the first 10,000 bushels of soybeans forgone "buys" the farmer 38,000 bushels of wheat, whereas the second 10,000 bushels of soybeans "buys" only 14,000 bushels of wheat. Figure 1 and Table 1 show that these returns continue to decline as wheat production expands: The next 10,000-bushel reduction in soybean production yields only 8,000 bushels of additional wheat, and so on.

If the farmer's objective is to maximize the amount of wheat or soybean product he gets out of his land and labor then, as we can see, the *slope* of the production possibilities frontier graphically represents the concept of *opportunity cost*. Between points C and B, for example, the opportunity cost of acquiring 10,000 additional bushels of soybeans is shown on the graph to be 14,000 bushels of forgone wheat; between points B and A, the opportunity cost of 10,000 bushels of soybeans is 38,000 bushels of forgone wheat. In general, as we move upward to the left along the production possibilities frontier (toward more soybeans and less wheat), the opportunity cost of soybeans in terms of wheat increases. Looking at the same thing the other way, as we move downward to the right, the opportunity cost of acquiring wheat by giving up soybeans increases—more and more soybeans must be forgone per added bushel of wheat and successive addition to wheat output occurs.

## 3-2b The Principle of Increasing Costs

The **principle of increasing costs** states that as the production of a good expands, the opportunity cost of producing another unit generally increases.

We have just described a very general phenomenon with applications well beyond farming. The **principle of increasing costs** states that as the production of one good expands, the opportunity cost of producing another unit of this good generally increases. This principle is not a universal fact—exceptions do arise—but it does seem to be a technological regularity that applies to a wide range of economic activities. As our farming example suggests, the principle of increasing costs is based on the fact that resources tend to be at least somewhat specialized. So we lose some of their productivity when those resources are transferred from doing what they are relatively *good* at to what they are relatively *bad* at. In terms of diagrams such as Figure 1, the principle simply asserts that the production possibilities frontier is bowed outward.

Perhaps the best way to understand this idea is to contrast it with a case in which no resources are specialized so costs do not increase as output proportion changes. Figure 2 depicts a production possibilities frontier for producing black shoes and brown shoes. Because the labor and machinery used to produce black shoes are just as good at producing brown shoes, the frontier is a straight line. If the firm cuts back its production of black shoes by 10,000 pairs, it can produce 10,000 additional pairs of brown shoes, no matter how big the shift between these two outputs. It loses no productivity in the switch because resources are not specialized.

More typically, however, as a firm concentrates more of its productive capacity on one commodity, it is forced to employ inputs that are better suited to making another commodity. The firm is forced to vary the proportions in which it uses inputs because of the limited quantities of some of those inputs. This fact also explains the typical curvature of the firm's production possibilities frontier.

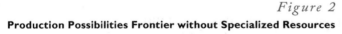

*Figure 2*

**Production Possibilities Frontier without Specialized Resources**

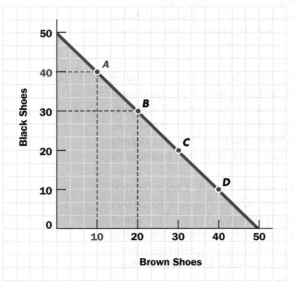

NOTE: Quantities are in thousands of pairs per week.

## 3-3 SCARCITY AND CHOICE FOR THE ENTIRE SOCIETY

Like an individual firm, the entire economy is also constrained by its limited resources and technology. If the public wants more aircraft and tanks, it will have to give up some boats and automobiles. If it wants to build more factories and stores, it will have to build fewer homes and sports arenas. In general:

**The position and shape of the production possibilities frontier that constrains society's choices are determined by the economy's physical resources, its skills and technology, its willingness to work, and how much it has devoted in the past to the construction of factories, research, and innovation.**

Because so many nations have long debated whether to reduce or augment military spending, let us exemplify the nature of society's choices by deciding between military might (represented by missiles) and civilian consumption (represented by automobiles). Just like a single firm, the economy as a whole faces a production possibilities frontier for missiles and autos, determined by its technology and the available resources of land, labor, capital, and raw materials. This production possibilities frontier may look like curve *BC* in Figure 3. If most workers are employed in auto plants, car production will be large, but the output of missiles will be small. If the economy transfers resources out of auto manufacturing when consumer demand declines, it can, by congressional action, alter the output mix toward more missiles (the move from *D* to *E*). However, something is likely to be lost in the process because physical resources are specialized. The fabric used to make car seats will not help much in missile production. The principle of increasing costs strongly suggests that the production possibilities frontier curves downward toward the axes.

We may even reach a point where the only resources left are not very useful outside of auto manufacturing. In that case, even a large sacrifice of automobiles will get the economy few additional missiles. That is the meaning of the steep segment, *FC*, on the frontier. At point *C*, there is little additional output of missiles as compared to point *F*, even though at *C* automobile production has been given up entirely.

**The downward slope of society's production possibilities frontier implies that hard choices must be made. Civilian consumption (automobiles) can be increased only by decreasing military expenditure, not by rhetoric or wishing. The curvature of the production possibilities frontier implies that as defense spending increases, it becomes progressively more expensive to "buy" additional military strength ("missiles") in terms of the resulting sacrifice of civilian consumption.**

### 3-3a Scarcity and Choice Elsewhere in the Economy

We have emphasized that limited resources force hard choices on business managers and society as a whole, but the same type of choices arises elsewhere—in households, universities, and other nonprofit organizations, as well as the government.

The nature of opportunity cost is perhaps most obvious for a household that must decide how to divide its income among the goods and services that compete for the family's attention. If the Simpson family buys an expensive new car, they may be forced to cut back sharply on some other purchases. This fact does not make it unwise to buy the car, but it does make it unwise to buy the car until the family considers the full implications for its overall budget. If the Simpsons are to utilize their limited resources most effectively, they must recognize the opportunity costs of the car—the things they will forgo as a result—perhaps a vacation and an expensive new TV. The decision to buy the car will be rational if the benefit to the family from the automobile (however measured) is greater than the opportunity cost—their benefit if they buy an equally expensive vacation or TV instead.

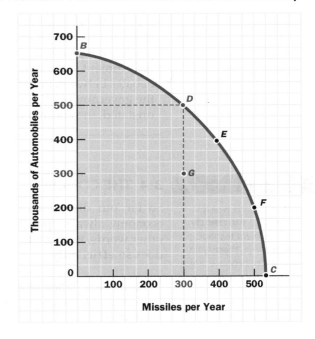

*Figure 3*

**Production Possibilities Frontier for the Entire Economy**

# Hard Choices in the Real World

This excerpt from a recent newspaper story brings home the realities of scarcity and choice:

"President Obama rolled out an election-year budget on Monday that would delay action to reduce the national debt in favor of fresh spending on Democratic priorities aimed at rebuilding the American middle class.

In his final budget request before facing voters in November, Obama called for $350 billion in new stimulus to maintain lower payroll taxes, bolster domestic manufacturing, lure jobs back from overseas, hire teachers, retrain workers and fix the nation's crumbling infrastructure. There would be only modest trims to federal health-care programs and no changes to Social Security, the biggest drivers of future borrowing, despite last year's raucous political debate over the federal debt.

Instead, Obama would reduce deficits by raising taxes by nearly $2 trillion over the next decade on corporations and the wealthy, in part by letting expire George W. Bush-era tax cuts on household income over $250,000 a year.

And the president is encouraging lawmakers to rewrite the tax code to eliminate the alternative minimum tax, which strikes many middle-class families, while requiring millionaires to pay at least 30 percent of their annual income to the Internal Revenue Service.

The $3.8 trillion spending request for fiscal 2013 would limit agency budgets according to limits agreed to during last year's

budget battles, forcing belt-tightening at the Pentagon and the lowest spending on domestic agencies as a percentage of the economy in at least a decade... ."

Alex Wong /Getty Images

SOURCE: Excerpted from Lori Montgomery, "Obama Budget: National Debt Will Be $1 Trillion Higher in a Decade than Forecast," *The Washington Post*, February 13, 2012. Reprinted by permission of The Wall Street Journal. Copyright © 2009 Dow Jones & Company, Inc. All Rights Reserved Worldwide.

---

**Issue Revisited** | *Coping with the Budget Deficit*

As already noted, even a rich and powerful nation like the United States must cope with the limitations implied by scarce resources. The necessity for choice imposed on governments by the limited amount they feel they can afford to spend is similar in character to the problems faced by business firms and households. For the goods and services that it buys from others, a government must prepare a budget similar to that of a very large household. For the items it produces itself—education, police protection, libraries, and so on—it faces a production possibilities frontier much like a business firm does. Even though the U.S. government spent almost $3.5 trillion in fiscal year 2013, some of the most acrimonious debates between President Obama and his critics arose from disagreements about how the government's limited resources should be allocated among competing uses. Even if unstated, the concept of opportunity cost was central to these debates.

---

## 3-4 THE CONCEPT OF EFFICIENCY

A set of outputs is said to be produced **efficiently** if, given current technological knowledge, there is no way one can produce larger amounts of any output without using larger input amounts or giving up some quantity of another output.

So far, our discussion of scarcity and choice has assumed that either the firm or the economy always operates on its production possibilities frontier rather than *below* it. In other words, we have tacitly assumed that whatever the firm or economy decides to do, it does so **efficiently**.

Economists define efficiency as the absence of waste. An efficient economy wastes none of its available resources and produces the maximum amount of output that its technology permits.

To see why any point on the economy's production possibilities frontier in Figure 3 (in a choice between missiles or automobiles or some combination of the two) represents an efficient decision, suppose for a moment that society has decided to produce 300 missiles. The production possibilities frontier tells us that if 300 missiles are to be produced, then the maximum number of automobiles that can be made is 500,000 (point *D* in Figure 3). The economy is, therefore, operating efficiently only if it produces 500,000 automobiles (when it manufactures 300 missiles) rather than some smaller number of cars, such as 300,000 (as at point *G*).

Point *D* is efficient, but point *G* is not, because the economy is capable of moving from *G* to *D*, thereby producing 200,000 more automobiles without giving up any missiles (or anything else). Clearly, failure to take advantage of the option of choosing point *D* rather than point *G* constitutes a wasted opportunity—an inefficiency.

Note that the concept of efficiency does not tell us which point on the production possibilities frontier is *best*. Rather, it tells us only that any point *below* the frontier cannot be best, because any such point represents wasted resources. For example, should society ever find itself at a point such as *G*, the necessity of making hard choices would (temporarily) disappear. It would be possible to increase production of *both* missiles *and* automobiles by moving to a point such as *E*.

Why, then, would a society ever find itself at a point below its production possibilities frontier? Why are resources wasted in real life? The most important reason in today's economy is *unemployment*. When many workers are unemployed, the economy must be at a point such as *G*, below the frontier, because by putting the unemployed to work in each industry, the economy could produce both more missiles *and* more automobiles. The economy would then move from point *G* to the right (more missiles) and upward (more automobiles) toward a point such as *E* on the production possibilities frontier. Only when no resources are wasted is the economy operating on the frontier.

Inefficiency occurs in other ways, too. A prime example is assigning inputs to the wrong task—as when wheat is grown on land best suited to soybean cultivation. Another important type of inefficiency occurs when large firms produce goods that smaller enterprises could make better because they can pay closer attention to detail, or when small firms produce outputs best suited to large-scale production. Some other examples are the outright waste that occurs because of favoritism (e.g., promotion of an incompetent brother-in-law to a job he cannot do very well) or restrictive labor practices (e.g., requiring a railroad to keep a fireman on a diesel-electric locomotive where there is no longer a fire to tend).

A particularly deplorable form of waste is caused by discrimination against minority and female workers. When a job is given, for example, to a white male in preference to an African-American woman who is more qualified, society sacrifices potential output and the entire community is apt to be affected adversely. Every one of these inefficiencies means that the community obtains less output than it could have, given the available inputs.

## 3-5 THE THREE COORDINATION TASKS OF ANY ECONOMY

In deciding how to **allocate its scarce resources**, every society must somehow make three sorts of decisions:

- First, as we have emphasized, it must figure out *how to utilize its resources efficiently*; that is, it must find a way to reach its production possibilities frontier.
- Second, it must decide *which of the possible combinations of goods to produce*—how many missiles, automobiles, and so on; that is, it must select one specific point on the production possibilities frontier among all of the points (i.e., all of the output combinations) on the frontier.
- Third, it must decide *how much of the total output of each good to distribute to each person*, doing so in a sensible way that does not assign meat to vegetarians and wine to teetotalers.

**Allocation of scarce resources** refers to society's decisions on how to divide its scarce input resources among the different outputs produced in the economy and among the different firms or other organizations that produce those outputs.

There are many ways in which societies can and do make each of these decisions—to which economists often refer as *how, what,* and *to whom.* For example, a central planner may tell people how to produce, what to produce, and what to consume, as the authorities used to do, at least to some extent, in the former Soviet Union. But in a market economy, no one group or individual makes all such resource allocation decisions explicitly. Rather, consumer demands and production costs allocate resources *automatically* and *anonymously* through a system of prices and markets. As the formerly socialist countries learned, markets do an impressively effective job in carrying out these tasks. For our introduction to the ways in which markets do all this, let's consider each task in turn.

## 3-6  TASK 1. HOW THE MARKET FOSTERS EFFICIENT RESOURCE ALLOCATION

Production efficiency is one of the economy's three basic tasks, and societies pursue it in many ways. However, one source of efficiency is so fundamental that we must single it out for special attention: the tremendous productivity gains that stem from *specialization.*

### 3-6a  The Wonders of the Division of Labor

**Division of labor** means breaking up a task into a number of smaller, more *specialized* tasks so that each worker can become more adept at a particular job.

Adam Smith, the founder of modern economics, first marveled at how **division of labor** raised efficiency and productivity when he visited a pin factory. In a famous passage near the beginning of his monumental book *The Wealth of Nations* (1776), he described what he saw:

> One man draws out the wire, another straightens it, a third cuts it, a fourth points it, a fifth grinds it at the top for receiving the head. To make the head requires two or three distinct operations; to put it on is a peculiar business, to whiten the pins is another; it is even a trade by itself to put them into the paper.[1]

Smith observed that by dividing the work to be done in this way, each worker became quite skilled in a particular specialty, and the productivity of the group of workers as a whole was greatly enhanced. As Smith related it:

> I have seen a small manufactory of this kind where ten men only were employed…. Those ten persons … could make among them upwards of forty-eight thousand pins in a day … . But if they had all wrought separately and independently … they certainly could not each of them have made twenty, *perhaps not one pin in a day.*[2]

In other words, through the miracle of division of labor and specialization, 10 workers accomplished what might otherwise have required thousands. This was one of the secrets of the Industrial Revolution, which helped lift humanity out of the abject poverty that had been its lot for centuries.

### 3-6b  The Amazing Principle of Comparative Advantage

Specialization in production fosters efficiency in an even more profound sense. Adam Smith noticed that *how* goods are produced can make a huge difference to productivity, but so can *which* goods are produced. The reason is that people (and businesses and nations) have different abilities. Some can repair automobiles, whereas others are wizards with numbers. Some are handy with computers, and others can cook. An economy will be most efficient if people specialize in doing what they do best and then trade with

Library of Congress Prints and Photographs Division

---

[1] Adam Smith, *The Wealth of Nations* (New York: Random House, 1937), p. 4.
[2] Ibid., p. 5.

one another, so that the accountant gets her car repaired and the computer programmer gets to eat tasty and nutritious meals.

This much is obvious. What is less obvious—and is one of the great ideas of economics—is that two people (or two businesses or two countries) can generally gain from trade *even if one of them is more efficient than the other in producing everything.* A simple example will help explain why.

Some lawyers can type better than their administrative assistants. Should such a lawyer fire her assistant and do her own typing? Not likely. Even though the lawyer may type better than the assistant, good judgment tells her to concentrate on practicing law and leave the typing to a lower-paid assistant. Why? Because the *opportunity cost* of an hour devoted to typing is the amount that she could earn from an hour less spent with clients, which is a far more lucrative activity.

This example illustrates the principle of **comparative advantage** at work. The lawyer specializes in arguing cases despite her advantage as a typist because she has a *still greater* advantage as an attorney. She suffers some direct loss by leaving the typing to a less efficient employee, but she more than makes up for that loss by the income she earns selling her legal services to clients.

> One country is said to have a **comparative advantage** over another in the production of a particular good *relative to other goods* if it produces that good less inefficiently than it produces other goods, as compared with the other country.

Precisely the same principle applies to nations. As we shall learn in greater detail in Chapter 5, comparative advantage underlies the economic analysis of international trade patterns. A country that is particularly adept at producing certain items—such as aircraft in the United States, coffee in Brazil, or oil in Saudi Arabia—should specialize in those activities, producing more than it wants for its own use. The country can then take the money it earns from its exports and purchase from other nations items that it does not make for itself. And this is still true if one of the trading nations is the most efficient producer of almost everything. The underlying logic is precisely the same as in our lawyer–typist example. The United States might, for example, be better than South Korea at manufacturing both computers and television sets. But if the United States is vastly more efficient at producing computers, but only slightly more efficient at making TV sets, it pays for the United States to specialize in computer manufacturing, for South Korea to specialize in TV production, and for the two countries to trade.

This principle, called the *law of comparative advantage,* was discovered by David Ricardo, another giant in the history of economic analysis, almost 200 years ago. It is one of the *Ideas for Beyond the Final Exam* introduced in Chapter 1.

**THE SURPRISING PRINCIPLE OF COMPARATIVE ADVANTAGE** Even if one country (or one worker) is worse than another country (or another worker) in the production of *every* good, it is said to have a *comparative advantage* in making the good at which it is *least inefficient*—compared to the other country. Ricardo discovered that two countries can gain by trading even if one country is more efficient than another in the production of *every* commodity. Precisely the same logic applies to individual workers or to businesses.

Ideas for Beyond the Final Exam

In determining the most efficient patterns of production and trade, it is *comparative* advantage that matters. Thus, a country can gain by importing a good from abroad even if that good can be produced more efficiently at home. Such imports make sense if they enable the country to specialize in producing those goods at which it is *even more efficient.* And the other, less efficient country should specialize in exporting the goods in whose production it is *least inefficient.*

## 3-7 TASK 2. MARKET EXCHANGE AND DECIDING HOW MUCH OF EACH GOOD TO PRODUCE

The gains from specialization are welcome, but they create a problem: With specialization, people no longer produce only what they want to consume themselves. The workers in Adam Smith's pin factory had no use for the thousands of pins they produced each day; they wanted to trade them for things like food, clothing, and shelter. Similarly, the administrative assistant in our law office example has no personal use for the legal briefs he types. Thus, specialization requires some mechanism by which workers producing pins can *exchange* their wares with workers producing such things as cloth and potatoes, and office workers can turn their typing skills into things they want to consume.

Without a system of exchange, the productivity miracle achieved by comparative advantage and the division of labor would do society little good, because each producer in an efficient arrangement would be left with only the commodities in whose production its comparative efficiency was greatest and would have no other goods to consume. With it, standards of living have risen enormously.

Although people can and do trade goods for other goods, a system of exchange works better when everyone agrees to use some common item (such as pieces of paper with unique markings printed on them) for buying and selling things. Enter *money*. Then workers in pin factories, for example, can be paid in money rather than in pins, and they can use this money to purchase cloth and potatoes. Textile workers and farmers can do the same.

In a market in which trading is carried out by means of exchange between money and goods or services, the market mechanism also makes the second of our three crucial decisions: how much of each good should be produced with the resources that are available to the economy. For what happens is that if more widgets are produced than consumers want to buy at current prices, those who make widgets will be left with unsold widgets on their hands. Widget price will be driven down, and manufacturers will be forced to cut production, with some being driven out of business altogether. The opposite will happen if producers supply fewer widgets than consumers want at the prevailing prices. Then prices will be driven up by scarcity, and manufacturers will be led to increase their output. In this way, the output and price of each and every commodity will be driven toward levels at which supply matches demand or comes very close to it. That is how the market automatically deals with the second critical decision: how much of each commodity will be produced by the economy given the economy's productive capacity (as shown by the production possibility frontier).

## 3-8 TASK 3. HOW TO DISTRIBUTE THE ECONOMY'S OUTPUTS AMONG CONSUMERS

These two phenomena—specialization and exchange (assisted by money)—working in tandem led to vast increases in the abundance that the more prosperous economies of the world were able to supply. But that leaves us with the third basic issue: What forces allow those outputs to be distributed among the population in reasonable ways? What forces establish a smoothly functioning system of exchange so that people can first exploit their comparative advantages and then acquire what they want to consume? One alternative is to have a central authority telling people what to do. Adam Smith explained and extolled yet another way of organizing and coordinating economic activity—markets and prices can coordinate those activities. Smith noted that people are adept at pursuing their own self-interests and that a **market system** harnesses this self-interest remarkably well. As he put it—with clear religious overtones—in doing what is best for themselves, people are "led by an invisible hand" to promote the economic well-being of society as a whole.

A **market system** is a form of economic organization in which resource allocation decisions are left to individual producers and consumers acting in their own best interests without central direction.

Those of us who live in a well-functioning market economy like that found in the United States tend to take the achievements of the market for granted, much like the daily rising and setting of the sun. Few bother to think about, say, the reason why Hawaiian pineapples show up daily in Vermont supermarkets in quantities desired by Vermont consumers. The market deals with this issue through the profit motive, which guides firms' output decisions, matching quantities produced to consumer preferences. A rise in the price of wheat because of increased demand for bread, for example, will persuade farmers to produce more wheat and devote less of their land to soybeans. Such a price system also distributes goods among consumers in accord with their tastes and preferences, using voluntary exchange to determine who gets what. Consumers spend their income on the things they like best (among those they can afford). Vegetarians do not waste their income on beef, and teetotalers do not spend money on gin. So consumers, by controlling their spending patterns, can ensure that the goods they buy at the supermarket are compatible with their preferences. That is how the market mechanism ensures that the products of the economy are divided among consumers in a rational manner, meaning that this distribution tends to fit in with the preferences of the different purchasers. But there is at least one problem here; the ability to buy goods is hardly divided equally. Workers with valuable skills and owners of scarce resources can sell what they have at attractive prices. With the incomes they earn, they can purchase generous amounts of goods and services. Those who are less successful in selling what they own receive lower incomes and so can afford to buy less. In extreme cases, they may suffer severe deprivation.

The past few pages explain, in broad terms, how a market economy solves the three basic problems facing any society: how to produce any given combination of goods efficiently, how to select an appropriate combination of goods to produce, and how to distribute these goods sensibly among people. As we proceed through the following chapters, you will learn much more about these issues. You will see that they constitute the central theme that permeates not only this text but the work of economists in general. As you progress through this book, keep in mind two questions:

- What does the market do well?
- What does it do poorly?

There are numerous answers to both questions, as you will learn in subsequent chapters.

**Society has many important goals. Some of them, such as producing goods and services with maximum efficiency (minimum waste), can be achieved extraordinarily well by letting markets operate more or less freely.**

Tim Rue/Bloomberg/Getty Images

Free markets will not, however, achieve all of society's goals. For example, they often have trouble keeping unemployment low. In fact, the unfettered operations of markets may even run counter to some goals, such as protection of the environment. Many observers also believe that markets do not necessarily distribute income in accord with ethical or moral norms. Even in cases in which markets do not perform well, there may be ways of harnessing the power of the market mechanism to remedy its own deficiencies, as you will learn in later chapters.

Economic debates often have political and ideological overtones. So we will close this chapter by emphasizing that the central theme we have just outlined is neither a *defense of* nor an *attack on* the capitalist system. Nor is it a "conservative" position. One does not have to be a conservative to recognize that the market mechanism can be an extraordinarily helpful instrument for the pursuit of economic goals. Most of the formerly socialist countries of Europe have been working hard to "marketize" their economies, and even the communist People's Republic of China has made huge strides in that direction.

The point is not to confuse ends with means in deciding how much to rely on market forces. Liberals and conservatives surely have different goals, but the means chosen to pursue these goals should, for the most part, be chosen on the basis of how effective the selected means are, not on some ideological prejudgments. Even Karl Marx emphasized that the market is remarkably efficient at producing an abundance of goods and services that had never been seen in precapitalist history. Such wealth can be used to promote conservative goals, such as reducing tax rates, or to facilitate goals favored by liberals, such as providing more generous public aid for the poor.

Certainly the market cannot deal with every economic problem. Indeed, we have just noted that the market is the *source* of a number of significant problems. Even so, the evidence accumulated over centuries leads economists to believe that most economic problems are best handled by market techniques. The analysis in this book is intended to help you identify both the objectives that the market mechanism can reliably achieve and those that it will fail to promote, or at least not promote very effectively. We urge you to forget the slogans you have heard—whether from the left or from the right—and make up your own mind after learning the material in this book.

## Summary

1. Supplies of all **resources** are limited. Because resources are **scarce**, an **optimal decision** is one that chooses the best alternative among the options that are possible with the available resources.

2. With limited resources, a decision to obtain more of one item is also a decision to give up some of another. The value of what we give up is called the **opportunity** cost of what we get. The opportunity cost is the true cost of any decision. This is one of the *Ideas for Beyond the Final Exam*.

3. When markets function effectively, firms are led to use resources efficiently and to produce the things that consumers want most. In such cases, opportunity costs and money costs (prices) correspond closely. When the market performs poorly, or when important, socially costly items are provided without charging an appropriate price, or are given away free, opportunity costs and money costs can diverge.

4. A firm's **production possibilities frontier** shows the combinations of goods it can produce, given the current technology and the resources at its disposal. The frontier is usually bowed outward because resources tend to be specialized.

5. The **principle of increasing costs** states that as the production of one good expands, the opportunity cost of producing another unit of that good generally increases.

6. Like a firm, the economy as a whole has a production possibilities frontier whose position is determined by its technology and by the available resources of land, labor, capital, and raw materials.

7. A firm or an economy that ends up at a point below its production possibilities frontier is using its resources inefficiently or wastefully. This is what happens, for example, when there is unemployment.

8. Economists define **efficiency** as the absence of waste. It is achieved primarily by the gains in productivity brought about through **specialization** that exploits **division of labor** and **comparative advantage** and by a system of exchange.

9. Two countries (or two people) can gain by specializing in the activity in which each has a *comparative* advantage and then trading with one another. These gains from trade remain available even if one country is inferior at producing everything but specializes in producing those items at which it is least inefficient. This so-called principle of comparative advantage is one of our *Ideas for Beyond the Final Exam*.

10. If an exchange between two individuals is voluntary, both parties must benefit, even if no additional goods are produced. This is another of the *Ideas for Beyond the Final Exam*.

11. Every economic system must find a way to answer three basic questions: How can goods be produced most efficiently? How much of each good should be produced? How should goods be distributed among users?

12. The **market system** works very well in solving some of society's basic problems, but it fails to remedy others and may, indeed, create some of its own. Where and how it succeeds and fails constitute the central theme of this book and characterize the work of economists in general.

## Key Terms

| | | |
|---|---|---|
| allocation of scarce resources   47 | inputs   42 | outputs   42 |
| comparative advantage   49 | market system   50 | principle of increasing costs   44 |
| division of labor   48 | opportunity cost   41 | production possibilities frontier   43 |
| efficiency   46 | optimal decision   42 | resources   40 |

## Test Yourself

1. A person rents a house for $24,000 per year. The house can be purchased for $200,000, and the tenant has this much money in a bank account that pays 4 percent interest per year. Is buying the house a good deal for the tenant? Where does opportunity cost enter the picture?

2. Graphically show the production possibilities frontier for the nation of Stromboli, using the data given in the following table. Does the principle of increasing cost hold in Stromboli?

### Stromboli's 2018 Production Possibilities

| Pizzas per Year | Pizza Ovens per Year |
|---|---|
| 75,000,000 | 0 |
| 60,000,000 | 6,000 |
| 45,000,000 | 11,000 |
| 30,000,000 | 15,000 |
| 15,000,000 | 18,000 |
| 0 | 20,000 |

3. Consider two alternatives for Stromboli in 2018. In case (a), its inhabitants eat 60 million pizzas and build 6,000 pizza ovens. In case (b), the population eats 15 million pizzas but builds 18,000 ovens. Which case will lead to a more generous production possibilities frontier for Stromboli in 2018?

4. Jasmine's Snack Shop sells two brands of potato chips. She produces them by buying them from a wholesale supplier. Brand X costs Jasmine $1 per bag, and Brand Y costs her $1.40. Draw Jasmine's production possibilities frontier if she has $280 budgeted to spend on the purchase of potato chips from the wholesaler. Why is it not "bowed out"?

## Discussion Questions

1. Discuss the resource limitations that affect
   a. the poorest person on earth
   b. the richest person in the United States
   c. a farmer in Kansas
   d. the government of Indonesia

2. If you were president of your college, what would you change if your budget were cut by 10 percent? By 25 percent? By 50 percent?

3. If you were to leave college, what things would change in your life? What, then, is the opportunity cost of your education?

4. Raising chickens requires several types of feed, such as corn and soy meal. Consider a farm in the former Soviet Union. Try to describe how decisions on the number of chickens to be raised, and the amount of each feed to use in raising them, were made under the old communist regime. If the farm is now privately owned, how does the market guide the decisions that used to be made by the central planning agency?

5. The United States is one of the world's wealthiest countries. Think of a recent case in which the decisions of the U.S. government were severely constrained by scarcity. Describe the trade-offs that were involved. What were the opportunity costs of the decisions that were actually made?

# SUPPLY AND DEMAND: AN INITIAL LOOK

4

*The free enterprise system is absolutely too important to be
left to the voluntary action of the marketplace.*

FLORIDA CONGRESSMAN RICHARD KELLY, 1979

In this chapter, we study the economist's most basic investigative tool: the mechanism of supply and demand. Whether your econ course concentrates on macroeconomics or microeconomics, you will find that the so-called law of supply and demand is a fundamental tool of economic analysis. Economists use supply and demand analysis to study issues as diverse as inflation and unemployment, the effects of taxes on prices, government regulation of business, and environmental protection. Supply and demand curves—graphs that relate price to quantity supplied and quantity demanded, respectively—show how prices and quantities are determined in a free market.[1]

A major theme of the chapter is that governments around the world and throughout recorded history have tampered with the price mechanism. As we will see, these bouts with Adam Smith's "invisible hand" have produced undesirable side effects that often surprised and dismayed the authorities. The invisible hand fights back!

## CONTENTS

| Puzzle | *What Happened to Oil Prices?* |

Since 1949, the dollars of purchasing power that a buyer had to pay to buy a barrel of oil had remained remarkably steady, and gasoline had generally remained a bargain. But during two exceptional time periods—one from about 1975 through 1985 and another beginning in 2009 and peaking in 2011—oil prices exploded, and filling the automobile gas tank became painful to consumers. Clearly, supply and demand changes must have been behind these

---

[1] This chapter, like much of the rest of this book, uses many graphs like those described in the appendix to Chapter 1. If you have difficulties with these graphs, we suggest that you review that material before proceeding.

developments, but what led them to change so much and so suddenly? Later in the chapter, we will provide excerpts from a newspaper story about how dramatic and unexpected events can suddenly shift supply, which will help to bring the analysis of this chapter to life.

SOURCE: U.S. Energy Information Administration (April 2014), Gasoline Regular Grade Retail Prices Including Taxes, U.S. Average, 1995 to 2014, *Short-Term Energy Outlook*, accessed online at www.eia.gov/forecasts/steo.

## 4-1 THE INVISIBLE HAND

**Invisible hand** is a phrase used by Adam Smith to describe how, by pursuing their own self-interests, people in a market system are "led by an invisible hand" to promote the well-being of the community.

Adam Smith, the father of modern economic analysis, greatly admired the price system. He marveled at its accomplishments—both as an efficient producer of goods and as a guarantor that consumers' preferences are obeyed. Although many people since Smith's time have shared his enthusiasm for the concept of the **invisible hand**, many have not. Smith's contemporaries in the American colonies, for example, were often unhappy with the prices produced by free markets and thought they could do better by legislative decree. Such attempts failed, as explained in the accompanying box "Price Controls at Valley Forge." In countless other instances, the public was outraged by the prices charged on the open market, particularly in the case of housing rents, interest rates, and insurance rates.

Attempts to control interest rates (which are the price of borrowing money) go back hundreds of years before the birth of Christ, at least to the code of laws compiled under the Babylonian king Hammurabi in about 1800 B.C. Our historical legacy also includes a rather long list of price ceilings on foods and other products imposed in the reign of Diocletian, emperor of the Roman Empire during its decline. More recently, Americans have been offered the "protection" of a variety of price controls. Laws have placed ceilings on some prices (such as rents) to protect buyers, whereas legislation has placed floors under other prices (such as farm products) to protect sellers. Yet, somehow, everything such regulation touches seems to end up in even greater disarray than it was before. Despite rent controls, rents in New York City have soared. Despite laws against "scalping," tickets for popular shows and sports events sell at tremendous premiums—tickets to the Super Bowl, for example, often fetch thousands of dollars on the "gray" market. To understand what goes wrong when we tamper with markets, we must first learn how they operate unfettered. This chapter takes a first step in that direction by studying the machinery of supply and demand. Then, at the end of the chapter, we return to the issue of price controls.

Every market has both buyers and sellers. We begin our analysis on the consumers' side of the market.

## 4-2 DEMAND AND QUANTITY DEMANDED

People commonly think of consumer demands as fixed amounts. For example, when product designers propose a new computer model, management asks: "What is its market potential?"; that is, just how many are likely to be sold? Similarly, government bureaus conduct studies to determine how many engineers or doctors the United States will require (demand) in subsequent years.

Economists respond that such questions are not well posed—that there is no single answer to such a question. Rather, they say, the "market potential" for computers or the

# Price Controls at Valley Forge

George Washington, the history books tell us, was beset by many enemies during the winter of 1777–1778, including the British, their Hessian mercenaries, and the merciless winter weather. However, he had another enemy that the history books ignore—an enemy that meant well but almost destroyed his army at Valley Forge. As the following excerpt explains, that enemy was the Pennsylvania legislature:

> In Pennsylvania, where the main force of Washington's army was quartered . . . the legislature . . . decided to try a period of price control limited to those commodities needed for use by the army. . . . The result might have been anticipated by those with some knowledge of the trials and tribulations of other states. The prices of uncontrolled goods, mostly imported, rose to record heights. Most farmers kept back their produce, refusing to sell at what they regarded as an unfair price. Some who had large families to take care of even secretly sold their food to the British, who paid in gold.
>
> After the disastrous winter at Valley Forge when Washington's army nearly starved to death (thanks largely to these well-intentioned but misdirected laws), the ill-fated experiment in price controls was finally ended. The Continental Congress on June 4, 1778, adopted the following resolution:
>
> "Whereas . . . it hath been found by experience that limitations upon the prices of commodities are not only ineffectual for the purposes proposed, but likewise productive of very evil consequences

. . . resolved, that it be recommended to the several states to repeal or suspend all laws or resolutions within the said states respectively limiting, regulating or restraining the Price of any Article, Manufacture or Commodity."

*Valley Forge.*

SOURCES: Engraving "Men Gathering Wood at Valley Forge," Metropolitan Museum of Art, bequest of Charles Allen Munn, 1924 [24.90.1828]. All Rights Reserved, The Metropolitan Museum of Art; Robert L. Schuettinger and Eamonn F. Butler, *Forty Centuries of Wage and Price Controls* (Washington, D.C.: Heritage Foundation, 1979), p. 41. Reprinted by permission.

Image copyright © The Metropolitan Museum of Art/Art Resource, NY

number of engineers that will be "required" depends on a great number of influences, including the price charged for each.

**The quantity demanded of any product normally depends on its price. Quantity demanded also depends on a number of other determinants, including population size, consumer incomes, tastes, and the prices of other products.**

Because prices play a central role in a market economy, we begin our study of demand by focusing on how quantity demanded depends on price. A little later, we will bring the other determinants of quantity demanded back into the picture. For now, we will consider all influences other than price to be fixed. This assumption, often expressed as "other things being equal," is used in much of economic analysis. As an example of the relationship between price and demand, let's think about the quantity of beef demanded. If the price of beef is very high, its "market potential" may be very small. People will find ways to get along with less beef, perhaps by switching to pork or fish. If the price of beef declines, people will tend to eat more beef. They may serve it more frequently or eat larger portions or switch away from fish. Thus:

**There is no one demand figure for beef, or for computers, or for engineers. Rather, there is a different quantity demanded at each possible price, all other influences being held constant.**

## 4-2a The Demand Schedule

Table 1 shows how such information for beef can be recorded in a **demand schedule**. It indicates how much beef consumers in a particular area are willing and able to buy at different possible prices during a specified period of time, other things held

The **quantity demanded** is the number of units of a good that consumers are willing and can afford to buy over a specified period of time.

A **demand schedule** is a table showing how the quantity demanded of some product during a specified period of time changes as the price of that product changes, holding all other determinants of quantity demanded constant.

## Table 1

**Demand Schedule for Beef**

| Price | Quantity Demanded | Label in Figure 1 |
|-------|-------------------|-------------------|
| $7.50 | 45 | A |
| 7.40 | 50 | B |
| 7.30 | 55 | C |
| 7.20 | 60 | E |
| 7.10 | 65 | F |
| 7.00 | 70 | G |
| 6.90 | 75 | H |

NOTE: Quantity is in pounds per year.

A **demand curve** is a graphical depiction of a demand schedule. It shows how the quantity demanded of some product will change as the price of that product changes during a specified period of time, holding all other determinants of quantity demanded constant.

A **shift in a demand curve** occurs when any relevant variable other than price changes. If consumers want to buy *more* at any and all given prices than they wanted previously, the demand curve shifts to the right (or outward). If they desire *less* at any given price, the demand curve shifts to the left (or inward).

equal. Specifically, the table shows the quantity of beef that will be demanded in a year at each possible price ranging from $6.90 to $7.50 per pound. At a relatively low price, such as $7.00 per pound, customers wish to purchase 70 (million) pounds per year. But if the price were to rise to, say, $7.40 per pound, quantity demanded would fall to 50 million pounds.

Common sense tells us why this happens.[2] First, as prices rise, some customers will reduce the quantity of beef they consume. Second, higher prices will induce some customers to drop out of the market entirely—for example, by switching to pork or fish. On both counts, quantity demanded will decline as the price rises.

> As the price of an item rises, the quantity demanded normally falls. As the price falls, the quantity demanded normally rises, all other things held constant.

### 4-2b  The Demand Curve

The information contained in Table 1 can be summarized in a graph like Figure 1, which is called a **demand curve**. Each point in the graph corresponds to a line in the table. This curve shows the relationship between price and quantity demanded. For example, it tells us that to sell 55 million pounds per year, the price must be $7.10 per pound. This relationship is shown at point $G$ in Figure 1. If the price were $7.40, however, consumers would demand only 50 million pounds (point $B$). Because the quantity demanded declines as the price increases, the demand curve has a negative slope.[3]

Notice the last phrase in the definitions of the demand schedule and the demand curve: "holding all other determinants of quantity demanded constant." What are some of these "other things," and how do they affect the demand curve?

### 4-2c  Shifts of the Demand Curve

The quantity of beef demanded is subject to a variety of influences other than the price of beef. Changes in population size and characteristics, consumer incomes and tastes, and the prices of alternative products such as pork and fish presumably change the quantity of beef demanded, even if the price of beef does not change.

Because the demand curve for beef depicts only the relationship between the quantity of beef demanded and the price of beef, holding all other factors constant, a change in beef price moves the market for beef from one point on the demand curve to another point on the same curve. However, a change in any of these other influences on demand causes a **shift of the entire demand curve**. More generally:

> A change in the price of a good produces a movement *along* a fixed demand curve. By contrast, a change in any other variable that influences quantity demanded produces a shift of the *entire* demand curve.

If consumers want to buy more beef at every given price than they wanted previously, the

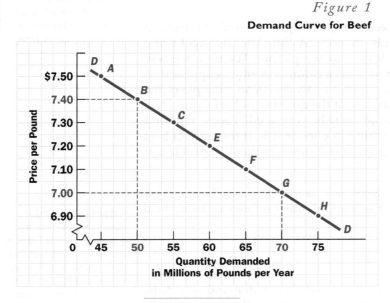

## Figure 1

**Demand Curve for Beef**

---

[2] This commonsense answer is examined more fully in later chapters.
[3] If you need to review the concept of slope, refer to the Chapter 1 appendix.

demand curve shifts to the right (or outward). If they desire less at every given price, the demand curve shifts to the left (or inward toward the origin).

Figure 2 shows this distinction graphically. If the price of beef falls from $7.30 to $7.10 per pound, and quantity demanded rises accordingly, we move along demand curve $D_0D_0$ from point $C$ to point $F$, as shown by the maroon arrow. If, on the other hand, consumers suddenly decide that they like beef better than before, or if they embrace a study that reports the health benefits of beef, the entire demand curve shifts outward from $D_0D_0$ to $D_1D_1$, as indicated by the blue arrow, meaning that at *any* given price consumers are now willing to buy more beef than

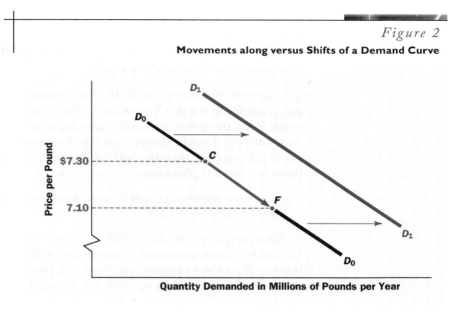

*Figure 2*

**Movements along versus Shifts of a Demand Curve**

before. To make this general idea more concrete, and to show some of its many applications, let us consider some specific examples of those "other things" that can shift demand curves.

**Consumer Incomes** If average incomes rise, consumers will purchase more of most goods, including beef, even if the prices of those goods remain the same. That is, increases in income normally shift demand curves outward to the right, as depicted in Figure 3(a), where the demand curve shifts outward from $D_0D_0$ to $D_1D_1$, establishing a new price and output quantity.

**Population** Population growth affects quantity demanded in more or less the same way as increases in average incomes. For instance, a larger population will presumably want to consume more beef, even if the price of beef and average incomes do not change, thus shifting the entire demand curve to the right, as in Figure 3(a). The equilibrium price and quantity both rise. Increases in particular population segments can also elicit shifts in demand—for example, the United States experienced a miniature population boom between the late 1970s and mid-1990s. This group (which is dubbed Generation Y and

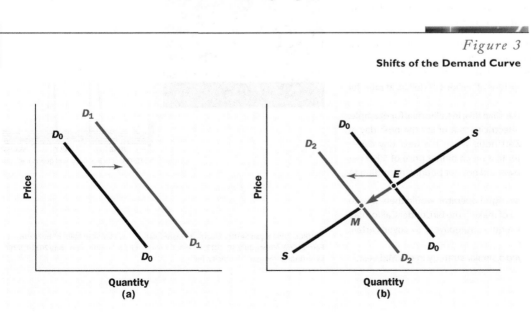

*Figure 3*

**Shifts of the Demand Curve**

Quantity
(a)

Quantity
(b)

includes most users of this book) has sparked higher demand for such items as cell phones and video games.

In Figure 3(b), we see that a decrease in population should shift the demand curve for beef to the left, from $D_0D_0$ to $D_2D_2$.

**Consumer Preferences** If the beef industry mounts a successful advertising campaign extolling the benefits of eating beef, families may decide to buy more at any given price. If so, the entire demand curve for beef would shift to the right, as in Figure 3(a). Alternatively, a medical report on the dangers of high cholesterol may persuade consumers to eat less beef, thereby shifting the demand curve to the left, as in Figure 3(b). Again, these are general phenomena:

> If consumer preferences shift in favor of a particular item, its demand curve will shift outward to the right, as in Figure 3(a).

An example is the ever-shifting "rage" in children's toys—be it Flutterbye Fairies, Yu-Gi-Oh! cards, electronic Elmo dolls, or the latest video game systems. These items become the object of desperate hunts as parents snap them up for their offspring, and stores are unable to keep up with the demand.

**Prices and Availability of Related Goods** Because pork, fish, and chicken are popular products that compete with beef, a change in the price of any of these other items can be expected to shift the demand curve for beef. If any of these alternative items becomes cheaper, some consumers will switch away from beef. Thus, the demand curve for beef will shift to the left, as in Figure 3(b). Other price changes may shift the demand curve for beef in the opposite direction. For example, suppose that hamburger buns and ketchup

## Manipulation of Electricity Prices

Although the industry was deregulated more than a decade ago, electricity prices have generally not fallen and, in many cases, have risen sharply. The Federal Energy Regulatory Commission contends that allowing competition among producers should guarantee the lowest possible price. Why have electricity prices not fallen, unlike other previously regulated industries?

Critics point to opportunities for suppliers to interfere in the market system, including the withholding of power or limiting of production during periods of high demand, leading to skyrocketing prices. The following news excerpt highlights the electricity industry's susceptibility to manipulation of the supply-demand mechanism.

"JPMorgan Chase will pay $410 million to settle charges it manipulated electricity markets in California and the Midwest....

The FERC alleged that the bank's bidding strategies in the power markets led to JPMorgan getting 'tens of millions of dollars at rates far above market prices.'

The strategies allegedly worked like this: In California, for example, the bank would bid to deliver electricity to a utility the next day at a low price of $30 per megawatt hour. When the next day came, JPMorgan would change its offer to a much higher price of $999 per megawatt hour, assuring the power did not get bought, according to the notice.

California ISO, the state's power-grid operator, would then have to compensate the bank for the cost of making the bid, under California's 'make whole provision,' which requires ratepayers to cover certain costs incurred by energy sellers.

JPMorgan allegedly employed a similar strategy in the Midwest."

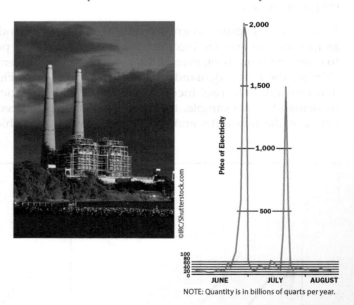

NOTE: Quantity is in billions of quarts per year.

SOURCE: "JPMorgan Settles Electricity Manipulation Case for $410 Million" by Maureen Farrell, *CNN Money*, July 30, 2013, accessed online at http://money.cnn.com/2013/07/30/investing/jp-morgan-electricity-fines.

become less expensive. This may induce some consumers to eat more beef and thus shift the demand curve for beef to the right, as in Figure 3(a). In general:

> **Increases in the prices of goods that are substitutes for the good in question (as pork, fish, and chicken are for beef) move the demand curve to the right. Increases in the prices of goods that are normally used together with the good in question (such as hamburger buns and beef) shift the demand curve to the left.**

This is just what happened when a frost wiped out almost half of Brazil's coffee bean harvest in 1995. The three largest U.S. coffee producers raised their prices by 45 percent, and as a result, the demand curve for alternative beverages such as tea shifted to the right. Then in 1998, coffee prices dropped about 34 percent, which in turn caused the demand curve for tea to shift toward the left (or toward the origin).

Although the preceding list does not exhaust the possible influences on quantity demanded, we have said enough to suggest the principles followed by demand and shifts of demand. Let's turn now to the supply side of the market.

> The **quantity supplied** is the number of units that sellers want to sell over a specified period of time.

## 4-3 SUPPLY AND QUANTITY SUPPLIED

Like quantity demanded, the quantity of beef that is supplied by business firms such as farms is not a fixed number; it also depends on many things. Obviously, we expect more beef to be supplied if there are more farms or more cows per farm. Cows may provide less meat if bad weather deprives them of their feed. As before, however, let's turn our attention first to the relationship between the price and quantity of beef supplied.

Economists generally suppose that a higher price calls forth a greater **quantity supplied**. Why? Remember our analysis of the principle of increasing costs in Chapter 3. According to that principle, as more of any farmer's (or the nation's) resources are devoted to beef production, the opportunity cost of obtaining another pound of beef increases. Farmers will therefore find it profitable to increase beef production only if they can sell the beef at a higher price—high enough to cover the additional costs incurred to expand production. In other words, it normally will take higher prices to persuade farmers to raise beef production. This idea is quite general and applies to the supply of most goods and services.[4] As long as suppliers want to make profits and the principle of increasing costs holds:

> **As the price of any commodity rises, the quantity supplied normally rises. As the price falls, the quantity supplied normally falls.**

> A **supply schedule** is a table showing how the quantity supplied of some product changes as the price of that product changes during a specified period of time, holding all other determinants of quantity supplied constant.
>
> A **supply curve** is a graphical depiction of a supply schedule. It shows how the quantity supplied of a product will change as the price of that product changes during a specified period of time, holding all other determinants of quantity supplied constant.

### 4-3a The Supply Schedule and the Supply Curve

Table 2 shows the relationship between the price of beef and its quantity supplied. Tables such as this one are called **supply schedules**; they show how much sellers are willing to provide during a specified period at alternative possible prices. This particular supply schedule tells us that a low price like $7.00 per pound will induce suppliers to provide only 50 million pounds, whereas a higher price like $7.30 will induce them to provide much more—55 million pounds.

As you might have guessed, when such information is plotted on a graph, it is called a **supply curve**. Figure 4 is the supply curve corresponding to the supply schedule in Table 2, showing the relationship between the price of beef and the quantity supplied. It slopes upward—it has a positive slope—because quantity supplied is higher when price is higher. Notice again the same phrase in the definition: "holding all other determinants of quantity supplied constant." What are these "other determinants"?

*Table 2*
**Supply Schedule for Beef**

| Price | Quantity Supplied | Label in Figure 4 |
|---|---|---|
| $7.50 | 90 | a |
| 7.40 | 80 | b |
| 7.30 | 70 | c |
| 7.20 | 60 | e |
| 7.10 | 50 | f |
| 7.00 | 40 | g |
| 6.90 | 30 | h |

NOTE: Quantity is in pounds per year.

---

[4] This analysis is carried out in much greater detail in later chapters.

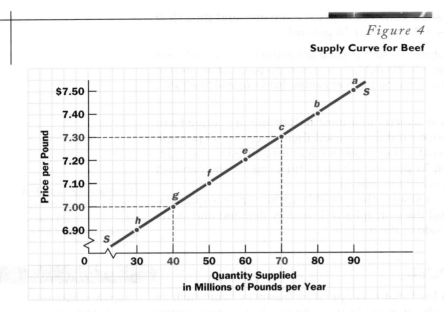

*Figure 4*

**Supply Curve for Beef**

## 4-3b  Shifts of the Supply Curve

Like quantity demanded, the quantity supplied in a market typically responds to many influences other than price. The weather, the cost of feed, the number and size of farms, and a variety of other factors all influence how much beef will be brought to market. Because the supply curve depicts only the relationship between the price of beef and the quantity of beef supplied, holding all other influences constant, a change in any of these other determinants of quantity supplied will cause the entire supply curve to shift. That is:

A change in the price of the good causes a movement *along* a fixed supply curve. Price is not the only influence on quantity supplied, however. If any of these other influences change, the *entire* supply curve shifts.

Figure 5 depicts this distinction graphically. A rise in price from $7.10 to $7.30 will raise quantity supplied by moving along supply curve $S_0S_0$ from point $f$ to point $c$. Any rise in quantity supplied attributable to an influence other than price, however, will shift the *entire* supply curve outward to the right, from $S_0S_0$ to $S_1S_1$, as shown by the blue arrows. Let us consider what some of these other influences are and how they shift the supply curve.

**Size of the Industry**  We begin with the most obvious influence. If more farmers enter the beef industry, the quantity supplied at any given price will increase. For example, if each farm provides 60,000 pounds of beef per year at a price of $7.10 per pound, then

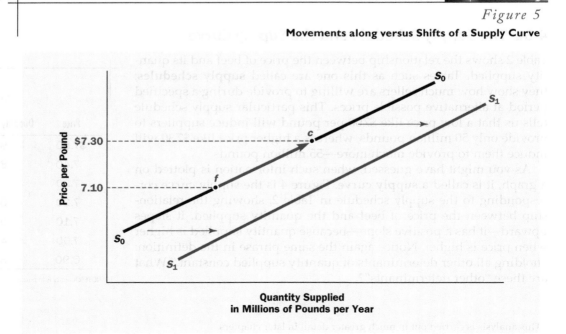

*Figure 5*

**Movements along versus Shifts of a Supply Curve**

**Quantity Supplied
in Millions of Pounds per Year**

100,000 farmers would provide 600 million pounds, but 130,000 farmers would provide 780,000 million. Thus, when more farms are in the industry, the quantity of beef supplied will be greater at any given price—and hence the supply curve will move farther to the right.

Figure 6(a) illustrates the effect of an expansion of the industry from 100,000 farms to 130,000 farms—a rightward shift of the supply curve from $S_0S_0$ to $S_1S_1$. Figure 6(b) illustrates the opposite case: a contraction of the industry from 100,000 farms to 62,500 farms. The supply curve shifts inward to the left, from $S_0S_0$ to $S_2S_2$. Even if no farmers enter or leave the industry, results like those depicted in Figure 6 can be produced by expansion or contraction of the *existing* farms.

**Technological Progress** Another influence that shifts supply curves is technological change. Suppose an enterprising farmer invents a new growth hormone that increases the body mass of cattle. Thereafter, at any given price, farms will be able to produce more beef; that is, the supply curve will shift outward to the right, as in Figure 6(a). This example, again, illustrates a general influence that applies to most industries:

> **Technological progress that reduces costs will shift the supply curve outward to the right.**

Automakers, for example, have been able to reduce production costs since industrial technology invented robots that can be programmed to work on several different car models. This technological advance has shifted the supply curve outward.

**Prices of Inputs** Changes in input prices also shift supply curves. Suppose a drought raises the price of animal feed. Farmers will have to pay more to keep their cows alive and healthy and consequently will no longer be able to provide the same quantity of beef at each possible price. This example illustrates that

> **Increases in the prices of inputs that suppliers must buy will shift the supply curve inward to the left.**

**Prices of Related Outputs** Ranchers sell hides as well as meat. If leather prices rise sharply, ranchers may decide not to fatten their cattle as much as they used to before bringing them to market, thereby reducing the quantity of beef supplied. On a supply-demand diagram, the supply curve would then shift inward, as in Figure 6(b).

Similar phenomena occur in other industries, and sometimes the effect goes the other way. For example, suppose that the price of beef goes up, which increases the quantity of meat supplied. That, in turn, will raise the number of cowhides supplied

*Figure 6*

**Shifts of the Supply Curve**

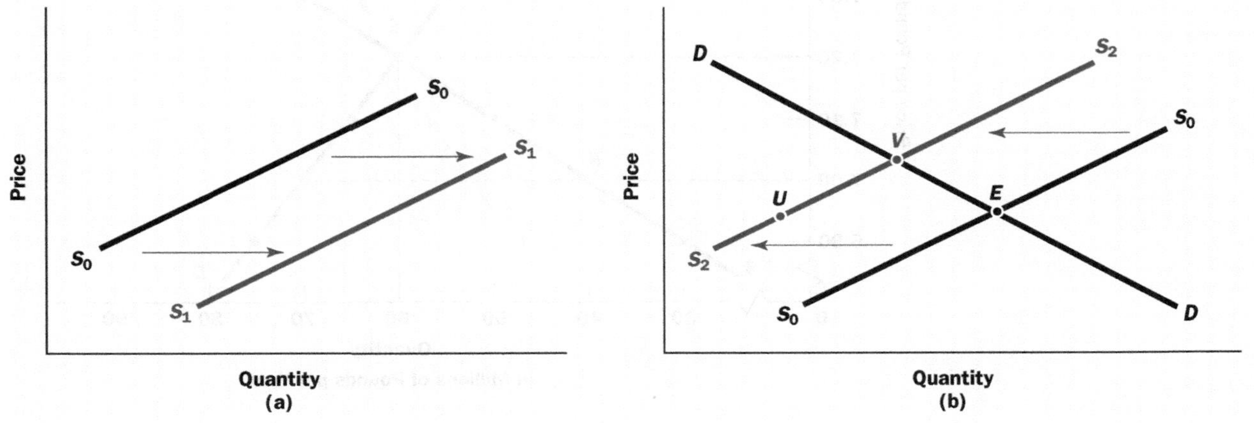

Quantity
(a)

Quantity
(b)

even if the price of leather does not change. Thus, a rise in the price of beef will lead to a rightward shift in the supply curve of leather. In general:

> A change in the price of one good produced by a multiproduct industry may be expected to shift the supply curves of other goods produced by that industry.

## 4-4 SUPPLY AND DEMAND EQUILIBRIUM

To analyze how the free market determines price, we must compare the desires of consumers (demand) with the desires of producers (supply) to see whether the two plans are consistent. Table 3 and Figure 7 help us do this.

A **supply-demand diagram** graphs the supply and demand curves together. It also determines the equilibrium price and quantity.

Table 3 brings together the demand schedule from Table 1 and the supply schedule from Table 2. Similarly, Figure 7 puts the demand curve from Figure 1 and the supply curve from Figure 4 on a single graph. Such graphs are called **supply-demand diagrams**, and you will encounter many of them in this book. Notice that, for reasons already discussed, the demand curve has a negative slope and the supply curve has a positive slope. That is generally true of supply-demand diagrams.

In a free market, price and quantity are determined by the intersection of the supply and demand curves. At only one point in Figure 7, point *E*, do the supply curve and the demand curve intersect. At the price corresponding to point *E*, which is $7.20 per pound, the quantity supplied and the quantity demanded are both 60 million pounds per year. This means that at a price of $7.20 per pound, consumers are willing to buy exactly what producers are willing to sell.

At a lower price, such as $7.00 per pound, only 40 million pounds of beef will be supplied (point *g*), whereas 70 million pounds will be

*Table 3*

**Determination of the Equilibrium Price and Quantity of Beef**

| Price per Pound | Quantity Demanded | Quantity Supplied | Surplus or Shortage | Price Direction |
|---|---|---|---|---|
| $7.50 | 45 | 90 | Surplus | Fall |
| 7.40 | 50 | 80 | Surplus | Fall |
| 7.30 | 55 | 70 | Surplus | Fall |
| 7.20 | 60 | 60 | Neither | Unchanged |
| 7.10 | 65 | 50 | Shortage | Rise |
| 7.00 | 70 | 40 | Shortage | Rise |
| 6.90 | 75 | 30 | Shortage | Rise |

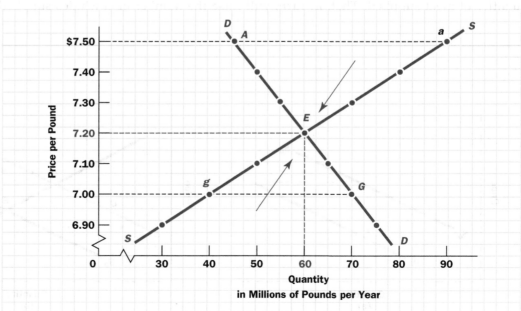

*Figure 7*

**Supply-Demand Equilibrium**

demanded (point *G*). Thus, quantity demanded will exceed quantity supplied. There will be a **shortage** equal to 70 minus 40, or 30 million pounds. Price will thus be driven up by unsatisfied demand. Alternatively, at a higher price, such as $7.50 per pound, quantity supplied will be 90 million pounds (point *a*) and quantity demanded will be only 45 million (point *A*). Quantity supplied will exceed quantity demanded—creating a **surplus** equal to 90 minus 45, or 45 million pounds. The unsold output can then be expected to push the price down.

Because $7.20 is the only price in this graph at which quantity supplied and quantity demanded are equal, we say that $7.20 per pound is the equilibrium price (or the "market clearing" price) in this market. Similarly, 60 million pounds per year is the equilibrium quantity of beef. The term **equilibrium** merits a little explanation, because it arises so frequently in economic analysis.

An equilibrium is a situation in which there are no inherent forces that produce change. Think, for example, of a pendulum resting at its center point. If no outside force (such as a person's hand) comes to push it, the pendulum will remain exactly where it is; it is therefore in equilibrium.

If you give the pendulum a shove, however, its equilibrium will be disturbed, and it will start to move. When it reaches the top of its arc, the pendulum will, for an instant, be at rest again. This point is not an equilibrium position, for the force of gravity will pull the pendulum downward. Thereafter, gravity and friction will govern its motion from side to side. Eventually, the pendulum will return to its original position. The fact that the pendulum tends to return to its original position is described by saying that this position is a *stable* equilibrium. That position is also the only equilibrium position of the pendulum. At any other point, inherent forces will cause the pendulum to move.

The concept of equilibrium in economics is similar and can be illustrated by our supply- and-demand example. Why is no price other than $7.20 an equilibrium price in Table 3 or Figure 7? What forces will change any other price?

Consider first a low price such as $7.00, at which quantity demanded (70 million pounds) exceeds quantity supplied (40 million pounds). If the price were this low, many frustrated customers would be unable to purchase the quantities they desired. In their scramble for the available supply of beef, some would offer to pay more. As customers sought to outbid one another, the market price would be forced up. Thus, a price below the equilibrium price cannot persist in a free market because a shortage sets in motion powerful economic forces that push the price upward.

Similar forces operate in the opposite direction if the market price exceeds the equilibrium price. If, for example, the price should somehow reach $7.50, Table 3 tells us that quantity supplied (90 million pounds) would far exceed the quantity demanded (45 million pounds). Producers would be unable to sell their desired quantities of beef at the prevailing price, and some would undercut their competitors by reducing price. Such competitive price cutting would continue as long as the surplus remained—that is, as long as quantity supplied exceeded quantity demanded. Thus, a price above the equilibrium price cannot persist indefinitely.

We are left with a clear conclusion. The price of $7.20 per pound and the quantity of 60 million pounds per year constitute the only price-quantity combination that does not sow the seeds of its own destruction. It is thus the only equilibrium for this market. Any lower price must rise, and any higher price must fall. It is as if natural economic forces place a magnet at point *E* that attracts the market, just as gravity attracts a pendulum.

The pendulum analogy is worth pursuing further. Most pendulums are more frequently in motion than at rest. However, unless they are repeatedly buffeted by outside forces (which, of course, is exactly what happens to economic equilibria in reality), pendulums gradually return to their resting points. The same is true of price and quantity in a free market. They are moved about by shifts in the supply and demand curves that we have already described. As a consequence, markets are not always in equilibrium. But, if nothing interferes with them, experience shows that they normally move toward equilibrium.

A **shortage** is an excess of quantity demanded over quantity supplied. When there is a shortage, buyers cannot purchase the quantities they desire at the current price.

A **surplus** is an excess of quantity supplied over quantity demanded. When there is a surplus, sellers cannot sell the quantities they desire to supply at the current price.

An **equilibrium** is a situation in which there are no inherent forces that produce change. Changes away from an equilibrium position will occur only as a result of "outside events" that disturb the status quo.

## 4-4a The Law of Supply and Demand

The **law of supply and demand** states that in a free market the forces of supply and demand generally push the price toward the level at which quantity supplied and quantity demanded are equal.

In a free market, the forces of supply and demand generally push the price toward its equilibrium level, the price at which quantity supplied and quantity demanded are equal. Like most economic "laws," some markets will occasionally disobey the **law of supply and demand**. Markets sometimes display shortages or surpluses for long periods of time. Prices sometimes fail to move toward equilibrium. But the "law" is a fair generalization that is right far more often than it is wrong.

## 4-5 EFFECTS OF DEMAND SHIFTS ON SUPPLY-DEMAND EQUILIBRIUM

Figure 3 showed how developments other than changes in price—such as increases in consumer income—can shift the demand curve. We saw that a rise in income, for example, will shift the demand curve to the right, meaning that at any given price, consumers—with their increased purchasing power—will buy more of the good than before. This, in turn, will move the equilibrium point, changing both market price and quantity sold.

This market adjustment is shown in Figure 8(a). It adds a supply curve to Figure 3(a) so that we can see what happens to the supply-demand equilibrium. In the example in the graph, the quantity demanded at the old equilibrium price of \$7.20 increases from 60 million pounds per year (point $E$ on the demand curve $D_0D_0$) to 75 million pounds per year (point $R$ on the demand curve $D_1D_1$). We know that \$7.20 is no longer the equilibrium price, because at this price quantity demanded (75 million pounds) exceeds quantity supplied (60 million pounds). To restore equilibrium, the price must rise. The new equilibrium occurs at point $T$, which is the intersection point of the supply curve and the shifted demand curve, where the price is \$7.30 per pound and both quantities demanded and supplied are 70 million pounds per year. This example illustrates a general result, which is true when the supply curve slopes upward:

> Any influence that makes the demand curve shift outward to the right, and does not affect an upward-sloped supply curve, will raise the equilibrium price and the equilibrium quantity.[5]

*Figure 8*

**The Effects of Shifts of the Demand Curve**

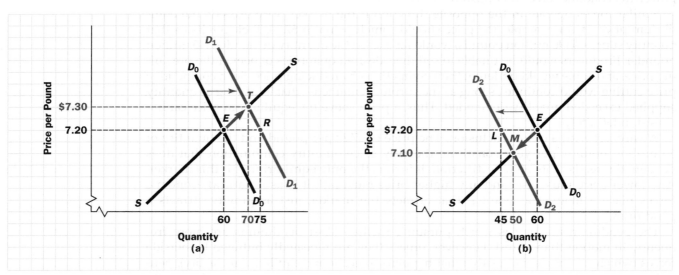

NOTE: Quantity is in millions of pounds per year.

---

[5] For example, when incomes rise rapidly, in many developing countries the demand curves for a variety of consumer goods shift rapidly outward to the right. In India, for example, the demand for high-end consumer goods, such as plasma screen TVs, air conditioners, and washing machines, has skyrocketed in recent decades as India's growing middle class searches for outlets for their rising incomes.

## The Ups and Downs of Milk Consumption

The following excerpt from a U.S. Department of Agriculture publication discusses some of the things that have affected the consumption of milk in the last century.

> Milk availability from 1909 to 2008 dramatically demonstrates the impact of health information on food choices. In 1918, Elmer McCollum, a leading nutritionist at Yale University, labeled milk a "protective" food. McCollum regarded milk, fruit, and vegetables—foods that contained newly discovered substances called vitamins—as critical for preventing specific diseases and promoting healthy growth.
>
> . . . Milk availability grew from a yearly average of 31.3 gallons per person in the 1910s to 39.2 gallons in the 1940s. Similarly, the shift from whole to lower fat milk over the past 30 years owes much to the nutritional advice to "choose lower fat foods."
>
> In 1946, President Harry Truman signed the National School Lunch Act, establishing USDA's National School Lunch Program. This and subsequent school feeding programs . . . included milk in their meals, propping up demand for milk, at least by schools. However, competition from soft drinks, fruit juices, and, more recently, bottled water,

has contributed to the decline in milk availability over the second half of the 20th century and into the first decade of the 21st century. Milk availability is down from its peak of 44.7 gallons per person in 1945 to 20.8 gallons in 2008.

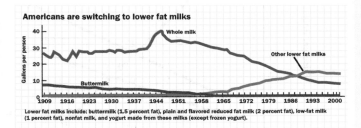

Americans are switching to lower fat milks

Lower fat milks include: buttermilk (1.5 percent fat), plain and flavored reduced fat milk (2 percent fat), low-fat milk (1 percent fat), nonfat milk, and yogurt made from these milks (except frozen yogurt).

SOURCE: Rosanna Mentzer Morrison, Jean C. Buzby, and Hodan Farah Wells, "Guess Who's Turning 100? Tracking a Century of American Eating," *Amber Waves: The Economics of Food, Farming, Natural Resources, and Rural America*, Vol. 8, Issue 1, March 2010, pp. 15–16, U.S. Department of Agriculture, available at http://www.ers.usda.gov/AmberWaves.

Everything works in reverse if consumer incomes fall. Figure 8(b) depicts a leftward (inward) shift of the demand curve that results from a decline in consumer incomes. For example, the quantity demanded at the previous equilibrium price ($7.20) falls from 60 million pounds (point $E$) to 45 million pounds (point $L$ on the demand curve $D_2D_2$). The initial price is now too high and must fall. The new equilibrium will eventually be established at point $M$, where the price is $7.10 and both quantity demanded and quantity supplied are 50 million pounds. In general:

> Any influence that shifts the demand curve inward to the left, and that does not affect the supply curve, will lower both the equilibrium price and the equilibrium quantity.

## 4-6  SUPPLY SHIFTS AND SUPPLY-DEMAND EQUILIBRIUM

A story precisely analogous to that of the effects of a demand shift on equilibrium price and quantity applies to supply shifts. Figure 6 described the effects on the supply curve of beef if the number of farms increases. Figure 9(a) now adds a demand curve to the supply curves of Figure 6 so that we can see the supply-demand equilibrium. Notice that at the initial price of $7.20, the quantity supplied after the shift is 780 million pounds (point $I$ on the supply curve $S_1S_1$), which is 30 percent more than the original quantity demanded of 600 million pounds (point $E$ on the supply curve $S_0S_0$). We can see from the graph that the price of $7.20 is too high to be the equilibrium price; the price must fall. The new equilibrium point is $J$, where the price is $7.10 per pound and the quantity is 650 million pounds per year. In general:

> Any change that shifts the supply curve outward to the right, and does not affect the demand curve, will lower the equilibrium price and raise the equilibrium quantity.

This must always be true if the industry's demand curve has a negative slope, because the greater quantity supplied can be sold only if the price is decreased so as to induce customers to buy more.[6] The cellular phone industry is a case in point. As more providers

---

[6] Graphically, whenever a positively sloped curve shifts to the right, its intersection point with a negatively sloping curve must always move lower. Just try drawing it yourself.

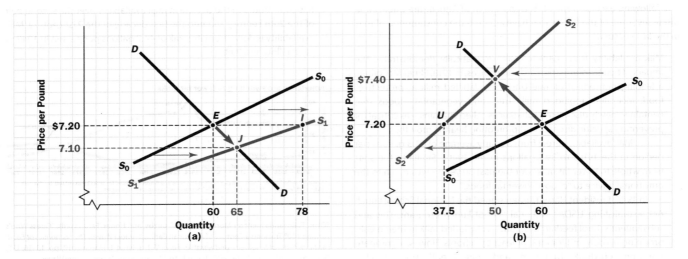

*Figure 9*

**Effects of Shifts of the Supply Curve**

have entered the industry, the cost of cellular service has plummeted. Some cellular carriers have even given away telephones as sign-up bonuses.

Figure 9(b) illustrates the opposite case: a contraction of the industry. The supply curve shifts inward to the left and equilibrium moves from point *E* to point *V*, where the price is $7.40 and quantity is 500 million pounds per year. In general:

> Any influence that shifts the supply curve to the left, and does not affect the demand curve, will raise the equilibrium price and reduce the equilibrium quantity.

Many outside forces can disturb equilibrium in a market by shifting the demand curve or the supply curve, either temporarily or permanently. Between 2006 and 2009, for example, U.S. home prices fell by roughly 30 percent because an oversupply of unsold homes, coupled with the larger effect of the economic crisis of 2007–2009, shifted the real estate demand curve downward.[7] In the fall of 2010, heavy rains ruined the napa cabbage crop in South Korea, shifting the supply curve downward and quadrupling prices of napa cabbage—the essential ingredient in kimchi, a staple of most Koreans' diets.[8] Such outside influences change the equilibrium price and quantity. If you look again at Figures 8 and 9, you can see clearly that any event that causes either the demand curve or the supply curve to shift will also change the equilibrium price and quantity.

---

**Puzzle Resolved** | *Those Leaping Oil Prices*

The disturbing increases in the price of gasoline, and of the oil from which it is made, is attributable to large shifts in both demand and supply conditions. In addition to Americans and their gas-guzzling vehicles, Indian and Chinese consumers are now using more oil, and the resulting upward shift in the demand curve raises the price of oil. At the same time, limits on the amount of oil supplied by the members of OPEC (Organization of the Petroleum Exporting Countries)—the petroleum cartel; instability in oil-rich countries like Iran, Iraq, Nigeria, and Russia; and refinery bottlenecks in the United States have undermined supply—also raising prices. We have seen the results at

---

[7] Les Christie, "Home Prices Sag in August," October 26, 2010, accessed online at http://CNNMoney.com.
[8] CNN Wire Staff, "Cabbage Shortage Leaves Koreans Hungry for Kimchi," October 6, 2010, accessed online at http://CNN.com.

the gas pumps. The following news story describes a sensational sort of change in supply conditions:

> July 28, 2010 (Reuters)—Heightened caution following the BP oil spill is prompting oil and gas producers in the Gulf of Mexico to shut more production faster as storms threaten, exacerbating energy price volatility this hurricane season.
>
> Comparing producers' precautions ahead of storms this year with preparations for more severe storms in previous years indicates that companies are taking tropical threats more seriously, even though predictions of a harsh hurricane season have yet to be borne out. . . .
>
> While interruptions have been temporary, the volumes of production cut have been high and can have a big impact on energy prices. Gulf production accounts for a third of U.S. oil output and more than 10 percent of U.S. natural gas output.
>
> Interruptions from Tropical Storm Bonnie last week helped push oil to 11-week highs near $80 a barrel.
>
> Bonnie cut nearly 52 percent of total Gulf production at its peak, even though it had weakened from a tropical storm to a tropical depression by the time it entered the Gulf and never restrengthened as forecast. . . .
>
> Total output lost to Bonnie was 2.7 million barrels of oil and more than 4.6 [billion cubic feet] of gas through Tuesday. By comparison, [Hurricane] Ida in 2009—crossing the same key Gulf production area—cost the market 1.4 million barrels of oil and 4.6 [billion cubic feet] of gas. . . .
>
> **Extra Caution Exhibited Early in Season** A similarly cautious approach could be seen with Hurricane Alex, which earlier this month took a more southerly route across the Gulf than Bonnie.
>
> At peak, Alex triggered evacuation of 11.7 percent of manned production platforms and 15.7 percent of drilling rigs. Production lost totalled 1.4 million barrels of oil and 3.2 [billion cubic feet] of gas. . . .
>
> Although this season has started slowly despite forecasts of a severe hurricane year, activity typically picks up in August and September and the season does not end until November 30. One weak hurricane and one tropical depression in July could be just the beginning for the Gulf oil patch this year.

SOURCE: Bruce Nichols, "Analysis: Oil Companies More Cautious on Storms after Gulf Spill," July 28, 2010, Reuters, accessed online at http://uk.reuters.com. All rights reserved. Republication or redistribution of Thomson Reuters content, including by framing or similar means, is expressly prohibited without the prior written consent of Thomson Reuters. Thomson Reuters and its logo are registered trademarks or trademarks of the Thomson Reuters group of companies around the world. © Thomson Reuters 2010. Thomson Reuters journalists are subject to an Editorial Handbook which requires fair presentation and disclosure of relevant interests.

## 4-6a  Application: Who Really Pays That Tax?

Supply-and-demand analysis offers insights that may not be readily apparent. Here is an example. Suppose your state legislature raises the gasoline tax by 10 cents per gallon. Service station operators will then have to collect 10 additional cents in taxes on every gallon they pump. They will consider this higher tax as an addition to their costs and will pass it on to you and other consumers by raising the price of gas by 10 cents per gallon. Right? No, wrong—or rather, partly wrong.

The gas station owners would certainly *like* to pass on the entire tax to buyers, but the market mechanism will allow them to shift only *part* of it—perhaps 6 cents per gallon. They will then be stuck with the remainder—4 cents, in our example. Figure 10, which is just another supply-demand graph, shows why.

The demand curve is the maroon curve $DD$. The supply curve before the tax is the black curve $S_0S_0$. Before the new tax, the equilibrium point is $S_0$, and the price is $2.54. We can interpret the supply curve as telling us at what price sellers are willing to provide any

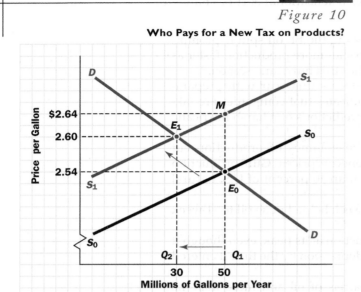

Figure 10

**Who Pays for a New Tax on Products?**

given quantity. For example, they are willing to supply quantity $Q_1 = 50$ million gallons per year if the price is $2.54 per gallon.

So what happens as a result of the new tax? Because they must now turn 10 cents per gallon over to the government, gas station owners will be willing to supply any given quantity only if they get 10 cents more per gallon than before. Therefore, to get them to supply quantity $Q_1 = 50$ million gallons, a price of $2.54 per gallon will no longer suffice. Only a price of $2.64 per gallon will now induce them to supply 50 million gallons. Thus, at quantity $Q_1 = 50$, the point on the supply curve will move up by 10 cents, from point $E_0$ to point $M$. Because firms will insist on the same 10-cent price increase for any other quantity they supply, the *entire* supply curve will shift up by the 10-cent tax—from the black curve $S_0S_0$ to the new blue-colored supply curve $S_1S_1$. And, as a result, the supply-demand equilibrium point will move from $E_0$ to $E_1$, and the price will increase from $2.54 to $2.60.

The supply curve shift may give the impression that gas station owners have succeeded in passing the entire 10-cent increase on to consumers—the distance from $E_0$ to $M$—but look again. The *equilibrium* price has only gone up from $2.54 to $2.60. That is, the price has risen by only 6 cents, not by the full 10-cent amount of the tax. The gas station will have to absorb the remaining 4 cents of the tax.

Now this really *looks* as though we have pulled a fast one on you—a magician's sleight of hand. After all, the supply curve has shifted upward by the full amount of the tax, and yet the resulting price increase has covered only part of the tax rise. However, a second look reveals that, like most apparent acts of magic, this one has a simple explanation. The explanation arises from the *demand* side of the supply-demand mechanism. The negative slope of the demand curve means that when prices rise, at least some consumers will reduce the quantity of gasoline they demand. That will force sellers to give up part of the price increase. In other words, firms must absorb the part of the tax—4 cents—that consumers are unwilling to pay. But note that the equilibrium quantity $Q_1$ has fallen from 50 million gallons to $Q_1 = 30$ million gallons—so both consumers and suppliers lose out in some sense.

This example is not an oddball case. Indeed, the result is almost always true. The cost of any increase in a tax on any commodity will usually be paid partly by the consumer and partly by the seller. This is so regardless of whether the legislature says that it is imposing the tax on the sellers or on the buyers. Whichever way it is phrased, the economics are the same: The supply-demand mechanism ensures that the tax will be shared by both of the parties.

---

## 4-7  BATTLING THE INVISIBLE HAND: THE MARKET FIGHTS BACK

Ideas for Beyond the Final Exam

As we noted in our *Ideas for Beyond the Final Exam* in Chapter 1, lawmakers and rulers have often been dissatisfied with the outcomes of free markets. From Rome to Reno, and from biblical times to the space age, they have battled the invisible hand. Sometimes, rather than trying to adjust the workings of the market, governments have tried to raise or lower the prices of specific commodities by decree. In many such cases, the authorities felt that market prices were, in some sense, immorally low or immorally high. Penalties were therefore imposed on anyone offering the commodities in question at prices above or below those established by the authorities. Such legally imposed constraints on prices are called "price ceilings" and "price floors." To see their result, we will focus on the use of price ceilings.

## 4-7a  Restraining the Market Mechanism: Price Ceilings

The market has proven itself a formidable foe that strongly resists attempts to get around its decisions. In case after case where legal **price ceilings** are imposed, virtually the same series of consequences ensues:

> A **price ceiling** is a maximum that the price charged for a commodity cannot legally exceed.

1. *A persistent shortage develops because quantity demanded exceeds quantity supplied.* Queuing (people waiting in lines), direct rationing (with everyone getting a fixed allotment), or any of a variety of other devices, usually inefficient and unpleasant, must substitute for the distribution process provided by the price mechanism. Example: Rampant shortages of even basic goods in Eastern Europe and the former Soviet Union helped precipitate the revolts that ended communism.
2. *An illegal, or "black," market often arises to supply the commodity.* Usually some individuals are willing to take the risks involved in meeting unsatisfied demands illegally. Example: Although most states ban the practice, ticket "scalping" (the sale of tickets at higher than regular prices) occurs at most popular sporting events and rock concerts.
3. *The prices charged on illegal markets are almost certainly higher than those that would prevail in free markets.* After all, lawbreakers expect some compensation for the risk of being caught and punished. Example: Illegal drugs are normally quite expensive. (See the accompanying box "Economic Aspects of the War on Drugs.")

## Policy Debate

### Economic Aspects of the War on Drugs

For years now, the U.S. government has engaged in a highly publicized "war on drugs." Billions of dollars have been spent on trying to stop illegal drugs at the country's borders. In some sense, interdiction has succeeded: Federal agents have seized literally tons of cocaine and other drugs. Yet these efforts have made barely a dent in the flow of drugs to America's city streets. Simple economic reasoning explains why.

When drug interdiction works, it shifts the supply curve of drugs to the left, thereby driving up street prices. But that, in turn, raises the rewards for potential smugglers and attracts more criminals into the "industry," which shifts the supply curve back to the right. The net result is that increased shipments of drugs to U.S. shores replace much of what the authorities confiscate. This is why many economists believe that any successful antidrug program must concentrate on reducing demand, which would lower the street price of drugs, not on reducing supply, which can only raise it.

Some people suggest that the government should go even further and legalize many drugs. (Indeed, as of 2014, Colorado and Washington State have legalized marijuana.) Although this idea remains a highly controversial position that few are ready to endorse, the reasoning behind it is straightforward. A stunningly high fraction of all the violent crimes committed in America—especially robberies and murders—are drug-related. One major reason is that

AP Images/Guillermo Arias

street prices of drugs are so high that addicts must steal to get the money, and drug traffickers are all too willing to kill to protect their highly profitable "businesses."

How would things differ if drugs were legal? Because South American farmers earn pennies for drugs that sell for hundreds of dollars on the streets of Los Angeles and New York, we may safely assume that legalized drugs would be vastly cheaper. In fact, according to one estimate, a dose of cocaine would cost less than 50 cents. That, proponents point out, would reduce drug-related crimes dramatically. When, for example, was the last time you heard of a gang killing connected with the distribution of cigarettes or alcoholic beverages?

The argument against legalization of drugs is largely moral: Should the state sanction potentially lethal substances? But there is an economic aspect to this position as well: The vastly lower street prices of drugs that would surely follow legalization would increase drug use. Thus, although legalization would almost certainly reduce crime, it may also produce more addicts. The key question here is, How many more addicts? (No one has a good answer.) If you think the increase in quantity demanded would be large, you are unlikely to find legalization an attractive option.

4. *A substantial portion of the price falls into the hands of the illicit supplier instead of going to those who produce the good or perform the service.* Example: A constant complaint during the public hearings that marked the history of theater-ticket price controls in New York City was that the "ice" (the illegal excess charge) fell into the hands of ticket scalpers rather than going to those who invested in, produced, or acted in the play.

5. *Investment in the industry generally dries up.* Because price ceilings reduce the monetary returns that investors can legally earn, less money will be invested in industries that are subject to price controls. Even fear of impending price controls can have this effect. Example: Price controls on farm products in Zambia have prompted peasant farmers and large agricultural conglomerates alike to cut back production rather than grow crops at a loss. The result has been thousands of lost jobs and widespread food shortages.

## 4-7b Case Study: Rent Controls in New York City

These points and others are best illustrated by considering a concrete example involving price ceilings. New York is the only major city in the United States that has continuously legislated rent controls in much of its rental housing and has done so since World War II. Rent controls, of course, are intended to protect the consumer from high rents. But most economists believe that rent control does not help the cities or their residents and that, in the long run, it leaves almost everyone worse off. Elementary supply-demand analysis shows us why.

Figure 11 is a supply-demand diagram for rental units in New York. Curve *DD* is the demand curve, and curve *SS* is the supply curve. Without controls, equilibrium would be at point *E*, where rents average $2,000 per month and 3 million housing units are occupied. If rent controls are effective, the ceiling price must be below the equilibrium price of $2,000. But with a low rent ceiling, such as $1,200, the quantity of housing demanded will be 3.5 million units (point *B*), whereas the quantity supplied will be only 2.5 million units (point *C*).

The diagram shows a shortage of 1 million apartments. This theoretical concept of a "shortage" manifests itself in New York City as an abnormally low vacancy rate, that is, a low share of unoccupied apartments available for rental—typically about half the national urban average. Naturally, rent controls have spawned a lively black market in New York. The black market raises the effective price of rent-controlled apartments in many ways, including bribes, so-called key money paid to move up on a waiting list, or the requirement that prospective tenants purchase worthless furniture at inflated prices.

According to Figure 11, rent controls reduce the quantity supplied from 3 million to 2.5 million apartments. How does this reduction show up in New York? First, some property owners, discouraged by the low rents, have converted apartment buildings into office space or other uses. Second, some apartments have been inadequately maintained. After all, rent controls create a shortage, which makes even dilapidated apartments easy to rent. Third, some landlords have actually abandoned their buildings rather than pay rising tax

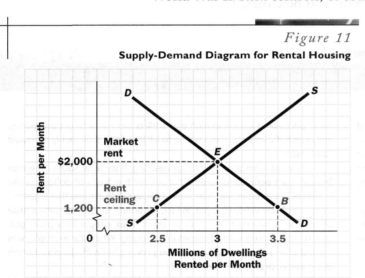

*Figure 11*

**Supply-Demand Diagram for Rental Housing**

*"If you leave me, you know, you'll never see this kind of rent again."*

Richard Cline/The New Yorker Collection/The Cartoon Bank

and fuel bills. These abandoned buildings rapidly become eyesores and eventually pose threats to public health and safety.

An important implication of these last observations is that rent controls—and price controls more generally—harm consumers in ways that offset part or all of the benefits to those who are fortunate enough to find and acquire at lower prices the product that the reduced prices has made scarce. Tenants must undergo long waits and undertake time-consuming searches to find an apartment. The apartment they obtain is likely to be poorly maintained or even decrepit, and normal landlord services are apt to disappear. Thus, even for the lucky beneficiaries, rent control is always far less of a bargain than the reduced monthly payments make them appear to be. The same problems generally apply with other forms of price control as well.

With all of these problems, why does rent control persist in New York City? And why do other cities sometimes move in the same direction?

Part of the explanation is that most people simply do not understand the problems that rent controls create. Another part is that landlords are unpopular politically. But a third, and very important, part of the explanation is that not everyone is hurt by rent controls—and those who benefit from controls fight hard to preserve them. In New York, for example, many tenants pay rents that are only a fraction of what their apartments would fetch on the open market. They are, naturally enough, quite happy with this situation. This last point illustrates another very general phenomenon:

Virtually every price ceiling or floor creates a class of people that benefits from the regulations. These people use their political influence to protect their gains by preserving the status quo, which is one reason why it is so difficult to eliminate price ceilings or floors.

## 4-7c Restraining the Market Mechanism: Price Floors

Interferences with the market mechanism are not always designed to keep prices low. Agricultural price supports and minimum wage laws are two notable examples in which the law keeps prices *above* free-market levels. Such **price floors** are typically accompanied by a standard series of symptoms:

> A **price floor** is a legal minimum below which the price charged for a commodity is not permitted to fall.

1. *A surplus develops because sellers cannot find enough buyers.* Example: Surpluses of various agricultural products have been a persistent—and costly—problem for the U.S. government. The problem is even worse in the European Union (EU), where the common agricultural policy holds prices even higher. One source estimates that this policy accounts for nearly half of all EU spending.[9]
2. *Where goods, rather than services, are involved, the surplus creates a problem of disposal.* Something must be done about the excess of quantity supplied over quantity demanded. Example: The U.S. government has often been forced to purchase, store, and then dispose of large amounts of surplus agricultural commodities.
3. *To get around the regulations, sellers may offer discounts in disguised—and often unwanted—forms.* Example: Back when airline fares were regulated by the government, airlines offered more and better food and more stylishly uniformed flight attendants instead of lowering fares. Today, the food is worse, but tickets cost much less.
4. *Regulations that keep prices artificially high encourage overinvestment in the industry.* Even inefficient businesses whose high operating costs would doom them in an unrestricted market can survive beneath the shelter of a generous price floor. Example: This is why the airline and trucking industries both went through painful "shakeouts" of the weaker companies in the 1980s, after they were deregulated and allowed to charge market-determined prices.

Once again, a specific example is useful for understanding how price floors work.

---

[9] Vivienne Walt, "Even in Hard Times, E.U. Farm Subsidies Roll On," *TIME*, May 14, 2010, accessed online at http://time.com.

### 4-7d  Case Study: Farm Price Supports and the Case of Sugar Prices

America's extensive program of farm price supports began in 1933 as a "temporary method of dealing with an emergency"—in the years of the Great Depression, farmers were going broke in droves. These price supports are still with us today, even though farmers account for less than 2 percent of the U.S. workforce.[10]

One of the consequences of these price supports has been the creation of unsellable surpluses—more output of crops than consumers were willing to buy at the inflated prices yielded by the supports. Warehouses were filled to overflowing. New storage facilities had to be built, and the government was forced to set up programs in which the unmanageable surpluses were shipped to poor foreign countries to combat malnutrition and starvation in those nations. Realistically, if price supports are to be effective in keeping prices above the equilibrium level, then *someone* must be prepared to purchase the surpluses that invariably result. Otherwise, those surpluses will somehow find their way into the market and drive down prices, undermining the price support program. In the United States (and elsewhere), the buyer of the surpluses has usually turned out to be the government, which makes its purchases at the expense of taxpayers who are forced to pay twice—once through taxes to finance the government purchases and a second time in the form of higher prices when they purchase the farm products.

One of the more controversial farm price supports involves the U.S. sugar industry. Sugar producers receive low-interest loans from the federal government and a guarantee that the price of sugar will not fall below a certain level.

In a market economy such as that found in the United States, Congress cannot simply set prices by decree; rather, it must take some action to enforce the price floor. In the case of sugar, that "something" is limiting both domestic production and foreign imports, thereby shifting the supply curve inward to the left. Figure 12 shows the mechanics involved in this price floor. Government policies shift the supply curve inward from $S_0S_0$ to $S_1S_1$ and drive the U.S. price up from 25¢ to 50¢ per pound. The more the supply curve shifts inward, the higher the price.

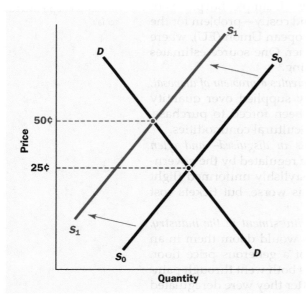

*Figure 12*

**Supporting the Price of Sugar**

The sugar industry obviously benefits from the price-control program, but consumers pay for it in the form of higher prices for sugar and sugar-filled products such as soft drinks, candy bars, and cookies. Although estimates vary, in 1998 the federal sugar price support program cost consumers approximately $1.9 billion. Changes to the program, implemented by the 2008 Farm Bill and continued in the 2014 bill, are likely to cost taxpayers $258 million each year.[11]

If all of this sounds a bit abstract to you, take a look at the ingredients in a U.S.-made soft drink. Instead of sugar, you will likely find "high-fructose corn syrup" listed as a sweetener. Foreign producers generally use sugar, but sugar is simply too expensive to be used for this purpose in the United States.

### 4-7e  A Can of Worms

Our two case studies—rent controls and sugar price supports—illustrate some of the major side effects of price floors and ceilings but barely hint at others. Difficulties arise that we have not even mentioned, for the market mechanism is a tough bird that imposes

---

[10] Under major legislation passed in 1996, many agricultural price supports were supposed to be phased out over a seven-year period. In reality, many support programs, especially that for sugar, have changed little.
[11] Senator John McCain, "Statement by Senator John McCain on Farm Bill Conference Report," February 3, 2014, accessed online at /www.mccain.senate.gov/public/index.cfm/2014/2/statement-by-senator-john-mccain-on-farm-bill-conference-report.

suitable retribution on those who seek to evade it by government decree. Here is a partial list of other problems that may arise when prices are controlled.

**Favoritism and Corruption** When price ceilings or floors create shortages or surpluses, someone must decide who gets to buy or sell the limited quantity that is available. This decision-making process can lead to discrimination along racial or religious lines, political favoritism, or corruption in government. For example, many prices were held at artificially low levels in the former Soviet Union, making queuing for certain goods quite common. Even so, Communist Party officials and other favored groups were somehow able to purchase the scarce commodities that others could not get.

**Unenforceability** Attempts to limit prices are almost certain to fail in industries with numerous suppliers, simply because the regulating agency must monitor the behavior of so many sellers. People will usually find ways to evade or violate the law, and something like the free-market price will generally reappear. However, there is an important difference: Because the evasion process, whatever its form, will have some operating costs, those costs must be borne by someone. Normally, that someone is the consumer, who must pay higher prices to the suppliers for taking the risk of breaking the law.

**Auxiliary Restrictions** Fears that a system of price controls will break down invariably lead to regulations designed to shore up the shaky edifice. Consumers may be told when and from whom they are permitted to buy. The powers of the police and the courts may be used to prevent the entry of new suppliers. Occasionally, an intricate system of market subdivision is imposed, giving each class of firms a protected sphere in which others are not permitted to operate. For example, in New York City, there are laws banning conversion of rent-controlled apartments to condominiums.

**Limitation of Volume of Transactions** To the extent that controls succeed in affecting prices, they can be expected to reduce the volume of transactions. Curiously, this is true regardless of whether the regulated price is above or below the free-market equilibrium price. If it is set above the equilibrium price, the quantity demanded will be below the equilibrium quantity. On the other hand, if the imposed price is set below the free-market level, the quantity supplied will be reduced. Because sales volume cannot exceed either the quantity supplied or the quantity demanded, a reduction in the volume of transactions is the result.[12]

**Misallocation of Resources** Departures from free-market prices are likely to result in misuse of the economy's resources because the connection between production costs and prices is broken. For example, Russian farmers used to feed their farm animals bread instead of unprocessed grains because price ceilings kept the price of bread ludicrously low. In addition, just as more complex locks lead to more sophisticated burglary tools, more complex regulations lead to the use of yet more resources for their avoidance.

Economists put it this way: Free markets are capable of dealing efficiently with the three basic coordination tasks outlined in Chapter 3: deciding what to produce, how to produce it, and to whom the goods should be distributed. Price controls throw a monkey wrench into the market mechanism. Although the market is surely not flawless, and government interferences often have praiseworthy goals, good intentions are not enough.

Any government that sets out to repair what it sees as a defect in the market mechanism runs the risk of causing even more serious damage elsewhere. As a prominent economist once quipped, societies that are too willing to interfere with the operation of free markets soon find that the invisible hand is nowhere to be seen.

---

[12] See Discussion Question 4 at the end of this chapter.

## 4-8  A SIMPLE BUT POWERFUL LESSON

Astonishing as it may seem, many people in authority do not understand the law of supply and demand, or they act as if it does not exist. For example, more than a decade ago *The New York Times* carried a dramatic front-page picture of the president of Kenya setting fire to a large pile of elephant tusks that had been confiscated from poachers. The accompanying story explained that the burning was intended as a symbolic act to persuade the world to halt the ivory trade.[13] One may certainly doubt whether the burning really touched the hearts of criminal poachers, but one economic effect was clear: By reducing the supply of ivory on the world market, the burning of tusks forced up the price of ivory, which raised the illicit rewards reaped by those who slaughter elephants. That could only encourage more poaching—precisely the opposite of what the Kenyan government sought to accomplish. Fortunately, more recent reports indicate that burning ivory is no longer seen as an effective means of curbing poaching. In 2010, for instance, Tanzania rejected calls for it to burn its stockpiles of confiscated ivory.[14]

## Summary

1. The quantity of a product that is demanded is not a fixed number. Rather, **quantity demanded** depends on such influences as the price of the product, consumer incomes, and the prices of other products.

2. The relationship between quantity demanded and price, holding all other things constant, can be displayed graphically on a **demand curve.**

3. For most products, the higher the price, the lower the quantity demanded. As a result, the demand curve usually has a negative slope.

4. The quantity of a product that is supplied depends on its price and many other influences. A **supply curve** is a graphical representation of the relationship between **quantity supplied** and price, holding all other influences constant.

5. For most products, supply curves have positive slopes, meaning that higher prices lead to supply of greater quantities.

6. A change in quantity demanded that is caused by a change in the price of the good is represented by a movement *along* a fixed demand curve. A change in quantity demanded that is caused by a change in any other determinant of quantity demanded is represented by a **shift of the demand curve.**

7. This same distinction applies to the supply curve: Changes in price lead to movements along a fixed supply curve; changes in other determinants of quantity supplied lead to shifts of the entire supply curve.

8. A market is said to be in **equilibrium** when quantity supplied is equal to quantity demanded. The equilibrium price and quantity are shown by the point on the supply-demand graph where the supply and demand curves intersect. The **law of supply and demand** states that price and quantity tend to gravitate to this point in a free market.

9. Changes in consumer incomes, tastes, technology, prices of competing products, and many other influences lead to shifts in either the demand curve or the supply curve and produce changes in price and quantity that can be determined from **supply-demand diagrams**.

10. A tax on a good generally leads to a rise in the price at which the taxed product is sold. The rise in price is generally less than the tax, so consumers usually pay less than the entire tax.

11. Consumers generally pay only part of a tax because the resulting rise in price leads them to buy less and the cut in the quantity they demand helps to force price down.

12. An attempt to use government regulations to force prices above or below their equilibrium levels is likely to lead to **shortages** or **surpluses,** to black markets in which goods are sold at illegal prices, and to a variety of other problems. The market always strikes back at attempts to repeal the law of supply and demand.

## Key Terms

| | | |
|---|---|---|
| demand curve  58 | price ceiling  71 | Shortage  65 |
| demand schedule  57 | price floor  73 | supply curve  61 |
| equilibrium  65 | quantity demanded  57 | supply schedule  61 |
| invisible hand  56 | quantity supplied  61 | supply-demand diagram  64 |
| law of supply and demand  66 | shift in a demand curve  58 | surplus  65 |

---

[13] *The New York Times*, July 19, 1989.
[14] Lucas Liganga, "Destroy Ivory to Curb Poaching, PM Urges Tanzania," *Daily Nation*, May 7, 2010.

## Test Yourself

1. What shapes would you expect for the following demand curves?

   a. A medicine that means life or death for a patient

   b. French fries in a food court with kiosks offering many types of food

2. The following are the assumed supply and demand schedules for hamburgers in Collegetown:

| Demand Schedule | | Supply Schedule | |
|---|---|---|---|
| Price | Quantity Demanded per Year (thousands) | Price | Quantity Supplied per Year (thousands) |
| $2.75 | 14 | $2.75 | 32 |
| 2.50 | 18 | 2.5 | 30 |
| 2.25 | 22 | 2.25 | 28 |
| 2 | 26 | 2 | 26 |
| 1.75 | 30 | 1.75 | 24 |
| 1.5 | 34 | 1.5 | 22 |

   a. Plot the supply and demand curves and indicate the equilibrium price and quantity.

   b. What effect would a decrease in the price of beef (a hamburger input) have on the equilibrium price and quantity of hamburgers, assuming all other things remained constant? Explain your answer with the help of a diagram.

   c. What effect would an increase in the price of pizza (a substitute commodity) have on the equilibrium price and quantity of hamburgers, assuming again that all other things remain constant? Use a diagram in your answer.

3. Suppose the supply and demand schedules for bicycles are as they appear in the following table.

| Price | Quantity Demanded per Year (millions) | Quantity Supplied per Year (millions) |
|---|---|---|
| $170 | 43 | 27 |
| 210 | 39 | 31 |
| 250 | 35 | 35 |
| 300 | 31 | 39 |
| 330 | 27 | 43 |
| 370 | 23 | 47 |

   a. Graph these curves and show the equilibrium price and quantity.

   b. Now suppose that it becomes unfashionable to ride a bicycle, so that the quantity demanded at each price falls by 8 million bikes per year. What is the new equilibrium price and quantity? Show this solution graphically. Explain why the quantity falls by less than 8 million bikes per year.

   c. Suppose instead that several major bicycle producers go out of business, thereby reducing the quantity supplied by 8 million bikes at every price. Find the new equilibrium price and quantity, and show it graphically. Explain again why quantity falls by less than 8 million.

   d. What are the equilibrium price and quantity if the shifts described in Test Yourself Questions 3(b) and 3(c) happen at the same time?

4. The following table summarizes information about the market for principles of economics textbooks:

| Price | Quantity Demanded per Year | Quantity Supplied per Year |
|---|---|---|
| $45 | 4,300 | 300 |
| 55 | 2,300 | 700 |
| 65 | 1,300 | 1,300 |
| 75 | 800 | 2,100 |
| 85 | 650 | 3,100 |

   a. What is the market equilibrium price and quantity of textbooks?

   b. To quell outrage over tuition increases, the college places a $55 limit on the price of textbooks. How many textbooks will be sold now?

   c. While the price limit is still in effect, automated publishing increases the efficiency of textbook production. Show graphically the likely effect of this innovation on the market price and quantity.

5. How are the following demand curves likely to shift in response to the indicated changes?

   a. The effect of a drought on the demand curve for umbrellas

   b. The effect of higher popcorn prices on the demand curve for movie tickets

   c. The effect on the demand curve for coffee of a decline in the price of Coca-Cola

6. The two accompanying diagrams show supply and demand curves for two substitute commodities: regular cell phones and smartphones.

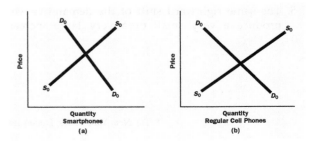

a. On the right-hand diagram, show what happens when rising raw material prices make it costlier to produce regular cell phones.

b. On the left-hand diagram, show what happens to the market for smartphones.

7. Consider the market for beef discussed in this chapter (Tables 1 through 3 and Figures 1 and 8). Suppose that the government decides to fight cholesterol by levying a tax of 50 cents per pound on sales of beef. Follow these steps to analyze the effects of the tax:

a. Construct the new supply schedule (to replace Table 2) that relates quantity supplied to the price that consumers pay.

b. Graph the new supply curve constructed in Test Yourself Question 7(a) on the supply-demand diagram depicted in Figure 7.

c. Does the tax succeed in its goal of reducing the consumption of beef?

d. Is the price rise greater than, equal to, or less than the 50-cent tax?

e. Who actually pays the tax, consumers or producers? (This may be a good question to discuss in class.)

8. **(More difficult)** The demand and supply curves for T-shirts in Touristtown, U.S.A., are given by the following equations:

$$Q = 24{,}000 - 500P \qquad Q = 6{,}000 + 1{,}000P$$

where $P$ is measured in dollars and $Q$ is the number of T-shirts sold per year.

a. Find the equilibrium price and quantity algebraically.

b. If tourists decide they do not really like T-shirts that much, which of the following might be the new demand curve?

$$Q = 21{,}000 - 500P \qquad Q = 27{,}000 - 500P$$

Find the equilibrium price and quantity after the shift of the demand curve.

c. If, instead, two new stores that sell T-shirts open up in town, which of the following might be the new supply curve?

$$Q = 4{,}000 + 1{,}000P \qquad Q = 9{,}000 + 1{,}000P$$

Find the equilibrium price and quantity after the shift of the supply curve.

## Discussion Questions

1. How often do you rent videos? Would you do so more often if a rental cost half as much? Distinguish between your demand curve for home videos and your "quantity demanded" at the current price.

2. Discuss the likely effects of the following:

a. Rent ceilings on the market for apartments

b. A price floor in the market for wheat

Use supply-demand diagrams to show what may happen in each case.

3. U.S. government price supports for milk led to an unceasing surplus of milk. In an effort to reduce the surplus about a decade ago, Congress offered to pay dairy farmers to slaughter cows. Use two diagrams, one for the milk market and one for the meat market, to illustrate how this policy should have affected the price of meat. (Assume that meat is sold in an unregulated market.)

4. It is claimed in this chapter that either price floors or price ceilings reduce the actual quantity exchanged in a market. Use a diagram or diagrams to test this conclusion, and explain the common sense behind it.

5. The same rightward shift of the demand curve may produce a very small or a very large increase in quantity, depending on the slope of the supply curve. Explain this conclusion with diagrams.

6. In 1981, when regulations were holding the price of natural gas below its free-market level, then-Congressman Jack Kemp of New York said the following in an interview with *The New York Times*: "We need to decontrol natural gas, and get production of natural gas up to a higher level so we can bring down the price."[15] Evaluate the congressman's statement.

7. From 2000 to 2010 in the United States, the number of working men fell by 0.6 percent, while the number of working women *grew* by almost 4 percent. During this time, average wages for men grew by roughly 3 percent, whereas average wages for women grew by slightly more than 6 percent. Which of the following two explanations seems more consistent with the data?

a. Women decided to work more, raising their relative supply (relative to men).

b. Discrimination against women declined, raising the relative (to men) demand for female workers.

---

[15] *The New York Times*, December 24, 1981.

# The Macroeconomy: Aggregate Supply and Demand

*Macroeconomics* is the headline-grabbing part of economics. When economic news appears on the front page of your daily newspaper, or is reported on some web site you read regularly, you are probably reading about some macroeconomic development in the national or world economy. The Federal Reserve has finally started raising interest rates. Inflation remains low. Jobs remain scarce. The federal government's large budget deficit is shrinking. The euro is rising in value. All of these developments are *macroeconomic* news. But what do they mean?

Part 2 begins your study of macroeconomics. It will first acquaint you with some of the major concepts of macroeconomics—things that you hear about every day, such as gross domestic product (GDP), inflation, unemployment, and economic growth (Chapters 5 and 6). Then it will introduce you to the basic theory that we use to interpret and understand macroeconomic events (Chapters 7 through 10). By the time you finish Chapter 10—which is only six chapters away—those newspaper articles will make a lot more sense.

CHAPTERS

2

# AN INTRODUCTION TO MACROECONOMICS

*Where the telescope ends, the microscope begins. Which of the two has the grander view?*

VICTOR HUGO

By time-honored tradition, economics is divided into two fields: *microeconomics* and *macroeconomics*. These inelegant words are derived from the Greek, where *micro* means something small and *macro* means something large. Chapters 3 and 4 introduced you to microeconomics. This chapter does the same for macroeconomics.

How do the two branches of the discipline differ? It is *not* a matter of using different tools. As we shall see in this chapter, supply and demand provide the basic organizing framework for constructing macroeconomic models, just as they do for microeconomic models. Rather, the distinction is based on the issues addressed. For an example of a macroeconomic question, take a look at the issue box "How Did the Housing Bust Lead to the Great Recession?" that begins this chapter.

## CONTENTS

## Issue | *How Did the Housing Bust Lead to the Great Recession?*

The U.S. economy expanded, albeit at highly variables rates, for 25 consecutive quarters starting in the fourth quarter of 2001 and continuing through the fourth quarter of 2007. Then the economy hit a wall, *declining* in five of the next six quarters before finally righting itself in mid-2009. What went wrong? Part of the answer is well known. An exceptional boom in homebuilding came to an abrupt end, and then turned into a severe housing bust that did not bottom out until the middle of 2009. Although housing was not the only factor at work, it was certainly a major contributor to the Great Recession.

But how? How does a housing bust push an entire economy downhill? After all, even at its peak, homebuilding amounted to just a bit more than 6 percent of the economy. There is, of course, no simple answer to questions like these. But beginning in this chapter and continuing through Parts 2 and 3, we will learn a great deal about the factors that determine whether an economy grows or declines—and how fast. Among those factors, we will see, are a number of government policy decisions.

## 5-1  DRAWING A LINE BETWEEN MACROECONOMICS AND MICROECONOMICS

In microeconomics, the spotlight is on *how individual decision-making units behave.* For example, the beef farmers of Chapter 4 are individual decision makers; so are the consumers who purchase the beef. How do they decide which actions are in their own best interests? How are these millions of decisions coordinated by the market mechanism, and with what consequences? Questions such as these lie at the heart of microeconomics.

Although Plato and Aristotle might wince at the abuse of their language, microeconomics applies to the decisions of some astonishingly large units. The annual sales of General Electric (GE) and Walmart, for example, exceed the total production of many nations. Yet, someone who studies GE's pricing policies is a microeconomist, whereas someone who studies inflation in a small country like Monaco is a macroeconomist. The micro–macro distinction in economics is certainly not based solely on size.

What, then, is the basis for this long-standing distinction? The answer is that microeconomics focuses on the *decisions of individual units,* no matter how large, while macroeconomics concentrates on *the behavior of entire economies,* no matter how small. Microeconomists might look at a single company's pricing and output decisions. Macroeconomists study the overall price level, unemployment rate, and other things that we call *economic aggregates.*

### 5-1a  Aggregation and Macroeconomics

An "economic aggregate" is simply an *abstraction* that people use to describe some salient feature of economic life. For example, although we observe the prices of gasoline, telephone calls, and movie tickets every day, we never actually see "the price level." Yet, many people—not just economists—find it meaningful to speak of "the cost of living." In fact, the government's attempts to measure it are widely publicized by the news media each month.

Among the most important of these abstract notions is the concept of *domestic product,* which represents the total production of a nation's economy. The process by which real objects such as software, new houses, and theater tickets are combined into an abstraction called total domestic product is called **aggregation**, and it is one of the foundations of macroeconomics. We can illustrate it by a simple example.

**Aggregation** means combining many individual markets into one overall market.

An imaginary nation called Agraria produces nothing but foodstuffs to sell to consumers. Rather than deal separately with the many markets for pizzas, candy bars, hamburgers, and so on, macroeconomists group them all into a single abstract "market for output." Thus, when macroeconomists announce that output in Agraria grew 10 percent last year, are they referring to more potatoes or hot dogs, more soybeans or green peppers? The answer is: They do not care. In the aggregate measures of macroeconomics, output is output, no matter what form it takes.

### 5-1b  The Foundations of Aggregation

Amalgamating many markets into one means ignoring distinctions among different products. Can we really believe that no one cares whether the national output of Agraria consists of $800,000 worth of pickles and $200,000 worth of ravioli rather than $500,000 each of lettuce and tomatoes? Surely this is too much to swallow.

Macroeconomists certainly do not believe that no one cares; instead, they rest the case for aggregation on two foundations:

1. Although the *composition* of demand and supply in the various markets may be terribly important for *some* purposes (such as how income is distributed and the diets people either enjoy or suffer through), it may be of little consequence for economy-wide issues like growth, inflation, and unemployment—the issues that concern macroeconomists.

2. During economic fluctuations, markets tend to move up or down together. When demand in the economy rises, there is more demand for potatoes *and* tomatoes, more demand for artichokes *and* pickles, more demand for ravioli *and* hot dogs.

Although there are exceptions to these two principles, both are serviceable enough as approximations. In fact, if they were not, there would be no discipline called macroeconomics, and a full-year course in economics could be reduced to a half-year. Lest this cause you a twinge of regret, bear in mind that many people believe that unemployment and inflation would be far more difficult to control without macroeconomics—which would be a lot worse.

## 5-1c  The Line of Demarcation Revisited

These two principles—that the composition of demand and supply may not matter for some purposes, and that markets normally move together—enable us to draw a different kind of dividing line between microeconomics and macroeconomics.

> In macroeconomics, we typically assume that most details of resource allocation and income distribution are relatively unimportant to the study of the overall rates of inflation and unemployment. In microeconomics, we generally ignore inflation, unemployment, and growth, focusing instead on how individual markets allocate resources and distribute income.

To use a well-worn metaphor, a macroeconomist analyzes the size of the proverbial economic "pie," paying scant attention to what is inside it or to how it gets divided among the dinner guests. A microeconomist, by contrast, assumes that the pie is of the right size and shape, and frets over its ingredients and who gets to eat it. If you have ever baked or eaten a pie, you will realize that either approach alone is a trifle myopic.

Economics is divided into macroeconomics and microeconomics largely for the sake of pedagogical clarity: We can't teach you everything at once. In reality, the crucial interconnection between macroeconomics and microeconomics is with us all the time. There is, after all, only one economy.

## 5-2  SUPPLY AND DEMAND IN MACROECONOMICS

Whether you are taking a course that concentrates on macroeconomics or one that focuses on microeconomics, the discussion of supply and demand in Chapter 4 served as an invaluable introduction. Supply and demand analysis is just as fundamental to macroeconomics as it is to microeconomics.

## 5-2a  A Quick Review

Figure 1 shows two diagrams that should look familiar from Chapter 4. In Figure 1(a), we find a downward-sloping demand curve, labeled $DD$, and an upward-sloping supply curve, labeled $SS$. Because the figure is a multipurpose diagram, the "Price" and "Quantity" axes do not specify any particular commodity. To start on familiar terrain, first imagine that this graph depicts the market for beef, so the vertical axis measures the price of a pound of beef and the horizontal axis measures the quantity of beef demanded and supplied. As we know, if nothing interferes with the operation of a free market, equilibrium will be at point $E$ with a price $P_0$ and a quantity of output $Q_0$.

Next, suppose something happens to shift the demand curve outward. For example, we learned in Chapter 4 that an increase in consumer incomes might do that.

*Figure 1*

**Two Interpretations of a Shift in the Demand Curve**

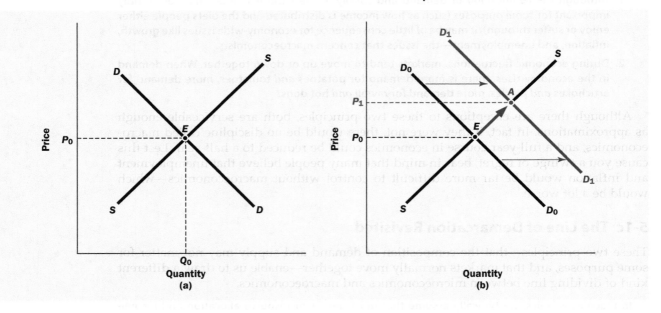

Figure 1(b) shows this shift as a rightward movement of the demand curve from $D_0D_0$ to $D_1D_1$. Equilibrium shifts from point $E$ to point $A$, so both price and output rise.

### 5-2b  Moving to Macroeconomic Aggregates

Now let's switch from microeconomics to macroeconomics. To do so, we reinterpret Figure 1 as representing the market for an abstract object called "domestic product"—one of those economic aggregates that we described earlier. No one has ever seen, touched, or eaten a unit of domestic product, but these are the kinds of abstractions we use in macroeconomic analysis.

Consistent with this reinterpretation, think of the price measured on the vertical axis as being another abstraction—the overall price index, or "cost of living."[1] Then the curve $DD$ in Figure 1(a) is called an **aggregate demand curve**, and the curve $SS$ is called an **aggregate supply curve**. We will develop an economic theory to derive these curves explicitly in Chapters 7 through 10. As we will see there, the curves have rather different origins from the microeconomic counterparts we encountered in Chapter 4.

The **aggregate demand curve** shows the quantity of domestic product that is demanded at each possible value of the price level.

The **aggregate supply curve** shows the quantity of domestic product that is supplied at each possible value of the price level.

**Inflation** refers to a sustained increase in the general price level.

### 5-2c  Inflation

With this macroeconomic reinterpretation, Figure 1(b) depicts the problem of **inflation**. We see from the figure that the outward shift of the aggregate demand curve, whatever its cause, pushes the price level up. If aggregate demand keeps shifting out month after month, the economy will suffer from inflation—meaning a sustained increase in the general price level.

### 5-2d  Recession and Unemployment

The second principal issue of macroeconomics, recession and unemployment, also can be illustrated on a supply–demand diagram, this time by shifting the demand curve in the opposite direction. Figure 2 repeats the supply and demand curves of Figure 1(a) and

---

[1] Chapter 6's appendix explains how such price indexes are calculated.

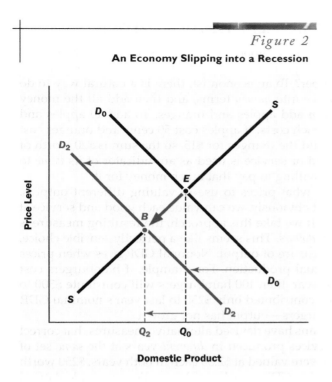

*Figure 2*

**An Economy Slipping into a Recession**

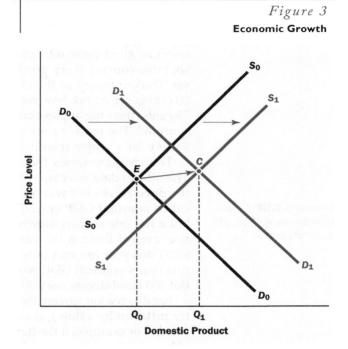

*Figure 3*

**Economic Growth**

in addition depicts a leftward shift of the aggregate demand curve from $D_0D_0$ to $D_2D_2$. Equilibrium now moves from point $E$ to point $B$ so that domestic product (total output) declines. This is what we normally mean by a **recession**—a period of time during which production falls and people lose jobs.

A **recession** is a period of time during which the total output of the economy declines.

## 5-2e Economic Growth

Figure 3 illustrates the third major concern of macroeconomics: the process of economic growth. Here the original aggregate demand and supply curves are, once again, $D_0D_0$ and $S_0S_0$, which intersect at point $E$. But now we consider the possibility that both curves shift to the right over time, moving to $D_1D_1$ and $S_1S_1$, respectively. The new intersection point is $C$, and the blue arrow running from point $E$ to point $C$ shows the economy's growth path. Over this period of time, domestic product grows from $Q_0$ to $Q_1$.

## 5-3 GROSS DOMESTIC PRODUCT

Up to now, we have been somewhat cavalier in using the phrase "domestic product." Let's now get more specific. Of the various ways to measure an economy's total output, the most popular choice by far is **gross domestic product**, or **GDP** for short—a term you have probably encountered in the news media. GDP is the most comprehensive measure of the output of all the factories, offices, and shops in the United States. Specifically, it is the sum of the *money values* of all *final* goods and services *produced* in the *domestic* economy within the year.

Several features of this definition need to be underscored.[2] First, you will notice that

**We add up the money values of things.**

**Gross domestic product (GDP)** is the sum of the money values of all final goods and services produced in the domestic economy and sold on organized markets during a specified period of time, usually a year.

_____

[2] Certain exceptions to the definition are dealt with in Chapter 8's appendix. Some instructors may prefer to take up that material here.

## 5-3a  Money as the Measuring Rod: Real versus Nominal GDP

The GDP consists of a bewildering variety of goods and services: computer chips and potato chips, tanks and textbooks, ballet performances and rock concerts. How can we combine all of these into a single number? To an economist, there is a natural way to do so: First, convert every good and service into *money* terms, and then add all the money up. Thus, contrary to the cliché, we *can* add apples and oranges. To add 10 apples and 20 oranges, first ask how much *money* each costs. If apples cost 50 cents and oranges cost 75 cents, then the apples count for $5 and the oranges for $15, so the sum is $20 worth of "output." The market *price* of each good or service is used as an indicator of its *value* to society for a simple reason: *Someone* is willing to pay that much money for it.

This decision raises the question of what prices to use in valuing different outputs. The official data offer two choices. Most obviously, we can value each good and service at the price at which it was actually sold. If we take this approach, the resulting measure is called **nominal GDP** or *GDP in current dollars*. This seems like a perfectly sensible choice, but it has one serious drawback as a measure of output: Nominal GDP rises when prices rise, even if there is no increase in actual production. For example, if hamburgers cost $3.00 this year but cost only $2.50 last year, then 100 hamburgers will contribute $300 to this year's nominal GDP, whereas they contributed only $250 to last year's nominal GDP. But 100 hamburgers are still 100 hamburgers—output has not grown.

For this reason, government statisticians have devised alternative measures that correct for inflation by valuing goods and services produced in *different* years at the *same* set of prices. For example, if the hamburgers were valued at $2.50 each in both years, $250 worth of hamburger output would be included in GDP *in each year*. In practice, such calculations can be quite complicated, but the details need not worry us in an introductory course. Suffice it to say that, when the calculations are done, we obtain **real GDP** or *GDP in constant dollars*. The news media often refer to this measure as "GDP corrected for inflation." Throughout most of this book, and certainly whenever we are discussing the nation's output, we will be concerned mainly with *real* GDP.

The distinction between nominal and real GDP leads us to a working definition of a *recession* as a period in which *real* GDP declines. For example, between the fourth quarter of 2007 and the second quarter of 2009, the period known as the Great Recession, real GDP *fell* from $14,992 billion to $14,356 billion. In fact, it has become conventional to say that a recession occurs when real GDP declines for two or more consecutive quarters. During the Great Recession, real GDP declined for four consecutive quarters and five out of six, making it the worst recession since the 1930s.

> **Nominal GDP** is calculated by valuing all outputs at current prices.

> **Real GDP** is calculated by valuing outputs of different years at common prices. Therefore, real GDP is a far better measure than nominal GDP of changes in total production.

## 5-3b  What Gets Counted in GDP?

The next important aspect of the definition of GDP is that

> The GDP for a particular year includes only goods and services produced in that year. Sales of items produced in previous years are explicitly excluded.

For example, suppose you buy a perfectly beautiful 1999 Corvette from a friend and are overjoyed by your purchase. The national income statistician will not share your glee. She counted that car in the GDP of 1999, when it was first produced and sold, and will never count it again. The same is true of houses. Even though houses often go *up* in value, the resale values of houses do not count in GDP because they were counted in the years they were built.

Next, you will note from the definition of gross domestic product that

> Only **final goods and services** count in the GDP.

> **Final goods and services** are those that are purchased by their ultimate users.

> An **intermediate good** is a good purchased for resale or for use in producing another good.

The adjective *final* is the key word here. For example, when Dell buys computer chips from Intel, the transaction is not included in the GDP because Dell does not want the chips for itself. It buys them only to manufacture computers, which it sells to consumers. Only the computers are considered a final product. When Dell buys chips from Intel, economists call the chips **intermediate goods**. GDP excludes sales of intermediate goods and services because, if they were included, we would wind up counting the same outputs several times.[3] For example, if chips sold to computer manufacturers were included in GDP, we would count the same chip when it was sold to the computer maker and then again as a component of the computer when it was sold to a consumer.

Next, note that

**The adjective *domestic* in the definition of GDP denotes production within the geographic boundaries of the United States.**

"*More and more, I ask myself what's the point of pursuing the meaning of the universe if you can't have a rising GNP.*"

Some Americans work abroad, and many American companies have offices or factories in foreign countries. For example, more than half of IBM's employees work outside the United States. Although all of these foreign employees of American firms produce valuable outputs, none of it counts in the GDP of the United States. (It counts, instead, in the GDPs of the other countries.) On the other hand, quite a few foreign companies produce goods and services in the United States. For example, if your family owns a Toyota or a Honda, it was most likely assembled in a factory here. All that activity of foreign firms on our soil does count in our GDP.[4]

Finally, the definition of GDP notes that

**For the most part, only goods and services that pass through organized markets count in the GDP.**

This restriction, of course, excludes many economic activities. For example, illegal activities are not included in the GDP. Thus, gambling services in Atlantic City are part of GDP, but gambling services in Chicago are not. Garage sales, although sometimes lucrative, are not included either. The definition reflects the statisticians' inability to measure the value of many of the economy's most important activities, such as housework, do-it-yourself repairs, and leisure time. These activities certainly result in currently produced goods or services, but they all lack that important measuring rod—a market price.

This omission results in certain oddities. For example, suppose that each of two neighboring families hired the other to clean house, generously paying $1,000 per week for the services. Each family could easily afford such generosity because it would collect an identical salary from its neighbor. Nothing real would change, but GDP would rise by $104,000 per year. If this example seems trivial, you may be interested to know that, according to one estimate made some years ago, America's GDP might be a stunning 44 percent higher if unpaid housework were valued at market prices and counted in GDP.[5]

## 5-3c Limitations of the GDP: What GDP Is Not

Now that we have seen in some detail what the GDP *is*, let's examine what it *is not*. In particular:

**Gross domestic product is not a measure of the nation's economic well-being.**

The GDP is not intended to measure economic well-being and does not do so for several reasons.

**Only Market Activity Is Included in GDP** As we have just seen, a great deal of work done in the home contributes to the nation's well-being but is not counted in GDP because it has no price tag. One important implication of this exclusion arises when we try to compare the GDPs of developed and less-developed countries. Americans are always amazed

---

[3] Actually, there is another way to add up the GDP by counting a portion of each intermediate transaction. This is explained in Chapter 8's appendix.

[4] There is another concept, called gross *national* product, which counts the goods and services produced by all Americans, regardless of where they work. For consistency, the outputs produced by foreigners working in the United States are not included in GNP. In practice, the two measures—GDP and GNP—are very close.

[5] Ann Chadeau, "What Is Households' Non-Market Production Worth?" *OECD Economic Studies*, 18 (1992), pp. 85–103.

to hear that the per capita GDPs of the poorest African countries are less than $250 per year. Surely, no one could survive in America on $5 per week. How can Africans do it? Part of the answer, of course, is that these people are terribly poor. But another part of the answer is that

> **International GDP comparisons are vastly misleading when the two countries differ greatly in the fraction of economic activity that each conducts in organized markets.**

This fraction is relatively large in the United States and relatively small in the poorest countries. So when we compare their respective measured GDPs, we are not comparing the same economic activities. Many things that get counted in the U.S. GDP are not counted in the GDPs of very poor nations because they do not pass through markets. It is ludicrous to think that these people, impoverished as they are, survive on what an American thinks of as $5 per week.

A second implication is that GDP statistics take no account of the so-called *underground economy*—a term that includes not just criminal activities, but also a great deal of legitimate business that is conducted in cash or by barter to escape the tax collector. Naturally, we have no good data on the size of the underground economy. Some observers, however, think that it may amount to 10 percent or more of U.S. GDP—and much more in some foreign countries.

**GDP Places No Value on Leisure**  As a country gets richer, its citizens normally take more and more leisure time. If that is true, a better measure of national well-being that included the value of leisure would display faster growth than conventionally measured GDP. For example, because the length of the typical workweek in the United States fell steadily for many decades, growth in GDP systematically *underestimated* the growth in national well-being because leisure time was increasing. But then this trend stopped and may even have reversed. (See "Are Americans Working More?")

## Are Americans Working More?

According to conventional wisdom, the workweek in the United States has been steadily shrinking over the decades, leaving Americans with more and more leisure time to enjoy. But a 1991 book by economist Juliet Schor overturned this conventional wisdom, pointing out that Americans were really working longer and longer hours. Her findings were both provocative and controversial at the time. And since then, the gap between the typical American and European workweek has widened.

In the last twenty years the amount of time Americans have spent at their jobs has risen steadily…. Americans report that they have only sixteen and a half hours of leisure a week, after the obligations of job and household are taken care of…. If present trends continue, by the end of the century Americans will be spending as much time at their jobs as they did back in the nineteen twenties.

The rise in worktime was unexpected. For nearly a hundred years, hours had been declining…. Equally surprising, but also hardly recognized, has been the deviation from Western Europe. After progressing in tandem for nearly a century, the United States veered off into a trajectory of declining leisure, while in Europe work has been disappearing…. U.S. manufacturing employees currently work 320 more hours [per year]—the equivalent of over two months—than their counterparts in West Germany or France…. We have paid a price for prosperity…. We are eating more, but we are burning up those

calories at work. We have color televisions and compact disc players, but we need them to unwind after a stressful day at the office. We take vacations, but we work so hard throughout the year that they become indispensable to our sanity.

SOURCE: Juliet B. Schor, *The Overworked American* (New York: Basic Books; 1991), pp. 1–2, 10–11.

**"Bads" as Well as "Goods" Get Counted in GDP**  There are also reasons why the GDP *overstates* how well-off a country is. Here is a tragic example. A powerful typhoon struck the Philippines in November 2013, killing thousands of people and leaving hundreds of thousands homeless. Entire towns were literally swept away. Millions of Filipinos suffered, and their economy was severely disrupted. No one doubts that this horrific natural disaster left the Philippines much worse off. Yet, many economists believe that, after an adjustment period, the disaster actually *raised* GDP in the Philippines. The cleanup and disaster relief alone resulted in huge expenditures. And the eventual rebuilding will account for even more. Much of this spending will be by government, but hundreds of billions of pesos will be spent by businesses and households as well. The Philippine GDP in 2014 and 2015 may well be higher because of the catastrophe. But that doesn't mean the country is better off.

Wars represent an even more extreme example. Mobilization for a war fought on some other nation's soil normally causes a country's GDP to rise rapidly. But men and women serving in the military could be producing civilian output instead. Factories assigned to produce armaments could instead be making cars, washing machines, and televisions. A country at war is surely worse off than a country at peace, but this fact will not be reflected in its GDP.

**Ecological Costs Are Not Netted Out of the GDP**  Many productive activities of a modern industrial economy have undesirable side effects on the environment. Automobiles provide an essential means of transportation, but they also despoil the atmosphere. Factories that manufacture valuable commodities also pollute rivers and lakes. Almost everything seems to produce garbage, which creates serious disposal problems. None of these ecological costs are deducted from the GDP in an effort to give us a truer measure of the *net* increase in economic welfare that our economy produces. Is this omission foolish? Not if we remember that national income statisticians are trying to measure economic activity conducted through organized markets, not national welfare.

Now that we have defined several of the basic concepts of macroeconomics, let us breathe some life into them by perusing the economic history of the United States.

## 5-4 THE ECONOMY ON A ROLLER COASTER

Like most countries, the macroeconomic history of the United States exhibits many ups and downs—booms and recessions, inflations, and even a few deflations.

### 5-4a  Growth, but with Fluctuations

The most salient fact about the U.S. economy has been its seemingly limitless *growth;* it gets bigger almost every year. Nominal gross domestic product in 2014 was around $17.5 trillion, more than 33 times as much as in 1959. The black curve in Figure 4 shows that extraordinary upward march. But, as the discussion of nominal versus real GDP suggests, a large part of this apparent growth was simply inflation. Because of higher prices, the *purchasing power* of each 2014 dollar was less than one-sixth of each 1959 dollar. Corrected for inflation, we see that *real GDP* (the maroon curve in the figure) was only about 5.3 times greater in 2014 than in 1959.

Another reason for the growth of GDP is population growth. A nation becomes richer only if its GDP grows *faster* than its population. To see how much richer the United States has actually become since 1959, we must divide real GDP by the size of the population to obtain **real GDP per capita**—which is the blue line in Figure 4. It turns out that real output per person in 2014 was roughly three times as much as in 1959. That is still not a bad performance.

If aggregate supply and demand grew smoothly from one year to the next, the economy would expand at a steady rate. But U.S. economic history displays a far less regular pattern—one of alternating periods of rapid and slow growth that are called *macroeconomic fluctuations,* or sometimes just *business cycles.* In some years—six since 1959, to be

**Real GDP per capita** is the ratio of real GDP divided by population.

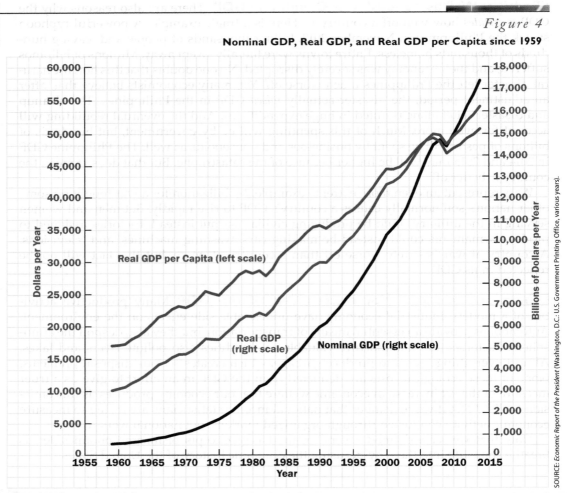

*Figure 4*

**Nominal GDP, Real GDP, and Real GDP per Capita since 1959**

NOTE: Real GDP figures are in 2009 dollars.

SOURCE: *Economic Report of the President* (Washington, D.C.: U.S. Government Printing Office, various years).

exact, with 2009 being the worst—real GDP actually declined. Such *recessions*, and their attendant problem of rising unemployment, have been a persistent feature of American economic performance—one to which we will pay much attention in the coming chapters.

The bumps encountered along the American economy's historic growth path stand out more clearly in Figure 5, which displays the same data in a different way and extends the time period back to 1870. Here we plot not the *level* of real GDP each year, but, rather, its *growth rate*—the percentage change from one year to the next. Now the booms and busts that delight and distress people—and swing elections—stand out clearly. For example, the fact that real GDP grew by more than 7 percent from 1983 to 1984 helped ensure Ronald Reagan's landslide reelection. Then, from 1990 to 1991, real GDP actually fell slightly, which helped Bill Clinton defeat George H. W. Bush. The recent recession stands out for its severity. The still-weak economy made Barack Obama's reelection in 2012 an uphill climb, though he won anyway.

## 5-4b Inflation and Deflation

**Deflation** refers to a sustained decrease in the general price level.

The history of the inflation rate depicted in Figure 6 also shows more positive numbers than negative ones—more inflation than **deflation**. Although the price level has risen roughly 18-fold since 1869, the upward trend is of rather recent vintage. Prior to World War II, Figure 6 displays periods of inflation and deflation, with little or no tendency for one to be more common than the other. Indeed, prices in 1940 were barely higher than those at the close of the Civil War. However, the figure does show some large gyrations in the inflation rate, including sharp bursts of inflation during and immediately after the

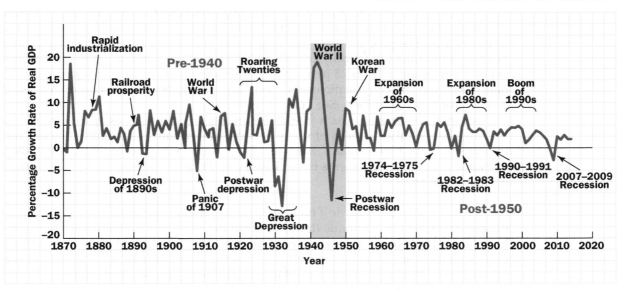

*Figure 5*

**The Growth Rate of U.S. Real GDP since 1870**

two world wars and dramatic deflations in the 1870s, the 1880s, 1921–1922, and 1929–1933. Recently, as you can see, inflation has been both low and stable.

In sum, although both real GDP, which measures the economy's output, and the price level have grown a great deal over the past 145 years, neither has grown smoothly. The ups and downs of both real growth and inflation are important economic events that need to be explained. The remainder of Part 2, which develops a model of aggregate supply and demand, and Part 3, which explains the tools the government uses to try to manage aggregate demand, will build a macroeconomic theory designed to do precisely that.

## 5-4c The Great Depression

As you look at these graphs, the Great Depression of the 1930s is bound to catch your eye. The decline in economic activity from 1929 to 1933 indicated in Figure 5 was the most severe in our nation's history, and the rapid deflation in Figure 6 was extraordinary.

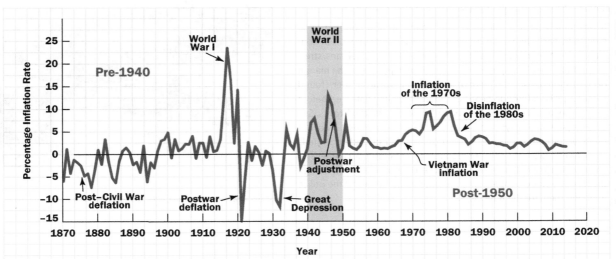

*Figure 6*

**The Inflation Rate in the United States since 1870**

SOURCE: Constructed by the authors from Commerce Department data since 1929. Data for 1869–1928 are based on research by Professor Christina Romer.

The  Depression is but a dim memory now, though for a while in 2008 and 2009, events started to rekindle those memories. There was even talk of "Great Depression 2.0."

**Human Consequences**  Statistics often conceal the human consequences and drama of economic events. But in the case of the Great Depression, they stand as bitter testimony to its severity. The production of goods and services dropped an astonishing 26 percent, business investment practically ceased, and the unemployment rate rose ominously from about 3 percent in 1929 to 25 percent in 1933—one person in four was jobless! From the data alone, you can conjure pictures of soup lines, beggars on street corners, closed factories, and homeless families. (See "Life in 'Hooverville.'")

The Great Depression was a worldwide event; no country was spared its ravages. It literally changed the histories of many nations. In Germany, it facilitated the ascendancy of Nazism. In the United States, it enabled Franklin Roosevelt to engineer one of the most dramatic political realignments in our history and to push through a host of political and economic reforms.

**A Revolution in Economic Thought**  The worldwide depression also caused a much-needed revolution in economic thinking. Until the 1930s, the prevailing economic theory held that a capitalist economy occasionally misbehaved but had a natural tendency to cure recessions or inflations by itself. The roller coaster bounced around but did not run off the tracks. But the stubbornness of the Great Depression shook almost everyone's faith in the ability of the economy to correct itself. In England, this questioning attitude led John Maynard Keynes, one of the world's most renowned economists, to write *The General Theory of Employment, Interest, and Money* (1936). Probably the most important economics book of the twentieth century, it carried a message that was considered revolutionary at the time and remains controversial to this day. Keynes rejected the idea that the economy naturally gravitated toward smooth growth and high levels of employment, asserting instead that if pessimism led businesses and consumers to curtail their spending, the economy might be condemned to years of stagnation.

In terms of our simple aggregate demand–aggregate supply framework, Keynes was suggesting that there were times when the aggregate demand curve shifted inward—as depicted in Figure 2. As that figure showed, the consequence would be declining output

## Life in "Hooverville"

During the worst years of the Great Depression, unemployed workers congregated in shantytowns on the outskirts of many major cities. With a heavy dose of irony, these communities were known as "Hoovervilles," in honor of the then–president of the United States, Herbert Hoover. A contemporary observer described a Hooverville in New York City as follows:

It was a fairly popular "development" made up of a hundred or so dwellings, each the size of a dog house or chickencoop, often constructed with much ingenuity out of wooden boxes, metal cans, strips of cardboard or old tar paper. Here human beings lived on the margin of civilization by foraging for garbage, junk, and waste lumber. I found some … picking through heaps of rubbish they had gathered before their doorways or cooking over open fires or battered oilstoves. Still others spent their days improving their rent-free homes.… Most of them, according to the police, lived by begging or trading in junk; when all else failed they ate at the soup kitchens or public canteens.… They lived in fear of being forcibly removed by the authorities, though the neighborhood people in many cases helped them and the police tolerated them for the time being.

SOURCE: Mathew Josephson, *Infidel in the Temple* (New York: Knopf, 1967), pp. 82–83.

and deflation. This doleful prognosis sounded all too realistic at the time. But Keynes closed his book on a hopeful note by showing how certain government actions—the things we now call monetary and fiscal policy—might prod the economy out of a depressed state. The lessons he taught the world then are among the lessons we will be learning in the rest of Part 2 and in Part 3—along with many qualifications that economists have learned since 1936. These lessons show how governments can manage their economies so that recessions will not turn into depressions and depressions will not last as long as the Great Depression, but they also show why this is not an easy task.

While Keynes was working on *The General Theory,* he wrote his friend George Bernard Shaw that "I believe myself to be writing a book on economic theory which will largely revolutionize … the way the world thinks about economic problems." In many ways, he was right.

*John Maynard Keynes*

© Pictorial Press Ltd/Alamy

## 5-4d  From World War II to 1973

The Great Depression finally ended when the United States mobilized for war in the early 1940s. As government spending skyrocketed, it gave aggregate demand a huge boost. Thus, **fiscal policy** was (accidentally) being used in a big way. The economy boomed, and the unemployment rate fell as low as 1.2 percent during the war.

> The government's **fiscal policy** is its plan for spending and taxation. It can be used to steer aggregate demand in the desired direction.

Figure 1(b) suggested that spending spurts such as this one should lead to inflation, but much of the potential inflation during World War II was contained by price controls. With prices held below the levels at which quantity supplied equaled quantity demanded, shortages of consumer goods were common. Sugar, butter, gasoline, cloth, and a host of other goods were strictly rationed. When controls were lifted after the war, prices shot up.

A period of strong growth marred by several recessions after the war then gave way to the fabulous 1960s, a period of unprecedented, noninflationary growth that was credited to the success of the economic policies that Keynes had prescribed in the 1930s. For a while, it looked as if we could avoid both unemployment and inflation, as aggregate demand and aggregate supply expanded in approximate balance. But the optimistic verdicts proved premature on both counts.

Inflation came first, beginning in about 1966. Its major cause, as it had been so many times in the past, was high wartime spending. The Vietnam War pushed aggregate demand up too fast. Despite a short and mild recession in 1970, inflation continued at more than 5 percent per year. Faced with persistent inflation, President Richard Nixon stunned the nation by instituting wage and price controls in 1971, the first time this tactic had ever been employed in peacetime. The controls program held inflation in check for a while, but inflation worsened dramatically in 1973, mainly because of an explosion in food prices caused by poor harvests around the world.

## 5-4e  The Great Stagflation, 1973–1980

Things began to get much worse in 1973, not only for the United States but for all oil-importing nations. A war between Israel and Arab nations precipitated a quadrupling of oil prices by the Organization of Petroleum Exporting Countries (OPEC). At the same time, continued poor harvests in many parts of the globe pushed world food prices higher. Prices of other raw materials also skyrocketed.

By unhappy coincidence, these events came just as the Nixon administration was lifting wage and price controls. As had happened after World War II, the elimination of controls led to a temporary acceleration of inflation as prices that had been held artificially low were allowed to rise. For all these reasons, the inflation rate in the United States soared above 12 percent during 1974.

Meanwhile, the U.S. economy was slipping into a severe recession. Real GDP fell between mid-1973 and early 1975, and the unemployment rate rose to nearly 9 percent. With both inflation and unemployment unusually virulent in 1974 and 1975, the press coined a new term—**stagflation**—to refer to the simultaneous occurrence of economic

> **Stagflation** is inflation that occurs while the economy is growing slowly ("stagnating") or in a recession.

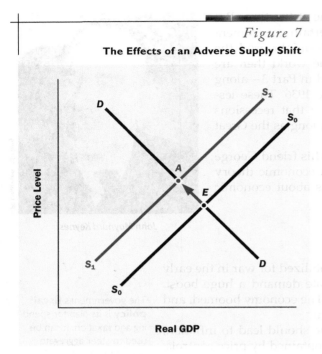

*Figure 7*

**The Effects of an Adverse Supply Shift**

*stag*nation and rapid *inflation*. Conceptually, what was happening in this episode is that the economy's aggregate *supply* curve, which normally moves outward from one year to the next, shifted *inward* instead. When this happens, the economy moves from a point like *E* to a point like *A* in Figure 7. Real GDP declines as the price level rises.

Thanks to a combination of government actions and natural economic forces, the economy recovered. Unfortunately, stagflation came roaring back in 1979 when the price of oil soared again. This time, inflation hit the astonishing rate of 16 percent in the first half of 1980, and the economy sagged.

## 5-4f Reaganomics and Its Aftermath

Recovery was already underway when President Ronald Reagan assumed office in January 1981, but high inflation seemed deeply ingrained. The new president promised to change things with a package of policies—mainly large tax cuts—that, he claimed, would both boost growth and reduce inflation.

However, the Federal Reserve under Chairman Paul Volcker was already deploying **monetary policy** to fight inflation—which meant using excruciatingly high interest rates to deter spending. So although inflation did fall, the economy also slumped—into an even deeper recession than 1973–1975. When the 1981–1982 recession finally hit bottom, the unemployment rate was approaching 11 percent, the financial markets were in disarray, and the word *depression* had reentered the American vocabulary. The U.S. government also acquired chronically large budget deficits, far larger than anyone had dreamed possible only a few years before.

**Monetary policy** refers to actions taken by the Federal Reserve to influence aggregate demand, mainly by changing interest rates.

Fortunately, the recovery that began in the winter of 1982–1983 proved to be vigorous and long-lasting. Unemployment fell more or less steadily for about 6 years, eventually dropping below 5.5 percent, while inflation remained tame. These developments provided an ideal economic platform on which George H. W. Bush ran to succeed Reagan—and to continue his policies.

Unfortunately for the first President Bush, the good times did not continue to roll. Shortly after he took office, inflation began to accelerate a bit, and Congress enacted a deficit-reduction package (including a tax increase) not entirely to the president's liking. Then, in mid-1990, the U.S. economy slumped again—yet another recession precipitated by a spike in oil prices. When the recovery from the 1990–1991 recession proved to be sluggish, candidate Bill Clinton hammered away at the lackluster economic performance of the Bush years. His message apparently resonated with American voters.

## 5-4g Clintonomics: Deficit Reduction and the "New Economy"

Although *candidate* Clinton ran on a platform that concentrated on spurring economic growth, the yawning budget deficit forced *President* Clinton to concentrate on deficit reduction instead.[6] A politically contentious package of tax increases and spending cuts barely squeaked through Congress in August 1993, and a second deficit-reduction package passed in 1997. Transforming the huge federal budget deficit into a large surplus turned out to be a crowning achievement of Clinton's economic policy.

Whether by cause or coincidence, the national economy boomed during the Clinton presidency. Business spending perked up, the stock market soared, unemployment fell rapidly, and even inflation drifted lower. Why did all these wonderful things happen at once? Some optimists explained the good news by heralding the arrival of a "New Economy"—a

---

[6] *Disclosure* One of the authors of this book was a member of President Clinton's original Council of Economic Advisers.

product of globalization and computerization—that naturally performed better than the economy of the past.

An alluring vision, but was it real? Most mainstream economists answered yes and no. On the one hand, advances in computer and information technology did lead to faster growth in the second half of the 1990s. In that respect, we got a New Economy. But something more mundane also happened: A variety of transitory factors pushed the economy's aggregate supply curve outward at an unusually rapid pace between 1996 and 1998. When this happens, the expected result is faster economic growth and lower inflation, as Figure 8 shows.

Figure 8 takes the graphical analysis of economic growth from Figure 3 and adds a new aggregate supply curve, $S_2S_2$, which lies to the right of $S_1S_1$. With supply curve $S_2S_2$ instead of $S_1S_1$, the economy moves from point $E$ not just to point $C$, as in the earlier figure, but all the way to point $B$. Comparing $B$ to $C$, we see that the economy winds up both farther to the right (i.e., it grows faster) and lower (i.e., it experiences less inflation). That, in a nutshell, is how our simple aggregate demand–aggregate supply framework explains this episode of U.S. economic history.

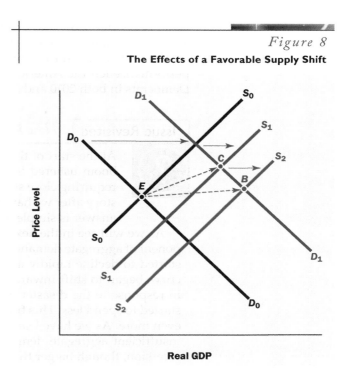

*Figure 8*

**The Effects of a Favorable Supply Shift**

## 5-4h  Tax Cuts and the Bush Economy

The Clinton boom ended around the middle of 2000—just before the election of President George W. Bush. Real GDP grew slowly in the second half of 2000 and then actually *declined* in two quarters of 2001, marking the first recession in the United States in 10 years. But it was a very minor one.

The tax cuts of 2001 turned out to be remarkably well timed, although they brought back large budget deficits. The war on terrorism also led to a burst of government spending. Both of these components of fiscal policy helped shift the aggregate demand curve outward, thereby mitigating the recession. (Refer back to Figure 1(b).) The Federal Reserve also lowered interest rates to encourage more spending. The recession ended late in 2001, but the recovery was extremely weak until the spring of 2003, when growth finally picked up—at least until late in 2007.

One sector of the U.S. economy that really boomed during the Bush years was housing. Both housing prices and new construction soared, especially between 2002 and 2006. Then the so-called housing "bubble" burst, and the economy started to slow down. The Great Recession began very late in 2007, with real GDP falling in five of the next six quarters despite more tax cuts under both Presidents Bush and Obama and several bursts of federal government spending.

## 5-4i  Obamanomics and the Great Recession

When President Obama took office in January 2009, the economy was sinking like a stone and jobs were disappearing at a rapid pace. Talk of depression was in the air. The new president reacted by recommending more tax cuts, a burst of federal spending, and large-scale aid to help state and local governments avoid painful budget cuts. In addition, the Bush and Obama administrations and the Federal Reserve each put in place a variety of unprecedented emergency measures designed to rescue the collapsing financial system. Virtually every one of these policies was politically unpopular; many will be discussed in coming chapters.

But the medicine seemed to work. By the summer of 2009, the Great Recession, the nation's worst since the 1930s, was over. The economy bottomed out and started growing again, albeit too slowly to create enough new jobs. However, the recovery proved to be agonizingly slow. Real GDP did not regain its previous peak level until the spring of 2011. Total employment did not recover to its previous peak until May 2014. This lackluster performance left the American public pretty unhappy. They turned strongly against the Democrats in both 2010 and 2014, though President Obama won reelection in 2012.

---

**Issue Revisited**  |  *How Did the Housing Bust Lead to the Great Recession?*

At the start of this chapter, we asked why and how the end of the housing boom ushered in such a severe recession. Much of the answer is complex, requiring close study of the financial system. We will revisit that part of that story after we have learned more about banking and finance. But part of the answer is simple enough.

As we will see in the next chapter, spending on new home construction is one component of aggregate demand. When the housing boom ended, that component naturally started to decline rapidly as companies built fewer houses. So the aggregate demand curve began to shift inward. In addition, as the financial system deteriorated—partly in response to the disaster in housing—consumers and investors lost confidence and started to spend less. This further pullback shifted the aggregate demand curve inward even more. As we have learned in this chapter, and will explore in greater depth later, insufficient aggregate demand is the typical cause of recessions (see Figure 2). This recession, though bigger than most, was no exception.

---

## 5-5  THE PROBLEM OF MACROECONOMIC STABILIZATION: A SNEAK PREVIEW

**Stabilization policy** is the name given to government programs designed to prevent or shorten recessions and to counteract inflation (i.e., to *stabilize* prices).

This brief look at the historical record shows that the U.S. economy has not generally produced steady growth without inflation. Rather, it has been buffeted by periodic bouts of unemployment or inflation; sometimes it has been plagued by both. We have also suggested several times that government policies may have had something to do with this performance. Let us now expand upon and systematize this suggestion.

To provide a preliminary analysis of **stabilization policy**, the name given to government programs designed to shorten recessions and to counteract inflation, we can once again use the basic tools of aggregate supply and demand analysis. To facilitate this discussion, we have reproduced as Figures 9 and 10 two diagrams found earlier in this chapter, but we now give them slightly different interpretations.

### 5-5a  Combating Unemployment

Figure 9 offers a simplified view of government policy to fight unemployment. Suppose that, in the absence of government intervention, the economy would reach an equilibrium at point $E$, where aggregate demand curve $D_0D_0$ crosses aggregate supply curve $SS$. If the output corresponding to point $E$ is too low, leaving many workers unemployed, *the government can reduce unemployment by increasing aggregate demand.* The year 2009 provided a dramatic example. Although subsequent chapters will consider in detail how this is done, our brief historical review has already mentioned three methods: Congress can spend more or reduce taxes (two varieties of "fiscal policy"), as it did with the 2009 "stimulus" bill; or the Federal Reserve can lower interest rates ("monetary policy"), as it also did throughout 2008. In the diagram, any of these

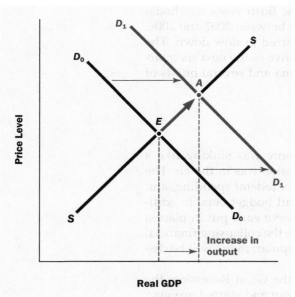

*Figure 9*

**Stabilization Policy to Fight Unemployment**

actions would shift the demand curve outward to $D_1D_1$, causing equilibrium to move to point $A$. In general:

> Recessions and unemployment are often caused by insufficient aggregate demand. When such situations occur, fiscal or monetary policies that successfully augment demand can be effective ways to increase output and reduce unemployment. They also normally raise prices.

## 5-5b Combating Inflation

The opposite type of demand management is called for when inflation is the main macroeconomic problem. Figure 10 illustrates this case. Here again, point $E$, the intersection of aggregate demand curve $D_0D_0$ and aggregate supply curve $SS$, is the equilibrium the economy would reach in the absence of government policy. But now suppose the price level corresponding to point $E$ is considered "too high," meaning that the price level would be rising too rapidly if the economy were to move to point $E$. Government policies that reduce demand from $D_0D_0$ to $D_2D_2$ can keep prices down and thereby reduce inflation. Some examples are reducing government spending or raising taxes, as done by the Clinton administration in the 1990s, or raising interest rates, which the Federal Reserve last did in 2004–2006. Thus,

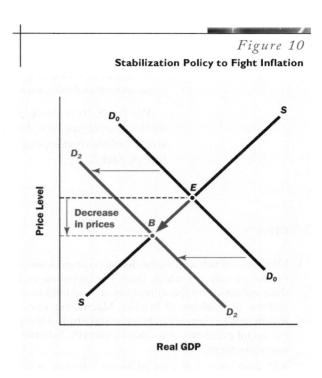

**Figure 10**

**Stabilization Policy to Fight Inflation**

> Inflation is frequently caused by aggregate demand racing ahead too fast. When this is the case, fiscal or monetary policies that reduce aggregate demand can be effective anti-inflationary devices. But such policies also decrease real GDP and raise unemployment.

This, in brief, summarizes the *intent* of stabilization policy. When aggregate demand fluctuations are the source of economic instability, the government can limit both recessions and inflations by pushing aggregate demand ahead when it would otherwise lag and restraining it when it would otherwise grow too quickly.

## 5-5c Does It Really Work?

Can the government actually stabilize the economy, as these simple diagrams suggest? That is a matter of some debate—a debate that is important enough to constitute one of our *Ideas for Beyond the Final Exam.*

We will deal with the pros and cons in Part 3, but a look back at Figures 5 and 6 may be instructive right now. First, cover the portions of the two figures that deal with the period after 1940, the portions from the shaded area rightward in each figure. The picture that emerges for the 1870–1940 period is that of an economy with frequent and sometimes quite pronounced fluctuations.

Now do the reverse. Cover the data before 1950 and look only at the postwar period. There is indeed a difference. Instances of negative real GDP growth are less common and business fluctuations look less severe—even counting the recent unhappy episode. Although government policies have not achieved perfection, things do look much better.

When we turn to inflation, however, matters look rather worse. Gone are the periods of deflation and price stability that occurred before World War II. Prices now seem only to rise. This quick tour through the data suggests that something *has* changed. The U.S. economy behaved differently from 1950 to 2014 than it did from 1870 to 1940.

> Although controversy over this point continues, many economists attribute this shift in the economy's behavior to lessons the government has learned about managing the economy—lessons you will be learning in the next part of this book. When you look at the prewar data, you see the fluctuations of an unmanaged economy that went through booms and recessions for "natural" economic reasons. The government did little about either. When you examine the

Ideas for Beyond the Final Exam

postwar data, on the other hand, you see an economy that has been managed by government policy—sometimes successfully and sometimes unsuccessfully. Although the recessions are less severe, this improvement has come at a cost: The economy appears to be more inflation-prone than it was in the more distant past. These two changes in our economy may be connected, but to understand why, we will have to provide some relevant economic theory.

We have, in a sense, spent much of this chapter running before we have learned to walk—that is, we have been using aggregate demand and aggregate supply curves extensively before developing the theory that underlies them. That is the task before us in the rest of Part 2.

## Summary

1. Microeconomics studies the decisions of individuals and firms, the ways in which these decisions interact, and their influence on the allocation of a nation's resources and the distribution of income. Macroeconomics looks at how entire economies behave and studies the pressing social problems of economic growth, inflation, and unemployment.

2. Although they focus on different subjects, microeconomics and macroeconomics rely on virtually identical tools. Both use the supply-and-demand analysis introduced in Chapter 4.

3. Macroeconomic models use abstract concepts like "the price level" and "gross domestic product" that are derived by combining many different markets into one. This process is known as **aggregation**; it should not be taken literally but rather viewed as a useful approximation.

4. The best specific measure of the nation's economic output is **gross domestic product (GDP)**, which is obtained by adding up the money values of all **final goods and services** produced in a given year. These outputs can be evaluated at current market prices (to get **nominal GDP**) or at some fixed set of prices (to get **real GDP**). Neither **intermediate goods** nor transactions that take place outside organized markets are included in GDP.

5. GDP measures an economy's production, not the increase in its well-being. For example, GDP places no value on housework, other do-it-yourself activities, or leisure time. On the other hand, even commodities that might be considered as "bads" rather than "goods" are counted in GDP (e.g., activities that harm the environment).

6. America's economic history shows steady growth punctuated by periodic **recessions**—that is, periods in which real GDP declined. Although the distant past included some periods of falling prices **(deflation)**, more recent history shows only rising prices **(inflation)**.

7. The Great Depression of the 1930s was the worst in U.S. history. It profoundly affected both our nation and countries throughout the world. It also led to a revolution in economic thinking, thanks largely to the work of John Maynard Keynes.

8. From World War II to the early 1970s, the American economy exhibited steadier growth than in the past. Many observers attributed this more stable performance to the implementation of the **monetary and fiscal policies** (collectively called **stabilization policy**) that Keynes had suggested. At the same time, however, the price level seems only to rise—never to fall—in the modern economy. The economy seems to have become more "inflation-prone."

9. Between 1973 and 1983, the U.S. economy suffered through several serious recessions. In the first part of that period, inflation was also unusually virulent. This unhappy combination of economic stagnation with rapid inflation was nicknamed **"stagflation."** Since 1982, however, inflation has been low.

10. The United States enjoyed a boom in the 1990s, and unemployment fell to its lowest level in 30 years. Yet, inflation also fell. One explanation for this happy combination of rapid growth and low inflation is that the **aggregate supply curve** shifted out unusually rapidly.

11. One major cause of inflation is that aggregate demand may grow more quickly than does aggregate supply. In such a case, a government policy that reduces aggregate demand may be able to stem the inflation.

12. Recessions often occur because aggregate demand grows too slowly. In this case, a government policy that stimulates demand may be an effective way to fight the recession.

13. Such policies were used to fight the Great Recession of 2007–2009, though with limited success.

## Key Terms

aggregate demand curve   84

aggregate supply curve   84

aggregation   82

deflation   90

final goods and services   86

fiscal policy   93

gross domestic product (GDP)   85

inflation   84

intermediate good   86

monetary policy   94

nominal GDP   86

real GDP   86

real GDP per capita   89

recession   85

stabilization policy   96

stagflation   93

## Test Yourself

1. Which of the following problems are likely to be studied by a microeconomist and which by a macroeconomist?

   a. The rapid growth of Twitter

   b. Why unemployment in the United States fell from 2010 to 2014

   c. Why Japan's economy grew faster than the U.S. economy in the 1980s, but slower in the 2000s

   d. Why the growth of health-care costs slowed down in recent years

2. Use an aggregate supply-and-demand diagram to study what would happen to an economy in which the aggregate supply curve never moved while the aggregate demand curve shifted outward year after year.

3. Which of the following transactions are included in gross domestic product, and by how much does each raise GDP?

   a. Smith pays a carpenter $50,000 to build a garage.

   b. Smith purchases $10,000 worth of materials and builds himself a garage, which is worth $50,000.

   c. Smith goes to the woods, cuts down a tree, and uses the wood to build himself a garage that is worth $50,000.

   d. The Jones family sells its old house to the Reynolds family for $400,000. The Joneses then buy a newly constructed house from a builder for $500,000.

   e. You purchase a used computer from a friend for $200.

   f. Your university purchases a new mainframe computer from IBM, paying $25,000.

   g. You win $100 in an Atlantic City casino.

   h. You make $100 in the stock market.

   i. You sell a used economics textbook to your college bookstore for $60.

   j. You buy a new economics textbook from your college bookstore for $100.

## Discussion Questions

1. You probably use "aggregates" frequently in everyday discussions. Try to think of some examples. (Here is one: Have you ever said, "The students at this college generally think …"? What, precisely, did you mean?)

2. Try asking a friend who has not studied economics in which year he or she thinks prices were higher: 1870 or 1900? 1920 or 1940? (In both cases, prices were higher in the earlier year.) Most people think that prices have always risen. Why do you think they have this opinion?

3. Give some reasons why gross domestic product is not a suitable measure of the well-being of the nation. (Have you noticed newspaper accounts in which journalists seem to use GDP for this purpose?)

# THE GOALS OF MACROECONOMIC POLICY

*When men are employed, they are best contented.*

BENJAMIN FRANKLIN

*Inflation is repudiation.*

CALVIN COOLIDGE

Someone once quipped that you could turn a parrot into an economist by teaching him just two words: *supply* and *demand*. And now that you have been through Chapters 4 and 5, you see what he meant. Sure enough, economists think of the process of economic growth as having two essential ingredients:

- The first ingredient is *aggregate supply*. Given the available supplies of **inputs** like labor and capital, and the technology at its disposal, an economy is able to produce a certain volume of **outputs**, measured by GDP. This capacity to produce normally increases from year to year as the supplies of inputs grow and the technology improves. The theory of aggregate supply will be our focus in Chapters 7 and 10.

- The second ingredient is *aggregate demand*. How much of the capacity to produce is actually utilized depends on how many goods and services people and businesses want to buy. We begin building a theory of aggregate demand in Chapters 8 and 9.

**Inputs** are the labor, machinery, buildings, and other resources used to produce outputs.

**Outputs** are the goods and services that the economy produces.

## CONTENTS

**Growth policy** refers to government policies intended to make the economy grow faster in the long run.

Corresponding to these two ingredients, economists visualize a dual task for those who make macroeconomic policy. First, *policy should create an environment in which the economy can expand its productive capacity rapidly*, because that is the ultimate source of higher living standards. This first task is the realm of **growth policy**, which is taken up in the next chapter. Second, *policy makers should manage aggregate demand so that it grows in line with the economy's capacity to produce*, avoiding as much as possible the cycles of boom and bust that we saw in the last chapter. This is the realm of *stabilization policy*. As we noted in that chapter, inadequate growth of aggregate demand can lead to high *unemployment*, whereas excessive growth of aggregate demand can lead to high *inflation*. Both are to be avoided.

Thus, the goals of macroeconomic policy can be summarized succinctly as *achieving rapid but relatively smooth economic growth with low unemployment and low inflation*. Unfortunately, that turns out to be a tall order, as events since 2007 have painfully illustrated. In chapters to come, we will explain why these goals cannot be attained with machine-like precision and why improvement on one front often spells deterioration on another. Along the way, we will pay a great deal of attention to both the *causes* of and *cures* for sluggish growth, high unemployment, and high inflation.

But before getting involved in such weighty issues of theory and policy, this chapter takes a close look at the three goals themselves. How fast can—or should—the economy grow? Why does a rise in unemployment cause such social distress? Why is inflation so loudly deplored? The answers to some of these questions may seem obvious at first. But, as you will see, there is more to them than meets the eye.

## 6-1 THE GOAL OF ECONOMIC GROWTH

To residents of a prosperous society like ours, economic growth—the notion that standards of living rise from one year to the next—seems like part of the natural order of things. But it is not. Historians tell us that living standards barely changed from the Roman Empire to the dawn of the Industrial Revolution—a period of some 16 centuries! Closer in time, per capita incomes tragically declined, on net, in most of the former Soviet Union in the 1990s and in some of the poorest countries of Africa in recent decades. Economic growth is *not* automatic.

In most advanced countries, growth is also a slow, and therefore barely noticeable, process. In a typical year, the average American consumes about 1 or 2 percent more goods and services than in the previous year. Can you perceive a difference that small? Perhaps not, but such tiny changes, when compounded over decades or even centuries, transform societies. During the twentieth century, for example, living standards in the United States increased by a factor of almost seven—which means that your ancestors in the year 1900 consumed less than one-seventh as much food, clothing, shelter, and other amenities as you do today. Try to imagine how your family would fare on one-seventh of its current income.

Small differences in growth rates make an enormous difference—*eventually*. To illustrate this point, think about the relative positions of three major nations—the United States, the United Kingdom, and Japan—at two points in history: 1870 and 1979. In 1870, the United States was a young, upstart nation. Although already among the most prosperous countries on earth, the United States was in no sense yet a major power. The United Kingdom, by contrast, was the preeminent economic and military power of the world. The Victorian era was at its height, and the sun never set on the British Empire. Meanwhile, somewhere across the Pacific was an inconsequential island nation called Japan. In 1870, Japan had only recently opened up to the West and was economically backward.

Now fast-forward more than a century. By 1979, the United States had become the world's preeminent economic power, Japan had emerged as the clear number two, and the United Kingdom had retreated into the second rank of nations. Obviously, the Japanese economy grew faster than the U.S. economy during this century, whereas the British economy grew more slowly, or else this stunning transformation of relative positions would not have occurred. But the magnitudes of the differences in growth rates may astound you.

# The Wonders of Compound Interest

Growth rates, like interest rates, *compound* so that, for example, 10 years of growth at 3 percent per year leaves the economy *more than* 30 percent larger. How much more? The answer is 34.4 percent. To see how we get this figure, start with the fact that $100 left in a bank account for one year at 3 percent interest grows to $103, which is 1.03 × $100. If left for a second year, that $103 will grow another 3 percent—to 1.03 × $103 = $106.09, which is already more than $106. Compounding has begun.

Notice that 1.03 × $103 = $(1.03)^2 \times $100$. Similarly, after three years the original $100 will grow to $(1.03)^3 \times $100 = $109.27. As you can see, each additional year adds another 1.03 growth factor to the multiplication. Now returning to answer our original question, after 10 years of compounding, the depositor will have $(1.03)^{10} \times $100 = $134.39 in the bank. Thus the balance will have grown by 34.4 percent. By identical logic, an economy growing at 3 percent per year for 10 years will expand 34.4 percent in total.

You may not be impressed by the difference between 30 percent and 34.4 percent. If not, follow the logic for longer periods. After 20 years of 3 percent growth, the economy will be 80.6 percent bigger (because $(1.03)^{20} = 1.806$), not just 60 percent bigger. After 50 years, cumulative growth will be 338 percent, not 150 percent. And after a century, it will be 1,822 percent, not just 300 percent. Now we are talking about large discrepancies! No wonder Einstein once said, presumably in jest, that compounding was the most powerful force in the universe.

The arithmetic of growth leads to a convenient "doubling rule" that you can do in your head. If something (the money in a bank account, the GDP of a country, and so on) grows at an annual rate of *g* percent, it will it take approximately 70/*g* years to double. So the rule is often called "the Rule of 70." For example, at a 2 percent growth rate, anything doubles in about 70/2 = 35 years. At a 3 percent growth rate, doubling takes roughly 70/3 = 23.33 years. Yes, small differences in growth rates can make a large difference.

Photo by Popperfoto/Getty Images

Over the 109-year period, GDP per capita in the United States grew at a 2.3 percent compound annual rate, whereas the United Kingdom's growth rate was 1.8 percent—a difference of merely 0.5 percent per annum, but compounded for more than a century. And what of Japan? What growth rate propelled it from obscurity into the front rank of nations? The answer is just 3.0 percent, a mere 0.7 percent per year faster than the United States. These numbers show vividly what a huge difference a 0.5 or 0.7 percentage point change in the growth rate makes, *if sustained for a long time.*

Economists define the *productivity* of a country's labor force (or **labor productivity**) as the amount of output a typical worker turns out in an hour of work. For example, if output is measured by GDP, productivity would be measured by GDP divided by the total number of hours of work. It is the growth rate of productivity that determines whether living standards will rise rapidly or slowly.

> **Labor productivity** is the amount of output a worker turns out in an hour (or a week, or a year) of labor. If output is measured by GDP, it is GDP per hour of work.

**PRODUCTIVITY GROWTH IS (ALMOST) EVERYTHING IN THE LONG RUN** As we pointed out in our list of *Ideas for Beyond the Final Exam*, only rising productivity can raise standards of living in the long run. Over long periods of time, small differences in rates of productivity growth compound like interest in a bank account and make an enormous difference to a society's prosperity. Nothing contributes more to material well-being, to the reduction of poverty, to increases in leisure time, and to a country's ability to finance education, public health, environmental improvement, and culture than its productivity growth rate.

Ideas for Beyond the Final Exam

**Issue** | *Is Faster Growth Always Better?*

How fast should the U.S. economy, or any economy, grow? At first, the question may seem silly. Isn't it obvious that we should grow as fast as possible? After all, that will make us all richer. In a sense, economists agree; faster growth is generally preferred to slower growth. But as we shall see in a few pages, further thought suggests that the apparently naive question is not quite as silly as it sounds. Growth comes at a cost. So more may not always be better.

## 6-2  THE CAPACITY TO PRODUCE: POTENTIAL GDP AND THE PRODUCTION FUNCTION

**Potential GDP** is the real GDP that the economy would produce if its labor and other resources were fully employed.

The **labor force** is the number of people holding or seeking jobs.

The economy's **production function** shows the volume of output that can be produced from given inputs (such as labor and capital), given the available technology.

Questions like how fast our economy can or should grow require quantitative answers. Economists have invented the concept of **potential GDP** to measure the economy's normal capacity to produce goods and services. Specifically, potential GDP is the real gross domestic product (GDP) an economy *could* produce if its **labor force** was fully employed.

Note the use of the word *normal* in describing capacity. Just as it is possible to push a factory beyond its normal operating rate (by, e.g., adding a night shift), it is possible to push an economy beyond its normal full-employment level by working it very hard. For example, we observed in the previous chapter that the unemployment rate dropped as low as 1.2 percent under abnormal conditions during World War II. So when we talk about employing the labor force fully, we do not mean a measured unemployment rate of zero.

Conceptually, we estimate potential GDP in two steps. First, we count up the available supplies of labor, capital, and other productive resources. Then we estimate how much *output* these *inputs* could produce if they were all fully utilized. This second step—the transformation of inputs into outputs—involves an assessment of the economy's *technology*. The more technologically advanced an economy, the more output it will be able to produce from any given bundle of inputs—as we emphasized in Chapter 3's discussion of the production possibilities frontier.

To help us understand how technology affects the relationship between inputs and outputs, it is useful to introduce a tool called the **production function**—which is simply a mathematical or graphical depiction of the relationship between inputs and outputs. We will use a graph in our discussion.

For a given level of technology, Figure 1 shows how output (measured by real GDP on the vertical axis) depends on labor input (measured by hours of work on the horizontal axis). To read these graphs, and to relate them to the concept of potential GDP, begin with the black curve $OK$ in Figure 1(a), which shows how GDP depends on labor input, *holding both capital and technology constant.* Naturally, output rises as labor inputs increase as we move outward along the curve $OK$, just as you would expect. If the country's labor force can supply $L_0$ hours of work when it is fully employed, then *potential GDP is $Y_0$* (see point $A$). If the technology improves, the production function will shift upward—say, to the blue

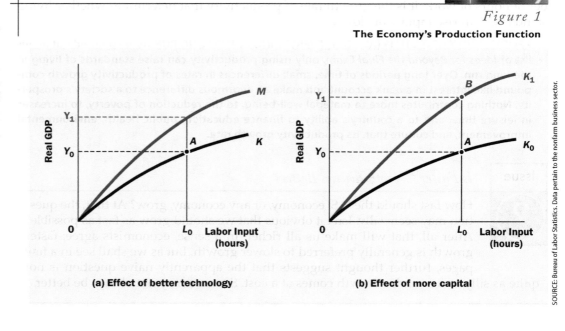

*Figure 1*

**The Economy's Production Function**

(a) Effect of better technology

(b) Effect of more capital

SOURCE: Bureau of Labor Statistics. Data pertain to the nonfarm business sector.

curve labeled *OM*—meaning that the *same* amount of labor input will now produce *more* output. The graph shows that potential GDP increases to $Y_1$.

Now what about capital? Figure 1(b) shows two production functions. The black curve $OK_0$ applies when the economy has some lower capital stock, $K_0$. The higher, blue curve $OK_1$ applies when the capital stock is some higher number, $K_1$. Thus, the production function tells us that potential GDP will be $Y_0$ if the capital stock is $K_0$ (point *A*) but $Y_1$ if the capital stock is $K_1$ instead (point *B*). Once again, this relationship is just what you would expect: The economy can produce *more* output with the *same* amount of labor if workers have more capital to work with.

You can hardly avoid noticing the similarities between the two panels of Figure 1: Better technology, as in Figure 1(a), or more capital, as in Figure 1(b), affects the production function in more or less the same way. In general:

**Either more capital or better technology will shift the production function upward and therefore raise potential GDP.**

## 6-3 THE GROWTH RATE OF POTENTIAL GDP

With this new tool, it is but a short jump to potential growth rates. If the *size* of potential GDP depends on the size of the economy's labor force, the amount of capital and other resources it has, and its technology, it follows that the *growth rate* of potential GDP must depend on

- The growth rate of the labor force
- The growth rate of the nation's capital stock
- The rate of technical progress

To sharpen the point, observe that real GDP is, by definition, the product of the total hours of work in the economy times the amount of output produced per hour—what we have just called *labor productivity*:

**GDP = Hours of work × Output per hour = Hours of work × Labor productivity**

For example, in the United States today, in round numbers, GDP is more than $17.5 trillion and total hours of work per year are about 240 billion. Thus labor productivity tops $17.5 trillion/240 billion hours, or about $73 per hour.

How fast can the economy increase its productive capacity? By transforming the preceding equation into growth rates, we have our answer: The growth rate of potential GDP is the *sum* of the growth rates of labor input (hours of work) and labor productivity:[1]

**Growth rate of potential GDP = Growth rate of labor input + Growth rate of labor productivity**

Prior to the Great Recession of 2007–2009, labor input in the United States was increasing at a rate of nearly 1 percent per year. But labor productivity growth, which was very slow until the mid-1990s, leaped upward after 1995—averaging about 2.6 percent per annum from 1995 to 2010. Together, these two figures would imply an estimated growth rate of potential GDP of about 3.5 percent over these years.

Do the growth rates of potential GDP and actual GDP match up? The answer is an important one to which we will return often in this book:

**Over long periods of time, the growth rates of actual and potential GDP are normally quite similar. However, the two often diverge sharply over short periods owing to cyclical fluctuations. The departure since 2007 is dramatic.**

---

[1] You may be wondering about what happened to capital. The answer, as we have just seen in our discussion of the production function, is that one of the main determinants of potential GDP, and thus of labor productivity, is the amount of capital that each worker has to work with. Accordingly, the role of capital is incorporated into the productivity number; that is, the growth rate of labor productivity depends on the growth rate of capital.

| Table 1 |
| Recent Growth Rates of Real GDP in the United States |

| Years | Growth Rate per Year |
|---|---|
| 1999–2001 | 2.5% |
| 2001–2003 | 2.3 |
| 2003–2005 | 3.6 |
| 2005–2007 | 2.2 |
| 2007–2009 | –1.6 |
| 2009–2011 | 2.2 |
| 2011–2013 | 2.3 |
| 1999–2013 | 1.9 |

SOURCE: U.S. Department of Commerce.

Table 1 illustrates this point with some recent U.S. data. Since 1999, GDP growth rates over 2-year periods have ranged from about 3.6 percent down to about –1.6 percent per annum. Over the entire 14-year period, GDP growth averaged just 1.9 percent, which is well below the suggested estimate of the growth rate of potential GDP—not surprisingly because performance was so poor in the years since 2007.

The next chapter is devoted to studying the *determinants* of economic growth and some *policies* that might speed it up. We already know from the production function that there are two basic ways to boost a nation's growth rate—other than faster population growth and simply working harder. One is accumulating more capital. Other things being equal, a nation that builds more capital for its future will grow faster. The other way is by improving technology. When technological breakthroughs are coming at a fast and furious pace, an economy will grow more rapidly. We will discuss both of these factors in detail in the next chapter. First, however, we need to address the more basic question posed earlier in this chapter.

---

**Issue Revisited** | *Is Faster Growth Always Better?*

It might seem that the answer to this question is obviously yes. After all, faster growth of either labor productivity or GDP per person is the route to higher living standards. But exceptions have been noted.

For openers, some social critics have questioned the desirability of faster economic growth as an end in itself, at least in the rich countries. Faster growth brings more wealth, and to most people the desirability of wealth is beyond question. "I've been rich and I've been poor. Believe me, honey, rich is better," singer Sophie Tucker once told an interviewer. And most people seem to share her sentiment. To those who hold this belief, a healthy economy is one that produces vast quantities of jeans, pizzas, cars, and smartphones.

Yet the desirability of further economic growth for a society that is already quite wealthy has been questioned on several grounds. Environmentalists worry that the sheer increase in the volume of goods imposes enormous costs on society in the form of crowding, pollution, global climate change, and proliferation of wastes that need disposal. It has, they argue, dotted our roadsides with junkyards, polluted our air, and poisoned our food with dangerous chemicals.

Furthermore, some psychologists and social critics argue that the never-ending drive for more and better goods has failed to make people happier. Instead, industrial progress has transformed the satisfying and creative tasks of the artisan into the mechanical and dehumanizing routine of the assembly-line worker. In the United States, it even seems to be driving people to want to work longer and longer hours. The question is whether the vast outpouring of material goods is worth all the stress and environmental damage. In fact, surveys of self-reported happiness show that happiness generally rises with income *within* a country, but residents of richer countries are no happier, on average, than residents of poorer countries.

But despite this, most economists continue to believe that more growth is better than less. For one thing, slower growth would make it extremely difficult to finance programs that improve the quality of life—including efforts to protect the environment. Such programs are costly, and the evidence suggests that people are willing to pay for them only after their incomes reach a certain level. Second, it would be difficult to prevent further economic growth even if we were so inclined. Mandatory controls are abhorrent to most Americans; we cannot order people to stop being inventive and hardworking. Third, slower economic growth would seriously hamper efforts to eliminate poverty—both within our own country and throughout the world. Much of the earth's population still lives in a state of extreme want. These unfortunate people are far less interested in clean air and fulfillment in the workplace than they are in more food, better clothing, and sturdier shelters.

All that said, economists concede that faster growth is not always better. One important reason will occupy our attention later in Parts 2 and 3: An economy that grows too fast may generate inflation. Why? You were introduced to the answer at the end of the last chapter: Inflation rises when aggregate demand races ahead of aggregate supply. In plain English, an economy will become inflationary when people's demands for goods and services expand faster than its capacity to produce them. So we probably do not want to grow faster than the growth rate of potential GDP for long—unless we are making up for lost ground in the aftermath of a recession, as was true in recent years.

Should society then seek the maximum possible growth rate of *potential* GDP? Maybe, but maybe not. After all, more rapid growth does not come for free. We have noted that building more capital is one good way to speed the growth of potential GDP. But the resources used to manufacture jet engines and computer servers could be used to make home air conditioners and video games instead. Building more capital imposes an obvious cost on a society: The citizens must consume less today. Saying this does not argue against investing for the future. Indeed, most economists believe that we Americans need to do more of that. But we must realize that faster growth through capital formation comes at a cost—an *opportunity cost*. Here, as elsewhere, you don't get something for nothing.

## 6-4 THE GOAL OF LOW UNEMPLOYMENT

We noted earlier that actual GDP growth can differ sharply from potential GDP growth over periods as long as several years. These *macroeconomic fluctuations* have major implications for employment and unemployment. In particular:

**When the economy grows more *slowly* than its potential, it fails to generate enough new jobs for its ever-growing labor force. So the unemployment rate *rises*. Conversely, GDP growth *faster* than the economy's potential leads to a *falling unemployment rate*.**

The **unemployment rate** is the number of unemployed people, expressed as a percentage of the labor force.

The Great Recession reminded us of this problem in a very painful way. When real GDP first declined sharply and then grew slowly, unemployment first soared and then remained stubbornly high for years.

High unemployment is socially wasteful. When the economy does not create enough jobs to employ everyone who is willing to work, a valuable resource is lost. Potential goods and services that might have been produced and enjoyed by consumers are lost forever. This lost output is the central economic cost of high unemployment, and we can measure it by comparing actual and potential GDP.

That cost is considerable. Table 2 summarizes the idleness of workers and machines, and the resulting loss of national output, for some of the years of lowest economic activity in recent decades. The second column lists the civilian unemployment rate and thus measures unused labor resources. The third lists the percentage of industrial capacity that U.S. manufacturers were actually using, which indicates the extent to which plant and equipment went unused. The fourth column estimates the shortfall between potential and actual real GDP. We see that unemployment has cost the people of the United States as much as an 8.1 percent reduction in their real incomes.

Although Table 2 shows extreme examples, our inability to utilize all of the nation's available resources has been a persistent economic problem on and off for decades. The maroon line in Figure 2 shows actual real GDP in the United States from 1960 to 2014, whereas the

*Table 2*

**The Economic Costs of High Unemployment**

| Year | Civilian Unemployment Rate | Capacity Utilization Rate | Real GDP Lost Due to Idle Resources |
|---|---|---|---|
| 1958 | 6.8% | 75.0% | 4.8% |
| 1961 | 6.7 | 77.3 | 4.1 |
| 1975 | 8.5 | 73.4 | 5.4 |
| 1982 | 9.7 | 71.3 | 8.1 |
| 1992 | 7.5 | 79.4 | 2.6 |
| 2003 | 6.0 | 73.4 | 2.2 |
| 2009 | 9.3 | 70.0 | 7.6 |
| 2010 | 9.6 | 74.3 | 6.5 |

SOURCES: Bureau of Labor Statistics, Federal Reserve System, and Congressional Budget Office.

NOTE: The Federal Reserve's capacity utilization index covers only the manufacturing, mining, and utility sectors—a minority of the economy.

*Figure 2*

**Actual and Potential GDP in the United States since 1960**

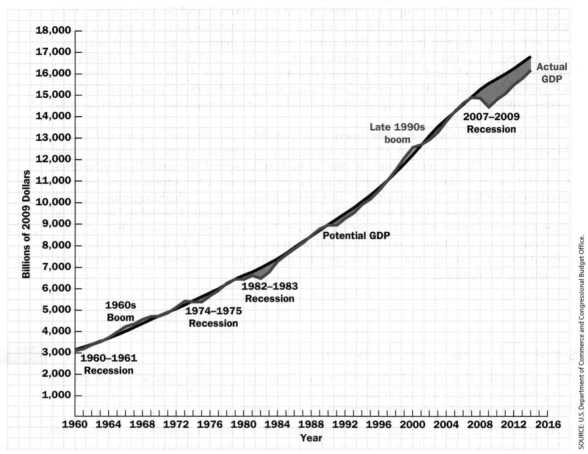

SOURCE: U.S. Department of Commerce and Congressional Budget Office.

black line shows potential GDP. The graph makes it clear that actual GDP has fallen short of potential GDP more often than it has exceeded it, and dramatically so in the period since 2007. In fact:

> A conservative estimate of the cumulative gap between actual and potential GDP over the seven years 2008 to 2014 (all evaluated in 2009 prices) exceeds $5.5 trillion. At 2014 levels, this loss in output as a result of unemployment amounted to about 4 months' worth of production. And there is no way to redeem those losses. The labor wasted in 2014 cannot be utilized in 2017.

## 6-5    THE HUMAN COSTS OF HIGH UNEMPLOYMENT

If these numbers seem a bit dry and abstract, think about the human costs of being unemployed. Years ago, job loss meant not only enforced idleness and a catastrophic drop in income, it often led to hunger, cold, ill health, even death. Here is how one unemployed worker during the Great Depression described his family's plight in a mournful letter to the governor of Pennsylvania:

> I have been out of work for over a year and a half. Am back almost thirteen months and the landlord says if I don't pay up before the 1 of 1932 out I must go, and where am I to go in the cold winter with my children? If you can help me please for God's sake and the children's sakes and like please do what you can and send me some

help, will you, I cannot find any work.... Thanksgiving dinner was black coffee and bread and was very glad to get it. My wife is in the hospital now. We have no shoes to were [sic]; no clothes hardly. Oh what will I do I sure will thank you.[2]

Nowadays, unemployment does not hold quite such terrors for most families, although its consequences remain dire enough. Our system of unemployment insurance (discussed later in this chapter) has taken part of the sting out of unemployment, as have other social welfare programs that support the incomes of the poor. Yet most families still suffer painful losses of income and, often, severe noneconomic consequences when a breadwinner becomes unemployed. And in the recent recession, *long-term* unemployment soared to heights not seen since the 1930s and became a major social problem.

Even families that are protected by unemployment compensation suffer when joblessness strikes. Ours is a work-oriented society. A man's place has always been in the office or shop, and in recent decades this has become just as true for women. A worker forced into idleness by a recession endures a psychological cost that is no less real for our inability to measure it. Martin Luther King, Jr., put it graphically: "In our society, it is murder, psychologically, to deprive a man of a job.... You are in substance saying to that man that he has no right to exist."[3] High unemployment has been linked to psychological and physical disorders, divorces, suicides, and crime.

It is important to realize that these costs, whether large or small in total, are distributed most unevenly across the population. In 2013, for example, the unemployment rate among all workers averaged 7.4 percent. But, as Figure 3 shows, 13.1 percent of black workers were unemployed. For teenagers, the situation was much worse, with unemployment at 22.9 percent, and that of black teenagers a shocking 38.8 percent. Married men had the lowest rate, at 4.3 percent. Overall unemployment varies from year to year, but these relationships are typical:

**In good times and bad, married men suffer the least unemployment and teenagers suffer the most; nonwhites are unemployed much more often than whites; blue-collar workers have above-average rates of unemployment; well-educated people have below-average unemployment rates.**[4]

It is worth noting that unemployment in the United States used to be much lower than in most other industrialized countries. As recently as 2006, when the U.S. unemployment rate averaged 4.6 percent, the comparable figures were 5.5 percent in Canada, 9.5 percent in France, 6.9 percent in Italy, and 10.4 percent in Germany. But by 2009, owing to the deep recession here, our unemployment rate had soared to 9.3 percent, while Canada's was 7.3 percent, France's was 9.1 percent, Italy's was 7.9 percent, and Germany's was 7.8 percent. By 2012, with a weak recovery here and continued recession in much of Europe, our unemployment rate of 8.1 percent far exceeded Germany's (5.5 percent) and Canada's (6.3 percent), but was well below that of France (10 percent) and Italy (10.8 percent).[5]

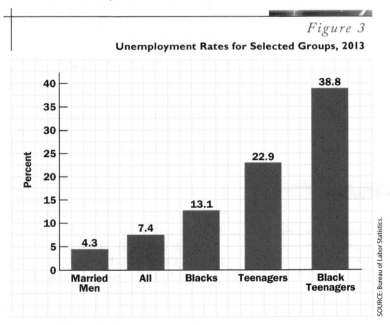

*Figure 3*

**Unemployment Rates for Selected Groups, 2013**

SOURCE: Bureau of Labor Statistics.

---

[2] From Milton Meltzer, *Brother, Can You Spare a Dime? The Great Depression 1929–1933*, p. 103. Copyright © 1969. Reprinted by permission of Alfred A. Knopf, Inc.

[3] Quoted in Coretta Scott King (ed.), *The Words of Martin Luther King* (New York: Newmarket Press, 1983), p. 45.

[4] Unemployment rates for men and women are about equal.

[5] The numbers for foreign countries are based (approximately) on U.S. unemployment concepts.

## 6-6  COUNTING THE UNEMPLOYED: THE OFFICIAL STATISTICS

We have been using unemployment figures without considering where they come from or how accurate they are. The basic data come from a monthly survey of about 72,000 households conducted for the U.S. Bureau of Labor Statistics. The census taker asks several questions about the employment status of each member of the household and, on the basis of the answers, classifies each person as *employed, unemployed,* or *not in the labor force.*[6]

**The Employed**  The first category is the simplest to define. It includes everyone currently at work, including part-time workers. Although some part-timers work less than a full week by choice, others do so only because they cannot find suitable full-time jobs. These workers are counted as employed, even though many would consider them "underemployed."

**The Unemployed**  The second category is a bit trickier. For persons not currently working, the survey first determines whether they are temporarily laid off from a job to which they expect to return. If so, they are counted as unemployed. The remaining workers are asked whether they actively sought work during the previous four weeks. If they did, they are also counted as unemployed.

**Out of the Labor Force**  If they failed to look for a job, they are classified as *out of the labor force* rather than unemployed. This seems a reasonable way to draw the distinction—after all, not everyone *wants* to work. But there is a problem: Research shows that many unemployed workers give up looking for jobs after a while. These so-called **discouraged workers** are victims of poor job prospects, just like the officially unemployed. When they give up hope, the measured unemployment rate—which is the ratio of the number of unemployed people to the total labor force—actually declines.

Involuntary part-time work, loss of overtime or shortened work hours, and discouraged workers are all examples of "hidden" or "disguised" unemployment. People concerned about such phenomena argue that we should include them in the official unemployment rate because, if we do not, the magnitude of the problem will be *under*estimated. In practice, however, more comprehensive measures of unemployment that include such phenomena normally rise or fall in lock step with the conventionally measured unemployment rate. Furthermore, some critics argue that measured unemployment *over*estimates the problem because, to count as unemployed, potential workers need only *claim* to be looking for jobs, even if they are not really interested in finding them.

> A **discouraged worker** is an unemployed person who gives up looking for work and is therefore no longer counted as part of the labor force.

## 6-7  TYPES OF UNEMPLOYMENT

Providing jobs for those willing to work is one principal goal of macroeconomic policy. But how are we to define this goal concretely?

We have already noted that zero measured unemployment would clearly be an *incorrect* answer. Ours is a dynamic, highly mobile economy. Households move from one state to another. Individuals quit jobs to seek better positions or retool for more attractive occupations. These and other decisions produce some minimal amount of unemployment—people who are literally *between* jobs. Economists call this **frictional unemployment**, and it is unavoidable in our market economy. The critical distinguishing feature of frictional unemployment is that it is short-lived. A frictionally unemployed person has every reason to expect to find a new job soon.

> **Frictional unemployment** is unemployment that is due to normal turnover in the labor market. It includes people who are temporarily between jobs because they are moving or changing occupations, or are unemployed for similar reasons.

---

[6] The survey is called the Current Population Survey (CPS). The Bureau of Labor Statistics web site has lots of information on how the CPS is conducted and how the data are used. If you are interested, start browsing on www.bls.gov/cps.

## Policy Debate

### Does the Minimum Wage Cause Unemployment?

Elementary economic reasoning—summarized in the simple supply-demand diagram in this box—suggests that setting a minimum wage (*W* in the graph) above the free-market wage (*w* in the graph) must cause unemployment. In the graph, unemployment is the horizontal gap between the quantity of labor supplied (point *B*) and the quantity demanded (point *A*) at the minimum wage. Indeed, the conclusion seems so elementary and compelling that generations of economists took it for granted. Indeed, early editions of this book confidently told students that a higher minimum wage must lead to higher unemployment.

But some surprising economic research published in the 1990s cast serious doubt on this conventional wisdom. For example, economists David Card and Alan Krueger compared employment changes at fast-food restaurants in New Jersey and nearby Pennsylvania after New Jersey, but not Pennsylvania, raised its minimum wage in 1992. To their surprise, the New Jersey stores did *more* net hiring than their Pennsylvania counterparts. Similar results were found for fast-food stores in Texas after the federal

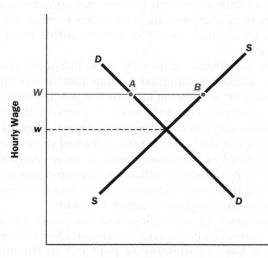

**Number of Workers**

minimum wage was raised in 1991 and in California after the statewide minimum wage was increased in 1988. In none of these cases did a higher minimum wage seem to reduce employment—in contrast to the implications of simple economic theory.

The research of Card and Krueger, and of others who reached similar conclusions, was controversial from the start, and remains so. Thus, a policy question that had been deemed closed now seems to be open: Does the minimum wage really cause unemployment?

Resolution of this debate is of more than academic interest. In 1996, President Clinton recommended and Congress passed an increase in the federal minimum wage—justifying its action, in part, by the new research suggesting that unemployment would not rise as a result. Something similar happened again in 2007, when Congress debated and enacted another increase. And the debate was reignited in 2013, when President Obama called upon Congress to raise the minimum wage again. (But Congress refused.) Economic research can have consequences.

---

A second type of unemployment can be difficult to distinguish from frictional unemployment but has very different implications. **Structural unemployment** arises when jobs are eliminated by changes in the economy, such as permanent changes in the technology of production or in the demand for particular products. The crucial difference between frictional and structural unemployment is that, unlike frictionally unemployed workers, structurally unemployed workers cannot realistically be considered "between jobs." Instead, their skills and experience may be unmarketable in the changing economy in which they live. They are thus faced with either prolonged periods of unemployment or the necessity of making major changes in their skills or occupations.

The remaining type of unemployment, **cyclical unemployment**, will occupy most of our attention. Cyclical unemployment rises when the level of economic activity declines, as it does in a recession. Thus, when macroeconomists speak of maintaining "full employment," they mean limiting unemployment to its frictional and structural components—which means, roughly, producing at potential GDP. A key question, therefore, is: How much measured unemployment constitutes full employment?

**Structural unemployment** refers to workers who have lost their jobs because they have been displaced by automation, because their skills are no longer in demand, or because of similar reasons.

**Cyclical unemployment** is the portion of unemployment that is attributable to a decline in the economy's total production. Cyclical unemployment rises during recessions and falls as prosperity is restored.

### 6-8  HOW MUCH EMPLOYMENT IS "FULL EMPLOYMENT"?

John F. Kennedy was the first president to commit the federal government to a specific numerical goal for unemployment. He picked a 4 percent target, which was subsequently rejected as being too ambitious. But no new number was put in its place. Instead, we have experienced a long-running national debate over how much measured unemployment corresponds to **full employment**. In 2014, the Federal Reserve estimated a range between 5.2 and 5.8 percent, but not everyone accepts that. The debate goes on.

**Full employment** is a situation in which everyone who is willing and able to work can find a job. At full employment, the measured unemployment rate is still positive.

## 6-9 UNEMPLOYMENT INSURANCE: THE INVALUABLE CUSHION

**Unemployment insurance** is a government program that replaces some of the wages lost by eligible workers who lose their jobs.

One major reason why America's unemployed workers no longer experience the complete loss of income that devastated so many during the 1930s is our system of **unemployment insurance**—one of the most valuable institutional innovations to emerge from the trauma of the Great Depression.

Each of the 50 states administers an unemployment insurance program under federal guidelines. Although the precise amounts vary, the average weekly benefit check in 2013 was about $310, which amounted to about 45 percent of average weekly earnings. Although a 55 percent drop in earnings poses very serious problems, the importance of this 45 percent income cushion can scarcely be exaggerated, especially because it may be supplemented by funds from other welfare programs. Families that are covered by unemployment insurance suffer, but they rarely go hungry when they lose their jobs.

Eligibility for benefits varies by state, but some criteria apply quite generally. Only experienced workers qualify, so persons just joining the labor force (such as recent college graduates) or re-entering after prolonged absences (such as women returning to the job market after years of child rearing) cannot collect benefits. Neither can those who quit their jobs, except under unusual circumstances. Also, benefits end after a stipulated period of time, normally six months. For all of these reasons, prior to the Great Recession only about a third of the unemployed actually received benefits. As the recession grew worse, however, Congress extended unemployment benefits several times—eventually extending them to a maximum of 99 weeks before cutting back. So in 2013, about 40 percent of the unemployed received benefits.

The importance of unemployment insurance to the unemployed is obvious, but significant benefits also accrue to citizens who never become unemployed. During recessions, billions of dollars are paid out in unemployment benefits. And because recipients probably spend most of their benefits, unemployment insurance limits the severity of recessions by providing additional purchasing power when and where it is most needed.

> The unemployment insurance system is one of several cushions built into our economy since 1933 to prevent another Great Depression. By giving money to those who become unemployed, the system helps prop up aggregate demand during recessions.

Although the U.S. economy is now probably "depression-proof," this should not be a cause for much rejoicing, for the many recessions we have had since the 1950s—and especially the devastating 2007–2009 recession—amply demonstrate that we are far from "recession-proof."

The fact that unemployment insurance and other social welfare programs replace a significant fraction of lost income has led some skeptics to claim that unemployment is no longer a serious problem. But unemployment insurance is just what the name says—an *insurance* program. Insurance never prevents catastrophes from occurring; it merely spreads the costs among many people instead of letting all the costs fall on an unfortunate few. As we noted earlier, unemployment robs the economy of output it could have produced, and no insurance policy can insure society against such losses.

> Our system of payroll taxes and unemployment benefits spreads the costs of unemployment over the entire population, but it does not eliminate the basic economic cost.

In that case, you might ask, why not cushion the blow even more by making unemployment insurance much more generous, as many European countries do? The answer is that there is also a downside to unemployment insurance. When unemployment benefits are very generous, people who lose their jobs may be less eager to look for new ones. The right level of unemployment insurance strikes an appropriate balance between the benefits of supporting the incomes of unemployed people and the costs of raising the unemployment rate a bit. In 2013, there was a vocal controversy in the United States over whether to reduce the generosity of unemployment insurance because the job market was improving.

# 6-10 THE GOAL OF LOW INFLATION

Both the human and economic costs of inflation are less obvious than the costs of unemployment. But this does not make them any less real, for if one thing is crystal clear about inflation, it is that people do not like it.

When inflation is low, as it has been for years now, it barely registers as a problem in national public opinion polls. However, when inflation is high, it often heads the list—often even ahead of unemployment. Surveys also find that inflation, like unemployment, makes people unhappy. Finally, studies of elections suggest that voters penalize the party that occupies the White House when inflation is high. The fact that people dislike inflation is beyond dispute. The question is: Why?

At first, the question may seem ridiculous. During inflationary times, people pay higher prices for the same goods and services they bought before. So more and more income is needed just to maintain their standards of living. Is it not obvious that this erosion of **purchasing power**—that is, the decline in what money will buy—makes everyone worse off?

> The **purchasing power** of a given sum of money is the volume of goods and services that it will buy.

## 6-10a  Inflation and Real Wages

Well, no—because of one very significant fact. The wages that people earn are also prices—prices for labor services. During a period of inflation, wages also rise. In fact, the average wage typically rises faster than prices. Thus, contrary to popular myth, workers as a group are not usually victimized by inflation.

> The real wage rate is the wage rate adjusted for inflation. Specifically, it is the nominal wage divided by the price index. The real wage thus indicates the volume of goods and services that the nominal wages will buy.

> The purchasing power of wages—what is called the **real wage rate**—is not systematically eroded by inflation. Sometimes wages rise faster than prices, and sometimes prices rise faster than wages. In the long run, wages tend to outstrip prices as new capital equipment and innovation increase output per worker.

Figure 4 illustrates this simple fact. The blue line shows the rate of increase of prices in the United States for each year since 1948, and the black line shows the rate of increase of wages. The difference between the two, shaded maroon in the diagram, indicates the rate of growth of *real* wages. Generally, wages rise faster than prices, reflecting the steady advance of labor productivity; therefore, real wages rise. But this is not always the case; the graph shows a few instances in which inflation outstripped wage increases.

The feature of Figure 4 that virtually jumps off the page is the way the two lines dance together. Wages normally rise rapidly when prices rise rapidly and slowly when prices rise slowly. But you should not draw any hasty conclusions from this association. It does not, for example, imply that rising prices *cause* rising wages or that rising wages *cause* rising prices.

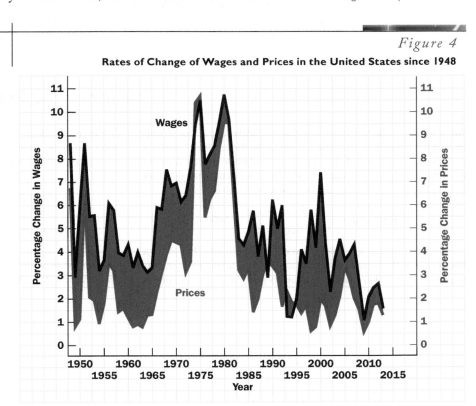

*Figure 4*

**Rates of Change of Wages and Prices in the United States since 1948**

*"Sure, you're raising my allowance. But am I actually gaining any purchasing power?"*

Remember the warnings given in Chapter 1 about trying to infer causation just by looking at correlations in data. But analyzing cause and effect is not our purpose right now. We merely want to dispel the myth that inflation inevitably erodes real wages.

Why is this myth so widespread? Imagine a world without inflation in which wages are rising 2 percent per year because of the increasing productivity of labor. Now imagine that, all of a sudden, inflation sets in and prices start rising 3 percent per year but nothing else changes. Figure 4 suggests that, with perhaps a small delay, wage increases will accelerate to $2 + 3 = 5$ percent per year. Will workers view this change with equanimity? Probably not. To each worker, the 5 percent wage increase will be seen as something he earned by the sweat of his brow. In his view, he *deserves* every penny of his 5 percent raise. In a sense, he is right because "the sweat of his brow" earned him a 2 percent increment in real wages that, when the inflation rate is 3 percent, can be achieved only by increasing his money wages by 5 percent. An economist would divide the wage increase in the following way:

| Reason for Wages to Increase | Amount |
| --- | --- |
| Higher productivity | 2% |
| Compensation for higher prices | 3% |
| Total | 5% |

But the worker will probably keep score differently. Feeling that he earned the entire 5 percent raise by his own merits, he will view inflation as having "robbed" him of three-fifths of his just deserts. The higher the rate of inflation, the more of his raise the worker will feel has been stolen from him.

Of course, nothing could be farther from the truth. Basically, the economic system rewards the worker with *the same 2 percent real wage increment for higher productivity, regardless of the rate of inflation.* The "evils of inflation" are often exaggerated because people fail to understand this point.

## Calculating the Real Wage: A Real Example

The *real* wage shows not how many dollars a worker is paid for an hour of work (i.e. called the *nominal* wage), but rather the *purchasing power* of that money. It indicates what an hour's worth of work can buy. As noted in the definition of the real wage in the margin, we calculate the real wage by *dividing* the nominal wage by the price level. The rule is[7]

$$\text{Real wage} = \frac{\text{Nominal wage}}{\text{Price level}} \times 100$$

Here's a concrete example. Between 1998 and 2013, the average hourly wage in the United States rose from $13.01 to $20.13, an increase of 55 percent over fifteen years. Sounds pretty good for American workers.

But over those same fifteen years, the Consumer Price Index (CPI), the most commonly used index of the price level, rose by 43 percent, from 163 to 233. This means that the real wages in the two years were

$$\text{Real wage in 1998} = \frac{\$13.01}{163} \times 100 = \$7.98$$

$$\text{Real wage in 2013} = \frac{\$20.13}{233} \times 100 = \$8.64$$

for an increase of just 8.3 percent over the fifteen years, which is both a small fraction of 55 percent and a very poor real wage performance.

---

[7] As explained in the appendix, it is conventional to multiply price index numbers by 100. That is the reason for the 100 in the formula. It does not alter the percentage change.

## 6-10b The Importance of Relative Prices

A related misperception results from failure to distinguish between a *rise in the general price level* and a change in **relative prices**, which is a rise in one price relative to another. To see the distinction most clearly, imagine first a *pure inflation* in which every price rises by 10 percent during the year, so that relative prices do not change. Table 3 gives an example in which the price of movie tickets increases from $6.00 to $6.60, the price of candy bars from 50 cents to 55 cents, and the price of cheap automobiles from $9,000 to $9,900. After the inflation, just as before, it will still take 12 candy bars to buy a movie ticket, 1,500 movie tickets to buy a car, and so on. A person who manufactures candy bars in order to purchase movie tickets is neither helped nor harmed by the inflation. Neither is a car dealer with a sweet tooth.

But real inflations are not like this. When there is 10 percent general inflation—meaning that the "average price" rises by 10 percent—some prices may jump 20 percent or more whereas others actually fall.[8]

Suppose that, instead of the price increases shown in Table 3, prices rise as shown in Table 4. Movie prices go up by 25 percent, but candy prices do not change. Surely, candy manufacturers who love movies will be disgruntled because it now costs 15 candy bars instead of 12 to get into the theater. They will blame inflation for raising the price of movie tickets, even though their real problem stems from the *increase in the price of movies relative to candy*. (They would have been hurt as much if movie tickets had remained at $6 while the price of candy fell to 40 cents.) Because car prices have risen by only 5 percent, theater owners in need of new cars will be delighted by the fact that an automobile now costs only 1,260 movie admissions—just as they would have cheered if car prices had fallen to $7,560 while movie tickets remained at $6. However, they are unlikely to attribute their good fortune to inflation. Indeed, they should not. What has actually happened is that *cars became cheaper relative to movies*.

Because real-world inflations proceed at uneven rates, relative prices are always changing. There are gainers and losers, just as some would gain and others lose if relative prices were to change without any general inflation. Inflation, however, gets a bad name because losers often blame inflation for their misfortune, whereas gainers rarely credit inflation for their good luck.

**Inflation is not usually to blame when some goods become more expensive *relative to others*.**

These two kinds of misconceptions help explain why respondents to public opinion polls often cite inflation as a major national issue, why higher inflation rates depress consumers, and why voters express their ire at the polls when inflation is high. But not all of the costs of inflation are mythical. Let us now turn to some of the real costs.

*Table 3*
**Pure Inflation**

| Item | Last Year's Price | This Year's Price | Increase |
|---|---|---|---|
| Candy bar | $ 0.50 | $ 0.55 | 10% |
| Movie ticket | 6.00 | 6.60 | 10 |
| Automobile | 9,000 | 9,900 | 10 |

*Table 4*
**Real-World Inflation**

| Item | Last Year's Price | This Year's Price | Increase |
|---|---|---|---|
| Candy bar | $ 0.50 | $ 0.50 | 0% |
| Movie ticket | 6.00 | 7.50 | 25 |
| Automobile | 9,000 | 9,450 | 5 |

An item's **relative price** is its price in terms of some other item rather than in terms of dollars.

## 6-11 INFLATION AS A REDISTRIBUTOR OF INCOME AND WEALTH

We have just seen that the *average* person is neither helped nor harmed by inflation. But almost no one is exactly average. Some people gain from inflation and others lose. For example, senior citizens trying to scrape by on pensions or other fixed incomes suffer badly from inflation. Because they earn no wages, it is little solace to them that wages keep pace with prices. Their pension incomes do not.[9]

---

[8] How statisticians figure out "average" price increases is discussed in the appendix to this chapter.
[9] This is not true of Social Security benefits, which are automatically increased to compensate recipients for changes in the price level.

This example illustrates a general problem. Think of pensioners as people who "lend" money to an organization (the pension fund) when they are young, expecting to be paid back with interest when they are old. Because of the rise in the price level during the intervening years, the unfortunate pensioners get back dollars that are worth less in purchasing power than those they originally loaned. In general:

**Those who lend money are often victimized by inflation.**

Although lenders may lose heavily, borrowers may do quite well. For example, homeowners who borrowed money from banks in the form of mortgages back in the 1950s, when interest rates were 3 or 4 percent, gained enormously from the surprisingly virulent inflation of the 1970s. They paid back dollars of much lower purchasing power than those that they borrowed. The same is true of other borrowers.

**Borrowers often gain from inflation.**

Because the redistribution caused by inflation generally benefits borrowers at the expense of lenders, and because both lenders and borrowers can be found at every income level, we conclude that

**Inflation does not systematically steal from the rich to aid the poor, nor does it do the reverse.**

Why, then, is the redistribution caused by inflation so widely condemned? Because its victims are selected capriciously. No one legislates the redistribution. No one enters into it voluntarily. The gainers do not earn their spoils, and the losers do not deserve their fate. Moreover, inflation robs particular classes of people of purchasing power year after year—people living on private pensions, families who save money and "lend" it to banks, and workers whose wages and salaries do not adjust to higher prices. Even if the average person suffers no income loss from inflation, that fact offers little consolation to those who are its victims. This is one fundamental indictment of inflation.

**Inflation redistributes income in an arbitrary way. Society's income distribution should reflect the interplay of the operation of free markets and the purposeful efforts of government to alter that distribution. Inflation interferes with and distorts this process.**

## 6-12   REAL VERSUS NOMINAL INTEREST RATES

But wait. Must inflation always rob lenders to bestow gifts upon borrowers? If both parties see inflation coming, won't lenders demand that borrowers pay a higher interest rate as compensation for the coming inflation? Indeed they will. For this reason, economists draw a sharp distinction between *expected* inflation and *unexpected* inflation.

What happens when inflation is fully expected by both parties? Suppose Diamond Jim wants to borrow $1,000 from Scrooge for one year, and both agree that, in the absence of inflation, a fair rate of interest would be 3 percent. This means that Diamond Jim would pay back $1,030 at the end of the year for the privilege of having $1,000 now.

If both men expect prices to increase by 6 percent, Scrooge may reason as follows: "If Diamond Jim pays me back $1,030 one year from today, that money will buy less than what $1,000 buys today. Thus, I'll really be *paying him* to borrow from me! I'm no philanthropist. If I charge him 9 percent instead, he'll pay back $1,090 at the end of the year. With prices 6 percent higher, this will buy roughly what $1,030 is worth today. So I'll get the same 3 percent increase in purchasing power that we would have agreed on in the absence of inflation and won't be any worse off. That's the least I'll accept."

Diamond Jim may follow a similar chain of logic. "With no inflation, I was willing to pay $1,030 one year from now for the privilege of having $1,000 today, and Scrooge was willing to lend it. He'd be crazy to do the same with 6 percent inflation. He'll want to charge me more. How much should I pay? If I offer him $1,090 one year from now, that will have roughly the same purchasing power as $1,030 today, so I won't be any worse off. That's the most I'll pay."

This kind of thinking may lead Scrooge and Diamond Jim to write a contract with a 9 percent interest rate—3 percent as the increase in purchasing power that Diamond Jim pays to Scrooge and 6 percent as compensation for expected inflation. Then, if the expected 6 percent inflation actually materializes, neither party will be made better or worse off by inflation.

This example illustrates a general principle. The 3 percent increase in purchasing power that Diamond Jim agrees to turn over to Scrooge is called the **real rate of interest**. The 9 percent contractual interest charge that Diamond Jim and Scrooge write into the loan agreement is called the **nominal rate of interest**. The nominal rate of interest is calculated by adding the *expected rate of inflation* to the real rate of interest. The general relationship is

> Nominal interest rate = Real interest rate + Expected inflation rate

Expected inflation is added to compensate the lender for the loss of purchasing power that the lender expects to suffer as a result of inflation. Because of this,

> **Inflation that is accurately predicted need not redistribute income between borrowers and lenders. If the *expected* rate of inflation that is embodied in the nominal interest rate matches the *actual* rate of inflation, no one gains and no one loses. However, to the extent that expectations prove incorrect, inflation will still redistribute income.[10]**

It need hardly be pointed out that errors in predicting the rate of inflation are the norm, not the exception. Published forecasts bear witness to the fact that economists sometimes have great difficulty in predicting the rate of inflation. The task is no easier for businesses, consumers, and banks. This is another reason why inflation is so widely condemned as unfair and undesirable. It sets up a guessing game that no one likes.

The **real rate of interest** is the percentage increase in purchasing power that the borrower pays to the lender for the privilege of borrowing. It indicates the increased ability to purchase goods and services that the lender earns.

The **nominal rate of interest** is the percentage by which the money the borrower pays back exceeds the money that was borrowed, making no adjustment for any decline in the purchasing power of this money that results from inflation.

## 6-13 INFLATION DISTORTS MEASUREMENTS

So inflation imposes costs on society because it is difficult to predict. But other costs arise even when inflation is predicted accurately. Many such costs stem from the fact that people are simply unaccustomed to thinking in inflation-adjusted terms and so make errors in thinking and calculation. Many laws and regulations that were designed for an inflation-free economy malfunction when inflation is high. Here are some important examples.

### 6-13a  Confusing Real and Nominal Interest Rates

People frequently confuse *real* and *nominal* interest rates. For example, most Americans viewed the 12 percent mortgage interest rates that banks charged in 1980 as scandalously high but saw the 4 percent mortgage rates of 2013 as great bargains. In truth, with inflation around 1 percent in 2013 and 10 percent in 1980, the real interest rate in 2013 (about 3 percent) was above the bargain-basement real rates in 1980 (about 2 percent).

### 6-13b  The Malfunctioning Tax System

The tax system is probably the most important example of inflation illusion at work. The law does not recognize the distinction between nominal and real interest rates; it simply taxes *nominal* interest regardless of how much real interest it represents. Similarly, **capital gains**—the difference between the price at which an investor sells an asset and the price paid for it—are taxed in nominal, not real, terms. As a result, our tax system can do strange things when inflation is high. An example will show why.

A **capital gain** is the difference between the price at which an asset is sold and the price at which it was bought.

---

[10] Exercise: Who gains and who loses if the inflation turns out to be only 4 percent instead of the 6 percent that Scrooge and Diamond Jim expected? What if the inflation rate is 8 percent?

Between 1988 and 2013, the price level nearly doubled. Consider some stock that was purchased for $20,000 in 1988 and sold for $36,000 in 2013. The investor actually *lost* purchasing power while holding the stock because $36,000 of 2013 money could buy roughly what $18,000 could buy in 1988. Yet because the law levies taxes on nominal capital gains, with no correction for inflation, the investor would have been taxed on the $16,000 *nominal* capital gain—despite suffering a *real* capital loss of about $4,000 (in 2013 dollars).

Many economists have proposed that this (presumably unintended) feature of the law be changed by taxing only real capital gains, that is, capital gains in excess of inflation. To date, Congress has not agreed. This little example illustrates a pervasive and serious problem:

> Because it fails to recognize the distinction between nominal and real capital gains, or between nominal and real interest rates, our tax system levies high, and presumably unintended, tax rates on capital income when inflation is high. Thus the laws that govern our financial system can become counterproductive in an inflationary environment, causing problems that were never intended by legislators. Some economists feel that the high tax rates caused by inflation discourage saving, lending, and investing—and therefore retard economic growth.

Thus, failure to understand that high *nominal* interest rates can still be low *real* interest rates has been known to make the tax code misfire, to impoverish savers, and to inhibit borrowing and lending. And it is important to realize that *these costs of inflation are not purely redistributive.* Society as a whole loses when mutually beneficial transactions are prohibited by dysfunctional legislation.

Why, then, do such harmful laws stay on the books? The main reason appears to be a lack of understanding of the difference between real and nominal interest rates. People fail to understand that it is normally the *real* rate of interest that matters in an economic transaction because that rate shows how much borrowers pay and lenders receive *in terms of the goods and services that money can buy.* They focus instead on the high *nominal* interest rates caused by inflation, even when those rates correspond to low real interest rates.

> The difference between real and nominal interest rates, and the fact that the real rate matters economically whereas the nominal rate is often more significant politically, are matters of the utmost importance and yet are understood by very few people—including many who make public policy decisions.

## 6-14    OTHER COSTS OF INFLATION

Another cost of inflation is that rapidly changing prices make it risky to enter into long-term contracts. In an extremely severe inflation, the "long term" may be only a few days from now, but even moderate inflations can have remarkable effects on long-term loans. Suppose a corporation wants to borrow $1 million to finance the purchase of some new equipment and needs the loan for 20 years. If inflation averages 2 percent over this period, the $1 million it repays at the end of 20 years will be worth $672,971 in today's purchasing power. If inflation averages 5 percent instead, it will be worth only $376,889.

Lending or borrowing for this long a period is obviously a big gamble. With the stakes so high, the outcome may be that neither lenders nor borrowers want to get involved in long-term contracts. But without long-term loans, business investment may become impossible. The economy may stagnate.

Inflation also makes life difficult for the shopper. You probably have a group of stores and web sites that you habitually patronize because they carry the items you want to buy at (roughly) the prices you want to pay. This knowledge saves you time and energy. But when prices are changing rapidly, your list quickly becomes obsolete. You return to your favorite clothing store to find that the price of jeans has risen drastically. Should you buy? Should you shop around at other stores? Will they have also raised their prices? Business firms have precisely the same problem with their suppliers. Rising prices force them to shop around more, which imposes costs on the firms and, more generally, reduces the efficiency of the entire economy.

## 6-15  THE COSTS OF LOW VERSUS HIGH INFLATION

The preceding litany of the costs of inflation alerts us to one very important fact: *Predictable inflation is far less burdensome than unpredictable inflation.* When is inflation most predictable? When it proceeds year after year at a modest and more or less steady rate. Thus, the *variability of the inflation rate* is a crucial factor. Inflation of 3 percent per year for three consecutive years will exact lower social costs than inflation that is 3 percent in the first year, zero in the second year, and 6 percent in the third year. In general:

> Steady inflation is more predictable than variable inflation and therefore has smaller social and economic costs.

But the *average level of inflation* also matters. Partly because of the inflation illusions mentioned earlier and partly because of the more rapid breakdown in normal customer relationships that we have just mentioned, steady inflation of 6 percent per year is more damaging than steady inflation of 3 percent per year.

Economists distinguish between *low inflation,* which is a modest economic problem, and *high inflation,* which can be a devastating one, partly on the basis of the average level of inflation and partly on its variability. If inflation remains steady and low, prices may rise for a long time, but at a moderate and fairly constant pace, allowing people to adapt. For example, inflation in the United States, as measured by the Consumer Price Index, was remarkably steady from 1991 through 2007, never dropping below 1.6 percent nor rising above 4.1 percent.

Very high inflations typically last for short periods of time and are often marked by highly variable inflation rates from month to month or year to year. In recent decades, for example, countries ranging from Argentina to Russia to Zimbabwe have experienced bouts of inflation exceeding 100 percent or even 1,000 percent per year (see "How to Make Hyperinflation Even Worse"). Each of these episodes severely disrupted the affected country's economy.

The German hyperinflation after World War I is perhaps the most famous episode of runaway inflation. Between December 1922 and November 1923, when a hard-nosed reform program finally broke the spiral, wholesale prices in Germany increased by almost 100 million percent! Even this experience was dwarfed by the great Hungarian inflation of 1945–1946. For a period of one year, the *monthly* rate of inflation averaged about 20,000 percent. In the final month, the price level skyrocketed 42 quadrillion percent!

If you review the costs of inflation that have been discussed in this chapter, you will see why the distinction between low and high inflation is so fundamental. Many economists think we can live just fine in an environment of steady, low inflation. No one believes we can survive very well under extremely high inflation. When inflation is steady and low, the rate at which prices rise is relatively easy to predict. It can therefore be taken into account in setting interest rates. Under high inflation, especially if prices are rising at ever-increasing or highly variable rates, this is extremely difficult, and perhaps impossible, to do. The potential redistributions become monumental, and lending and borrowing may cease entirely.

Any inflation makes it difficult to write long-term contracts. Under low, creeping inflation, the "long term" may be 20 years, or 10 years, or 5 years. By contrast, under high, galloping inflation, the "long term" may be measured in days or weeks. Restaurant prices may change daily. Airfares may go up while you are in flight. When it is impossible to enter into contracts of any duration longer than a few days, economic activity becomes paralyzed. We conclude that

> The horrors of hyperinflation are very real. But they are either absent in low, steady inflations or present in such muted forms that they can scarcely be considered horrors.

## How to Make Hyperinflation Even Worse[11]

True hyperinflations are rare; only about 30 have been recorded in history. But one of them happened quite recently: the stunning 2006–2009 episode in Zimbabwe.

After averaging around 20–30 percent per year in the mid-1990s, Zimbabwean inflation began to accelerate at the end of that decade and really took off starting in 2002. According to the International Monetary Fund (IMF), consumer prices in Zimbabwe rose 132 percent in 2002, 350 percent in 2004, and a stunning 1,017 percent in 2006. Then things really got out of control, with the inflation rate rising month after month. The IMF estimated that inflation in Zimbabwe reached the astonishing rate of 16,000 percent for 2007 as a whole, topping 66,000 percent at an annual rate by December.

But that was just the beginning, as it turned out. By July 2008, when the official data end, Zimbabwean inflation exceeded 231 *million* percent per annum. And it was still rising! Two scholars have estimated that inflation was up to almost 90 *sextillion* percent (yes, that's 90,000,000,000,000,000,000,000) per year by November. That's almost 100 percent a day. And it still wasn't over. This page isn't wide enough to show all the zeroes in the inflation rates of early 2009. The system finally crashed entirely—with the Zimbabwean dollar abandoned—in April 2009.

The root cause of this amazing hyperinflation, of course, was what it always is in hyperinflations: The Zimbabwean government was printing colossal amounts of money to pay its bills. By the end, ordinary notes of $100 trillion Zimbabwean dollars were in circulation.

Although printing too much money was bad enough, Zimbabwe's dictator, Robert Mugabe, compounded the sin by instituting price controls in July 2007. After all, if inflation is running too high, he apparently reasoned, why not just decree that it stop? Well, even an absolute dictator must contend with the laws of economics—especially if he keeps running the printing presses at full tilt. The result was predictable: Commodities, including basic foodstuffs, quickly disappeared from the shelves. Long queues and even riots developed as Zimbabwe's starved citizens scrambled to purchase what little there was to buy. Neighboring South Africa reported Zimbabweans pouring over the border—some to flee the chaos, but many just to shop.

A newspaper story in July 2007 reported that "buying meat in Zimbabwe these days is like buying an illegal substance." And meat was by no means a special case. Within weeks after price controls were instituted, such basics as bread, cornmeal, sugar, salt, flour, and even matches were difficult to find; thousands of shopkeepers had been arrested; and many stores were opening only at night to avoid the inspectors. Zimbabwe was barreling full-speed-ahead toward economic chaos.

SOURCES: "Zimbabwe's Shopping Nightmare," *The Scotsman*, July 26, 2007; Steve Hanke and Alex Kwok, "On the Measurement of Zimbabwe's Hyperinflation," *Cato Journal*, 2009, pp. 353–364.

## 6-16 LOW INFLATION DOES NOT NECESSARILY LEAD TO HIGH INFLATION

*These children in Germany during the hyperinflation of the 1920s are building a pyramid with cash, worth no more than the sand or sticks used by children elsewhere.*

We noted earlier that inflation is surrounded by a mythology that bears precious little relation to reality. It seems appropriate to conclude this chapter by disposing of one particularly persistent myth: that low inflation is a slippery slope that invariably leads to high inflation.

**There is neither statistical evidence nor theoretical support for the belief that low inflation inevitably leads to high inflation. To be sure, inflations sometimes speed up. At other times, however, they slow down.**

Although creeping inflations have many causes, runaway inflations have occurred only when the government has printed incredible amounts of money, usually to finance wartime expenditures. In the German inflation of 1923, the government finally found that its printing presses could not produce enough paper money to keep pace with the exploding prices. Not that it did not try—by the end of the inflation, the *daily* output of currency exceeded 400 quadrillion marks! The Hungarian authorities in 1945–1946 tried even harder: The average growth rate of the money supply was more than 12,000 percent *per month*. Needless to say, these are not the kinds of inflation problems that are likely to face industrialized countries in the foreseeable future.

---

[11] You may find the Wikipedia entry "Hyperinflation in Zimbabwe" interesting.

But that does not mean there is nothing wrong with low inflation. We have spent much time analyzing the very real costs of even modest inflation. A case against moderate inflation can indeed be built. But slogans like "Creeping inflation always leads to galloping inflation" are simply not true.

## Summary

1. Macroeconomic policy strives to achieve rapid and reasonably stable growth while keeping both unemployment and inflation low.

2. Only rising productivity can raise standards of living in the long run. And seemingly small differences in productivity growth rates can compound to enormous differences in living standards. This is one of our *Ideas for Beyond the Final Exam.*

3. The **production function** tells us how much output the economy can produce from the available supplies of labor and capital, given the state of technology.

4. The growth rate of **potential GDP** is the sum of the growth rate of the **labor force** plus the growth rate of **labor productivity.** The latter depends on, among other things, technological change and investment in new capital.

5. Over long periods of time, the growth rates of actual and potential GDP match up well. But, owing to macroeconomic fluctuations, the two can diverge sharply over short periods.

6. Although some psychologists, environmentalists, and social critics question the merits of faster economic growth, economists generally assume that faster growth of potential GDP is socially beneficial.

7. When GDP is below its potential, unemployment is above **full employment.** High unemployment exacts heavy financial and psychological costs from those who are its victims, costs that are borne quite unevenly by different groups in the population.

8. **Frictional unemployment** arises when people are between jobs for normal reasons. Thus, most frictional unemployment is desirable.

9. **Structural unemployment** is due to shifts in the pattern of demand or to technological change that makes certain skills obsolete.

10. **Cyclical unemployment** is the portion of unemployment that rises when real GDP grows more slowly than potential GDP and falls when the opposite is true.

11. Today, after some years of extremely high unemployment, economists are unsure where full employment lies. Many think it may be at a measured unemployment rate around 5.5 percent.

12. **Unemployment insurance** replaces almost half of the lost income of unemployed persons who are insured. But in normal times, barely more than one-third of the unemployed actually collect benefits, and no insurance program can bring back the lost output that could have been produced had these people been working.

13. People have many misconceptions about inflation. For example, many believe that inflation systematically erodes **real wages** and blame inflation for any unfavorable changes in relative prices. Both of these ideas are myths.

14. Other costs of inflation are real, however. For example, inflation often redistributes income from lenders to borrowers.

15. This redistribution is ameliorated by adding the expected rate of inflation to the interest rate, but such expectations often prove to be inaccurate.

16. The **real rate of interest** is the **nominal rate of interest** minus the **expected rate of inflation**.

17. Because the real rate of interest indicates the command over real resources that the borrower surrenders to the lender, it is of primary economic importance. But public attention often is riveted on nominal rates of interest, and this confusion can lead to costly policy mistakes.

18. Because nominal—not real—**capital gains** and interest are taxed, our tax system levies heavy taxes on income from capital when inflation is high.

19. Low inflation that proceeds at moderate and fairly predictable rates year after year carries far lower social costs than does high or variable inflation. But even low, steady inflations entail costs.

20. The notion that low inflation inevitably accelerates into high inflation is a myth with no foundation in economic theory and no basis in historical fact.

## Key Terms

| | | |
|---|---|---|
| capital gain   117 | labor force   104 | real rate of interest   117 |
| cyclical unemployment   111 | labor productivity   103 | real wage rate   113 |
| discouraged workers   110 | nominal rate of interest   117 | relative prices   115 |
| frictional unemployment   110 | outputs   101 | structural unemployment   111 |
| full employment   111 | potential GDP   104 | unemployment insurance   112 |
| growth policy   102 | production function   104 | unemployment rate   107 |
| inputs   101 | purchasing power   113 | |

## Test Yourself

1. Two countries start with equal GDPs. The economy of Country A grows at an annual rate of 3 percent, whereas the economy of Country B grows at an annual rate of 4 percent. After 25 years, how much larger is Country B's economy than Country A's economy? Why is the answer *not* 25 percent?

2. If output rises by 35 percent while hours of work increase by 40 percent, has productivity increased or decreased? By how much?

3. Most economists believe that from 2010 to 2013, actual GDP in the United States grew slightly faster than potential GDP. What, then, should have happened to the unemployment rate over those three years? Before that, from 2006 to 2010, actual GDP grew slower than potential GDP, even contracting for several quarters. What should have happened to the unemployment rate over those three years? (Check the data on the inside back cover of this book to see what actually happened.)

4. Country A and Country B have identical population growth rates of 1 percent per annum, and everyone in each country always works 40 hours per week. Labor productivity grows at a rate of 2 percent in Country A and a rate of 2.5 percent in Country B. What are the growth rates of potential GDP in the two countries?

5. What is the *real interest rate* paid on a credit card loan bearing 12 percent nominal interest per year, if the rate of inflation is

   a. zero?

   b. 4 percent?

   c. 8 percent?

   d. 15 percent?

6. Suppose you agree to lend money to your friend on the day you both enter college at what you both expect to be a zero *real* rate of interest. Payment is to be made at graduation, with interest at a fixed *nominal* rate. If inflation proves to be *lower* during your college years than what you both had expected, who will gain and who will lose?

## Discussion Questions

1. If an earthquake destroys some of the factories in Poorland, what happens to Poorland's potential GDP? What happens to Poorland's potential GDP if it acquires some new advanced technology from Richland and starts using it?

2. Why is it not as terrible to become unemployed nowadays as it was during the Great Depression?

3. "Unemployment is no longer a social problem because unemployed workers receive unemployment benefits and other benefits that make up for most of their lost wages." Comment.

4. Why is it so difficult to define *full employment?* What unemployment rate should the government be shooting for today?

5. Show why each of the following complaints is based on a misunderstanding about inflation:

   a. "Inflation must be stopped because it robs workers of their purchasing power."

   b. "Inflation makes it impossible for working people to afford many of the things they were hoping to buy."

   c. "Inflation must be stopped today, for if we do not stop it, it will surely accelerate to ruinously high rates and lead to disaster."

## Appendix  *How Statisticians Measure Inflation*

### Index Numbers for Inflation

Inflation is generally measured by the change in some index of the general price level. For example, between 1982 and 2013, the Consumer Price Index (CPI), the most widely used measure of the price level, rose from 96.5 to 233.0—an increase of 141 percent over 31 years. The meaning of the *change* is clear enough. But what are the meanings of the 96.5 figure for the price level of 1982 and the 233 figure for 2013? Both are **index numbers**.

**A price index** expresses the cost of a market basket of goods relative to its cost in some "base" period, which is simply the year used as a basis of comparison.

Because the CPI currently uses 1982–1984 as its base period, the CPI of 233 for 2013 means that it cost $233 in 2013 to purchase the same basket of several hundred goods and services that cost $100, on average, over 1982–1984.

Now in fact, the particular list of consumer goods and services under scrutiny did not actually cost $100 in 1982–1984. When constructing index numbers, the index is set at 100 in the base period by convention. This figure is then used to obtain index numbers for other years in a very simple way. Suppose that the budget needed to buy the hundreds of items included in the CPI was $2,000 per month in 1982–1984 and $4,660 per month in 2013. Then the index is defined by the following rule:

$$\frac{\text{CPI in 2013}}{\text{CPI in 1982–1984}} = \frac{\text{Cost of market basket in 2013}}{\text{Cost of market basket in 1982–1984}}$$

Because the CPI in 1982–1984 is set at 100:

$$\frac{\text{CPI in 2013}}{100} = \frac{\$4,660}{\$2,000} = \$2.33$$

or

$$\text{CPI in 2013} = 233$$

Exactly the same sort of equation enables us to calculate the CPI in any other year. We have the following rule:

$$\text{CPI in given year} = \frac{\text{Cost of market basket in given year}}{\text{Cost of market basket in base year}} \times 100$$

Of course, not every combination of consumer goods that cost $2,000 in 1982–1984 rose to $4,660 by 2013. For example, a TV set that cost $400 in 1982–1984 might still have cost $400 in 2013, but a $400 hospital bill in 1982–1984 might have ballooned to $4,000. For this reason, there is no perfect cost-of-living index because no two families buy precisely the same bundle of goods and services, and hence no two families suffer precisely the same increase in prices. Economists call this the **index number problem**:

> When relative prices are changing, there is no such thing as a "perfect price index" that is correct for every consumer. Any statistical index will understate the increase in the cost of living for some families and overstate it for others. At best, the index can represent the situation of an "average" family.

## The Consumer Price Index

The **Consumer Price Index (CPI)**, which is calculated and announced each month by the Bureau of Labor Statistics (BLS), is surely the most closely watched price index. When you read in the newspaper or see on television that the "cost of living rose by 0.1 percent last month," chances are the reporter is referring to the CPI.[12]

> The **Consumer Price Index (CPI)** is measured by pricing the items on a list representative of a typical urban household budget.

To know which items to include and in what amounts, the BLS conducts periodic surveys of the spending habits of American households, including what they buy, where they buy it, and so on. A simple example will help us understand how the CPI is constructed.

Imagine that college students purchase only three items—hamburgers, jeans, and movie tickets—and that we want to devise a cost-of-living index (call it SPI, or "Student Price Index") for them. First, we would conduct a survey of spending habits in the base year. (Suppose it is 1983.) Table 5 represents the hypothetical results. You will note that the frugal students of that day spent only $100 per month: $56 on hamburgers, $24 on jeans, and $20 on movies.

*Table 5*

**Results of Student Expenditure Survey, 1983**

| Item | Average Price | Average Quantity Purchased per Month | Average Expenditure per Month |
|---|---|---|---|
| Hamburger | $ 0.80 | 70 | $ 56 |
| Jeans | 24.00 | 1 | 24 |
| Movie ticket | 5.00 | 4 | 20 |
| Total | | | $100 |

Table 6 presents hypothetical prices of these same three items in 2013. Each price has risen by a different amount, ranging from 25 percent for jeans up to 50 percent for hamburgers. By how much has the SPI risen?

*Table 6*

**Prices In 2013**

| Item | Price | Increase over 1983 |
|---|---|---|
| Hamburger | $ 1.20 | 50% |
| Jeans | 30.00 | 25 |
| Movie ticket | 7.00 | 40 |

Pricing the 1983 student budget at 2013 prices, we find that what once cost $100 now costs $142, as the calculation in Table 7 shows. Thus, the SPI, based on 1983 = 100, is

$$\text{SPI} = \frac{\text{Cost of budget in 2013}}{\text{Cost of budget in 1983}} \times 100$$
$$= \frac{\$142}{\$100} \times 100 = 142$$

[12] A great deal of information about the CPI can be found on the Bureau of Labor Statistics web site, www.bls.gov. Just click on the pages pertaining to the CPI.

*Table 7*

**Cost of 1983 Student Budget in 2013 Prices**

| | |
|---|---|
| 70 hamburgers at $1.20 | $ 84 |
| 1 pair of jeans at $30 | 30 |
| 4 movie tickets at $7 | 28 |
| Total | $142 |

So, the SPI in 2013 stands at 142, meaning that students' cost of living has increased 42 percent over the 30 years.

## Using a Price Index to "Deflate" Monetary Figures

One of the most common uses of price indexes is in the comparison of monetary figures relating to two different points in time. The problem is that if there has been inflation, the dollar is not a good measuring rod because it can buy less now than it did in the past.

Here is a simple example. Suppose the average student spent $100 per month in 1983 but $140 per month in 2013. If there was an outcry that students had become spendthrifts, how would you answer the charge?

The obvious answer is that a dollar in 2013 does not buy what it did in 1983. Specifically, our SPI shows us that it takes $1.42 in 2013 to purchase what $1 would purchase in 1983. To compare the spending habits of students in the two years, we must divide the 2013 spending figure by 1.42. Specifically, *real* spending per student in 2013 (where "real" is defined by 1983 dollars) is:

$$\text{Real spending in 2013} = \frac{\text{Nominal spending in 2013}}{\text{Price index of 2013}} \times 100$$

$$\text{Real spending in 2013} = \frac{\$140}{142} \times 100 = \$98.59$$

This calculation shows that, despite appearances to the contrary, the change in nominal spending from $100 to $140 actually represented a small *decrease* in real spending.

This procedure of dividing by the price index is called **deflating**, and it serves to translate noncomparable monetary figures into more directly comparable real figures.

**Deflating** is the process of finding the real value of some monetary magnitude by dividing by some appropriate price index.

A good practical illustration is the real wage, a concept we have discussed in this chapter. As we saw in the box "Calculating the Real Wage: A Real Example,"

we obtain the real wage by dividing the nominal wage by the price level.

## Using a Price Index to Measure Inflation

In addition to deflating nominal magnitudes, price indexes are commonly used to measure *inflation*, that is, the *rate of increase* of the price level. The procedure is straightforward. The data on the inside back cover (column 13) show that the CPI was 49.3 in 1974 and 44.4 in 1973. The ratio of these two numbers, 49.3/44.4, is 1.11, which means that the 1974 price level was 11 percent greater than the 1973 price level. Thus, the *inflation rate* between 1973 and 1974 was 11 percent. The same procedure holds for any two adjacent years. More recently, the CPI rose from 229.6 in 2012 to 233 in 2013. The ratio of these two numbers is 233/229.6 = 1.015, meaning that the inflation rate from 2012 to 2013 was 1.5 percent.

## The GDP Deflator

In macroeconomics, one of the most important of the monetary magnitudes that we have to deflate is the nominal gross domestic product (GDP).

The price index used to deflate nominal GDP is called the **GDP deflator**. It is a broad measure of economy-wide inflation that includes the prices of all goods and services in the economy.

Our general principle for deflating a nominal magnitude tells us how to go from nominal GDP to real GDP:

$$\text{Real GDP} = \frac{\text{Nominal GDP}}{\text{GDP deflator}} \times 100$$

As with the CPI, the 100 simply serves to establish the base of the index as 100, rather than 1.00.

Some economists consider the GDP deflator to be a better measure of overall inflation than the Consumer Price Index. The main reason is that the GDP deflator is based on a broader market basket. As mentioned earlier, the CPI is based on the budget of a typical urban family. By contrast, the GDP deflator is constructed from a market basket that includes *every* item in the GDP—that is, every final good and service produced by the economy. Thus, in addition to prices of consumer goods, the GDP deflator includes the prices of airplanes, lathes, and other goods purchased by businesses—especially computers, which fall in price every year. It also includes government services. For this reason, the two indexes rarely give the same measure of inflation. Usually the discrepancy is minor, but sometimes it can be noticeable, as in 2009 when the CPI recorded a 2.7 percent inflation rate over 2008 while the GDP deflator recorded an inflation rate of merely 0.8 percent.

## Summary

1. Inflation is measured by the percentage increase in an **index number** of prices, which shows how the cost of some basket of goods has changed over a period of time.

2. Because relative prices are always changing, and because different families purchase different items, no price index can represent precisely the experience of every family.

3. The **Consumer Price Index (CPI)** tries to measure the cost of living for an average urban household by pricing a typical market basket every month.

4. Price indexes such as the CPI can be used to **deflate** nominal figures to make them more comparable. Deflation amounts to dividing the nominal magnitude by the appropriate price index.

5. The inflation rate between two adjacent years is computed as the percentage change in the price index between the first year and the second year.

6. The **GDP deflator** is a broader measure of economy-wide inflation than the CPI because it includes the prices of all goods and services in the economy.

## Key Terms

Consumer Price Index (CPI)  123

deflating  124

GDP deflator  124

index numbers  122

index number problem  123

price index  122

## Test Yourself

1. Below you will find the yearly average values of the Dow Jones Industrial Average, the most popular index of stock market prices, for five different years. The Consumer Price Index for each year (on a base of 1982–1984 = 100) can be found on the inside back cover of this book. Use these numbers to deflate all five stock market values. Do real stock prices always rise every decade?

| Year | Dow Jones Industrial Average |
|------|------------------------------|
| 1970 | 753 |
| 1980 | 891 |
| 1990 | 2,679 |
| 2000 | 10,735 |
| 2010 | 10,663 |

2. Below you will find nominal GDP and the GDP deflator (based on 2009 = 100) for the years 1992, 2002, and 2012.

   a. Compute real GDP for each year.

   b. Compute the percentage change in nominal and real GDP from 1992 to 2002, and from 2002 to 2012.

   c. Compute the percentage change in the GDP deflator over these two periods.

| GDP Statistics | 1992 | 2002 | 2012 |
|----------------|------|------|------|
| Nominal GDP | 6,539 | 10,980 | 16,245 |
| Real GDP | | | |
| GDP deflator | 70.6 | 85.1 | 105.0 |

3. Fill in the blanks in the following table of GDP statistics:

| | 2010 | 2011 | 2012 |
|--|------|------|------|
| Nominal GDP | 14,958 | | 16,245 |
| Real GDP | 14,779 | 15,052 | |
| GDP deflator | | 103.2 | 105.0 |

4. Use the following data to compute the College Price Index for 2013 using the base 1983 = 100.

| Item | Price in 1983 | Quantity per Month in 1983 | Price in 2013 |
|------|------|------|------|
| Button-down shirts | $10 | 1 | $25 |
| Loafers | 25 | 1 | 55 |
| Sneakers | 10 | 3 | 35 |
| Textbooks | 12 | 12 | 40 |
| Jeans | 12 | 3 | 30 |
| Restaurant meals | 5 | 11 | 14 |

5. Average hourly earnings in the U.S. economy during several past years were as follows:

| 1970 | 1980 | 1990 | 2000 | 2010 |
|------|------|------|------|------|
| $3.40 | $6.85 | $10.20 | $14.02 | $19.07 |

Use the CPI numbers provided on the inside back cover of this book to calculate the real wage (in 1982–1984 dollars) for each of these years. Which decade had the fastest growth of money wages? Which had the fastest growth of real wages?

6. The example in the appendix showed that the Student Price Index (SPI) rose by 42 percent from 1983 to 2013. You can understand the meaning of this better if you do the following:

a. Use Table 5 to compute the fraction of total spending accounted for by each of the three items in 1983. Call these values the "expenditure weights."

b. Compute the weighted average of the percentage increases of the three prices shown in Table 6, using the expenditure weights you just computed.

You should get 42 percent as your answer. This shows that inflation, as measured by the SPI, is a weighted average of the percentage price increases of all the items that are included in the index.

# ECONOMIC GROWTH: THEORY AND POLICY

*Once one starts to think about ... [differences in growth rates among countries], it is hard to think about anything else.*

ROBERT E. LUCAS, JR., 1995 NOBEL PRIZE WINNER IN ECONOMICS

W hy do some economies grow rapidly while others grow slowly—or not at all? As the opening quotation suggests, there is probably no more important question in all of economics. From 2002 to 2012, according to the International Monetary Fund (IMF), the American economy grew at a 1.8 percent average annual rate despite the terrible recession. But China's economy grew 10.4 percent per year while Zimbabwe's *declined* 2.5 percent per year. Those are very large differences. What factors account for such disparities?

The previous chapter's discussion of the goal of economic growth focused our attention on two crucial but distinct tasks for macroeconomic policy makers, both of which are quite difficult to achieve:

- *Growth policy:* Ensuring that the economy sustains a high long-run growth rate of potential GDP (although not necessarily the *highest possible* growth rate)
- *Stabilization policy:* Keeping actual GDP reasonably close to potential GDP in the short run, so that society is plagued by neither high unemployment nor high inflation

This chapter is devoted to the first of these: the theory of economic growth and the policies that this theory suggests.

Corresponding to the two tasks just listed, there are two ways to think about what is to come in this and subsequent chapters. The two views of the macroeconomy complement one another. In discussing *growth policy* in this chapter, we study the factors that determine an economy's *long-run* growth rate of *potential GDP*, and we consider how policy makers can try to speed it up. When we turn to *stabilization policy,* starting in the next chapter, we will investigate how and why *actual GDP* may deviate from potential GDP in the *short run* and how policy makers can try to minimize these deviations—two questions that have consumed the nation's attention for years now.

## CONTENTS

| Puzzle | *Why Does College Education Keep Getting More Expensive?* |

Have you ever wondered why the cost of a college education rises more rapidly than most other prices year after year? If you have not, your parents surely have! And it's not a myth. Between 1982 and 2012, the component of the Consumer Price Index (CPI) that measures college tuition costs rose by 678 percent—compared to 138 percent for the overall CPI. That is, the *relative* price of college tuition increased massively.

Economists understand at least part of the reason, and it has little, if anything, to do with the efficiency (or lack thereof) with which colleges are run. Rather, it is a natural corollary of the economy's long-run growth rate. Furthermore, there is good reason to expect the relative price of college tuition to keep rising, and to rise more rapidly in faster-growing societies. Economists believe that the same explanation for the unusually rapid growth in the cost of attending college applies to services as diverse as visits to the doctor, theatrical performances, and restaurant meals—all of which also have become relatively more expensive over time. What is that explanation? We will see later in this chapter.

© bikeriderlondon/Shutterstock.com

## 7-1 THE THREE PILLARS OF PRODUCTIVITY GROWTH

As we learned in the previous chapter, the growth rate of potential GDP is the *sum* of the growth rates of *hours of work* and *labor productivity*. It is hardly mysterious that an economy will grow if its people keep working harder and harder, year after year. A few societies have followed that recipe successfully for relatively brief periods of time, but there is a limit to how much people can work or, more important, to how much they want to work. In fact, people typically want more leisure time, not longer hours of work, as they get richer. In consequence, the natural focus of growth policy is on enhancing productivity— on working *smarter* rather than working *harder*.

The last chapter introduced a tool called the *production function*, which tells us how much *output* the economy can produce from specified *inputs* of labor and capital, given the state of *technology*. The discussion there focused on two of the three main determinants of productivity growth:[1]

- The rate at which the economy builds up its stock of *capital*
- The rate at which *technology* improves

Before introducing the third determinant, let us review how these first two pillars work.

### 7-1a Capital

Figure 1 resembles Figure 1 of the last chapter. The lower curve $0K_1$ is the production function when the capital stock is some low number $K_1$. Its upward slope indicates, naturally enough, that more labor input produces more output. (Remember, technology

---

[1] If you need review, see Chapter 6 sections "The Capacity to Produce: Potential GDP and the Production Function" and "The Growth Rate of Potential GDP."

is held constant in this graph.) The middle curve $0K_2$ is the production function corresponding to some larger capital stock $K_2$, and the upper curve $0K_3$ pertains to an even larger capital stock $K_3$.

To keep things simple at first, suppose hours of work do not grow over time, but rather remain fixed at $L_1$. However, the nation's businesses invest in new plant and equipment, so the capital stock grows from $K_1$ in the first year to $K_2$ in the second year and $K_3$ in the third year. Then the economy's capacity to produce will move up from point *a* in year 1 to point *b* in year 2 and point *c* in year 3. Potential GDP will therefore rise from $Y_a$ to $Y_b$ to $Y_c$. Because hours of work do not change in this example (by assumption), every bit of this growth comes from rising *productivity*, which is in turn due to the accumulation of more capital.[2] In general:

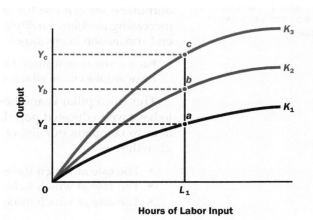

Figure 1

**Production Functions Corresponding to Three Different Capital Stocks**

> For a given technology and a given labor force, labor productivity will rise as the capital stock increases.

This conclusion is hardly surprising. Employees who work with more capital can obviously produce more goods and services. Just imagine manufacturing a desk, first with only hand tools, then with power tools, and finally with all the equipment available in a modern furniture factory. Or think about selling books from a sidewalk stand, in a bookstore, or over the Internet. Your productivity would rise in each case. Furthermore, workers with *more* capital are almost certainly blessed with *newer*—and, hence, *better*—capital as well. This advantage, too, makes them more productive. Again, compare one of Henry Ford's assembly-line workers of a century ago to an autoworker in a Ford plant today.

## 7-1b Technology

In Chapter 6, we saw that a graph like Figure 1 can also be used to depict the effects of *improvements in technology*. So now imagine that curves $0K_1$, $0K_2$, and $0K_3$ all correspond to the *same* capital stock, but to *different* levels of technology. Specifically, the economy's technology improves as we move up from $0K_1$ to $0K_2$ to $0K_3$. The graphical (and commonsense) conclusion is exactly the same: Labor becomes more productive from year 1 to year 2 to year 3, so improving technology leads directly to growth. In general:

> For given inputs of labor and capital, labor productivity will rise as technology improves.

Once again, this conclusion hardly comes as a surprise—indeed, it is barely more than the definition of technical progress. When we say that a nation's technology improves, we mean, more or less, that firms in the country can produce *more output* from the *same inputs*. Superior technology is a major factor behind the vastly higher productivity of workers in rich countries versus poor ones. Textile plants in North Carolina, for example, use technologies that are far superior to those employed in Africa.

## 7-1c Labor Quality: Education and Training

It is now time to introduce the third pillar of productivity growth, the one not mentioned in Chapter 6: *workforce quality*. It is generally assumed—and supported by reams of evidence—that better-educated workers can produce more goods and services in an hour than can less-educated workers. And the same lesson applies to training that takes place outside the schools, such as on the job: Better-trained workers are more productive.

---

[2] Because productivity is the ratio $Y/L$, it is shown on the graph by the slope of the straight line connecting the origin to point *a*, or point *b*, or point *c*. Clearly, that slope is rising over time.

**Human capital** is the amount of skill embodied in the workforce. It is most commonly measured by the amount of education and training.

The amount of education and training embodied in a nation's labor force is often referred to as its stock of **human capital**. Conceptually, an increase in human capital has the same effect on productivity as an increase in physical capital or an improvement in technology; that is, the same *quantity* of labor input becomes capable of producing more output. So we can use the ever-adaptable Figure 1 for yet a third purpose—to represent increasing *workforce quality* as we move up from $0K_1$ to $0K_2$ to $0K_3$. Once again, the general conclusion is obvious:

> For a given capital stock, labor force, and technology, labor productivity will rise as the workforce acquires more education and training.

This third pillar is another source of large disparities between rich nations, which tend to have well-educated populations, and poor nations, which do not. So we can add a third item to complete our list of the three principal determinants of a nation's productivity growth rate:

- The rate at which the economy builds up its stock of *capital*
- The rate at which *technology* improves
- The rate at which *workforce quality* (or "human capital") is improving

In rich countries like the United States, average educational attainment is high and workforce quality changes little from year to year. But in some rapidly developing countries, improvements in education have been an important engine of growth. For example, average years of schooling in South Korea soared from less than five in 1970 to more than nine in 1990, which contributed mightily to South Korea's remarkably rapid economic development.

Although there is no unique formula for growth, the most successful growth strategies of the post–World War II era, beginning with Japan's "economic miracle," made ample use of all three pillars. Starting from a base of extreme deprivation after World War II, Japan showed the world how a combination of high investment, a well-educated workforce, and the adoption of state-of-the-art technology could catapult a poor nation into the leading ranks within a few decades. The lessons were not lost on the so-called Asian Tigers—including Taiwan, South Korea, Singapore, and Hong Kong—which developed rapidly using their own versions of the Japanese model.

Today, a host of other countries are applying variants of this growth formula once again. The most notable example, of course, is China, which is investing like mad; educating its workforce at all levels, from kindergarten through graduate school; and adopting technologies from the rich countries rapidly. The formula is working again—spectacularly well. In just a few decades, it has helped lift hundreds of millions of Chinese out of poverty and has made China one of the world's biggest economies.

## 7-2 LEVELS, GROWTH RATES, AND THE CONVERGENCE HYPOTHESIS

Notice that where productivity *growth rates* are concerned, it is the *rates of increase* of capital, technology, and workforce quality that matter, rather than their current *levels*. This distinction may sound boring, but it is important.

Productivity *levels* are vastly higher in the rich countries—that is why they are called rich. The wealthy nations have more bountiful supplies of capital, more highly skilled workers, and superior technologies. So naturally, they produce more output per hour of work. Table 1 shows, for example, that an hour of labor in France in 2011 produced 95 percent as much output as an hour of labor in the United States, when evaluated in U.S. dollars, whereas the corresponding figure for Singapore was only 68 percent. And Singapore is considered a rich country. Corresponding figures for poor African countries are a mere fraction of U.S. productivity.

But the *growth rates* of capital, workforce skills, and technology are not necessarily higher in the rich countries. For example, Country A might have abundant capital, but the amount might be increasing at a snail's pace, whereas in Country B capital might be scarce but growing rapidly. When it comes to determining the long-run growth rate, it is the *growth rates* rather than the current *levels* of these three pillars that matter.

In fact, GDP per hour of work actually grew faster over the 32 years covered in Table 1 in several countries that had and still have lower average incomes than the United States. For example, productivity in each of the other countries listed in the table grew faster than in the United States. Why? Although a typical Japanese worker in 1979 had less physical and human capital than a typical American worker, and used less-advanced technology, the capital stock, average educational attainment, and level of technology all *increased* faster in Japan than in the United States.

> The level of productivity in a nation depends on its supplies of human and physical capital and the state of its technology. But the growth rate of productivity depends on the *rates of increase* of these three factors.

The distinction between productivity levels and productivity growth rates may strike you as pedantic, but it has many important practical applications. Here is a particularly striking one. *If the productivity growth rate is higher in poorer countries than in richer ones, then poor countries will close the gap on rich ones.* The so-called **convergence hypothesis** suggests that this is what normally happens.

> *Convergence hypothesis:* **The productivity growth rates of poorer countries tend to be higher than those of richer countries.**

The idea behind the convergence hypothesis, as illustrated in Figure 2, is that productivity growth typically will be faster where the initial level of productivity is lower. In this hypothetical example, the poorer country starts out with a per capita GDP of $2,000, just one-fifth that of the richer country. But the poor country's real GDP per capita grows faster, so it gradually narrows the relative income gap.

Why might we expect such convergence to be the norm? In some poor countries, the supply of capital may be growing very rapidly. In others, educational attainment may be rising quickly, albeit from a low base. But the main reason to expect convergence in the long run is that *low-productivity countries should be able to learn from high-productivity countries* as scientific and managerial know-how spreads around the world.

A country that is operating at the technological frontier can improve its technology only by *innovating*. It must constantly figure out ways to do things better. But a less-advanced country can boost its productivity simply by *imitating*, by adopting technologies that are already in common use in the advanced countries. Not surprisingly, it is much easier to "look it up" than to "think it up."

Modern communications assist the convergence process by speeding the flow of information around the globe. The Internet was invented mainly in the United States and the United Kingdom, but it quickly spread to almost every corner of the world. Likewise, advances in human genomics and stem-cell research are now originating in several advanced countries, but they are being communicated rapidly to scientists all over the world. A poor country that is well-organized and adept at importing scientific and engineering advances from the rich countries can achieve very rapid productivity growth. Indeed, when Japan was a poor

*Table 1*

**Productivity Levels and Productivity Growth Rates in Selected Countries**

| Country | GDP per Hour of Work 1979 (as percentage of U.S.) | GDP per Hour of Work 2011 (as percentage of U.S.) | Growth Rate (1979–2011) |
|---|---|---|---|
| **United States** | 100 | 100 | 1.6 |
| France | 88 | 95 | 1.9 |
| Spain | 78 | 79 | 1.7 |
| United Kingdom | 65 | 77 | 2.2 |
| Japan | 51 | 66 | 2.4 |
| Singapore | 38 | 68 | 3.5 |

NOTE: All productivity data are measured in constant U.S. dollars.

SOURCE: Bureau of Labor Statistics.

The **convergence hypothesis** holds that nations with low levels of productivity tend to have high productivity growth rates, so that international productivity differences shrink over time.

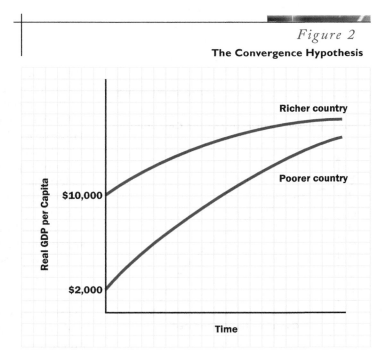

*Figure 2*

**The Convergence Hypothesis**

### Table 2

**Levels and Growth Rates of GDP per Capita in Selected Poor Countries**

| Country | GDP per Capita, 2012* | GDP per Capita Growth Rate, 1992–2012 |
|---|---|---|
| Yemen | 1,367 | 0.3 |
| Ukraine | 3,877 | −0.2 |
| Haiti | 759 | −1.1 |
| Sierra Leone | 615 | −0.3 |
| Burundi | 282 | −1.0 |

* In U.S. dollars.

SOURCE: International Monetary Fund

nation, successful imitation was one of its secrets to getting rich. India and China are doing that now—with considerable success. India, once famous for call centers (and still running them), is now also engaged in the most high-tech computer applications. China, once synonymous with producing low-end goods (and still producing many), has lately begun producing automobiles, cutting-edge energy-saving technologies, and the like.

Unfortunately, many poor countries seem unable to participate in the convergence process. For a variety of reasons (some of which will be mentioned later in this chapter), a number of developing countries seem incapable of adopting and adapting advanced technologies. And that is one major reason why real incomes have stagnated or even fallen in some of the poorest countries of the world, especially in parts of Africa, the Middle East, and some former communist countries (see Table 2). Convergence certainly cannot be taken for granted.

**Technological laggards can, and sometimes do, close the gap with technological leaders by imitating and adapting existing technologies. Within this "convergence club," productivity *growth rates* are higher where productivity *levels* are lower. Unfortunately, some of the world's poorest nations have been unable to join the club.**

## 7-3  GROWTH POLICY: ENCOURAGING CAPITAL FORMATION

A nation's **capital** is its available supply of plant, equipment, and software. It is the result of past decisions to make *investments* in these items.

**Investment** is the *flow* of resources into the production of new capital. It is the labor, steel, and other inputs devoted to the *construction* of factories, warehouses, railroads, and other pieces of capital during some period of time.

Let us now see how the government might spur growth by working on these three pillars, beginning with capital.

First, we need to clarify some terminology. We have spoken of the supply of **capital**, by which we mean the volume of plant (factories, office buildings, and so on), equipment (drill presses, computers, and so on), and software currently available. Businesses *add* to the existing supply of capital whenever they make **investment** expenditures—purchases of new plant, equipment, and software. In this way, the *growth* of the capital stock depends on how much businesses spend on investment. That process is called **capital formation**—literally, forming new capital.

But you don't get something for nothing. Devoting more of society's resources to producing investment goods generally means devoting fewer resources to producing consumer goods. The *production possibilities frontier* introduced in Chapter 3 can be used to depict the nature of this trade-off—and the choices open to a nation. Given its technology and existing resources of labor, capital, and so on, the country can in principle select any point on the production possibilities frontier *AICD* in Figure 3. If it picks a point like *C*, its citizens will enjoy many consumer goods, but it will not be investing much for the future. *So it will grow slowly.* If, on the other hand, it selects a point like *I*, its citizens will consume less today, but the nation's higher level of investment means *it will grow more quickly.* Thus, at least within limits, the amount of capital formation and growth can be chosen.

Now suppose the government wants the capital stock to grow faster; that is, it wants to move from a point like *C* toward a point like *I* in Figure 3. In a capitalist market economy such as ours, private businesses make almost all investment decisions—how many factories to build, how many computers to purchase, and so on. To speed up the process of capital formation, the government must somehow persuade private businesses to invest more. How?

### Figure 3

**Choosing between Investment and Consumption**

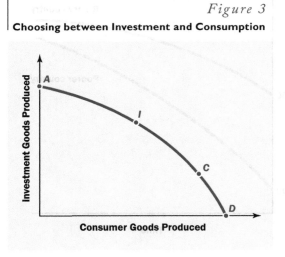

**Real Interest Rates**  The most obvious way to increase investment by private businesses is to lower real interest rates. When real interest rates fall, investment normally rises. Why? Because businesses often borrow to finance their investments, and the real interest rate indicates how much firms must pay for that privilege. An investment project that looks unattractive at an interest rate of 10 percent may look highly profitable if the firm has to pay only 6 percent.

**The amount that businesses invest depends on the real interest rate they pay to borrow funds. The lower the real rate of interest, the more investment there will be.**

In subsequent chapters, we will learn how government policy, especially monetary policy, influences interest rates—which gives policy makers some leverage over private investment decisions. That relationship, in fact, is the main reason why monetary policy will play such a crucial role in subsequent chapters. But we might as well come clean right now: For reasons to be examined later, the government's ability to control real interest rates is imperfect. Furthermore, the rate of interest is only one of several determinants of investment spending. So policy makers have only a limited ability to affect the level of investment by manipulating interest rates.

**Tax Provisions** The government also can influence investment spending by altering various provisions of the tax code. For example, President Barack Obama proposed more generous tax write-offs for businesses that invested in equipment in 2010, arguing that lower taxes would lead to greater investment spending. In addition, the United States imposes a tax on corporate profits and can reduce that tax to spur investment as well. Congress discussed that option extensively in 2014, but did not act on it. There are other, more complicated tax provisions relating to investment, too.[3] To summarize:

**The tax law gives the government several ways to influence business spending on investment goods, but *influence* is far from *control*. Business decisions are dominant in capital formation, and these decisions depend on many factors other than taxes.**

**Technical Change** Technology, which we have listed as a separate pillar of growth, also drives investment. New business opportunities suddenly appear when a new product such as the smartphone or e-book reader is invented or when a technological breakthrough makes an existing product much cheaper or better, as with 3-D printers and LED television sets. In a capitalist system, entrepreneurs pounce on such opportunities—building new factories, stores, and offices, and buying new equipment. Thus, if the government can figure out how to spur technological progress (a subject discussed later in this chapter), those same policies will probably boost investment.

**The Growth of Demand** Rapid growth itself can induce businesses to invest more. When demand presses against capacity, executives are likely to believe that new factories and machinery can be employed profitably—which creates strong incentives to build new capital. Thus it was no coincidence that investment soared in the United States during the boom years of the 1990s, and collapsed during the sharp slump of 2008–2009. By contrast, if machinery and factories stand idle, businesses may find new investments unattractive. In summary:

**High levels of sales and expectations of rapid economic growth create an atmosphere conducive to investment.**

This situation creates a kind of virtuous cycle in which high rates of investment boost economic growth, and rapid growth boosts investment. Of course, the same process can also operate in reverse—as a vicious cycle: When the economy stagnates, firms do not want to invest much, damaging prospects for further growth.

**Capital formation** is synonymous with investment. It refers to the process of building up the capital stock.

[3] Any kind of a tax cut will reduce government revenue. Unless that revenue is made up by a spending cut or by some other tax, the government's budget deficit will rise—which will also affect investment. We will study that channel in Chapter 16.

**Property rights** are laws and/or conventions that assign owners the rights to use their property as they see fit (within the law)—for example, to sell the property or to reap the benefits (such as rents or dividends) while they own it.

**Political Stability and Property Rights** There is one other absolutely critical determinant of investment spending that Americans simply take for granted but many people in poor countries certainly do not.

A business thinking about committing funds to, say, build a factory faces any number of risks. Construction costs might run higher than estimates. Interest rates might rise. Demand for the product might prove weaker than expected. The list goes on and on. These are the normal hazards of entrepreneurship, an activity that is not for the faint of heart. But, at a minimum, business executives contemplating a long-term investment want assurances that their property will not be taken from them for capricious or political reasons. Republican businesspeople in the United States do not worry that their property will be seized if the Democrats win the next election. Nor do they worry that court rulings will deprive them of their **property rights** without due process.

By contrast, in many less well-organized societies, the rule of law is regularly threatened by combinations of arbitrary government actions, political instability, anti-capitalist ideology, rampant corruption, or runaway crime. Such problems have posed serious impediments to long-term investment in many poor countries throughout history. They are among the chief reasons these countries have remained poor. And the litany of problems that threaten property rights is not just a matter of history—these issues remain relevant in Russia, much of Africa, and parts of Latin America today. A drop in interest rates of a few percentage points will not encourage much investment if businesses fear that their property may be expropriated.

Needless to say, the strength of property rights, adherence to the rule of law, the level of corruption, and the like are not easy things to measure. Anyone who attempts to rank countries on such criteria must make many subjective judgments. Nevertheless, due to its recent interest in the subject, the World Bank currently ranks countries on various aspects of their business climate, including their degree of investor protection. Some of their data are displayed in Table 3. The ranking of the various countries holds a few surprises but is mainly what you might expect.

*Table 3*

**Selected Countries Ranked by Level of Investor Protection**

| Country | Rating (0–10 scale) |
| --- | --- |
| Singapore | 9.3 |
| Canada | 8.7 |
| United States | 8.3 |
| United Kingdom | 8.0 |
| Japan | 7.0 |
| Sweden | 6.3 |
| India | 6.3 |
| Italy | 6.0 |
| Mexico | 5.7 |
| Brazil | 5.3 |
| China | 5.0 |
| Swaziland | 4.3 |

SOURCE: World Bank web site, www.doingbusiness.org, accessed December 2013. The index is constructed by rating countries on transparency of transactions, liability for self-dealing, and shareholders' ability to sue for misconduct.

# To Grow Fast, Get the Institutions Right

Some years ago, the World Bank surveyed the ways the governments of around 100 countries either encourage or discourage market activity. Its conclusion, as summarized in *The Economist*, was that "when poor people are allowed access to the institutions richer people enjoy, they can thrive and help themselves. A great deal of poverty, in other words, may be easily avoidable."

The World Bank study highlighted the importance of making simple institutions accessible to the poor—such as protection of property rights (especially over land), access to the judicial system, and a free and open flow of information—as key ingredients in successful economic development. *The Economist* put it graphically:

If it is too expensive and time-consuming, for example, to open a bank account, the poor will stuff their savings under the mattress. When it

takes 19 steps, five months and more than an average person's annual income to register a new business in Mozambique, it is no wonder that aspiring, cash-strapped entrepreneurs do not bother.

The Bank's conclusion reminded many people of the central message of a best-selling 2000 book by Peruvian economist and businessman Hernando de Soto—who found to his dismay that, in his own country, it took 700 bureaucratic steps to obtain legal title to a house!

SOURCES: "Now, Think Small," *The Economist*, September 15, 2001, pp. 40–42; and Hernando de Soto, *The Mystery of Capital: Why Capitalism Triumphs in the West and Fails Everywhere Else* (New York: Basic Books, 2000).

## 7-4 GROWTH POLICY: IMPROVING EDUCATION AND TRAINING

Numerous studies in many countries confirm the fact that more educated and better-trained workers earn higher wages. Economists naturally assume that the people who earn more are also more productive. Thus, more education and training presumably contribute to higher productivity. Although private institutions play a role in the educational process, in most societies the state bears the primary responsibility for educating the population. So *education policy* is an obvious and critical component of growth policy.

A modern industrial society is built more on brains than on brawn. Even ordinary blue-collar jobs often require a high school education. For this reason, policies that raise rates of high school attendance and completion and, perhaps as important, improve the *quality* of secondary education can make genuine contributions to growth. Unfortunately, such policies have proven difficult to devise and implement. President Obama's "Race to the Top" initiative is only the latest in a long list of educational reforms. The debate over how to improve our public schools goes on and on, with no resolution in sight.

Finally, if knowledge is power in the Information Age, then sending more young people to college and graduate school may be crucial to economic success. It is well documented that the earnings gap between high school and college graduates in the United States has risen dramatically since the late 1970s. One graphical depiction of this rising disparity is shown in Figure 4. It shows that the job market has been rewarding the skills acquired in college ever more generously since about 1978. To the extent that high wages reflect high productivity, low-cost tuition (such as that paid at many state colleges and universities), student loans to low-income families, and other policies that encourage college attendance may yield society rich dividends.

Devoting more resources to education should, therefore, raise an economy's growth rate. By suitable reinterpretation, Figure 3 can again be used to illustrate the trade-off between present and future. Because expenditures on education are naturally thought of as *investments in human capital*, just interpret the vertical axis as now representing educational investments. If a society spends more on them and less on consumer goods (thus moving from point C toward point I), it should grow faster. China, to cite the most prominent recent example, is doing that with great enthusiasm. It is upgrading its domestic school system, from top to bottom, and sending many of its brightest students to universities abroad.

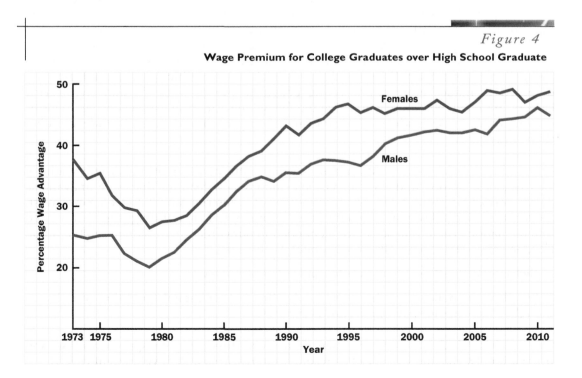

*Figure 4*

**Wage Premium for College Graduates over High School Graduate**

But education is not a panacea for all of an economy's ills. Education in the former Soviet Union was outstanding in some respects, but proved insufficient to prevent the Soviet economy from falling ever further behind the capitalist economies in terms of economic growth.

**On-the-job training**
refers to skills that workers acquire while at work, rather than in school or in formal vocational training programs.

**On-the-job training** may be just as important as formal education in raising productivity, but it is less amenable to influence by the government. For the most part, private businesses decide how much, and in what ways, to train their workers. Various public policy initiatives—ranging from government-run training programs, to subsidies for private-sector training, to mandated minimum training expenditures by firms—have been tried in various countries with mixed results. In the United States, mandates on companies have always been viewed as improper interferences with private business decisions, and they have been avoided. The government runs some training programs, though the biggest by far is the armed forces.

## 7-5 GROWTH POLICY: SPURRING TECHNOLOGICAL CHANGE

Our third pillar of growth is *technology*, or getting more output from given supplies of inputs. Some of the most promising policies for speeding up the pace of technical progress have already been mentioned.

**Expanding Higher Education** Although some inventions and innovations are the product of dumb luck, most result from the sustained application of knowledge, resources, and brainpower to scientific, engineering, and managerial problems. We have just noted that more educated workers appear to be more productive *per se*. In addition, a society is likely to be more innovative if it has a greater supply of scientists, engineers, and skilled business managers who are constantly on the prowl for new opportunities. Modern growth theory emphasizes the pivotal role in the growth process of committing more human, physical, and financial resources to the acquisition of knowledge.

> High levels of education, especially scientific, engineering, and managerial education, contribute to the advancement of technology.

There is little doubt that the United States leads the world in the quality of its graduate programs in business and in many scientific and engineering disciplines. For evidence of this superiority, one need only look at the tens of thousands of foreign students who flock to our shores to attend graduate school—many of whom remain in America. It seems reasonable to suppose that America's unquestioned leadership in scientific and business education contributes to our leadership in productivity. On this basis, many economists and politicians endorse policies—such as scholarships, fellowships, and research grants—designed to induce more bright young people to pursue scientific and engineering careers. Yet many observers worry that too few young Americans are choosing scientific careers. Indeed, our graduate programs are often packed with foreign students rather than Americans.

**Invention** is the act of discovering new products or new ways of making products.

**Innovation** is the act of putting new ideas into effect, for example, by bringing new products to market, changing product designs, and improving the way in which things are done.

**More Capital Formation** We are all familiar with the fact that the latest versions of smartphones, laptops, and even televisions embody new features that were unavailable a year or even six months ago. The same is true of industrial capital. Indeed, new investment is the principal way in which the latest technological breakthroughs get hard-wired into the nation's capital stock. As we mentioned in our earlier discussion of capital formation, newer capital is normally better capital. In this way,

> High rates of investment contribute to rapid technical progress.

So all of the policies we discussed earlier that bolster capital formation can also be thought of as ways to speed up technical progress.

**Research and development (R&D)** refers to activities aimed at inventing new products or processes, or improving existing ones.

**Research and Development** There is a more direct way to spur **invention** and **innovation**: Devote more of society's resources to **research and development (R&D)**.

Driven by the profit motive, American businesses have long invested heavily in industrial R&D. According to the old saying, "Build a better mousetrap, and the world will beat a path to your door." And innovative companies in the United States and elsewhere have been engaged in research on "better mousetraps" for decades. Polaroid invented instant photography, Xerox developed photocopying, and Apple and IBM pioneered the desktop computer. Boeing improved jet aircraft several times. U.S.-based pharmaceutical companies have discovered many new, life-enhancing drugs. Intel has developed generation after generation of ever-faster microprocessors. The list goes on and on, with new entries like Google, Twitter, and Facebook transforming our world.

All these companies and others have spent untold billions of dollars on R&D to discover new products, to improve old ones, and to make their industrial processes more efficient. Although many research dollars are inevitably "wasted" on false starts and experiments that don't pan out, numerous studies have shown that the average dollar invested in R&D has yielded high returns to society. Heavy spending on R&D is, indeed, one of the keys to high productivity growth.

The U.S. government supports and encourages R&D in several ways. First, it subsidizes private R&D spending through the tax code. For example, the Research and Experimentation Tax Credit reduces the taxes of companies that spend money on R&D.

Second, the government sometimes joins with private companies in collaborative research efforts. The Human Genome Project was perhaps the most spectacular example of such a public–private partnership (some called it a race). There also have been cooperative ventures in new automotive technology, alternative energy sources, and elsewhere.

Last, and certainly not least, the federal government has over the years spent a great deal of taxpayer money directly on R&D. Much of this spending has been funneled through the Department of Defense, but the National Aeronautics and Space Administration (NASA), the National Science Foundation (NSF), the National Institutes of Health (NIH), and many other agencies have also played important roles. Inventions as diverse as atomic energy, advanced ceramic materials, and the Internet were originally developed in federal laboratories. Federal government R&D spending in fiscal year 2014 amounted to almost $150 billion, nearly half of which went through the Pentagon.

Our multipurpose Figure 3 again illustrates the choice facing society. Now interpret the vertical axis as measuring investments in R&D. Devoting more resources to R&D—that is, choosing point *I* rather than point *C*—leads to less current consumption but more growth.

## 7-6 THE PRODUCTIVITY SLOWDOWN AND SPEED-UP IN THE UNITED STATES

Around 1973, productivity growth in the United States suddenly and mysteriously slowed down—from the rate of about 2.8 percent per year that had characterized the 1948–1973 period to about 1.5 percent thereafter (see Figure 5). Hardly anyone anticipated this productivity slowdown. Then, starting around 1995, productivity growth suddenly speeded up again—from about 1.5 percent per year during the 1973–1995 period back to about 2.6 percent between 1995 and 2010 (see Figure 5 again). Once again, the abrupt change in the growth rate caught most people by surprise.

Since 2010, productivity growth seems to have dropped again—sharply. This is a bit worrisome, but there are too few observations to make a judgment about a new trend. So let's concentrate on the notable changes in 1973 and 1995.

Recall from the discussion of compounding in Chapter 6 that a change in the productivity growth rate of under 1 percentage point, if sustained for decades, makes an enormous difference in living standards. So understanding these two major events is of critical importance. Yet even now economists remain puzzled about the 1973 productivity slowdown, and the reasons behind the 1995 productivity speed-up are only partly understood. Let us see what economists know about these two episodes.

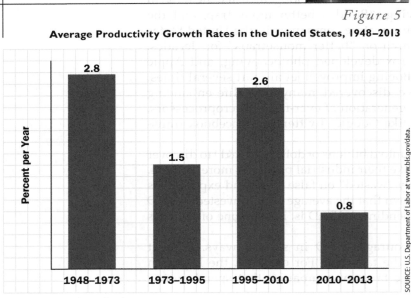

*Figure 5*

**Average Productivity Growth Rates in the United States, 1948–2013**

NOTE: Data pertain to the non-farm business sector.

SOURCE: U.S. Department of Labor at www.bls.gov/data.

## 7-6a The Productivity Slowdown, 1973–1995

The productivity slowdown after 1973 was a disconcerting development, and economists have been struggling to explain it ever since. Among the explanations that have been offered are the following.

**Lagging Investment** During the 1980s and early 1990s, many people suggested that inadequate investment was behind America's productivity problem. Countries such as Germany and Japan, these critics observed, saved and invested far more than America did, thereby equipping their workers with more modern equipment that boosted labor productivity. United States tax policy, they argued, should create stronger incentives for business to invest and for households to save. Indeed, you still hear this case made today.

Although the argument is logical, the facts never supported it. For example, the share of U.S. GDP accounted for by business investment did not decline during the period of slow productivity growth. Nor did the contribution of capital formation to growth fall. (See the box "Growth Accounting in the United States.")

**High Energy Prices** A second explanation begins with a tantalizing fact: The productivity slowdown started around 1973, just when the Organization of Petroleum Exporting Countries (OPEC) first jacked up the price of oil. As a matter of logic, higher oil prices should reduce business use of energy, which should make labor less productive. Furthermore, productivity growth fell when energy prices rose all over the world, not just in the United States—which is a striking coincidence. This circumstantial evidence points the finger at oil prices. The argument sounds persuasive until you remember another important fact: When energy prices dropped sharply in the mid-1980s, productivity growth did not revive. So the energy explanation for the productivity slowdown has many skeptics.

**Inadequate Workforce Skills** Could it be that the skills of the U.S. labor force failed to keep pace with the demands of new technology after 1973? Although workforce skills are notoriously difficult to measure, there was and is a widespread feeling that the quality of education in the United States has declined. For example, SAT scores peaked in the late 1960s and then declined for about 20 years.[4] Yet standard measures such as school attendance rates, graduation rates, and average levels of educational attainment all continued to register gains in the 1970s and 1980s. Clearly, the proposition that the quality of the U.S. workforce declined is at least debatable.

**A Technological Slowdown?** Could the pace of innovation have slowed in the 1973–1995 period? Most people instinctively answer "no." After all, the microchip and the personal computer were invented in the 1970s, opening the door to what can only be called a revolution in computing and information technology (IT). Workplaces were transformed beyond recognition. Entirely new industries (such as those related to PCs) were spawned. Didn't these technological marvels raise productivity by enormous amounts?

The paradox of seemingly rapid technological advance coupled with sluggish productivity performance puzzled economists for years. How could the contribution of technology to growth have *fallen*? A satisfactory answer was never given. And then, all of a sudden, the facts changed.

---

[4] The SAT was rescaled more than a decade ago to reflect this decline in average scores.

## Growth Accounting in the United States

In this chapter, we have learned that labor productivity (output per hour of work) rises because more capital is accumulated, because technology improves, and because workforce quality rises. The last of these three pillars is minor in the modern United States because average educational attainment has been high for a long time and has not changed much recently, but the other two pillars are very important.

The table breaks down the growth rate of labor productivity into its two main components over three different periods of time. We see that the productivity slowdown after 1973 was entirely accounted for by slower technological improvement; the contribution of capital formation did not decline at all.* Similarly, the productivity speed-up after 1995 was mostly accounted for by faster technical progress; higher rates of investment played a much smaller role.

|  | 1948–1973 | 1973–1995 | 1995–2010 |
|---|---|---|---|
| Growth rate of labor productivity | 2.8% | 1.5% | 2.6% |
| Contribution of capital formation | 0.9 | 1.0 | 1.1 |
| Contribution of technology | 1.9 | 0.5 | 1.5 |

* Changes in workforce quality are included in the technology component.

SOURCE: Bureau of Labor Statistics at www.bls.gov/data.

## 7-6b The Productivity Speed-Up 1995–2010

Figure 5 shows that productivity growth speeded up remarkably after 1995, rising from about 1.5 percent per annum before that year to about 2.6 percent from 1995 to 2010. This time, the causes are better understood—and most of them relate to the IT revolution.

**Surging Investment** Bountiful new business opportunities in the IT sector and elsewhere, coupled with a strong national economy, led to a surge in business investment spending in the 1990s. Business investment rose sharply as a percentage of real GDP from 1995 to 2000, and most of the increase was concentrated in computers, software, and telecommunications equipment. We have observed several times in this chapter that the productivity growth rate should rise when the capital stock grows faster, and that's exactly what happened in the late 1990s. But then investment fell after the stock market crashed in 2000. Over the entire 1995–2010 period, the table in the "Growth Accounting in the United States" box shows only a slightly larger contribution of capital formation to productivity growth than over 1973–1995. So investment is only a small part of the answer.

**Falling Energy Prices?** For part of this period, especially the years 1996–1998, energy prices were falling. By the same logic used earlier, falling energy prices should have enhanced productivity growth. But, as we noted earlier, this argument did not seem to work so well when energy prices fell in the 1980s. Why, then, should we believe it for the 1990s? In addition, productivity continued to surge in the early years of this decade, as energy prices soared.

**Advances in Information Technology** We seem to be on safer ground when we look to technological progress, especially in computers and semiconductors, to explain the speed-up in productivity growth. First, innovation seemed to explode in the 1990s. Computers became faster and much, much cheaper—as did telecommunications equipment and services. Corporate intranets became commonplace. The Internet grew from a scientific curiosity into a commercial reality, and so on. We truly entered the Information Age.

Second, it probably took American businesses some time to learn how to use the computer and telecommunications technologies that were invented and adopted between, say, 1980 and the early 1990s. It was only in the late 1990s, some observers argue, that U.S. industry was positioned to reap the benefits of these advances in the form of higher productivity. Such long delays are not unprecedented. Research has shown, for example, that it took a long time for the availability of electric power at the end of the nineteenth century to contribute much to productivity growth. Like electric power, computers were a novel input to production, and it may have taken years for prospective users to find the most productive ways to employ them.

In summary:

**The biggest pillar of productivity growth—technological change—seems to do most of the work of explaining why productivity accelerated in the United States after 1995.**

| Puzzle Resolved | *Why the Relative Price of College Tuition Keeps Rising* |
|---|---|

Earlier in this chapter, we observed that the relative prices of services such as college tuition, medical care, and theater tickets seem to rise year after year. And we suggested that one main reason for this perpetual increase is tied to the economy's long-run growth rate. We are now in a position to understand precisely how that mechanism works. Rising productivity is the key. The argument is based on three simple ideas.

**Idea 1** It stands to reason, and is verified by historical experience, that over long periods of time *economy-wide real wages tend to rise at the same rate as labor productivity*. This relationship makes sense: Labor normally gets paid more when it produces more. Thus real wages will rise most rapidly in economies with the fastest productivity growth.

**Idea 2** *Real wages in different occupations must rise at similar rates in the long run.* This point may sound wrong at first: Haven't the wages of software engineers risen faster than those of schoolteachers in recent years? Yes they have, and that is the market's way of attracting more young people into software development. In the long run, however, these growth rates must (more or less) equilibrate, or else virtually no one would want to be a schoolteacher any more.

**Idea 3** Although average labor productivity in the economy increases from year to year, *there are a number of personally provided services for which productivity (output per hour) cannot or does not grow*. We have already mentioned several of them. Your college or university can increase the "productivity" of its faculty by increasing class size, but most students and parents would view that as a decrease in educational quality. Similarly, a modern doctor takes roughly as long to give a patient a physical as his counterparts did 25 or 50 years ago. It also takes *exactly* the same time for an orchestra to play one of Beethoven's symphonies today as it did in Beethoven's time.

There is a common ingredient in each of these diverse examples: The major sources of higher labor productivity that we have studied in this chapter—more capital and better technology—are completely or nearly irrelevant. It still takes one lecturer to teach a class, one doctor to examine a patient, and four musicians to play a string quartet—just as it did 100 years ago. Saving on labor by using more and better equipment is more or less out of the question.[5] These so-called *personal services* stand in stark contrast to, say, working on an automobile assembly line or in a semiconductor plant, or even to working in service industries such as telecommunications—all instances in which both capital formation and technical progress regularly raise labor productivity.

Now let's bring the three ideas together. College teachers are no more productive than they used to be, but autoworkers are much more productive (Idea 3). In the long run, however, the real wages of college teachers and autoworkers must grow at roughly the same rate (Idea 2), which is the economy-wide productivity growth rate (Idea 1). As a result, wages of college teachers and doctors will rise *faster* than their productivity does, and so their services must grow ever more expensive compared to, say, computers and phone calls.

That is, indeed, the way things seem to have worked out. Compared to the world in which your parents grew up, computers and telephone calls are now unimaginably cheap, whereas college tuition and doctors' bills are extremely expensive. The same logic applies to the services of police officers (two per squad car), baseball players (nine per team), chefs,

---

[5] However, MOOCs (massive open online courses) are beginning to boost productivity in higher education enormously by delivering lectures long distance over the Internet. No one yet knows how far this process will go.

and many other occupations where productivity improvements are either impossible or undesirable. All of these services have grown much more expensive over time. This phenomenon has been called the **cost disease of the personal services**.

Ironically, the villain of the piece is actually the economy's strong productivity growth. If manufacturing and telecommunications workers had *not* become more productive over time, their real wages would not have risen. In that case, the real wages of teachers and doctors would not have had to keep pace, so their services would not have grown ever more expensive. Paradoxically, the enormous productivity gains that have blessed our economy and raised our standard of living also account for the problem of rising tuition costs. In the most literal sense, we are the victims of our own success.

According to the **cost disease of the personal services**, service activities that require direct personal contact tend to rise in price relative to other goods and services.

## 7-7 GROWTH IN THE DEVELOPING COUNTRIES[6]

Ernest Hemingway once answered a query of F. Scott Fitzgerald's by agreeing that, yes, the rich *are* different—they have more money! Similarly, whereas the main determinants of economic growth—increases in capital, improving technology, and rising workforce skills—are the same in both rich and poor countries, they look quite different in the developing countries. So far, this chapter has focused on growth in the industrialized countries. Let us now review the three pillars of productivity growth from the standpoint of the developing nations, using China as the most recent, and most spectacular, success story.

### 7-7a The Three Pillars Revisited

Capital We noted earlier that many poor countries are poorly endowed with capital. Given their low incomes, they simply have been unable to accumulate the volumes of business capital (factories, equipment, and the like) and public capital (roads, bridges, airports, and so on) that we take for granted in the industrialized world. In a rich country like the United States, more than $150,000 worth of capital stands behind a typical worker, whereas in a poor African country the corresponding figure may be less than $500. No wonder the American worker is vastly more productive than his African counterpart.

Accumulating more capital can be exceptionally difficult in the developing world. We noted earlier that rich countries have a *choice* about how much of their resources to devote to current consumption versus investment for the future. But building capital for the future is a far more difficult task in poor countries, where much of the population may be living on the edge of survival, literally unable to save for the future. For this reason, it has long been believed that **development assistance**, sometimes called *foreign aid*, is a crucial ingredient for growth in the developing world. Indeed, the World Bank was established in 1944 precisely to make low-interest development loans to poor countries.

Development assistance has always been controversial. Critics of foreign aid argue that the money is often not well spent. Without honest and well-functioning governments, well-defined property rights, and so on, they argue, the developing countries cannot and will not make good use of the assistance they receive. Supporters of foreign aid counter that the donor countries have been far too stingy. The United States, for example, donates only about 0.1 percent of its GDP each year. Can grants that amount to $60 per person—which is a fairly typical figure for the recipient countries—really be expected to make much difference?

Although foreign aid can be critical in certain instances, it has certainly *not* been the secret to China's success. Instead, the Chinese have shown a remarkable willingness and ability to save and invest—around half of GDP in recent years—despite their relatively low incomes. This is part of the tried-and-true formula that Japan employed decades ago. But in addition, China has welcomed **foreign direct investment**, often by **multinational corporations**, which it has received in great volume.

Technology You need only visit a poor country to see that the level of technology is generally far below what we are accustomed to in the West. In principle, this handicap

**Development assistance** ("foreign aid") refers to outright grants and low-interest loans to poor countries from both rich countries and multinational institutions like the World Bank. The purpose is to spur economic development.

**Foreign direct investment** is the purchase or construction of real business assets—such as factories, offices, and machinery—in a foreign country.

**Multinational corporations** are corporations, generally large ones, that do business in many countries. Most, but not all, of these corporations have their headquarters in developed countries.

---

[6] This section can be skipped in shorter courses.

should be easy to overcome. As noted in our discussion of the convergence hypothesis, people in poor countries don't have to invent anything; they can just adopt technologies that have already been invented in the rich countries. And indeed, a number of formerly poor countries have followed this strategy with great success. South Korea, which was destitute in the mid-1950s, is a prime example. China is doing this very successfully today and on a massive scale. Indeed, much of the foreign direct investment flowing into China brings Western technology along with it.

As we observed earlier, many of the developing nations, especially the poorest ones, seem unable to join this "convergence club." They may lack the necessary scientific and engineering know-how. They may be short on educated workers. They may be woefully undersupplied with the necessary infrastructure, such as transportation and communications systems. Or they may simply be plagued by incompetent or corrupt governments. Whatever the reasons, they have been unable emulate the technological advances of the West.

There are no easy solutions to this problem. One common suggestion is to encourage foreign direct investment by multinational corporations. Industrial giants like Toyota (Japan), IBM (United States), Siemens (Germany), and others bring their advanced technologies with them when they open a factory or office in a developing nation. They can train local workers and improve local transportation and communications networks. But, of course, these companies are *foreign*, and they come to make a *profit*—both of which can cause resentment in the local population.

For this and other reasons, many developing countries have not always welcomed foreign investment. China, as mentioned, is a big exception: It has welcomed foreign investment with enthusiasm, especially for the technology it brings, and it has learned avidly and openly from the West. However, multinational companies are rarely tempted to open factories in the poorest developing countries, such as those in sub-Saharan Africa, where skilled labor is in short supply, transportation systems may be inadequate, and governments are often unstable and unreliable.

**Education and Training** Huge discrepancies exist between the average levels of educational attainment in the rich and poor countries. Table 4 shows some data on average years of schooling in selected countries, both developed and developing, in 2000. The differences were dramatic—ranging from a high of 12.3 years in the United States to less than 5 years in India and less than 2 years in the Sudan. In most industrialized countries, universal primary education and high rates of high school completion are already realities. In many poor countries, even completing grade school may be the exception, leaving rudimentary skills such as reading, writing, and basic arithmetic in short supply. In such cases, expanding and improving primary education—including keeping children in school until they reach the age of 12—may be among the most cost-effective growth policies available. The problem is particularly acute in many traditional societies, where women are second-class citizens—or worse. In such countries, the education of girls may be considered unimportant or even inappropriate.

China, again, offers a stunning contrast. It is raising the educational attainment of its population rapidly—including girls. It is sending legions of students abroad to study science, engineering, business, and economics (among other things), including tens of thousands to America. And it is developing world-class universities of its own.

## 7-7b  Some Special Problems of Developing Countries

Accumulating capital, improving technology, and enhancing workforce skills are common ingredients of growth in rich and poor countries alike. But many Third World countries also must contend with some special handicaps to growth that are mostly absent in the West.

**Geography** Americans often forget how blessed we are geographically. We live in a temperate climate zone, on a land mass that has literally millions of acres of flat, fertile land that is ideal for agriculture.

*Table 4*

**Average Educational Attainment in Selected Countries, 2000***

| United States | 12.3 |
| --- | --- |
| Canada | 11.4 |
| South Korea | 10.5 |
| Japan | 9.7 |
| United Kingdom | 9.4 |
| Italy | 7.0 |
| Mexico | 6.7 |
| India | 4.8 |
| Brazil | 4.6 |
| Sudan | 1.9 |

* For people older than 25 years of age.

SOURCE: Web site accompanying Robert J. Barro and Jong-Wha Lee, "International Data on Educational Attainment: Updates and Implications," CID Working paper No. 42, Harvard University, 2000, www.cid.harvard.edu/ciddata/ciddata.html.

The fact that our nation literally stretches "from sea to shining sea" also means we have many fine seaports. Contrast this splendid set of geographical conditions with the situation of the world's poorest region: sub-Saharan Africa. Many African nations are landlocked, have extremely hot climates, and/or are terribly short on arable land.

**Health** People in the rich countries rarely think about debilitating tropical diseases such as malaria, dengue fever, and sleeping sickness that are rampant in many developing nations, especially in Africa. The AIDS pandemic, of course, has ravaged that continent (and other countries). In 2010, Haiti was afflicted by a cholera epidemic. In 2014, the dread Ebola virus broke out in several African nations. Although improvements in public health are important in all countries, they are literally matters of life and death in the poorest nations. And there is a truly vicious cycle here: Poor health is a serious impediment to economic growth, and poverty makes it hard to improve health standards.

**Governance** Complaining about low-quality or dishonest government is a popular pastime in many Western democracies. Americans do it every day. But most governments in industrialized nations are paragons of virtue and efficiency compared to the governments of some (though certainly not all) developing nations. Just as political stability, the rule of law, and respect for property rights are critical requirements for economic growth, corruption, overregulation of business, and capricious government are obvious deterrents to investment. Lawlessness, tyrannical rule, and war are even worse, of course. Unfortunately, too many poor nations have been victimized by a succession of corrupt dictators and tragic wars—quite a few are raging as this edition goes to press. It need hardly be said that those conditions are not conducive to economic growth.

## 7-8 FROM THE LONG RUN TO THE SHORT RUN

Most of this chapter has been devoted to explaining and evaluating the factors underpinning the growth rate of *potential* GDP. Over long periods of time, the growth rates of actual and potential GDP match up pretty well. But, just like people, economies do not always live up to their potential. As we observed in the previous chapter, GDP in the United States often diverges from potential GDP as a result of macroeconomic fluctuations. Sometimes it is higher; sometimes, as in recent years, it is lower. Indeed, whereas this chapter has studied the factors that determine the rate at which the GDP of a particular country can *grow* from one year to the next, we have been reminded since 2007 that GDP occasionally *shrinks*—during periods we call *recessions*. To study these fluctuations, we must supplement the long-run theory of *aggregate supply*, which we have just described, with a short-run theory of *aggregate demand*—a task that begins in the next chapter.

## Summary

1. More **capital**, improved workforce quality (which is normally measured by the amount of education and training), and better technology all raise labor productivity and therefore shift the production function upward. They constitute the three main pillars of growth.

2. The growth rate of labor productivity depends on the rate of capital formation, the rate of improvement of workforce quality, and the rate of technical progress. So growth policy concentrates on speeding up these processes.

3. **Capital formation** can be encouraged by low real interest rates, favorable tax treatment, rapid technical change, rapid growth of demand, and a climate of political stability that respects **property rights**. Each of these factors is at least influenced by policy.

4. Policies that increase education and training—the second pillar of growth—can be expected to make a country's workforce more productive. They range from universal primary education to postgraduate fellowships in science and engineering.

5. Technological advances can be encouraged by more education, by higher rates of **investment**, and also by direct expenditures—both public and private—on **research and development (R&D)**.

6. The **convergence hypothesis** holds that countries with lower productivity levels tend to have higher productivity growth rates, so that poor countries gradually close the gap on rich ones.

7. One major reason to expect convergence is that technological know-how can be transferred quickly from the leading

nations to the laggards. Unfortunately, not all countries seem able to benefit from this information transfer.

8. Productivity growth slowed precipitously in the United States around 1973, and economists are still not sure why.

9. Productivity growth in the United States sped up again in 1995, largely as a result of the information technology (IT) revolution.

10. Because many personal services—such as education, medical care, and police protection—are essentially handicraft activities that are not amenable to labor-saving innovations, they suffer from a **cost disease** that makes them grow ever more expensive over time.

11. The same three pillars of economic growth—capital, technology, and education—apply in the developing countries. But on all three fronts, conditions are much more difficult there—and improvements are harder to obtain.

12. The rich countries try to help with all three pillars by providing **development assistance**, and **multinational corporations** sometimes provide capital and better technology via **foreign direct investment**. But both of these mechanisms are surrounded by controversy.

13. Growth in many of the poor countries is also held back by adverse geographical conditions and/or corrupt governments.

## Key Terms

| | | |
|---|---|---|
| capital   132 | development assistance   141 | investment   132 |
| capital formation   132 | foreign direct investment   141 | multinational corporations   141 |
| convergence hypothesis   131 | human capital   130 | on-the-job training   136 |
| cost disease of the personal services   141 | innovation   136 | property rights   134 |
| | invention   136 | research and development (R&D)   136 |

## Test Yourself

1. The following table shows real GDP per hour of work in four imaginary countries in the years 2004 and 2014. By what percentage did labor productivity grow in each country? Is it true that productivity *growth* was highest where the initial *level* of productivity was the lowest? For which countries?

|  | Output per Hour | |
|---|---|---|
|  | 2004 | 2014 |
| Country A | $40 | $48 |
| Country B | 25 | 35 |
| Country C | 2 | 3 |
| Country D | 0.50 | 0.60 |

2. Imagine that new inventions in the computer industry affect the growth rate of productivity as follows:

| Year of Invention | Following Year | 5 Years Later | 10 Years Later | 20 Years Later |
|---|---|---|---|---|
| 0% | −1% | 0% | +2% | +4% |

Would such a pattern help explain U.S. productivity performance since the mid-1970s? Why?

3. Which of the following prices would you expect to rise rapidly over long periods of time? Why?

    a. Cable television rates

    b. Football tickets

    c. Internet access

    d. Household cleaning services

    e. Driving lessons

4. Two countries have the production possibilities frontier (PPF) shown in Figure 3. Consumia chooses point C, whereas Investia chooses point I. Which country will have the higher PPF the following year? Why?

5. Show on a graph how capital formation shifts the production function. Use this graph to show that capital formation increases labor productivity. Explain in words why labor is more productive when the capital stock is larger.

## Discussion Questions

1. Explain the different objectives of (long-run) growth policy versus (short-run) stabilization policy.

2. Explain why economic growth might be higher in a country with well-established property rights and a stable political system compared with a country where property rights are uncertain and the government is unstable.

3. The previous chapter pointed out that, because faster capital formation comes at a cost (reduced current consumption), it is possible for a country to invest too much. Suppose the government of some country decides that its businesses are investing too much. What steps might it take to slow the pace of capital formation?

4. Explain why the best educational policies to promote faster growth might be different in the following countries.

   a. Mozambique
   b. Brazil
   c. France

5. Comment on the following: "Sharp changes in the volume of investment in the United States help explain both the productivity slowdown in 1973 and the productivity speed-up in 1995."

6. Discuss some of the pros and cons of increasing development assistance, both from the point of view of the donor country and the point of view of the recipient country.

# AGGREGATE DEMAND AND THE POWERFUL CONSUMER

**8**

*Men are disposed, as a rule and on the average, to increase their consumption as their income increases, but not by as much as the increase in their income.*

JOHN MAYNARD KEYNES

The last chapter focused on the determinants of *potential GDP*—the economy's capacity to produce. We turn our attention now to the factors determining *actual GDP*—how much of that potential is actually utilized. Will the economy be pressing against its capacity, and therefore perhaps also be having trouble with inflation? Or will there be a great deal of unused capacity, and therefore high unemployment, as has been the case in the United States for years?

The theory that economists use to answer such questions is based on the two central concepts we introduced in Chapter 5: aggregate demand and supply. The last chapter examined the long-run determinants of *aggregate supply*, a topic to which we will return in Chapter 10. In this chapter and the next, we will construct a simplified model of *aggregate demand* and learn the origins of the aggregate demand curve.

Although aggregate supply rules the roost in the long run, Chapter 5's whirlwind tour of U.S. economic history suggested that the strength of aggregate demand holds the key to the economy's condition in the short run. When aggregate demand grows briskly, the economy booms, as in the late 1990s. When aggregate demand is weak, the economy stagnates or declines, as in 2007–2009.

The model we develop to understand aggregate demand in this chapter and the next will teach us much about this process. But it is too simple to deal directly with policy issues, because the government and the financial system are largely ignored. We remedy these two big omissions in Part 3, where we give government spending, taxation, and interest rates appropriately prominent roles. The influence of the exchange rate between the U.S. dollar and foreign currencies is then considered in Part 4.

## CONTENTS

| Issue |
|---|
| **?** |

## Demand Management and the Ornery Consumer

In Chapter 5, we suggested that the government sometimes wants to shift the aggregate demand curve. It can do so a number of ways. One direct approach is to alter its own purchases, spending freely when private demand is weak and tightening its belt when private demand is strong. Alternatively, the government can take a more indirect route by using taxes and other policy tools to influence *private* spending decisions. Because consumer expenditures constitute more than two-thirds of gross domestic product, the consumer presents the most tempting target.

Indeed, the U.S. government tried that several times during and after the 2007–2009 recession, when economic growth first slowed to a crawl and then collapsed. Both President George W. Bush in 2008 and President Barack Obama in 2009 decided that consumer spending needed a boost, and in each case Congress passed a *temporary* income tax cut to help accomplish that. When the recovery proved weak, the medicine was then repeated again in late 2010.

There should be no mystery about how changes in personal income taxes are expected to affect consumer spending. Any *reduction* in personal taxes leaves consumers with *more* after-tax income to spend; any tax *increase* leaves them with *less*. The linkage from taxes to spendable income to consumer spending seems direct and unmistakable, and in a certain sense, it is.

Yet the congressional debates over the tax bills in both 2008 and 2009 sent legislators and journalists scurrying to the scholarly evidence on a similar episode more than 30 years earlier. In the spring of 1975, as the U.S. economy hit a recessionary bottom, Congress enacted a tax rebate to spur consumer spending. That time consumers did not follow the wishes of the president and Congress. They saved a substantial share of their tax cuts, rather than spending them. As a result, the economy did not receive the expected boost.

Perhaps the legislators should have taken the 1975 episode to heart. Early estimates of the effects of the 2008 and 2009 tax cuts suggested that consumers spent less money than would have been expected if the tax cuts were permanent. (But not zero, as some critics claimed.) Thus, at least in a limited sense, history repeated itself. But why? Why did these temporary tax cuts seem to have weaker effects on spending than permanent tax cuts? This chapter attempts to provide some answers. But before getting involved in such complicated issues, we must build some vocabulary and learn some basic concepts.

## 8-1   AGGREGATE DEMAND, DOMESTIC PRODUCT, AND NATIONAL INCOME

First, some vocabulary. We have already introduced the concept of gross domestic product as the standard measure of the economy's total output.[1]

For the most part, firms in a market economy produce goods only if they think they can sell them. **Aggregate demand** is the total amount that all consumers, business firms, government agencies, and foreigners spend on U.S. final goods and services. The downward-sloping aggregate demand curve of Chapter 5 alerted us to the fact that *aggregate demand is a schedule, not a fixed number*—the actual numerical value of aggregate demand depends on the price level. Several reasons for this dependence will emerge in coming chapters.

The level of aggregate demand also depends on a variety of other factors—such as consumer incomes, various government policies, and events in foreign countries. To understand the nature of aggregate demand, it is best to break it up into its major components.

**Consumer expenditure** (*consumption*, for short) is simply the total value of all consumer goods and services demanded. Because consumer spending constitutes more than two-thirds of total spending, it is the main focus of this chapter. We represent it by the letter C.

**Aggregate demand** is the total amount that all consumers, business firms, government agencies, and foreigners spend on final goods and services.

**Consumer expenditure (C)** is the total amount spent by consumers on newly produced goods and services (excluding purchases of new homes, which are considered investment goods).

---

[1] See the section entitled "Gross Domestic Product" in Chapter 5.

**Investment spending**, represented by the letter *I*, was discussed in the last chapter. It is the amount that firms spend on factories, machinery, software, and the like, plus the amount that families spend on new houses. Notice that this usage of the word *investment* differs from common parlance. Most people speak of "investing" in the stock market or in a bank account, but that kind of investment merely swaps one form of financial asset (such as money) for another form (such as a share of stock). When economists speak of *investment,* they mean instead the purchase of some *new physical asset,* such as a drill press, a computer, or a house. The distinction is important here because only investments like these constitute direct additions to the demand for newly produced goods.

The third major component of aggregate demand, **government purchases** of goods and services, includes items such as paper, computers, airplanes, ships, and labor bought by all levels of government. We use the symbol *G* for this variable.

The final component of aggregate demand, **net exports**, is simply defined as U.S. exports *minus* U.S. imports. The reasoning here is simple. Part of the demand for American goods and services originates beyond our borders—as when foreigners buy our wheat, software, and banking services. So to obtain total demand for U.S. products, these goods and services must be *added* to U.S. domestic demand. Similarly, some items included in *C* and *I* are made abroad. Think, for example, of beer from Germany, cars from Japan, and shirts from Malaysia. These must be *subtracted* from the total amount demanded by U.S. consumers if we want to measure total spending *on U.S. products.* The addition of exports, *X*, and the subtraction of imports, *IM*, leads to the following shorthand definition of aggregate demand:

Aggregate demand is the sum of $C + I + G + (X - IM)$.

The last concept we need for our vocabulary is a way to measure the total *income* of all individuals in the economy. It comes in two versions: one for before-tax incomes, called **national income**, and one for after-tax incomes, called **disposable income**.[2] The term *disposable income,* which we will abbreviate *DI*, is meant to be descriptive—it tells us how much consumers actually have available to spend or to save. For that reason, it will play a prominent role in this chapter and in subsequent discussions.

**Investment spending (*I*)** is the sum of the expenditures of business firms on new plant, equipment, software and households on new homes. Financial "investments" are not included and neither are resales of existing physical assets.

**Government purchases (*G*)** refer to the goods (such as airplanes and paper clips) and services (such as school teaching and police protection) purchased by all levels of government.

**Net exports,** or **(*X − IM*)**, is the difference between exports (*X*) and imports (*IM*). It indicates the difference between what we sell to foreigners and what we buy from them.

"When I refer to it as disposable income, don't get the wrong idea."

From *The Wall Street Journal.* Reprinted with the permission of Cartoon Features Syndicate.

## 8-2  THE CIRCULAR FLOW OF SPENDING, PRODUCTION, AND INCOME

Enough definitions. How do these three concepts—domestic product, total expenditure, and national income—interact in a market economy? We can answer this best with the rather elaborate diagram seen in Figure 1. For obvious reasons, Figure 1 is called a circular flow diagram. It depicts a large tube in which an imaginary fluid circulates in a clockwise direction. At several points along the way, some of the fluid leaks out or some additional fluid is injected into the tube.

To examine this system, start on the far left. At point 1 on the circle, we find consumers. Disposable income (*DI*) flows into their pockets, and two things flow out: consumption (*C*), which stays in the circular flow, and saving (*S*), which "leaks out." This outflow depicts the fact that consumers normally spend less than they earn and save the balance. The "leakage" to saving, of course, does not disappear; it flows into the financial system via banks, mutual funds, and so on. A lot happens there, but we defer consideration of that important subject until Chapters 12 and 13.

**National income** is the sum of the incomes that all individuals in the economy earn in the forms of wages, interest, rents, and profits. It excludes government transfer payments and is calculated before any deductions are taken for income taxes.

**Disposable income (*DI*)** is the sum of the incomes of all individuals in the economy after all taxes have been deducted and all transfer payments have been added.

---

[2] More detailed information on these and other concepts is provided in the appendix to this chapter.

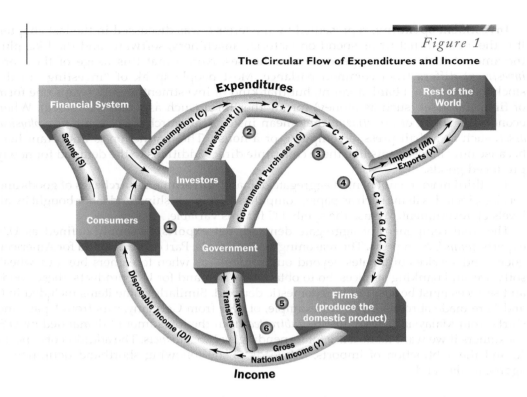

*Figure 1*

**The Circular Flow of Expenditures and Income**

The upper loop of the circular flow represents expenditures, and as we move clockwise to point 2, we encounter the first "injection" into the flow: investment spending (*I*). The diagram shows this injection as coming from "investors"—a group that includes both business firms and home buyers. Remember that expenditure on housing, which is where the Great Recession started, is part of *I*, not part of *C*. As the circular flow moves past point 2, it is bigger than it was before: Total spending has increased from *C* to *C* + *I*.

At point 3, there is yet another injection. The government adds its demand for goods and services (*G*) to those of consumers and investors (*C* + *I*). Now aggregate demand has grown to *C* + *I* + *G*.

The next leakage and injection come at point 4. Here we see export spending entering the circular flow from abroad and import spending leaking out. The net effect of these two forces may increase or decrease the circular flow, depending on whether net exports are positive or negative. (In the United States in recent years, they have been strongly negative.) In either case, by the time we pass point 4, we have accumulated the full amount of aggregate demand, *C* + *I* + *G* + (*X* − *IM*).

The circular flow diagram shows this aggregate demand for goods and services arriving at the business firms, which are located at point 5. Responding to this demand, firms produce the domestic product. As the circular flow emerges from the firms, however, we rename it *gross national income*. Why? The reason is that, except for some complications explained in this chapter's appendix,

**National income and domestic product must be equal.**

Why is this so? When a firm produces and sells $100 worth of output, it pays most of the proceeds to its workers, to people who have lent it money, and to the landlord who owns the property on which the plant is located. All of these payments represent *income* to some individuals. But what about the rest? Suppose, for example, that the firm pays wages, interest, and rent totaling $90 million and sells its output for $100 million. What happens to the remaining $10 million? The firm's owners receive it as *profits*. Because these owners are citizens of the country, their incomes also count in national income.[3] Thus, when

---

[3] Some of the income paid out by American companies goes to noncitizens. Similarly, some Americans earn income from foreign firms. This complication is discussed in the appendix to this chapter.

we add up all the wages, interest, rents, *and profits* in the economy to obtain the *national income,* we must arrive at the *value of output.*

The lower loop of the circular flow diagram shows national income leaving firms and heading for consumers. But some of the flow takes a detour along the way. At point 6, the government siphons off a portion of the national income in the form of *taxes.* But it also adds back government **transfer payments**, such as unemployment compensation and Social Security benefits, which government agencies give to certain individuals as out-right *grants* rather than as payments for goods or services rendered.

By subtracting taxes from gross domestic product (GDP) and adding transfer payments, we obtain disposable income:[4]

$$DI = \text{GDP} - \text{Taxes} + \text{Transfer payments}$$
$$= \text{GDP} - (\text{Taxes} - \text{Transfers})$$
$$= Y - T$$

where $Y$ represents GDP and $T$ represents taxes *net of transfers* or simply *net taxes*. Disposable income flows unimpeded to consumers at point 1, and the cycle repeats.

Figure 1 raises several complicated questions, which we pose now but will not try to answer until subsequent chapters:

- Does the flow of spending and income grow larger or smaller as we move clock-wise around the circle? Why?
- Is the output that firms produce at point 5 (the GDP) equal to aggregate demand? If so, what makes these two quantities equal? If not, what happens?

The next chapter provides the answers to these two questions.

- Do the government's accounts balance, so that what flows in at point 6 (net taxes) is equal to what flows out at point 3 (government purchases)? What happens if they do not balance?

This important question is first addressed in Chapter 11 and then recurs many times, especially in Chapter 16, which discusses budget deficits and surpluses in detail.

- Is our international trade balanced, so that exports equal imports at point 4? More generally, what factors determine net exports, and what consequences arise from trade deficits or surpluses?

We take up these questions in the next two chapters but deal with them more fully in Part 4.

However, we cannot dig very deeply into any of these issues until we first understand what goes on at point 1, where consumers make decisions. So we turn next to the deter-minants of consumer spending.

**Transfer payments** are sums of money that the government gives certain individuals as outright grants rather than as payments for services rendered to employers. Some common examples are Social Security and unemployment benefits.

## 8-3 CONSUMER SPENDING AND INCOME: THE IMPORTANT RELATIONSHIP

Recall that we started the chapter with a puzzle: Why did consumers seem to respond relatively weakly to temporary cuts in income taxes in 1975, 2008, and 2009? An econo-mist interested in predicting how consumer spending will respond to a change in taxes must first ask how consumption ($C$) relates to disposable income ($DI$), because a tax increase decreases after-tax income and a tax reduction increases it. So this section examines what we know about how consumer spending is influenced by changes in disposable income.

Figure 2 depicts the historical paths of $C$ and $DI$ for the United States since 1929. The association is extremely close, suggesting that consumption will rise whenever disposable income rises and fall whenever income falls. The vertical distance between the two lines

---

[4] This definition omits a few minor details, which are explained in the appendix to this chapter.

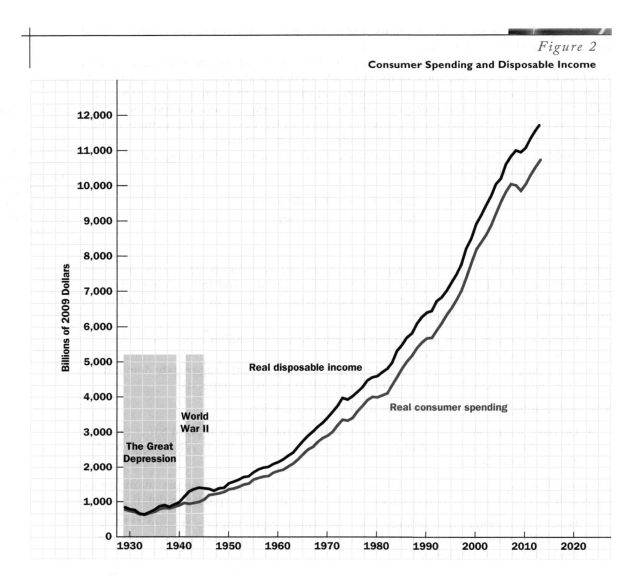

*Figure 2*

**Consumer Spending and Disposable Income**

represents personal saving: disposable income minus consumption. Notice how little saving consumers did during the Great Depression of the 1930s (when the two lines run very close together); how much they did during World War II, when many consumer goods were either unavailable or rationed; and how little saving consumers did just prior to the Great Recession. Lately, personal saving has risen a bit.

Of course, knowing that *C* will move in the same direction as *DI* is not enough for policy planners. They need to know *how much* one variable will go up when the other rises a given amount. Figure 3 presents the same data as in Figure 2, but in a way designed to help answer the "how much" question.

A **scatter diagram** is a graph showing the relationship between two variables (such as consumer spending and disposable income). Each year is represented by a point in the diagram, and the coordinates of each year's point show the values of the two variables in that year.

Economists call such pictures **scatter diagrams**, and they are very useful in predicting how one variable (in this case, consumer spending) will change in response to a change in another variable (in this case, disposable income). Each dot in the diagram represents the data on *C* and *DI* corresponding to a particular year. For example, the point labeled "1996" shows that real consumer expenditures in 1996 were $6,756 billion (which we read off the vertical axis), whereas real disposable incomes amounted to $7,476 billion (which we read off the horizontal axis). Similarly, each year from 1929 to 2013 is represented by its own dot in Figure 3.

To see how such a diagram can assist fiscal policy planners, imagine that you were a member of Congress way back in 1964, contemplating a tax cut. (In fact, Congress did cut

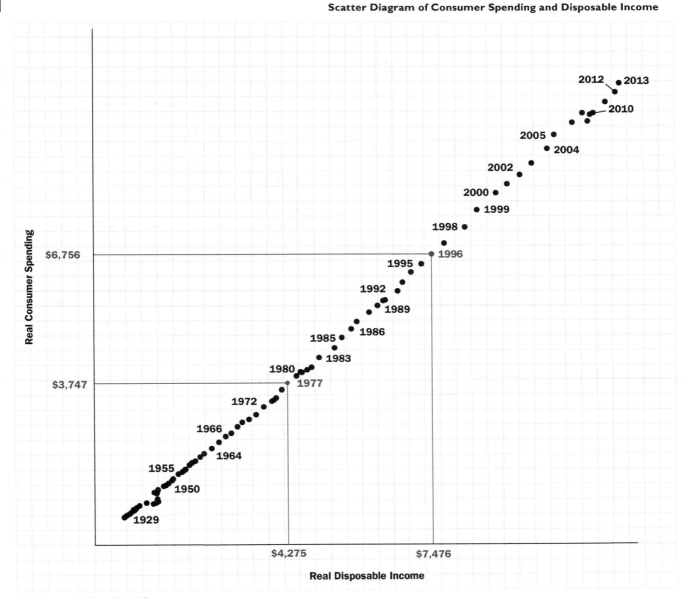

*Figure 3*

**Scatter Diagram of Consumer Spending and Disposable Income**

NOTE: Figures are in billions of 2009 dollars.

taxes that year.) Legislators want to know how much additional consumer spending may be stimulated by tax cuts of various sizes. To assist your imagination, the scatter diagram in Figure 4 removes the points for 1964 through 2013 that appear in Figure 3; after all, these data were unknown in 1964. Years prior to 1947 have also been removed because, as Figure 2 showed, both the Great Depression and wartime rationing disturbed the normal relationship between *DI* and *C*. With no more training in economics than you have right now, what would you suggest?

One rough-and-ready approach is to get a ruler, set it down on Figure 4, and sketch a straight line that comes as close as possible to hitting all the points. That has been done for you in the figure, and you can see that the resulting line comes remarkably close to touching all the points. The line summarizes, in a very rough way, the normal relationship between income and consumption. The two variables certainly appear to be closely related.

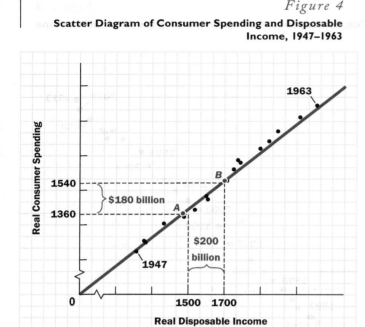

*Figure 4*

**Scatter Diagram of Consumer Spending and Disposable Income, 1947–1963**

NOTE: Figures are in billions of 2009 dollars.

The *slope* of the straight line in Figure 4 is very important.[5] Chapter 1 Specifically, we note that it is

$$\text{Slope} = \frac{\text{Vertical change}}{\text{Horizontal change}} = \frac{\$180 \text{ billion}}{\$200 \text{ billion}} = 0.90$$

Because the horizontal change involved in the move from *A* to *B* represents a rise in disposable income of $200 billion (from $1500 billion to $1700 billion), and the corresponding vertical change represents the associated $180 billion rise in consumer spending (from $1360 billion to $1540 billion), the slope of the line indicates how consumer spending responds to changes in disposable income. In this case, we see that each additional $1 of income leads to 90 cents of additional spending.

Now let us return to tax policy. First, recall that each dollar of tax cut increases disposable income by exactly $1. Next, apply the finding from Figure 4 that each additional dollar of disposable income increases consumer spending by about 90 cents. The conclusion is that a tax cut of, say, $9 billion—which is about what happened in 1964—would be expected to increase consumer spending by about $9 × 0.9 = $8.1 billion.

## 8-4 THE CONSUMPTION FUNCTION AND THE MARGINAL PROPENSITY TO CONSUME

The **consumption function** shows the relationship between total consumer expenditures and total disposable income in the economy, holding all other determinants of consumer spending constant.

The **marginal propensity to consume (MPC)** is the ratio of the change in consumption relative to the change in disposable income that produces the change in consumption. On a graph, it appears as the slope of the consumption function.

It has been said that economics is just systematized common sense. So let us now organize and generalize what has been a completely intuitive discussion up to now. One thing we have discovered is the apparently close relationship between consumer spending, *C*, and disposable income, *DI*. Economists call this relationship the **consumption function**.

A second fact we have gleaned from these figures is that the *slope* of the consumption function is quite constant. This constancy is demonstrated by the fact that the straight line drawn in Figure 4 comes so close to touching every point. If the slope of the consumption function had varied widely, we could not have done so well with a single straight line.[6] Because of its importance in applications such as the tax cut, economists have given this slope a special name—the **marginal propensity to consume**, or **MPC** for short. The MPC tells us how much more consumers will spend if disposable income rises by $1.

$$\text{MPC} = \frac{\text{Change in } C}{\text{Change in } DI \text{ that produces the change in } C}$$

The MPC is best illustrated by an example, and for this purpose we turn away from U.S. data for a moment and look at consumption and income in a hypothetical country whose data come in nice round numbers—which facilitates computation.

Columns (1) and (2) of Table 1 show annual consumer expenditure and disposable income, respectively, from 2009 to 2014. These two columns constitute the consumption function, and they are plotted in Figure 5. Column (3) in the table shows the marginal propensity to consume (MPC), which is the slope of the line in Figure 5; it is derived from the first two columns. We can see that, between 2011 and 2012, *DI* rose by $400 billion

---

[5] To review the concept of *slope*, see Chapter 1's appendix.

[6] Figure 4 is limited to 17 years of data, so try fitting a single straight line to all of the data in Figure 3. You will find that you can still do that rather well.

Table 1

**Consumption and Income in a Hypothetical Economy**

| Year | (1) Consumption, C | (2) Disposable Income, DI | (3) Marginal Propensity to Consume, MPC |
|------|------|------|------|
| 2009 | $2,700 | $3,200 | |
| 2010 | 3,000 | 3,600 | 0.75 |
| 2011 | 3,300 | 4,000 | 0.75 |
| 2012 | 3,600 | 4,400 | 0.75 |
| 2013 | 3,900 | 4,800 | 0.75 |
| 2014 | 4,200 | 5,200 | 0.75 |

NOTE: Amounts are in billions of dollars.

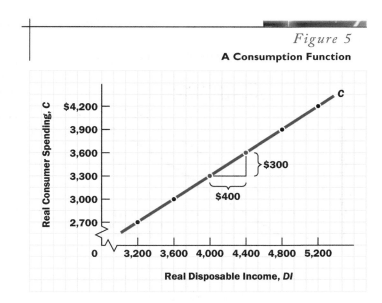

Figure 5

**A Consumption Function**

(from $4,000 billion to $4,400 billion) while C rose by $300 billion (from $3,300 billion to $3,600 billion). Thus, the MPC was

$$\text{MPC} = \frac{\text{Change in } C}{\text{Change in } DI} = \frac{\$300}{\$400} = 0.75$$

As you can easily verify, the MPC between any other pair of years in Table 1 is also 0.75. This relationship explains why the slope of the line in Figure 4 was so crucial in estimating the effect of a tax cut. This slope, which we found there to be 0.90, is simply the MPC for the United States. The MPC tells us how much *additional* spending will be induced by each dollar *change* in disposable income. For each $1 of tax cut, economists expect consumption to rise by $1 times the marginal propensity to consume.

To estimate the *initial* effect of a tax cut on consumer spending, economists must first estimate the MPC and then multiply the amount of the tax cut by the estimated MPC.[7] Because they never know the true MPC with certainty, their prediction is always subject to some margin of error.

## 8-5 FACTORS THAT SHIFT THE CONSUMPTION FUNCTION

Unfortunately for policy planners, the consumption function does not always stand still. Recall from Chapter 4 the important distinction between a *movement along* a demand curve and a *shift* of the curve. A demand curve depicts the relationship between quantity demanded and one of its many determinants—price. Thus a change in price causes a movement *along* the demand curve. But a change in any other factor that influences quantity demanded causes a *shift* of the entire demand curve.

Because several factors other than disposable income influence consumer spending, a similar distinction is vital to understanding real-world consumption functions. Look back at the definition of the consumption function in the margin. A change in disposable income leads to a *movement along the consumption function* precisely because the consumption function depicts the relationship between C and DI. Such movements, which are what we have been considering so far, are indicated by the blue arrows in Figure 6.

But consumption also has other determinants, and a change in any of them will *shift the entire consumption function*—as indicated by the maroon arrows in Figure 6. Such shifts

---

[7] The word *initial* in this sentence is an important one. The next chapter will explain why the effects discussed in this chapter are only the beginning of the story.

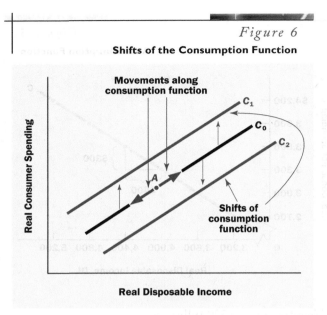

Figure 6

**Shifts of the Consumption Function**

Real Consumer Spending

Movements along consumption function

$C_1$

$C_0$

$C_2$

A

Shifts of consumption function

Real Disposable Income

account for many of the errors in forecasting consumption. To summarize:

> Any change in disposable income moves us *along a given consumption function*. A change in any of the other determinants of consumption *shifts the entire consumption schedule* (see Figure 6).

Because disposable income is far and away the main determinant of consumer spending, the real-world data in Figure 3 come *close* to lying along a straight line. However, if you use a ruler to draw such a line, you will find that it misses a number of points notably. These deviations reflect the influence of the "other determinants" just mentioned. Let us see what some of them are.

**Wealth**  One key factor affecting spending is consumers' *wealth*, which is a source of purchasing power in addition to income. Wealth and income are two different things. Think of a wealthy retiree with a huge bank balance earning very little current *income* because interest rates are so low. Or think of a high-flying investment banker who spends every penny of her high income, thereby accumulating little *wealth*.

To appreciate the importance of the distinction, imagine two recent college graduates, each of whom earns $50,000 per year. If one of them has $100,000 in the bank and the other has no assets at all, who do you think will spend more? Presumably the one with the big bank account. The general point is that current income is not the only source of spendable funds; households can also finance spending by cashing in some of the wealth they have previously accumulated.

One important implication of this analysis is that the stock market can exert a major influence on consumer spending. A stock market boom adds to wealth and thus raises the consumption function, as depicted by the shift from $C_0$ to $C_1$ in Figure 6. That is what happened, for example, during the bull market that began in 2009, when the stock market soared, helping American consumers maintain their spending. Correspondingly, a sharp collapse of stock prices, like the one that occurred in the 2008–2009 crisis, should shift the consumption function down (see the shift from $C_0$ to $C_2$).

Although stock market wealth is by far the most volatile part of wealth, it is not the whole story. In fact, American households hold a great deal of their wealth in the form of houses—though less than they once did. Using the same logic as before, falling house prices make consumers less wealthy and therefore less willing to spend. This is not hypothetical. Between 2006 and 2009, the values of American houses fell by trillions of dollars, and that reduced consumer spending.

The financial crisis brought in its wake a collapse of asset prices—not only for stocks and houses, as just mentioned, but also for many forms of bonds and other securities. In total, the loss of wealth was enormous—estimates run close to $20 trillion dollars. Most economists believe that this huge destruction of wealth was the main reason why the **personal saving rate**—the ratio of saving to disposable income—increased from about 3 percent before the Great Recession to about 5 percent more recently.

The **personal saving rate** is the ratio of consumer saving to disposable income.

**The Price Level**  In addition to stocks and houses, people hold a great deal of wealth in forms that are fixed in money terms. Bank accounts are the most obvious example, but government and corporate bonds also have fixed face values in money terms. The purchasing power of such **money-fixed assets** obviously declines whenever the price level rises, which means that the asset can buy less. For example, if the price level rises by 10 percent, a $1,000 government bond will buy about 10 percent less than it could when prices were lower. This is no trivial matter. Consumers in the United States hold money-fixed assets worth over $9 *trillion,* so that each 1 percent rise in the price level reduces the purchasing power of consumer wealth by more than $90 billion, a tidy sum. This process,

A **money-fixed asset** is an asset whose value is a fixed number of dollars.

## Policy Debate

### Using the Tax Code to Spur Saving

Even though the saving rate has risen in recent years, Americans still save very little compared to the citizens of virtually every other industrial nation. Many policy makers consider this lack of saving to be a serious problem, so they have proposed numerous changes in the tax laws to increase incentives to save. In 2001, for example, Congress expanded Individual Retirement Accounts (IRAs), which allow taxpayers to save tax-free. In 2003, the taxation of dividends was reduced. Further tax incentives for saving seem to be proposed every year.

All of these tax changes are designed to increase the *after-tax* return on saving. For example, if you put away money in a bank at a 3 percent rate of interest and your income is taxed at a 30 percent rate, your after-tax rate of return on saving is just 2.1 percent (70 percent of 3 percent). However, if the interest is earned tax-free, as in an IRA, you get to keep the full 3 percent. Over long

© PTstock/Shutterstock.com

periods of time, this seemingly small interest differential can compound to make an enormous difference in returns. For example, $100 invested for 20 years at 2.1 percent interest grows to $151. At 3 percent, it grows to $199. Members of Congress who advocate tax incentives for saving argue that lower tax rates will therefore induce Americans to save more.

This idea seems reasonable and has many supporters. Unfortunately, the evidence runs squarely against it. Economists have conducted many studies of the effect of higher rates of return on saving. With very few exceptions, they detect little or no impact. Although the evidence fails to support the "common-sense" solution to the undersaving problem, the debate goes on. Many people, it seems, refuse to believe the evidence.

of course, operates equally well in reverse, because a decline in the price level increases the purchasing power of money-fixed assets.

**The Real Interest Rate**  A higher real rate of interest raises the rewards for saving. For this reason, many people believe it is "obvious" that higher real interest rates encourage saving and therefore discourage spending. Surprisingly, however, statistical studies of this relationship suggest otherwise. With few exceptions, they show that interest rates have negligible effects on consumption decisions in the United States and other countries. Hence, in developing our model of the economy, we will assume that changes in real interest rates do *not* shift the consumption function. (See the box "Using the Tax Code to Spur Saving.")

**Future Income Expectations**  It is hardly earth-shattering to suggest that consumers' expectations about their *future* incomes should affect how much they spend today. This final determinant of consumer spending holds the key to resolving the puzzle posed at the beginning of the chapter: Why did tax policy designed to boost consumer spending apparently fail in 1975 and succeed only modestly in 2008 and 2009?

| Issue Revisited | *Why Temporary Tax Cuts Have Only Modest Effects on* |
| --- | --- |

*Spending*

To understand how expectations of future incomes affect current consumer expenditures, consider the abbreviated life histories of three consumers given in Table 2. (The reason for giving our three imaginary individuals such odd names will be apparent shortly.) The consumer named "Constant" earned $100 in each of the years considered in the table. The consumer named "Temporary" earned $100 in three of the four years but had a good year in 1975. The consumer named "Permanent" enjoyed a permanent increase in income in 1975 and was therefore clearly the most well-off.

*Table 2*

**Incomes of Three Consumers**

| Consumer | Incomes in Each Year | | | | |
|---|---|---|---|---|---|
| | 1974 | 1975 | 1976 | 1977 | Total Income |
| Constant | $100 | $100 | $100 | $100 | $400 |
| Temporary | 100 | 120 | 100 | 100 | 420 |
| Permanent | 100 | 120 | 120 | 120 | 460 |

Now let us use common sense to think about how much each of these consumers might have spent in 1975. Temporary and Permanent had the same income that year. Do you think they spent the same amount? Not if they had some ability to foresee their future incomes, because Permanent was richer in the long run.

Now compare Constant and Temporary. Temporary had 20 percent higher income in 1975 ($120 versus $100), but only 5 percent more over the entire four-year period ($420 versus $400). Do you think his spending in 1975 was closer to 20 percent above Constant's or closer to 5 percent above it? Most people guess the latter.

The point of this example is that consumers probably decide on their current consumption spending by looking at their long-run income prospects. This should come as no surprise to a college student. You are probably spending more than you earn this year, but that does not make you a foolish spendthrift. On the contrary, your college education will likely give you a much higher income in the future, and you are spending with that in mind.

To relate this example to the failure of the 1975 income tax cut, now imagine that the three rows in Table 2 represent the entire economy under three different government policies. Recall that 1975 was the year of the temporary tax cut. The first row (Constant) shows the unchanged path of disposable income in the absence of a tax cut. The second (Temporary) shows an increase in disposable income attributable to a tax cut for one year only. The bottom row (Permanent) shows a policy that increases *DI* in every future year by cutting taxes permanently in 1975. Which of the two lower rows do you imagine would have generated more consumer spending in 1975? The bottom row (Permanent), of course. What we have concluded, then, is this:

> **Permanent cuts in income taxes cause greater increases in consumer spending than do temporary cuts of equal magnitude.**

The application of this analysis to the 1975, 2008, and 2009 tax cuts is immediate. Each was advertised as a one-time increase in after-tax income, like that experienced by Temporary in Table 2. No future income was affected, so consumers did not increase their spending as much as government officials had hoped.

We have, then, what appears to be a general principle, backed up by both historical evidence and common sense. Permanent changes in income taxes have more significant effects on consumer spending than do temporary ones. This conclusion may seem obvious, but it is not a lesson you would have learned from an introductory textbook prior to 1975. It is one we learned the hard way, through bitter experience.

## 8-6 THE EXTREME VARIABILITY OF INVESTMENT

Next, we turn to the most *volatile* component of aggregate demand: investment spending.[8] Although Figure 2 showed that consumer spending follows movements in disposable income quite closely, investment spending swings from high to low levels with astonishing speed. For example, when real GDP in the United States slowed abruptly from a 1.8 percent growth rate in 2007 to a *minus* 2.8 percent rate in 2009, a drop of 4.6 percentage points in two years, the growth rate of real business investment spending dropped from 5.9 percent to *minus* 15.6 percent, a swing of 21.5 percentage points. What accounts for such dramatic changes in investment spending?

---

[8] We repeat the warning given earlier about the meaning of the word *investment*. It *includes* spending by businesses and individuals on newly produced factories, machinery, software, and houses, but it *excludes* sales of used industrial plants, equipment, and homes as well as purely financial transactions, such as the purchases of stocks and bonds.

Several factors that influence how much businesses want to invest were discussed in the previous chapter, including interest rates, tax provisions, technical change, and the strength of the economy. Sometimes these determinants change abruptly, leading to dramatic variations in investment.

Perhaps the most important factor accounting for the volatility of investment spending was not discussed much in the previous chapter: the *state of business confidence*, which in turn depends on *expectations about the future*. Although confidence is tricky to measure, it does seem obvious that businesses will build more factories and purchase more new machines when they are optimistic. Correspondingly, their investment plans will be very cautious if the economic outlook appears bleak. Keynes pointed out that psychological perceptions such as these are subject to abrupt shifts, so that fluctuations in investment can be a major cause of instability in aggregate demand.

Unfortunately, neither economists nor, for that matter, psychologists have many good ideas about how to *measure*—much less *control*—business confidence. So economists usually focus on several more objective determinants of investment that are easier to quantify and even influence—factors such as interest rates and tax provisions.

What about investment in housing, which led the economy downhill in 2007–2009? Consumer incomes are obviously a major determinant of spending on new houses, just as they are of C. But so are interest rates, especially the interest rates on home mortgages, because most people borrow money to buy their homes. Finally, the expected rate of price appreciation (or depreciation!) of houses influences people's willingness to buy them.

As recent events illustrated, each of these determinants of expenditures on housing—especially the last—can change abruptly. During the housing boom from 2001 to 2006, prices climbed rapidly, convincing consumers that housing was a great investment. Homebuilding naturally soared. But when the bust came and house prices declined, building fell by more than 55 percent from its peak. While the economy experienced a severe recession, the homebuilding industry experienced a depression.

## 8-7   THE DETERMINANTS OF NET EXPORTS

Another highly variable source of demand for U.S. products is foreign purchases of U.S. goods—our *exports*. As we observed earlier in this chapter, we obtain the *net* contribution of foreigners to U.S. aggregate demand by subtracting *imports*, which is the portion of domestic demand that is satisfied by foreign producers, from our exports to get *net exports*. What determines net exports?

### 8-7a   National Incomes

Although both exports and imports depend on many factors, the predominant one is *income levels in different countries*. When American consumers and firms spend more on consumption and investment, some of this new spending goes toward the purchase of foreign goods. Therefore:

**Our imports rise when our GDP rises and fall when our GDP falls.**

Similarly, because our *exports* are the *imports* of other countries, our exports depend on *their* GDPs, not on our own. Thus:

**Our exports are relatively insensitive to our own GDP, but are quite sensitive to the GDPs of other countries.**

Putting these two ideas together leads to a clear implication: When our economy grows faster than the economies of our trading partners, our net exports tend to shrink. Conversely, when foreign economies grow faster than ours, our net exports tend to rise. Recent events illustrate these points dramatically. As the U.S. economy grew rapidly from 2003 to 2006, our real net exports fell from –$501 billion to –$762 billion. But then, as our economy first slowed and then plunged into a deep recession, U.S. net exports rose dramatically from –$762 billion in 2006 to –$392 billion in 2009. (Remember, –392 is a *larger* number than –762.)

## 8-7b Relative Prices and Exchange Rates

Although GDP levels here and abroad are important influences on a country's net exports, they are not the only relevant factors. International prices matter, too.

To make things concrete, let's focus on trade between the United States and Japan. Suppose American prices rise while Japanese prices fall, making U.S. goods more expensive *relative to Japanese goods*. If American consumers react to these new relative prices by buying more Japanese goods, U.S. *imports rise*. If Japanese consumers react to the same relative price changes by buying fewer American products, U.S. *exports fall*. Both reactions reduce America's *net* exports.

Naturally, a decline in American prices (or a rise in Japanese prices) does precisely the opposite. Thus:

> A rise in the prices of a country's goods will lead to a reduction in that country's net exports. Analogously, a decline in the prices of a country's goods will raise that country's net exports. Similarly, price increases abroad raise the home country's net exports, whereas price decreases abroad have the opposite effect.

This simple idea holds the key to understanding how exchange rates among the world's currencies influence exports and imports—an important topic that we will consider in depth in Chapters 19 and 20. The reason is that exchange rates translate foreign prices into terms that are familiar to home country customers—their own currencies.

Consider, for example, Americans interested in buying Japanese cars that cost ¥3,000,000. If it takes ¥100 to buy a dollar, these cars cost American buyers $30,000. But if the dollar is worth ¥150, those same cars cost Americans just $20,000, and consumers in the United States are likely to buy more of them. These sorts of responses help explain why American automakers lost market share to Japanese imports when the dollar rose against the yen in the late 1990s. They also explain why, today, so many U.S. manufacturers want to see the value of the Chinese yuan rise. With such a low yuan, Chinese goods look cheap to Americans, and American goods look expensive to the Chinese.

## 8-8 HOW PREDICTABLE IS AGGREGATE DEMAND?

We have now learned enough to see why economists often have difficulty predicting aggregate demand. Consider the four main components, starting with consumer spending.

Because wealth affects consumption, forecasts of spending can be thrown off by unexpected movements of the stock market, house prices, or by poor forecasts of future prices. It can also be difficult to anticipate how taxpayers will view changes in the income tax law. If the government says that a tax cut is permanent (as, e.g., in 1964), will consumers take the government at its word and increase their spending accordingly? Perhaps not, if the government has a history of raising taxes after promising to keep them low. Similarly, when (as in 2008) the government explicitly announces that a tax cut is temporary, will consumers always believe the announcement? Or might they greet it with a hefty dose of skepticism? Such a reaction is quite possible if there is a history of "temporary" tax changes that stayed on the books indefinitely.

Swings in investment spending are even more difficult to predict, partly because they are tied so closely to business confidence and expectations. Developments abroad also often lead to surprises in the net export account. Even the final component of aggregate demand, government purchases (G), is subject both to the vagaries of politics and to sudden military and national security events such as 9/11 and the wars in Iraq and Afghanistan.

We could say much more about the determinants of aggregate demand, but it is best to leave the rest to more advanced courses—for we are now ready to apply our knowledge of aggregate demand to the construction of the first model of the economy. Although it is true that income determines consumption, the consumption function in turn helps to determine the level of income. If that sounds like circular reasoning, read the next chapter!

## Summary

1. **Aggregate demand** is the total volume of goods and services purchased by consumers, businesses, government units, and foreigners. It can be expressed as the sum $C + I + G + (X - IM)$, where $C$ is consumer spending, $I$ is investment spending, $G$ is **government purchases**, and $X - IM$ is **net exports.**

2. Aggregate demand is a schedule: The aggregate quantity demanded depends on (among other things) the price level. But, for any given price level, aggregate demand is a number.

3. Economists reserve the term **investment spending** to refer to purchases of newly produced factories, machinery, software, and houses.

4. Gross domestic product is the total volume of final goods and services produced in the country.

5. **National income** is the sum of the before-tax wages, interest, rents, and profits earned by all individuals in the economy. By necessity, it must be approximately equal to domestic product.

6. **Disposable income** is the sum of the incomes of all individuals in the economy after taxes and transfers. It is the chief determinant of **consumer expenditures.**

7. All of these concepts, and others, can be depicted in a **circular flow diagram** that shows expenditures on all four sources flowing into business firms and national income flowing out.

8. The close relationship between consumer spending ($C$) and disposable income ($DI$) is called the **consumption function.** Its slope, which is used to predict the change in consumption that will be caused by a change

in income taxes, is called the **marginal propensity to consume (MPC).**

9. Changes in disposable income move us along a given consumption function. Changes in any of the other variables that affect $C$ shift the entire consumption function. Among the most important of these other variables are total consumer wealth, the price level, and expected future incomes.

10. Because consumers hold so many **money-fixed assets,** they lose purchasing power when prices rise, which leads them to reduce their spending.

11. The government often tries to manipulate aggregate demand by influencing private consumption decisions, usually through changes in the personal income tax. But this policy did not work so well in 1975, 2008, or 2009.

12. Future income prospects help explain why. The 1975 tax cut was temporary and therefore left future incomes unaffected. The tax cuts in 2008 and 2009 were also advertised as one-time events.

13. Investment is the most volatile component of aggregate demand, largely because business investment is closely tied to confidence and expectations and because housing investment depends on the likely future behavior of house prices.

14. Policy makers cannot influence confidence in any reliable way, so policies designed to spur investment focus on more objective, although possibly less important, determinants of investment—such as interest rates and taxes.

15. Net exports depend on GDPs and relative prices both domestically and abroad.

## Key Terms

aggregate demand    148

consumer expenditure (C)    148

consumption function    154

disposable income (DI)    149

government purchases (G)    149

investment spending (I)    149

marginal propensity to consume (MPC)    154

money-fixed assets    156

movement along versus shift of the consumption function    155

national income    149

net exports (X − IM)    149

personal saving rate    156

scatter diagram    152

temporary versus permanent tax change    160

transfer payments    151

## Test Yourself

1. What are the four main components of aggregate demand? Which is the largest? Which is the smallest?

2. Which of the following acts constitute *investment* according to the economist's definition of that term?

   a. Pfizer builds a new factory in the United States to manufacture pharmaceuticals.

   b. You buy 100 shares of Pfizer stock.

   c. A small drugmaker goes bankrupt, and Pfizer purchases its factory and equipment.

   d. Your family buys a newly constructed home from a developer.

   e. Your family buys an older home from another family. (*Hint:* Are any *new* products demanded by this action?)

3. On a piece of graph paper, construct a consumption function from the data given here and determine the MPC.

| Year | Consumer Spending | Disposable Income |
|------|-------------------|-------------------|
| 2010 | $1,200 | $1,500 |
| 2011 | 1,440 | 1,800 |
| 2012 | 1,680 | 2,100 |
| 2013 | 1,920 | 2,400 |
| 2014 | 2,160 | 2,700 |

4. In which direction will the consumption function shift if the price level rises? Show this on your graph from the previous question.

## Discussion Questions

1. Explain the difference between *investment* as the term is used by most people and *investment* as defined by an economist.

2. What would the circular flow diagram (Figure 1) look like in an economy with no government? Draw one for yourself.

3. The marginal propensity to consume (MPC) for the United States as a whole is roughly 0.90. Explain in words what this means. What is your personal MPC at this stage in your life? How might that change by the time you are your parents' age?

4. Look at the scatter diagram in Figure 3. What does it tell you about what was going on in this country in the years 1942 to 1945?

5. What is a consumption function, and why is it a useful device for government economists planning a tax cut?

6. Explain why permanent tax cuts are likely to lead to bigger increases in consumer spending than temporary tax cuts do.

7. In 2001 and again in 2003, Congress enacted changes in the tax law designed to promote saving. If such saving incentives had been successful, how would the consumption function have shifted?

8. **(More difficult)** Between 2008 and 2009, real disposable income (in 2009 dollars) declined slightly (by $51 billion), owing to a recession. Use the data on real consumption expenditures given on the inside back cover of this book to compare the change in C to this $51 billion decline in DI. Explain why dividing the two does *not* give a good estimate of the marginal propensity to consume.

## Appendix  *National Income Accounting*

The type of macroeconomic analysis presented in this book dates from the publication of John Maynard Keynes's *The General Theory of Employment, Interest, and Money* in 1936. At that time, there was really no way to test Keynes's theories because the necessary data did not exist. It took some years for the theoretical notions used by Keynes to find concrete expression in real-world data.

The system of measurement devised for collecting and expressing macroeconomic data is called **national income accounting.**

The development of this system of accounts ranks as a great achievement in applied economics, perhaps as important in its own right as was Keynes's theoretical work. Without it, the practical value of Keynesian analysis would be severely limited. Many economists spent long hours wrestling with the difficult conceptual questions that arose as they translated the theory into numbers. Along the way, some more or less arbitrary decisions and conventions had to be made. You may not agree with all of them, but the accounting framework that they devised, though imperfect, is eminently serviceable.

## Defining GDP: Exceptions to the Rules

We first encountered the concept of **gross domestic product (GDP)** in Chapter 5:

**Gross domestic product (GDP)** is the sum of the money values of all final goods and services produced during a specified period of time, usually one year.

However, the definition of GDP has certain exceptions that we have not yet noted.

First, the treatment of government output involves a minor departure from the principle of using market prices. Unlike private products, the "outputs" of government offices are rarely sold; indeed, it is sometimes even difficult to define what those outputs are. Lacking prices for outputs, national income accountants fall back on the only prices they have: prices for the inputs from which the outputs are produced. Thus:

> Government outputs are valued at the cost of the inputs needed to produce them.

This means, for example, that if a clerk at the Department of Motor Vehicles who earns $20 per hour spends one-half hour torturing you with explanations of why you cannot get a driver's license, that particular government "service" increases GDP by $10. Never mind that you wouldn't pay $10 for it.

Second, some goods that are produced but not sold during the year are nonetheless counted in that year's GDP. Specifically, goods that firms add to their *inventories* count in the GDP even though they do not (yet) pass through markets.

> National income statisticians treat inventories as if they were "bought" by the firms that produced them, even though these "purchases" do not actually take place.

Finally, the treatment of investment goods can be thought of as running slightly counter to the rule that GDP includes only final goods. In a broad sense, factories, generators, machine tools, and the like might be considered intermediate goods. After all, their owners want them only for use in producing other goods, not for any innate value that they possess. But this classification would present a real problem. Because factories and machines normally are never sold to consumers, when would we count them in GDP? National income statisticians avoid this problem by defining investment goods as final products demanded by the *firms* that buy them.

Now that we have a more complete definition of what the GDP is, let us turn to the problem of actually measuring it. National income accountants have devised three ways to perform this task, and we consider each in turn.

## GDP as the Sum of Final Goods and Services

The first way to measure GDP is the most natural, because it follows so directly from the circular flow diagram (Figure 1). It also turns out to be the most useful definition for macroeconomic analysis. We simply add up the final demands of all consumers, business firms, government, and foreigners. Using the symbols $Y$, $C$, $I$, $G$, and $(X - IM)$ as we did in the chapter, we have:

$$Y = C + I + G + (X - IM)$$

The $I$ that appears in the actual U.S. national accounts is called **gross private domestic investment.** We will explain the word *gross* presently. *Private* indicates that government investment is considered part of $G$, and *domestic* means that, say, machinery sold by American firms to foreign companies is included in exports rather than in $I$ (investment).

> **Gross private domestic investment ($I$) includes business investment in plant, equipment, software, and other intellectual property products; residential construction (new houses); and inventory investment.**

We repeat again that *only* these things are *investment* in national income accounting terminology.

> **As defined in the national income accounts,** *investment* **includes only newly produced capital goods, such as machinery, factories, and new homes. It does not include exchanges of existing assets.**

The symbol $G$, for government purchases, represents the volume of *current goods and services purchased by all levels of government.* Thus, all government payments to its employees are counted in $G$, as are all of its purchases of goods. Few citizens realize, however, that the federal government spends most of its money, not for purchases of goods and services, but rather on *transfer payments*—literally, giving away money—either to individuals or to other levels of government.

The importance of this conceptual distinction lies in the fact that $G$ represents the part of the national product that government uses up for its own purposes—to pay for armies, bureaucrats, paper, and ink—whereas transfer payments merely shuffle purchasing power from one group of citizens to another. Except for the administrators needed to run these programs, real economic resources are not used up in this process.

In adding up the nation's total output as the sum of $C + I + G + (X - IM)$, we sum the shares of GDP that are used up by consumers, investors, government, and foreigners, respectively. Because transfer payments merely give someone the capability to spend on $C$, it is logical to exclude transfers from our definition of $G$, including in $C$ only the portion of these transfer payments that consumers spend. If we included transfers in $G$, the same spending would get counted twice: once in $G$ and then again in $C$.

The final component of GDP is net exports, which are simply exports of goods and services minus imports of goods and services. Table 3 shows GDP for 2013, in both nominal and real terms, computed as the sum of $C + I + G + (X - IM)$. Note that the numbers for net exports in the table are actually negative. We will say much more about America's trade deficit in Part 4.

*Table 3*

**Gross Domestic Product in 2013 as the Sum of Final Demands**

| Item | Nominal Amount* | Real Amount† |
|---|---|---|
| Personal consumption expenditures (C) | $11,484 | $10,700 |
| Gross private domestic investment (I) | 2,648 | 2,543 |
| Government purchases of goods and services (G) | 3,144 | 2,895 |
| Net exports (X–IM) | –508 | –420 |
| Exports (X) | 2,262 | 2,020 |
| Imports (IM) | 2,770 | 2,440 |
| **Gross domestic product (Y)** | **16,768** | **15,710** |

\* In billions of current dollars.
† In billions of 2009 dollars.

SOURCE: U.S. Department of Commerce. Totals do not add up precisely due to rounding and method of deflating.

## GDP as the Sum of All Factor Payments

We can count up the GDP another way: by *adding up all incomes in the economy*. Let's see how this method handles some typical transactions. Suppose General Electric (GE) builds a generator and sells it to General Motors (GM) for $1 million. The first method of calculating GDP simply counts the $1 million as part of *I*. The second method asks: What incomes resulted from producing this generator? The answer might be something like this:

| | |
|---|---|
| Wages of GE employees | $400,000 |
| Interest to bondholders | 50,000 |
| Rentals of buildings | 50,000 |
| Profits of GE stockholders | 100,000 |

The total is $600,000. The remaining $400,000 is accounted for by inputs that GE purchased from other companies: steel, circuitry, tubing, rubber, and so on. If we traced this $400,000 back even further, we would find that it is accounted for by the wages, interest, and rentals paid by these other companies, *plus* their profits, *plus* their purchases from other firms. In fact, for *every* firm in the economy, there is an accounting identity that says:

$$\text{Revenue from sales} = \begin{cases} \text{Wages paid} + \\ \text{Interest paid} + \\ \text{Rentals paid} + \\ \text{Profits earned} + \\ \text{Purchases from} \\ \text{other firms} \end{cases}$$

Why must this always be true? Because profits are the balancing item; they are what is *left over* after the firm has made all other payments. In fact, this accounting identity really reflects the definition of profits: sales revenue less all costs.

Now apply this accounting identity to *all firms in the economy*. Total purchases from other firms are precisely what we call *intermediate goods*. What, then, do we get if we subtract these intermediate transactions from both sides of the equation?

$$\text{Revenue from sales minus} \atop \text{purchases from other firms} = \begin{cases} \text{Wages paid} + \\ \text{Interest paid} + \\ \text{Rentals paid} + \\ \text{Profits earned} \end{cases}$$

On the right-hand side, we have the sum of all factor incomes: payments to labor, land, and capital. On the left-hand side, we have total sales minus sales of intermediate goods. This means that we have sales of *final goods*, which is precisely our definition of GDP. Thus, the accounting identity for the entire economy can be rewritten as follows:

**GDP = Wages + Interest + Rents + Profits**

This definition gives national income accountants another way to measure the GDP.

Table 4 shows how to obtain GDP from the sum of all incomes. Once again, we have omitted a few details in our discussion. By adding up wages, interest, rents, and profits, we obtain only $13,385 billion, whereas nominal GDP in 2013 was $16,768 billion. When sales taxes, excise taxes, and the like are added to the sum of wages, interest, rents, and profits, we obtain what is called **national income**—the sum of all factor payments, including indirect business taxes.

> **National income** is the sum of the incomes that all individuals in the country earn in the forms of wages, interest, rents, and profits. It includes indirect business taxes but excludes transfer payments and makes no deduction for income taxes.

Notice that national income is a measure of the factor incomes of all Americans, regardless of whether they work in this country or somewhere else. Likewise, incomes earned by foreigners in the United States are excluded from (our) national income. We will return to this distinction shortly.

But, reading down Table 4, we next encounter a new concept: **net national product (NNP)**, a measure of *production*. For reasons explained in the chapter, NNP is conceptually identical to national income. However, in practice, national income accountants estimate *income* and *production* independently; and so the two measures are never precisely equal. The difference in 2013 was $212 billion, or about 1.5 percent of NNP; it is called the statistical discrepancy.

*Table 4*

**Gross Domestic Product in 2013 as the Sum of Incomes**

| Item | Amount |
|---|---|
| Compensation of employees (wages) | $ 8,845 |
| plus | |
| Net interest | 500 |
| plus | |
| Rental income | 596 |
| plus | |
| Profits | 3,444 |
| Corporate profits | 2,107 |
| Proprietors' income | 1,337 |
| plus | |
| Indirect business taxes and misc. items | 1,192 |
| equals | |
| National income | 14,577 |
| plus | |
| Statistical discrepancy | −212 |
| equals | |
| Net national product | 14,365 |
| plus | |
| Depreciation | 2,627 |
| equals | |
| Gross national product | 16,992 |
| minus | |
| Income received from other countries | 810 |
| plus | |
| Income paid to other countries | 586 |
| equals | |
| Gross domestic product | 16,768 |

NOTE: Amounts are in billions of current dollars.

SOURCE: U.S. Department of Commerce. Due to rounding, totals do not add up precisely.

Moving further down the table, the only difference between NNP and **gross national product (GNP)** is **depreciation** of the nation's capital stock. Thus the adjective "net" means excluding depreciation, and "gross" means including it. GNP is thus a measure of *all* final production, making no adjustment for the fact that some capital is used up each year and thus needs to be replaced. NNP deducts the required replacements to arrive at a net production figure.

---

[9] If the capital stock is used for consumption, it will decline, and the nation will wind up poorer than it was before.

**Depreciation** is the value of the portion of the nation's capital equipment that is used up within the year. It tells us how much output is needed just to maintain the economy's capital stock.

From a conceptual point of view, most economists feel that NNP is a more meaningful indicator of the economy's output than is GNP. After all, the depreciation component of GNP represents the output that is needed just to repair and replace worn-out factories and machines; it is not available for anybody to consume.[9] Therefore, NNP seems to be a better measure of production than GNP.

Alas, GNP is much easier to measure because depreciation is a particularly tricky item. What fraction of his tractor did Farmer Jones "use up" last year? How much did the Empire State Building depreciate during 2013? If you ask yourself difficult questions like these, you will understand why most economists believe that we can measure GNP more accurately than NNP. For this reason, most economic models are based on GNP.

The final two adjustments that bring us to GDP return to a fact mentioned earlier. Some American citizens earn their incomes abroad, and some of the payments made by American companies are paid to foreign citizens. Thus, to obtain a measure of total production in the U.S. *domestic* economy (which is GDP) rather than a measure of the total production by U.S. *nationals* (which is GNP), we must *subtract* the income that Americans receive for factors supplied abroad and *add* the income that foreigners receive for factors supplied here. The net of these two adjustments is usually a small number, as it is in Table 4. Thus, GDP and GNP are close to equal.

In Table 4, you can hardly help noticing the preponderant share of employee compensation in total factor payments—almost two-thirds. Labor is by far the most important factor of production. The return on land is about 4½ percent of factor payments, and interest accounts for about 3½ percent. Profits account for the remaining 25½ percent—among the highest shares ever. Still, the size of *corporate* profits (just one-eighth of GDP in 2013) is much less than the public thinks. If, by some magic stroke, we could convert all corporate profits into wages without upsetting the economy's performance, the average worker would get a raise of about 24 percent!

## GDP as the Sum of Values Added

It may strike you as strange that national income accountants include only *final* goods and services in GDP. Aren't *intermediate* goods part of the nation's production? Of course they are. The problem is that, if all intermediate goods were included in GDP, we would wind up double- and triple-counting certain goods and services and therefore get an exaggerated impression of the actual level of economic activity.

To explain why, and to show how national income accountants cope with this difficulty, we must introduce a new concept, called **value added**.

The **value added** by a firm is its revenue from selling a product minus the amount paid for goods and services purchased from other firms.

The intuitive sense of this concept is clear: If a firm buys some inputs from other firms, does something to them, and sells the resulting product for a price higher than it paid for the inputs, we say that the firm has "added value" to the product. If we sum up the values added by all firms in the economy, we must get the total value of all final products. Thus:

GDP can be measured as the sum of the values added by all firms.

To verify this fact, look back at the second accounting identity introduced in the "GDP as the Sum of All Factor Payments" section. The left-hand side of this equation, sales revenue minus purchases from other firms, is precisely the firm's value added. Thus:

$$\text{Value added} = \text{Wages} + \text{Interest} + \text{Rents} + \text{Profits}$$

Because the second method we gave for measuring GDP is to add up wages, interest, rents, and profits, we see that the value-added approach must yield the same answer.

The value-added concept is useful in avoiding double-counting. Often, however, intermediate goods are difficult to distinguish from final goods. Paint bought by a painter, for example, is an intermediate good. But paint bought by a do-it-yourselfer is a final good. What happens, then, if the professional painter buys some paint to refurbish his own garage? The intermediate good becomes a final good. You can see that the

line between intermediate goods and final goods is a fuzzy one in practice.

If we measure GDP by the sum of values added, however, we need not make such subtle distinctions. In this method, every purchase of a new good or service counts, but we do not count the entire selling price, only the portion that represents value added.

To illustrate this idea, consider the data in Table 5 and how they would affect GDP as the sum of final products. Our example begins when a farmer who grows soybeans sells them to a mill for $3 per bushel. This transaction does *not* count in the GDP because the miller does not purchase the soybeans for her own use. The miller then grinds up the soybeans and sells the resulting bag of soy meal to a factory that produces soy sauce. The miller receives $4, but GDP still has not increased because the ground beans are also an intermediate product. Next, the factory turns the beans into soy sauce, which it sells to your favorite Chinese restaurant for $8. Still no effect on GDP.

Then the big moment arrives: The restaurant sells the sauce to you and other customers as a part of your meals, and you eat it. At this point, the $10 worth of soy sauce becomes part of a final product and *does* count in the GDP. Notice that if we had also counted the three intermediate transactions (farmer to miller, miller to factory, factory to restaurant), we would have come up with $25—2½ times too much.

Why is it too much? The reason is straightforward. Neither the miller, the factory owner, nor the

Table 5

**An Illustration of Final and Intermediate Goods**

| Item | Seller | Buyer | Price |
|---|---|---|---|
| Bushel of soybeans | Farmer | Miller | $ 3 |
| Bag of soy meal | Miller | Factory | 4 |
| Gallon of soy sauce | Factory | Restaurant | 8 |
| Gallon of soy sauce used as seasoning | Restaurant | Consumers | 10 |
| | | | **Total: $25** |
| **Addendum: Contribution to GDP** | | | $10 |

Table 6

**An Illustration of Value Added**

| Item | Seller | Buyer | Price | Value Added |
|---|---|---|---|---|
| Bushel of soybeans | Farmer | Miller | $ 3 | $ 3 |
| Bag of soy meal | Miller | Factory | 4 | 1 |
| Gallon of soy sauce | Factory | Restaurant | 8 | 4 |
| Gallon of soy sauce used as seasoning | Restaurant | Consumers | 10 | 2 |
| | | | Total: $ 25 | $10 |

**Addendum: Contribution to GDP**

| | |
|---|---|
| Final Products | $10 |
| Sum of values added | $10 |

restaurateur values the product we have been considering *for its own sake*. Only the customers who eat the final product (the soy sauce) have increased their material well-being, so only this last transaction counts in the GDP. However, as we shall now see, value-added calculations enable us to come up with the right answer ($10) by counting only *part* of each transaction. The basic idea is to count at each step only the contribution to the value of the ultimate final product that is made at that step, excluding the values of items produced at other steps.

Ignoring the minor items (such as fertilizer) that the farmer purchases from others, the entire $3 selling price of the bushel of soybeans is new output produced by the farmer; that is, the whole $3 is value added. The miller then grinds the beans and sells them for $4. She has added $4 minus $3, or $1 to the value of the beans. When the factory turns this soy meal into soy sauce and sells it for $8, it has added $8 minus $4, or $4 more in value. Finally, when the restaurant sells it to hungry customers for $10, a further $2 of value is added.

The last column of Table 6 shows this chain of creation of value added. We see that the total value added by all four firms is $10, exactly the same as the restaurant's selling price. This is as it must be, for only the restaurant sells the soybeans as a final product.

## Summary

1. **Gross domestic product (GDP)** is the sum of the money values of all final goods and services produced during a year and sold on organized markets. There are, however, certain exceptions to this definition.

2. One way to measure the GDP is to add up the final demands of consumers, investors, government, and foreigners: $GDP = C + I + G + (X - IM)$.

3. A second way to measure the GDP is to start with all factor payments—wages, interest, rents, and profits—that constitute the **national income** and then add indirect business taxes and **depreciation.**

4. A third way to measure the GDP is to sum up the **values added** by every firm in the economy (and then once again add indirect business taxes and depreciation).

5. Except for possible bookkeeping and statistical errors, all three methods must give the same answer.

## Key Terms

depreciation  165

gross domestic product (GDP)  162

gross national product (GNP)  165

gross private domestic investment (I)  163

national income  164

national income accounting  162

net national product (NNP)  164

value added  166

## Test Yourself

1. Which of the following transactions are included in the gross domestic product, and by how much does each raise GDP?

   a. You buy a new Toyota, made in the United States, paying $25,000.

   b. You buy a new Toyota, imported from Japan, paying $25,000.

   c. You buy a used Cadillac, paying $12,000.

   d. Google spends $500 million to increase its Internet capacity.

   e. Your grandmother receives a Social Security check for $1,500.

   f. Chrysler manufactures 1,000 automobiles at a cost of $15,000 each. Unable to sell them, the company holds the cars as inventories.

   g. Mr. Black and Mr. Blue, each out for a Sunday drive, have a collision in which their cars are destroyed. Black and Blue each hire a lawyer to sue the other, paying the lawyers $5,000 each for services rendered. The judge throws the case out of court.

   h. You sell a used computer to your friend for $100.

2. The following outline provides a complete description of all economic activity in Trivialand for 2014. Draw up versions of Tables 3 and 4 for Trivialand showing GDP computed in two different ways.[10]

   i. There are thousands of farmers but only two big business firms in Trivialand: Specific Motors (an auto company) and Super Duper (a chain of food markets). There is no government and no depreciation.

---

[10] In Trivialand, net national product and net domestic product are the same. So there are no entries corresponding to "income received from other countries" or "income paid to other countries" as in Table 4.

ii. Specific Motors produced 1,000 small cars, which it sold at $6,000 each, and 100 trucks, which it sold at $8,000 each. Consumers bought 800 of the cars, and the remaining 200 cars were exported to the United States. Super Duper bought all the trucks.

iii. Sales at Super Duper markets amounted to $14 million, all of it sold to consumers.

iv. All farmers in Trivialand are self-employed and sell all of their wares to Super Duper.

v. The costs incurred by all of Trivialand's businesses were as follows:

| | Specific Motors | Super Duper | Farmers |
|---|---|---|---|
| Wages | $3,800,000 | $4,500,000 | $ 0 |
| Interest | 100,000 | 200,000 | 700,000 |
| Rent | 200,000 | 1,000,000 | 2,000,000 |
| Purchases of food | 0 | 7,000,000 | 0 |

3. **(More difficult)** Now complicate Trivialand in the following ways and answer the same questions. In addition, calculate national income and disposable income.[11]

a. The government bought 50 cars, leaving only 150 cars for export. In addition, the government spent $800,000 on wages and made $1,200,000 in transfer payments.

b. Depreciation for the year amounted to $600,000 for Specific Motors and $200,000 for Super Duper. (The farmers had no depreciation.)

c. The government levied sales taxes amounting to $500,000 on Specific Motors and $200,000 on Super Duper (but none on farmers). In addition, the government levied a 10 percent income tax on all wages, interest, and rental income.

d. In addition to the food and cars mentioned in Test Yourself Question 2, consumers in Trivialand imported 500 computers from the United States at $2,000 each.

## Discussion Questions

1. Explain the difference between final goods and intermediate goods. Why is it sometimes difficult to apply this distinction in practice? In this regard, why is the concept of value added useful?

2. Explain the difference between government spending and government purchases of goods and services (G). Which is larger?

3. Explain why national income and gross domestic product would be essentially equal if there were no depreciation.

---

[11] In this context, disposable income is national income plus transfer payments minus taxes.

# DEMAND-SIDE EQUILIBRIUM: UNEMPLOYMENT OR INFLATION?

*A definite ratio, to be called the Multiplier, can be established between income and investment.*

JOHN MAYNARD KEYNES

Let's briefly review where we have just been. In Chapter 5, we learned that the interaction of aggregate demand and aggregate supply determines whether the economy will stagnate or prosper, whether our labor and capital resources will be fully employed or substantially unemployed. In Chapter 8, we learned that aggregate demand has four components: consumer expenditure (*C*), investment (*I*), government purchases (*G*), and net exports (*X − IM*). It is now time to start building a theory that puts the pieces together so we can see where the aggregate demand and aggregate supply curves come from.

Because it is best to walk before you try to run, our approach is sequential. We begin in this chapter by assuming that taxes, the price level, the rate of interest, and the international value of the dollar are all constant. None of these assumptions is true, of course, and we will dispense with all of them in subsequent chapters. But we reap two important pedagogical benefits from making these unrealistic assumptions now. First, they enable us to construct a simple but useful model of how the strength of aggregate demand influences the level of gross domestic product (GDP)—a model we will use to derive specific numerical solutions. Second, this simple model enables us to obtain an initial answer to a question of great policy importance: Can we expect the economy to achieve full employment if the government does not intervene?

## CONTENTS

| Issue | *Why Does the Market Permit High Unemployment?* |
| --- | --- |

Economists are fond of pointing out the amazing achievements of free markets. Without central direction, they somehow get businesses to produce just the goods and services that consumers want—and to do so cheaply and efficiently. If consumers want less meat and more fish, markets respond. If people subsequently change their minds, markets respond again. Free markets seem able to coordinate literally millions of decisions effortlessly and seamlessly.

Yet for hundreds of years and all over the globe, market economies have stumbled over one particular coordination problem: the periodic bouts of mass unemployment that we call *recessions* and *depressions*. Widespread unemployment represents a failure to coordinate economic activity in the following sense. If the unemployed were hired, they would be able to buy the goods and services that businesses cannot sell. The revenues from those sales would, in turn, allow firms to hire—and pay—many workers who otherwise would not have jobs. So a seemingly straightforward "deal" offers jobs for the unemployed and sales for the firms. Yet, somehow, this deal is not made. Workers remain unemployed, and firms get stuck with unsold output.

Thus while free markets manage to get rough diamonds dug out of the ground in South Africa and turned into beautiful rings that grooms buy for brides in Los Angeles, they cannot solve the coordination problem posed by unemployment. Why not? For centuries, economists puzzled over this question. By the end of the chapter, we will be well on the way toward providing an answer.

## 9-1 THE MEANING OF EQUILIBRIUM GDP

First, let's put the four components of aggregate demand together to see how they interact, using as our organizing framework the circular flow diagram from the last chapter. In doing so, we initially ignore a possibility raised in earlier chapters: that the government might use monetary and fiscal policy to steer the economy in some desired direction. Aside from simplicity, there is an important reason for ignoring these policies at first: One crucial question about stabilization policy is whether the economy would *automatically* gravitate toward full employment if the government simply left it alone.

Keynes claimed it would not, thereby contradicting the teachings of generations of economists before him. But Keynes's views have always been controversial. Even today, after years of high unemployment, there are those who claim the lessons Keynes taught in the 1930s should be unlearned, that we should rely instead on the economy's ability to cure unemployment by itself. We can study this conceptual issue best by imagining an economy in which the government never tries to manipulate aggregate demand, which is what we do in this chapter.

To begin to construct such a model, we must first understand what we mean by *equilibrium GDP*. Figure 1, which repeats the circular flow diagram from the last chapter, will help us do this. As explained there, total *production* and total *income* must be equal, but the same need not be true of total *spending*. Imagine that, for some reason, the total expenditures made by the time we reach point 4 in the figure, $C + I + G + (X - IM)$, exceed the output produced by the business firms at point 5. What happens then?

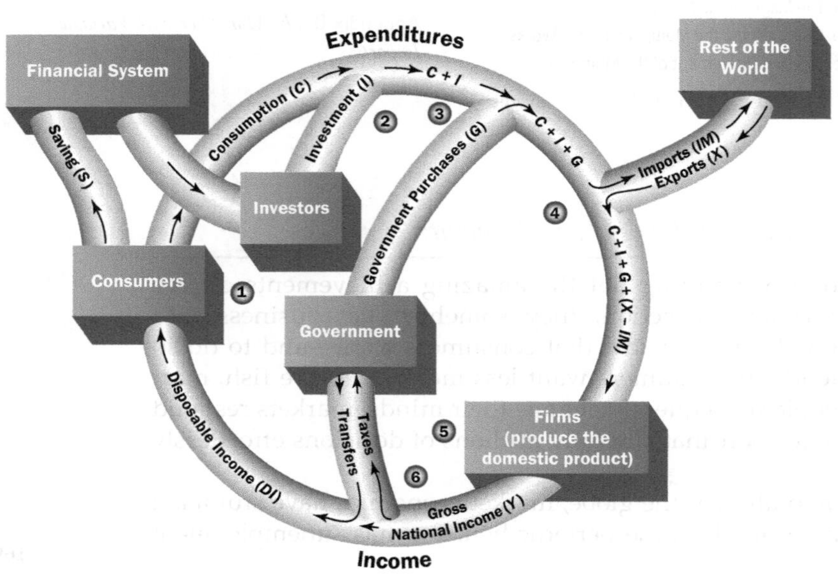

Because consumers, businesses, government, and foreigners together are buying more than firms are producing, firms will start pulling goods out of their warehouses to meet demand. Thus, inventory stocks will fall—which signals retailers that they need to increase their orders and signals manufacturers that they need to step up production. Output is therefore likely to rise.

At some later date, if evidence indicates that the high level of spending is not just a temporary aberration, manufacturers and retailers may also respond to buoyant sales by raising their prices. Economists therefore say that

*Figure 1*

**The Circular Flow Diagram**

neither output nor the price level is in **equilibrium** when total spending exceeds current production.

The definition of *equilibrium*, found in the margin, tells us that the economy cannot be in equilibrium when total spending exceeds production, because falling inventories demonstrate to firms that their production and pricing decisions were not quite right.[1] Thus, because we normally use GDP to measure output:

> **The equilibrium level of GDP on the demand side cannot be one at which total spending exceeds output because firms will be depleting their inventory stocks. They may first decide to increase production sufficiently to meet the higher demand. Later they may decide to raise prices.**

Now imagine the other case, in which the flow of spending reaching firms falls short of current production. The unsold output winds up as additional inventories. That inventory pile-up, in turn, signals firms that either their pricing or output decisions were wrong. Once again, they will probably react first by cutting back on production, causing GDP to fall (at point 5 in Figure 1). If the imbalance persists, they may also lower prices to stimulate sales. However, they certainly will not be content with things as they are. Thus:

> **The equilibrium level of GDP on the demand side cannot be one at which total spending is less than output, because firms will not allow inventories to pile up. They may decide to decrease production, or they may decide to cut prices in order to stimulate demand.**

We have now determined, by process of elimination, the only level of output that is consistent with people's desires to spend. We have reasoned that GDP will *rise* whenever it is *less* than total spending, $C + I + G + (X - IM)$ and that GDP will *fall* whenever it *exceeds* $C + I + G + (X - IM)$. Equilibrium can occur, then, only when there is just enough spending to absorb the current level of production. Under such circumstances, producers conclude that their price and output decisions are correct and have no incentive to change. We conclude that:

> **The equilibrium level of GDP on the demand side is the level at which total spending equals production. In such a situation, firms find their inventories remaining at desired levels, so they have no incentive to change output or prices.**

Thus, the circular flow diagram has, first, helped us understand the concept of equilibrium GDP and, second, shown us how the economy is driven toward this equilibrium. However, it leaves three important questions unanswered:

- How large is the equilibrium level of GDP?
- Will the economy suffer from unemployment, inflation, or both?
- Is the equilibrium level of GDP on the demand side also consistent with firms' desires to produce? That is, is it also an equilibrium on the supply side?

The first two questions will occupy our attention in this chapter; the third is reserved for the next.

**Equilibrium** refers to a situation in which neither consumers nor firms have any incentive to change their behavior. They are content to continue with things as they are.

## 9-2 THE MECHANICS OF INCOME DETERMINATION

Our first objective is to determine precisely the equilibrium level of GDP on the demand side. To make the analysis more concrete, we turn to a numerical example. Specifically, we examine the relationship between total spending and GDP in the hypothetical economy we introduced in the last chapter.

Columns 1 and 2 of Table 1 repeat the relationship between consumption and GDP that we first encountered in the preceding chapter, showing how consumer spending, $C$, depends on GDP, which we symbolize by the letter $Y$. Columns 3 through 5 provide the other three components of total spending—$I$, $G$, and $X - IM$—through the simplifying assumptions that each is just a fixed number regardless of the level of GDP. Specifically, we assume that investment spending is $900 billion, government purchases are $1,300

---

[1] All the models in this book assume, strictly for simplicity, that firms seek constant inventories. Deliberate inventory changes are treated in more advanced courses.

*Table 1*

**The Expenditure Schedule**

| (1)<br>GDP (Y) | (2)<br>Consumption<br>(C) | (3)<br>Investment<br>(I) | (4)<br>Government<br>Purchases<br>(G) | (5)<br>Net<br>Exports<br>(X – IM) | (6)<br>Total<br>Expenditure |
|---|---|---|---|---|---|
| 4,800 | 3,000 | 900 | 1,300 | –100 | 5,100 |
| 5,200 | 3,300 | 900 | 1,300 | –100 | 5,400 |
| 5,600 | 3,600 | 900 | 1,300 | –100 | 5,700 |
| 6,000 | 3,900 | 900 | 1,300 | –100 | 6,000 |
| 6,400 | 4,200 | 900 | 1,300 | –100 | 6,300 |
| 6,800 | 4,500 | 900 | 1,300 | –100 | 6,600 |
| 7,200 | 4,800 | 900 | 1,300 | –100 | 6,900 |

An **expenditure schedule** shows the relationship between national income (GDP) and total spending.

billion, and net exports are –$100 billion—meaning that in this hypothetical economy, as in the United States at present, imports exceed exports.

By adding columns 2 through 5, we calculate $C + I + G + (X - IM)$ or total expenditure, which appears in column 6 of Table 1. Columns 1 and 6 are highlighted in color to show how total expenditure depends on income. We call this relationship the **expenditure schedule**.

Figure 2 shows the construction of the expenditure schedule graphically. The black line labeled $C$ is the consumption function; it plots on the graph the numbers given in columns 1 and 2 of Table 1.

The maroon line, labeled $C + I$, displays our assumption that investment is fixed at $900 billion. It lies a fixed distance (corresponding to $900 billion) above the $C$ line. If investment were not always $900 billion, the two lines would either move closer together or grow farther apart. For example, our analysis of the determinants of investment spending suggested that $I$ might be larger when GDP is higher. Such added

*Figure 2*

**Construction of the Expenditure Schedule**

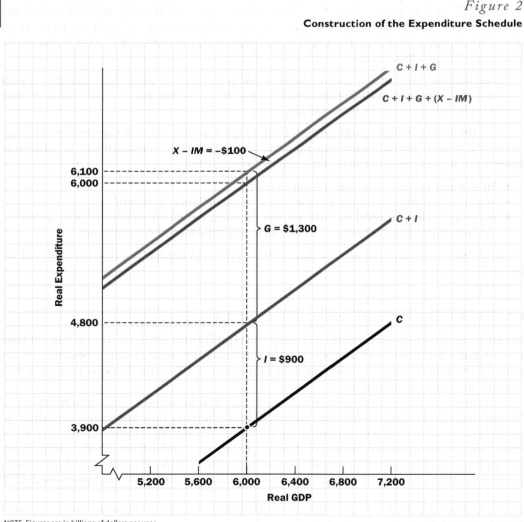

NOTE: Figures are in billions of dollars per year.

investment as GDP rises—which is called **induced investment**—would give the resulting $C + I$ line a steeper slope than the $C$ line. We ignore that possibility here for simplicity.

The green line, labeled $C + I + G$, adds government purchases. Because they are assumed to be $1,300 billion regardless of the size of GDP, the green line is parallel to the maroon line and $1,300 billion higher.

*Table 2*

**The Determination of Equilibrium Output**

| (1) | (2) | (3) | (4) | (5) |
|-----|-----|-----|-----|-----|
| Output (Y) | Total Spending [C + I + G (X − IM)] | Balance of Spending and Output | Inventory Status | Producer Response |
| 4,800 | 5,100 | Spending exceeds output | Falling | Produce more |
| 5,200 | 5,400 | Spending exceeds output | Falling | Produce more |
| 5,600 | 5,700 | Spending exceeds output | Falling | Produce more |
| 6,000 | 6,000 | Spending = output | Constant | No change |
| 6,400 | 6,300 | Output exceeds spending | Rising | Produce less |
| 6,800 | 6,600 | Output exceeds spending | Rising | Produce less |
| 7,200 | 6,900 | Output exceeds spending | Rising | Produce less |

NOTE: Amounts are in billions of dollars.

Finally, the blue line labeled $C + I + G + (X - IM)$ adds in net exports. It is parallel to the green line and $100 billion lower, reflecting our assumption that net exports are always *negative* $100 billion. Once again, if imports depended on GDP, as Chapter 8 suggested, the $C + I + G + (X - IM)$ lines would not be parallel. We deal with this complication in Appendix B.

**Induced investment** is the part of investment spending that rises when GDP rises and falls when GDP falls.

We are now ready to determine demand-side equilibrium in our hypothetical economy. Table 2 presents the logic of the circular flow argument in tabular form. The first two columns reproduce the *expenditure schedule* that we have just constructed. The other columns explain the process by which the economy approaches equilibrium. Let us see why equilibrium must come at a GDP of $6,000 billion.

Consider first any output level below $6,000 billion. For example, at output level $Y = $5,200 billion, total expenditure is $5,400 billion, as shown in column 2. This is $200 billion more than production. With spending greater than output, as noted in column 3, inventories will fall (column 4). As the table suggests in column 5, this will signal producers to raise their output. Clearly, then, no output level below $Y = $6,000 billion can be an equilibrium, because output is too low.

Equilibrium GDP on the demand side occurs where $Y = C + I + G + (X - IM)$

A similar line of reasoning eliminates any output level above $6,000 billion. Consider, for example, $Y = $6,800 billion. The table shows that total spending would be $6,600 billion if output were $6,800 billion, so $200 billion would go unsold. This would raise producers' inventory stocks and signal them that their rate of production was too high.

Just as we concluded from our circular flow diagram, equilibrium will be achieved only when total spending, $C + I + G + (X - IM)$, exactly equals GDP, $Y$. In symbols, our condition for equilibrium GDP is

$$Y = C + I + G + (X - IM)$$

Table 2 shows that this equation holds only at a GDP of $6,000 billion, which must therefore be the equilibrium level of GDP.

Figure 3 depicts the same conclusion graphically, by adding a 45° line to Figure 2. Why a 45°

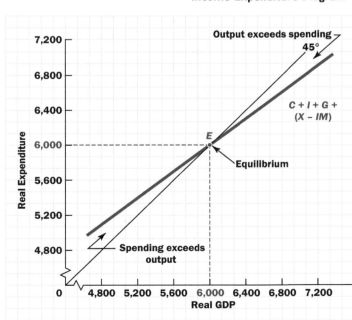

*Figure 3*

**Income-Expenditure Diagram**

NOTE: Figures are in billions of dollars per year.

line? Recall from the appendix to Chapter 1 that a $45°$ line marks all points on a graph at which the value of the variable measured on the horizontal axis (in this case, GDP) equals the value of the variable measured on the vertical axis (in this case, total expenditure).[2] Thus, the $45°$ line in Figure 3 shows all the points at which output and spending are equal—that is, where $Y = C + I + G + (X - IM)$. *The $45°$ line therefore displays all the points at which the economy can possibly be in demand-side equilibrium*, for firms will be content with current output levels only if total spending equals production.

Now we must compare these *potential* equilibrium points with the *actual* combinations of spending and output that are consistent with the behavior of consumers and investors. That behavior is described by the $C + I + G + (X - IM)$ line in Figure 3, which shows how total expenditure varies as income changes. *The economy will always be on the expenditure line* because only points on the $C + I + G + (X - IM)$ line are consistent with the spending plans of consumers and investors. Similarly, *if* the economy is in equilibrium, it *must* be on the $45°$ line. As Figure 3 shows, these two requirements imply that the only viable equilibrium comes at point $E$, where the $C + I + G + (X - IM)$ line intersects the $45°$ line. Only this point is consistent with both equilibrium and people's desires to consume and invest.

Notice that to the left of the equilibrium point, $E$, the expenditure line lies *above* the $45°$ line. This means that total spending exceeds total output, as we have already noted. Hence, inventories will be falling, and firms will conclude that they should increase production. Thus, production will rise toward the equilibrium point, $E$. The opposite is true to the right of point $E$. Here spending falls short of output, inventories rise, and firms will cut back production—thereby moving closer to $E$.

In other words, whenever production is *above* the equilibrium level, market forces will drive output *down*. And whenever production is *below* equilibrium, market forces will drive output *up*. In either case, deviations from demand-side equilibrium will gradually be eliminated.

Diagrams such as Figure 3 will recur so frequently in this and coming chapters that it is convenient to have a special name for them. We call them **income-expenditure diagrams**, because they show how expenditures vary with income, or simply **$45°$ line diagrams**.

An **income-expenditure diagram** (or **$45°$ line diagram**), plots total real expenditure (on the vertical axis) against real income (on the horizontal axis). The $45°$ line marks off points where income and expenditure are equal.

## 9-3 THE AGGREGATE DEMAND CURVE

Chapter 5 introduced aggregate demand and aggregate supply curves relating aggregate quantities demanded and supplied to the price level. The expenditure schedule graphed in Figure 3 is *not* the aggregate demand curve, for we have yet to bring the price level into our discussion. It is now time to remedy this omission and derive the **aggregate demand curve**.

To do so, we need only recall something we learned in the last chapter. As we noted, households own a great deal of *money-fixed assets* whose real value declines when the price level rises. The money in your bank account is a prime example. If prices rise, that money will buy less. Because of that fact, consumers' *real* wealth declines whenever the price level rises—and that decreases their spending. Specifically:

The **aggregate demand curve** shows the quantity of domestic product that is demanded at each possible value of the price level.

Higher prices decrease the demand for goods and services because they erode the purchasing power of consumer wealth. Conversely, lower prices increase the demand for goods and services by enhancing the purchasing power of consumer wealth.

For these reasons, a change in the price level will shift the entire consumption function. To represent this shift graphically, Figure 4 (which looks just like Figure 6 from the previous chapter) shows that:

A higher price level leads to lower real wealth and therefore to less spending *at any given level of real income*. Thus, a higher price level leads to a lower consumption function (such as $C_1$ in Figure 4), and a lower price level leads to a higher consumption function (such as $C_2$ in Figure 4).

---

[2] If you need review, see the appendix to Chapter 1.

Because students are sometimes confused by this point, it is worth repeating that the depressing effect of the price level on consumer spending works through real *wealth*, not through real *income*. The consumption function displays the relationship between *real consumer income* and *real consumer spending*. Thus, if real income declines for any reason, the economy moves leftward *along a fixed consumption function*. By contrast, a decline in *real wealth* will *shift the entire consumption function downward*, meaning that people spend less at any given level of real income.

In terms of the $45°$ line diagram, a rise in the price level will therefore pull down the consumption function depicted in Figure 2 and hence will pull down the total expenditure schedule as well. Conversely, a fall in the price level will raise both the $C$ and $C + I + G + (X - IM)$ schedules in the diagram. The two panels of Figure 5 illustrate both of these shifts.

How, then, do changes in the price level affect the equilibrium level of real GDP on the demand side? Common sense says that, with lower spending, equilibrium GDP should fall, and Figure 5 shows that this conclusion is correct. Figure 5(a) shows that a rise in the price level, by shifting the expenditure schedule downward, leads to a reduction in the equilibrium quantity of real GDP demanded from $Y_0$ to $Y_1$. Figure 5(b) shows that a fall in the price level, by shifting the expenditure schedule upward, leads to a rise in the equilibrium quantity of real GDP demanded from $Y_0$ to $Y_2$. In summary:

A rise in the price level leads to a lower equilibrium level of real aggregate quantity demanded. This relationship between the price level and real GDP (depicted in Figure 6) is precisely what we called the aggregate demand curve in earlier chapters. It comes directly from the $45°$ line diagrams in Figure 5. Thus, points $E_0$, $E_1$, and $E_2$ in Figure 6 correspond precisely to the points bearing the same labels in Figure 5.

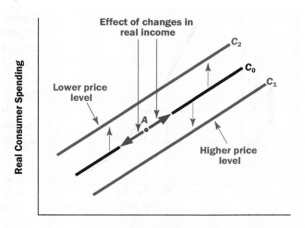

*Figure 4*

**How the Price Level Shifts the Consumption Function**

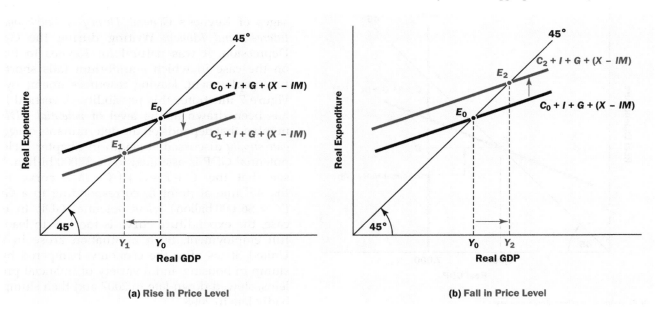

*Figure 5*

**The Effect of the Price Level on Equilibrium Aggregate Quantity Demanded**

(a) Rise in Price Level

(b) Fall in Price Level

## Figure 6
### The Aggregate Demand Curve

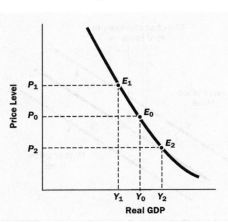

The effect of higher prices on consumer wealth is just one of several reasons why the aggregate demand curve slopes downward. A second reason comes from international trade. In Chapter 8's discussion of the determinants of net exports, we pointed out that higher U.S. prices (holding foreign prices constant) will depress exports $(X)$ and stimulate imports $(IM)$. That means that, holding other things equal, a higher U.S. price level will reduce the $(X - IM)$ component of total expenditure, thereby shifting the $C + I + G + (X - IM)$ line downward and lowering real GDP, as depicted in Figure 5(a).

Later in this book, after we have studied interest rates and exchange rates, we will encounter still more reasons for a downward-sloping aggregate demand curve. All of them imply that:

> An income-expenditure diagram like Figure 3 can be drawn only for a *specific* price level. At different price levels, the $C + I + G + (X - IM)$ schedule will be different and, hence, the equilibrium quantity of GDP demanded will also be different.

As we will now see, this seemingly technical point is critical to understanding the genesis of unemployment and inflation.

## 9-4 DEMAND-SIDE EQUILIBRIUM AND FULL EMPLOYMENT

We now turn to the second major question posed earlier in this chapter: Will the economy's equilibrium be at full employment without inflation, or will we see unemployment, inflation, or both? This question is a crucial one for stabilization policy, for if the economy always gravitates toward full employment *automatically*, then the government should simply leave it alone.

In the income-expenditure diagrams used so far, the equilibrium level of GDP demanded appears as the intersection of the expenditure schedule and the 45° line, regardless of the GDP level that corresponds to full employment. However, as we will see now, when equilibrium GDP falls above potential GDP, the economy probably will be plagued by inflation, and when equilibrium falls below potential GDP, unemployment and recession will result.

## Figure 7
### A Recessionary Gap

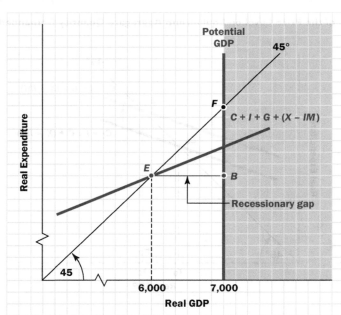

NOTE: Figures are in billions of dollars per year.

This notable fact was one of the principal messages of Keynes's *General Theory of Employment, Interest, and Money*. Writing during the Great Depression, it was natural for Keynes to focus on the case in which equilibrium falls short of full employment, leaving resources unemployed. Figure 7 illustrates this possibility. A vertical line has been drawn at the level of *potential GDP*, a number that depends on the determinants of *aggregate supply* discussed at length in Chapter 7. Here, potential GDP is assumed to be $7,000 billion. We see that the $C + I + G + (X - IM)$ curve cuts the 45° line at point $E$, corresponding to a GDP $(Y = \$6,000 \text{ billion})$ *below* potential GDP. In this case, the expenditure curve is too low to lead to full employment. Such a situation arose in the United States after the economy, hampered by a slump in housing and a variety of financial problems, slowed down late in 2007 and then slumped badly late in 2008.

An equilibrium below potential GDP can arise when consumers or investors are unwilling to spend at normal rates, when government spending is low, when foreign demand is weak, or when the price level is "too high." Any of these events would depress the $C + I + G + (X - IM)$ curve. Unemployment then occurs because not enough output is demanded to keep the entire labor force at work.

The distance between the *equilibrium* level of output demanded and the *full-employment* level of output (i.e., potential GDP) is called the **recessionary gap**, or sometimes just the *output gap*. It is shown by the horizontal distance from point $E$ to point $B$ in Figure 7. Although the figure is entirely hypothetical, real-world gaps of precisely this sort were shown shaded in maroon in Figure 2 of Chapter 6. They have been a frequent feature of U.S. economic history and have been especially large of late.

Figure 7 clearly shows that full employment can be reached by raising the total expenditure schedule to eliminate the recessionary gap. Specifically, the $C + I + G + (X - IM)$ line must move upward until it cuts the $45°$ line at point $F$. Can this happen without government intervention? We know that a sufficiently large drop in the price level can do the job. But is that a realistic prospect? We will return to this important question in the next chapter, after we bring the supply side into the picture, for we cannot discuss prices without bringing in *both* supply *and* demand. First, however, let us briefly consider the other case—when equilibrium GDP exceeds full employment.

Figure 8 illustrates this possibility, which many people believe characterized the U.S. economy in 2006 and into 2007, when the unemployment rate dipped down to about $4\frac{1}{2}$ percent. Now the expenditure schedule intersects the $45°$ line at point $E$, where GDP is \$8,000 billion. But this exceeds the full-employment level, $Y = \$7,000$ billion. Such a case can arise when consumer or investment spending is unusually buoyant, when foreign demand is particularly strong, when the government spends too much, or when a "low" price level pushes the $C + I + G + (X - IM)$ curve upward.

To reach an equilibrium at full employment, the price level would have to rise enough to drive the expenditure schedule *down* until it passed through point $F$. The horizontal distance $BE$—which indicates the amount by which the quantity of GDP demanded exceeds potential GDP—is now called the **inflationary gap**. If there is an inflationary gap, a higher price level or some other means of reducing total expenditure is necessary to create an equilibrium at full employment. Rising prices will eventually pull the $C + I + G + (X - IM)$ line down until it passes through point $F$. Real-world inflationary gaps were shown shaded in blue in Figure 2 of Chapter 6. In sum:

**Only if the price level and spending plans are "just right" will the expenditure curve intersect the $45°$ line precisely at full employment, so that neither a recessionary gap nor an inflationary gap occurs.**

Are there reasons to expect this outcome? Does the economy have a self-correcting mechanism that automatically eliminates recessionary or inflationary gaps and propels it toward full employment? We are not yet ready for full answers to these questions because we have not yet brought *aggregate supply* into the picture. However, it is not too early to see why things go wrong during a recession like the recent one.

The **recessionary gap** is the amount by which the equilibrium level of real GDP falls short of potential GDP.

The **inflationary gap** is the amount by which equilibrium real GDP exceeds the full-employment level of GDP.

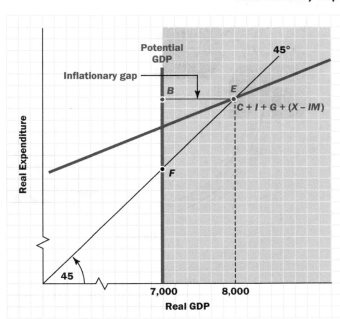

*Figure 8*

**An Inflationary Gap**

NOTE: Figures are in billions of dollars per year.

## 9-5 THE COORDINATION OF SAVING AND INVESTMENT

**Full employment** is a situation in which everyone who is willing and able to work can find a job. At full employment, the measured unemployment rate is still positive.

To do so, it is useful to pose the following question: Must the **full-employment level of GDP** be a demand-side equilibrium? Decades ago, economists thought the answer was "yes." Since Keynes, most economists believe the answer is "not necessarily."

To help us see why, Figure 9 offers a simplified circular flow diagram that ignores exports, imports, and the government. In this version, income can "leak out" of the circular flow only at point 1, where consumers save some of their income. Similarly, lost spending can be replaced only at point 2, where investment enters the circular flow.

What happens if firms produce exactly the full-employment level of GDP at point 3 in the diagram? Will this income level be maintained as we move around the circle, or will it shrink or grow? The answer is that full-employment income will be maintained *only* if the spending by investors at point 2 exactly balances the saving done by consumers at point 1. In other words:

> The economy will be in demand-side equilibrium at full employment only if the amount that consumers wish to save out of their full-employment incomes happens to equal the amount that investors want to invest. If these two magnitudes are unequal, full employment will not be an equilibrium.

Thus, the basic answer to the puzzle we posed at the start of this chapter is:

> The market will permit unemployment when total spending is too low to employ the entire labor force.

But how can that occur? The circular flow diagram shows that if saving exceeds investment at full employment, the total demand received by firms at point 3 will fall short of total output because the added investment spending will not be enough to replace the leakage to saving. If demand is inadequate to support production at full employment, GDP must fall below potential. There will be a recessionary gap. Conversely, if investment exceeds saving when the economy is at full employment, then total demand will exceed potential GDP and production will rise above the full-employment level. There will be an inflationary gap.

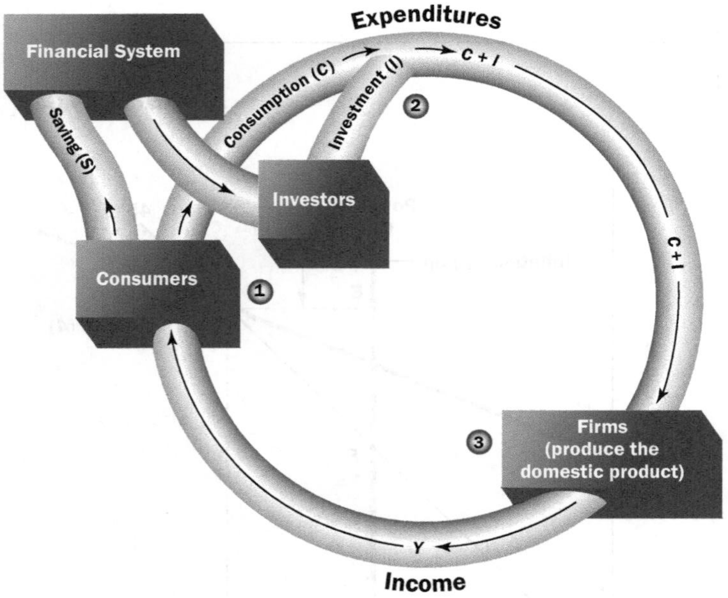

This discussion merely restates what we already know in different words.[3] But these words provide the key to understanding why the economy sometimes finds itself stuck above or below full employment, for *the people who invest are not the same as the people who save.* In a modern capitalist economy, investing is done by one group of individuals (primarily corporate executives and home buyers), whereas saving is done by another group.[4] It is easy to imagine that their plans may not be well coordinated. If they are not, we have just seen how either unemployment or inflation can result.

Neither of these problems would arise if the acts of saving and investing were perfectly coordinated. Although perfection is never attainable, the analysis in the box "Unemployment and Inflation as Coordination Failures" raises a tantalizing possibility. If both high unemployment and high

*Figure 9*

**A Simplified Circular Flow**

---

[3] In symbols, our equilibrium condition without government or foreign trade is $Y = C + I$. If we note that $Y$ is also the sum of consumption plus saving, $Y = C + S$, then it follows that $C + S = C + I$, or $S = I$, is a restatement of the equilibrium condition.

[4] In a modern economy, not only do households save but businesses also save in the form of retained earnings. Nonetheless, households are the ultimate source of the saving needed to finance investment.

## Unemployment and Inflation as Coordination Failures

The idea that unemployment stems from a lack of coordination between the decisions of savers and investors may seem abstract, but we encounter coordination failures in the real world quite frequently. The following familiar example may bring the idea down to earth.

Picture a crowd watching a football game, all seated. Now something exciting happens, and the fans rise from their seats. People in the front rows begin standing first, and those seated behind them are forced to stand if they want to see the game. Soon everyone in the stadium is on their feet.

With everyone standing, though, no one can see any better than when everyone was sitting. And the fans are enduring the further discomfort of being on their feet. (Never mind that stadium seats are uncomfortable!) Everyone in the stadium would be better off if everyone sat down, which sometimes happens. But then the crowd rises to its feet again on every exciting play. There is simply no way to coordinate the individual decisions of tens of thousands of football fans.

Unemployment poses a similar coordination problem. During a deep recession, workers are unemployed, and businesses cannot sell their wares. Figuratively speaking, everyone is "standing" and unhappy about it. If only the firms could agree to hire more workers, those newly employed people could afford to buy more of the goods and services the firms want to produce. However, as at the football stadium, there is no central authority to coordinate these millions of decisions.

The coordination failure idea also helps to explain why it is so difficult to stop inflation. Virtually everyone prefers stable prices to rising prices. Now think of yourself as the seller of a product. If all other participants in the economy would hold their prices steady, you would happily hold yours steady, too. If you believe that others will continue to raise their prices at a rate of, say, 5 percent per year, you may find it dangerous not to increase your prices apace. Hence, society may get stuck with 5 percent inflation even though everyone agrees that zero inflation is better.

Ezra Shaw/Getty Images

inflation arise from **coordination failures**, might the government be able to do something about the problem? Keynes suggested that it could, by using its powers over monetary and fiscal policy. His ideas, which constitute one of our *Ideas for Beyond the Final Exam*, will be examined in detail in later chapters. However, even the simple football analogy described in the box reminds us that a central authority may not find it easy to solve a coordination problem.

> A **coordination failure** occurs when party A would like to change his behavior if party B would change his, and vice versa, and yet the two changes do not take place because the decisions of A and B are not coordinated.

## 9-6 CHANGES ON THE DEMAND SIDE: MULTIPLIER ANALYSIS

We have just learned how demand-side equilibrium depends on the consumption function and on the amounts spent on investment, government purchases, and net exports. But none of these are constants of nature; they all change from time to time. How does equilibrium GDP change when the consumption function shifts or when $I$, $G$, or $(X - IM)$ changes? As we will see now, the answer is simple: *by more!* A remarkable result, called the **multiplier**, says that a change in spending will bring about an *even larger* change in equilibrium GDP on the demand side. Let us see why.

> The **multiplier** is the ratio of the change in equilibrium GDP ($Y$) divided by the original change in spending that causes the change in GDP.

### 9-6a The Magic of the Multiplier

Because it is subject to abrupt swings, investment spending often causes business fluctuations in the United States and elsewhere. So let us ask what would happen if firms suddenly decided to spend more on investment goods. As we will see next, such a decision would have a *multiplied* effect on GDP; that is, each $1 of additional investment spending would add *more* than $1 to GDP.

To see why, refer first to Table 3, which looks very much like Table 1. The only difference is that we now assume that firms want to invest $200 billion more than previously—for a

*Table 3*

**Total Expenditure after a $200 Billion Increase in Investment Spending**

| (1)<br>Income (Y) | (2)<br>Consumption (C) | (3)<br>Investment<br>(I) | (4)<br>Government<br>Purchases (G) | (5)<br>Net Exports<br>(X – IM) | (6)<br>Total<br>Expenditure |
|---|---|---|---|---|---|
| 4,800 | 3,000 | 1,100 | 1,300 | –100 | 5,300 |
| 5,200 | 3,300 | 1,100 | 1,300 | –100 | 5,600 |
| 5,600 | 3,600 | 1,100 | 1,300 | –100 | 5,900 |
| 6,000 | 3,900 | 1,100 | 1,300 | –100 | 6,200 |
| 6,400 | 4,200 | 1,100 | 1,300 | –100 | 6,500 |
| 6,800 | 4,500 | 1,100 | 1,300 | –100 | 6,800 |
| 7,200 | 4,800 | 1,100 | 1,300 | –100 | 7,100 |

NOTE: Figures are in billions of dollars per year.

total of $1,100 billion. As indicated by the green numbers, only income level $Y = \$6,800$ billion is an equilibrium on the demand side of the economy now, because only at this level is total spending, $C + I + G + (X - IM)$, equal to production ($Y$).

The *multiplier* principle says that GDP will rise by *more than* the $200 billion increase in investment. Specifically, the multiplier is defined as the ratio of the change in equilibrium GDP ($Y$) to the original change in spending that caused GDP to change. In shorthand, when we deal with the multiplier for investment ($I$), the formula is

$$\text{Multiplier} = \frac{\text{Change in } Y}{\text{Change in } I}$$

Let us verify that the multiplier is, indeed, greater than 1. Table 3 shows how the new expenditure schedule is constructed by adding up $C$, $I$, $G$, and $(X - IM)$ at each level of $Y$, just as we did earlier—only now $I$ is $1,100 billion rather than $900 billion. If you compare the last columns of Table 1 and Table 3, you will see that the new expenditure schedule lies uniformly above the old one by $200 billion.

Figure 10 depicts this change graphically. The black curve marked $C + I_0 + G + (X - IM)$ is derived from the last column of Table 1, whereas the higher blue curve marked $C + I_1 + G + (X - IM)$ is derived from the last column of Table 3. The two expenditure lines are parallel and $200 billion apart.

So far things look just as you might expect, but one more step will bring the multiplier rabbit out of the hat. Let us see what the upward shift of the expenditure line does to equilibrium income. In Figure 10, equilibrium moves outward from point $E_0$ to point $E_1$, or from $6,000 billion to $6,800 billion. The difference is an increase of $800 billion in GDP. All this from a $200 billion stimulus to investment? That is the magic of the multiplier.

Because the change in $I$ is $200 billion and the change in equilibrium $Y$ is $800 billion, by applying our definition, the multiplier is

$$\text{Multiplier} = \frac{\text{Change in } Y}{\text{Change in } I} = \frac{\$800}{\$200} = 4$$

This tells us that, in our example, each additional $1 of investment demand will add $4 to equilibrium GDP!

This result does, indeed, seem mysterious. Can something be created from nothing? Let's first check that the graph has not deceived us. The first and last columns of Table 3 show in numbers what Figure 10 shows graphically. Notice that equilibrium now comes at $Y = \$6,800$ billion, because only at that point is total expenditure equal to production ($Y$). This equilibrium level of GDP is $800 billion higher than the $6,000 billion level found when investment was $200 billion lower. Thus, a $200 billion rise in investment does indeed lead to an $800 billion rise in equilibrium GDP. The multiplier really is 4.

*Figure 10*

**Illustration of the Multiplier**

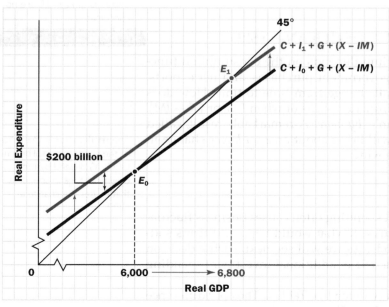

NOTE: Figures are in billions of dollars per year.

## 9-6b  Demystifying the Multiplier: How It Works

The multiplier result seems strange at first, but it loses its mystery once we recall the circular flow of income and expenditure and the simple fact that one person's spending is another person's income. To illustrate the logic of the multiplier and see why it is exactly 4 in our example, think about what happens when businesses decide to spend $1 million on investment goods.

Suppose that Microhard—a major corporation in our hypothetical country—decides to spend $1 million to upgrade an office building. Its $1 million expenditure goes to construction workers and owners of construction companies as wages and profits. That is, the $1 million becomes their *income.*

The construction firm's owners and workers will not keep all of their $1 million in the bank; instead, they will spend most of it. If they are "typical" consumers, their spending will be $1 million times the marginal propensity to consume (MPC). In our example, the MPC is 0.75, so assume they spend $750,000 and save the rest. *This $750,000 expenditure is a net addition to the nation's demand for goods and services,* just as Microhard's original $1 million expenditure was. So, at this stage, the $1 million investment has already pushed GDP up by some $1.75 million—and the process is by no means over.

Shopkeepers receive the $750,000 spent by construction workers, and they in turn also spend 75 percent of their new income. This activity accounts for $562,500 (75 percent of $750,000) in additional consumer spending in the "third round." Next follows a fourth round in which the recipients of the $562,500 spend 75 percent of this amount, or $421,875, and so on. At each stage in the spending chain, people spend 75 percent of the additional income they receive, and the process continues—with consumption growing in every round.

Where does it all end? Does it all end? The answer is that, yes, it does eventually end—with GDP a total of $4 million higher than it was before Microhard spent the original $1 million. The multiplier is indeed 4.

Table 4 displays the basis for this conclusion. In the table, "Round 1" represents Microhard's initial investment, which creates $1 million in income for construction workers. "Round 2" represents the construction workers' spending, which creates $750,000 in income for shopkeepers. The rest of the table proceeds accordingly; each entry in column 2 is 75 percent of the previous entry. Column 3 tabulates the running sum of column 2.

We see that after 10 rounds of spending, the initial $1 million investment has mushroomed to $3.77 million—and the sum is still growing. After 20 rounds, the total increase in GDP is more than $3.98 million—near its eventual value of $4 million. Although it takes quite a few rounds of spending before the multiplier chain nears 4, we see from the table that it hits 3 rather quickly. If each income recipient in the chain waits, say, two months before spending his new income, the multiplier will reach 3 in about ten months.

Figure 11 provides a graphical presentation of the numbers in the last column of Table 4. Notice how the multiplier builds up rapidly at first and then tapers off to approach its ultimate value (4 in this example) gradually.

*Table 4*

**The Multiplier Spending Chain**

| (1) | (2) | (3) |
|---|---|---|
| Round Number | Spending in This Round | Cumulative Total |
| 1 | $1,000,000 | $1,000,000 |
| 2 | 750,000 | 1,750,000 |
| 3 | 562,500 | 2,312,500 |
| 4 | 421,875 | 2,734,375 |
| 5 | 316,406 | 3,050,781 |
| 6 | 237,305 | 3,288,086 |
| 7 | 177,979 | 3,466,065 |
| 8 | 133,484 | 3,599,549 |
| 9 | 100,113 | 3,699,662 |
| 10 | 75,085 | 3,774,747 |
| ⋮ | ⋮ | ⋮ |
| 20 | 4,228 | 3,987,317 |
| ⋮ | ⋮ | ⋮ |
| "Infinity" | 0 | 4,000,000 |

*Figure 11*

**How the Multiplier Builds**

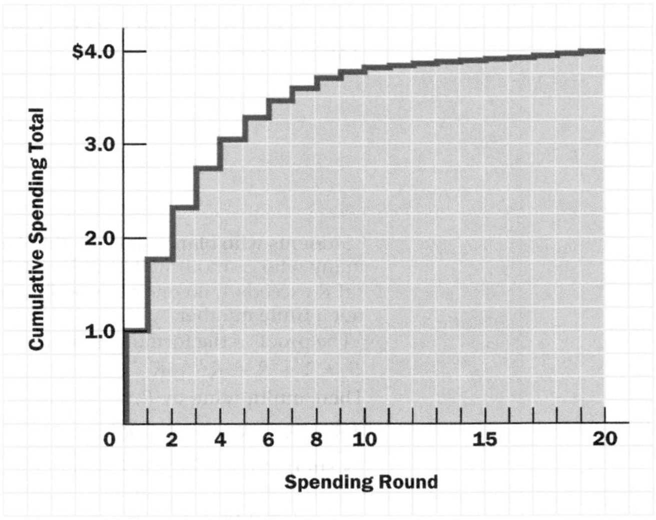

NOTE: Amounts are in millions of dollars.

And, of course, all this operates exactly the same—but in the opposite direction—when spending falls. For example, when the housing boom in America ended in 2006, spending on new houses (a component of *I*) began to decline. As this process progressed, the slow-down in housing created a negative multiplier effect on everything from appliances and furniture to carpeting and insulation. Indeed, the downward pull of housing on overall GDP was so strong that it pushed the whole economy into a recession.

### 9-6c  Algebraic Statement of the Multiplier

Figure 11 and Table 4 probably make a persuasive case that the multiplier eventually reaches 4, but for the remaining skeptics, we offer a simple algebraic proof.[5] Most of you learned about something called an *infinite geometric progression* in high school. This term refers to an infinite series of numbers, each one of which is a fixed fraction of the previous one. The fraction is called the *common ratio*. A geometric progression beginning with 1 and having a common ratio of 0.75 looks like this:

$$1 + 0.75 + (0.75)^2 + (0.75)^3 + \ldots$$

More generally, a geometric progression beginning with 1 and having a common ratio $R$ would be

$$1 + R + R^2 + R^3 + \ldots$$

A simple formula enables us to sum such a progression as long as $R$ is less than 1.[6] The formula is[7]

$$\text{Sum of infinite geometric progression} = \frac{1}{1 - R}$$

We now recognize that the multiplier chain in Table 4 is just an infinite geometric progression with 0.75 as its common ratio. That is, each \$1 that Microhard spends leads to a $(0.75) \times \$1$ expenditure by construction workers, which in turn leads to a $(0.75) \times (0.75 \times \$1) = (0.75)^2 \times \$1$ expenditure by the shopkeepers, and so on. Thus, for each initial dollar of investment spending, the progression is

$$1 + 0.75 + (0.75)^2 + (0.75)^3 + (0.75)^4 + \ldots$$

Applying the formula for the sum of such a series, we find that

$$\text{Multiplier} = \frac{1}{1 - 0.75} = \frac{1}{0.25} = 4$$

Notice how this result can be generalized. If we did not have a specific number for the marginal propensity to consume, but simply called it MPC, the geometric progression in Table 4 would have been

$$1 + \text{MPC} + (\text{MPC})^2 + (\text{MPC})^3 + \ldots$$

---

[5] Students who blanch at the sight of algebra should not be put off. Anyone who can balance a checkbook (even many who cannot!) will be able to follow the argument.

[6] If $R$ exceeds 1, no one can possibly sum it—not even with the aid of a modern computer—because the sum is not a finite number.

[7] The proof of the formula is simple. Let the symbol $S$ stand for the (unknown) sum of the series:

$S = 1 + R + R^2 + R^3 + \ldots$

Then, multiplying by $R$,

$RS = R + R^2 + R^3 + R^4 + \ldots$

By subtracting $RS$ from $S$, we obtain

$S - RS = 1 \text{ or } S = \dfrac{1}{1 - R}$

This progression uses the MPC as its common ratio. Applying the formula for summing a geometric progression to this more general case gives us the following general result:

**Oversimplified Multiplier Formula**

$$\text{Multiplier} = \frac{1}{1 - \text{MPC}}$$

We call this formula "oversimplified" because it ignores many factors that are important in the real world. You can begin to appreciate just how unrealistic the oversimplified formula is by considering some real numbers for the U.S. economy. The MPC is more than 0.90. From our oversimplified formula, then, it would seem that the multiplier should be at least

$$\text{Multiplier} = \frac{1}{1 - 0.90} = \frac{1}{0.1} = 10$$

In fact, the actual multiplier for the U.S. economy is less than 2. That is quite a discrepancy!

This discrepancy does not mean that anything we have said about the multiplier so far is incorrect. Our story is simply incomplete. As we progress through this and subsequent chapters, you will learn several reasons why the multiplier in the United States is less than 2 even though the country's MPC is more than 0.90. One such reason relates to *international trade*—in particular, the fact that a country's imports depend on its GDP. We deal with this complication in Appendix B to this chapter. A second factor is *inflation*, a complication we will address in the next chapter. A third factor is *income taxation*, a point we will emphasize in Chapter 11. The last important reason arises from the *financial system* and, after we discuss money and banking in Chapters 12 and 13, we will explain in Chapter 15 how the financial system influences the multiplier. As you will see, each of these factors *reduces* the size of the multiplier. So:

> The multiplier in the real world cannot be calculated accurately with the oversimplified multiplier formula. The actual multiplier is much *lower* than the formula suggests.

## 9-7 THE MULTIPLIER IS A GENERAL CONCEPT

Although we have used business investment to illustrate the workings of the multiplier, it should be clear from the logic that *any* increase in spending can kick off a multiplier chain. To see how the multiplier works when the process is initiated by an upsurge in consumer spending, we must distinguish between two types of change in consumer spending.

To do so, look back at Figure 4. When C rises because income rises—that is, when consumers move outward *along a fixed consumption function*—we call the increase in C an **induced increase in consumption**. (See the blue arrows in the figure.) When C rises because the entire consumption function *shifts upward* (such as from $C_0$ to $C_2$ in the figure), we call it an **autonomous increase in consumption**. The name indicates that consumption changes *independently* of income. The discussion of the consumption function in Chapter 8 pointed out that a number of events, such as a change in the value of the stock market, can initiate such a shift.

If consumer spending were to rise autonomously by $200 billion, we would revise our table of aggregate demand to look like Table 5. Comparing this new table to Table 3, we note that each entry in column 2 is $200 billion *higher* than the corresponding entry in Table 3 (because consumption is higher), and each entry in column 3 is $200 billion *lower* (because in this case investment is only $900 billion).

Column 6, the expenditure schedule, is identical in both tables, so the equilibrium level of income is clearly $Y = \$6,800$ billion once again. The initial rise of $200 billion in *consumer* spending leads to an eventual rise of $800 billion in GDP, just as it did in the case of higher *investment* spending. In fact, Figure 10 applies directly to this case once we note that the upward shift is now caused by an autonomous change in C rather than in I. The multiplier for autonomous changes in consumer spending, then, is also 4 (= $800/$200).

The reason is straightforward. It does not matter who injects an additional dollar of spending into the economy—investors or consumers. Whatever the source of the extra

An **induced increase in consumption** is an increase in consumer spending that stems from an increase in consumer incomes. It is represented on a graph as a movement along a fixed consumption function.

An **autonomous increase in consumption** is an increase in consumer spending without any increase in consumer incomes. It is represented on a graph as a shift of the entire consumption function.

*Table 5*

**Total Expenditure after Consumers Decide to Spend $200 Billion More**

| (1) | (2) | (3) | (4) | (5) | (6) |
|---|---|---|---|---|---|
| Income (Y) | Consumption (C) | Investment (I) | Government Purchases (G) | Net Exports (X − IM) | Total Expenditure |
| 4,800 | 3,200 | 900 | 1,300 | −100 | 5,300 |
| 5,200 | 3,500 | 900 | 1,300 | −100 | 5,600 |
| 5,600 | 3,800 | 900 | 1,300 | −100 | 5,900 |
| 6,000 | 4,100 | 900 | 1,300 | −100 | 6,200 |
| 6,400 | 4,400 | 900 | 1,300 | −100 | 6,500 |
| 6,800 | 4,700 | 900 | 1,300 | −100 | 6,800 |
| 7,200 | 5,000 | 900 | 1,300 | −100 | 7,100 |

NOTE: Figures are in billions of dollars per year.

dollar, 75 percent of it will be re-spent if the MPC is 0.75, and the recipients of this second round of spending will, in turn, spend 75 percent of their additional income, and so on. That continued spending constitutes the multiplier process. Thus a $200 billion increase in government purchases (G) or in net exports (X − IM) would have the same multiplier effect as depicted in Figure 10. The multipliers are identical because the logic behind them is identical.

The idea that changes in G have multiplier effects on GDP will play a central role in the discussion of government stabilization policy that begins in Chapter 11. So it is worth noting here that:

> Changes in the volume of government purchases of goods and services will change the equilibrium level of GDP on the demand side in the same direction, but by a multiplied amount.

To cite a recent example, additional *federal* government spending was used to fight the recession in 2009 by boosting the G component of C + I + G + (X − IM). This spending presumably had a multiplier effect on GDP, but part of that effect was canceled by declines in state and local government purchases. (See the accompanying box "The Multiplier in Practice.")

Applying the same multiplier idea to exports and imports teaches us another important lesson: *Booms and recessions tend to be transmitted across national borders.* Why is that? Suppose a boom abroad raises GDPs in foreign countries. With rising incomes, foreigners will buy more American goods—which means that U.S. exports will increase. An increase in our exports will, via the multiplier, raise GDP in the United States. By this mechanism,

## The Multiplier in Practice

One component of the so-called "fiscal stimulus" package recommended by President Barack Obama and enacted by Congress in early 2009 was an increase in real federal G, which rose from $1,180 billion (at annual rates) in the first quarter of 2009 to $1,285 billion by the third quarter of 2010—an increase of $105 billion in a year and a half. According to the logic of this chapter, this additional spending should have had a multiplied effect on GDP. Did it? Maybe not, for two reasons.

The first is simple arithmetic. While the federal government was busy raising its G, hard-pressed state and local governments were *cutting* theirs. Those cutbacks directly offset about 40 percent of the increase in federal G.

As to the rest, real-world estimates of the multiplier for G in the United States tend to cluster in the 0.8 to 1.5 range—not the much higher numbers suggested by the Oversimplified Multiplier Formula. (Remember, it is greatly oversimplified!) Using a multiplier of 1.2 and a net increase in G of $63 billion leads to an estimated impact on real GDP of just $76 billion, less than the original $105 billion and only about 0.5 percent of GDP at the time. That's not exactly a strong dose of medicine.[8]

David R. Frazier Photolibrary, Inc. / Alamy

---

[8] It is important to note that the 2009 fiscal package contained much more than just increases in G.

rapid economic growth abroad contributes to rapid economic growth here. And, of course, the same mechanism also operates in reverse. Thus:

> **The GDPs of the major economies are linked by trade. A boom in one country tends to raise its imports and hence push up exports and GDP in other countries. Similarly, a recession in one country tends to pull down GDP in other countries.**

A painful illustration of this idea came in late 2008, when a sharp decline of U.S. GDP after the failure of the giant investment bank Lehman Brothers quickly led to recessions in many other countries.

## 9-8 THE MULTIPLIER AND THE AGGREGATE DEMAND CURVE

One last mechanical point about the multiplier: Recall that income-expenditure diagrams such as Figure 3 can be drawn only for a given price level. Different price levels lead to different total expenditure curves. This means that our oversimplified multiplier formula indicates *the increase in real GDP demanded that would occur if the price level were fixed*. Graphically, this means that it measures the *horizontal shift* of the economy's aggregate demand curve.

Figure 12 illustrates this conclusion by supposing that the price level that underlies Figure 3 is $P = 100$. The top panel simply repeats Figure 10 and shows how an increase in investment spending from $900 to $1,100 billion leads to an increase in GDP from $6,000 to $6,800 billion.

The bottom panel shows two downward-sloping aggregate demand curves. The first, labeled $D_0 D_0$, depicts the situation when investment is $900 billion. Point $E_0$ on this curve corresponds exactly to point $E_0$ in the top panel. It indicates that, at the given price level $(P = 100)$, the equilibrium quantity of GDP demanded is $6,000 billion. The second aggregate demand curve, $D_1 D_1$, depicts the situation after investment has risen to $1,100 billion. Point $E_1$ on this curve indicates that the equilibrium quantity of GDP demanded when $P = 100$ has risen to $6,800 billion, which corresponds exactly to point $E_1$ in the top panel.

As Figure 12 shows, the horizontal distance between the two aggregate demand curves is exactly equal to the increase in real GDP shown in the income-expenditure diagram—in this case, $800 billion. Thus:

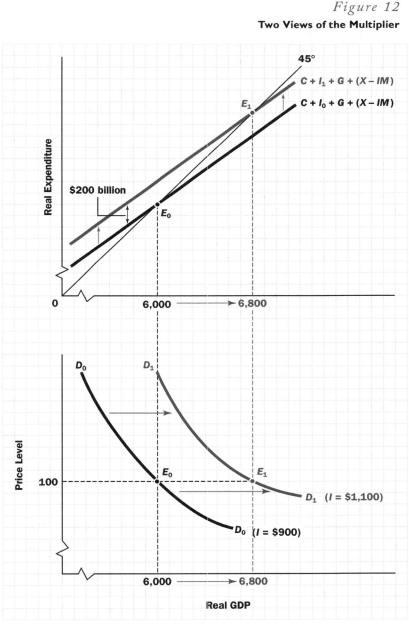

*Figure 12*

**Two Views of the Multiplier**

NOTE: Figures are in billions of dollars per year.

An autonomous increase in spending leads to a horizontal shift of the aggregate demand curve by an amount given by the oversimplified multiplier formula.

So everything we have just learned about the multiplier applies to *shifts of the economy's aggregate demand curve*. If businesses decide to increase their investment spending, if the consumption function shifts upward, or if the government or foreigners decide to buy more goods, then the aggregate demand curve moves horizontally to the right—as indicated in Figure 12. If any of these variables moves downward instead, the aggregate demand curve moves horizontally to the left.

Thus, the economy's aggregate demand curve cannot be expected to stand still for long. Autonomous changes in one or another of the four components of total spending will cause it to move around. But to understand the *consequences* of such shifts of aggregate demand, we must bring the *aggregate supply* curve back into the picture. That is the task for the next chapter.

## Summary

1. The **equilibrium level of GDP on the demand side** is the level at which total spending just equals production. Because total spending is the sum of consumption, investment, government purchases, and net exports, the condition for equilibrium is $Y = C + I + G + (X - IM)$.

2. Output levels below **equilibrium** are bound to rise because when spending exceeds output, firms will see their inventory stocks being depleted and will react by stepping up production.

3. Output levels above equilibrium are bound to fall because when total spending is insufficient to absorb total output, inventories will pile up and firms will react by curtailing production.

4. The determination of the equilibrium level of GDP on the demand side can be portrayed on a convenient **income-expenditure diagram** as the point at which the **expenditure schedule**—defined as the sum of $C + I + G + (X - IM)$—crosses the 45° line. The 45° line is significant because it marks off points at which spending and output are equal—that is, at which $Y = C + I + G + (X - IM)$, which is the basic condition for equilibrium.

5. An income-expenditure diagram can be drawn only for a specific price level. Thus, the equilibrium GDP so determined depends on the price level.

6. Because higher prices reduce the purchasing power of consumers' wealth, they reduce total expenditures on the 45° line diagram. Equilibrium real GDP demanded is therefore lower when prices are higher.

This downward-sloping relationship is known as the **aggregate demand curve**.

7. Equilibrium GDP can be above or below **potential GDP**, which is defined as the GDP that would be produced if the labor force were fully employed.

8. If equilibrium GDP exceeds potential GDP, the difference is called an **inflationary gap**. If equilibrium GDP falls short of potential GDP, the resulting difference is called a **recessionary gap**.

9. Such gaps can occur because of the problem of **coordination failure**: The saving that consumers want to do at full-employment income levels may differ from the investing that investors want to do.

10. Any **autonomous increase in expenditure** has a multiplier effect on GDP; that is, it increases GDP by more than the original increase in spending.

11. The **multiplier** effect occurs because one person's additional expenditure constitutes a new source of income for another person, and this additional income leads to still more spending, and so on.

12. The multiplier is the same for an autonomous increase in consumption, investment, government purchases, or net exports.

13. A simple formula for the multiplier says that its numerical value is $1/(1 - MPC)$. This formula is much too simple to give accurate results, however.

14. Rapid (or sluggish) economic growth in one country contributes to rapid (or sluggish) growth in other countries because one country's imports are other countries' exports.

## Key Terms

aggregate demand curve     174

autonomous increase in consumption   183

coordination failure     179

equilibrium   171

expenditure schedule     172

full-employment level of GDP (or potential GDP)     178

income-expenditure (or 45° line) diagram     174

induced increase in consumption     183

induced investment     173

inflationary gap     177

multiplier     179

recessionary gap     177

$Y = C + I + G + (X - IM)$     173

## Test Yourself

1. From the following data, construct an expenditure schedule on a piece of graph paper. Then use the income-expenditure ($45°$ line) diagram to determine the equilibrium level of GDP.

| Income | Consumption | Investment | Government Purchases | Net Exports |
|---|---|---|---|---|
| $3,600 | $3,220 | $240 | $120 | $40 |
| 3,700 | 3,310 | 240 | 120 | 40 |
| 3,800 | 3,400 | 240 | 120 | 40 |
| 3,900 | 3,490 | 240 | 120 | 40 |
| 4,000 | 3,580 | 240 | 120 | 40 |

Now suppose investment spending rises to $260, and the price level is fixed. By how much will equilibrium GDP increase? Derive the answer both numerically and graphically.

2. From the following data, construct an expenditure schedule on a piece of graph paper. Then use the income-expenditure ($45°$ line) diagram to determine the equilibrium level of GDP. Compare your answer with your answer to the previous question.

| Income | Consumption | Investment | Government Purchases | Net Exports |
|---|---|---|---|---|
| $3,600 | $3,280 | $180 | $120 | $40 |
| 3,700 | 3,340 | 210 | 120 | 40 |
| 3,800 | 3,400 | 240 | 120 | 40 |
| 3,900 | 3,460 | 270 | 120 | 40 |
| 4,000 | 3,520 | 300 | 120 | 40 |

3. Suppose that investment spending is always $250, government purchases are $100, net exports are always $50, and consumer spending depends on the price level in the following way:

| Price Level | Consumer Spending |
|---|---|
| 90 | $740 |
| 95 | 720 |
| 100 | 700 |
| 105 | 680 |
| 110 | 660 |

On a piece of graph paper, use these data to construct an aggregate demand curve. Why do you think this example supposes that consumption declines as the price level rises?

4. **(More difficult)**[9] Consider an economy in which the consumption function takes the following simple algebraic form:

$$C = 300 + 0.75DI$$

and in which investment ($I$) is always $900 and net exports are always −$100. Government purchases are fixed at $1,300 and taxes are fixed at $1,200. Find the equilibrium level of GDP, and then compare your answer to Table 1 and Figure 2. (*Hint:* Remember that disposable income is GDP minus taxes: $DI = Y - T = Y - 1,200$.)

5. **(More difficult)** Keep everything the same as in Test Yourself Question 4 *except* change investment to $I = $1,100$. Use the equilibrium condition $Y = C + I + G + (X - IM)$ to find the equilibrium level of GDP on the demand side. (In working out the answer, assume the price level is fixed.) Compare your answer to Table 3 and Figure 10. Now compare your answer to the answer to Test Yourself Question 4. What do you learn about the multiplier?

6. **(More difficult)** An economy has the following consumption function:

$$C = 200 + 0.8DI$$

The government budget is balanced, with government purchases and taxes both fixed at $1,000. Net exports are $100. Investment is $600. Find equilibrium GDP. What is the multiplier for this economy? If $G$ rises by $100, what happens to $Y$? What happens to $Y$ if both $G$ and $T$ rise by $100 at the same time?

7. Use both numerical and graphical methods to find the multiplier effect of the following shift in the consumption function in an economy in which investment is always $220, government purchases are always $100, and net exports are always −$40. (*Hint:* What is the marginal propensity to consume?)

| Income | Consumption before Shift | Consumption after Shift |
|---|---|---|
| $1,080 | $ 880 | $ 920 |
| 1,140 | 920 | 960 |
| 1,200 | 960 | 1,000 |
| 1,260 | 1,000 | 1,040 |
| 1,320 | 1,040 | 1,080 |
| 1,380 | 1,080 | 1,120 |
| 1,440 | 1,120 | 1,160 |
| 1,500 | 1,160 | 1,200 |
| 1,560 | 1,200 | 1,240 |

---

[9] The answer to this question is provided in Appendix A to this chapter.

## Discussion Questions

1. For more than 30 years, imports have consistently exceeded exports in the U.S. economy. Many people consider this imbalance to be a major problem. Does this chapter give you any hints about why? (You may want to discuss this issue with your instructor. You will learn more about it in later chapters.)

2. Look back at the income-expenditure diagram in Figure 3 and explain why some level of real GDP other than $6,000 (say, $5,000 or $7,000) is *not* an equilibrium on the demand side of the economy. Do not give a mechanical answer to this question. Explain the economic mechanism involved.

3. Does the economy this year seem to have an inflationary gap or a recessionary gap? (If you do not know the answer from news reports, ask your instructor.)

4. Try to remember where you last spent a dollar. Explain how this dollar will lead to a multiplier chain of increased income and spending. (Who received the dollar? What will he or she do with it?)

## Appendix A  *The Simple Algebra of Income Determination and the Multiplier*

The model of demand-side equilibrium that the chapter presented graphically and in tabular form can also be handled with some simple algebra. Written as an equation, the consumption function in our example is

$$C = 300 + 0.75DI$$
$$= 300 + 0.75(Y - T)$$

because, by definition, $DI = Y - T$. This is simply the equation of a straight line with a slope of 0.75 and an intercept of $300 - 0.75T$. Because $T = 1,200$ in our example, the intercept is $-600$ and the equation can be written more simply as follows:

$$CD = -600 + 0.75Y$$

Investment in the example was assumed to be 900, regardless of the level of income, government purchases were 1,300, and net exports were $-100$. So the sum $C + I + G + (X - IM)$ is

$$C+I+G+(X-IM)=-600+0.75Y+900+1,300-100$$
$$= 1,500 + 0.75Y$$

This equation describes the expenditure curve in Figure 3. Because the equilibrium quantity of GDP demanded is defined by

$$Y = C + I + G + (X - IM)$$

we can solve for the equilibrium value of $Y$ by substituting $1,500 + 0.75\,Y$ for $C + I + G + (X - IM)$ to get

$$Y = 1,500 + 0.75Y$$

To solve this equation for $Y$, first subtract $0.75Y$ from both sides to get

$$0.25Y = 1,500$$

Then divide both sides by 0.25 to obtain the answer:

$$Y = 6,000$$

This, of course, is precisely the solution we found by graphical and tabular methods in the chapter.

We can easily generalize this algebraic approach to deal with any set of numbers in the equations. Suppose that the consumption function is:

$$C = a + bDI = a + b(Y - T)$$

(In the example, $a = 300$, $T = 1,200$, and $b = 0.75$.) Then the equilibrium condition that $Y = C + I + G + (X - IM)$ implies that

$$Y = a + bDI + I + G + (X - IM)$$
$$= a + bY - bT + I + G + (X - IM)$$

Subtracting $bY$ from both sides leads to

$$(1 - b)Y = a - bT + I + G + (X - IM)$$

and dividing through by $1 - b$ gives

$$Y = \frac{a - bT + I + G + (X - IM)}{1 - b}$$

This formula is valid for any numerical values of $a$, $b$, $T$, $G$, $I$, and $(X - IM)$ (so long as $b$ is between 0 and 1).

From this formula, it is easy to derive the oversimplified multiplier formula algebraically and to show that it applies equally well to a change in investment, autonomous consumer spending, government purchases, or net exports. To do so, suppose that *any* of the symbols in the numerator of the multiplier formula increases by one unit. Then GDP would rise from the previous formula to

$$Y = \frac{a - bT + I + G + (X - IM) + 1}{1 - b}$$

By comparing this expression with the previous expression for $Y$, we see that a one-unit change in any component of spending changes equilibrium GDP by

$$\text{Change in } Y = \frac{a - bT + I + G + (X - IM) + 1}{1 - b}$$
$$-\frac{a - bT + I + G + (X - IM)}{1 - b}$$

or

$$\text{Change in } Y = \frac{1}{1 - b}$$

Recalling that $b$ is the marginal propensity to consume, we see that this is precisely the oversimplified multiplier formula.

## Test Yourself

1. Find the equilibrium level of GDP demanded in an economy in which investment is always $300, net exports are always –$50, the government budget is balanced with purchases and taxes both equal to $400, and the consumption function is described by the following algebraic equation:

$$C = 150 + 0.75DI$$

   (*Hint:* Remember that $DI = Y - T$.)

2. Referring to Test Yourself Question 1, do the same for an economy in which investment is $250, net exports are zero, government purchases and taxes are both $400, and the consumption function is as follows:

$$C = 250 + 0.5DI$$

3. In each of these cases, how much saving is there in equilibrium? (*Hint:* Income not consumed must be saved.) Is saving equal to investment?

4. Imagine an economy in which consumer expenditure is represented by the following equation:

$$C = 50 + 0.75DI$$

Imagine also that investors want to spend $500 at every level of income ($I = $500$), net exports are zero ($X - IM = 0$), government purchases are $300, and taxes are $200.

   a. What is the equilibrium level of GDP?

   b. If potential GDP is $3,000, is there a recessionary or inflationary gap? If so, how much?

   c. What will happen to the equilibrium level of GDP if investors become optimistic about the country's future and raise their investment to $600?

   d. After investment has increased to $600, is there a recessionary or inflationary gap? How much?

5. Fredonia has the following consumption function:

$$C = 100 + 0.8DI$$

Firms in Fredonia always invest $700 and net exports are zero, initially. The government budget is balanced with spending and taxes both equal to $500.

   a. Find the equilibrium level of GDP.

   b. How much is saved? Is saving equal to investment?

   c. Now suppose that an export-promotion drive succeeds in raising net exports to $100. Answer (a) and (b) under these new circumstances.

## Discussion Questions

1. Explain the basic logic behind the multiplier in words. Why does it require $b$, the marginal propensity to consume, to be between 0 and 1?

2. (**More difficult**) What would happen to the multiplier analysis if $b = 0$? If $b = 1$?

## Appendix B  *The Multiplier with Variable Imports*

In the chapter, we assumed that net exports were a fixed number, $-100$ in the example. In fact, a nation's imports vary along with its GDP for a simple reason: Higher GDP leads to higher incomes, some of which is spent on foreign goods. Thus:

**Our imports rise as our GDP rises and fall as our GDP falls.**

Similarly, our *exports* are the *imports* of other countries, so it is to be expected that our exports depend on *their* GDPs, not on our own. Thus:

**Our exports are relatively insensitive to our own GDP, but are quite sensitive to the GDPs of other countries.**

This appendix derives the implications of these rather elementary observations. In particular, it shows that once we recognize the dependence of a nation's imports on its GDP,

**International trade lowers the value of the multiplier.**

To see why, we begin with Table 6, which adapts the example of our hypothetical economy to allow imports to depend on GDP. Columns 1 through 4 are the same as in Table 1; they show $C$, $I$, and $G$ at alternative levels of GDP. Columns 5 and 6 record revised assumptions about the behavior of exports and imports. Exports are fixed at $650 billion regardless of GDP. But imports are assumed to rise by $60 billion for every $400 billion rise in GDP, which is a simple numerical example of the idea that imports depend on GDP. Column 7 subtracts imports from exports to get net exports, $(X - IM)$, and column 8 adds up the four components of total expenditure, $C + I + G + (X + IM)$.

The equilibrium, you can see, occurs at $Y = \$6,000$ billion, just as it did in the chapter.

Figures 13 and 14 display the same conclusion graphically. The upper panel of Figure 13 shows that exports are fixed at $650 billion regardless of GDP, whereas imports increase as GDP rises, just as in Table 6. The difference between exports and imports, or net exports, is positive until GDP approaches $5,300 billion, and negative once GDP surpasses that amount. The bottom panel of Figure 13 shows the subtraction explicitly by displaying *net exports*. It shows clearly that

**Net exports decline as GDP rises.**

Figure 14 carries this analysis over to the $45°$ line diagram. We begin with the familiar $C + I + G + (X - IM)$ line in black. Previously, we simply assumed that net exports were fixed at –$100 billion regardless of GDP. Now that we have amended our model to note that net exports decline as GDP rises, the sum $C + I + G + (X - IM)$ rises more slowly than we previously assumed. This change is shown by the blue line in Figure 14. Note that it is less steep than the black line.

Let us now consider what happens if exports rise by $160 billion while imports remain as in Table 6. Table 7 shows that equilibrium now occurs at a GDP of $Y = \$6,400$ billion. Naturally, higher exports have raised domestic GDP, but consider the magnitude. A $160 billion increase in exports (from $650 billion to $810 billion) leads to an increase of $400 billion in GDP (from $6,000 billion to $6,400 billion). So the multiplier is 2.5 ($= \$400/\$160$).[10]

*Table 6*

**Equilibrium Income with Variable Imports**

| (1) | (2) | (3) | (4) | (5) | (6) | (7) | (8) |
|---|---|---|---|---|---|---|---|
| Gross Domestic Product (Y) | Consumer Expenditures (C) | Investment (I) | Government Purchases (G) | Exports (X) | Imports (IM) | Net Exports (X − IM) | Total Expenditure [C + I = G + (X − IM)] |
| 4,800 | 3,000 | 900 | 1,300 | 650 | 570 | +80 | 5,280 |
| 5,200 | 3,300 | 900 | 1,300 | 650 | 630 | +20 | 5,520 |
| 5,600 | 3,600 | 900 | 1,300 | 650 | 690 | −40 | 5,760 |
| 6,000 | 3,900 | 900 | 1,300 | 650 | 750 | −100 | 6,000 |
| 6,400 | 4,200 | 900 | 1,300 | 650 | 810 | −160 | 6,240 |
| 6,800 | 4,500 | 900 | 1,300 | 650 | 870 | −220 | 6,480 |
| 7,200 | 4,800 | 900 | 1,300 | 650 | 930 | −280 | 6,720 |

NOTE: Figures are in billions of dollars per year.

[10] EXERCISE: Construct a version of Table 6 to show what would happen if imports rose by $160 billion at every level of GDP and exports remained at $650 billion. You should be able to show that the new equilibrium would be $Y = \$5,600$.

*Figure 13*

**The Dependence of Net Exports on GDP**

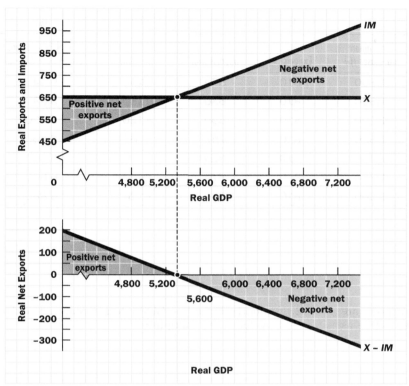

NOTE: Figures are in billions of dollars per year.

This same conclusion is shown graphically in Figure 15, where the line $C + I + G + (X_0 - IM)$ represents the original expenditure schedule and the line $C + I + G + (X_1 - IM)$ represents the expenditure schedule after the $160 billion increase in exports. Equilibrium shifts from point $E$ to point $A$, and GDP rises by $400 billion.

Notice that the multiplier in this example is 2.5, whereas in the chapter, with net exports taken to be a fixed number, it was 4. This simple example illustrates the general point made earlier: *International trade lowers the numerical value of the multiplier.* Why is this so? Because, in an open economy, any autonomous increase in spending is partly dissipated in purchases of foreign goods, which creates additional income for *foreigners* rather than for domestic citizens.

Thus, international trade gives us the first of what will eventually be several reasons why the oversimplified multiplier formula overstates the true value of the multiplier.

*Figure 14*

**Equilibrium GDP with Variable Imports**

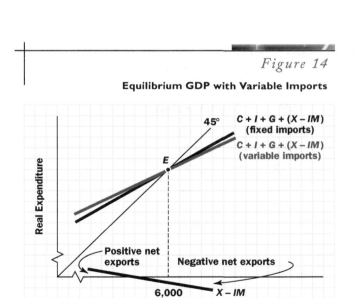

*Figure 15*

**The Multiplier with Variable Imports**

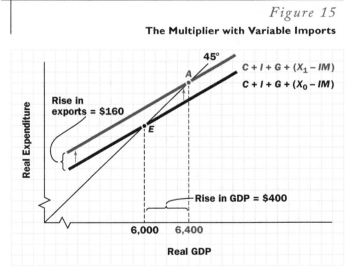

*Table 7*

**Equilibrium Income after a $160 Billion Increase in Exports**

| (1) | (2) | (3) | (4) | (5) | (6) | (7) | (8) |
|---|---|---|---|---|---|---|---|
| Gross Domestic Product (Y) | Consumer Expenditures (C) | Investment (I) | Government Purchases (G) | Exports (X) | Imports (IM) | Net Exports (X − IM) | Total Expenditure [C + I = G + (X − IM)] |
| 4,800 | 3,000 | 900 | 1,300 | 810 | 570 | +240 | 5,440 |
| 5,200 | 3,300 | 900 | 1,300 | 810 | 630 | +180 | 5,680 |
| 5,600 | 3,600 | 900 | 1,300 | 810 | 690 | +120 | 5,920 |
| 6,000 | 3,900 | 900 | 1,300 | 810 | 750 | +60 | 6,160 |
| 6,400 | 4,200 | 900 | 1,300 | 810 | 810 | 0 | 6,400 |
| 6,800 | 4,500 | 900 | 1,300 | 810 | 870 | −60 | 6,640 |
| 7,200 | 4,800 | 900 | 1,300 | 810 | 930 | −120 | 6,880 |

NOTE: Figures are in billions of dollars per year.

## Summary

1. Because imports rise as GDP rises, while exports are insensitive to (domestic) GDP, net exports decline as GDP rises.

2. If imports depend on GDP, international trade reduces the value of the multiplier.

## Test Yourself

1. Suppose exports and imports of a country are given by the following:

| GDP | Exports | Imports |
|---|---|---|
| $2,500 | $400 | $250 |
| 3,000 | 400 | 300 |
| 3,500 | 400 | 350 |
| 4,000 | 400 | 400 |
| 4,500 | 400 | 450 |
| 5,000 | 400 | 500 |

Calculate net exports at each level of GDP

2. If domestic expenditure (the sum of $C + I + G$ in the economy described in Test Yourself Question 1) is as shown in the following table, construct a $45°$ line diagram and locate the equilibrium level of GDP.

| GDP | Domestic Expenditures |
|---|---|
| $2,500 | $3,100 |
| 3,000 | 3,400 |
| 3,500 | 3,700 |
| 4,000 | 4,000 |
| 4,500 | 4,300 |
| 5,000 | 4,600 |

3. Now raise exports to $650 and find the equilibrium again. How large is the multiplier?

# BRINGING IN THE SUPPLY SIDE: UNEMPLOYMENT *AND* INFLATION?

# 10

*We might as well reasonably dispute whether it is the upper or the under blade of a pair of scissors that cuts a piece of paper, as whether value is governed by [demand] or [supply].*

ALFRED MARSHALL

The previous chapter taught us that the position of the economy's total expenditure $(C + I + G + X - IM)$ schedule governs whether the economy will experience a recessionary or an inflationary gap. Too little spending leads to a *recessionary gap*. Too much leads to an *inflationary gap*. Which sort of gap actually occurs is of considerable practical importance, because a recessionary gap translates into *unemployment* whereas an inflationary gap leads to *inflation*.

The tools we have provided so far are not sufficient to tell us which sort of gap will arise because, as we learned, the position of the expenditure schedule depends on the price level—and the price level is determined by *both* aggregate demand *and* aggregate supply. So this chapter has a clear task: to bring the supply side of the economy back into the picture.

Doing so will put us in a position to deal with the crucial question raised, but not answered, in earlier chapters: Does the economy have an efficient self-correcting mechanism? We shall see that the answer is "yes, but": Yes, but it works slowly. The chapter will also enable us to explain the vexing problem of *stagflation*—the simultaneous occurrence of high unemployment *and* high inflation—which plagued the economy in the 1980s and which some people worry may stage a comeback.

## CONTENTS

 Puzzle | *What Causes Stagflation?*

When the inflation rate briefly topped 5 percent in 2008, the financial press was full of stories about the possible return of the dread disease of stagflation, which plagued the U.S. economy in the 1970s and early 1980s. Many economists, however, found this talk unduly alarming. (And, in fact, inflation fell very quickly.)

On the surface, the very existence of stagflation—the combination of economic *stagnation* and *inflation*—seems to contradict one of our *Ideas for Beyond the Final Exam* from Chapter 1: that there is a *trade-off* between inflation and unemployment. Low unemployment is supposed to make the inflation rate rise, and high unemployment is supposed to make inflation fall. (This trade-off will be discussed in more detail in Chapter 17.) Yet things do not always work out this way. For example, both unemployment and inflation rose together in the early 1980s and then fell together in the late 1990s. Why is that? What determines whether inflation and unemployment move in opposite directions (as in the trade-off view) or in the same direction (as during a stagflation)? This chapter will provide some answers.

## 10-1   THE AGGREGATE SUPPLY CURVE

In earlier chapters, we noted that aggregate demand is a schedule, not a fixed number. The idea that the quantity of real gross domestic product (GDP) that will be demanded depends on the price level is summarized in the economy's *aggregate demand curve*. Precisely the same point applies to *aggregate supply:* The concept of aggregate supply does not refer to a fixed number, but rather to a schedule—an *aggregate supply curve.*

The volume of goods and services that profit-seeking enterprises provide depends on the prices they obtain for their outputs, on wages and other production costs, on the capital stock, on the state of technology, and on other things. The relationship between the price level and the quantity of real GDP supplied, *holding all other determinants of quantity supplied constant,* is called the economy's **aggregate supply curve**.

> The **aggregate supply curve** shows, for each possible price level, the quantity of goods and services that all the nation's businesses are willing to produce during a specified period of time, holding all other determinants of aggregate quantity supplied constant.

Figure 1 shows a typical aggregate supply curve. It slopes upward, meaning that as prices rise, more output is produced, *other things held constant.* Let's see why.

### 10-1a   Why the Aggregate Supply Curve Slopes Upward

Most producers are motivated by profit. The profit made by producing and selling an additional unit of output is simply the difference between the price at which it is sold and the unit cost of production:

$$\text{Unit profit} = \text{Price} - \text{Unit cost}$$

The response of output to a rising price level—which is what the slope of the aggregate supply curve shows—depends on the response of costs. So the question is: Do costs rise along with selling prices, or not?

The answer is: Some do, and some do not. Many of the prices that firms pay for labor and other inputs remain fixed for lengthy periods of time—although certainly not forever. For example, workers and firms often enter into long-term labor contracts that set nominal wages a year or more in advance. Even where no explicit contracts exist, wage rates typically adjust only annually. Similarly, a variety of material inputs are delivered to firms under long-term contracts at prearranged prices.

This fact is significant because firms decide how much to produce by comparing their selling prices with their costs of production. If the selling prices of the firm's products rise while its nominal wages and other factor costs are fixed, production becomes more profitable, and firms will presumably produce more.

A simple example will illustrate the idea. Suppose that, given the scale of its operations, a particular firm needs one

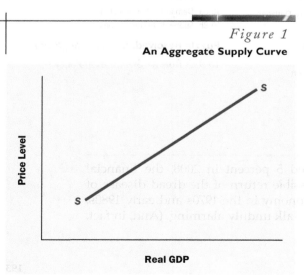

*Figure 1*

**An Aggregate Supply Curve**

Price Level

S

S

Real GDP

hour of labor to manufacture one additional gadget. If the gadget sells for $9, workers earn $8 per hour, and the firm has no other costs, its profit on this unit will be

$$\text{Unit profit} = \text{Price} - \text{Unit cost}$$
$$= \$9 - \$8 = \$1$$

If the price of the gadget then rises to $10, but wage rates remain constant, the firm's profit on the unit becomes

$$\text{Unit profit} = \text{Price} - \text{Unit cost}$$
$$= \$10 - \$8 = \$2$$

With production more profitable, the firm presumably will supply more gadgets.

The same process operates in reverse. If selling prices fall while input costs remain relatively fixed, profit margins will be squeezed and production cut back. This behavior is summarized by the upward slope of the aggregate supply curve: Production rises when the price level (henceforth, $P$) rises, and falls when $P$ falls. In other words,

> The aggregate supply curve slopes upward because firms normally can purchase labor and other inputs at prices that are fixed for some period of time. Thus, higher selling prices for output make production more attractive.[1]

The phrase "for some period of time" alerts us to the important fact that the aggregate supply curve may not stand still for long. If wages or prices of other inputs change, as they surely will during inflationary times, then the aggregate supply curve will shift.

## 10-1b  Shifts of the Aggregate Supply Curve

So let's consider what happens when input prices change.

**The Nominal Wage Rate**  The most obvious determinant of the position of the aggregate supply curve is the *nominal wage rate* (also called the "money wage rate"). Wages are the major element of cost in the economy, accounting for about 70 percent of all input costs. Because higher wage rates mean higher production costs, they spell lower profits at any given selling prices. This is why companies have been known to dig in their heels when workers demand increases in wages and benefits—or even to insist on give-backs by workers under extreme circumstances. For example, negotiations between Verizon Communications and two unions broke down in August 2011 over a list of wage and benefit concessions demanded by the company—leading to a two-week strike by 45,000 repairers and installers.

Returning to our hypothetical example, consider what would happen to a gadget producer if the nominal wage rate rose to $8.75 per hour while the gadget's price remained $9. Unit profit would decline from $1 to

$$\$9.00 - \$8.75 = \$0.25$$

With profits thus squeezed, the firm would probably cut back on production.

Thus, a wage increase leads to a decrease in aggregate quantity supplied at current prices. Graphically, the aggregate supply curve *shifts to the left* (or inward) when nominal wages rise, as shown in Figure 2. In this diagram, firms are willing to supply $6,000 billion in goods and services at a price level of 100 when wages are low (point *A*). But after

---

[1] There are both differences and similarities between the *aggregate* supply curve and the *microeconomic* supply curves studied in Chapter 4. Both are based on the idea that quantity supplied depends on how output prices move relative to input prices. But the aggregate supply curve pertains to the behavior of *the overall price level*, whereas a microeconomic supply curve pertains to the *price of some particular commodity*.

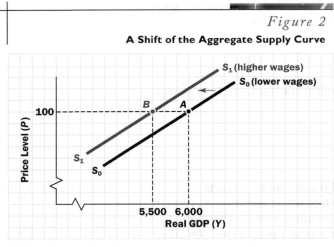

*Figure 2*

**A Shift of the Aggregate Supply Curve**

NOTE: Amounts are in billions of dollars per year.

wages increase, the same firms are willing to supply only $5,500 billion at this price level (point *B*). By similar reasoning, the aggregate supply curve will shift to the right (or outward) if wages fall.

> An increase in the nominal wage shifts the aggregate supply curve *inward*, meaning that the quantity supplied at any price level *declines*. A decrease in the nominal wage shifts the aggregate supply curve *outward*, meaning that the quantity supplied at any price level *increases*.

The logic behind these shifts is straightforward. Consider a wage increase, as indicated by the blue line in Figure 2. With selling prices fixed, at 100 in the illustration, an increase in the nominal wage means that wages rise *relative to prices*. In other words, the *real wage rate* rises. It is this increase in the firms' real production costs that induces a contraction of quantity supplied—from *A* to *B* in the diagram.

**Prices of Other Inputs** In this regard, wages are not unique. An increase in the price of *any* input that firms buy will shift the aggregate supply curve in the same way. That is,

> The aggregate supply curve is shifted to the left (or inward) by an increase in the price of any input to the production process, and it is shifted to the right (or outward) by any decrease.

The logic is exactly the same.

Although producers use many inputs other than labor, the one that has attracted the most attention in recent decades is energy. Increases in the prices of imported energy, such as those that took place during the political turmoil in the Middle East in 2011, push the aggregate supply curve inward—as shown in Figure 2. By the same token, decreases in the price of oil, such as the ones we enjoyed in the fall of 2014, shift the aggregate supply curve outward.

**Technology and Productivity** Another factor that can shift the aggregate supply curve is the state of technology. The idea that technological progress increases the **productivity** of labor is familiar from earlier chapters. Holding wages constant, any increase of productivity will *decrease* business costs, improve profitability, and encourage more production.

**Productivity** is the amount of output produced by a unit of input.

Once again, our gadget example will help us understand how this process works. Suppose the price of a gadget stays at $9 and the hourly wage rate stays at $8, but gadget workers become more productive. Specifically, suppose the labor input required to manufacture a gadget *decreases* from one hour (which costs $8) to three-quarters of an hour (which costs just $6). Then unit profit rises from $1 to

$$\$9 - (\tfrac{3}{4})\,\$8 = \$9 - \$6 = \$3$$

The lure of higher profits should induce gadget manufacturers to increase output—which is, of course, why companies constantly strive to raise their productivity. In brief, we have concluded that

> Improvements in productivity shift the aggregate supply curve outward.

We can therefore interpret Figure 2 as illustrating the effect of a *decline* in productivity. As we mentioned in Chapter 7, a slowdown in productivity growth was a persistent problem for the United States for more than two decades starting in 1973.

**Available Supplies of Labor and Capital** The last determinants of the position of the aggregate supply curve are the ones we studied in Chapter 7: The bigger the economy—as measured by its available supplies of labor and capital—the more it is capable of producing. Thus:

> **As the labor force grows or improves in quality, and as investment increases the capital stock, the aggregate supply curve shifts *outward* to the right, meaning that more output can be produced at any given price level.**

So, for example, the great investment boom of the late 1990s, by boosting the supply of capital, left the U.S. economy with a greater capacity to produce goods and services—that is, it shifted the aggregate supply curve outward. The investment slump of the late 2000s did precisely the reverse.

These factors, then, are the major "other things" that we hold constant when drawing an aggregate supply curve: nominal wage rates, prices of other inputs (such as energy), technology, labor force, and capital stock. A change in the price level moves the economy *along a given supply curve*, but a change in any of these determinants of aggregate quantity supplied *shifts the entire supply schedule.*

## 10-2 EQUILIBRIUM OF AGGREGATE DEMAND AND SUPPLY

The previous chapter taught us that the price level is a crucial determinant of whether equilibrium GDP falls below full employment (a "recessionary gap"), precisely at full employment, or above full employment (an "inflationary gap"). We can now analyze which type of gap, if any, will occur in any particular case by combining the analysis of aggregate supply we just completed with the analysis of aggregate demand from the last chapter.

Figure 3 displays the simple mechanics. In the figure, the aggregate demand curve *DD* and the aggregate supply curve *SS* intersect at point *E*, where real GDP (*Y*) is $6,000 billion and the price level (*P*) is 100. As can be seen in the graph, at any higher price level, such as 120, aggregate quantity supplied would exceed aggregate quantity demanded. In such a case, there would be a glut of goods on the market as firms found themselves unable to sell all their output. As inventories piled up, firms would compete more vigorously for the available customers, thereby forcing prices down. Both the price level and production would fall.

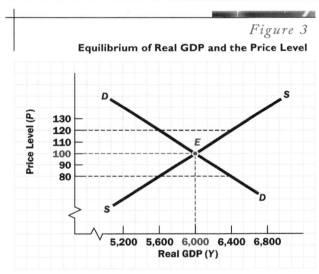

*Figure 3*

**Equilibrium of Real GDP and the Price Level**

NOTE: Amounts are in billions of dollars per year.

At any price level lower than 100, such as 80, quantity demanded would exceed quantity supplied. There would be a shortage of goods on the market. With inventories disappearing and customers knocking on their doors, firms would be encouraged to raise prices. The price level would rise, and so would output. Only when the price level is 100 are the quantities of real GDP demanded and supplied equal. Therefore, only the combination $P = 100$ and $Y = \$6,000$ is an equilibrium.

Table 1 illustrates this conclusion via a tabular analysis similar to the one in the previous chapter. Columns (1) and (2) constitute an aggregate demand schedule corresponding to curve *DD* in Figure 3. Columns (1) and (3) constitute an aggregate supply schedule corresponding to aggregate supply curve *SS*.

*Table 1*

**Determination of the Equilibrium Price Level**

| (1) | (2) | (3) | (4) | (5) |
|---|---|---|---|---|
| Price Level | Aggregate Quantity Demanded | Aggregate Quantity Supplied | Balance of Supply and Demand | Prices will be: |
| 80 | $6,400 | $5,600 | Demand exceeds supply | Rising |
| 90 | 6,200 | 5,800 | Demand exceeds supply | Rising |
| 100 | 6,000 | 6,000 | Demand equals supply | Unchanged |
| 110 | 5,800 | 6,200 | Supply exceeds demand | Falling |
| 120 | 5,600 | 6,400 | Supply exceeds demand | Falling |

NOTE: Quantities are in billions of dollars.

The table clearly shows that equilibrium occurs only at $P = 100$. At any other price level, aggregate quantities supplied and demanded would be unequal, with consequent upward or downward pressure on prices. For example, at a price level of 90, customers demand \$6,200 billion worth of goods and services, but firms wish to provide only \$5,800 billion. In this case, the price level is too low and will be forced upward. Conversely, at a price level of 110, quantity supplied (\$6,200 billion) exceeds quantity demanded (\$5,800 billion), implying that the price level must fall.

## 10-3  INFLATION AND THE MULTIPLIER

To illustrate the importance of the slope of the aggregate supply curve, we return to a question we posed in the previous chapter: What happens to equilibrium GDP if the aggregate demand curve shifts outward? We saw there that such changes have a *multiplier* effect, and we noted that the actual numerical value of the multiplier is considerably smaller than suggested by the oversimplified multiplier formula. One of the reasons, variable imports, was discussed in Appendix B to Chapter 9. We are now in a position to understand a second reason:

**Inflation reduces the size of the multiplier.**

The basic idea is simple. The last chapter described a multiplier process in which one person's spending becomes another person's income, which leads to further spending by the second person, and so on. But this story was confined to the *demand* side of the economy; it ignored what is likely to be happening on the *supply* side. The question is: As the multiplier process unfolds, will firms meet the additional demand without raising prices?

An upward-sloping aggregate supply curve means that the answer is no: More goods will be provided only at *higher* prices. Thus, as the multiplier chain progresses, pulling income and employment up, prices will rise, too. This development, as we know from earlier chapters, will reduce net exports and dampen consumer spending because rising prices erode the purchasing power of consumers' wealth. As a consequence, the multiplier chain will not proceed as far as it would have in the absence of inflation.

How much inflation results from a given rise in aggregate demand? How much is the multiplier chain muted by inflation? The answers to these questions depend on the *slope* of the economy's aggregate supply curve.

For a concrete example, let us return to the \$200 billion increase in investment spending studied in the previous chapter. There we found (see especially Figure 10) that \$200 billion in additional investment spending would eventually lead to \$800 billion in additional spending *if the price level did not rise*, meaning that the analysis there tacitly assumed that *the aggregate supply curve was horizontal*—which is not so. The slope of the aggregate supply curve tells us how any expansion of aggregate demand gets apportioned between higher output and higher prices.

Figure 4 shows the \$800-billion rightward shift of the aggregate demand curve, from $D_0D_0$ to $D_1D_1$, that we derived from the oversimplified multiplier formula in the last chapter. We see that, as the economy's equilibrium moves from point $E_0$ to point $E_1$ (instead of to point $A$), real GDP does not rise by \$800 billion. Instead, rising prices cancel out part of the increase in quantity demanded. As a result, output rises from \$6,000 billion to \$6,400 billion—an increase of only \$400 billion. Thus, in the example, inflation reduces the multiplier from \$800/\$200 = 4 to \$400/\$200 = 2. In general:

> **As long as the aggregate supply curve slopes upward, any increase in aggregate demand will push up the price level. Higher prices, in turn, will drain off some of the higher real demand by eroding the purchasing power of consumer wealth and by reducing net exports. Thus, inflation reduces the value of the multiplier below what is suggested by the oversimplified formula.**

Notice also that the price level in this example has been pushed up (from 100 to 120, or by 20 percent) by the rise in investment demand. This, too, is a general result:

> As long as the aggregate supply curve slopes upward, any outward shift of the aggregate demand curve will increase the price level.

The economic behavior behind these results is certainly not surprising. Faced with large increases in quantity demanded at their original prices, firms respond in two natural ways: They raise production (so that real GDP rises), and they raise prices (so the price level rises). This rise in the price level, in turn, reduces the purchasing power of the bank accounts and bonds held by consumers, and they, too, react in the natural way: They reduce their spending. Such a reaction amounts to a movement *along* aggregate demand curve $D_1 D_1$ in Figure 4 from point $A$ to point $E_1$.

Figure 4 also shows us exactly where the oversimplified multiplier formula goes wrong. By ignoring the effects of the higher price level, the oversimplified formula erroneously pretends that the economy moves horizontally from point $E_0$ to point $A$—which it will not do unless the aggregate supply curve is horizontal. As the diagram clearly shows, output actually rises by less, which is one reason why the oversimplified formula exaggerates the size of the multiplier.

*Figure 4*

**Inflation and the Multiplier**

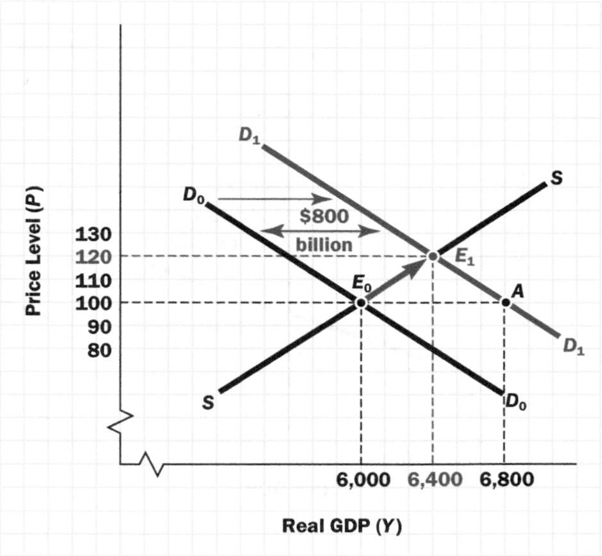

NOTE: Amounts are in billions of dollars per year.

## 10-4   RECESSIONARY AND INFLATIONARY GAPS REVISITED

With this understood, let us now reconsider the question we have been deferring: Will equilibrium occur at, below, or beyond potential GDP?

We could not answer this question in the last chapter because we had no way to determine the equilibrium price level, and therefore no way to tell which type of gap, if any, would arise. The aggregate supply-and-demand analysis presented in this chapter now gives us what we need, but we find that our answer is the same: Anything can happen.

Why? Because Figure 3 tells us nothing about where *potential* GDP falls. The factors determining the economy's capacity to produce were discussed extensively in Chapter 7, but that analysis could leave potential GDP above the $6,000 billion equilibrium level or below it. Depending on the locations of the aggregate demand and aggregate supply curves, then, we can reach equilibrium *beyond* potential GDP (an **inflationary gap**), exactly *at* potential GDP, or *below* potential GDP (a **recessionary gap**). All three possibilities are illustrated in Figure 5.

The three upper panels duplicate diagrams from the last chapter.[2] Start with the upper-middle panel, in which the expenditure schedule $C + I_1 + G + (X - IM)$ crosses the 45° line exactly at potential GDP—which we take to be $7,000 billion in the example. Equilibrium is at point $E$, with neither a recessionary nor an inflationary gap. Now suppose that total expenditures either *fall* to $C + I_0 + G + (X - IM)$ (producing the upper-left diagram) or *rise* to $C + I_2 + G + (X - IM)$ (producing the upper-right diagram). As we read across the page from left to right, we see equilibrium occurring with a recessionary gap, exactly at full employment, or with an inflationary gap—depending on the position of the $C + I + G + (X - IM)$ line. In the previous chapter, we learned of several variables that might shift the expenditure schedule up and down in this way. One of them was the price level.

The **inflationary gap** is the amount by which equilibrium real GDP exceeds the full-employment level of GDP.

The **recessionary gap** is the amount by which the equilibrium level of real GDP falls short of potential GDP.

---

[2] Recall that each income-expenditure diagram considers *only* the demand side of the economy by treating the price level as fixed.

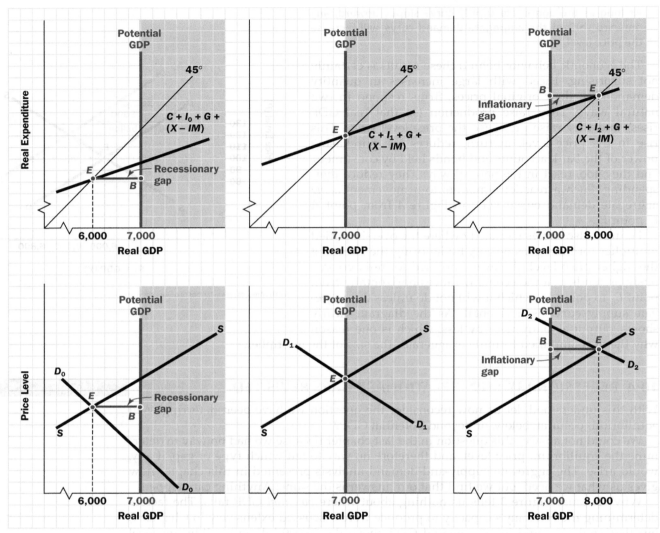

Figure 5

**Recessionary and Inflationary Gaps Revisited**

NOTE: Real GDP is in billions of dollars per year.

The three lower panels portray the same three cases differently—in a way that can tell us what the price level will be. These diagrams consider *both* aggregate demand *and* aggregate supply, and therefore simultaneously determine *both* the equilibrium price level *and* the equilibrium GDP at point *E*—where the aggregate supply curve *SS* and the aggregate demand curve *DD* intersect. However, there are still three possibilities.

In the lower-left panel, aggregate demand is too low to provide jobs for the entire labor force, so we have a recessionary gap equal to distance *EB*, or $1,000 billion. This situation corresponds precisely to the one depicted on the income-expenditure diagram immediately above it.

In the lower-right panel, aggregate demand is so high that the economy reaches equilibrium beyond potential GDP. An inflationary gap equal to *BE*, or $1,000 billion, arises, just as in the diagram immediately above it.

In the lower-middle panel, the aggregate demand curve $D_1D_1$ is at just the right level to produce an equilibrium at potential GDP. There is neither an inflationary gap nor a recessionary gap, as in the diagram just above it.

It may seem, therefore, that we have simply restated our previous conclusions. But, in fact, we have done much more. For now that we have studied the determination of the equilibrium price level, we are able to examine how the economy adjusts to either a recessionary gap or an inflationary gap. Specifically, because wages are fixed in the short run, any one of the three cases depicted in Figure 5 can occur. In the long run, however, wages will adjust to labor market conditions, which will shift the aggregate supply curve. It is to that adjustment that we now turn.

## 10-5  ADJUSTING TO A RECESSIONARY GAP: DEFLATION OR UNEMPLOYMENT?

Suppose the economy starts with a recessionary gap—that is, at an equilibrium *below* potential GDP—as depicted in the lower-left panel of Figure 5. Such a situation might be caused, for example, by inadequate consumer spending or by anemic investment spending. When the last recession started at the end of 2007, the U.S. economy was pretty close to full employment. Then the recessionary gap began to grow, reaching a peak estimated to be around 8 percent of GDP by late 2009—the biggest GDP gap this country has seen since the 1930s. What happens when an economy experiences such a recessionary gap?

With equilibrium GDP below potential (point *E* in Figure 6), jobs will be difficult to find. The ranks of the unemployed will exceed the number of people who are jobless because of moving, changing occupations, and so on. In the terminology of Chapter 6, the economy will experience a considerable amount of *cyclical unemployment*. Businesses, by contrast, will have little trouble finding workers, and their current employees will be eager to hang on to their jobs.

Such an environment makes it difficult for workers to win wage increases. Indeed, in extreme situations, wages may even fall—thereby shifting the aggregate supply curve *outward*. (Remember: An aggregate supply curve is drawn for a *given* nominal wage.) But as the aggregate supply curve shifts to the right—eventually moving from $S_0S_0$ to $S_1S_1$ in Figure 6—prices decline and the recessionary gap shrinks. By this process, deflation gradually erodes the recessionary gap—leading eventually to an equilibrium at potential GDP (point *F* in Figure 6).

There is an important catch, however. In our modern economy, this adjustment process proceeds slowly—painfully slowly. Our brief review of the historical record in Chapter 5 showed that the history of the United States includes several examples of *deflation* before World War II but none since then. Not even severe recessions have forced average prices and wages down except fleetingly, although they have certainly slowed inflation to a crawl. The only protracted episode of deflation in any advanced economy since the 1930s is the experience of Japan over roughly the last 20 years, and even there the rate of deflation was quite mild. That said, deflation in Japan was still painful, and some observers have worried that the United States and Europe could be headed the way of Japan.

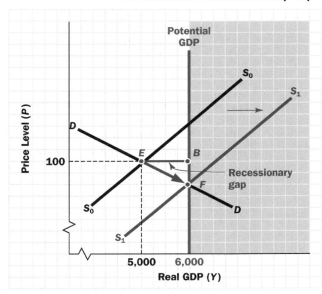

*Figure 6*

**The Elimination of a Recessionary Gap**

NOTE: Amounts are in billions of dollars per year.

## 10-5a  Why Nominal Wages and Prices Won't Fall (Easily)

Exactly why wages and prices rarely fall in a modern economy is still a subject of intense debate among economists. Some economists emphasize institutional factors such as minimum wage laws, union contracts, and a variety of government regulations that place legal floors under particular wages and prices. Because most of these institutions are of recent vintage, this theory successfully explains why wages and prices fall less frequently now than they did before World War II. But only a small fraction of the U.S. economy is subject to legal restraints on wage and price cutting. So it seems doubtful that legal

## Recessionary Gaps in Practice

According to the theory taught in this book, a recessionary gap should bring inflation down—but it takes a while and it doesn't always work. The accompanying table lists the ten years over the past half century with the largest recessionary gaps. (Notice, sadly, that six of the ten were 2008 through 2013.) In each case, the table shows the *change* in the core CPI inflation rate from the indicated year *to the following year*. Although that is a pretty crude "test" of the theory, the data by and large support the idea that large recessionary gaps pull inflation down. There are just three small exceptions: Inflation rose from 1983 to 1984 and then again from 2010 to 2011 to 2012, despite large GDP gaps.

| Year | Recessionary Gap (percent of GDP)* | Change in Inflation (from year shown to following year, in percentage points)** |
|------|-----------------------------------|--------------------------------------------------------------------------------|
| 1975 | 4.3 | −2.6 |
| 1982 | 7.0 | −3.4 |
| 1983 | 5.5 | +1.0 |
| 1991 | 3.1 | −1.2 |
| 2008 | 2.7 | 0 |
| 2009 | 7.1 | −0.6 |
| 2010 | 6.1 | −0.7 |
| 2011 | 5.8 | +0.7 |
| 2012 | 4.6 | +0.4 |
| 2013 | 4.5 | −0.3 |

*Authors' calculations from Congressional Budget Office data.
**Bureau of Labor Statistics.

restrictions can take us far in explaining sluggish wage-price adjustments in the United States. In Europe, however, such institutional factors are much more important.

Other observers suggest that workers have a profound psychological resistance to accepting a wage reduction. This theory has roots in psychological research that finds people to be far more aggrieved when they suffer an absolute loss (e.g., a nominal wage reduction) than when they receive only a small gain. So, for example, businesses may find it relatively easy to cut the rate of wage increase from 3 percent to 1 percent, but excruciatingly hard to cut it from 1 percent to *minus* 1 percent. This psychological theory has the ring of truth. Think how you might react if your boss announced he was cutting your hourly wage rate. You might quit, or you might devote less care to your job. If the boss suspects you will react this way, he may be reluctant to cut your wage. In recent decades, genuine wage reductions have been rare enough to be newsworthy. Although no one doubts that wage cuts can damage morale, the psychological theory still must explain why the resistance to wage cuts apparently started only after World War II.

A third explanation is based on a fact we emphasized in Chapter 5: At least until the Great Recession, business cycles have been less severe in the postwar period than they were in the prewar period. As workers and firms came to realize that recessions would not turn into depressions, the argument goes, they decided to wait out the bad times rather than accept wage or price reductions that they would later regret.

Yet another theory is based on the old adage, "You get what you pay for." The idea is that workers differ in productivity but that the productivities of individual employees are difficult to identify. Firms therefore worry that, if they reduce wages, they will lose their best employees—because these workers have the best opportunities elsewhere in the economy. Rather than take this chance, the argument goes, firms prefer to maintain high wages even in recessions.

Other theories have been proposed, but none commands a clear majority of professional opinion. Regardless of the cause, however, we might as well accept it as a well-established fact that wages fall only sluggishly, if at all, when demand is weak.

The implications of this rigidity are serious, for a recessionary gap cannot cure itself without some deflation. And if wages and prices will not fall, recessionary gaps like *EB* in Figure 6 will linger for a long time. That is,

> When aggregate demand is low, the economy may get stuck with a recessionary gap for a long time. If wages and prices fall very slowly, the economy will endure a prolonged period of production below potential GDP.

## 10-5b  Does the Economy Have a Self-Correcting Mechanism?

A situation like the one just described would, presumably, not last forever. As the recession lengthened and perhaps deepened, more and more workers would be unable to find jobs at the prevailing "high" wages. Eventually, their need to be employed would overwhelm their resistance to wage cuts. Firms, too, would become increasingly willing to cut prices as the period of weak demand persisted and managers became convinced that the slump was not merely a temporary aberration. Prices and wages did, in fact, fall in many countries during the Great Depression of the 1930s; they fell in Japan for almost 20 years, albeit slowly; and some wages have even fallen in the United States since the Great Recession.

Thus, starting from a recessionary gap, the economy will *eventually* return to potential GDP—following a path something like the blue arrow from *E* to *F* in Figure 6. For this reason, economists think of the vertical line at potential GDP as representing the economy's long-run aggregate supply curve. But this "long run" might be long indeed.

Nowadays, political leaders of both parties—and in virtually all countries—believe that it is folly to wait for falling wages and prices to eliminate a recessionary gap. They agree that government action is both necessary and appropriate under recessionary conditions. Nevertheless, vocal—and highly partisan—debate continues over how much and what kind of intervention is warranted, as has been abundantly clear in this country since 2008. One reason for the disagreement is that the **self-correcting mechanism** does operate—if only weakly—to cure recessionary gaps.

The economy's **self-correcting mechanism** refers to the way money wages react to either a recessionary gap or an inflationary gap. Wage changes shift the aggregate supply curve and therefore change equilibrium GDP and the equilibrium price level.

## 10-5c  An Example from Recent History: Deflation Worries in the United States

The world's largest economy has flirted with deflation several times in the past dozen years or so, in each case driven there by recessionary gaps.

To measure the economy's underlying inflationary tendencies, most analysts focus on what is called "core" inflation, meaning the inflation rate for all items other than food and energy. Core inflation, as measured by the Consumer Price Index (CPI), fell steadily in the weak economy of 2002 and 2003, eventually dropping to barely over 1 percent per annum by late 2003. Watching the inflation rate fall then, more and more people began worrying about deflation. It didn't happen, however. But after rising as high as 2.5 percent as the economy strengthened, the inflation rate fell steadily again during and after the Great Recession. Core CPI inflation first dropped below 1 percent in September 2010, and remained there for the rest of the year. Later, as the recessionary gap persisted, inflation drifted down again in 2013–2014. Qualitatively, this is just the sort of behavior the theoretical model of the self-correcting mechanism predicts.

## 10-6  ADJUSTING TO AN INFLATIONARY GAP: INFLATION

Let us now turn to what happens when the economy finds itself *beyond* full employment—that is, with an *inflationary* gap like that shown in Figure 7. When the aggregate supply curve is $S_0S_0$ and the aggregate demand curve is *DD*, the economy will initially reach equilibrium (point *E*) with an inflationary gap, shown by the segment *BE*.

By most reckonings, the last time we had a situation like this in the United States was in 2006 and 2007, when the unemployment rate dipped below 5 percent. What should happen under such circumstances? As we shall see now, the tight labor market should produce an inflation that eventually eliminates the inflationary gap, although perhaps in a slow and painful way.

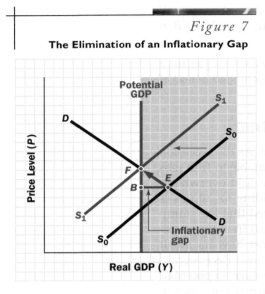

*Figure 7*

**The Elimination of an Inflationary Gap**

When equilibrium GDP exceeds potential GDP, jobs are plentiful and labor is in great demand. Firms are likely to have trouble recruiting new workers or even holding onto their old ones as other firms try to lure workers away with higher wages.

Rising nominal wages add to business costs, which shift the aggregate supply curve to the left. As the aggregate supply curve moves from $S_0S_0$ to $S_1S_1$ in Figure 7, the inflationary gap shrinks. In other words, inflation eventually erodes the inflationary gap and brings the economy to an equilibrium at potential GDP (point $F$).

There is a straightforward way of looking at the economics behind this process. Inflation arises because buyers are demanding more output than the economy can produce at normal operating rates. To paraphrase an old cliché, there is too much demand chasing too little supply. Such an environment encourages price hikes.

Ultimately, rising prices eat away at the purchasing power of consumers' wealth, forcing them to cut back on consumption, as explained in Chapter 8. In addition, exports fall and imports rise, as we learned in Chapter 9. Eventually, aggregate quantity demanded is scaled back to the economy's capacity to produce—graphically, the economy moves back along curve $DD$ from point $E$ to point $F$. At this point the self-correcting process stops. In brief:

If aggregate demand is exceptionally high, the economy may reach a short-run equilibrium above full employment (an *inflationary gap*). When this occurs, the tight situation in the labor market soon forces nominal wages to rise. Because rising wages increase business costs, prices increase; there is inflation. As higher prices cut into consumer purchasing power and net exports, the inflationary gap begins to close.

As the inflationary gap closes, output falls and prices continue to rise. When the gap is finally eliminated, a long-run equilibrium is established with a higher price level and with GDP equal to potential GDP.

This scenario is precisely what seems to have happened in 2006 and 2007. Because the U.S. economy had a small inflationary gap then, economists expected inflation to rise slightly—which it did, before receding again. Remember that *the self-correcting mechanism takes time* because wages and prices do not adjust quickly. Thus, although an inflationary gap sows the seeds of its own destruction, the seeds germinate slowly. So, once again, policy makers may want to speed up the process.

## 10-6a  Demand Inflation and Stagflation

Simple as it is, this model of how the economy adjusts to an inflationary gap teaches us a number of important lessons about inflation in the real world. First, Figure 7 reminds us that the real culprit is *too much aggregate demand* relative to potential GDP. The aggregate demand curve is initially so high that it intersects the aggregate supply curve well beyond full employment. The resulting intense demand for goods and labor pushes prices and wages higher. Although aggregate demand in excess of potential GDP is not the only possible cause of inflation, it certainly is the cause in our example.

Nonetheless, business managers and journalists may blame inflation on rising wages. In a superficial sense, of course, they are right, because higher wages do indeed lead firms to raise product prices. But in a deeper sense they are wrong. Both rising wages and rising prices are symptoms of the same underlying malady: too much aggregate demand. Blaming labor for inflation in such a case is a bit like blaming high doctor bills for making you ill.

Second, notice that output *falls* while prices *rise* as the economy adjusts from point $E$ to point $F$ in Figure 7. This is our first (but not our last) explanation of the phenomenon of **stagflation**—the conjunction of in*flation* and economic *stag*nation. Specifically:

**Stagflation** is inflation that occurs while the economy is growing slowly or having a recession.

A period of stagflation is part of the normal aftermath of a period of excessive aggregate demand.

It is easy to understand why. When aggregate demand is excessive, the economy will temporarily produce beyond its normal capacity. Labor markets tighten and wages rise. Machinery and raw materials may also become scarce and so start rising in price. Faced with higher costs, business firms quite naturally react by producing less and charging higher prices. That is stagflation.

## 10-6b  A U.S. Example

The stagflation that follows a period of excessive aggregate demand is, you will note, a rather benign form of the dreaded disease. After all, even though output is falling, it still remains above potential GDP. And unemployment is low. The U.S. economy last experienced such an episode at the end of the 1980s.

The long economic expansion of the 1980s brought the unemployment rate down to a 15-year low of 5 percent by March 1989. Almost all economists believed at the time that 5 percent was below the full-employment unemployment rate; that is, the U.S. economy had an *inflationary gap*. As the theory suggests, inflation began to accelerate—from 4.4 percent in 1988 to 4.6 percent in 1989 and then to 6.1 percent in 1990.

In the meantime, the economy was stagnating. Real GDP growth fell from 3.7 percent during 1989 to 1.9 percent in 1990 and down to −0.1 percent in 1991. Inflation was eating away at the inflationary gap, which had virtually disappeared by mid-1990, when the recession started. Yet inflation remained high through the early months of the recession. The U.S. economy was in a *stagflation* phase.

Our overall conclusion about the economy's ability to right itself seems to run something like this:

> The economy does, indeed, have a self-correcting mechanism that tends to eliminate either unemployment or inflation. But this mechanism works slowly and unevenly. In addition, its beneficial effects on either inflation or unemployment are sometimes swamped by strong forces pushing in the opposite direction (such as rapid increases or decreases in aggregate demand). Thus, the self-correcting mechanism is not always reliable.

## A Tale of Two Graduating Classes: 2007 versus 2009

Timing matters. The college graduates of 2007 were extremely fortunate. The unemployment rate was a low 4.5 percent in May and June of that year—close to its lowest level in a generation. With employers on the prowl for new hires, starting salaries rose and many graduating seniors had numerous job offers.

Things were starkly different for the Class of 2009 when it hit the job market just two years later. The U.S. economy was in a deep recession, and job offers were scarce. The unemployment rate in May–June 2009 averaged 9.5 percent. Most companies were less than eager to hire more workers, salary increases were modest, and "perks" were being trimmed. Similar job market conditions have greeted every graduating class since then, although the market has been gradually improving. The Class of 2009 had it worst.

This accident of birth meant that the college grads of 2009 started their working careers in a less advantageous position than their more fortunate brothers and sisters who graduated just two years earlier. What's more, research suggests that the initial job market advantage of the Class of 2007, compared to the Class of 2009, is likely to be maintained for many years to come.

## 10-7 STAGFLATION FROM A SUPPLY SHOCK

*Figure 8*

**Stagflation from an Adverse Shift in Aggregate Supply**

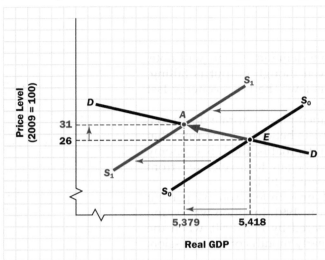

**Real GDP**

NOTE: Amounts are in billions of 2009 dollars per year.

We have just discussed the type of stagflation that follows in the wake of an inflationary boom. However, that is not what happened when unemployment and inflation both soared to shocking heights in the 1970s and early 1980s. This more virulent strain of stagflation had several causes, though the principal culprit was rising energy prices.

In 1973, the Organization of Petroleum Exporting Countries (OPEC) quadrupled the price of crude oil. American consumers soon found the prices of gasoline and home heating fuels increasing sharply, and American businesses saw an important cost of doing business—energy prices—rising drastically. OPEC struck again in the period 1979–1980, this time doubling the price of oil. Then the same thing happened again, albeit on a smaller scale, when Iraq invaded Kuwait in 1990. More recently, oil prices went on an irregular but impressive upward climb from 2002 to 2008 because of the Iraq war, other political issues in the Middle East and elsewhere, problems with refining capacity, and surging energy demand from China. Something similar happened again in 2011, spurred on by political turmoil in several Middle Eastern countries.

Higher energy prices, we observed earlier, shift the economy's aggregate supply curve *inward* in the manner shown in Figure 8. If the aggregate supply curve shifts inward, as it did following each of these "oil shocks," production will decline. To reduce demand to the available supply, prices will have to rise. The result is the worst of both worlds: falling production and rising prices.

This conclusion is displayed graphically in Figure 8, which shows an aggregate demand curve, *DD*, and two aggregate supply curves. When the supply curve shifts inward, the economy's equilibrium shifts from point *E* to point *A*. Thus, output falls while prices rise—which is precisely our definition of stagflation. In sum:

**Stagflation is the typical result of adverse shifts of the aggregate supply curve.**

The numbers used in Figure 8 are meant to indicate what the big energy shock in late 1973 might have done to the U.S. economy. Between 1973 (represented by supply curve $S_0S_0$ and point *E*) and 1975 (represented by supply curve $S_1S_1$ and point *A*), real GDP is shown falling by nearly 1 percent while the price level rises about 19 percent over the two years. The general lesson to be learned from the U.S. experience with supply shocks is both clear and important:

**The typical results of an adverse supply shock are lower output and higher inflation. This is one reason why the world economy was plagued by stagflation in the mid-1970s and early 1980s. And it can happen again if another series of supply-reducing events takes place.**

## 10-8 APPLYING THE MODEL TO A GROWING ECONOMY

You may have noticed that we have been using the simple aggregate supply and aggregate demand model since Chapter 5 to determine the equilibrium *price level* and the equilibrium *level of real GDP*, as depicted in several graphs in this chapter. But in the real world, neither the price level nor real GDP remains constant for long. Instead, both normally rise from one year to the next.

The growth process is illustrated in Figure 9, which is a scatter diagram of the U.S. price level and the level of real GDP for every year from 1972 to 2013. The labeled points show the clear upward march of the economy through time—toward higher prices and higher levels of output.

## Why Was There No Stagflation in 2006–2008?

As noted earlier, oil prices climbed steeply, if irregularly, from early 2002 through mid-2008. Yet this succession of "oil shocks" seems not to have caused much, if any, stagflation in the United States or in other industrial economies. This recent experience stands in sharp contrast to the 1970s and early 1980s. What was different this time around?

In truth, economists do not have a complete answer to this question, and research on it continues. But we do understand a few things. Most straightforwardly, the world has learned to live with less energy (relative to GDP). In the United States and many other countries, for example, the energy content of $1 worth of GDP is now less than half of what it was in the 1970s. That alone cuts the impact of an oil shock in half.

In addition, for reasons that are not entirely understood, the United States and other economies seemed to become less volatile from the mid-1980s until the Great Recession hit in late 2007. Sound macroeconomic policies probably contributed to the reduction in volatility, as did a variety of structural changes that made these economies more flexible.

Gary Gladstone/Getty Images

However, in the view of most researchers who have studied the question, part of the story is plain old good luck. Naturally, we cannot expect good luck to continue forever.

This upward trend is hardly mysterious, for both the aggregate demand curve and the aggregate supply curve normally shift to the right each year. Aggregate supply grows because more workers join the workforce each year and because investment and technology improve productivity (Chapter 7). Aggregate demand grows because a growing population generates more demand for both consumer and investment goods and because the government increases its purchases (Chapters 8 and 9). We can think of each point in Figure 9

*Figure 9*

**The Price Level and Real GDP in the United States, 1972–2013**

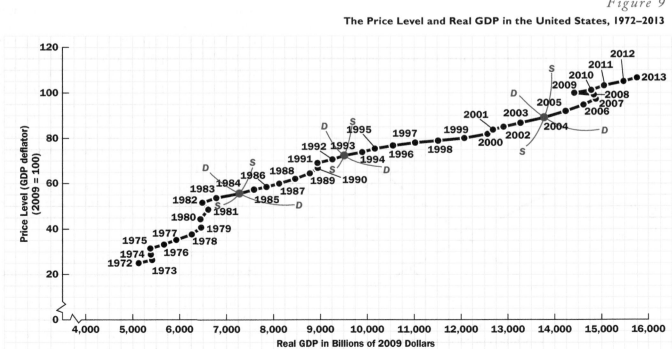

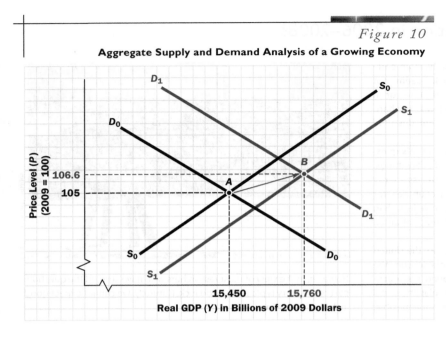

*Figure 10*

**Aggregate Supply and Demand Analysis of a Growing Economy**

Real GDP (Y) in Billions of 2009 Dollars

as the intersection of an aggregate supply curve and an aggregate demand curve for that particular year. To help you visualize this idea, the curves for 1984, 1993, and 2004 are sketched in the diagram.

Figure 10 is a more realistic version of the aggregate supply-and-demand diagram that illustrates how our theoretical model applies to a growing economy. We have chosen the numbers so that the black curves $D_0D_0$ and $S_0S_0$ roughly represent the year 2012, and the blue curves $D_1D_1$ and $S_1S_1$ roughly represent 2013—except that we use nice round numbers to facilitate computations. Thus, the equilibrium in 2012 was at point $A$, with a real GDP of $15,450 billion (in 2009 dollars) and a price level of 105. A year later, the equilibrium was at point $B$, with real GDP at $15,760 billion and the price level at 106.6. The maroon arrow in the diagram shows how equilibrium moved from 2012 to 2013. It points upward and to the right, meaning that both prices and output increased. In this case, the economy grew by about 2 percent and prices rose about 1.5 percent, which is just about what happened in the United States over that year.

## 10-8a  Demand-Side Fluctuations

Let us now use our theoretical model to rewrite history. Suppose that aggregate demand grew *faster* than it actually did between 2012 and 2013. What difference would this have made to the performance of the U.S. economy? Figure 11 provides answers. Here the black demand curve $D_0D_0$ is exactly the same as in the previous diagram, as are the two supply curves, indicating a given rate of aggregate supply growth. But the blue demand curve $D_2D_2$ lies farther to the right than the demand curve $D_1D_1$ in Figure 10. Equilibrium is at point $A$ in 2012 and point $C$ in 2013. Comparing point $C$ in Figure 11 with point $B$ in Figure 10, you can see that *both* output *and* prices would have increased more over the year—that is, the economy would have experienced faster *growth* and more *inflation*. This is generally what happens when the growth rate of aggregate demand speeds up.

> For any given growth rate of aggregate supply, a faster growth rate of aggregate demand will lead to more inflation and faster growth of real output.

Figure 12 illustrates the opposite case. Here we imagine that the aggregate demand curve shifted out *less* than in Figure 10. That is, the blue demand curve $D_3D_3$ in Figure 12 lies to the left of the demand curve $D_1D_1$ in Figure 10. The consequence, we see, is that the shift of the economy's equilibrium

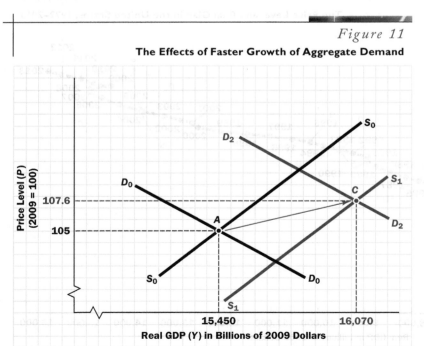

*Figure 11*

**The Effects of Faster Growth of Aggregate Demand**

Real GDP (Y) in Billions of 2009 Dollars

from 2012 to 2013 (from point *A* to point *E*) would have entailed *less inflation* and *slower growth* of real output than actually took place. Again, that is generally the case when aggregate demand grows more slowly.

> For any given growth rate of aggregate supply, a slower growth rate of aggregate demand will lead to less inflation and slower growth of real output.

Putting these two findings together gives us a clear prediction:

> If fluctuations in the economy's real growth rate from year to year arise primarily from variations in the rate at which *aggregate demand* increases, then the data should show the most rapid inflation occurring when output grows most rapidly and the slowest inflation occurring when output grows most slowly.

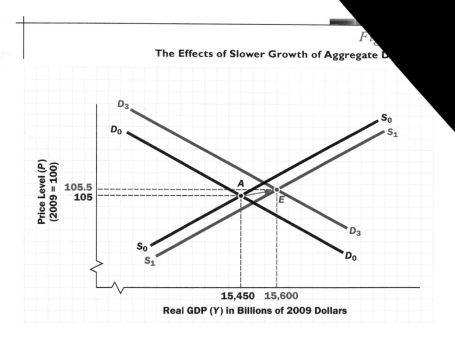

The Effects of Slower Growth of Aggregate D

Is it true? For the most part, yes. Our brief review of U.S. economic history back in Chapter 5 found that most episodes of high inflation came with rapid growth. But not all. Some surges of inflation resulted from the kinds of supply shocks we have considered in this chapter.

## 10-8b Supply-Side Fluctuations

For a stark historical example, let's return to the events of 1973 to 1975 that were depicted in Figure 8. But now let's add in something we ignored there: While the aggregate supply curve was shifting *inward* because of the oil shock, the aggregate demand was shifting *outward*. In Figure 13, the black aggregate demand curve $D_0 D_0$ and aggregate supply curve $S_0 S_0$ represent the economic situation in 1973. Equilibrium was at point *E*, with a price level of 26 (based on 2009 = 100) and real output of $5,418 billion. By 1975, the aggregate demand curve had shifted out to the position indicated by the blue curve $D_1 D_1$, but the aggregate supply curve had shifted *inward* from $S_0 S_0$ to the blue curve $S_1 S_1$. The equilibrium for 1975 (point *B* in the figure), therefore, wound up to the left of the equilibrium point for 1973 (point *E* in the figure). Real output declined slightly and prices—led by energy costs—rose rapidly.

What about the opposite case? Suppose the economy experiences a *favorable* supply shock, as it did in the late 1990s, so the aggregate supply curve shifts *outward* at an unusually rapid rate.

Figure 14 depicts the consequences, which are now much happier. The aggregate demand curve shifts out from $D_0 D_0$ to $D_1 D_1$ as usual, but the aggregate supply curve shifts all the way out to $S_1 S_1$. (The dotted line indicates what would happen in a "normal" year.) So the economy's equilibrium winds up at point *B* rather than at point *C*. Compared to *C*, point *B* represents *faster economic growth* (*B* is to the right of *C*) and *lower inflation* (*B* is lower than *C*). In brief, the economy wins on both fronts: Inflation falls while GDP grows rapidly, as happened in the late 1990s.

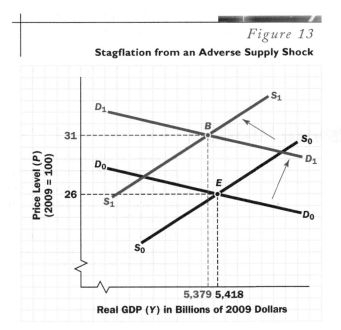

*Figure 13*

Stagflation from an Adverse Supply Shock

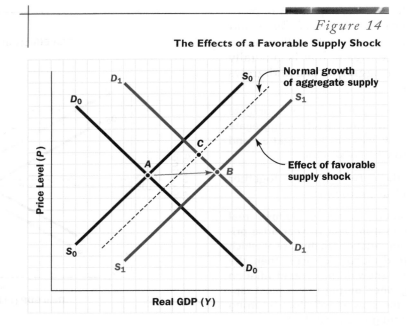

*Figure 14*

**The Effects of a Favorable Supply Shock**

Combining these two cases, we conclude that

If fluctuations in economic activity emanate mainly from the supply side, higher rates of inflation will be associated with *lower* rates of economic growth.

---

**Puzzle Resolved** | *Explaining Stagflation*

What we have learned in this chapter helps us to understand why the U.S. economy performed so poorly in the 1970s and early 1980s, when both unemployment and inflation rose together. The OPEC cartel first flexed its muscles in 1973–1974, when it quadrupled the price of oil, thereby precipitating the first bout of serious stagflation in the United States and other oil-importing nations. Then OPEC struck again in 1979–1980, this time doubling the price of oil, and stagflation returned. Unlucky? Yes. But mysterious? No. What was happening was that the economy's aggregate supply curve was shifted *inward* by the rising price of energy, rather than moving *outward* from one year to the next, as it normally does.

Unfavorable supply shocks tend to push unemployment and inflation up at the same time. It was mainly unfavorable supply shocks that accounted for the stunningly poor economic performance of the 1970s and early 1980s.[3]

---

## 10-9 A ROLE FOR STABILIZATION POLICY

Chapter 8 emphasized the volatility of investment spending, and Chapter 9 noted that changes in investment have multiplier effects on aggregate demand. This chapter took the next step by showing how shifts in the aggregate demand curve cause fluctuations in *both* real GDP *and* prices—fluctuations that are widely decried as undesirable. It also suggested that the economy's self-correcting mechanism works, but slowly, thereby leaving room for government stabilization policy to improve the workings of the free market. Can the government really accomplish this goal? If so, how? These are some of the important questions for Part 3.

---

[3] As we mentioned in the box "Why Was There No Stagflation in 2006–2008?" questions have been raised, and only partially answered, about why stagflation did not return in the 2006–2008 period.

## Summary

1. The economy's **aggregate supply curve** relates the quantity of goods and services that will be supplied to the price level. It normally slopes upward to the right because the costs of labor and other inputs remain relatively fixed in the short run, meaning that higher selling prices make input costs relatively cheaper and therefore encourage greater production.

2. The position of the aggregate supply curve can be shifted by changes in money wage rates, prices of other inputs, technology, or quantities or qualities of labor and capital.

3. The **equilibrium price level and the equilibrium level of real GDP** are jointly determined by the intersection of the economy's aggregate supply and aggregate demand schedules.

4. Among the reasons why the oversimplified multiplier formula is wrong is the fact that it ignores the inflation that is caused by an increase in aggregate demand. Such inflation decreases the multiplier by reducing both consumer spending and net exports.

5. The equilibrium of aggregate supply and demand can come at full employment, below full employment (a **recessionary gap**), or above full employment (an **inflationary gap**).

6. The economy has a **self-correcting mechanism** that erodes a recessionary gap. Specifically, a weak labor market reduces wage increases and, in extreme cases, may even drive wages down. Lower wages shift the aggregate supply curve outward, but it happens very slowly.

7. If an inflationary gap occurs, the economy has a mechanism that erodes the gap through a proce inflation. Unusually strong job prospects push wa up, which shifts the aggregate supply curve to the le and reduces the inflationary gap.

8. One consequence of this self-correcting mechanism is that, if a surge in aggregate demand opens up an inflationary gap, the economy's subsequent natural adjustment will lead to a period of **stagflation**—that is, a period in which prices are rising while output is falling.

9. An inward shift of the aggregate supply curve will cause output to fall while prices rise—that is, it will produce stagflation. Among the events that have caused such a shift are abrupt increases in the price of foreign oil.

10. Adverse supply shifts like this plagued the U.S. economy when oil prices skyrocketed in 1973–1974, in 1979–1980, and again in 1990, leading to stagflation each time.

11. Things reversed in 1997–1998, when falling oil prices and rising productivity shifted the aggregate supply curve out more rapidly than usual, thereby boosting real growth and reducing inflation simultaneously.

12. Inflation can be caused either by rapid growth of aggregate demand or by sluggish growth of aggregate supply. When fluctuations in economic activity emanate from the demand side, prices will rise rapidly when real output grows rapidly. However, when fluctuations in economic activity emanate from the supply side, output will grow slowly when prices rise rapidly.

## Key Terms

| | | |
|---|---|---|
| aggregate supply curve   194 | productivity   196 | self-correcting mechanism   203 |
| inflationary gap   199 | recessionary gap   199 | stagflation   204 |

## Test Yourself

1. In an economy with the following aggregate demand and aggregate supply schedules, find the equilibrium levels of real output and the price level. Graph your solution. If full employment comes at $2,800 billion, is there an inflationary or a recessionary gap?

| Aggregate Quantity Demanded | Price Level | Aggregate Quantity Supplied |
|---|---|---|
| $3,200 | 90 | $2,750 |
| 3,100 | 95 | 2,900 |
| 3,000 | 100 | 3,000 |
| 2,900 | 105 | 3,050 |
| 2,800 | 110 | 3,075 |

NOTE: Amounts are in billions of dollars.

2. Suppose a worker receives a wage of $20 per hour. Compute the real wage (money wage deflated by the price index) corresponding to each of the following possible price levels: 85, 95, 100, 110, 120. What do you notice about the relationship between the real wage and the price level? Relate your finding to the slope of the aggregate supply curve.

3. Add the following aggregate supply-and-demand schedules to the example in Test Yourself Question 1 of Chapter 9 to see how inflation affects the multiplier.

| | (3) | (4) |
|---|---|---|
| | Aggregate Demand When Investment Is $260 | Aggregate Supply |
| .40 | $3,860 | $4,060 | $3,660 |
| 95 | 3,830 | 4,030 | 3,730 |
| 100 | 3,800 | 4,000 | 3,800 |
| 105 | 3,770 | 3,970 | 3,870 |
| 110 | 3,740 | 3,940 | 3,940 |
| 115 | 3,710 | 3,910 | 4,010 |

Draw these schedules on a piece of graph paper.

a. Notice that the difference between columns (2) and (3), which show the aggregate demand schedule at two different levels of investment, is always $200. Discuss how this constant gap of $200 relates to your answer in the previous chapter.

b. Find the equilibrium GDP and the equilibrium price level both before and after the increase in investment. What is the value of the multiplier? Compare that to the multiplier you found in Test Yourself Question 1 of Chapter 9.

4. Use an aggregate supply-and-demand diagram to show that multiplier effects are smaller when the aggregate supply curve is steeper. Which case gives rise to more inflation—the steep aggregate supply curve or the flat one? What happens to the multiplier if the aggregate supply curve is vertical?

## Discussion Questions

1. Explain why a decrease in the price of foreign oil shifts the aggregate supply curve outward to the right. What are the consequences of such a shift?

2. Comment on the following statement: "Inflationary and recessionary gaps are nothing to worry about because the economy has a built-in mechanism that cures either type of gap automatically."

3. Give two different explanations of how the economy can suffer from stagflation.

4. Why do you think wages tend to be rigid in the downward direction?

5. Explain in words why rising prices reduce the multiplier effect of an autonomous increase in aggregate demand.

# FISCAL AND MONETARY POLICY

In Part 2, we constructed a framework for understanding the macroeconomy. The basic theory came in three parts. We started with the determinants of the long-run growth rate of *potential* GDP in Chapter 7, added some analysis of short-run fluctuations in *aggregate demand* in Chapters 8 and 9, and finally considered short-run fluctuations in *aggregate supply* in Chapter 10. Part 3 uses that framework to consider a variety of public policy issues—the sorts of things that make headlines daily.

At several points in earlier chapters, beginning with our list of *Ideas for Beyond the Final Exam* in Chapter 1, we suggested that the government may be able to manage aggregate demand by using its *fiscal and monetary policies*. Chapters 11–13 pick up and build on that suggestion. You will learn how the government tries to promote rapid growth and low unemployment while simultaneously limiting inflation—and why its efforts do not always succeed. This material will enable us to understand better the unhappy events that damaged the U.S. economy so severely in 2008–2009—which we do in Chapter 14. Then, in Chapters 15–17, we turn explicitly to a number of important controversies related to the government's *stabilization policy*. How should the Federal Reserve do its job? Why is it considered so important to reduce the budget deficit? Is there a trade-off between inflation and unemployment?

By the end of Part 3, you will be in an excellent position to understand most of the important debates over national economic policy—not only today but also in the years to come. You may be amazed to learn that you understand these issues better than most public figures do.

# MANAGING AGGREGATE DEMAND: FISCAL POLICY

**11**

*Next, let us turn to the problems of our fiscal policy. Here the myths are legion and the truth hard to find.*

JOHN F. KENNEDY

The government played a rather passive role in the model of the economy we have constructed so far. It did some spending and collected taxes, but that was about it. We concluded that such an economy has only a weak tendency to move toward an equilibrium with high employment and low inflation. Furthermore, we hinted that well-designed government policies might improve the economy's performance. It is now time to expand on that hint—and to learn about some of the difficulties that must be overcome if stabilization policy is to succeed.

We begin in this chapter with **fiscal policy**, which was employed in 2008, 2009, and 2010—amidst much controversy—to shorten the Great Recession and to speed up the recovery. Three of the next four chapters take up the government's other main tool for managing aggregate demand, *monetary policy*, which was used for precisely the same purpose, and which has also provoked a great deal of controversy. Both of these controversies continue to this day.

> The government's **fiscal policy** is its plan for spending and taxation. It is designed to steer aggregate demand in some desired direction.

## CONTENTS

| Issue | *The Great Debate over Fiscal Stimulus* |
| --- | --- |

When President Barack Obama assumed office in January 2009, the U.S. economy was sliding downhill fast. One of the new president's first actions was to ask Congress to pass a large fiscal stimulus bill (originally costed-out at $787 billion) consisting of a combination of tax cuts, new federal spending, and substantial aid to state and local governments. The aim of the Recovery Act was clear: to increase aggregate demand and, thereby, to moderate the economic decline and speed up the recovery. It was precisely the sort of *fiscal policy* response that we will study in this chapter.

The Recovery Act was controversial—and highly partisan—from the start. It passed Congress in February 2009 with almost no Republican support, and many Republicans subsequently clamored for its repeal. They objected on several grounds: that the bill had too much spending and not enough tax cuts, that it would increase the federal budget deficit, and that it would not even give the economy a boost. Democrats countered that new government spending would affect the economy sooner and more surely than some of the tax cuts advocated by Republicans, and that larger deficits, although undesirable *per se*, were part of the price we had to pay to prevent "Great Depression 2.0." They also asked a simple question: How in the world could this much government spending *not* stimulate the economy?

© Frontpage/Shutterstock.com

Thus the great fiscal stimulus debate revolved around three concepts that we will study in this chapter:

- The multiplier effects of tax cuts versus higher government spending
- The multiplier effects of different types of tax cuts
- The incentive effects of tax cuts

By the end of the chapter, you will be in a much better position to form your own opinion on this important, and ongoing, public policy issue.

## 11-1    INCOME TAXES AND THE CONSUMPTION SCHEDULE

Part of the stimulus debate was about tax cuts. To understand how taxes affect equilibrium gross domestic product (GDP), we begin by recalling that taxes ($T$) are subtracted from gross domestic product ($Y$) to obtain disposable income ($DI$):

$$DI = Y - T$$

and that disposable income, not GDP, is the amount actually available to consumers and is therefore the principal determinant of consumer spending ($C$). Thus, at any given level of GDP, if taxes rise, disposable income falls—and hence so does consumption. What we have just described in words is summarized graphically in Figure 1.

**Any increase in taxes shifts the consumption schedule downward, and any tax reduction shifts the consumption schedule upward.**

Of course, if the $C$ schedule moves up or down, so does the $C + I + G + (X - IM)$ schedule that is built on top of it. And we know from Chapter 9 that such a shift will have a multiplier effect on aggregate demand. So it follows that:

**An increase or decrease in taxes will have a multiplier effect on equilibrium GDP on the demand side. Tax reductions increase equilibrium GDP, and tax increases reduce it.**

So far, this analysis just echoes our previous analysis of the multiplier effects of government spending, but there is one important difference. Government purchases of goods and services add to total spending *directly*—through the $G$ component of $C + I + G + (X - IM)$. Taxes reduce total spending only *indirectly*—by lowering disposable income and thus reducing the $C$ component. As we will now see, that little detail turns out to be important.

*Figure 1*

**How Tax Policy Shifts the Consumption Schedule**

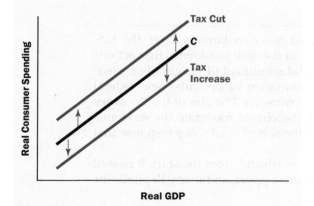

Real Consumer Spending

Tax Cut

C

Tax Increase

Real GDP

## 11-2 THE MULTIPLIER REVISITED

To understand why, let us return to the example used in Chapter 9, in which we learned that the multiplier works through a chain of spending and responding as one person's expenditure becomes another's income. In the example, the spending chain was initiated by Microhard's decision to spend an additional $1 million on investment. With a marginal propensity to consume (MPC) of 0.75, the complete multiplier chain was

$$\$1,000,000 + \$750,000 + \$562,500 + \$421,875 + \dots.$$
$$= \$1,000,000\left(1 + 0.75 + (0.75)^2 + (0.75)^3 + \dots\right)$$
$$= \$1,000,000 \times 4 = \$4,000,000.$$

Thus, each dollar originally spent by Microhard eventually produced $4 in additional spending.

### 11-2a The Tax Multiplier

Now suppose the initiating event was a $1 million tax cut instead. As we just noted, a tax cut affects spending only indirectly. By adding $1 million to disposable income, it increases consumer spending by $750,000 (assuming that the MPC is 0.75). Thereafter, the chain of spending and responding proceeds exactly as before, to yield:

$$\$750,000 + \$562,500 + \$421,875 + \dots.$$
$$= \$750,000\left(1 + 0.75 + (0.75)^2 + \dots\right)$$
$$= \$750,000 \times 4 = \$3,000,000.$$

Notice that the multiplier effect of each dollar of tax cut is three, not four. The reason is straightforward. Each new dollar of additional autonomous spending—regardless of whether it is $C$ or $I$ or $G$—has a multiplier of four, but each dollar of tax cut creates only 75 cents of new consumer spending. Applying the basic expenditure multiplier of four to the 75 cents of first-round spending leads to a multiplier of three for each dollar of tax cut. This numerical example illustrates a general result:[1]

**The multiplier for changes in taxes is smaller than the multiplier for changes in government purchases because not every dollar of tax cut is spent.**

### 11-2b Income Taxes and the Multiplier

This is not the only way in which taxes require us to modify the multiplier analysis of Chapter 9. If the volume of taxes collected depends on GDP—which, of course, it does in reality—there is another way.

To understand this new wrinkle, return again to our Microhard example, but now assume that the government levies a 20 percent income tax—meaning that individuals pay 20 cents in taxes for each $1 of income they receive. Now when Microhard spends $1 million on salaries, its workers receive only $800,000 in after-tax (i.e., disposable) income. The rest goes to the government in taxes. If workers spend 75 percent of the $800,000 (because the MPC is 0.75), spending in the next round will be only $600,000. Notice that this is only 60 percent of the original expenditure, not 75 percent—as was the case before.

Thus, the multiplier chain for each original dollar of spending *shrinks* from

$$1 + 0.75 + (0.75)^2 + (0.75)^3 \dots = \frac{1}{1 - 0.75} = \frac{1}{0.25} = 4$$

---

[1] You may notice that the tax multiplier of three is the spending multiplier of four times the marginal propensity to consume, which is 0.75. See Appendix B for an algebraic explanation.

in Chapter 9's example to

$$1 + 0.6 + (0.6)^2 + (0.6)^3 \ldots = \frac{1}{1 - 0.6} = \frac{1}{0.4} = 2.5$$

now. This is clearly a large reduction in the multiplier. Although this is just a numerical example, the two appendixes to this chapter show that the basic finding is quite general:

> The multiplier is reduced by an income tax because an income tax reduces the fraction of each dollar of GDP that consumers actually receive and spend.

We thus have a third reason why the oversimplified multiplier formula of Chapter 9 exaggerates the size of the multiplier: It ignores income taxes.

**REASONS WHY THE OVERSIMPLIFIED FORMULA OVERSTATES THE MULTIPLIER**

1. It ignores variable imports, which reduce the multiplier.
2. It ignores price-level changes, which reduce the multiplier.
3. It ignores income taxes, which also reduce the multiplier.

The last of these three reasons is the most important one quantitatively.

This conclusion about the multiplier is shown graphically in Figure 2, which can usefully be compared to Figure 10 in Chapter 9. Here we draw our $C + I + G + (X - IM)$ schedules with a slope of 0.6, reflecting an MPC of 0.75 and a tax rate of 20 percent, rather than the 0.75 slope we used in Chapter 9. Figure 2 then illustrates the effect of a \$400 billion increase in government purchases of goods and services, which shifts the total expenditure schedule from $C + I + G_0 + (X - IM)$ to $C + I + G_1 + (X - IM)$.

Equilibrium moves from point $E_0$ to point $E_1$—a GDP increase from $Y = \$6,000$ billion to $Y = \$7,000$ billion.

Thus, if we ignore for the moment any increases in the price level (which would further reduce the multiplier), a \$400-billion increment in government spending leads to a \$1,000-billion increment in GDP. So, when a 20 percent income tax is included in our model, the multiplier is only $\$1,000/\$400 = 2.5$, as we concluded before.

We now have noted two different ways in which taxes modify the multiplier analysis:

- Tax changes have a smaller multiplier effect than spending changes by government or others.
- An income tax reduces the multipliers for *both* tax changes *and* changes in spending.

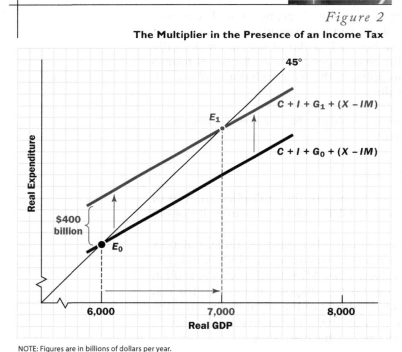

*Figure 2*

**The Multiplier in the Presence of an Income Tax**

45°

$E_1$

$C + I + G_1 + (X - IM)$

$C + I + G_0 + (X - IM)$

Real Expenditure

\$400 billion

$E_0$

6,000        7,000        8,000

**Real GDP**

NOTE: Figures are in billions of dollars per year.

An **automatic stabilizer** is a feature of the economy that reduces its sensitivity to shocks, such as sharp increases or decreases in spending.

## 11-2c Automatic Stabilizers

The size of the multiplier may seem to be a rather abstract notion with little practical importance, but it is not. Fluctuations in one or another component of total spending—$C$, $I$, $G$, or $(X - IM)$—occur all the time. Some come unexpectedly; some are even difficult to explain after the fact. We know from Chapter 9 that any such fluctuation will move GDP up or down by a multiplied amount. Thus, if the multiplier is smaller, GDP will be less sensitive to such shocks—that is, the economy will be less volatile.

Features of the economy that reduce its sensitivity to shocks are called **automatic stabilizers**. The most obvious example is the one we have just been discussing: the personal income tax. The income tax acts as a shock absorber because it makes disposable income, and thus consumer spending, less sensitive to fluctuations in GDP. As we have just seen, when GDP rises, disposable income (*DI*) rises *less* because part of the increase in GDP is siphoned off by the U.S. Treasury. This leakage helps limit any increase in consumption spending. When GDP falls, *DI* falls less sharply because part of the loss is absorbed by the Treasury rather than by consumers. So consumption does not drop as much as it otherwise might. Thus, the personal income tax, unloved though it may be, is one of the main features of our modern economy that help ensure against a repeat performance of the Great Depression.

Our economy has other automatic stabilizers as well. For example, Chapter 6 discussed the U.S. system of unemployment insurance. This program also serves as an automatic stabilizer. When GDP drops and people lose their jobs, unemployment benefits prevent disposable incomes from falling as dramatically as earnings. As a result, unemployed workers can maintain their spending better, and consumption fluctuates less than employment.

The list could continue, but the basic principle remains the same: Each automatic stabilizer serves, in one way or another, as a shock absorber, thereby lowering the multiplier. And each does so quickly, without the need for any decision maker to take action. In a word, they work *automatically.*

A dramatic example arose when the U.S. economy sagged in fiscal years 2008 and 2009. The budget deficit naturally rose sharply as tax receipts came in far lower than had been expected and unemployment insurance payments soared. There was much consternation over the rising deficit, but most economists viewed it as a good thing in the short run: The automatic stabilizers were propping up spending.

## 11-2d  Government Transfer Payments

To complete our discussion of multipliers for fiscal policy, let us now turn to the last major fiscal tool: *government transfer payments.* Transfers, as you will remember, are payments to individuals that are not compensation for any direct contribution to production. How are transfers treated in models of income determination—like purchases of goods and services (*G*) or like taxes (*T*)?

The answer to this question follows readily from the circular flow diagram (Figure 1) in Chapter 8 or the accounting identity: DI = GDP − Taxes + Transfer payments. The important thing to understand about transfer payments is that they intervene between gross domestic product (*Y*) and disposable income (*DI*) in precisely the *opposite* way from income taxes. They add to earned income rather than subtract from it.

Specifically, starting with the wages, interest, rents, and profits that constitute national income, we *subtract* income taxes to calculate disposable income. We do so because these taxes represent the portion of incomes that consumers *earn* but never *receive*. But we must then *add* transfer payments because they represent sources of income that are *received* although they were not *earned* in the process of production. Thus:

**Transfer payments function basically as negative taxes.**

As you may recall from Chapter 8, we use the symbol *T* to denote taxes *minus* transfers. Thus, giving consumers $1 in the form of transfer payments is treated in the 45° line diagram in the same way as a $1 decrease in taxes.

---

**Issue Revisited** | *The Stimulus Debate in 2009–2010*

What we have learned already has some bearing on the partisan debate between Democrats and Republicans over President Obama's proposed fiscal stimulus package in 2009. Remember, one of the main bones of contention was that Republicans wanted more tax cuts and less spending. We have just learned that the multiplier for *T* is smaller than the multiplier for *G.* That means that removing some government spending from the stimulus package and replacing it with more tax cuts would probably have weakened the overall impact on aggregate demand. So does that mean the Democrats were right?

Well, not quite. Our simple analysis so far has focused solely on the effects of fiscal stimulus on *aggregate demand*; it leaves out any possible incentive effects of tax cuts on *aggregate supply*. It is precisely these incentive effects, Republicans argue, that tip the scales in favor of tax cuts. We will return to that question later in this chapter.

## 11-3 PLANNING EXPANSIONARY FISCAL POLICY

We will have more to say about the stimulus debate later, but first imagine that you were a member of Congress trying to decide whether to use fiscal policy to stimulate the economy in 2009—and, if so, by how much. Suppose the economy would have had a GDP of $6,000 billion if the government simply reenacted the previous year's budget. Suppose further that your goal was to achieve a fully employed labor force and that staff economists told you that a GDP of approximately $7,000 billion was needed to reach this target. Finally, to keep the calculations simple, imagine that the price level was fixed. What sort of budget would you have voted for?

This chapter has taught us that the government has three ways to raise GDP by $1,000 billion. Congress can close the recessionary gap between actual and potential GDP by

- Raising government purchases
- Reducing taxes
- Increasing transfer payments

Figure 3 illustrates the problem, and its cure through higher government spending, on our 45° line diagram. Figure 3(a) shows the equilibrium of the economy if no changes are made in the budget. With an expenditure multiplier of 2.5, you can figure out that an additional $400 billion of government spending would be needed to push GDP up by $1,000 billion and eliminate the recessionary gap ($400 \times 2.5 = $1,000$).

So you might vote to raise $G$ by $400 billion, hoping to move the $C + I + G + (X - IM)$ line in Figure 3(a) up to the position indicated in Figure 3(b), thereby achieving full employment at point $F$. Or you might prefer to achieve the same amount of fiscal stimulus by lowering taxes. Or you might opt for more generous transfer payments. The point is that a variety of budgets are capable of increasing GDP by $1,000 billion. Figure 3 applies equally well to any of them. President George W. Bush favored tax cuts, which is the tool the U.S. government relied on in both 2001 and 2008. In 2009 and after, President Barack Obama has preferred a mixture of tax cuts, increases in transfers, and direct government spending.

*Figure 3*

**Fiscal Policy to Eliminate a Recessionary Gap**

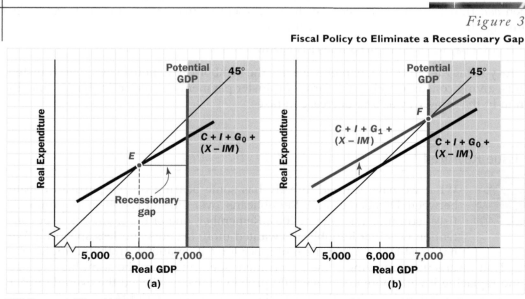

NOTE: Figures are in billions of dollars per year.

## 11-4 PLANNING CONTRACTIONARY FISCAL POLICY

The preceding example assumed that the basic problem of fiscal policy is to close a recessionary gap, as has surely been the case since 2008. But a decade earlier, in 1999, the major macroeconomic problem in the United States was just the opposite: Real GDP exceeded potential GDP, producing an inflationary gap. And a small inflationary gap probably emerged once again in 2006 and 2007, when the unemployment rate dropped to around 4.5 percent. In such cases, the government might wish to adopt more restrictive fiscal policies to reduce aggregate demand.

It does not take much imagination to run our previous analysis in reverse. If an inflationary gap would arise from a continuation of current budget policies, contractionary fiscal policy tools can eliminate it. By cutting spending, raising taxes, or by a combination of the two, the government can pull the $C + G + I + (X - IM)$ schedule down to a noninflationary position and achieve an equilibrium at full employment.

Notice the difference between this way of eliminating an inflationary gap and the natural self-correcting mechanism that we discussed in the last chapter. There we observed that, if the economy were left to its own devices, a cumulative but self-limiting process of inflation would eventually eliminate the inflationary gap and return the economy to full employment. Here we see that we need not put the economy through the inflationary wringer. Instead, a restrictive fiscal policy can avoid inflation by limiting aggregate demand to the level that the economy can produce at full employment.

## 11-5 THE CHOICE BETWEEN SPENDING POLICY AND TAX POLICY

In principle, fiscal policy can nudge the economy in the desired direction equally well by changing government spending or by changing taxes. For example, if the government wants to spur faster growth, it can raise $G$ or lower $T$. Either policy would shift the total expenditure schedule upward, as depicted in Figure 3(b), thereby raising equilibrium GDP on the demand side.

In terms of our aggregate demand-and-supply diagram, either policy shifts the aggregate demand curve outward, as illustrated in the shift from $D_0D_0$ to $D_1D_1$ in Figure 4. As a result, the economy's equilibrium moves from point $E$ to point $A$; both real GDP and the price level rise. As this diagram points out,

> Any combination of higher spending and lower taxes that produces the same aggregate demand curve leads to the same increases in real GDP and prices.

How, then, do policy makers decide whether to raise spending or to cut taxes? The answer depends mainly on how large a public sector they want, which has been a recurring theme in the long-running debate over the proper size of government in the United States.

The small-government point of view, typically advocated by conservatives, says that we are foolish to rely on the public sector to do what private individuals and businesses can do better. Conservatives believe that the growth of government interferes too much in our everyday lives, thereby curtailing our freedom. Those who hold this view can argue for *tax cuts* when macroeconomic considerations call for expansionary fiscal policy, as President George W. Bush did, and for *lower public spending* when contractionary policy is required.

An opposing opinion, expressed more often by liberals, holds that something is amiss when a country as wealthy as the United States has such an impoverished public sector. In this view, America's most pressing needs are not for more fast food and video games but, rather, for better schools, better

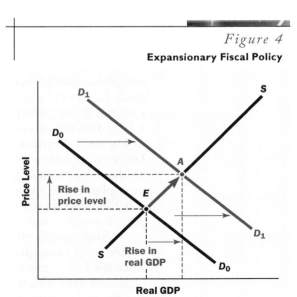

*Figure 4*

**Expansionary Fiscal Policy**

transportation infrastructure, and health insurance for all of our citizens—all priorities of President Obama. People on this side of the debate can advocate *increased* spending when the economy needs stimulus and favor paying for these improved public services by *increasing taxes* when it is necessary to rein in the economy.

It is important not to confuse the fiscal stabilization issue with the "big-government" issue. In fact,

> Individuals who favor a smaller public sector can advocate an active fiscal policy just as well as those who favor a larger public sector. Advocates of bigger government can seek to expand demand (when appropriate) through higher government spending and to contract demand (when appropriate) through tax increases. Advocates of smaller government can seek to expand demand by cutting taxes and to reduce demand by cutting expenditures.

*"Free gifts to every kid in the world? Are you a Keynesian or something?"*

Indeed, our two most conservative recent presidents, Ronald Reagan and George W. Bush, each pursued activist fiscal policies, as has the more liberal President Obama.

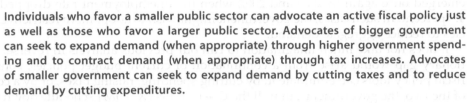

| Issue Redux | *Democrats versus Republicans on Stimulus* |

Although both parties wanted to stimulate the economy in 2009, the choice between tax cuts and more government spending played a central role in the highly partisan debate that broke out over President Obama's proposed stimulus package. The bill that the Democrats eventually passed, with hardly any Republican support, consisted, very roughly, of one-third tax cuts, one-third federal spending, and one-third aid to state and local governments. Clearly, those choices made government "bigger," at least temporarily. (It would shrink later because the spending was temporary.) Republicans objected to those proportions. They wanted more tax cuts and less spending—a "smaller" government—and, on those grounds, voted almost unanimously against the bill.

## 11-6 SOME HARSH REALITIES

The mechanics outlined so far in this chapter make the fiscal policy planner's job look deceptively simple. The elementary diagrams make it appear that policy makers can drive GDP to any level they please simply by manipulating spending and tax programs. It seems they should be able to hit the full-employment bull's-eye every time. In fact, a better analogy is to a poor rifleman shooting through dense fog at an erratically moving target with an inaccurate gun and slow-moving bullets.

The target is moving because, in the real world, the investment, net exports, and consumption schedules constantly shift about as expectations, technology, events abroad, and other factors change. For all of these reasons and others, the policies decided on today, which will take effect at some future date, may no longer be appropriate by the time that future date rolls around.

The second misleading feature of our diagrams (the "inaccurate gun") is that we do not know multipliers as precisely as in our numerical examples. Although our best guess may be that a $20 billion increase in government purchases will raise GDP by $30 billion (a multiplier of 1.5), the actual outcome may be as little as $10 billion or as much as $40 billion. It is therefore impossible to "fine-tune" every little wobble out of the economy's growth path. Economic science is simply not that precise.

A third complication is that our target—full-employment GDP—may be only dimly visible, as if through a fog. The present time is a great example. It has been a long time since the U.S. economy operated at anything close to full employment. When the unemployment rate, which had risen as high as 10 percent during the worst of the recession, finally dropped to around 6 percent in the fall of 2014, there was a vigorous debate over how far the U.S. economy was from full employment. Some argued we were basically there already. Others insisted that full employment came at a rate substantially lower than 6 percent. That debate goes on.

A fourth complication is that fiscal policy "bullets" travel slowly: Tax and spending policies affect aggregate demand only after some time elapses. Consumer spending, for example, may take months to react to an income-tax cut. Because of these time lags, fiscal policy decisions must be based on *forecasts* of the future state of the economy—forecasts that are often inaccurate. The combination of long lags and poor forecasts may occasionally leave the government fighting the last recession just as the new inflation gets under way.

And, finally, the people aiming the fiscal "rifle" are not skilled economic technicians; they are politicians. Sometimes political considerations lead to policies that deviate markedly from what textbook economics would suggest. Even when they do not, the wheels of Congress grind slowly.

In addition to all of these operational problems, legislators trying to decide whether to push the unemployment rate lower would like to know the answers to two further questions. First, because either higher spending or lower taxes will increase the government's budget deficit, what are the long-run costs of running large budget deficits? This is a question we will take up in depth in Chapter 16. Second, how large is the inflationary cost likely to be? As we know, an expansionary fiscal policy that reduces a recessionary gap by increasing aggregate demand will lower unemployment. As Figure 4 reminds us, it also tends to be inflationary. This undesirable side effect may make the government hesitant to use fiscal policy to combat recessions.

Is there a way out of this dilemma? Can we pursue the battle against unemployment without aggravating inflation? For more than 30 years now, a small but influential minority of economists, journalists, and politicians have argued that we can. They call their approach "supply-side economics." The idea helped sweep Ronald Reagan to smashing electoral victories in 1980 and 1984 and was revived under President George W. Bush. Just what is supply-side economics?

## 11-7 THE IDEA BEHIND SUPPLY-SIDE TAX CUTS

The central idea of supply-side economics is that certain types of tax cuts increase aggregate supply. For example, taxes can be cut in ways that raise the rewards for working, saving, and investing. Then, *if people actually respond to these incentives,* such tax cuts will increase the total supplies of labor and capital in the economy, thereby increasing aggregate supply.

Figure 5 illustrates the idea on an aggregate supply-and-demand diagram. If policy measures can shift the economy's aggregate supply to position $S_1S_1$, then prices will be lower and output higher than if the aggregate supply curve remained at $S_0S_0$. Policy makers will have reduced inflation and raised real output at the same time—as shown by point $B$ in the figure. The trade-off between inflation and unemployment will have been defeated, which is the goal of supply-side economics.

What sorts of policies do supply-siders advocate? Mostly tax cuts. Here is a sampling:

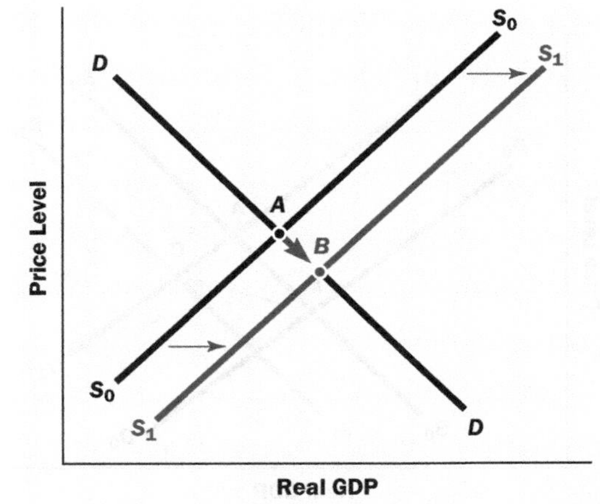

**Lower Personal Income-Tax Rates** Sharp cuts in personal taxes were the cornerstone of the economic strategy of George W. Bush, just as they had been 20 years earlier for Ronald Reagan. Starting in 2001, tax rates on individuals were reduced in stages. The four upper tax bracket rates were cut, and some very low income taxpayers saw their tax rate fall from 15 percent to 10 percent. Later, taxes on income from dividends and capital gains were cut. Lower tax rates, supply-siders argue, augment the supplies of both labor and capital.

When the Bush tax cuts reached their scheduled expiry in late 2010, there was a vigorous national debate over what to do about them. Republicans wanted to extend them all, indeed, to make

*Figure 5*

**The Goal of Supply-Side Tax Cuts**

them permanent features of the tax code. Most Democrats, including President Obama, wanted to let the upper-income tax cuts expire on schedule. A political compromise was struck under which all the cuts were extended, but only for two more years. Then, in 2012, another political compromise was reached under which most of the Bush tax cuts were made permanent but the rate cuts for very high income households were rescinded.

**Reduce Taxes on Income from Savings** One extreme form of this proposal would simply exempt all income from interest and dividends from taxation. Because income must be either consumed or saved, doing so would change our present personal income tax into a tax on consumer spending. Several such proposals for radical tax reform have been considered over the years, but none have been adopted. However, Congress did reduce the tax rate on dividends to just 15 percent as part of the Bush tax cuts in 2003.

**Reduce Taxes on Capital Gains** When an investor sells an asset for a profit, that profit is called a *capital gain*. Supply-siders argue that the government can encourage more investment by taxing capital gains at lower rates than ordinary income. This proposal was also acted upon in 2003, when the top rate on capital gains was cut to 15 percent. In 2011, President Obama—a Democrat!—proposed eliminating capital gains taxes on small businesses entirely.

**Reduce the Corporate Income Tax** By reducing the tax burden on corporations, proponents argue, the government can provide both greater investment incentives (by raising the profitability of investment) and more investable funds (by letting companies keep more of their earnings). Supply-siders (and others) have noted that the U.S. corporate income tax rate is higher than those of most other countries, which, they argue, puts American firms at a disadvantage in international competition. They are constantly seeking to reduce the rate.

Let us suppose, for the moment, that a successful supply-side tax cut is enacted. Because *both* aggregate demand *and* aggregate supply increase simultaneously, the economy may be able to avoid the inflationary consequences of an expansionary fiscal policy shown in Figure 4.

Figure 6 illustrates this conclusion. The two aggregate demand curves and the initial aggregate supply curve $S_0S_0$ carry over directly from Figure 4. But we have introduced an additional supply curve, $S_1S_1$, to reflect the successful supply-side tax cut depicted in Figure 5. The equilibrium point for the economy moves from $E$ to $C$, whereas with a conventional demand-side tax cut it would have moved from $E$ to $A$. As compared with point $A$, which reflects only the demand-side effects of a tax cut, output is higher and prices are lower at point $C$.

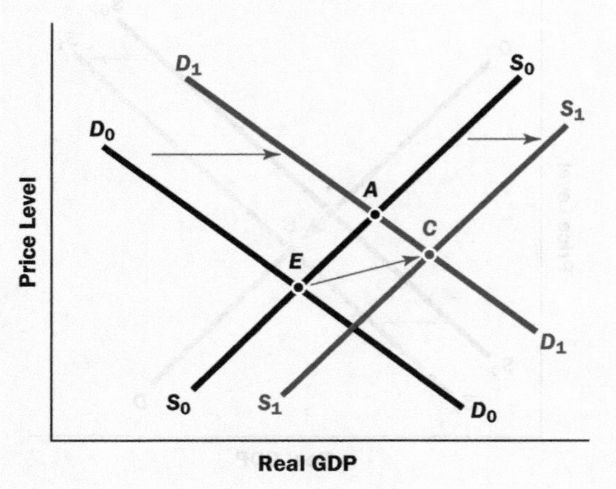

A good deal, you say. And indeed it is. The supply-side argument is extremely attractive *in principle*. The question is: Does it work *in practice*? Can we actually do what is depicted in Figure 6? Let us consider some of the difficulties.

*Figure 6*

**A Successful Supply-Side Tax Reduction**

### 11-7a  Some Flies in the Ointment

Critics of supply-side economics rarely question its goals or the basic idea that lower taxes improve incentives. They argue, instead, that supply-siders exaggerate the beneficial effects of tax cuts and ignore some undesirable side effects. Here is a brief rundown of some of their main objections.

**Small Magnitude of Supply-Side Effects** The first objection is that supply-siders are simply too optimistic: No one really knows how to do what Figure 5 shows. Although it is easy, for example, to design tax incentives that make saving more *attractive* financially, people may not actually respond to these incentives.

In fact, most of the statistical evidence suggests that we should not expect much from tax incentives for saving. As economist Charles Schultze quipped years ago: "There's nothing wrong with supply-side economics that division by 10 couldn't cure."

**Demand-Side Effects** The second objection is that supply-siders ignore the effects of tax cuts on aggregate demand. If you cut personal taxes, for example, individuals *may possibly* work more, but they *will certainly* spend more.

The joint implications of these two objections appear in Figure 7. This figure depicts a *small* outward shift of the aggregate supply curve (which reflects the first objection) and a *large* outward shift of the aggregate demand curve (which reflects the second objection). The result is that the economy's equilibrium moves from point $E$ (the intersection of $S_0 S_0$ and $D_0 D_0$) to point $C$ (the intersection of $S_1 S_1$ and $D_1 D_1$). Prices rise as output expands. The outcome differs only a little from the straight "demand-side" fiscal stimulus depicted in Figure 4.

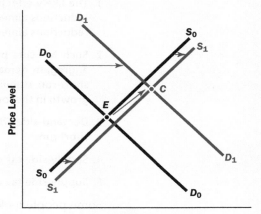

*Figure 7*

**A More Pessimistic View of Supply-Side Tax Cuts**

**Problems with Timing** Investment incentives are the most promising type of supply-side tax cuts, but the benefits from greater investment do not arrive by Instagram. In particular, the *expenditures* on investment goods almost certainly come before any *expansion of capacity*. Thus, supply-side tax cuts have their primary short-run effects on aggregate demand. Effects on aggregate supply come later.

**Effects on Income Distribution** The preceding objections all pertain to the likely effects of supply-side policies on aggregate supply and demand. However, a different problem bears mentioning: Most supply-side initiatives increase income inequality. Indeed, some tilt toward the rich is an almost inescapable corollary of supply-side logic. Why? Because the basic aim of supply-side economics is to increase the incentives for working and investing—that is, to increase the gap between the rewards of those who succeed in the economic game (by working hard, investing well, or just being lucky) and those who fail. It is not surprising, therefore, that supply-side policies tend to increase economic inequality.

**Losses of Tax Revenue** You can hardly help but notice that most of the policies suggested by supply-siders involve cutting one tax or another. For this reason, supply-side tax cuts are bound to increase the government budget deficit. This problem proved to be the Achilles' heel of supply-side economics in the United States in the 1980s. The Reagan tax cuts left in their wake a legacy of budget deficits that took 15 years to overcome. Twenty years later, President George W. Bush's tax cuts left us in a similar position: The tax cuts used up the budget surpluses of the late Clinton years and turned them into large deficits. So, when the tax cuts came up for renewal at the end of 2010, at a time of huge budget deficits, there was some sentiment to let them lapse. But as noted, that argument lost out to the counterargument that raising taxes when the economy is weak is bad macroeconomic policy.

---

| Issue | *The Partisan Debate Once More* |
|---|---|

Several items on the preceding list have played prominent roles in the continuing debate over fiscal stimulus. Many Democrats argue that the supply-side effects of many Republican-proposed tax cuts are small and uncertain and that, at any rate, the U.S. economy's real problem is too little *demand*, not too little *supply*. Many Republicans counter that business tax incentives are the best way to spur real, lasting job creation and that the fiscal multiplier is small, or even zero. Implicitly, they believe more in supply-side effects than demand-side effects.

## 11-7b  Toward an Assessment of Supply-Side Economics

On balance, most economists have reached the following conclusions about supply-side tax initiatives:

1. The likely effectiveness of supply-side tax cuts depends on what kinds of taxes are cut. Tax reductions aimed at stimulating business investment are likely to pack more punch than tax reductions aimed at getting people to work longer hours or to save more.

2. Such tax cuts probably increase aggregate supply much more slowly than they increase aggregate demand. Thus, supply-side policies should not be regarded as a substitute for short-run stabilization policy, but rather, as a way to promote (slightly) faster economic growth in the long run.

3. Demand-side effects of supply-side tax cuts are likely to overwhelm supply-side effects in the short run.

4. Supply-side tax cuts are likely to widen income inequalities.

5. Supply-side tax cuts are almost certain to lead to larger budget deficits.

Some people look over this list and decide that they favor supply-side tax cuts; others, perusing the same facts, reach the opposite conclusion. We cannot say that either group is wrong because, like almost every economic policy, supply-side economics has its pros and cons and involves value judgments that color people's conclusions.

Why, then, have so many economists and politicians reacted so negatively to supply-side economics over the years? The main reason seems to be that the claims made by the most ardent supply-siders were clearly excessive. Naturally, these claims proved wrong. But showing that wild claims are wild does not eliminate the kernel of truth in supply-side economics: Reductions in marginal tax rates *do* improve economic incentives. Any specific supply-side tax cut must be judged on its individual merits.

## Supply-Side Economics and Presidential Elections

Ronald Reagan won landslide victories in 1980 and 1984 by running on a supply-side platform. In 1992, candidate Bill Clinton attacked supply-side economics as "trickle-down economics," arguing that it had failed. He emphasized two of the drawbacks of such a fiscal policy: the effects on income inequality and on the budget deficit. The voters apparently agreed with him.

The hallmark of Clintonomics was, first, reducing the budget deficit that President Clinton had inherited from the first President George Bush, and second, building up a large surplus. This policy succeeded—for a while. The huge budget deficit turned into a large surplus, the economy boomed, and Clinton, like Reagan before him, was reelected easily.

Then, in the 2000 presidential election, the voters once again switched their allegiance. During that campaign, Democratic candidate Al Gore promised to continue the "fiscal responsibility" of the Clinton years, whereas Republican candidate George W. Bush echoed Reagan by offering large tax cuts. Bush won in what was virtually a dead heat. In 2004, Senator John Kerry ran a losing campaign against the incumbent George W. Bush on what amounted to a promise to roll back some of the Bush tax cuts and return to Clintonomics.

In the 2008 campaign, the tax issue was on the agenda again. Then-Senator Barack Obama wanted to repeal most of the Bush tax cuts because, he argued, the government needed the tax revenue. Republican Senator John McCain wanted to make the tax cuts permanent. Obama, of course, won the election—but eventually wound up agreeing to make most (though not all) of the Bush tax cuts permanent. Then, in 2012, Obama defeated the tax-cutting Mitt Romney.

So which approach do American voters prefer? They appear to be fickle. But one thing is clear: The debate over taxes, and fiscal policy more generally, played a major role in each of the last nine presidential elections.

Top left, AAP Images/ REAGAN FOR PRESIDENT; top right, AP Images/Greg Wahl-Stephens; bottom left, Wally McNamee/Corbis News/Corbis; bottom middle, AP Images/J. Scott Applewhite; bottom right, AP Images/Rick Bowmer

## Summary

1. The government's **fiscal policy** is its plan for managing aggregate demand through its spending and taxing programs. This policy is made jointly by the president and Congress.

2. Because consumer spending (C) depends on disposable income (DI), and DI is GDP minus taxes, any change in taxes will shift the consumption schedule on a 45° line diagram. Such shifts in the consumption schedule have multiplier effects on GDP.

3. The multiplier for changes in taxes is smaller than the multiplier for changes in government purchases because each $1 of tax cuts leads to less than $1 of increased consumer spending.

4. An income tax reduces the size of the multiplier.

5. Because an income tax reduces the multiplier, it reduces the economy's sensitivity to shocks. It is therefore considered an **automatic stabilizer**.

6. Government transfer payments are like negative taxes, rather than like government purchases of goods and services, because they influence total spending only indirectly through their effect on consumption.

7. If the multipliers were known precisely, it would be possible to plan a variety of fiscal policies to eliminate either a recessionary gap or an inflationary gap. Recessionary gaps can be cured by raising G or cutting T. Inflationary gaps can be cured by cutting G or raising T.

8. Active stabilization policy can be carried out either by means that tend to expand the size of government (by raising either G or T when appropriate) or by means that reduce the size of government (by reducing either G or T when appropriate).

9. Expansionary fiscal policy can mitigate recessions, but it also raises the budget deficit.

10. Expansionary fiscal policy also normally exacts a cost in terms of higher inflation. This last dilemma has led to a great deal of interest in "supply-side" tax cuts designed to stimulate aggregate supply.

11. **Supply-side tax cuts** aim to push the economy's aggregate supply curve outward to the right. When successful, they can expand the economy and reduce inflation at the same time—a highly desirable outcome.

12. Critics point out at least five serious problems with supply-side tax cuts: They also stimulate aggregate demand; the beneficial effects on aggregate supply may be small; the demand-side effects occur before the supply-side effects; they make the income distribution more unequal; and large tax cuts lead to large budget deficits.

## Key Terms

automatic stabilizer   218

fiscal policy   215

## Test Yourself

1. Consider an economy in which tax collections are always $400 and in which the four components of aggregate demand are as follows:

| GDP | Taxes | DI | C | I | G | (X−IM) |
|---|---|---|---|---|---|---|
| $1,360 | $400 | $960 | $720 | $200 | $500 | $30 |
| 1,480 | 400 | 1,080 | 810 | 200 | 500 | 30 |
| 1,600 | 400 | 1,200 | 900 | 200 | 500 | 30 |
| 1,720 | 400 | 1,320 | 990 | 200 | 500 | 30 |
| 1,840 | 400 | 1,440 | 1,080 | 200 | 500 | 30 |

Find the equilibrium of this economy graphically. What is the marginal propensity to consume? What is the multiplier? What would happen to equilibrium GDP if government purchases were reduced by $60 and the price level remained unchanged?

2. Consider an economy similar to that in the preceding question in which investment is also $200, government purchases are also $500, net exports are also $30, and the price level is also fixed. But taxes now vary with income, and as a result, the consumption schedule looks like the following:

| GDP | Taxes | DI | C |
|---|---|---|---|
| $1,360 | $320 | $1,040 | $810 |
| 1,480 | 360 | 1,120 | 870 |
| 1,600 | 400 | 1,200 | 930 |
| 1,720 | 440 | 1,280 | 990 |
| 1,840 | 480 | 1,360 | 1,050 |

Find the equilibrium of this economy graphically. What is the marginal propensity to consume? What is the multiplier? What would happen to equilibrium GDP if government purchases were reduced by $60 and the price level remained unchanged?

3. Return to the hypothetical economy in Test Yourself Question 1, and now suppose that *both* taxes and government purchases are increased by $120. Find the new equilibrium under the assumption that consumer spending continues to be exactly three-quarters of disposable income (as it is in Test Yourself Question 1).

4. Suppose you are put in charge of fiscal policy for the economy described in Test Yourself Question 1. There is an inflationary gap, and you want to reduce income by $120. What specific actions can you take to achieve this goal?

5. Now put yourself in charge of the economy in Test Yourself Question 2, and suppose that full employment comes at a GDP of $1,840. How can you push income up to that level?

## Discussion Questions

1. The federal government spending (relative to the size of the economy) was cut back in several dimensions after the gigantic budget deficits of 2009 and 2010. How would GDP in the United States have been affected if this lower spending led to
   a. smaller budget deficits?
   b. more spending elsewhere in the budget, so that total government purchases remained the same?

2. Explain why G has the same multiplier as I, but taxes have a different multiplier.

3. If the government decides that aggregate demand is excessive and is causing inflation, what options are open to it? What if the government decides that aggregate demand is too weak instead?

4. Which of the proposed supply-side tax cuts appeals to you most? Draw up a list of arguments for and against enacting such a cut right now.

5. **(More difficult)** Advocates of lower taxes on capital gains argue that this type of tax cut will raise aggregate supply by spurring business investment. Compare the effects on investment, aggregate supply, and tax revenues of three different ways to cut the capital gains tax:
   a. Reduce capital gains taxes on *all* investments, including those that were made before tax rates were cut.
   b. Reduce capital gains taxes only on investments made after tax rates are cut.
   c. Reduce capital gains taxes only on certain types of investments, such as corporate stocks and bonds.

   Which of the three options seems most desirable to you? Why?

## Appendix A    *Graphical Treatment of Taxes and Fiscal Policy*

Most of the taxes collected by the U.S. government—indeed, by all national governments—rise and fall with GDP. In some cases, the reason is obvious: *Personal* and *corporate income-tax* collections, for example, depend on how much income there is to be taxed. *Sales tax* receipts depend on GDP because consumer spending is higher when GDP is higher. However, other types of tax receipts—such as property taxes—do not vary with GDP. We call the first kind of tax **variable taxes** and the second kind **fixed taxes**.

Many tax policies actually change disposable income by larger amounts when incomes are higher. That is true, for example, whenever Congress alters the tax rates imposed by the personal income tax, as it did in 2012. Because higher tax rates decrease disposable income *more* when GDP is *higher*, the C schedule shifts down more sharply at higher income levels than at lower ones, as depicted in Figure 8. The same relationships apply for tax decreases, as the upward shift in the figure shows.

Figure 9 illustrates the second reason why the distinction between fixed and variable taxes is important. This diagram shows two different consumption lines. $C_1$ is

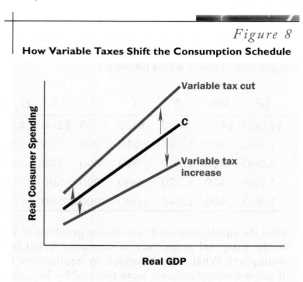

*Figure 8*

**How Variable Taxes Shift the Consumption Schedule**

the consumption schedule used in earlier chapters; it reflects the assumption that tax collections are fixed—the same regardless of GDP. $C_2$ depicts a more realistic case in which the government collects taxes equal to

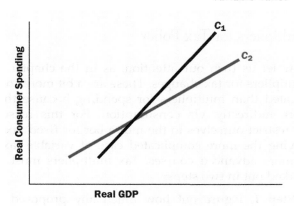

## Figure 9

### The Consumption Schedule with Fixed versus Variable Taxes

## Table 2

### The Relationship between Consumption and GDP

| With Fixed Taxes ($T = \$1,200$) (from Table 1, Chapter 9) | | With a 20 Percent Income Tax (from Table 1) | |
|---|---|---|---|
| $Y$ | $C$ | $Y$ | $C$ |
| $4,800 | $3,000 | $4,500 | $3,000 |
| 5,200 | 3,300 | 5,000 | 3,300 |
| 5,600 | 3,600 | 5,500 | 3,600 |
| 6,000 | 3,900 | 6,000 | 3,900 |
| 6,400 | 4,200 | 6,500 | 4,200 |
| 6,800 | 4,500 | 7,000 | 4,500 |
| 7,200 | 4,800 | 7,500 | 4,800 |
| Line $C_1$ in Figure 9 | | Line $C_2$ in Figure 9 | |

20 percent of GDP. Notice that $C_2$ is flatter than $C_1$. This is no accident. In fact, as pointed out in the chapter:

> Variable taxes such as the income tax flatten the consumption schedule in a 45° line diagram.

We can easily understand why. Column (1) of Table 1 shows alternative values of GDP ranging from $4.5 trillion to $7.5 trillion. Column (2) then indicates that taxes are always one-fifth of this amount. Column (3) subtracts column (2) from column (1) to arrive at disposable income (*DI*). Column (4) then gives the amount of consumer spending corresponding to each level of *DI*. The schedule relating *C* to *Y*, which we need for our 45° line diagram, is therefore found in columns (1) and (4).

Notice that each $500 billion increase in GDP in Table 1 leads to a $300 billion rise in consumer spending. Thus, the slope of line $C_2$ in Figure 9 is $300/$500,

or 0.60, as we observed in the chapter. But in our earlier example in Chapter 9, consumption rose by $300 billion each time GDP increased $400 billion—making the slope $300/$400, or 0.75. (See the steeper line $C_1$ in Figure 9.) Table 2 compares the two cases explicitly. In the Chapter 9 example, taxes were fixed at $1,200 billion and each $400 billion rise in *Y* led to a $300 billion rise in *C*—as in the left-hand panel of Table 2. But now, with taxes variable (equal to 20 percent of GDP), each $500 billion increment to *Y* gives rise to a $300 billion increase in *C*—as in the right-hand panel of Table 2.

These differences sound terribly mechanical, but the economic reasoning behind them is both intuitive and vital to understanding tax policies. When taxes are fixed, as in line $C_1$, each additional dollar of GDP raises disposable income (*DI*) by $1. Consumer spending then rises by $1 times the marginal propensity to consume (MPC), which is 0.75 in our example. Hence, each additional dollar of GDP leads to 75 cents more spending. But when taxes vary with income, each additional dollar of GDP raises *DI* by less than $1 because the government takes a share in taxes. In our example, taxes are 20 percent of GDP, so each additional $1 of GDP generates just 80 cents more *DI*. With an MPC of 0.75, then, spending rises by only 60 cents (75 percent of 80 cents) for each $1 of additional GDP. Thus, the slope of line $C_2$ in Figure 9 is only 0.60, instead of 0.75.

Table 3 and Figure 10 take the next step by replacing the old consumption schedule with this new one in the tabular presentation of income determination and in the 45° line diagram. We see immediately that the equilibrium level of GDP is at point *E*. Here gross domestic product is $6,000 billion, consumption is $3,900 billion, investment is $900 billion, net exports are –$100 billion, and government purchases are $1,300 billion. As we

## Table 1

### The Effects of an Income Tax on the Consumption Schedule

| (1) Gross Domestic Product | (2) Taxes | (3) Disposable Income (GDP minus taxes) | (4) Consumption |
|---|---|---|---|
| $4,500 | $900 | $3,600 | $3,000 |
| 5,000 | 1,000 | 4,000 | 3,300 |
| 5,500 | 1,100 | 4,400 | 3,600 |
| 6,000 | 1,200 | 4,800 | 3,900 |
| 6,500 | 1,300 | 5,200 | 4,200 |
| 7,000 | 1,400 | 5,600 | 4,500 |
| 7,500 | 1,500 | 6,000 | 4,800 |

NOTE: Figures are in billions of dollars per year.

Table 3

**Total Expenditure Schedule with a 20 Percent Income Tax**

| (1) | (2) | (3) | (4) | (5) | (6) |
|---|---|---|---|---|---|
| Gross Domestic Product $Y$ | Consumption $C$ | Investment $I$ | Government Purchases $G$ | Net Exports $(X - IM)$ | Total Expenditures $C + I + G + (X - IM)$ |
| $4,500 | $3,000 | $900 | $1,300 | -$100 | $5,100 |
| 5,000 | 3,300 | 900 | 1,300 | -100 | 5,400 |
| 5,500 | 3,600 | 900 | 1,300 | -100 | 5,700 |
| 6,000 | 3,900 | 900 | 1,300 | -100 | 6,000 |
| 6,500 | 4,200 | 900 | 1,300 | -100 | 6,300 |
| 7,000 | 4,500 | 900 | 1,300 | -100 | 6,600 |
| 7,500 | 4,800 | 900 | 1,300 | -100 | 6,900 |

Figure 10

**Income Determination with a Variable Income Tax**

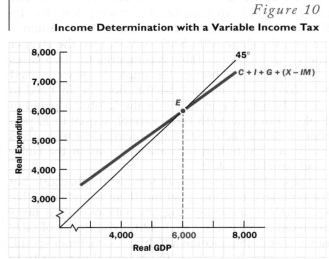

NOTE: Figures are in billions of dollars per year.

know from previous chapters, full employment may occur above or below $Y = \$6,000$ billion. If it is below this level, an inflationary gap arises. Prices will probably start to rise, pulling the expenditure schedule down and reducing equilibrium GDP. If it is above this level, a recessionary gap results, and history suggests that prices will fall only slowly. In the interim, the economy will suffer a period of high unemployment.

In short, once we adjust the expenditure schedule for variable taxes, the determination of national income proceeds exactly as before. The effects of government spending and taxation, therefore, are fairly straightforward and can be summarized as follows:

Government purchases of goods and services add to total spending *directly* through the $G$ component of $C + I + G + (X - IM)$. Higher taxes reduce total spending *indirectly* by lowering disposable income and thus reducing

the $C$ component of $C + I + G + (X - IM)$. On balance, then, the government's actions may raise or lower the equilibrium level of GDP, depending on how much spending and taxing it does.

## Multipliers for Tax Policy

Now let us turn our attention, as in the chapter, to multipliers for tax changes. These are a bit more complicated than multipliers for spending because they work indirectly, via consumption. For this reason, we restrict ourselves to the multiplier for fixed taxes, leaving the more complicated case of variable taxes to more advanced courses. Tax multipliers must be worked out in two steps:

**Step 1.** Figure out how much any proposed or actual changes in the tax law will affect consumer spending.

**Step 2.** Enter this vertical shift of the consumption schedule in the 45° line diagram and see how it affects output.

To create a simple and familiar numerical example, suppose income taxes fall by a fixed amount at each level of GDP—say, by $400 billion. Step 1 instructs us to multiply the $400 billion tax cut by the marginal propensity to consume (MPC), which is 0.75, to get $300 billion as the increase in consumer spending—that is, as the vertical shift of the consumption schedule.

Step 2 then instructs us to multiply this $300 billion increase in consumption by the expenditure multiplier—which is 2.5 in our example—giving $750 billion as the rise in GDP. Figure 11 verifies that this is correct by depicting a $300 billion upward shift of the consumption function in the 45°

Figure 11

**The Multiplier for a Reduction in Fixed Taxes**

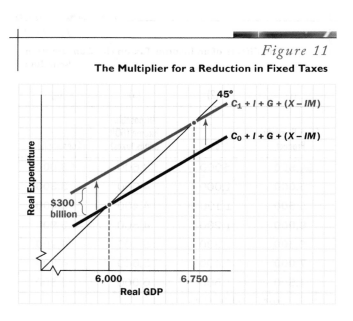

line diagram and noting that GDP does indeed rise by $750 billion as a consequence—from $6,000 billion to $6,750 billion.

Notice that the $400 billion tax cut raises GDP by $750 billion, whereas the multiplier effect of the $400 billion increase in government purchases depicted in the chapter in Figure 2 raised GDP by $1,000 billion.

This is a specific numerical example of a lesson learned in the chapter. Because some of the change in disposable income affects *saving* rather than *spending*, a dollar of tax cut does not pack as much punch as a dollar of G. That is why we multiplied the $400 billion change in taxes by 0.75 to get the $300 billion shift of the C schedule shown in Figure 11.

## Summary

1. Precisely *how* a tax change affects the consumption schedule depends on whether **fixed taxes** or **variable taxes** are changed.

2. Shifts of the consumption function caused by tax policy are subject to the same multiplier as autonomous shifts in $G$, $I$, or $X - IM$.

3. Because tax changes affect $C$ only indirectly, the multiplier for a change in $T$ is smaller than the multiplier for a change in $G$.

4. The government's net effect on aggregate demand—and hence on equilibrium output and prices—depends on whether the expansionary effects of its spending are greater or smaller than the contractionary effects of its taxes.

## Key Terms

**fixed taxes**   228

**variable taxes**   228

## Test Yourself

1. Which of the following is considered a fixed tax and which a variable tax?
   a. The gasoline tax
   b. The corporate income tax
   c. The estate tax
   d. The payroll tax

2. In a certain economy, the multiplier for government purchases is 2 and the multiplier for changes in fixed taxes is 1.5. The government then proposes to raise both spending and taxes by $100 billion. What should happen to equilibrium GDP on the demand side?

3. (**More difficult**) Suppose real GDP is $10,000 billion and the basic expenditure multiplier is two. If two tax changes are made at the same time:
   a. fixed taxes are raised by $100 billion
   b. the income-tax *rate* is reduced from 20 percent to 18 percent
   will equilibrium GDP on the demand side rise or fall?

## Discussion Questions

1. When the income-tax rate declines, as it did in the United States in the early 2000s, does the multiplier go up or down? Explain why.

2. Discuss the pros and cons of having a higher or lower multiplier.

## Appendix B *Algebraic Treatment of Taxes and Fiscal Policy*

In this appendix, we explain the simple algebra behind the fiscal policy multipliers discussed in the chapter. In so doing, we deal only with a simplified case in which prices do not change. Although it is possible to work out the corresponding algebra for the more realistic aggregate demand-and-supply analysis with variable prices, the analysis is rather complicated and is best left to more advanced courses.

We start with the example used both in the chapter and in Appendix A. The government spends $1,300 billion on goods and services ($G = 1,300$) and levies an income tax equal to 20 percent of GDP. So, if the symbol $T$ denotes tax receipts,

$$T = 0.20Y$$

Because the consumption function we have been working with is

$$C = 300 + 0.75DI$$

where $DI$ is disposable income, and because disposable income and GDP are related by the accounting identity

$$DI = Y - T,$$

it follows that the $C$ schedule used in the $45°$ line diagram is described by the following algebraic equation:

$$
\begin{aligned}
C &= 300 + 0.75(Y - T) \\
&= 300 + 0.75(Y - 0.20Y) \\
&= 300 + 0.75(0.80Y) \\
&= 300 + 0.60Y
\end{aligned}
$$

We can now apply the equilibrium condition:

$$Y = C + I + G + (X - IM)$$

Because investment in this example is $I = 900$, $G = 1,300$, and net exports are –100, substituting for $C, I, G,$ and $(X - IM)$ into this equation gives:

$$
\begin{aligned}
Y &= 300 + 0.60Y + 900 + 1,300 - 100 \\
0.40Y &= 2,400 \\
Y &= 6,000
\end{aligned}
$$

This is all there is to finding equilibrium GDP in an economy with a government.

To find the multiplier for government spending, increase $G$ by one and solve the problem again:

$$
\begin{aligned}
Y &= C + I + G + (X - IM) \\
Y &= 300 + 0.60Y + 900 + 1,301 - 100 \\
0.40Y &= 2,401 \\
Y &= 6,002.5
\end{aligned}
$$

Thus, the multiplier is $6,002.5 - 6,000 = 2.5$, as stated in the text.

To find the multiplier for an increase in fixed taxes, change the tax schedule as follows:

$$T = 0.20Y + 1$$

Disposable income is then

$$DI = Y - T = Y - (0.20Y + 1) = 0.80Y - 1$$

so the consumption function is

$$
\begin{aligned}
C &= 300 + 0.75DI \\
&= 300 + 0.75(0.80Y - 1) \\
&= 299.25 + 0.60Y
\end{aligned}
$$

Solving for equilibrium GDP as usual gives:

$$
\begin{aligned}
Y &= C + I + G + (X - IM) \\
Y &= 299.25 + 0.60Y + 900 + 1,300 - 100 \\
0.40Y &= 2,399.25 \\
Y &= 5,998.125
\end{aligned}
$$

So a $1 increase in fixed taxes lowers $Y$ by $1.875. The tax multiplier is –1.875, which is 75 percent of –2.5.

Now let us proceed to a more general solution, using symbols rather than specific numbers. The equations of the model are as follows:

$$Y = C + I + G + (X - IM) \qquad (1)$$

is the usual equilibrium condition.

$$C = a + bDI \qquad (2)$$

is the same consumption function we used in Appendix A of Chapter 9.

$$DI = Y - T \qquad (3)$$

is the accounting identity relating disposable income to GDP.

$$T = T_0 + tY \qquad (4)$$

is the tax function, where $T_0$ represents fixed taxes (which are zero in our numerical example) and $t$ represents the tax rate (which is 0.20 in the example). Finally, $I, G,$ and $(X - IM)$ are just fixed numbers.

We begin the solution by substituting Equations (3) and (4) into Equation (2) to derive the consumption schedule relating C to Y:

$$C = a + bDI$$
$$C = a + b(Y - T)$$
$$C = a + b(Y - T_0 - tY)$$
$$C = a - bT_0 + b(1 - t)Y \qquad (5)$$

Notice that a change in fixed taxes ($T_0$) shifts the *intercept* of the C schedule, whereas a change in the tax rate ($t$) changes its *slope*, as explained in Appendix A.

Next, substitute Equation (5) into Equation (1) to find equilibrium GDP:

$$Y = C + I + G + (X - IM)$$
$$Y = a - bT_0 + b(1 - t)Y$$
$$+ I + G + (X - IM)$$
$$[1 - b(1 - t)]Y = a - bT_0 + I + G + (X - IM)$$

or

$$Y = \frac{a - bT_0 + I + G + (X - IM)}{1 - b(1 - t)} \qquad (6)$$

Equation (6) shows us that the multiplier for G, I, a, or $(X - IM)$ is

$$\text{Multiplier} = \frac{1}{1 - b(1 - t)}$$

To see that this is in fact the multiplier, raise any of G, I, a, or $(X - IM)$ by one unit. In each case, Equation (6) would be changed to read:

$$Y = \frac{a - bT_0 + I + G + (X - IM) + 1}{1 - b(1 - t)}$$

Subtracting Equation (6) from this expression gives the change in Y stemming from a one-unit change in G, I, or a:

$$\text{Change in } Y = \frac{1}{1 - b(1 - t)}$$

In Chapter 9 ("Algebraic Statement of the Multiplier" section), we noted that if there were no income tax ($t = 0$), a realistic value for b (the marginal propensity to consume) would yield a multiplier of 10, which is much bigger than the true multiplier. Now that we have added taxes to the model, our multiplier formula produces much more realistic numbers. Approximate values for these parameters for the U.S. economy are $b = 0.9$ and $t = 1/3$. The multiplier formula then gives

$$\text{Multiplier} = \frac{1}{1 - 0.9\left(1 - \frac{1}{3}\right)}$$
$$= \frac{1}{1 - 0.6} = \frac{1}{0.4} = 2.5$$

which is much closer to its actual estimated value of around 1.5.

Finally, we can see from Equation (6) that the multiplier for a change in fixed taxes $(T_0)$ is

$$\text{Tax Multiplier} = \frac{-b}{1 - b(1 - t)}$$

For the example considered in the text and earlier in this appendix, $b = 0.75$ and $t = 0.20$, so the formula gives

$$\frac{-0.75}{1 - 0.75(1 - 0.20)} = \frac{-0.75}{1 - 0.75(0.8)}$$
$$= \frac{-0.75}{1 - 0.60} = \frac{-0.75}{0.40} = -1.875$$

According to these figures, each \$1 *increase* in $T_0$ *reduces* Y by \$1.875.

## Test Yourself

1. Consider an economy described by the following set of equations:

$$C = 120 + 0.80DI$$
$$I = 320$$
$$G = 480$$
$$(X - IM) = -80$$
$$T = 200 + 0.25Y$$

Find the equilibrium level of GDP. Next, find the multipliers for government purchases and for fixed taxes. If full employment comes at $Y = 1,800$, what are some policies that would move GDP to that level?

2. This question is a variant of the previous problem that approaches things in the way that a fiscal policy planner might. In an economy whose consumption function and tax function are as given in Test Yourself Question 1, with investment fixed at 320 and net exports

fixed at −80, find the value of $G$ that would make GDP equal to 1,800.

3. You are given the following information about an economy:

$$C = 0.90DI$$
$$I = 100$$
$$G = 540$$
$$(X - IM) = -40$$
$$T = \tfrac{1}{3}Y$$

a. Find equilibrium GDP and the budget deficit.

b. Suppose the government, unhappy with the budget deficit, decides to cut government spending by precisely the amount of the deficit you just found. What actually happens to GDP and the budget deficit, and why?

4. **(More difficult)** In the economy considered in Test Yourself Question 3, suppose the government, seeing that it has not wiped out the deficit, keeps cutting $G$ until it succeeds in balancing the budget. What level of GDP will then prevail?

# MONEY AND THE BANKING SYSTEM

12

> *[Money] is a machine for doing quickly and commodiously what would be done, though less quickly and commodiously, without it.*
>
> JOHN STUART MILL

The circular flow diagrams of earlier chapters show a "financial system" in the upper-left corner. (Look back, e.g., at Figure 1 of Chapter 9.) Saving flows into this system and investment flows out. Obviously, many things happen inside the financial system to channel the saving back into investment, and it is time we learned what some of them are.

Doing so is essential to understanding how *monetary policy* works—the subject of the next two chapters. It is also essential to understanding what happened to our economy when the financial crisis struck, especially in 2008. Our banks and other financial institutions clearly stopped doing their work "quickly and commodiously," as John Stuart Mill so quaintly put it. Instead, the financial system, which is supposed to *facilitate* economic activity (which is what Mill meant), started to *impede* it, and we experienced the worst recession since the 1930s. The after-effects of that recession linger on, as does the bitter memory. So it is imperative that we understand what hit us and why. The lessons of this chapter should help.

## CONTENTS

---

| Issue | *Why Are Banks So Heavily Regulated?* |
|---|---|

Banking has long been one of the most heavily regulated industries in America, but the pendulum of bank regulation has swung back and forth.

In the late 1970s and early 1980s, the United States eased several restrictions on interest rates and permissible bank activities. Then, after a large number of banks and savings institutions went bankrupt in the 1980s, Congress and the bank regulatory agencies cracked down with stiffer regulation and much closer scrutiny. Later, the pendulum swung back toward deregulation, with two landmark banking laws passed in the 1990s. The good times rolled for a while, but then the near meltdown of the financial system that began in 2007 raised new questions about what further regulations might be needed. Many were proposed, and Congress eventually enacted a sweeping financial regulation bill in 2010. The Dodd-Frank Act restricts banks' activities, subjects them to much tougher regulation, establishes a new consumer protection agency, and more. Today, some people are saying that Dodd-Frank went too far, while others claim it did not go far enough.

Thus, although we have spent decades wrestling with the question of how much bank regulation is enough, we are certainly not finished with that debate. To address this question intelligently, we must first answer a more basic question: Why are banks so heavily regulated in the first place?

A first reason is something we will learn in the next chapter: that one major "output" of the banking industry—*the nation's money supply*—is *an important determinant of aggregate demand*. Bank managers are paid to do what is best for their stockholders. But as we will see, what is best for bank stockholders is not always best for the economy as a whole. Consequently, the government does not allow bankers to determine the money supply and interest rates on profit considerations alone. Instead, it tries to influence, or even control, the process.

A second reason for the extensive web of bank regulation is concern for the *safety of depositors*. In a free-enterprise system, new businesses are born and die every day, and no one other than the people immediately involved takes much notice. When a firm goes bankrupt, stockholders lose money, and employees may lose their jobs. However, except for the case of very large firms, that is about all that happens.

But banking is different. If banks were treated like other firms, depositors would lose money whenever a bank went bankrupt. That outcome is bad enough, but the real dangers emerge in the case of a **run on a bank**. When depositors get nervous about the security of their money, they may all rush to cash in their accounts. For reasons we will learn in this chapter, most banks could not survive such a "run" and would be forced to shut their doors.

> A **run on a bank** occurs when many depositors withdraw cash from their accounts all at once.

Worse yet, this disease is highly contagious. If one family hears that their neighbors just lost their life savings because their bank went broke, they are likely to rush to their own bank to withdraw their funds. In fact, fear of contagion is precisely what prompted British bank regulators to act in September 2007 when Northern Rock, a bank specializing in home mortgages, experienced a highly publicized run. (See the box "It Wasn't Such a Wonderful Life" later in this chapter.) They first guaranteed all deposits in Northern Rock and later extended the guarantee to all British banks.[1]

Without modern forms of bank regulation, therefore, one bank failure might lead to another. And indeed, bank failures were common for most of U.S. history. (See Figure 1(a).) But after the 1930s, bank failures became far less common—until recently. (See Figure 1(b), and notice the sharply different scales.) And they have rarely been precipitated by runs because the government has taken steps to ensure that such an infectious disease will not spread. It has done so in several ways that we will study in this chapter.

## 12-1 THE NATURE OF MONEY

> **Barter** is a system of exchange in which people directly trade one good for another, without using money as an intermediate step.

Money is so much a part of our daily existence that we take it for granted, failing to appreciate all that it accomplishes. But money is in no sense "natural." Like the wheel, it had to be invented.

The most obvious way to trade commodities is not by using money, but by **barter**—a system in which people exchange one good directly for another. And the best way to appreciate what monetary exchange accomplishes is to imagine a world without it.

---

[1] At the time, the United Kingdom did not have a deposit insurance system like the Federal Deposit Insurance Corporation (FDIC) in the United States.

SOURCE: Federal Deposit Insurance Corporation.

*Figure 1*

**Bank Failures in the United States, 1915–2013**

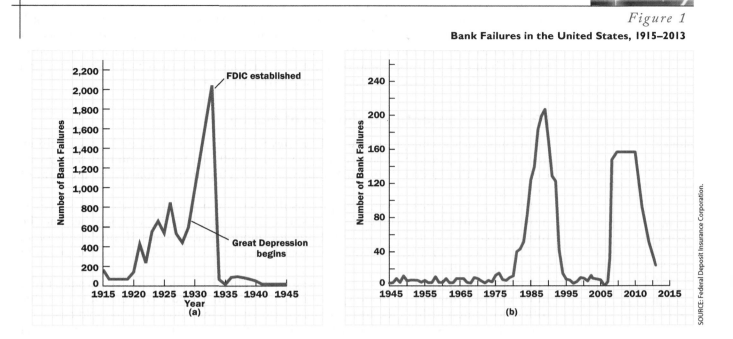

## 12-1a  Barter versus Monetary Exchange

Under a system of direct barter, if Farmer Jones grows corn and has a craving for peanuts, he has to find a peanut farmer, say, Farmer Smith, with a taste for corn. If he finds such a person (a situation called the *double coincidence of wants*), the two farmers make the trade. If that sounds easy, try to imagine how busy Farmer Jones would be if he had to repeat the sequence for everything he consumed in a week. For the most part, the desired double coincidences of wants are more likely to turn out to be double wants of coincidence. (See the cartoon below.) Jones gets no peanuts and Smith gets no corn. Worse yet, with so much time spent looking for trading partners, Jones would have far less time to grow corn. In brief:

> Money greases the wheels of exchange and thus makes the whole economy more productive.

Reprinted with permission of Johnny Hart and Creators Syndicate, Inc.

Under a monetary system, Farmer Jones gives up his corn for money. He does so not because he wants the money *per se,* but because of what that money can buy. With cash in hand, he simply needs to locate a peanut farmer who wants money. And what peanut farmer does not? For these reasons, monetary exchange replaced barter at a very early stage of human civilization, and only extreme circumstances, such as massive wars and runaway inflations, have been able to bring barter back—temporarily.

## 12-1b The Conceptual Definition of Money

**Money** is the standard object used in exchanging goods and services. In short, money is the medium of exchange.

The **medium of exchange** is the object or objects used to buy and sell other items such as goods and services.

The **unit of account** is the standard unit for quoting prices.

A **store of value** is an item used to store wealth from one point in time to another.

Under monetary exchange, people trade **money** for goods when they purchase something, and they trade goods for money when they sell something, but they do not trade goods directly for other goods. This practice defines money's principal role as the **medium of exchange**.

But once money has become accepted as the medium of exchange, whatever serves as money is bound to serve other functions as well. For one, it will inevitably become the **unit of account**—that is, the standard unit for quoting prices. Thus, if inhabitants of an idyllic tropical island use coconuts as money, they would be foolish to quote prices in terms of seashells.

Money may also come to be used as a **store of value**. If Farmer Jones's corn sales bring him more cash than he wants to spend right away, he may find it convenient to store the difference temporarily in the form of money. He knows that money can be sold easily for goods and services at a later date, whereas land, gold, and other stores of value might not be. Of course, if inflation is substantial, he may decide to forgo the convenience of money and store his wealth in some other form rather than see its purchasing power eroded. So money's role as a store of value is far from inevitable.

Because money may not always serve as a store of value, and because other commodities may act as stores of value, we will not include the store-of-value function as part of our conceptual definition of money. Instead, we simply label as "money" whatever serves as the medium of exchange.

## 12-1c What Serves as Money?

Anthropologists and historians can testify that a bewildering variety of objects have served as money in different times and places. Cattle, stones, candy bars, cigarettes, woodpecker scalps, porpoise teeth, and giraffe tails provide a few of the more colorful examples. (For another example, see the accompanying box "Dealing by Wheeling on Yap.")

**Commodity money** is an object in use as a medium of exchange that also has a substantial value in alternative (nonmonetary) uses.

In primitive or less-organized societies, the commodities that served as money generally had value in themselves. If not used as money, cattle could be slaughtered for food, cigarettes could be smoked, and so on. Such **commodity money** generally runs into several severe difficulties. To be useful as a medium of exchange, a commodity must be easily divisible—which makes cattle a poor choice. It must also be of uniform, or at least readily identifiable, quality so that inferior substitutes are easy to recognize. This shortcoming may be why woodpecker scalps never achieved great popularity. The medium of exchange must also be storable and durable, which presents a serious problem for candy-bar money. Finally, because people will carry and store commodity money, it is helpful if the item is compact—that is, has high value per unit of volume and weight.

All of these traits make it natural that gold and silver have circulated as money since the first coins were struck about 2,500 years ago. Because they have high value in nonmonetary uses, a lot of purchasing power can be carried without too much weight. Pieces of gold are also storable, divisible (with a little trouble), and of identifiable quality (with a little more trouble).

The same characteristics suggest that paper money would be even better. The Chinese invented paper money in the eleventh century, and Marco Polo brought the idea to Europe. Because we can print any number on it that we please, we can make paper money as divisible as we like. People can also carry a large value of paper money in a lightweight and compact form. Paper is easy to store, and with a little

# Dealing by Wheeling on Yap

Primitive forms of money still exist in some remote places, as this extract from an old newspaper article shows.

> Yap, Micronesia—On this tiny South Pacific Island … the currency is as solid as a rock. In fact, it is rock. Limestone to be precise.
>
> For nearly 2,000 years the Yapese have used large stone wheels to pay for major purchases, such as land, canoes and permission to marry. Yap is a U.S. trust territory, and the dollar is used in grocery stores and gas stations. But reliance on stone money … continues.
>
> Buying property with stones is "much easier than buying it with U.S. dollars," says John Chodad, who recently purchased a building lot with a 30-inch stone wheel. "We don't know the value of the U.S. dollar."
>
> Stone wheels don't make good pocket money, so for small transactions, Yapese use other forms of currency, such as beer.… .
>
> Besides stone wheels and beer, the Yapese sometimes spend *gaw*, consisting of necklaces of stone beads strung together around a whale's tooth. They also can buy things with *yar*, a currency made from large seashells. But these are small change.
>
> The people of Yap have been using stone money ever since a Yapese warrior named Anagumang first brought the huge stones over from limestone caverns on neighboring Palau, some 1,500 to 2,000 years ago. Inspired by the moon, he fashioned the stone into large circles. The rest is history.… .

By custom, the stones are worthless when broken. You never hear people on Yap musing about wanting a piece of the rock.

SOURCE: Excerpted from Art Pine, "Hard Assets, or Why a Loan in Yap Is Hard to Roll Over," *The Wall Street Journal*, March 29, 1984, p. B1. Reprinted by permission of *The Wall Street Journal.* Copyright © 1984 Dow Jones & Company, Inc. All Rights Reserved Worldwide.

© Michael DeFreitas/Robert Harding World Imagery/Getty Images

cleverness, we can make counterfeiting challenging, though never impossible. (See the box "Remaking America's Paper Money.")

Paper cannot, however, serve as commodity money because its value per square inch in alternative uses is so low. A paper currency that is repudiated by its issuer can, perhaps, be used as wallpaper or to wrap fish, but these uses will surely represent only a small fraction of the paper's value as money. Contrary to the popular expression, such a currency literally *is* worth the paper it is printed on—which is to say that it is not worth much.[2] Thus, paper money is always **fiat money**.

All money in the contemporary United States is fiat money. Look at a dollar bill. Next to George Washington's picture it states: "This note is legal tender for all debts, public and private." Nowhere on the certificate is there a promise, stated or implied, that the U.S. government will exchange it for anything else. A dollar bill is convertible into, say, four quarters or ten dimes—but not into gold, chocolate, or any other commodity.

Why do people hold these pieces of paper? Because they know that others are willing to accept them for things of intrinsic value—food, rent, shoes, and so on. If this confidence ever evaporated, dollar bills would cease serving as a medium of exchange and, given that they make ugly wallpaper, would become virtually worthless.

But don't panic. That is hardly likely. Our current monetary system has evolved over hundreds of years, during which *commodity money* was first replaced by *full-bodied paper money*—paper certificates that were backed by gold or silver of equal value held in the issuer's vaults. Then the full-bodied paper money was replaced by certificates that were only partially backed by gold or silver. Finally, we arrived at our present system, in which

**Fiat money** is money that is decreed as such by the government. It is of little value as a commodity, but it maintains its value as a medium of exchange because people have faith that the issuer will stand behind the pieces of printed paper and limit their production.

---

[2] The first paper money issued by the U.S. federal government, the Continental dollar, was essentially repudiated. (Actually, the new government of the United States redeemed the Continentals for 1 cent on the dollar in the 1790s.) This event gave rise to the derisive expression, "It's not worth a Continental."

## Remaking America's Paper Money

In recent decades, the U.S. Treasury has periodically replaced portions of America's paper money with new notes designed to be increasingly more difficult to counterfeit. Several of the new anti-counterfeiting features are visible to the naked eye. By inspecting one of the new $20 bills—the ones with the big picture of Andrew Jackson that looks like it's been through a washing machine—you can easily see several of them. (Others are harder to detect.)

Most obvious are the various shades of coloration, including the silver blue eagle to Jackson's left. Next, hold the bill up to a light, with Jackson facing you. Near the left edge, you will find some small type set vertically, rather than horizontally. If your eyesight is very good, you will be able to read what it says. If you were a counterfeiter, you would find this line devilishly difficult to duplicate. Third, twist the bill and see how the gold numeral "20" in the lower-right corner glistens and changes color. An optical illusion? No, a clever way to make life hard on counterfeiters.

AP Images/Treasury Department

paper money has no "backing" whatsoever. Like hesitant swimmers who first dip their toes, then their legs, then their whole body into a cold swimming pool, we have "tested the water" at each step of the way—and found it to our liking. It is unlikely that we will ever take a step back in the other direction.

## 12-2 HOW THE QUANTITY OF MONEY IS MEASURED

Because the amount of money in circulation is important for the determination of real GDP and the price level, the government must know how much money there is. Thus we must devise some *measure* of the money supply.

Our conceptual definition of money as the medium of exchange raises difficult questions about which items to include and which items to exclude when we count up the money supply. Such questions have long made the statistical definition of money a subject of dispute. In fact, the U.S. government has several official definitions of the money supply, two of which we will meet shortly.

Some components are obvious. All of our coins and paper money—the small change of our economic system—clearly should count as money. But we cannot stop there if we want to include the main vehicle for making payments in our society, for the lion's share of our nation's payments are made neither in metal nor in paper money, but rather by either electronic or physical checks.

Checking deposits are actually bookkeeping entries on bank ledgers. Many people think of checks as a convenient way to pass coins or dollar bills to someone else, but that is not so. For example, when you pay your heating bill by check, dollar bills rarely change hands. Instead, the check for, say, $150 normally travels back to your bank, where $150 is deducted from the bookkeeping entry that records your account, and $150 is added to the bookkeeping entry for the utility that provides the heat. (If you and the company hold accounts at different banks, more books get involved, but still no coins or bills will likely move.) Indeed, when you pay bills electronically, physical checks don't even move—just electrons, which debit your account and credit the company's account. The volume of money held in the form of checkable deposits far exceeds the volume of currency.

## 12-2a  M1

So it seems imperative to include checkable deposits in any useful definition of the money supply. Unfortunately, this is not an easy task nowadays, because of the wide variety of ways to transfer money by check. Traditional checking accounts in commercial banks are the most familiar vehicle, but many people can also write checks on their savings accounts, on their deposits at credit unions, on their mutual funds, on their accounts with stockbrokers, and so on.

One popular definition of the money supply draws the line early and includes only coins, paper money, traveler's checks, conventional checking accounts, and certain other checkable deposits in banks and savings institutions. In the official U.S. statistics, this narrow concept of money is called **M1**. The upper part of Figure 2 shows the composition of M1 as of September 2014.

## 12-2b  M2

Other types of accounts allow withdrawals by check, so they are also candidates for inclusion in the money supply. Most notably, *money market deposit accounts* allow their owners to write only a few checks per month but pay higher, market-determined interest rates. Consumers have found these accounts attractive, and balances in them exceed all the checkable deposits included in M1.

In addition, many mutual fund organizations and brokerage houses offer *money market mutual funds*. These funds sell shares and use the proceeds to purchase a variety of short-term securities. The important point for our purposes is that owners of shares in money market mutual funds can withdraw their funds by writing checks. Thus, depositors can use their holdings of fund shares just like checking accounts.

Finally, although you cannot write a check on a *savings account*, modern banking procedures have blurred the distinction between checking balances and savings balances. For example, most banks these days offer convenient electronic transfers of funds from one account to another, by telephone, Internet, or by pushing buttons on an automatic teller machine (ATM). Consequently, savings balances can become checkable almost instantly. For this reason, savings accounts are included—along with money market deposit accounts and money market mutual fund shares—in the broader definition of the money supply known as **M2**.

The composition of M2 as of September 2014 is shown in the lower part of Figure 2. You can see that savings deposits predominate, dwarfing M1. Figure 2 illustrates that our money supply comes not only from banks but also from savings institutions, brokerage houses, and mutual fund organizations. Even so, banks still play a predominant role.

## 12-2c  Other Definitions of the Money Supply

Some economists do not want to stop counting at M2; they prefer still broader definitions of money (M3, and so on), which include more types of bank deposits and other closely related assets. (Even bitcoins?) The inescapable problem, however, is that there is no obvious place to stop, no clear line of demarcation between those assets that *are* money and those that are merely *close substitutes* for money—so-called **near moneys**.

If we define an asset's **liquidity** as the ease with which its holder can convert it into cash, there is a spectrum of assets of varying degrees of liquidity. Everything in M1 is completely liquid, the money market fund shares and passbook savings accounts included in M2 are a bit less so, and so on, until we encounter items such as short-term government

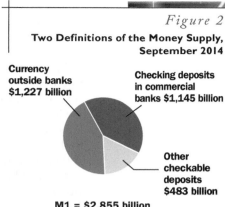

*Figure 2*

**Two Definitions of the Money Supply, September 2014**

M1 = $2,855 billion

Currency outside banks $1,227 billion; Checking deposits in commercial banks $1,145 billion; Other checkable deposits $483 billion

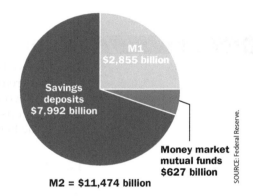

M2 = $11,474 billion

Savings deposits $7,992 billion; M1 $2,855 billion; Money market mutual funds $627 billion

SOURCE: Federal Reserve.

The narrowly defined money supply, usually abbreviated **M1**, is the sum of all coins and paper money in circulation, plus certain checkable deposit balances at banks and savings institutions.[3]

The broadly defined money supply, usually abbreviated **M2**, is the sum of all coins and paper money in circulation, plus all types of checking account balances, plus most forms of savings account balances, plus shares in money market mutual funds.

**Near moneys** are liquid assets that are close substitutes for money.

An asset's **liquidity** refers to the ease with which it can be converted into cash.

---

[3] This amount includes traveler's checks and NOW (negotiable order of withdrawal) accounts.

bonds, which, while still quite liquid, would not be included in anyone's definition of the money supply. Any number of different *M*s can be defined—and have been—by drawing the line in different places.

Yet more complexities arise. For example, credit cards clearly serve as a medium of exchange. Should they be included in the money supply? Of course, you say. But how much *money* does your credit card represent? Is it the amount you currently owe on the card, which may be zero? Or is it your entire line of credit, even though you may never use it all? Neither choice seems sensible. Furthermore, you will probably wind up writing a check or making an electronic funds transfer (which are included in M1) to pay your credit card bill. These are some reasons why economists have so far ignored credit cards in their definitions of money.

We could mention further complexities, but an introductory course in economics is not the place to get bogged down in complex definitional issues. So we will simply adhere to the convention that:

**"Money" consists only of coins, paper money, and checkable deposits.**

## 12-3 THE BANKING SYSTEM

Now that we have defined money and seen how to measure it, we turn our attention to the principal creators of money: the banks. Banking is a complicated business—and getting more so. If you go further in your study of economics, you will probably learn more about the operations of banks. But a few simple principles will suffice for present purposes. Let's start at the beginning.

### 12-3a How Banking Began

When Adam and Eve left the Garden of Eden, they did not encounter an ATM. Banking had to be invented. With a little imagination, we can see how the first banks must have begun.

When money was made of gold or other metals, it was inconvenient for consumers and merchants to carry it around and weigh and assay its purity every time they made a transaction. So the practice developed of leaving gold in a goldsmith's safe storage facilities and carrying in its place a receipt stating that John Doe did indeed own five ounces of gold. When people began trading goods and services for the goldsmiths' receipts, rather than for the gold itself, the receipts became an early form of paper money.

At this stage, paper money was fully backed by gold. Gradually, however, the gold-smiths began to notice that the amount of gold they were actually required to pay out in a day was but a small fraction of the total gold they had stored in their warehouses. Then one day some enterprising goldsmith hit upon a momentous idea that must have made him fabulously wealthy.

His thinking probably ran something like this: "I have 2,000 ounces of gold stored away in my vault, for which I collect storage fees from my customers. I am never called upon to pay out more than 100 ounces on a single day. What harm could it do if I lent out, say, half the gold I now have? I'll still have more than enough to pay off any depositors who come in for withdrawals, so no one will ever know the difference. And I could earn 30 additional ounces of gold each year in interest on the loans I make (at 3 percent interest on 1,000 ounces). With this profit, I could lower my service charges to depositors and so attract still more deposits. I think I'll do it."

**Fractional reserve banking** is a system under which bankers keep as reserves only a fraction of the funds they hold on deposit.

With this resolution, the modern system of **fractional reserve banking** was born. This system has three features that are crucially important to this chapter—and which will help us understand some aspects of the 2007–2009 financial crisis.

**Bank Profitability**   By getting deposits at zero interest and lending some of them out at positive interest rates, goldsmiths made profits. The history of banking as a profit-making industry was begun and has continued to this date. *Banks, like other enterprises, are in* *business to earn profits.* That's a perfectly legitimate goal. But as we shall see, what is in a bank's best interest is not always what's in society's best interest.

**Bank Discretion over the Money Supply** When goldsmiths decided to keep only fractions of their total deposits on reserve and lend out the balance, they acquired the ability to *create money.* As long as they kept 100 percent reserves, each gold certificate represented exactly 1 ounce of gold. So whether people decided to carry their gold or leave it with their goldsmiths did not affect the money supply, which was set by the volume of gold.

With the advent of fractional reserve banking, however, new paper certificates appeared whenever goldsmiths lent out some of the gold they held on deposit. The loans, in effect, created new money. In this way, the total amount of money came to depend on the amount of gold that each goldsmith felt compelled to keep in his vault. For any given volume of gold on deposit, the lower the reserves the goldsmiths kept, the more loans they could make, and therefore the more money would circulate.

Although we no longer use gold to back our money, the same principle applies today. *Bankers' decisions on how much to hold in reserves influence the supply of money.* A substantial part of the rationale for modern monetary policy is, as we have mentioned, that profit-seeking bankers might not create the amount of money that is best for society. For example, when bankers got frightened in the financial crisis of 2007–2009, they decided to hold vastly more idle reserves. Had the Federal Reserve not supplied these additional reserves, the money supply would have contracted violently and the recession would have been far worse than it was.[4]

**Exposure to Runs** A goldsmith who kept 100 percent reserves never had to worry about a run on his vault. Even if all his depositors showed up at the door at once, he could always convert their paper receipts back into gold. But as soon as the first goldsmith decided to get by with only fractional reserves, the possibility of a run on the bank (actually, on the vault) became a real concern. If the first goldsmith who lent out half his gold had found 51 percent of his customers at his door one unlucky day, he would have had a lot of explaining to do. Similar problems have worried bankers for centuries. *The danger of a run on the bank has induced bankers to keep prudent reserves and to lend out money carefully.*

Runs on banks are, for the most part, a relic of the past. You probably have seen the famous bank-run scene in Frank Capra's 1946 movie classic *It's a Wonderful Life,* with Jimmy Stewart playing a young banker named George Bailey. But you've probably never seen an actual bank run. Hardly anyone in America has. In September 2007, however, quite a few people in England did witness a run on Northern Rock, a large mortgage bank. (See the box "It Wasn't Such a Wonderful Life.") As we observed earlier, one of the main rationales for bank regulation is avoiding bank runs, which have not happened in the United States recently even though hundreds of banks have failed. We will see why shortly.

## 12-3b  Principles of Bank Management: Profits versus Safety

Bankers have a reputation for conservatism in politics, dress, and business affairs—though the latter was badly tarnished by the crisis. From what has been said so far, the economic rationale for this traditional conservatism should be clear. Checking deposits are pure fiat money. Years ago, these deposits were "backed" by nothing more than a particular bank's promise to convert them into currency on demand. If people lost trust in a bank, it was doomed.

---

[4] When something similar happened in 1929–1930, the Federal Reserve did not supply enough additional bank reserves and the money supply contracted sharply. That failure is why many economists, including the former chairman of the Federal Reserve Board, Ben Bernanke, blame the Fed for the severity of the Great Depression.

# It Wasn't Such a Wonderful Life

The subprime mortgage crisis that started in 2007 (described in the "What Happened to the Subprime Mortgage Market?" box) quickly spread beyond the borders of the United States. One of its victims was a large British mortgage lender called Northern Rock. In mid-September 2007, rumors that the bank was in trouble precipitated the first bank run in England since the nineteenth century. Here is the scene as described in the online version of *The Times* (of London) as it was happening:

Long queues formed outside branches of Northern Rock today as anxious customers waited to withdraw savings after the bank was forced to seek an emergency bailout from the Bank of England. Savers went in person to Northern Rock's branches to withdraw their money, after facing difficulties contacting the bank on the phone or via the internet.

William Gough, 75, arriving at a Northern Rock branch in Central London this morning, said he did not believe the bank's assurances that his savings were safe and intended to withdraw his funds. "At the time I put the money in I wouldn't have imagined something like this would happen," Mr. Gough said while joining the back of a 40-strong queue.

Customers queued for up to an hour and, as news of the Bank of England bailout spread, the throng inside the branch was so dense that some struggled to open the door.

Gary Diamond beat the crowd by arriving early. "I came down here to withdraw my funds because I'm concerned that Northern Rock are not still going to be in existence," he said after closing his accounts. He added that there was a danger that if others followed suit it could worsen Northern Rock's position. "But I don't want to be the mug left without my savings," he said.

[Other] customers said they were not concerned about the stability of the bank but had been forced to act over fears of a bank run. Paul De Lamare, a 46-year-old consultant, said: "I don't think the Bank of England would allow anything to happen. But I'm just trying to avoid getting caught short, so I've taken out cash."

SOURCE: Joe Bolger and Marcus Leroux, "Northern Rock Savers Rush to Empty Accounts," *Times Online,* September 14, 2007.

Thus, bankers have long relied on a reputation for prudence, which they achieved in two principal ways. First, they maintained a sufficiently generous level of reserves to minimize their vulnerability to runs. Second, they were cautious in making loans and investments, because large losses on their loans could undermine their depositors' confidence.

This second method of establishing prudence was, unfortunately, abandoned by too many banks during the housing boom of 2003–2006 when millions of home mortgages were granted to people of questionable creditworthiness. Not surprisingly, when the boom ended, millions of households could not meet their mortgage payments and lost their homes. The loans losses, in turn, dragged down the banks, many of which failed, too. (See Figure 1(b) again.)

It is important to realize something that too many bankers apparently forgot: that banking under a system of fractional reserves is an inherently risky business that is rendered safe only by cautious and prudent management. America's long history of bank failures bears sober testimony to the fact that many bankers were neither cautious nor prudent. Why not? Because caution is not the route to high profits. Bank profits are maximized by keeping reserves as low as possible and by making at least some loans to borrowers with questionable credit standing who will pay higher interest rates. Many such loans, particularly mortgages, were made between 2003 and 2007.

The art of bank management is to strike the appropriate balance between the lure of profits and the need for safety. If a banker errs by being too stodgy, his bank will earn inadequate profits. If he errs by taking unwarranted risks, his bank may not survive at all.

## 12-3c Bank Regulation

As we have suggested, governments in virtually all societies have decided that profit-minded bankers will not necessarily strike the balance between profits and safety exactly where society wants it. So they have constructed a web of regulations designed to ensure depositors' safety and to control the money supply.

## 12-3d Deposit Insurance

The principal innovation that guarantees the safety of bank deposits is **deposit insurance**. Today, most U.S. bank deposits are insured against loss by the Federal Deposit Insurance Corporation—an agency of the U.S. government. If your bank belongs to the FDIC, as almost all do, your account is insured for up to $250,000 regardless of what happens to the bank. Thus, although bank failures may spell disaster for the bank's stockholders, they do not create concern for many depositors. Deposit insurance eliminates the motive for customers to rush to their bank just because they hear some bad news about the bank's finances. Many observers give this innovation much of the credit for the pronounced decline in bank failures after the FDIC was established in 1933—a decline that is evident in Figure 1(a)—and the virtual disappearance of bank runs.

> **Deposit insurance** is a system that guarantees that depositors will not lose money even if their bank goes bankrupt.

Despite these achievements, some critics of FDIC insurance worry that depositors who are freed from any risk of loss from a failing bank will not bother to shop around for safer banks. This problem is an example of what is called **moral hazard**. The general idea is that, when people are well insured against a particular risk, they will put little effort into making sure that the risk does not occur. (Example: A business with good fire insurance may not install an expensive sprinkler system.) In this context, some of the FDIC's critics argue that high levels of deposit insurance actually make the banking system less safe.

> **Moral hazard** is the idea that, when people are insured against the consequences of a risk, they will engage in riskier behavior.

## 12-3e Bank Supervision

Partly for this reason, the government takes several steps to see that banks do not get into financial trouble. For one thing, various regulatory authorities conduct periodic *bank examinations* to keep tabs on the financial conditions and business practices of the banks under their purview.

After a rash of bank failures in the late 1980s and early 1990s (plainly visible in Figure 1(b)), U.S. bank supervision was tightened by legislation that permits the authorities to intervene early in the affairs of financially troubled banks. The more recent rash of bank failures since 2006 (also visible in Figure 1(b)) brought in its wake even tighter regulations, especially over the riskier activities of large banks. In addition, the government established a new bureau of consumer financial protection and a new mechanism for dealing with potential failures of giant banks.

Other laws and regulations *limit the kinds and quantities of assets in which banks may invest*. For example, banks are permitted to own only limited amounts of common stock. And the Dodd-Frank Act, passed in 2010, places new restrictions on banks' ability to engage in what is called "proprietary trading," that is, buying and selling assets to make a profit. All of these forms of regulation, and others, are aimed at making banks safer. That said, there is no such thing as perfect safety, as the subprime mortgage debacle vividly illustrated.

## 12-3f Reserve Requirements

A final type of regulation also has some bearing on safety but is motivated primarily by the government's desire to control the money supply. We have seen that the amount of money any bank will issue depends on the amount of reserves it elects to keep. For this reason, most banks are forced by law to hold minimum **required reserves**. Although banks may keep reserves in excess of these legal minimums, they may not keep less. So this regulation places an upper limit on the money supply.

> **Required reserves** are the minimum amount of reserves (in cash or the equivalent) required by law. Normally, required reserves are proportional to the volume of deposits.

# What Happened to the Subprime Mortgage Market?

One valuable, but also somewhat risky, innovation in American banking during the previous decade was the rapid expansion of so-called subprime mortgages, meaning loans to prospective homeowners with less-than-stellar credit histories. Often, these borrowers had low incomes and were poorly educated. Naturally, bankers expected higher default rates on subprime loans than on prime loans, and so they charged higher interest rates to compensate for expected future losses. That was all perfectly sound banking practice.

But a few things went badly wrong, especially in 2005 and 2006. For one thing, subprime loans started being made with little or no evidence that the homeowners had enough regular income to meet their monthly payments (e.g., a large-enough paycheck). That is *not* sound banking practice. Second, many subprime loans carried "adjustable rates," which in practice meant that the monthly mortgage payment could skyrocket after, say, two years. That created a ticking time bomb that should have raised serious questions about affordability of the mortgages—but apparently did not. Third, about half of these risky loans were not made by regulated banks at all, but rather by mortgage brokers—who were not regulated by the federal government and who sometimes followed unscrupulous sales practices. Finally, the general euphoria over housing (the housing "bubble") led many people to believe that all these dangers would be papered over by ever-rising home prices.

When house prices stopped rising so fast in 2006, the game of musical chairs ended abruptly. Default rates on subprime mortgages soared.

Then, in 2007, the subprime market virtually shut down, precipitating a near panic in financial markets in the United States and around the world. In the United States, the Federal Reserve stepped in to quell the panic by lending massively to banks and then cutting interest rates.

The medicine helped a bit, but losses from the housing downturn continued, banks contracted and some failed, and credit became harder to obtain. By early 2008, the economy was in recession.

Most of the rest of this chapter is concerned with the details of bank reserves and money creation, at least as the mechanism operates in normal times—when banks hold virtually no excess reserves. But due to the extremely *abnormal* circumstances created by the financial crisis and the Great Recession, U.S. banks have been holding unprecedented amounts of excess reserves in recent years. We will deal with the normal case before explaining the current abnormal situation. But first, a few final words on bank regulation.

## 12-4 SYSTEMIC RISK AND THE "TOO BIG TO FAIL" DOCTRINE

**Systemic risk** refers to risks to the entire *system* of banks or financial institutions. It arises because these institutions, especially the largest ones, are interlinked in many ways.

One particular type of banking risk has occupied the minds of policy makers in the United States and across the world since the financial crisis exploded. It is called **systemic risk**. The basic idea is simple, although practical applications can be excruciatingly complex.

The underlying notion is that no bank operates in a vacuum. Each is part of a national, and in many cases international, banking *system;* and the banking system, in turn, is an important part of the broader *financial system*. Just as with diseases spreading through populations, a "sick" bank can transmit its "disease" to others via a number of channels. We have encountered one already: bank runs, which were highly contagious prior to the advent of deposit insurance.

But there are other contagion mechanisms. For example, banks are constantly collecting funds from, and disbursing them to, other banks and non-bank financial institutions (e.g., stockbrokers). If an important link in this chain should fail, the whole payments system could be in danger. Or consider what are called "fire sales." If a bank suffers large losses and needs to raise cash rapidly, it may be forced to sell a large volume of assets quickly, which in turn would depress the prices of those assets and impose losses on other banks. Events like these pose potential *systemic* risks, that is, risks to the entire financial *system* and, via the financial system, to the whole economy.

These are risks that no government takes lightly. But how do you safeguard against them? That is a complicated question that would require a book in itself—and much more complicated analysis—to answer fully. But one aspect is obvious:

**Systemic risks inhere mainly in the largest financial institutions.**

If the Third National Bank of Littletown goes bankrupt, or fails to make payments, or "fire sells" some securities it owns, that will cause barely a ripple in the overall banking system. But if any of these things should happen to, say, Bank of America or Citibank, a worldwide financial panic would probably ensue. Indeed, that is exactly what happened when the investment bank Lehman Brothers failed in September 2008—and the memory lingers on.

Concern over systemic risk has led to the designation of some large financial institutions as **systemically important**, or in the colloquial expression as **"too big to fail."** One of the most vexing questions in bank regulation, both here and abroad, is how to deal with institutions that are too big to fail.

During the worst of the financial crisis, the U.S. government decided that Lehman Brothers was *not* too big to fail. But its chaotic bankruptcy precipitated a worldwide financial panic that no one wants to repeat. Then, a few days later, the same U.S. government decided that American International Group (AIG), then the world's largest global insurance company, *was* too big to fail. It kept AIG alive with massive loans from the Federal Reserve and then from the U.S. Treasury, that is, from the U.S. taxpayer—which seemingly everyone hated. These two very different "solutions" to problems in too-big-to-fail institutions left the doctrine in a state of confusion.

One major focus of the financial regulatory reform law enacted in 2010 (the Dodd-Frank Act) was to try to bring an end this confusion. Dodd-Frank empowers the Federal Reserve to supervise financial institutions that are deemed to be systemically important. It subjects these large institutions to a tougher regulatory regime than ordinary banks face. And it creates a new procedure, short of bankruptcy, to quietly lay to rest any of these institutions if it should fail—thus changing the doctrine from "too big to fail" to "too big to fail messily." Needless to say, it will be years before we know how well these regulatory innovations work in practice.

> A **systemically important** (or **"too big to fail"**) financial institution is one that, by virtue of its size or interconnectedness, can threaten the entire system if it runs into trouble.

## 12-5 THE ORIGINS OF THE MONEY SUPPLY

We turn now to our next objective: understanding the process by which the banking system "creates money" in normal times. To do that, we must first acquire at least a nodding acquaintance with elementary accounting and the mechanics of modern banking.

### 12-5a How Bankers Keep Books

The first thing to know is how to distinguish assets from liabilities. An **asset** of a bank is something of value that the bank *owns*. This "thing" may be a physical object, such as the bank building or a computer, or it may be a piece of paper, such as an IOU signed by a customer to whom the bank has made a loan (e.g., a mortgage). A **liability** of a bank is something of value that the bank *owes*. For example, if you have an account in the Main Street Bank, your bank balance is a liability of the bank. (It is an asset to you.) Most bank liabilities take the form of bookkeeping entries.

There is an easy test for whether some piece of paper or bookkeeping entry is a bank's *asset* or *liability*. Ask yourself this simple question: If the paper were converted into cash, would the bank receive the cash (if so, it is an asset) or pay it out (if so, it is a liability)? This test makes it clear that loans to customers are assets of the bank (when a loan is repaid, the bank collects), whereas customers' deposits are bank liabilities (when a deposit is cashed in, the bank pays). Of course, things are just the opposite to the bank's customers: The loans are liabilities, and the deposits are assets.

When accountants draw up a complete list of all the bank's assets and liabilities, the resulting document is called the bank's **balance sheet**. Typically, the value of all the bank's

> An **asset** of an individual or business firm is an item of value that the individual or firm owns.

> A **liability** of an individual or business firm is an item of value that the individual or firm owes. Many liabilities are known as *debts*.

> A **balance sheet** is an accounting statement listing the values of all assets on the left side and the values of all liabilities and *net worth* on the right side.

*Table 1*

**Balance Sheet of Bank-a-Mythica, December 31, 2014**

| Assets | | Liabilities and Net Worth | |
|---|---|---|---|
| Assets | | Liabilities | |
| Reserves | $1,000,000 | Checking deposits | $5,000,000 |
| Loans outstanding | 4,500,000 | | |
| Total | $5,500,000 | Net Worth | |
| Addendum: Bank Reserves | | Stockholders' equity | 500,000 |
| Actual reserves | $1,000,000 | | |
| Required reserves | 1,000,000 | Total | $5,500,000 |
| Excess reserves | $          0 | | |

assets exceeds the value of all its liabilities. (On the rare occasions when this is not so, the bank is in serious trouble.) In what sense, then, do balance sheets "balance"?

They balance because accountants have invented the concept of **net worth** to balance the books. Specifically, they define the net worth of a bank to be the *difference* between the value of all its assets and the value of all its liabilities. Thus, by definition, when accountants add net worth to liabilities, the sum they get must be equal to the value of the bank's assets:

$$\text{Assets} = \text{Liabilities} + \text{Net worth}$$

**Net worth** is the value of all assets minus the value of all liabilities.

Table 1 illustrates these ideas with the balance sheet of a fictitious bank, Bank-a-Mythica, whose finances are extremely simple. On December 31, 2014, it had only two kinds of assets (listed on the left side of the balance sheet)—$1 million in cash reserves and $4.5 million in outstanding loans to its customers, that is, in customers' IOUs. And it had only one type of liability (listed on the right side)—$5 million in checking deposits. The difference between total assets ($5.5 million) and total liabilities ($5.0 million) was the bank's net worth ($500,000), also shown on the right side of the balance sheet.

## 12-6 BANKS AND MONEY CREATION

Let us now turn to the process of deposit creation. Many bankers will deny that they have any ability to "create" money. The very phrase has a suspiciously hocus-pocus sound to it. But the protesting bankers are not quite right. Although any individual bank's ability to create money is severely limited, the banking system as a whole can achieve much more than the sum of its parts. Through the modern alchemy of **deposit creation**, it can turn one dollar into many dollars. To understand this important process, we had best proceed step-by-step, beginning with the case of a single bank, our hypothetical Bank-a-Mythica.

**Deposit creation** refers to the process by which a fractional reserve banking system turns $1 of bank reserves into several dollars of bank deposits.

### 12-6a The Limits to Money Creation by a Single Bank

According to the balance sheet in Table 1, Bank-a-Mythica holds cash reserves of $1 million, equal to 20 percent of its $5 million in deposits. Assume that this is the reserve ratio prescribed by law and that the bank strives to keep its reserves down to the legal minimum; that is, it strives to keep its **excess reserves** at zero—which is the normal case.

**Excess reserves** are any reserves held in excess of the legal minimum.

Now let us suppose that on January 2, 2015, an eccentric widower comes into Bank-a-Mythica and deposits $100,000 in cash into his checking account. The bank now has $100,000 more in cash reserves and $100,000 more in checking deposits. Because deposits are up by $100,000, *required* reserves rise by only $20,000, leaving $80,000 in *excess* reserves. Table 2 illustrates the effects of this transaction on Bank-a-Mythica's balance sheet. Tables such as this one, which show *changes* in balance sheets rather than the balance sheets themselves, are called "T-accounts" because of their characteristic shape. They will help us follow the money-creation process.[5]

Bank-a-Mythica is unlikely to be happy with the situation illustrated in Table 2, for it is holding $80,000 in excess reserves on which it earns little or no interest. So as soon

---

[5] Since T-accounts record *changes* in assets and *changes* in liabilities, they must also balance if the balance sheet is to balance both before and after the transaction.

as possible, it will lend out the extra $80,000—let us say to Hard-Pressed Construction Company. This loan leads to the balance sheet changes shown in Table 3: Bank-a-Mythica's loans rise by $80,000 while its holdings of cash reserves fall by $80,000.

By combining Tables 2 and 3, we arrive at Table 4, which summarizes the bank's transactions for the week. Reserves are up $20,000, loans are up $80,000, and now that the bank has had a chance to adjust to the inflow of deposits, it no longer holds excess reserves.

Looking at Table 4 and keeping in mind our specific definition of money, it appears at first that the chairman of Bank-a-Mythica is right when he claims not to have engaged in the nefarious-sounding practice of "money creation." All that happened was that, in exchange for the $100,000 in cash it received, the bank issued the widower a checking balance of $100,000. This transaction does not change M1; it merely converts one form of money (currency) into another (checking deposits).

But wait. What happened to the $100,000 in cash that the eccentric man brought to the bank? The table shows that Bank-a-Mythica retained $20,000 in its vault. Because this currency is no longer in circulation, it no longer counts in the official money supply, M1. (Notice that Figure 2 includes only "currency outside banks.") But the other $80,000, which the bank lent out, is still in circulation. It is held by Hard-Pressed Construction Company, which probably will redeposit it in some other bank. Even before this new deposit is made, the original $100,000 in cash has supported an increase in the money supply. There is now $100,000 in checking deposits and $80,000 of cash in circulation, making a total of $180,000—whereas prior to the original deposit there was only the $100,000 in cash. The money-creation process has begun.

*Table 2*

**Changes in Bank-a-Mythica's Balance Sheet, January 2, 2015**

| Assets | | Liabilities | |
|---|---|---|---|
| Reserves | +$100,000 | Checking deposits | +$100,000 |
| **Addendum: Changes in Reserves** | | | |
| Actual reserves | +$100,000 | | |
| Required reserves | +    20,000 | | |
| Excess reserves | +$  80,000 | | |

*Table 3*

**Changes in Bank-a-Mythica's Balance Sheet, January 3–6, 2015**

| Assets | | Liabilities | |
|---|---|---|---|
| Loans outstanding | +$  80,000 | Checking deposits | No Change |
| Reserves | −$  80,000 | | |
| **Addendum: Changes in Reserves** | | | |
| Actual reserves | −$  80,000 | | |
| Required reserves | No Change | | |
| Excess reserves | −$  80,000 | | |

*Table 4*

**Changes in Bank-a-Mythica's Balance Sheet, January 2–6, 2015**

| Assets | | Liabilities | |
|---|---|---|---|
| Reserves | +$  20,000 | Checking deposits | +$100,000 |
| Loan outstanding | +$  80,000 | | |
| **Addendum: Changes in Reserves** | | | |
| Actual reserves | +$  20,000 | | |
| Required reserves | +$  20,000 | | |
| Excess reserves | No Change | | |

## 12-6b  Multiple Money Creation by a Series of Banks

By tracing the $80,000 in cash, we can see how the process of money creation gathers momentum. Suppose Hard-Pressed Construction Company deposits the $80,000 in its bank account at the First National Bank. First National's reserves increase by $80,000.

**Table 5**

**Changes in First National Bank's Balance Sheet**

| Assets | | Liabilities | |
|---|---|---|---|
| Reserves | +$16,000 | Checking deposits | +$80,000 |
| Loans outstanding | +$64,000 | | |
| Addendum: Changes in Reserves | | | |
| Actual reserves | +$16,000 | | |
| Required reserves | +$16,000 | | |
| Excess reserves | No Change | | |

**Table 6**

**Changes in Second National Bank's Balance Sheet**

| Assets | | Liabilities | |
|---|---|---|---|
| Reserves | +$12,800 | Checking deposits | +$64,000 |
| Loans outstanding | +$51,200 | | |
| Addendum: Changes in Reserves | | | |
| Actual reserves | +$12,800 | | |
| Required reserves | +$12,800 | | |
| Excess reserves | No Change | | |

Because its deposits rise by $80,000, its *required* reserves increase by 20 percent of this amount, or $16,000. If First National Bank behaves like Bank-a-Mythica, it will lend out the $64,000 of excess reserves.

Table 5 shows the effects of these events on First National Bank's balance sheet. (We do not show the preliminary steps corresponding to Tables 2 and 3 separately.) At this stage in the chain, the original $100,000 in cash has led to $180,000 in deposits—$100,000 at Bank-a-Mythica and $80,000 at First National Bank—plus $64,000 in cash, which is still in circulation (in the hands of the recipient of First National's loan—say, Al's Auto Shop). Thus, from the original $100,000, a total of $244,000 worth of money ($180,000 in checking deposits plus $64,000 in cash) has been created so far.

But to coin a phrase, the bucks do not stop there. Al's Auto Shop will presumably deposit the proceeds from its loan into its own account at Second National Bank, leading to the balance sheet adjustments shown in Table 6 when Second National makes an additional loan of $51,200 rather than hold on to excess reserves. You can see how the money-creation process continues.

Figure 3 summarizes the balance sheet changes of the first five banks in the chain (from Bank-a-Mythica through the Fourth National Bank) graphically, based on the assumptions that (1) each bank holds exactly the 20 percent required reserves, and (2) each loan recipient redeposits the proceeds in the next bank. But the chain does not end there. The Main Street Movie Theatre, which received the $32,768 loan from the Fourth National Bank, deposits these funds into the Fifth National Bank. Fifth National has to keep only 20 percent of this deposit, or $6,553.60, on reserve and will lend out the balance. And so the chain continues.

Where does it all end? The running sums on the right side of Figure 3 show what eventually happens to the entire banking system. The initial deposit of $100,000 in cash is ultimately absorbed in bank reserves (column 1), leading to a total of $500,000 in new deposits (column 2) and $400,000 in new loans (column 3). The money supply rises by $400,000 because the non-bank public eventually holds $100,000 *less* in currency and $500,000 *more* in checking deposits.

As we see, there really is some hocus-pocus. Somehow, an initial deposit of $100,000 leads to $500,000 in new bank deposits—a multiple expansion of $5 for every original dollar—and a net increase of $400,000 in the money supply. We need to understand *why* this is so, but first let us verify that the calculations in Figure 3 are correct.

If you look carefully at the numbers, you will see that each column forms a geometric progression; specifically, each entry is equal to exactly 80 percent of the entry before it. Recall that in our discussion of the multiplier in Chapter 9 we learned how to sum an infinite geometric progression, which is just what each of these chains is. In particular, if the common ratio is $R$, the sum of an infinite geometric progression is:

$$1 - R + R^2 + R^3 + \ldots = \frac{1}{1 - R}$$

*Figure 3*

**The Chain of Multiple Deposit Creation**

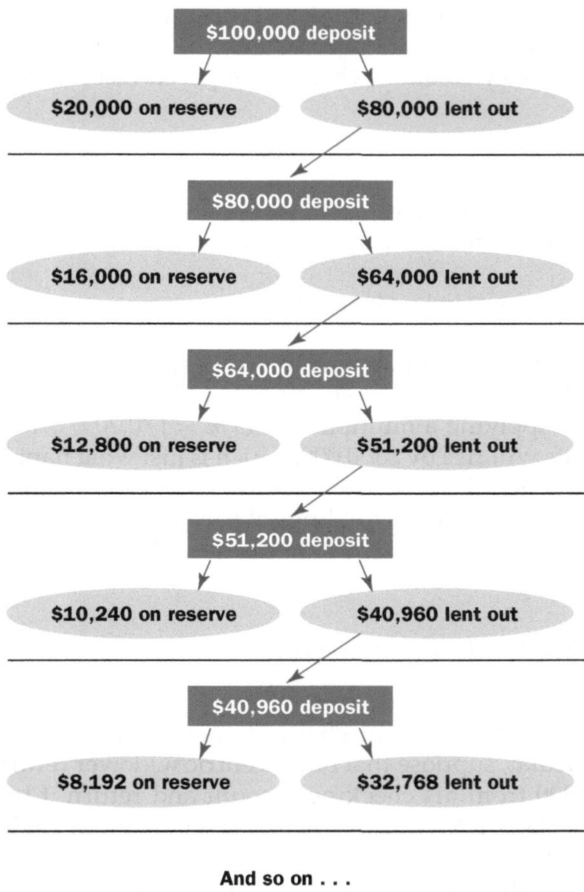
$100,000 deposit
$20,000 on reserve
$80,000 lent out
$80,000 deposit
$16,000 on reserve
$64,000 lent out
$64,000 deposit
$12,800 on reserve
$51,200 lent out
$51,200 deposit
$10,240 on reserve
$40,960 lent out
$40,960 deposit
$8,192 on reserve
$32,768 lent out
And so on . . .

| Running Sums | | |
|---|---|---|
| (1) *Reserves* | (2) *Deposits* | (3) *Loans* |
| | $100,000 | |
| $20,000 | | $80,000 |
| | $180,000 | |
| $36,000 | | $144,000 |
| | $244,000 | |
| $48,800 | | $195,200 |
| | $295,200 | |
| $59,040 | | $236,160 |
| | $336,160 | |
| $67,232 | | $268,928 |
| ⋮ | ⋮ | ⋮ |
| $100,000 | $500,000 | $400,000 |

SOURCE: This schematic diagram was suggested to us by Dr. Ivan K. Cohen, whom we thank.

By applying this formula to the chain of checking deposits in Figure 3, we get:

$$\begin{aligned}&\$100{,}000 + \$80{,}000 + \$64{,}000 + \$51{,}200 + \ldots\\ &= \$100{,}000 \times (1 + 0.80 + 0.64 + 0.512 + \ldots)\\ &= \$100{,}000 \times (1 + 0.80 + 0.80^2 + 0.80^3 + \ldots)\\ &= \$100{,}000 \times \frac{1}{1 - 0.80} = \frac{\$100{,}000}{0.20} = \$500{,}000\end{aligned}$$

Proceeding similarly, we can verify that the new loans sum to $400,000 and that the new required reserves sum to $100,000. (Check these figures as exercises.) Thus the numbers at the bottom of Figure 3 are correct. Let us, therefore, think through the logic behind them.

The chain of deposit creation ends only when there are no more *excess* reserves to be loaned out—that is, when the entire $100,000 in cash is tied up in *required* reserves. That explains why the last entry in column (1) of Figure 3 must be $100,000. With a reserve ratio of 20 percent, excess reserves disappear only when checking deposits expand by $500,000—which is the last entry in column (2). Finally, because balance sheets must balance, the sum of all newly created assets (reserves plus loans) must equal the sum of all newly created liabilities ($500,000 in deposits). That leaves $400,000 for new loans—which is the last entry in column (3).

More generally, if the reserve ratio is some number $m$ (rather than the one-fifth in our example), each dollar of deposits requires only a fraction $m$ of a dollar in reserves. The common ratio in the preceding formula is, therefore, $R = 1 - m$, and deposits must expand by $1/m$ for each dollar of new reserves that are injected into the system. This suggests the general formula for multiple money creation when the required reserve ratio is some number $m$:

### OVERSIMPLIFIED MONEY MULTIPLIER FORMULA

The **money multiplier** is the ratio of newly created bank deposits to new reserves.

If the required reserve ratio is some fraction, $m$, the banking system as a whole can convert each $1 of reserves into $1/m$ in new money. That is, the so-called **money multiplier** is given by:

$$\text{Change in money supply} = (1/m) \times \text{Change in reserves}$$

Although this formula correctly describes what happens in our example, it leaves out an important detail. The initial deposit of $100,000 in cash at Bank-a-Mythica constitutes $100,000 in new reserves (see Table 2). Applying a multiplier of $1/m = 1/0.20 = 5$ to this $100,000, we conclude that bank deposits will rise by $500,000, which is just what happens. But remember that the process started when the eccentric widower took $100,000 in cash and deposited it in his bank account. Thus the public's holdings of *money*—which includes both checking deposits and cash—increase by only $400,000 in this case: There is $500,000 more in deposits, but $100,000 less in cash.

## 12-6c  The Process in Reverse: Multiple Contractions of the Money Supply

Let us now briefly consider how this deposit-creation mechanism operates in reverse—as a system of deposit *destruction*. In particular, suppose that our eccentric widower returned to Bank-a-Mythica to withdraw $100,000 from his checking account and return it to his mattress, where it rightfully belongs. Bank-a-Mythica's *required* reserves would fall by $20,000 as a result of this transaction (20 percent of $100,000), but its *actual* reserves would fall by $100,000. The bank would be $80,000 short, as indicated in Table 7(a).

How will the bank react to this discrepancy? As some of its outstanding loans are routinely paid off, it will cease granting new ones until it has accumulated the necessary $80,000 in required reserves. The data for Bank-a-Mythica's contraction are shown in Table 7(b), assuming that borrowers pay off their loans in cash.[6]

Where did the borrowers get this money? Probably by making withdrawals from other banks. In this case, assume that the funds came from First National Bank, which loses $80,000 in deposits and $80,000 in reserves. It finds itself short some $64,000 in reserves, as shown in Table 8(a), and therefore must reduce its loan commitments by $64,000, as in Table 8(b). This reaction, of course, causes some other bank to suffer a loss of reserves and deposits of $64,000, and the whole process repeats just as it did in the case of deposit expansion.

After the entire banking system had become involved, the picture would be just as shown in Figure 3, except that all the numbers would have *minus signs* in front of them. Deposits would shrink by $500,000, loans would fall by $400,000, bank reserves would be reduced by $100,000, and the M1 money supply would fall by $400,000. As suggested by our money multiplier formula with $m = 0.20$, the decline in the bank deposit component of the money supply is $1/0.20 = 5$ times as large as the decline in reserves.

---

[6] In reality, the borrowers would probably pay with checks drawn on other banks. Bank-a-Mythica would then cash these checks to acquire the reserves.

Table 7

**Changes in the Balance Sheet of Bank-a-Mythica**

**(a)**

| Assets | | Liabilities | |
|---|---|---|---|
| Reserves | −$100,000 | Checking deposits | −$100,000 |

Addendum: Changes in Reserves

| Actual reserves | −$100,000 |
|---|---|
| Required reserves | −20,000 |
| Excess reserves | −$ 80,000 |

**(b)**

| Assets | | Liabilities | |
|---|---|---|---|
| Reserves | +$80,000 | No Change | |
| Loans outstanding | −$80,000 | | |

Addendum: Changes in Reserves

| Actual reserves | +$80,000 |
|---|---|
| Required reserves | No Change |
| Excess reserves | +$80,000 |

Table 8

**Changes in the Balance Sheet of First National Bank**

**(a)**

| Assets | | Liabilities | |
|---|---|---|---|
| Reserves | −$80,000 | Checking deposits | −$80,000 |

Addendum: Changes in Reserves

| Actual reserves | −$80,000 |
|---|---|
| Required reserves | −16,000 |
| Excess reserves | −$64,000 |

**(b)**

| Assets | | Liabilities | |
|---|---|---|---|
| Reserves | +$64,000 | No Change | |
| Loans outstanding | −$64,000 | | |

Addendum: Changes in Reserves

| Actual reserves | +$64,000 |
|---|---|
| Required reserves | No Change |
| Excess reserves | +$64,000 |

## 12-7 WHY THE MONEY-CREATION FORMULA IS OVERSIMPLIFIED

So far, our discussion of the process of money creation has been rather mechanical. If everything proceeds according to formula, each $1 in new reserves injected into the banking system leads to a $1/m$ increase in new deposits. In reality, things are not so simple—especially nowadays. Just as in the case of the expenditure multiplier, the over-simplified money multiplier is accurate only under very particular circumstances. These circumstances require that

1. Every recipient of cash must redeposit the cash into another bank rather than hold it.
2. Every bank must hold reserves no larger than the legal minimum.

It is the second of these conditions that has gone badly wrong in recent years.

The "chain" diagram in Figure 3 can teach us what happens if either of these assumptions is violated. Suppose first that the business firms and individuals who receive bank loans decide to redeposit only a fraction of the proceeds into their bank accounts, holding the rest in cash. Then, for example, the first $80,000 loan would lead to a deposit of less than $80,000—and similarly down the chain. The whole chain of deposit creation would therefore shrink. Thus:

> If individuals and business firms decide to hold more cash, the multiple expansion of bank deposits will be curtailed because fewer dollars of cash will be available for use as reserves to support checking deposits. Consequently, the money supply will be smaller.

The basic idea here is simple. Each $1 of cash held *inside* a bank can support several dollars (specifically, $1/m$) of money. But each $1 of cash held *outside* the banking system constitutes exactly $1 of money; it supports no deposits. Hence, when cash moves from inside the banking system into the hands of households or businesses, the money supply will decline. And when new cash enters the banking system, the money supply will rise.

The second of our conditions (no excess reserves) holds the key to understanding one aspect of the financial crisis and one reason why it has been so hard to revive the economy. Suppose bank managers become frightened about the outlook for loan repayments, perhaps because economic conditions have deteriorated—which is exactly what happened after 2008. In such a nervous environment, banks might decide to hold on to more reserves than their legal requirements, which means they will lend out less than the amounts assumed in Figure 3. Instead of being "put to work" financing lending, reserves will sit idle on banks' books instead. When this happens, each bank in the chain will receive a smaller deposit and, once again, the whole chain of deposit creation will be curtailed. Thus:

> If banks wish to hold excess reserves, the multiple expansion of bank deposits will be limited. A given amount of cash will support a smaller supply of money than in the case when banks hold no excess reserves.

To see the mechanics, look back at Table 2 and suppose now that Bank-a-Mythica wants to accumulate excess reserves. It might just hold on to the $80,000 in excess reserves it receives—in which case the money-creation process would be stopped in its tracks. Or it might keep, say, $60,000 in excess reserves and lend out just $20,000 (instead of the $80,000 shown in Table 3)—in which case the money multiplier would be sharply reduced.

This is exactly what happened—on a grand scale—in the United States after September 2008, when the collapse of Lehman Brothers set off a financial panic. Banks clung to reserves as if they were life preservers, and excess reserves exploded from a mere $2 billion just before Lehman to an astonishing $267 billion by October 2008 and almost $800 billion by January 2009. As of this writing, they stand at over $2.6 *trillion*. (See Figure 4.) In consequence, although *total* bank reserves rose over 260-fold between August 2008 and September 2014 (a period of about six years), the M1 money supply roughly doubled. Because the vast majority of bank reserves were sitting idle, rather than being used to create money, the oversimplified money multiplier formula missed by a country mile.

## 12-8  THE NEED FOR MONETARY POLICY

If we pursue these two points a bit farther, we will see why the government must regulate the money supply in an effort to maintain economic stability. We have just suggested that banks will keep excess reserves when they do not foresee profitable and secure opportunities to make loans. This scenario is most likely to arise when business conditions are depressed, such as in a recession. In times like that, the propensity of banks to hold excess reserves can turn the deposit-creation process into one of deposit destruction—which would have happened in the United States in 2008 and 2009 had the Federal Reserve not flooded the banking system with reserves (see Figure 4 again). In addition, if depositors become nervous, they may decide to hold on to more cash. Thus:

> During a recession, profit-oriented banks would be prone to reduce the money supply by increasing their excess reserves and declining to lend to less creditworthy applicants—if the government did not intervene. As we will learn in subsequent chapters, the money supply is an important influence on aggregate demand, so such a contraction of the money supply would aggravate the recession.

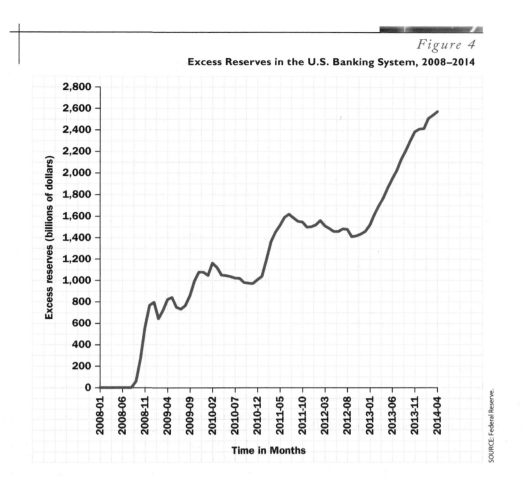

*Figure 4*

**Excess Reserves in the U.S. Banking System, 2008–2014**

SOURCE: Federal Reserve.

This is precisely what happened—with a vengeance—during the Great Depression of the 1930s. Although total bank reserves grew somewhat, the money supply contracted because banks preferred to hold excess reserves rather than make loans that might not be repaid. And something similar has happened in recent years: As noted earlier, the supply of reserves expanded much more rapidly than the money supply because nervous bankers held on to their excess reserves. But this time, the Federal Reserve kept the money supply growing by using policy tools we will describe in the next chapter. For example, it made sure that bank reserves were in ample supply.

By contrast, banks want to squeeze the maximum money supply possible out of any given amount of cash reserves by keeping their reserves at the bare minimum when the demand for bank loans is buoyant, profits are high, and secure investment opportunities abound. This reduced incentive to hold excess reserves in prosperous times means that

> During an economic boom, profit-oriented banks will likely make the money supply expand, adding undesirable momentum to the booming economy and paving the way for inflation. The authorities must intervene to prevent this rapid money growth.

Regulation of the money supply, then, is necessary because profit-oriented bankers might otherwise provide the economy with a money supply that dances to and amplifies the tune of the business cycle. Precisely how the authorities control the money supply is the subject of the next chapter.

## Summary

1. It is more efficient to exchange goods and services by using **money** as a medium of exchange than by **bartering** them directly.

2. In addition to being the **medium of exchange,** whatever serves as money is likely to become the standard **unit of account** and a popular **store of value.**

3. Throughout history, all sorts of items have served as money. **Commodity money** gave way to full-bodied paper money (certificates backed 100 percent by some commodity, such as gold), which in turn gave way to partially backed paper money. Nowadays, our paper money has no commodity backing whatsoever; it is pure **fiat money.**

4. One popular definition of the U.S. money supply is **M1,** which includes coins, paper money, and several types of checking deposits. Most economists prefer the **M2** definition, which adds to M1 other types of checkable accounts and most savings deposits. Much of M2 is held outside of banks by investment houses, credit unions, and other financial institutions.

5. Under our modern system of fractional reserve banking, banks keep cash reserves equal to only a fraction of their total deposit **liabilities.** This practice is the key to their profitability, because the remaining funds can be loaned out at interest. It also leaves banks potentially vulnerable to **runs.**

6. Because of this vulnerability, bank managers are generally conservative in their investment strategies. They also keep a prudent level of reserves. Even so, the government keeps a watchful eye over banking practices.

7. Before 1933, bank failures were common in the United States. They declined sharply when **deposit insurance** was instituted.

8. Some large banks and other financial institutions pose **systemic risk,** meaning that their failure would threaten the entire financial system. For that reason, such **systemically important** institutions are often considered **"too big to fail."**

9. Because it holds only fractional reserves, the banking system as a whole can create several dollars of deposits for each dollar of reserves it receives. Under certain assumptions, the ratio of new bank deposits to new reserves will be $1/m$, where $m$ is the **required reserve** ratio.

10. The same process works in reverse, as a system of money destruction, when cash is withdrawn from the banking system.

11. Because banks and individuals may want to hold more cash when the economy is shaky, the money supply would probably contract under such circumstances if the government did not intervene. Similarly, the money supply would probably expand rapidly in boom times if it were unregulated.

12. **Excess reserves** have proven to be a huge problem in the United States since the financial panic of September 2008. When excess reserves increase, the **money multiplier** is reduced, so the money supply (however measured) grows less rapidly than bank reserves do.

## Key Terms

| | | |
|---|---|---|
| asset 247 | liability 247 | net worth 248 |
| balance sheet 247 | liquidity 241 | required reserves 245 |
| barter 236 | M1 241 | run on a bank 236 |
| commodity money 238 | M2 241 | store of value 238 |
| deposit creation 248 | medium of exchange 238 | systemic risk 246 |
| deposit insurance 245 | money 238 | systemically important ("too big to fail") 247 |
| excess reserves 248 | money multiplier 252 | unit of account 238 |
| fiat money 239 | moral hazard 245 | |
| fractional reserve banking 242 | near moneys 241 | |

## Test Yourself

1. Suppose banks keep no excess reserves and no individuals or firms hold on to cash. If someone suddenly discovers $12 million in buried treasure and deposits it in a bank, explain what will happen to the money supply if the required reserve ratio is 10 percent.

2. How would your answer to Test Yourself Question 1 differ if the reserve ratio were 25 percent? If the reserve ratio were 100 percent?

3. Use tables such as Tables 2 and 3 to illustrate what happens to bank balance sheets when each of the following transactions occurs:

   a. You withdraw $100 from your checking account to buy concert tickets.

   b. Sam finds a $100 bill on the sidewalk and deposits it into his checking account.

   c. Mary Q. Contrary withdraws $500 in cash from her account at Hometown Bank, carries it to the city, and deposits it into her account at Big City Bank.

4. For each of the transactions listed in Test Yourself Question 3, what will be the ultimate effect on the money supply if the required reserve ratio is one-eighth (12.5 percent)? Assume that the oversimplified money multiplier formula applies.

## Discussion Questions

1. If ours were a barter economy, how would you pay your tuition bill? What if your college did not want the goods or services you offered in payment?

2. How is "money" defined, both conceptually and in practice? Does the U.S. money supply consist of commodity money, full-bodied paper money, or fiat money?

3. What is fractional reserve banking, and why is it the key to bank profits? (*Hint:* What opportunities to make profits would banks lose if reserve requirements were 100 percent?) Why does fractional reserve banking give bankers discretion over how large the money supply will be? Why does it make banks potentially vulnerable to runs?

4. After 2007, a rash of bank failures occurred in the United States. Explain why these failures did not lead to runs on banks.

5. Each year during the Christmas shopping season, consumers and stores increase their holdings of cash. Explain how this development could lead to a multiple contraction of the money supply. (As a matter of fact, the authorities prevent this contraction from occurring by methods explained in the next chapter.)

6. Excess reserves make a bank less vulnerable to runs. Why, then, don't bankers like to hold excess reserves? What circumstances might persuade them that it would be advisable to hold excess reserves?

7. If the government takes over a failed bank with liabilities (mostly deposits) of $2 billion, pays off the depositors, and sells the assets for $1.5 billion, where does the missing $500 million come from? Why?

# MONETARY POLICY: CONVENTIONAL AND UNCONVENTIONAL

# 13

*Victorians heard with grave attention that the Bank Rate had been raised. They did not know what it meant. But they knew that it was an act of extreme wisdom.*

JOHN KENNETH GALBRAITH

Armed with our newly acquired understanding of the rudiments of banking, we are now ready to bring money and interest rates into our macroeconomic model. Up to now, we have treated investment (*I*) as a fixed number, which is a poor assumption. Not only is investment highly variable, but it also depends on interest rates—which are, in turn, heavily influenced by **monetary policy**. The main task of this chapter is to explain how monetary policy affects interest rates, investment, and aggregate demand. By the end of the chapter, we will have constructed a complete macroeconomic model and used it to understand some of what has happened in the United States in the last decade. In subsequent chapters, we will use that same model to investigate a number of other important policy issues.

> **Monetary policy** refers to actions that the Federal Reserve System takes to change interest rates and the money supply. It is aimed at affecting the economy.

## CONTENTS

| Issue | *Why Resort to "Unconventional" Monetary Policies?* |
|---|---|

Ben Bernanke, the former Princeton University professor who was chairman of the Federal Reserve Board from 2006 to 2014, became a controversial figure, both at home and abroad. Why? Largely because he led the Federal Reserve into a variety of "unconventional" monetary policies designed to fight the financial crisis and the Great Recession. Just what were those unconventional policies? How are they supposed to work? Why did the Federal Reserve resort to them? And why is the Fed now seeking to "exit" from them?

To answer questions like these, we must first understand what *conventional* monetary policy is, how it works under normal conditions, and why it might not be enough under extremely adverse circumstances. That is the agenda for this chapter.

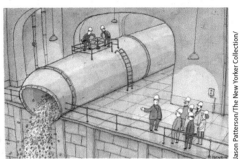

"*And this is where we adjust the interest rate.*"

## 13-1  MONEY AND INCOME: THE IMPORTANT DIFFERENCE

But first we must get some terminology straight. The words *money* and *income* are used almost interchangeably in common parlance. For example, people often say they work to earn *money*. Here, however, we must be more precise.

*Money* is a snapshot concept. It answers questions such as "How much money do you have right now?" or "How much money did you have at 3:32 P.M. on Friday, November 5?" To answer such questions, you would add up the cash you are (or were) carrying and whatever checkable balances you have (or had), and answer something like: "I have $126.33," or "On Friday, November 5, at 3:32 P.M., I had $31.43."

*Income*, by contrast, is more like a motion picture; it accrues over a period of time. If you are asked, "What is your income?" you would respond by saying "$1,000 *per week*," or "$4,000 *per month*," or "$50,000 *per year*," or something like that. Notice that a unit of time is attached to each of these responses. If you just answer, "My income is $45,000," without indicating whether it is per week, per month, or per year, no one will understand what you mean.

That the two concepts are very different is easy to see. A typical American family has an *income* of about $50,000 per year, but its *money* holdings at any point in time (using the M1 definition) are probably under $2,000. Similarly, at the national level, nominal GDP at the end of 2014 was around $18 trillion, whereas the money stock (M1) was around $3 trillion. In economic parlance, we say that people work to earn *income*, which, as a matter of convenience, is typically paid to them in the form of *money*.

Although money and income are conceptually different, they are certainly related. This chapter focuses on that relationship. Specifically, we will look at both how the Federal Reserve "creates money" and how interest rates and the stock of money influence the rate at which people earn income—that is, how *monetary policy* affects GDP.

## 13-2  AMERICA'S CENTRAL BANK: THE FEDERAL RESERVE SYSTEM

A **central bank** is a bank for banks. The United States' central bank is the *Federal Reserve System.*

The *Federal Reserve System* is America's **central bank**. Early in the nineteenth century, the First and Second Banks of the United States were established by the U.S. government, but they were soon abolished. The United States, traditionally distrustful of centralized economic power, was almost the only important nation without a central bank for many decades. When Congress established "the Fed," as it is commonly called, in 1914, the United States joined the company of most other advanced industrial nations. The Bank of England, for example, dates from 1694.

## 13-2a Origins and Structure

It was not the power of economic logic, but rather painful experiences with economic reality that finally persuaded Congress to establish a central bank for the United States. Four severe banking panics between 1873 and 1907, in which many banks failed, convinced legislators and bankers alike that a central bank that would regulate credit conditions was not a luxury but a necessity. The last of these, the Panic of 1907, led Congress to study the shortcomings of the U.S. banking system and, eventually, to establish the Federal Reserve System.

Although the basic ideas of central banking came from Europe, the United States made some changes when it imported the idea, making the Federal Reserve System a uniquely American institution.[1] Because of the vastness of our country, the extraordinarily large number of commercial banks, and our tradition of shared state-federal responsibilities, Congress decided that the United States should have not one central bank but twelve.

Technically, each Federal Reserve Bank is a corporation; its stockholders are its member banks. But your bank, if it is a member of the system, does not enjoy the privileges normally accorded to stockholders. It receives only a token share of the Federal Reserve's immense profits (the bulk is turned over to the U.S. Treasury), and it has virtually no say in corporate decisions. In fact, the banks are more like customers of the Fed than owners.

Who, then, controls the Fed? Most of the power resides in the seven-member Board of Governors of the Federal Reserve System in Washington, D.C., and especially in its chair, who is now Janet Yellen, a former economics professor at the University of California, Berkeley. The seven governors are appointed by the president of the United States, with the advice and consent of the Senate, for fourteen-year terms. The president also designates one member to serve a four-year term as chair of the board and thus to be the most powerful central banker in the world.

The Federal Reserve is independent of the rest of the government. As long as it stays within its statutory authority, it alone has responsibility for determining the nation's monetary policy. The power of appointment, however, gives the president some long-run influence over Federal Reserve policy. For example, it was President George W. Bush who first selected Ben Bernanke to be the Fed's chairman in 2006, although President Barack Obama reappointed him four years later. As of this writing, President Obama has appointed all of the Fed's governors (including Chair Yellen).

Closely allied with the Board of Governors is the powerful Federal Open Market Committee (FOMC), which meets eight times a year in Washington. For reasons to be explained in this chapter, FOMC decisions largely determine short-term interest rates and the size of the U.S. money supply. This twelve-member committee consists of the seven governors of the Federal Reserve System, the president of the Federal Reserve Bank of New York, and, on a rotating basis, four of the other eleven district bank presidents.[2]

"*I'm sorry, sir, but I don't believe you know us well enough to call us the Fed.*"

## 13-2b Central Bank Independence

For decades debates raged around the world over the pros and cons of **central bank independence**.

Proponents of central bank independence argued that it enables the central bank to take the long view and make monetary policy decisions on objective, technical

**Central bank independence** refers to the central bank's ability to make decisions without political interference.

---

[1] Ironically, when the European Central Bank was established in 1999, its structure was patterned on that of the Federal Reserve.

[2] Alan Blinder served as the vice chairman of the Federal Reserve Board, and thus a member of the Federal Open Market Committee, from 1994 to 1996.

# A Meeting of the Federal Open Market Committee

Meetings of the Federal Open Market Committee are serious and formal affairs. All nineteen members—seven governors and twelve reserve bank presidents—sit around a mammoth table in the Fed's cavernous but austere board room. A limited number of top Fed staffers join them at and around the table, for access to FOMC meetings is strictly controlled.

At precisely 9 A.M.—for punctuality is a high virtue at the Fed—the doors are closed and the chair calls the meeting to order. No press is allowed and, unlike most important Washington meetings, nothing said there will leak. Secrecy is another high virtue at the Fed.

After hearing a few routine staff reports, the chair calls on each of the members in turn to give their views of the current economic situation. District bank presidents offer insights into their local economies, and all members comment on the outlook for financial markets and the national economy. Committee members also offer their views on what changes in monetary policy, if any, are appropriate. Disagreements are raised, but voices are not, for politeness is another high virtue at the Fed. Strikingly, in this most political of cities, politics is almost never mentioned.

Once she has heard from all the others, the chair summarizes the discussion, offers her own views of the economic situation and of the policy options, and recommends a course of action. Most members normally agree with the chair, though some note differences of opinion. Then the chair asks the secretary to call the roll. Only the twelve voting members

answer, saying yes or no and perhaps elaborating on their reasons. Negative votes are rare, for the FOMC tries to operate by consensus and a dissent is considered a loud objection.

The meeting adjourns, and at precisely 2 P.M. the Fed's spokesperson announces its decision to the public. Within seconds, financial markets around the world react.

Board of Governors of the Federal Reserve System

criteria—thus keeping politics out of monetary policy. Without this independence, they argued, politicians with short time horizons might try to force the central bank to expand the money supply too rapidly before elections, thereby contributing to chronic inflation and undermining faith in the country's financial system. They pointed to historical evidence showing that countries with more independent central banks—such as the United States and Germany—had, on average, experienced lower inflation.

Opponents of this view countered that there is something profoundly undemocratic about letting a group of unelected bankers and economists make decisions that affect every citizen's well-being. Monetary policy, they argued, should be formulated by the elected representatives of the people, just like fiscal policy.

The high inflation of the 1970s and 1980s helped resolve this issue by convincing governments around the world that an independent central bank was essential to controlling inflation. Thus, one country after another made its central bank independent over the next 20 to 30 years. For example, the Maastricht Treaty (1992), which committed members of the European Union to both low inflation and a single currency (the euro), required that each member state make its central bank independent. All did so, even though several have not joined the monetary union. Japan also decided to make its central bank independent in 1998. In Latin America, several formerly high-inflation countries like Brazil and Mexico found that giving their central banks more independence helped them control inflation. And most of the formerly socialist countries of Europe, finding themselves saddled with high inflation and "unsound" currencies, made their central banks more independent for similar reasons. Thus, for practical purposes, the debate over central bank independence was all but over by 2000.

The new debate is over how to hold such independent and powerful institutions *accountable* to the political authorities and the broad public. For example, most central banks have now abandoned their former traditions of imperious secrecy and have become far more open to public scrutiny. Many now post specific numerical targets for inflation, thereby making it easy for outside observers to judge how well the central bank is doing its job. The Federal Reserve's stated target, for example, is 2 percent per year, which is a common choice around the world.

## 13-3 IMPLEMENTING MONETARY POLICY IN NORMAL TIMES: OPEN-MARKET OPERATIONS

When it wants to change interest rates, the Fed normally relies on **open-market operations**. In an open-market operation, the central bank either gives banks more reserves or takes reserves away, thereby triggering the sort of multiple expansion or contraction of the money supply described in the previous chapter.

> **Open-market operations** refer to the Fed's purchases or sales of government securities, normally Treasury bills, through transactions in the open market.

How does this process work? If the Federal Open Market Committee decides to lower interest rates, it can bring them down by providing banks with more reserves. Specifically, the Federal Reserve would normally *purchase* a particular kind of short-term U.S. government security called a *Treasury bill* from any individual or bank that wished to sell them, paying with newly created bank reserves. To see how such an open-market operation affects interest rates, we must understand that there is a market in which banks trade reserves among themselves, which is depicted in Figure 1.

### 13-3a The Market for Bank Reserves

The main sources of supply and demand in the market for reserves are straightforward. On the supply side, the Fed decides how many dollars of reserves to provide. Thus the label on the supply curve in Figure 1 indicates that *the position of the supply curve depends on Federal Reserve policy*. The Fed's decision on how many bank reserves to supply is the essence of normal monetary policy, and we will consider how the Fed makes that decision shortly.

On the demand side of the market, the main reason why banks hold reserves under normal circumstances is something we learned in the previous chapter: Government regulations *require* them to do so. In Chapter 12, we used the symbol $m$ to denote the required reserve ratio (which is 0.1 in the United States). So if the volume of transaction deposits is $D$, the demand for *required reserves* is simply $m \times D$. The demand for reserves thus reflects the underlying demand for transactions deposits in banks.

> The **federal funds rate** is the interest rates that banks pay and receive when they borrow reserves from one another.

The demand for transaction deposits, in turn, depends on many factors, but the principal determinant is the volume of transactions. After all, people and businesses hold checking deposits in order to conduct transactions. Real GDP ($Y$) is typically used as a convenient indicator of the *number* of transactions, and the price level ($P$) is a natural measure of the *average price* per transaction. So the volume of bank deposits, $D$, and therefore *the demand for bank reserves, depends on both Y and P*—as indicated in Figure 1.

There is more to the story, however, for we have not yet explained why the demand curve $DD$ slopes down and the supply curve $SS$ slopes up. The particular interest rate measured along the vertical axis of Figure 1 is called the **federal funds rate**. It is the rate that applies when banks borrow and lend reserves. When you hear on the evening news that "the Federal Reserve today raised interest rates by $\frac{1}{4}$ of a point," it is the federal funds rate that the reporter is talking about.

But where does this borrowing and lending come from? As we mentioned in the previous chapter, banks sometimes find themselves with either insufficient or excess reserves. Normally, either situation leaves them unhappy. Holding reserves in excess of requirements is perfectly permissible. But because reserves pay little interest, a bank normally can put excess reserves to better use by lending them out rather than

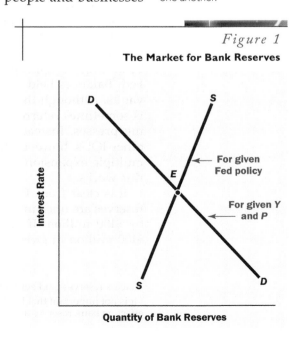

*Figure 1*

**The Market for Bank Reserves**

For given Fed policy

For given Y and P

Quantity of Bank Reserves

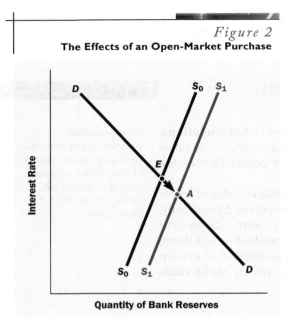

*Figure 2*
**The Effects of an Open-Market Purchase**

keeping them idle.[3] Keeping actual reserves below the required level is not allowed. So banks have developed an active market in which those with excess reserves lend them to those with reserve deficiencies. These bank-to-bank loans provide an additional source of *both* supply *and* demand—and one that (unlike required reserves) is interest sensitive. That's why the two curves in Figure 1 have slope.

Any bank that wants to borrow reserves must pay the federal funds rate for the privilege. Naturally, as the funds rate rises, borrowing looks more expensive and so fewer reserves are demanded. In a word, the demand curve for reserves (*DD*) slopes downward. Similarly, the supply curve for reserves (*SS*) slopes upward because lending reserves becomes more attractive as the federal funds rate rises.

The equilibrium federal funds rate is established, as usual, where the demand and supply curves cross—at point *E* in Figure 1. Now suppose the Federal Reserve wants to push the federal funds rate *down*. It can provide additional reserves to the market by purchasing Treasury bills (often abbreviated *T-bills*) from banks.[4] This *open-market purchase* would shift the supply curve of bank reserves outward, from $S_0S_0$ to $S_1S_1$, in Figure 2. Equilibrium would therefore shift from point *E* to point *A*, which, as the diagram shows, implies a lower interest rate and more bank reserves. That is precisely what the Fed does under normal conditions. We will deal with abnormal conditions later.

## 13-3b  The Mechanics of an Open-Market Operation

The bookkeeping behind such an open-market purchase is illustrated by Table 1, which imagines that the Fed purchases $100 million worth of T-bills from commercial banks. When the Fed buys the securities, the ownership of the T-bills shifts from the banks to the Fed—as indicated by the black arrows in Table 1. Next, *the Fed makes payment by giving the banks $100 million in new reserves,* that is, by adding $100 million to the bookkeeping entries that represent the banks' accounts at the Fed—called "bank reserves" in the table. These reserves, shown in teal in the table, are liabilities of the Fed and assets of the banks.

You may be wondering where the Fed gets the money to pay for the securities. It could pay in cash, but it normally does not. Instead, it manufactures the funds out of thin air or, more literally, by punching a keyboard. Specifically, the Fed pays the banks by adding the appropriate sums to the reserve accounts that the banks maintain at the Fed. Balances held in these accounts constitute bank reserves, just like cash in bank vaults. Although this process of adding to bookkeeping entries at the Federal Reserve is sometimes referred to as "printing money," the Fed does not literally run any printing presses. Instead, it simply trades its IOUs for an existing asset (a T-bill). Unlike other IOUs, however, the Fed's IOUs constitute bank reserves and thus can support a multiple expansion of the money supply just as cash does. Let's dig deeper into how this works.

It is clear from Table 1 that bank deposits have not increased at all—yet. So *required* reserves are unchanged by the open-market operation. But *actual* reserves have increased by $100 million. If banks want to hold only their required reserves, they now have $100 million in *excess reserves*. As the banks rid themselves of these excess reserves by

---

[3] Excess reserves paid zero interest until the law was changed in 2008.

[4] It is not important that banks be the sellers. Test Yourself Question 3 at the end of the chapter shows that the effect on bank reserves and the money supply is the same if bank customers sell the securities.

*Table 1*

**Effects of an Open-Market Purchase of Securities on the Balance Sheets of Banks and the Fed**

| Banks | | | | Federal Reserve System | | |
|---|---|---|---|---|---|---|
| **Assets** | | | **Liabilities** | **Assets** | **Liabilities** | |
| Reserves | +$100 million | | | Treasury | Bank | |
| Treasury bills | −$100 million | | | bills  +$100 million | reserves  +$100 million | |
| **Addendum: Changes in Reserves** | | | Banks get reserves | | | |
| Actual reserves | +$100 million | | Fed gets T-bills | | | |
| Required reserves | No change | | | | | |
| **Excess reserves** | +$100 million | | | | | |

making more loans, a multiple expansion of the banking system is set in motion—just as described in the previous chapter. In normal times, it is not difficult for the Fed to estimate the ultimate increase in the money supply that will result from its actions. As we learned in the previous chapter, each dollar of newly created bank reserves can support up to $1/m$ dollars of checking deposits, if $m$ is the required reserve ratio. In the example in the last chapter, $m = 0.20$; hence, $100 million in new reserves would support $100 million $\div$ 0.2 = $500 million in new money.

However, *estimating* the ultimate monetary expansion is a far cry from *knowing* it. We learned in the previous chapter that the oversimplified money multiplier formula is predicated on two critical assumptions: that people will hold no more cash, and that banks will hold no more excess reserves, as the monetary expansion proceeds. In practice, these assumptions are unlikely to be literally true. In fact, as we noted, the second assumption (zero excess reserves) has been spectacularly false recently, with excess reserves soaring above $2.5 *trillion*. So to predict the eventual effect of its action on the money supply, the Fed must *estimate* both the amount that firms and individuals will add to their currency holdings and the amount that banks will add to their excess reserves. Neither of these can be estimated with precision. In summary:

> When the Federal Reserve wants to lower interest rates, it purchases U.S. government securities in the open market. It pays for these securities by creating new bank reserves, which lead to a multiple expansion of the money supply. Because of fluctuations in people's desires to hold cash and banks' desires to hold excess reserves, the Fed cannot predict the consequences of these actions for the money supply with perfect accuracy. However, the Fed can always put the federal funds rate where it wants by buying just the right volume of securities.[5]

For this reason we will simply proceed as if the Fed controls the federal funds rate directly—with one big exception. When the economy is very weak, and monetary policy has already cut interest rates aggressively, the federal funds rate may reach or approximate zero—as it has since December 2008. In such a case, the Fed cannot push the funds rate down further; it gets "stuck" at zero. It is precisely under such unusual circumstances that the Fed may have to resort to any of a variety of "unconventional" monetary policies that we will discuss shortly.

---

[5] Why? Because the federal funds rate is observable in the market every minute and hence need not be estimated. If interest rates do not fall as much as the Fed wants, it can simply purchase more securities. If interest rates fall too much, the Fed can purchase fewer. Such adjustments can be made very quickly.

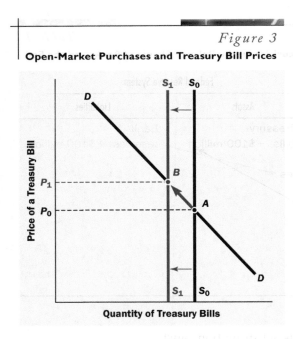

*Figure 3*

**Open-Market Purchases and Treasury Bill Prices**

Quantity of Treasury Bills

But first let's note an obvious point: The procedures followed when the FOMC wants to *raise* interest rates are exactly the opposite of those we have just explained. In brief, it normally *sells* Treasury bills in the open market. This takes reserves *away* from banks, because banks pay for the T-bills by drawing down their deposits at the Fed. A multiple *contraction* of the banking system should ensue. The principles are exactly the same—and so are the uncertainties.

### 13-3c  Open-Market Operations, Bond Prices, and Interest Rates

The *expansionary monetary policy* action we have been using as an example begins with the Federal Reserve buying more Treasury bills. When it goes into the open market to purchase more of these bills, the Fed naturally drives up their prices. This process is illustrated by Figure 3, which shows an *inward shift* of the (vertical) supply curve of T-bills *available to private investors*—from $S_0S_0$ to $S_1S_1$—indicating that the Fed's action takes some of the bills off the private market. With an unchanged (private) demand curve, *DD*, the price of T-bills rises from $P_0$ to $P_1$ as equilibrium in the market shifts from point *A* to point *B*.

Rising prices for Treasury bills—or for any other type of bond—translate directly into falling interest rates. Why? The reason is simple arithmetic. Bonds pay a fixed number of dollars of interest per year. For concreteness, consider a bond that pays $60 each year. If the bond sells for $1,000, bondholders earn a 6 percent return on their investment (the $60 interest payment is 6 percent of $1,000). We therefore say that *the interest rate on the bond is 6 percent*. Now suppose the price of the bond rises to $1,200. Because the annual interest payment is still $60, bondholders now earn just 5 percent on their money ($60 is 5 percent of $1,200). *Thus the effective interest rate on the bond has declined to 5 percent*. The inverse relationship between bond prices and interest rates is completely general:

> When bond prices rise, interest rates fall because the purchaser of a bond spends more money than before to earn a given number of dollars of interest per year. Similarly, when bond prices fall, interest rates rise.

In fact, the relationship amounts to nothing more than two ways of saying the same thing. Higher interest rates *mean* lower bond prices; lower interest rates *mean* higher bond prices.[6] Thus Figure 3 is another way to look at the fact that Federal Reserve open-market operations influence short-term interest rates. Specifically:

> An open-market purchase of Treasury bills by the Fed not only raises the money supply but also drives up T-bill prices and pushes their interest rates down. Conversely, an open-market sale of bills, which reduces the money supply, lowers T-bill prices and raises interest rates.

### 13-3d  Which Interest Rate?

The interest rate determined in Figures 1 and 2 is the federal funds rate. The interest rate that underlies Figure 3 is the Treasury bill rate. Those two rates are pretty easy for the Federal Reserve to control within small margins of error. But there are many other interest rates in our, or any other, economy—such as the rates paid on credit card balances, student loans, home mortgages, and corporate bonds. For these rates, literal *control* by the central bank is out of the question; even the Fed's *influence* can be muted at times.

Under normal conditions, this is one of those real-world "details" that can be ignored in an introductory course. The reason is simple: Virtually all interest rates tend to move

---

[6] For further discussion and examples, see Test Yourself Question 4 at the end of the chapter.

## You Now Belong to a Distinctive Minority Group

An amazing number of investors do not understand even the elementary facts about bond investing—including the relationship between bond prices and interest rates.

*The Wall Street Journal* reported back in November 2001 that "One of the bond basics about which many investors are clueless, for instance, is the fundamental seesaw relationship between interest rates and bond prices. Only 31% of 750 investors participating in the American Century [a mutual fund company] telephone survey knew that when interest rates rise, bond prices generally fall."* Imagine how many fewer, then, could explain *why* this is so.

*"When interest rates go up, bond prices go down. When interest rates go down, bond prices go up. But please don't ask me why."*

\* Karen Damato, "Investors Love Their Bond Funds—Too Much?" *The Wall Street Journal*, November 9, 2001, p. C1.

up and down together most of the time. Thus, when earlier editions of this book spoke of "the" interest rate going up or down, it did not matter much whether students thought of "the" interest rate as being the federal funds rate or the credit card rate or the home mortgage rate. When any one of those rates rose or fell, so did the others, albeit by different amounts.

But normal relationships among interest rates broke down spectacularly during the financial crisis. Why? Mainly because securities and loans differ in their **risk of default**, that is, in the risk that the borrower will fail to repay the loan fully. There is no such risk in U.S. government securities. Dating back to fundamental decisions made by Alexander Hamilton, the nation's first Secretary of the Treasury, the U.S. government has always paid its debts in full and on time. Investors assume it always will. So Treasury securities are considered *risk-free*.

Moving slightly up the risk spectrum, bank-to-bank borrowing and lending of reserves at the federal funds rate carries some tiny risk of default; the debts of the nation's leading corporations carry a bit more risk; so-called "junk bonds" (the debts of lesser corporations) carry more; and so on. Similarly, the bonds of emerging-market nations typically carry far higher risk than the bonds of the U.S. government because emerging-market debt sometimes falls into default. In order to induce investors to buy any of these riskier securities, rather than Treasuries, corporations, emerging-market nations, and mortgagees must pay higher interest rates than the U.S. Treasury does. In general:

> **Riskier borrowers pay higher interest rates than safer borrowers, in order to persuade lenders to accept the higher risk of default.**

The gap between the interest rate on any bond (or loan) and the corresponding risk-free interest rate on a Treasury security is called the **risk premium**, or sometimes just the "**spread**" (over Treasuries), on that bond:

$$\text{Interest rate (on any bond)} = \text{Risk-free (Treasury) interest rate} + \text{Risk premium}$$

Here's a real-world example: In September 2014, top-rated corporate bonds paid about 4.1 percent per annum while Treasury bonds paid about 2.5 percent. So we say that the *spread* on that particular bond was $4.1 - 2.5 = 1.6$ percentage points over Treasuries. Notice that this spread, which is determined by supply and demand every day in the

The **risk of default** on any loan or security is the risk that the borrower may not pay in full or on time.

Market interest rates generally include a **risk premium** (or **"spread"** over Treasuries) to compensate the lender for the probability of loss if the borrower fails to repay the loan in full or on time.

### Table 2

**Selected U.S. Interest Rates, September 2014 (in percent)**

| Security | Interest Rate | Spread over Treasuries |
|---|---|---|
| Three-month Treasury bill | 0.02 | — |
| Federal funds | 0.09 | 0.07 |
| Three-month commercial paper[a] | 0.10 | 0.08 |
| 10-year Treasury bond | 2.53 | — |
| Home mortgage | 4.25 | 1.72 |
| Baa corporate bond[b] | 4.80 | 2.27 |

[a] Commercial paper is a form of short-term borrowing by blue-chip companies.
[b] From Moody's. Bonds are rated by quality, with Aaa the highest rating.

SOURCE: Federal Reserve.

marketplace, compensates the investor for a 1.6 percent annual expected loss on the corporate bond. The clear implication is that:

> When the perceived risk of default increases, risk spreads widen. When the perceived risk of default decreases, risk spreads narrow.

Table 2 displays a few selected U.S. interest rates, and their corresponding spreads over Treasuries, in September 2014. The risk premiums clearly vary quite a lot.

When the financial crisis struck in 2008, investors altered their views of risk sharply. Suddenly, seemingly safe investments like mortgages or even the bonds of large banks looked far riskier than they had before. So the risk premiums on these and other instruments soared. At the same time, anxious investors from around the world started demanding huge volumes of U.S. Treasury securities, thereby driving their prices up and the corresponding interest rates down. The net result was that Treasury rates fell while risky interest rates rose. It was no longer true that all rates moved up and down together.

Returning to our previous numerical example, suppose the probable loss on corporate bonds in the minds of investors rises from 1.6 percent to 3.6 percent per annum. One possibility is that the Treasury interest rate could fall from 2.5 percent to 1.5 percent while the corporate bond rate could rise from 4.1 percent to 5.1 percent. Thus the two rates could move in opposite directions. Later, when the crisis passed and spreads returned to normal, the corporate interest rate might fall even as the Treasury rate rose. Such things did, in fact, happen during and after the financial crisis. Departures from the usual pattern, in which all interest rates rise or fall together, constitute another aspect of what constitutes "abnormal conditions." (See the box "Risk Spreads during the Financial Crisis.")

## 13-4 OTHER INSTRUMENTS OF MONETARY POLICY

When the Federal Reserve System was first established, its founders did not intend it to manipulate interest rates actively to stabilize the economy. The basic ideas of stabilization policy weren't even known at the time. Instead, the Fed's founders viewed it as a means of preventing the supplies of money and credit from drying up during banking panics, as had happened so often in the pre-1914 period—and as happened again in 2007–2009.

### 13-4a  Lending to Banks

One of the principal ways in which Congress intended the Fed to provide such insurance against financial panics was to act as a "lender of last resort." When risky business prospects made commercial banks hesitant to extend new loans, or when banks ran into trouble, the Fed was supposed to step in by lending money to the banks so that banks, in turn, could lend more to their customers. If that sounds familiar, it should, because it is exactly what the Fed and other central banks did in massive amounts at the beginning of the financial crisis in the summer of 2007. While the crisis made commercial banks wary of lending, huge central bank loans to banks helped keep the financial system functioning and eased the panic for a time. Later, in 2008, the Fed actually began a temporary program of lending directly to securities firms—something it had not done since the 1930s.

The mechanics of Federal Reserve lending are illustrated in Table 3. When the Fed makes a loan to a bank in need of reserves, that bank receives a credit in its deposit account

*Table 3*

**Balance Sheet Changes for Borrowing from the Fed**

| Banks | | | | Federal Reserve System | | | |
|---|---|---|---|---|---|---|---|
| Assets | | Liabilities | | Assets | | Liabilities | |
| Reserves | +$5 million | Loan from Fed +$5 million | | Loan to bank +$5 million | | Bank reserves | +$5 million |
| **Addendum: Changes in Reserves** | | | | | | | |
| Actual reserves | +$5 million | | | | | | |
| Required reserves | No change | | | | | | |
| **Excess reserves** | **+$5 million** | | | | | | |

Bank borrows $5 million

and

the proceeds are credited

to its reserve account

at the Fed—$5 million in the example. Because that $5 million represents newly created reserves, it expands the supply of reserves just as was shown in Figure 2. Furthermore, because bank deposits, and hence required reserves, are not increased by this operation, the additional bank reserves are all *excess reserves*, which should lead to a multiple expansion of the money supply.

## Risk Spreads during the Financial Crisis

Everything was abnormal during the worst of the financial crisis, certainly including risk spreads. The accompanying graph shows one particular example: the spread between what it cost major financial institutions to borrow for three months (called the "commercial paper rate") and what it cost the U.S. Treasury to borrow for three months (the three-month T-bill rate) over the years 2007–2009.

In the calm markets of early 2007, the spread between the two borrowing rates was only about 0.3 percentage point, reflecting the market's assessment that the probabilities of loss in lending to companies like Goldman Sachs, Citigroup, JPMorgan Chase, and the like were negligible. Then it began to creep up—slightly at first, but then dramatically when the financial crisis broke out in August 2007. After that, the graph resembles the electrocardiogram of a very sick person for a while, fluctuating wildly between about 0.8 percent and 2 percent, before leaping upward (to an amazing peak of 3.25 percent) in the aftermath of the bankruptcy of Lehman Brothers in September 2008. After that, markets began to calm down, and by the spring of 2009 the spread was back down to where it began.

Although this is just one example, virtually every interest rate spread displayed a similar pattern over the years 2007–2009, rising to an unprecedented peak and then declining.

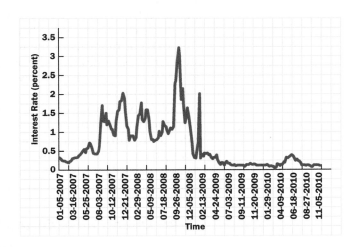

The **discount rate** is the interest rate the Fed charges on loans that it makes to banks.

Federal Reserve officials can try to influence the amount banks borrow by altering the *rate of interest charged on these loans*, which is known as the **discount rate**. If the Fed wants banks to have more reserves, it can reduce the interest rate it charges on loans, thereby tempting banks to borrow more—which is exactly what it did repeatedly in 2007 and 2008. In the other direction, it can soak up reserves by raising the discount rate and inducing the banks to borrow less.

But when it changes the discount rate, the Fed cannot know for sure how banks will react. Sometimes they respond vigorously to a cut in the rate, borrowing a great deal from the Fed and lending a correspondingly large amount to their customers. At other times, they essentially ignore the change in the discount rate. In fact, when it first cut the discount rate in 2007, the Fed was disappointed in the banks' meager response because it wanted to add reserves to the system. So it cut the rate more and became more aggressive about offering loans for longer periods of time and to different institutions. This episode graphically illustrated that the link between the discount rate and the volume of bank reserves can be a loose one.

Some foreign central banks use their versions of the discount rate *actively* as the centerpiece of monetary policy. However, prior to the crisis, the Federal Reserve normally lent money infrequently and in very small amounts. It relied instead on open-market operations to conduct monetary policy. For example, in August 2007, on the eve of the crisis, the Fed's total lending to all banks was a mere $250 *million*. By April 2008, however, it was up to $145 *billion*, and it peaked at over $735 billion in November 2008. These were lending volumes that no one at the Federal Reserve had ever contemplated before. (As this edition went to press, Federal Reserve lending to banks was again down to negligible amounts.)

### 13-4b  Changing Reserve Requirements

In principle, the Federal Reserve has a third way to conduct monetary policy: varying the minimum required reserve ratio. To see how this works, imagine that banks hold reserves that just match their required minimums; excess reserves are zero. If the Fed decides that lower interest rates are warranted, it can reduce the required reserve ratio, thereby transforming some previously *required* reserves into *excess* reserves. No new reserves are created directly by this action. But we know that such a change normally will set in motion a multiple expansion of the banking system.

Looked at in terms of the market for bank reserves (Figure 1), a reduction in reserve requirements would shift the demand curve *inward* (because banks would no longer need as many reserves), thereby lowering interest rates. Similarly, raising the required reserve ratio would raise interest rates and set off a multiple contraction of the banking system.

Such hypotheticals are quite unrealistic in the United States, however. The Fed has not used the reserve ratio as an instrument of monetary policy for decades. Current law provides for required reserves equal to 10 percent of *transactions deposits*—a ratio that has not changed since 1992. And over the years, banks have figured out many ways to transform "transactions deposits" into "non-transactions deposits," which have no reserve requirements at all. Required reserves these days are only about $75 billion.

### 13-4c  Quantitative Easing

**Unconventional monetary policy** is a generic term referring to unusual forms (or volumes) of central bank lending and to unusual types of open-market operations.

We mentioned at the start of this chapter that former Federal Reserve Chairman Ben Bernanke became a controversial figure by promulgating a series of **unconventional monetary policies** designed to fight the financial crisis and the Great Recession. A few of these unconventional policies have been mentioned already: pushing the federal funds rate down to virtually zero,[7] lending to banks in unprecedented volume, and even lending

---

[7] Actually, the federal funds rate never quite hit zero. The Fed maintained it in a range between zero and $\frac{1}{4}$ percent.

to some companies that are not banks. But some of the Fed's most controversial policy initiatives came under the awkward heading **quantitative easing**, which refers to some unusual kinds of open-market operations.

**Quantitative easing** refers to open-market purchases of assets other than Treasury bills.

Unusual in what respect? Look back at Table 1, which displayed the mechanics of a *conventional* open-market operation. There the Fed created new bank reserves by purchasing more Treasury bills; and as we explained, doing so drove the prices of T-bills up (see Figure 3) and their interest rates down. *Unconventional* open-market operations do essentially the same thing—except that the Fed starts the process by purchasing something other than T-bills.

What? The simplest case is when the Federal Reserve buys longer-dated (e.g., five- or ten-year) Treasury *bonds* instead of short-term (e.g., three-month) Treasury *bills*. Then Table 1 and Figure 3 apply with only one minor change: Just replace "Treasury bills" by "Treasury bonds" everywhere. Everything else is exactly the same. In particular, bank reserves rise and interest rates on Treasury bonds fall. Yet a furor arose in November 2010 when the FOMC decided to do precisely this. Several members of Congress even urged the Fed to rescind its decision.

In yet more unconventional versions of quantitative easing, the Fed might purchase assets other than Treasury securities, as it did during some of the worst months of the crisis in 2008 and 2009 in order to stabilize the mortgage market. Once again, however, the objectives were exactly the same: to increase bank reserves and drive down interest rates. (More on this in the next chapter.)

## 13-5 HOW MONETARY POLICY WORKS IN NORMAL TIMES

Let's now return to monetary policy in normal times, which we will define as times when the federal funds rate is *not* hovering close to zero, when risk spreads are roughly constant so that different interest rates rise and fall *together*, and when banks are *not* holding many excess reserves. Under these circumstances, Federal Reserve open-market operations are done mostly in Treasury bills. (We will investigate the "abnormal" case shortly.)

The two panels of Figure 4 illustrate the effects of *expansionary monetary policy* (an open-market purchase of T-bills) and *contractionary monetary policy* (an open-market sale). Panel (a) looks just like Figure 2. Expansionary monetary policy actions lower interest rates, and contractionary monetary policy actions raise interest rates. Then what happens?

To find out, let's go back to the analysis of earlier chapters, where we learned that aggregate demand is the sum of consumption spending (C), investment spending (I), government purchases of goods and services (G), and net exports $(X - IM)$. We know that *fiscal policy* controls G directly and influences both C and I through the tax laws. We now want to understand how *monetary policy* affects spending.

Most economists agree that, of the four components of aggregate demand, investment and net exports are the most sensitive to monetary policy. We will study the effects of monetary and fiscal policy on net exports in Chapter 20, after we have learned about international exchange rates. For now, we assume that net exports are *fixed* and focus on monetary policy's influence on investment.

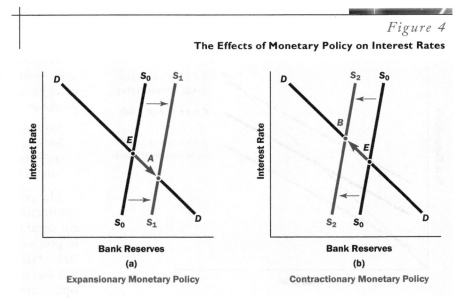

*Figure 4*

**The Effects of Monetary Policy on Interest Rates**

(a) Expansionary Monetary Policy
Bank Reserves — Interest Rate

(b) Contractionary Monetary Policy
Bank Reserves — Interest Rate

### 13-5a  Investment and Interest Rates

Given the stunning events in the housing market over the last decade, it is important to remember that the $I$ in $C + I + G + (X - IM)$ includes both *business investment* in new factories and machinery and *investment in housing*. Because the interest cost of a home mortgage is typically a major component of the total cost of owning a house, fewer families will purchase new homes as mortgage interest rates rise. Thus, higher interest rates reduce expenditures on housing. Business investment is also sensitive to interest rates, for reasons explained in earlier chapters. Because the rates of interest that must be paid on business borrowings are part of the cost of any investment, business executives will find investment prospects less attractive as interest rates rise. Therefore, they will spend less. We conclude that

> Higher interest rates lead to lower investment spending. But investment (*I*) is a component of total spending, $C + I + G + (X - IM)$. Therefore, when interest rates rise, total spending falls. In terms of the 45° line diagram of previous chapters, a higher interest rate leads to a lower expenditure schedule. Conversely, a lower interest rate leads to a higher expenditure schedule.

Figure 5 depicts these reactions graphically.

### 13-5b  Monetary Policy and Total Expenditure

The effect of interest rates on spending provides the chief channel through which monetary policy affects the economy. We know from our analysis of the market for bank reserves (Figure 4) that monetary policy can move interest rates up or down. Let us, therefore, trace the impacts of conventional monetary policy, starting there.

Suppose the Federal Reserve, worried that the economy might slip into a recession, decides to increase the supply of bank reserves. It would normally do so by purchasing T-bills in the open market, thereby shifting the supply schedule for reserves outward—as indicated by the shift from the black line $S_0S_0$ to the blue line $S_1S_1$ in Figure 4(a). This is essentially what the Fed did in the early stages of the financial crisis in 2007 and 2008.

With the demand schedule for bank reserves, *DD,* temporarily fixed, such a shift in the supply curve has the effect that an increase in supply always has in a free market: It lowers the price, as Figure 4(a) shows. In this case, the relevant price is the federal funds rate, the rate of interest that must be paid for to borrow reserves, *r.* So *r* falls, as do other interest rates.

Next, for reasons we have just outlined, investment spending on housing and business equipment (*I*) rises in response to the lower interest rates. But, as we learned in Chapter 9, such an autonomous rise in investment kicks off a multiplier chain of increases in output and employment.

This sequence of events summarizes the linkages from the supply of bank reserves to the level of aggregate demand. In brief, monetary policy works as follows:

> Expansionary monetary policy leads to lower interest rates (*r*), and these lower interest rates encourage more investment spending (*I*), which has multiplier effects on aggregate demand.

The process operates equally well in reverse. By contracting bank reserves and the money supply, the central bank can push interest rates up, which is precisely what the Fed did between 2004 and 2006. Higher rates cause investment spending to fall and pull down aggregate demand via the multiplier mechanism.

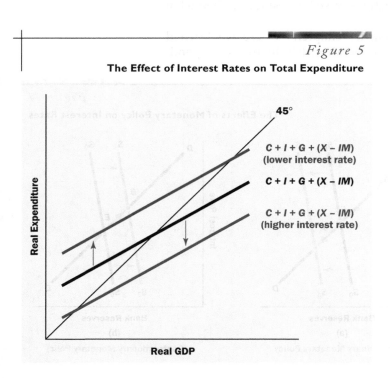

*Figure 5*

**The Effect of Interest Rates on Total Expenditure**

45°

$C + I + G + (X - IM)$
(lower interest rate)

$C + I + G + (X - IM)$

$C + I + G + (X - IM)$
(higher interest rate)

Real Expenditure

Real GDP

This, in outline form, is how monetary policy influences the economy in normal times. Because the chain of causation is fairly long, the following schematic diagram may help clarify it:

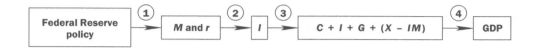

In this causal chain, Link 1 indicates that the Federal Reserve's open-market operations affect both interest rates and the money supply. Link 2 stands for the effect of interest rates on investment. Link 3 simply notes that investment is one component of total spending. Link 4 is the multiplier, relating an autonomous change in investment to the ultimate change in aggregate demand. To see what economists must study if they are to estimate the effects of monetary policy, let us briefly review what we know about each of these four links.

Link 1 is the main subject of this chapter. It was depicted in Figure 4(a), which shows how injections of bank reserves by the Federal Reserve push the interest rate down. Thus, the first thing an economist must know is how sensitive interest rates are to changes in the supply of bank reserves.

Link 2 translates the lower interest rate into higher investment spending. To estimate this effect in practice, economists must study the sensitivity of investment to interest rates—a topic we took up in Chapter 7.

Link 3 instructs us to enter the rise in $I$ as an autonomous upward shift of the $C + I + G + (X - IM)$ schedule in a 45° line diagram. Figure 6 carries out this next step. The expenditure schedule rises from $C + I_0 + G + (X - IM)$ to $C + I_1 + G + (X - IM)$.

Finally, Link 4 applies multiplier analysis to this vertical shift in the expenditure schedule to obtain the eventual increase in real GDP demanded. This change is shown in Figure 6 as a shift in equilibrium from $E_0$ to $E_1$, which raises real GDP by $500 billion in the example. Of course, the size of the multiplier itself must also be estimated. To summarize:

**The effect of monetary policy on aggregate demand depends on the sensitivity of interest rates to open-market operations, on the responsiveness of investment spending to the rate of interest, and on the size of the basic expenditure multiplier.**

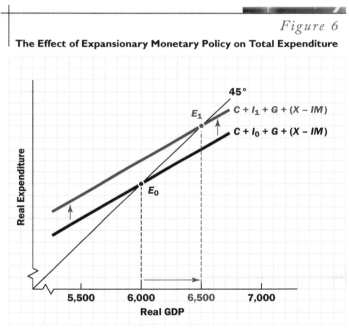

*Figure 6*

**The Effect of Expansionary Monetary Policy on Total Expenditure**

NOTE: Figures are in billions of dollars per year.

## 13-6  MONEY AND THE PRICE LEVEL

Our analysis up to now leaves one important question unanswered: What happens to the price level? To find the answer, we must recall that aggregate demand *and* aggregate supply *jointly* determine prices and output. Our analysis of monetary policy so far has shown us how expansionary monetary policy boosts total spending: It increases the *aggregate quantity demanded at any given price level*. To learn what happens to the price level and to real output, we must consider *aggregate supply* as well.

Specifically, when considering shifts in aggregate demand caused by *fiscal policy* in Chapter 11, we noted that an upsurge in total spending normally induces firms to increase output somewhat *and* to raise prices somewhat. These two reactions are summarized in

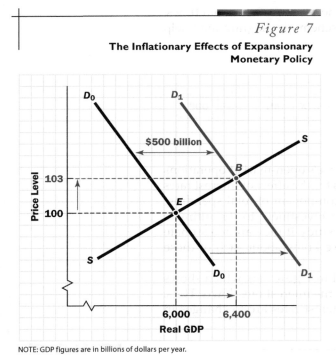

*Figure 7*

**The Inflationary Effects of Expansionary Monetary Policy**

NOTE: GDP figures are in billions of dollars per year.

the upward-sloping aggregate supply curve. Whether the responses come more in the form of real output or more in the form of prices depends on the slope of the aggregate supply curve (see Figure 7). Exactly the same analysis of output and price responses applies to monetary policy or, for that matter, to anything that raises the aggregate demand curve. So we conclude that

> **Expansionary monetary policy normally causes some inflation. But exactly how much inflation it causes depends on the slope of the aggregate supply curve.**

The effect of expansionary monetary policy on the price level is shown graphically on an aggregate supply and demand diagram in Figure 7. In the example depicted in Figure 6, the Fed's actions lowered interest rates enough to increase aggregate demand (through the multiplier) by $500 billion. We enter this increase as a $500 billion *horizontal* shift of the aggregate demand curve in Figure 7, from $D_0D_0$ to $D_1D_1$. The diagram then shows that this expansionary monetary policy pushes the economy's equilibrium from point $E$ to point $B$—the price level therefore rises from 100 to 103, or 3 percent. The diagram also shows that real GDP rises by only $400 billion, which is less than the $500 billion stimulus to aggregate demand. The reason, as we know from earlier chapters, is that rising prices stifle some aggregate demand and reduce the multiplier.

By taking account of the effect of an increase in the money supply on the price level, we have now completed our story about how monetary policy works. We can thus expand our schematic diagram of monetary policy to:

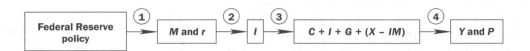

The last link now recognizes that *both* output *and* prices normally are affected by changes in interest rates and the money supply.

## 13-7  APPLICATION: WHY THE AGGREGATE DEMAND CURVE SLOPES DOWNWARD[8]

This analysis of the effect of monetary policy on the price level puts us in a better position to understand why higher prices reduce aggregate quantity demanded—that is, why the aggregate demand curve slopes downward. In earlier chapters, we explained this phenomenon in two ways. First, we observed that rising prices reduce the purchasing power of money-fixed assets held by consumers, such as money itself and government bonds, and that falling real wealth in turn reduces consumption spending. Second, we noted that higher domestic prices depress exports and stimulate imports.

There is nothing wrong with this analysis; it is just incomplete. Higher prices have an even more important effect on aggregate demand through a channel we are now in a position to understand.

Bank deposits are demanded primarily to conduct transactions. As we noted earlier in this chapter, an increase in the *average money cost* of each transaction—that is, in the

---

[8] This section contains somewhat more difficult material, which can be skipped in shorter courses.

price level—will increase the quantity of deposits demanded, and hence increase the demand for bank reserves. Thus, when spending rises for any reason, the price level will also rise, and more reserves will therefore be demanded at any given interest rate—that is, the demand curve for bank reserves will shift outward to the right, as shown in Figure 8.

If the Fed does not increase the *supply* of reserves, this outward shift of the demand curve will force the cost of borrowing reserves—the federal funds rate—to rise, as Figure 8 makes clear. As we know, increases in interest rates reduce investment and, hence, reduce aggregate demand. This is the main reason why the economy's aggregate demand curve has a negative slope, meaning that aggregate quantity demanded is lower when prices are higher. In sum:

> At higher price levels, the quantity of bank reserves demanded is greater. If the Fed holds the supply schedule fixed, a higher price level must therefore lead to higher interest rates. Because higher interest rates discourage investment, aggregate quantity demanded is lower when the price level is higher—that is, the aggregate demand curve has a negative slope.

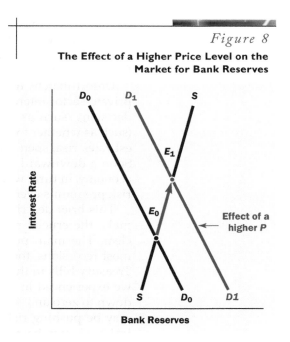

*Figure 8*

**The Effect of a Higher Price Level on the Market for Bank Reserves**

## 13-8 UNCONVENTIONAL MONETARY POLICIES

Events during and since the financial crisis dramatically point out one major omission from our analysis of monetary policy thus far: What happens if the Federal Reserve uses garden-variety open-market operations to push the federal funds rate all the way down to zero, and yet the economy still needs more stimulus? Such a possibility no longer seems remote because it actually happened in the United States in December 2008.

Once the federal funds rate hits zero, a central bank seeking to stimulate its economy further must turn to *unconventional* monetary policies. One option is massive lending to banks, or even to companies other than banks—both of which the Fed did in 2008 and 2009. Another option is open-market purchases of assets *other than Treasury bills* in order to drive their prices up and their interest rates down. But which assets should the central bank buy? When the Fed first faced this question in 2009 and 2010, the mortgage market had crumbled, and mortgage-related securities had few buyers. That made what are called *mortgage-backed securities*, a kind of bond backed by mortgages (and explained more in the next chapter), a natural choice. There are other choices as well. But unfortunately for the Fed, the evidence suggests that all of these unusual options have weaker effects than reducing the federal funds rate—something the Fed can no longer do once the funds rate hits zero.

## 13-9 FROM FINANCIAL DISTRESS TO RECESSION

Let's now use what we have learned in this chapter to gain some understanding of how a financial crisis can lead to a recession.

The story starts when something goes wrong in the financial markets, causing a loss of confidence in some financial assets. That "something" could be the failure of a major financial institution (such as, Lehman Brothers in 2008), or a stock market crash (as in 2000), or a collapse of real estate prices (as after 2006). There are other possibilities as well.

Whatever the cause, the resulting financial market distress often raises concerns about the abilities of a variety of debtors (mortgage holders, banks, corporations, etc.) to make payments on time or in full.[9] As the panic gains momentum, the *risk premiums* embedded in interest rates rise far above their "normal" levels, reflecting the new (higher) estimated probabilities of loss. So even if interest rates on *riskless* Treasury securities hold steady or fall, interest rates on *risky* securities are liable to rise—perhaps sharply.

Unfortunately, no person or company can borrow at riskless Treasury rates. Higher private-sector interest rates, which now embody higher risk premiums, guide household decisions (such as whether to buy a new car or a new house) and business decisions (such as whether to invest in new office buildings and equipment). As these private interest rates rise, spending on the interest-sensitive components of aggregate demand falls. Soon a downward multiplier process is pulling the entire economy down. The sagging economy, in turn, worsens the prospects for loan repayments even more, thereby pushing risk premiums even higher, and the vicious cycle continues.

This brief description of how rising interest rate spreads can cause recessions should make the crucial role of monetary policy—whether conventional or unconventional—clear. The main purpose of *expansionary monetary policy* is to reduce interest rates. In most recessions, the central bank can do that job by purchasing only riskless assets like Treasury bills in the open market. But in a particularly severe recession, such as the one we experienced in 2008 and 2009, the central bank may drive the T-bill rate all the way down to zero and yet still not revive the economy. Furthermore, rising perceptions of risk may be pushing risky interest rates up at the same time. When that happens, the central bank may have to resort to unconventional monetary policies, such as open-market operations in something other than Treasury bills. But remember, whether conventional or unconventional, the central idea behind expansionary monetary policy is the same: to fight the recession by lowering interest rates.

## 13-10  FROM MODELS TO POLICY DEBATES

You will no doubt be relieved to hear that we have now provided just about all the technical apparatus we need to analyze stabilization policy. To be sure, you will encounter many graphs in the next few chapters. Most of them, however, will be repeats of diagrams with which you are already familiar. Our attention now turns from *building* a theory to *using* that theory to address several important policy issues.

The next four chapters begin by taking up some of the stunning events of 2007–2009 (Chapter 14). Then we turn to a trio of controversial policy debates that surface regularly in the media: the debate over the conduct of stabilization policy (Chapter 15), the continuing debate over budget deficits and the effects of fiscal and monetary policy on growth (Chapter 16), and the controversy over the trade-off between inflation and unemployment (Chapter 17).

## Summary

1. "Money" and "income," though related, are two different concepts. A country's **central bank** creates its money supply. A central bank is a bank for banks.

2. The Federal Reserve System is America's central bank. There are 12 Federal Reserve banks, but most of the power is held by the Board of Governors in Washington and by the Federal Open Market Committee.

3. The Federal Reserve acts independently of the rest of the government. By now, many countries have decided that **central bank independence** is a good idea and have moved in this direction.

4. The Fed has three major monetary policy weapons: **open-market operations,** reserve requirements, and its lending policy toward banks. Normally, it relies on open-market operations but during the financial crisis it lent massive amounts to banks.

5. In normal times, the Fed increases the supply of bank reserves by purchasing Treasury bills (a type of short-term government security) in the open market. When it pays banks for such purchases by creating new reserves, the Fed lowers interest rates and induces a multiple expansion of the money supply. Conversely,

---

[9] How we got into such a situation in 2007 and 2008 will be discussed in detail in the next chapter.

open-market sales of Treasury bills take reserves away from banks, raise interest rates, and lead to a contraction of the money supply.

6. When the Fed buys bills or bonds, their prices rise and their interest rates fall. When the Fed sells bills or bonds, their prices fall and their interest rates rise.

7. There are many interest rates in a modern economy. In normal times, they all rise or fall together.

8. **Risk premiums** (or "**spreads**") in interest rates reflect buyers' perceptions of the risk of loss. Riskier borrowers must pay higher interest rates in order to secure credit.

9. Risk premiums are likely to rise sharply in a financial crisis. When that happens, all borrowers except the U.S. Treasury face higher borrowing costs. These higher interest rates can, in turn, depress economic activity.

10. In addition to conventional open-market purchases of T-bills, the Fed can also pursue a more expansionary monetary policy by allowing banks to borrow more reserves, perhaps by reducing the interest rate it charges on such loans (the **discount rate**) or by reducing **reserve requirements**. These are the three conventional weapons of monetary policy.

11. None of these weapons, however, give the Fed perfect control over the money supply in the short run, because it cannot predict perfectly how far the process of deposit creation or destruction will go. The Fed can, however, control the interest rate banks pay to borrow reserves, which is called the **federal funds rate,** quite precisely.

12. If the economy is weak for a long time, the central bank might reduce its interest rate all the way to zero, and yet still not stimulate growth sufficiently. In such a case, it might turn to one or more **unconventional monetary policies.** These policies include massive lending to banks, or even to firms that are not banks, and open-market purchases of securities other than Treasury bills. The latter is sometimes called **quantitative easing.**

13. Investment spending ($I$), including business investment and investment in new homes, is sensitive to interest rates ($r$). Specifically, $I$ is lower when $r$ is higher.

14. Conventional **monetary policy** works in the following way: Raising the supply of bank reserves leads to lower interest rates; the lower interest rates stimulate investment spending; and this investment stimulus, via the multiplier, raises aggregate demand.

15. Prices are likely to rise as output rises. The amount of inflation caused by expansionary monetary policy depends on the slope of the aggregate supply curve. Much inflation will occur if the supply curve is steep, but little inflation if it is flat.

16. The main reason why the aggregate demand curve slopes downward is that higher prices increase the demand for bank deposits, and hence for bank reserves. Given a fixed supply of reserves, this higher demand pushes interest rates up, which, in turn, discourages investment.

## Key Terms

central bank   260

central bank independence   261

discount rate   270

federal funds rate   263

monetary policy   259

open-market operations   263

quantitative easing   271

risk of default   267

risk premium (or "spread")   267

unconventional monetary policy   270

## Test Yourself

1. Suppose there is $120 billion of cash and that half of this cash is held in bank vaults as reserves, all of which are *required* (i.e., banks hold no *excess* reserves). How large will the money supply be if the required reserve ratio is 10 percent? 12½ percent? 16⅔ percent?

2. Show the balance sheet changes that would take place if the Federal Reserve Bank of New York purchased an office building from Citigroup for a price of $100 million. Compare this effect to the effect of an open-market purchase of securities shown in Table 1. What do you conclude?

3. Suppose the Fed purchases $5 billion worth of government bonds from Bill Gates, who banks at the Bank of America in San Francisco. Show the effects on the balance sheets of the Fed, the Bank of America, and Gates. (*Hint:* Where will the Fed get the $5 billion to pay Gates?) Does it make any difference if the Fed buys bonds from a bank or an individual?

4. Treasury bills have a fixed face value (say, $1,000) and pay interest by selling at a discount. For example, if a one-year bill with a $1,000 face value sells today for $950, it will pay $1,000 – $950 = $50 in interest over its life. The interest rate on the bill is therefore $50 / $950 = 0.0526, or 5.26 percent.

   a. Suppose the price of the Treasury bill falls to $925. What happens to the interest rate?

   b. Suppose, instead, that the price rises to $975. What is the interest rate now?

   c. **(More difficult)** Now generalize this example. Let $P$ be the price of the bill and $r$ be the interest rate. Develop an algebraic formula expressing $r$ in terms of $P$. (*Hint:* The interest earned is $1,000 – $P$. What is the *percentage* interest rate?) Show that this formula illustrates the point made in the text: Higher bond prices mean lower interest rates.

5. Explain what a $5 billion increase in bank reserves will do to real GDP under the following assumptions:

  a. Each $1 billion increase in bank reserves reduces the rate of interest by 0.5 percentage point.

  b. Each 1 percentage point decline in interest rates stimulates $30 billion worth of new investment.

  c. The expenditure multiplier is two.

  d. The aggregate supply curve is so flat that prices do not rise noticeably when demand increases.

6. Explain how your answers to Test Yourself Question 5 would differ if each of the assumptions changed. Specifically, what sorts of changes in the assumptions would weaken the effects of monetary policy?

7. Explain how your answers to Test Yourself Question 5 would differ if banks decided to hold onto the $5 billion in new reserves as excess reserves.

8. **(More difficult)** Consider an economy in which government purchases, taxes, and net exports are all zero. The consumption function is

$$C = 300 + 0.75Y$$

and investment spending ($I$) depends on the rate of interest ($r$) in the following way:

$$I = 1,000 - 100r$$

Find the equilibrium GDP if the Fed makes the rate of interest (a) 2 percent $(r = 0.02)$, (b) 5 percent, and (c) 10 percent.

## Discussion Questions

1. Why does a modern industrial economy need a central bank?

2. What are some reasons behind the worldwide trend toward greater central bank independence? Are there arguments on the other side?

3. Explain why the quantity of bank reserves supplied normally is higher and the quantity of bank reserves demanded normally is lower at higher interest rates.

4. From September 2007 through December 2008, the Fed believed that interest rates needed to fall and took steps to reduce them, eventually cutting the federal funds rate from 5.25 percent to nearly zero. How did the Fed reduce the federal funds rate? Illustrate your answer on a diagram.

5. Once the federal funds rate reached (approximately) zero, which happened in December 2008, what options were still open to the Fed. What did it actually do? (*Note*: This may be a good question to discuss with your instructor.)

6. Explain why both business investments and purchases of new homes rise when interest rates decline.

7. From 2003 to 2011, the federal government's budget deficit rose sharply because of tax cuts and increased spending. If the Federal Reserve wanted to maintain the same level of aggregate demand in the face of large increases in the budget deficit, what should it have done? What would you expect to happen to interest rates?

# THE FINANCIAL CRISIS AND THE GREAT RECESSION

# 14

*We came very, very close to a global financial meltdown.*

FORMER FEDERAL RESERVE CHAIRMAN BEN BERNANKE

If you have read the book thus far, you have learned a great deal about the causes and consequences of recessions. But the United States had not experienced a recession as severe as the last one since the 1930s. The recession of 2007–2009 clearly merits being called the "Great Recession." You have also learned, especially in the last few chapters, how fiscal and monetary policies can be used to combat recessions by raising aggregate demand. But the nation had never witnessed a policy response as powerful or multifaceted as what the U.S. government did to fight the Great Recession. Finally, although you have learned some important lessons about banking and the financial markets in Chapters 12 and 13, we have not yet provided nearly enough material on finance to understand the incredible series of events that shook the United States and the world financial system to its foundations in 2007 and 2008.

This chapter remedies some of these omissions. We review the history of the crisis, starting from its antecedents in the financial markets in 2003–2004 and finishing with a snapshot of where things stand late in 2014. Our focus is not so much on the chronology of events as on the "missing pieces" that are necessary to understand the crisis—concepts such as *asset bubbles, subprime mortgages, mortgage-backed securities,* and *leverage*—and on some of the lessons that have been learned. Indeed, the chapter closes with a list of such lessons.

## CONTENTS

| Issue | *Did the Fiscal Stimulus Work?* |
|---|---|

The Federal Reserve, the administration, and Congress responded to the financial crisis and the Great Recession with massive doses of monetary and fiscal stimulus, some of them quite unconventional. Yet, despite this unprecedented effort, real GDP declined for four consecutive quarters (the last two quarters of 2008 and the first two of 2009), and employment dropped for 23 consecutive months. The unemployment rate reached a high of 10 percent in October 2009—a figure not seen since June 1983.

Some critics interpret the severity of the recession as evidence that the Obama administration's prodigious efforts to save or create jobs through fiscal stimulus failed. How, they ask, can you claim to have saved jobs when more than 8 million jobs were lost? The stimulus bill enacted in February 2009 has been subjected to particularly vehement criticism on these grounds. More than two years after its enactment, some politicians were still clamoring for its repeal. But supporters of stimulus argued then that the critics ignored something important: Without the stimulus, they insist, the economy would have performed even worse, and job losses would have been even more severe.

Which side of the argument comes closer to the truth? Read this chapter and then decide.

## 14-1 ROOTS OF THE CRISIS

A home **mortgage** is a particular type of loan used to buy a house. The house normally serves as the collateral for the mortgage.

The rolling series of financial crises that began in the summer of 2007 traces its roots back further in the decade. Indeed, to understand the length and breadth of the crisis, it is important to understand that the problems that beset the market for home **mortgages** were just one manifestation of a broader set of forces that swept through America's credit markets during the years 2003–2006, leaving the financial system terribly vulnerable.

When the U.S. economy failed to snap back from the mild recession of 2001 and employment kept falling, the Federal Reserve made borrowing cheaper by pushing the federal funds rate all the way down to 1 percent in June 2003 in an effort to stimulate the economy. It then held the rate there for an entire year. Although this super-low interest rate policy was promulgated for valid macroeconomic reasons, it produced several notable side effects that came back to haunt us later.

A **bubble** is an increase in the price of an asset or assets that goes far beyond what can be justified by improving *fundamentals*, such as dividends and earnings for shares of stock or incomes and interest rates for houses.

Most obviously, it pushed up the demand for houses, and therefore house prices—after all, lower mortgage interest rates make it cheaper, and therefore more attractive, to own a home. This boost from monetary policy helped fuel the burgeoning house price **bubble**—pushing house prices well beyond what could be justified by the fundamentals. Indeed, that very fact illustrates how hard it can be to distinguish between a bubble and improvements in one or more of the fundamental factors that determine an asset's value. Mortgage rates are certainly an important *fundamental* factor, so lower rates should have led to higher house prices. But they also seem to have inflated the bubble.

An **interest rate spread** is the difference between an interest rate on a risky asset and the corresponding interest rate on a risk-free Treasury security.

The paltry returns on safe assets such as Treasury bills also encouraged investors to "reach for yield" by purchasing riskier securities that paid correspondingly higher interest rates. This behavior increased the demands for assets such as "junk" bonds, emerging-market debt, mortgage-backed securities (which will be explained later in this chapter), and others, thus pushing up their prices and reducing their yields.[1] In other words, the gaps between interest rates on risky assets and interest rates on safe Treasury securities—the **interest rate spreads** we studied in the last chapter—were compressed as investors poured money into riskier securities.

A mortgage is classified as **subprime** if the borrower fails to meet the traditional credit standards of "prime" borrowers.

This trend was compounded by the fact that the delinquencies (late payments) and defaults (nonpayments) on virtually all sorts of lending, including home mortgages, fell to extraordinarily low levels during the years 2004–2006. Low defaults, in turn, deluded bankers and other lenders into believing that these riskier assets were not so risky after all. And that cavalier attitude, coupled with lax regulation, encouraged and permitted careless lending standards across the board. So, for example, we witnessed an explosion of so-called **subprime mortgages** and even the notorious "NINJA" loans—made to people with "no income, no job or assets." Many of these subprime mortgages were granted with low or negligible down payments to borrowers of questionable credit standing who could barely afford their monthly payments. The borrowers hoped that rising home values would bail them out of excessive debt burdens.

When an asset is bought with **leverage**, the buyer uses borrowed money to supplement his or her own funds. Leverage is typically measured by the ratio of assets to equity. For example, if the buyer commits $100,000 of his or her own funds and borrows $900,000 to purchase a $1 million asset, we say that leverage is 10-to-1 ($1 million divided by $100,000).

The narrowing of interest rate spreads meant, as a matter of arithmetic, that lower financial rewards were being paid for bearing risk. The same amount of risk that used to earn investors, say, a 3 percent premium over Treasury rates, now earned them only, say, a 1 percent premium. That compression, in turn, led yield-hungry investors to make heavy use of **leverage** as a way to boost returns. All that leverage created tremendous vulnerabilities in our financial system, which made the subsequent crisis far worse than it otherwise would have been. Because leverage played such a central role in the financial crisis, we need to understand how it works.

---

[1] Remember from the last chapter that when the price of a bond goes up, the effective interest rate it pays goes down.

## 14-2 LEVERAGE, PROFITS, AND RISK

*Leverage* refers to the use of borrowed funds to purchase assets. The word itself derives from Archimedes, who famously declared that, if given a large enough lever, he could move the earth. (One wonders where he imagined he would place the fulcrum!) There is nothing wrong with leverage *per se*. However, just as with consumption of alcoholic beverages, excesses can lead to disaster, as we shall see presently.

We have encountered leverage before. In Chapter 12, we studied the balance sheet of the hypothetical Bank-a-Mythica, which is repeated for convenience here as Table 1. Notice that this tiny bank owns $5.5 million worth of assets on an equity base (the stockholders' investment) of only $500,000. Because the degree of leverage is conventionally measured by the ratio of assets to net worth, we say that this bank is leveraged 11-to-1, which is pretty typical of U.S. commercial banks.

Leverage is a major source of Bank-a-Mythica's, or any bank's, profitability. To see why, suppose the bank's deposits carry an average annual interest cost of 2 percent, or $100,000 per year in total, whereas its loans yield, on average, 4 percent a year, or $180,000.[2] The bank is nicely profitable because of the wide spread between its lending and deposit rates. It returns $80,000 per year ($180,000 − $100,000) in profit to its investors, which is a 16 percent rate of return on their invested capital of $500,000.

Now suppose the bank was forced to operate without borrowed funds, which, in this simple case, means without deposits.[3] In that case, the bank's far-smaller balance sheet would look like Table 2. A 4 percent return on its $500,000 loan portfolio would now net the bank just $20,000 per year, which is, of course, also a 4 percent rate of return on its $500,000 equity. With such low prospective returns, investors would probably find better uses for their money. So this bank would never exist. Thus:

**Leverage is essential to a bank's profitability, but leverage also exacerbates risk.**

Using the *unleveraged* balance sheet of Table 2, now suppose that loans decline in value by 10 percent, creating the new balance sheet shown in Table 3. The stockholders have lost 10 percent of their investment, which is bad but not devastating. By contrast, consider

*Table 1*

**Balance Sheet of Bank-a-Mythica, December 31, 2014**

| Assets | | Liabilities and Net Worth | |
|---|---|---|---|
| **Assets** | | **Liabilities** | |
| Reserves | $1,000,000 | Checking deposits | $5,000,000 |
| Loans outstanding | 4,500,000 | | |
| Total | **$5,500,000** | **Net Worth** | |
| | | Stockholders' equity | 500,000 |
| | | Total | **$5,500,000** |

*Table 2*

**Unleveraged Balance Sheet**

| Assets | | Liabilities and Net Worth | |
|---|---|---|---|
| Loans outstanding | $ 500,000 | Stockholders' equity | $ 500,000 |

---

[2] For example, the average loan rate might be 7 percent with an average 3 percent loss rate. Alas, not all loans get paid back!

[3] Remember from Chapter 12 that bank deposits are *liabilities* to banks because, if they are cashed in, the bank must pay out the cash. Thus, you *lend* money to your bank, and the bank *borrows* money from you, when you make a deposit.

*Table 3*

**Unleveraged Balance Sheet after 10 Percent Loan Losses**

| Assets | | Liabilities and Net Worth | |
|---|---|---|---|
| Loans outstanding | $ 450,000 | Stockholders' equity | $ 450,000 |

*Table 4*

**Leveraged Balance Sheet after 10 Percent Loan Losses**

| Assets | | Liabilities and Net Worth | |
|---|---|---|---|
| **Assets** | | **Liabilities** | |
| Reserves | $1,000,000 | Deposits | $5,000,000 |
| Loans outstanding | 4,050,000 | | |
| Total | $5,050,000 | **Net Worth** | |
| | | Stockholders' equity | 50,000 |
| | | Total | $5,050,000 |

the same 10 percent loan losses (which now amount to $450,000) in the highly leveraged balance sheet we started with in Table 1. We would then get the result shown in Table 4. Notice that the bank's shareholders have now lost 90 percent of their $500,000 investment. They are almost wiped out.

Thus leverage is the proverbial double-edged sword. It magnifies returns on the upside, which is what investors want, but it also magnifies losses on the downside, which can be fatal. The moral of this story is *not* that leverage must be shunned. Leverage is, for example, inherent in the very idea of banking, where an "unlevered bank" is an oxymoron because every dollar of deposits is "borrowed" from its customers. Rather, the true moral of the story is that any company operating with high leverage should be labeled "Fragile: Handle with Care." Its shock absorbers are not very resilient.

Unfortunately, too many banks and other financial institutions forgot this elementary lesson during the heady days of the real estate boom. Commercial banks employed legal and accounting gimmicks to push their leverage above the traditional ratio of 10-to-1 or so. Some investment banks operated with 30-to-1 or even 40-to-1 leverage. With 40-to-1 leverage, for example, a mere 2.5 percent decline in the value of your assets is enough to destroy all shareholder value.[4] That's a risky way to run a business. And when asset values dropped after the housing bubble burst, many of these firms were ill prepared to absorb losses and became **insolvent**.

A company is **insolvent** when the value of its liabilities exceeds the value of its assets, that is, when its net worth is negative.

So those were the four main ingredients in the dangerous witches' brew that existed *before* the housing bubble burst: the house-price bubble itself, lenient lending standards, compressed risk spreads, and high leverage.

But none of this mattered much as long as house prices continued to inflate.

## 14-3 THE HOUSE PRICE BUBBLE AND THE SUBPRIME MORTGAGE CRISIS

But they didn't. Cracks in the system began to emerge when house prices stopped rising in either 2006 or 2007, depending on the particular measure you use. Over the period from 2000 until 2006 or 2007, house prices in the United States soared by 60 to 90 percent, which constituted a faster rate of increase than we had ever seen before on a nationwide basis.

---

[4] EXERCISE: Demonstrate this conclusion with a hypothetical balance sheet both before and after a 2.5 percent loss.

## Leverage and Returns: An Example

**Leverage magnifies gains on the way up but also magnifies losses on the way down.**

To illustrate this general principle, consider the contrasting investment behaviors of Jane Doe and John Dough.

Jane invests $1,000,000 in corporate bonds paying 6 percent interest, which she plans to hold for one year. If, at the end of the year, the bond's price is still $1,000,000, she gets back her $1,000,000 in principal plus $60,000 in interest. Because what she receives is 6 percent more than what she originally paid, her rate of return is, naturally, 6 percent.

Now consider John Dough. He also commits $1,000,000 of his own money to these same bonds, but *leverages* his investment by borrowing another $9,000,000 from a bank, at 3 percent interest. Thus his investment in bonds is $10,000,000. Again assuming that the bond's price does not change, John gets back his $10,000,000 in principal plus $600,000 in interest at year's end, or $10,600,000 in total. He repays the bank $9,000,000 in principal plus $270,000 in interest (3% of the principal), or $9,270,000 in total. Hence, his net earnings are $10,600,000 - $9,270,000 = $1,330,000 on his original $1,000,000 investment. John's rate of return is therefore 33 percent—more than five times higher than Jane's.

So is John, who uses high leverage, a smarter investor than Jane, who does not? Well, maybe not. Suppose now that the bonds fall 5 percent in value during the year in which Jane and John own them. Jane will now receive $950,000 in principal plus $60,000 in interest, or $1,010,000 in total. Her rate of return is thus a paltry 1 percent. John, on the other hand, will get back $9,500,000 in principal plus $600,000 in interest, or $10,100,000 in total. But he will still have to pay the bank $9,270,000, leaving him with only $830,000 of his original $1,000,000 investment. John's rate of return is therefore *minus* 17 percent. (He has lost 17 percent of his money.)

So maybe John wasn't so smart after all.

© HIP/Art Resource, NY

Many observers believed that such sharp price increases far outstripped what could be justified by the fundamentals, such as rising incomes and falling mortgage interest rates; hence the term *bubble*. Their warnings were not heeded, however.

Once the bubble burst, house prices began to fall, especially severely in previous boom markets in California, Florida, Arizona, and Nevada. Again, depending on how you measure it, the price of an average American home fell by 12 to 25 percent over the next two to three years; in some areas, prices fell 50 percent or more. These sharp declines had a number of obvious effects on the economy, plus a few that were not so obvious.

First, plunging prices made both buying and building new homes far less attractive than when prices were soaring. For-sale signs sprouted up everywhere, and inventories of unsold houses piled up, driving prices down further. Think about the profitability of a builder whose construction costs for a certain type of home are $250,000. At a selling price of $300,000, the business is nicely profitable, inducing a great deal of new construction. But if the market price drops to $200,000, that's a signal to stop building, which is precisely what many construction companies did. Residential construction tumbled by a remarkable 56 percent between the winter of 2005–2006 and the spring of 2009, when it hit rock bottom. Remember, spending on newly constructed homes is part of investment, *I*, so this sharp decline starting dragging down GDP growth in late 2005.

Second, a great deal of consumer wealth was destroyed in the process. After all, a house is far and away the most valuable asset for most American families. If the value of the family house falls from, say, $300,000 to $200,000, which happened in many markets, the family is substantially poorer. As we learned in Chapter 8, reduced wealth normally leads to lower consumer spending, *C*. It did so in 2008 and 2009. The roots of recession were being sown.

But there was much more. Most houses are purchased mainly with borrowed funds—mortgages. A typical mortgage obligates the homeowner to make fixed monthly payments over a certain number of years (often 30). Obviously, the more a household borrows, the

**Collateral** is the asset or assets that a borrower pledges in order to guarantee repayment of a loan. If the borrower fails to pay, the collateral becomes the property of the lender.

**Foreclosure** is the legal process through which a mortgage lender obtains control of the property after the mortgage goes into default.

larger its monthly mortgage payment will be. If the homeowner fails to make the monthly payments, the bank can take back the house—which is the **collateral** on the loan—through a legal process called **foreclosure**. Notice that as falling home values reduce the value of the collateral, the bank finds itself in a more precarious position. If it forecloses on a homeowner who fails to make the required payments, the bank might not get all of its money back because the house might be worth less than the mortgage.

Let's think about some numbers that typified "the good old days" prior to the housing bubble. Down payments of about 20 percent were normal. So a $200,000 house would be bought with about $40,000 in cash and a mortgage of $160,000. The down payment served as a cushion. Because the original mortgage debt amounted to only 80 percent of the value of the house, even a 10 to 15 percent drop in price, which was a very rare event, would leave the property worth more than the mortgage. If the mortgage interest rate was, say, 7.5 percent per annum, the monthly payment would be about $1,120. By traditional banking rules of thumb, a household should have income of three to four times that amount to qualify for such a mortgage—say, $40,000 to $55,000 a year.

But mortgage lending standards dropped like a stone during the housing boom, in three main ways. The reason in each case was the same: As the bubble inflated, both borrowers and lenders came to believe that house prices would rise forever.

First, the rule of thumb just mentioned came to be viewed as hopelessly old-fashioned. Housing was such a fine investment, it was thought, that families could safely afford to devote more than 25 to 33 percent of their incomes to mortgage payments.

Second, banks and other lenders started to grant loans with small or even zero down payments. Both of these changes enabled households to purchase even more expensive homes—homes that ultimately proved to be beyond their means. But that meant that leverage rose.

Third, banks and other lenders started offering more and more mortgages to families with less-than-stellar credit ratings—the notorious subprime mortgages—often in amounts that borrowers could not afford. Under normal market conditions, such loans would have been considered too risky by borrowers and lenders alike. But as the bubble continued to grow, lenders reasoned (incorrectly, as it turned out) that ever-rising house prices would make their loans secure even if borrowers defaulted because the value of the collateral (the house) would keep rising. The corresponding delusion for households went something like this: "I know I shouldn't borrow $200,000 to buy a $200,000 house that I can't afford on my $25,000 annual income. But if I can muddle through the first two or three years, the house will be worth $300,000. Then I can pay off my old $200,000 loan, replacing it with a much safer $240,000 mortgage with $60,000 down (20 percent of $300,000)—leaving $40,000 in cash in my pocket."[5]

That all sounded good—until it didn't. When house prices stopped rising, subprime mortgages began to default in large numbers. The house of cards was beginning to crumble.

## 14-4 FROM THE HOUSING BUBBLE TO THE FINANCIAL CRISIS

At first, most observers thought the damage from the impending subprime mortgage debacle would be too small to cause a recession. That proved wrong for two main reasons. The first mistake was simple: Most people underestimated the scale of the subprime mortgage market, where volume had soared during the late stages of the bubble. The second mistake is harder to explain, and doing so requires a detour through a once-arcane aspect of finance called **securitization**. A simple example will illustrate how securitization works.

Loans are **securitized**—that is, transformed into marketable securities—when they are packaged together into a bond-like instrument that can be sold to investors, potentially all over the world.

Suppose Risky Bank (RB) has made 1,000 subprime mortgage loans averaging $200,000—all, let us say, in the Las Vegas area. RB's highly concentrated loan portfolio of $200 million is, well, risky. Should an economic downturn or natural disaster hit its local market, many of these loans would likely default, potentially driving RB into bankruptcy.

---

[5] Here is the arithmetic: If Bank Two will lend $240,000 against the $300,000 house—a safe loan with a 20 percent down payment, the homeowner can take $200,000 of the newly borrowed $240,000 and pay off his original loan from Bank One, keeping $40,000 for himself.

Enter Friendly Investment Bank (FIB), a *securitizer*. FIB offers the bank an attractive deal. "Sell us your $200 million in subprime mortgages. We will pay you cash immediately, which you can use to make loans to other borrowers. We'll then take your mortgages, combine them with others from banks around the country, and package them all into more diversified **mortgage-backed securities (MBS)**. These securities will be less risky than the underlying mortgages because they will be backed by payments emanating from several different geographical areas. Then we will spread the risk further by selling pieces of the MBS to investors all over the world." FIB, of course, would earn fees for all of its services.

A **mortgage-backed security (MBS)** is a type of bond whose interest payments and principal repayments derive from the monthly mortgage payments of many households.

On the surface, this little bit of "financial engineering," as it is called, seems to make good sense. RB is relieved of a substantial risk that could threaten its very existence. FIB's securitization of all those mortgages reduces risk in the two ways claimed. The first is geographical diversification: Even if Las Vegas real estate prices plummet, it is unlikely that real estate prices would drop simultaneously in Los Angeles, Chicago, Orlando, and so forth. Second, the risks that remain in the (diversified) MBS are then parceled out to hundreds or even thousands of investors all over the world, rather than being concentrated in a few banks. Thus no one bank is left "holding the bag" if mortgage defaults rise unexpectedly.

At least, that was the theory. However, it didn't work out that way in practice. Why not? The preceding paragraph contains the first two clues.

First, when the *national* housing bubble burst, home prices actually did fall almost everywhere—an "impossible" event that had not occurred since the Great Depression of the 1930s. For decades, Americans had witnessed periodic house-price bubbles in particular areas of the country. But when prices fell in, say, Boston, they kept rising in, say, Los Angeles—and vice versa. The period after 2006–2007 was different. With house prices falling all over the map, the expected gains from geographical diversification disappeared just when they were most needed. (See the box "A National Housing Bubble Bursts.") For this reason alone, the MBS turned out to be riskier than investors thought—and their market values declined. Remember from the previous chapter that greater perceived risk induces lenders to demand higher interest rates as compensation—and higher interest rates mean lower bond prices.

Second, we learned in the crisis that the securities were not as widely distributed as had been thought. On the contrary, many of the world's leading financial institutions apparently found MBS and other mortgage-related assets so attractive during the boom that they were left holding large concentrations of such assets when the markets collapsed. The failures and near failures of such venerable firms as Bear Stearns, Lehman Brothers,

## A National Housing Bubble Bursts

No one had seen anything like it since the Great Depression of the 1930s: House prices dropped virtually everywhere in America at the same time. The graph displays the changes in the S&P/Case-Shiller home price indexes (January 2000 = 100) for six different geographical markets at two different dates: June 2006, which was close to the market peak, and June 2010, which was close to the market bottom. The direction was the same coast to coast: down. But the magnitude of the price decline varied hugely from market to market. It was dramatic in the boom-and-bust markets of Las Vegas, Phoenix, and Miami; modest in the New York City area; and smaller in the relatively calm real estate markets of Cleveland and Denver.

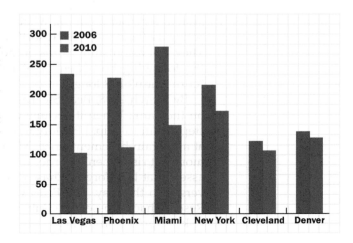

*"Stop! Wait! Government's no longer the problem—it's the solution."*

© The New Yorker Collection, 2009 David Sipress from cartoonbank.com. All rights reserved.

Merrill Lynch, Wachovia, Citigroup, Bank of America, and others were all traceable, directly or indirectly, to excessive concentrations of mortgage-related risks. When the panic hit, and one institution after another tried to unload their now-unwanted securities in a market with many sellers and few buyers, prices fell further.[6]

There is more to the story. We have already mentioned that excessive leverage is dangerous and that mortgages with less collateral behind them (less valuable houses) are riskier and therefore command lower prices in the marketplace. But there was another important factor: Many of the MBS and related assets were far more *complex* than our simple example suggests.

During the boom, Wall Street firms created and sold a dizzying array of financial securities that, in effect, offered investors complicated combinations of shares of mortgage loans—securities so complex that few investors really understood what they owned. As more and more of the underlying mortgages started to look like they might default, the values of all mortgage-backed securities naturally plummeted. In the cases of the most complex and opaque securities, this fear was exacerbated by the fact that nobody knew what they were really worth. That is a surefire cause for panic once the seeds of doubt are sown. The panic simmered for a while and then burst into the open in the summer of 2007. The financial crisis had begun.

The creaky system began to crack in July 2007, when Bear Stearns—a large investment bank that would later become infamous—told investors that there was "effectively no value left" in one of its mortgage funds. Not exactly reassuring. Soon a variety of financial markets were acting extremely nervous. The big bang came on August 9, 2007, when BNP Paribas, a huge French bank, halted withdrawals on three of its subprime mortgage funds—citing as its reason the inability to put values on the securities the funds owned. This reminded those acquainted with American history of the banking panics of the nineteenth century, which were often triggered by some bank "suspending specie payments"—that is, refusing to exchange its bank notes for gold or silver. BNP Paribas had just refused to exchange its fund shares for cash. Whether you were French or American, that was a signal to panic. And markets promptly did so, all over the world.

At first, the Federal Reserve and the European Central Bank (ECB) tried to hold the system together by doing what central banks have done since the seventeenth century—acting as "lenders of last resort" as described in the last chapter (see "Lending to Banks"). They lent astonishing sums of money to commercial banks within a matter of days. (See the following box "Lender of Last Resort.") Although that helped settle markets, the "cure" didn't last long.

By March 2008, Bear Stearns was suffering from the modern-day equivalent of a run on the bank. When it became clear that Bear had only days to live, the Federal Reserve stepped in to help. J.P. Morgan Chase, a giant commercial bank, purchased Bear Stearns at a bargain-basement price. Most surprisingly, the Federal Reserve put some of its own money at risk when, in order to seal the deal, it agreed to buy some of Bear Stearns's risky assets that J.P. Morgan Chase did not want. These unprecedented actions remain controversial to this day. The Fed's vice chairman at the time, Donald Kohn, said the Federal Reserve had "crossed the Rubicon" with the Bear Stearns deal, alluding to Julius Caesar's risky approach to Rome.

---

[6] EXERCISE: Draw a supply-and-demand diagram for mortgage-backed securities. Show what happens when the demand curve shifts in and the supply curve shifts out.

## Lender of Last Resort

Prior to the advent of the financial crisis, Federal Reserve lending was negligible—and confined to commercial banks. Lending started to rise after the problems at BNP Paribas surfaced in August, and people at the time thought this was a big increase in Federal Reserve lending. But compared to what happened after Lehman Brothers failed in September 2008, it was tiny—too small to show up on the scale of the accompanying graph. Not only did the Fed lend massively as lender of last resort, but it also went beyond commercial banks to lend money to investment banks and even to a giant insurance company! By 2010, almost all of this had been repaid.

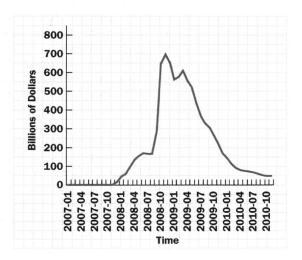

Not all of the anti-recessionary policies were financial. Conventional fiscal policy, as described in Chapter 11, was also employed to fight the recession. This process started in early 2008, when Congress enacted a one-time "tax rebate" to put more disposable income into the hands of consumers, just as it had done in 1975 and 2001.[7] As the economy worsened, it became clear that this modest fiscal stimulus (roughly 1 percent of GDP) was far too small, given the deteriorating economy.[8] In addition, many economists argued (as in Chapter 8, "Issue Revisited: Why Temporary Tax Cuts Have Only Modest Effects on Spending") that temporary tax cuts have smaller effects on consumer spending than permanent cuts do. So the first major action of the new Obama administration in 2009 was to recommend far more fiscal stimulus—as we have mentioned.

## 14-5 FROM THE FINANCIAL CRISIS TO THE GREAT RECESSION

A financial crisis does not remain purely financial for long. Soon the real economy gets dragged down. As we have learned in this book, all economies depend on credit. Borrowed funds are used to finance not only home purchases but also several types of consumer expenditures, $C$, such as automobile purchases, and most forms of business investment, $I$. Credit is also vital to exporting and importing, $X - IM$, and to financing substantial chunks of government spending, $G$. That list takes in every component of $C + I + G + (X - IM)$. So when credit contracts, so does aggregate demand. And as we have learned, declining aggregate demand is the most common cause of recessions.

Furthermore, banks are central to the credit system. If banks, feeling imperiled, become cautious about lending, businesses may find themselves starved for credit to finance inventories, households may be unable to obtain mortgages or auto loans, and local governments may find it hard to float their bonds. In worst-case scenarios—which nearly became a reality in the fall of 2008—firms may not even be able to obtain the short-term credit they need to make weekly payrolls. Such a situation is what former Federal Reserve Chairman Ben Bernanke feared when he spoke of a "global financial meltdown."

---

[7] These two episodes were analyzed in Chapter 8.
[8] The calculations behind such conclusions are more elaborate versions of the multiplier analysis presented in Chapters 9 and 11.

The Fed's job was not just to stop the financial bleeding, which was hard enough. It also had to find ways to repair the broken financial system and to get credit flowing again. In addition, it had to offset the drag on aggregate demand caused by the credit-market disruptions. The first two tasks were virtually unprecedented and required the Fed to improvise. But the last one was familiar. Central banks know how to stimulate (or contract) aggregate demand.

We learned in the previous chapter that monetary policy makers normally boost demand by cutting interest rates. In the case of the Federal Reserve, that meant lowering the *federal funds rate*, which stood at 5.25 percent when the crisis began. The Fed began cutting the funds rate in September 2007, cautiously at first. However, it soon realized that timidity would not do and accelerated its rate cutting enormously during the first quarter of 2008—including a dramatic reduction of 0.75 percent right after the Bear Stearns deal. By the end of April 2008, the federal funds rate stood at just 2 percent, where the Fed decided to leave it. Or so it thought.

Then came the demise of Lehman Brothers in September 2008. The Lehman bankruptcy changed everything by triggering the biggest financial panic yet. And panics are contagious. Within days, many other large financial firms were collapsing or teetering on the brink. Investors seemed unwilling to bear any risk at all, and risk premiums in interest rates soared. Everyone, it seemed, wanted to stash their funds in safe havens such as Treasury bills or FDIC-insured bank deposits. So, as we mentioned earlier, interest rates on Treasury bills *fell* even while most other rates were *rising*. The problem was that businesses and households were unable to borrow at the lower Treasury interest rates. If they could borrow at all, it was at the higher rates on bank loans, bonds, mortgages, and credit cards.

## The Collapse of Lehman Brothers: The Turning Point

The collapse of Lehman Brothers, a venerable Wall Street "brand name" that had survived the Great Depression, two world wars, and much else, marked a turning point in the crisis—and not just financially. The real economy also took a sharp turn for the worse immediately after Lehman filed for bankruptcy on September 15, 2008. Virtually all indicators of the health of the economy plunged downwards. Two of them are depicted here.

The right-hand panel shows the growth rate of *real GDP*, quarterly, from the fourth quarter of 2007 (the official start of the recession) through the second quarter of 2009, when the recession officially ended. Notice that GDP actually *grew* slightly, on balance, over the first three quarters shown in the graph, but then began plummeting just when Lehman fell. The left-hand panel depicts, in this case month by month, the rate of *job*

*loss* over approximately the same time period. Once again, we see only modest monthly job losses through August, and then stunningly large ones in the months after Lehman's collapse.

It's no wonder that the fall of Lehman Brothers is considered a milestone—and not a happy one—in the history of the financial and economic crisis of 2007–2009.

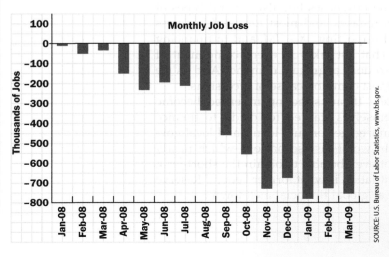

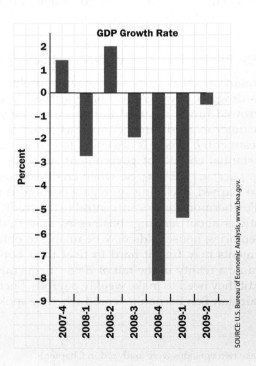

Banks, in turn, started hoarding *excess reserves* rather than lending them out. As we know from Chapter 12, unusual behavior like that would have led to a sharp contraction of the money supply had the Fed not intervened to prevent it from happening. It is no exaggeration to say that most of the economy's credit-granting mechanisms froze. It seemed that no one wanted to lend money to anyone. Within weeks, the real economy, starved of credit, looked like it was falling off a cliff. (See the box "The Collapse of Lehman Brothers: The Turning Point.")

These developments posed a huge new problem for the Fed. We learned in Chapters 12 and 30 that an injection of new bank reserves normally sets in motion a multiple expansion of the money supply and bank lending, which is how the Fed pushes the economy forward. In late 2008, the need for expansionary monetary policy was clear. But, as you will recall, the main reason why the multiple expansion process works is that banks do not hold excess reserves, which earn them little or nothing. Instead, they lend the funds out. Or at least that is what they do in normal times.

However, when banks fear a "run" by their depositors and/or worry that loans will not be repaid, it becomes rational for them to hang onto excess reserves.[9] Even if idle balances at the Federal Reserve pay them little or nothing, they are at least safe from loss. However, idle cash balances sitting on banks' balance sheets do not increase aggregate demand. Thus, conventional monetary policy loses much of its power. In fact, the Fed had to increase bank reserves massively to keep the money supply growing.

The Fed, the Treasury, the FDIC, and others reacted to this frightening state of affairs in multiple ways. First, the Fed added huge amounts of reserves and resumed cutting interest rates, pushing the federal funds rate all the way down to virtually zero by December 2008. But, for the reasons just mentioned, this additional dose of expansionary monetary policy may have had only minor effects.

Second, the Fed and the Treasury together mounted a rapid-fire series of dramatic rescue operations to prevent what was threatening to become "a global financial meltdown." They encouraged several gigantic mergers via which "strong" companies acquired "weak" ones. The Fed threw a big lifeline to AIG, a giant *insurance* company (not a bank) that was closely linked to Wall Street firms and banks, by lending it an enormous amount of money. In the process, the Fed effectively "nationalized" AIG without ever using the word—and without a vote in Congress. This operation eventually proved to be one of the most controversial of them all. The Fed is still being accused of making grievous errors in the AIG case, even though the company survived and is now in private hands again.

The Fed also declared the two surviving Wall Street giants, Goldman Sachs and Morgan Stanley, to be "banks" so that it could lend them money as necessary. The Treasury, which had previously denied it had any funds to commit to rescue operations, and hence left that task to the Fed, suddenly discovered a large pot of money that it used to stop runs on money market mutual funds.[10] The FDIC, which had long guaranteed bank deposits, extended its guarantee to larger accounts and also invented a new program to guarantee some of the bonds that banks issued. These examples are only a few of the attempted rescue operations. No living person had ever seen anything like it.

Despite these prodigious and unprecedented efforts, the financial markets remained in a state of shock, and the economy teetered on the brink of disaster. Against that background, Federal Reserve Chairman Bernanke and Secretary of the Treasury Henry Paulson locked arms (pretty much literally) and persuaded Congress (on the second try) to pass the **Troubled Assets Relief Program (TARP)** on October 3, 2008—just four weeks before the 2008 election.

The main idea behind TARP, for which Congress appropriated the astonishing sum of $700 billion,[11] was that MBS and other, more complicated, securities based on mortgages

The **Troubled Assets Relief Program (TARP)** enabled the U.S. Treasury to purchase assets and equity from banks and other financial institutions as a means of strengthening the financial sector.

---

[9] We discussed this possibility near the end of Chapter 12.

[10] Money market mutual fund deposits are very much like bank accounts; depositors can even write checks on them. Although not insured by the FDIC, millions of Americans considered the money in these funds to be totally safe—until one large money fund, which had invested in Lehman's debt instruments, suffered losses. That stunning event precipitated a run on money market funds in general.

[11] To put that number into perspective, the entire federal budget deficit for fiscal year 2008, which ended three days before the TARP legislation passed, was $459 billion.

were clogging up the financial system. With no buyers, the markets for these assets had pretty much shut down. Although most financial institutions owned mortgage-related securities, and some owned huge amounts, no one knew what they were worth because there were hardly any transactions. That ignorance engendered a nervous environment in which investors tended to assume the worse—including that most large financial institutions were hiding big losses. Few lenders were willing to extend credit to institutions that might prove to be insolvent.

The original purpose of TARP was to allow the Treasury Department to buy up some of the unwanted securities, hold them until the storm passed, and then sell them back into the market, hopefully at a profit. But that did not happen. Instead, Secretary Paulson utilized a catchall provision in the bill to divert TARP money to an entirely different purpose: to **recapitalize** the banks.[12] What does that mean?

Look back at the simplified balance sheet of the nearly insolvent bank we considered in Table 4. This bank is barely alive; the slightest further loss on its holdings of loans and securities will render it insolvent. Now suppose the bank receives $1 million in new cash when the government purchases $1 million worth of the bank's stock. The new balance sheet is shown in Table 5. The bank now has plenty of capital and plenty of capacity to lend. It's just that most of the new capital is owned by the government. Part of the idea, of course, is that the government will sell its shares later—as did indeed happen.

What Secretary Paulson actually did was a good deal more complicated than this simple example. But the balance sheets in Tables 4 and 5 give you the basic idea: Recapitalizations saved the banks by making the government a part owner. Many financial experts applauded the secretary's actions; others did not. However, the public at large felt it was fundamentally unfair to funnel all that money to the very banks that had caused the problems, while so many families and other businesses were struggling. The recapitalization of the banks, and the TARP itself, became wildly unpopular—hated by Republicans and Democrats alike. That attitude prevails to this day, even though the banks repaid the TARP funds with a profit to the government. Indeed, saying that some idea is "like the TARP" is a good way to kill it politically.

Politics aside, the recapitalizations did save the banks and proved to be the first step on the long, bumpy road to recovery. Unfortunately, as we traveled along this road, the economy was tanking. Look back at the boxed insert "The Collapse of Lehman Brothers: The Turning Point." The right-hand diagram shows that real GDP *declined* at an annualized rate of nearly 7 percent during the final quarter of 2008 and the first quarter of 2009, which were two of the worst quarters in the history of the U.S. economy since the 1930s. Commensurately, the unemployment rate rose from 4.8 percent in February 2008 to 6.1 percent at the time Lehman failed to 8.5 percent by March 2009—and rose further as 2009 progressed, peaking at 10 percent in October.

As we know, governments normally fight rising unemployment with expansionary monetary and fiscal policies. But the Fed was more or less out of ammunition after

> A bank is said to be **recapitalized** when some investor, private or government, provides new equity capital in return for partial ownership.

*Table 5*

**Balance Sheet after Recapitalization**

| Assets | | Liabilities and Net Worth | |
|---|---|---|---|
| **Assets** | | **Liabilities** | |
| Reserves | $2,000,000 | Deposits | $5,000,000 |
| Loans and securities | $4,050,000 | Stockholders' equity | $1,050,000 |
| Total | **$6,050,000** | Total | **$6,050,000** |

[12] This catchall provision authorized the secretary of the Treasury to purchase any asset he decided was "necessary to promote financial market stability."

December 2008, when it had lowered the federal funds rate to virtually zero. Policy makers worried: What if all that expansionary monetary policy was not enough?

When President Barack Obama took office in January 2009, his first major policy initiative was the massive fiscal stimulus bill we have mentioned, including both tax cuts and increases in government spending. The overall magnitude of the February 2009 fiscal package was announced as $787 billion, or about 5.5 percent of GDP, although it was spread out over several years. The idea, of course, was to close the sizable *recessionary gap* between potential and actual GDP—precisely as explained in Chapter 11. The bill passed, but with virtually no Republican support.

## 14-6 HITTING BOTTOM AND RECOVERING

Financial markets appeared to hit bottom around March 2009. The low point of the stock market came in March, and the subsequent recovery was spectacular: Stock prices soared more than 60 percent between March and November 2009. The interest rate spreads that we emphasized earlier also peaked in March, and they narrowed sharply after that. It was probably no coincidence that real GDP began to grow again in the third quarter of 2009—only modestly at first, but then more rapidly in the fourth quarter. However, job growth did not resume until 2010.

By mid- to late 2010, the recession was clearly behind us, and the economy was on the mend. But the pace of recovery was and remains disappointing. While growth in both real GDP and jobs has continued, virtually unbroken since the upturn began, progress has been slow. In consequence, the Fed continued its unconventional monetary policies: holding the federal funds rate at virtually zero and engaging in several rounds of purchases of MBS and long-term Treasury bonds right through October 2014. Despite these efforts, the U.S. economy was still not back to normal when this edition went to press.

| Issue Revisited | *Did the Fiscal Stimulus Work?* |
|---|---|

Did the monetary and fiscal policy stimulus work, especially President Obama's controversial $787 billion fiscal stimulus package of early 2009? Controversy still swirls around that question, but here are a few facts. First, real GDP growth moved from the *minus* 7 percent range to the *plus* 3 percent range within a few quarters. Not all of this sharp improvement can be traced to fiscal stimulus, of course, but quantitative models of the U.S. economy say that a sizable chunk can be. Second, job losses, which were running over 700,000 a month during January–February 2009, started to diminish immediately, and positive job growth resumed in January 2010. Third, some of the sectors specifically targeted by the stimulus and related policies—such as state and local government spending, automobiles, and housing—showed notable improvements. These developments seem to provide at least circumstantial evidence that the fiscal policy worked.

Skeptics point out, however, that employment continued to fall throughout 2009 even though the stimulus bill passed in February. That's a long lag, they argue. They also point out that the economy did considerably worse than the Obama administration had forecast when it asked for the stimulus bill. Furthermore, the economy has a natural *self-correcting mechanism* that we discussed in earlier chapters. Even without fiscal and monetary stimulus, recessions and depressions do eventually come to an end. Finally, some people give more credit to monetary policy than to fiscal policy for giving the economy a boost. Ironically, however, many of the sternest congressional critics of the 2009 stimulus bill strongly supported tax cuts when they were proposed and passed late in 2010, arguing that tax cuts stimulate the economy but government spending "kills jobs."

The debate rages on. What do you think?

## 14-7 LESSONS FROM THE FINANCIAL CRISIS

Historians will debate many aspects of the incredible events of 2007–2011 for decades to come, but we know a few things already.[13] First, most observers think financial *regulation* was too lax prior to the crisis; that is, that regulators did not properly perform the functions discussed in Chapter 12.

Second, these regulatory failures extended well beyond poor job performance by regulatory personnel. The crisis made it painfully clear that there were myriad weaknesses in the *regulatory structure*. In consequence, Congress set about the task of rewriting many of the laws that govern financial regulation in the United States, culminating in the passage of the massive Dodd-Frank Act of 2010. The governments of many other countries have engaged in similar exercises.

Third, virtually everyone agrees that we allowed the financial system to operate with far too much *leverage*, a point discussed extensively in this chapter. In part, excessive leverage can be traced to lax regulation and inadequate laws—which Dodd-Frank tries to fix. But a great deal of it reflected poor business (and household) judgments. Alas, we humans—even when armed with powerful computers—are a highly fallible lot, prone to wishful thinking.

Fourth, and closely related, we learned that excessive *complexity* and opacity in the securities markets can make a financial system fragile, and therefore dangerous. When investors don't understand what they are buying, they are prone to panic when they hear bad news. When companies don't understand the assets on their books, they may leave themselves exposed to larger losses than they realize.

Fifth, what had become almost a consensus view—that the job of stabilizing aggregate demand should be assigned to *monetary policy*, not to *fiscal policy*—is no longer the consensus. With its arsenal of weapons for reviving the moribund economy badly depleted in 2008 and 2009, the Fed found that it needed help from the president and Congress. And the fiscal authorities delivered on a timely basis—more than once. Although still controversial (as noted in this chapter), it looks as if expansionary fiscal policy really worked in 2008 and 2009, helping to shorten and moderate the Great Recession.

Sixth, we learned that expansionary monetary policy is not necessarily finished once the Fed reduces the federal funds rate to zero. The central bank under then-Chairman Ben Bernanke invented a number of "unconventional" monetary policies—unorthodox ways to lend to banks and non-banks, to guarantee lending by others, and, when necessary, to buy unwanted assets itself.

Seventh, we were rudely reminded that the *business cycle* is by no means dead. Each time our economy enjoys a lengthy period without serious recessions—such as during the long booms of the 1960s, the 1980s, and the 1990s—some analysts start waxing poetic about the death of the business cycle. But to paraphrase Mark Twain, the reports of its death have been greatly exaggerated. That means, among other things, that the lessons you have been learning about macroeconomics in Parts 2 and 3 are not historical relics. They remain tremendously useful in understanding the world in which we all live.

## Summary

1. An asset-price **bubble** occurs when the prices of some assets rise far above their fundamental values. Most observers believe that a large house-price bubble ended in the United States in 2006–2007, helping to bring on both the financial crisis and the worst recession since the 1930s.

2. A second major cause of the financial crisis was that **interest rate spreads,** which had narrowed to unsustainably low levels in the years 2004–2006, widened dramatically in 2007–2008, driving down the corresponding

bond prices. One prominent example was **mortgage-backed securities,** which tumbled in value.

3. As house prices fell, the **collateral** behind many mortgages declined in value, making these mortgages (and hence the securities based on them) riskier and therefore less valuable in the market.

4. A third major cause of the crisis was the large volume of **subprime mortgages** that were granted during the housing boom, often to borrowers who were not

---

[13] One of the authors of this book has written a best-selling history of the episode: Alan S. Blinder, *After the Music Stopped: The Financial Crisis, the Response, and the Work Ahead* (Penguin Press: 2013; paperback edition, 2014).

creditworthy. The explosion of subprime mortgages was enabled by both poor banking practices and lax regulation.

5. Perhaps the biggest and broadest cause of the financial crisis was the excessive amounts of **leverage** that developed all over the financial system. Because leverage magnifies both gains and losses, it boosted profits during the boom but inflicted tremendous damage when asset prices started falling.

6. The financial crisis began in earnest in the summer of 2007 when several funds based on complex mortgage-related securities lost most of their value. That development, in turn, led investors to question the values of similar securities.

7. The crisis entered a whole new phase in March 2008, when the Federal Reserve arranged and helped finance an emergency merger so that Bear Stearns, a large investment bank, would not fail. Six months later, Lehman Brothers, a much larger investment bank, did fail; and for the next several weeks there was utter panic in financial markets around the world.

8. The collapse of the housing bubble and the severe damage to the financial system brought on a serious recession for four main reasons: a great deal of wealth was destroyed, spending on new homes collapsed, confidence was utterly shattered, and businesses and households found it extremely difficult to borrow.

9. The U.S. government fought the recession with a tax rebate in 2008, a vastly larger fiscal stimulus in 2009, and a round of tax cuts in 2010. Congress also appropriated $700 billion for the controversial **Troubled Assets Relief Program (TARP)** in October 2008. Much of the TARP money was used to **recapitalize** banks.

10. At first, the Federal Reserve fought the recession in the usual way: by cutting interest rates. Eventually, the federal funds rate was reduced to nearly zero. After that, the Fed had to resort to a variety of *unconventional monetary policies.*

11. The U.S. economy hit bottom in the second quarter of 2009; after that, real GDP growth resumed. But jobs did not start growing again until months later. Many, but not all, observers credit the wide-ranging fiscal and monetary policy actions with bringing the recession to a more rapid conclusion. But the recovery has been slow.

## Key Terms

| | | |
|---|---|---|
| bubble   280 | interest rate spread   280 | recapitalize   290 |
| collateral   284 | leverage   280 | securitization   284 |
| foreclosure   284 | mortgage   280 | subprime mortgage   280 |
| insolvent   282 | mortgage-backed securities (MBS)   285 | Troubled Assets Relief Program (TARP)   289 |

## Test Yourself

1. If the expected default rate on a particular mortgage-backed security is 4 percent per year, and the corresponding Treasury security carries a 3 percent annual interest rate, what should be the interest rate on the mortgage-backed security? What happens if the expected default rate rises to 8 percent?

2. Create your own numerical example to illustrate how leverage magnifies returns both on the upside and on the downside.

3. Why do we say that deposits are "liabilities" of banks?

4. During the financial crisis and recovery, stock market prices first fell by about 55 percent and then rose by about 65 percent. Did investors therefore come out ahead? Explain why not.

## Discussion Questions

1. If you were watching house prices rise during the years 2000–2006, how might you have decided whether or not you were witnessing a "bubble"?

2. What factors do you think bankers normally use to distinguish "prime" borrowers from "subprime" borrowers?

3. Explain why a mortgage-backed security becomes riskier when the values of the underlying houses decline. What, as a result, happens to the price of the mortgage-backed security?

4. Explain how a collapse in house prices might lead to a recession.

5. Explain how a collapse of the economy's credit-granting mechanisms might lead to a recession.

6. Explain the basic idea behind the TARP legislation. Was that idea carried out in practice?

7. **(More difficult)** In March 2008, the Fed helped prevent the bankruptcy of Bear Stearns. However, in September 2008, the Fed and the Treasury let Lehman Brothers go bankrupt. What accounts for the different decisions? (*Note:* You may want to discuss this question with your instructor and/or do some research. The answer is *not* straightforward and continues to be debated.)

# THE DEBATE OVER MONETARY AND FISCAL POLICY

*The love of money is the root of all evil.*

THE NEW TESTAMENT

*Lack of money is the root of all evil.*

GEORGE BERNARD SHAW

U p to now, our discussion of stabilization policy has been almost entirely objective and technical. In seeking to understand how the national economy works and how government policies affect it, we have mostly ignored the intense economic and political controversies that swirl around the conduct of monetary and fiscal policy. Chapters 15 through 17 are meant to remedy this deficiency.

This chapter begins with a look at an alternative theory of how monetary policy affects the economy, known as *monetarism*. Although the monetarist and Keynesian *theories* seem to contradict one another, we will see that the conflict is more apparent than real. However, important differences *do* arise among economists over the appropriate design and execution of monetary *policy*. These differences are the central concern of the chapter. We will learn about the continuing debates over the nature of aggregate supply, over the relative virtues of monetary versus fiscal policy, and over when and if the Federal Reserve should engage in unconventional monetary policies—including whether it should try to burst asset price "bubbles." As we will see, the resolutions of these issues are crucial to the proper conduct of stabilization policy and, indeed, to the decision of whether the government should try to stabilize the economy at all.

## CONTENTS

### Issue  *Should We Forsake Stabilization Policy?*

We have suggested several times in this book, especially in the previous chapter, that well-timed changes in fiscal or monetary policy can mitigate fluctuations in inflation and unemployment. When the U.S. economy slumped badly in 2008–2009, both fiscal policy and monetary policy turned sharply expansionary. Congress cut taxes and raised spending substantially. The Federal Reserve not only cut interest rates dramatically but also engaged in a variety of "unconventional" monetary policies. These actions constituted "textbook responses" to the recession. They were completely consistent with the lessons you learned in Chapters 11 and 13.

But some economists argue that these lessons are best forgotten. In practice, they claim, attempts at macroeconomic stabilization are likely to do more harm than good. Policy makers are therefore best advised to follow fixed *rules* rather than use their best judgment on a case-by-case basis. In fact, several prominent economists who adhere to this dissenting view opposed almost every policy action taken by the Bush and Obama administrations and the Federal Reserve in 2008–2010.

Nothing we have said so far leads to such a conclusion. But we have not yet told the whole story. By the end of this chapter, you will have encountered several arguments in favor of rules and will be in a better position to make up your own mind.

## 15-1 VELOCITY AND THE QUANTITY THEORY OF MONEY

The previous chapter explained the *Keynesian* view of how monetary policy influences real output and the price level. But another, older model provides a different way of looking at these matters. This model, known as the *quantity theory of money*, is easy to understand once we introduce one new concept: **velocity**.

In Chapter 12, we learned that because barter is so cumbersome, virtually all economic transactions in advanced economies use money. Thus, if there are $15 trillion worth of transactions in an economy during a particular year, and there is an average money stock of $3 trillion during that year, then each dollar of money must have been used an average of five times during the year.

The number five in this example is called *velocity* because it indicates the *speed* at which money circulates. For example, a particular dollar bill might be used to buy a haircut in January; the barber might use it to purchase a sweater in March; the storekeeper might then use it to pay for gasoline in May; the gas station owner could pay it out to a house painter in October; and the painter might spend it on a Christmas present in December. In this way, the same dollar is used five times during the year. If it were used only four times during the year, its velocity would be four, and so on.

However, no one has data on every transaction in the economy. To make velocity an operational concept, economists need a workable measure of the dollar volume of all transactions. As we know from previous chapters, the most popular choice is nominal gross domestic product (GDP), even though it ignores many transactions that use money, such as the huge volume of activity in financial markets. If we accept nominal GDP as our measure of the money value of transactions, we are led to a concrete definition of velocity as the ratio of nominal GDP to the number of dollars in the money stock. Because nominal GDP is the product of real GDP ($Y$) times the price level ($P$), we can write this definition in symbols as follows:

$$\text{Velocity} = \frac{\text{Value of transactions}}{\text{Money stock}} = \frac{\text{Nominal GDP}}{M} = \frac{P \times Y}{M}$$

By multiplying both sides of the equation by $M$, we arrive at an identity called the **equation of exchange**, which relates the money supply and nominal GDP:

$$\text{Money supply} \times \text{Velocity} = \text{Nominal GDP}$$

Alternatively, stated in symbols, we have:

$$M \times V = P \times Y$$

The equation of exchange provides an obvious link between the stock of money, $M$, and the nominal value of the nation's output, $P \times Y$. But this connection is merely a matter of arithmetic, not of economics. For example, it does not imply that the Fed can raise nominal GDP by increasing $M$. Why not? Because $V$ might simultaneously fall enough to prevent

**Velocity** indicates the number of times per year that an "average dollar" is spent on goods and services. It is the ratio of nominal gross domestic product (GDP) to the number of dollars in the money stock. That is:

$$\text{Velocity} = \frac{\text{Nominal GDP}}{\text{Money stock}}$$

The **equation of exchange** states that the money value of GDP transactions must be equal to the product of the average stock of money times velocity. That is: $M \times V = P \times Y$

the product $M \times V$ from rising. In other words, if more dollar bills circulated than before, but each bill changed hands more slowly, total spending might not rise. Thus, we need an auxiliary assumption to change the arithmetic identity into an economic theory.

The **quantity theory of money** transforms the equation of exchange from an arithmetic identity into an economic model by assuming that changes in velocity are so minor that velocity can be taken to be virtually constant.

The **quantity theory of money** assumes that velocity is (approximately) constant. In that case, nominal GDP is proportional to the money stock.

You can see that if $V$ never changed, the equation of exchange would be a marvelously simple model of the determination of nominal GDP—far simpler than the Keynesian model that took us several chapters to develop. To see this, just rewrite the equation of exchange in terms of growth rates:

$$\%\triangle M + \%\triangle V = \%\triangle P + \%\triangle Y$$

If $V$ either never changed, making $\%\triangle V$ equal to zero, or grew at a constant rate from year to year, making $\%\triangle V$ a constant, then, for example, if the Federal Reserve wanted to raise the annual growth rate of nominal GDP by 2 percentage points, it need merely raise the growth rate of the money supply by 2 percentage points. In such a simple world, economists could use the equation of exchange to *predict* nominal GDP growth by predicting the growth rate of money. And policy makers could *control* nominal GDP growth by controlling the growth rate of the money supply.

Things are not so simple in the real world, however, because velocity is not a fixed number. But variable velocity does not necessarily destroy the usefulness of the quantity theory. As we explained in Chapter 1, all economic models make assumptions that are at least mildly unrealistic. Without such assumptions, they would not be models at all, just tedious descriptions of reality. The operational question is whether the assumption of constant velocity is a useful abstraction from annoying detail or a gross distortion of the facts.

Figure 1 sheds some light on this question by showing the behavior of velocity since 1929. Note that the figure includes two different measures of velocity, labeled $V_1$ and $V_2$. Why? Recall from Chapter 12 that we can measure money in several ways, the most popular of which are M1 and M2. Because velocity ($V$) is simply nominal GDP divided by the money stock ($M$), we get a *different* measure of $V$ for *each* measure of $M$. Figure 1 shows annual data on the velocities of both M1 and M2.

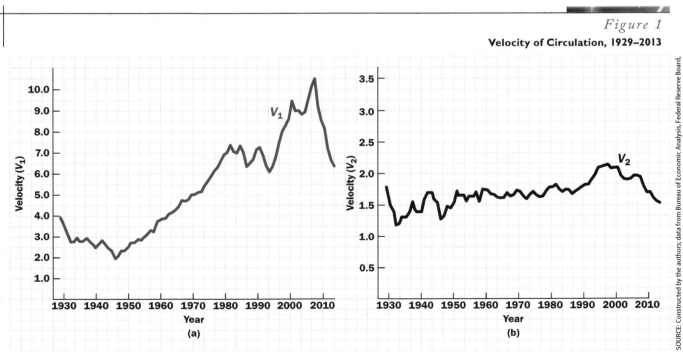

*Figure 1*

**Velocity of Circulation, 1929–2013**

SOURCE: Constructed by the authors; data from Bureau of Economic Analysis, Federal Reserve Board, and Robert Rasche.

You will undoubtedly notice the stark difference in the behavior of $V_1$ versus $V_2$. $V_1$ has obviously moved quite erratically, especially recently; $V_2$ is much more stable. But closer examination of monthly or quarterly data reveals substantial fluctuations both in velocity and the growth rate of velocity, by either measure. Because of this, predictions of nominal GDP growth based on assuming either constant or constantly growing velocity have not fared well, regardless of how $M$ is measured. So the strict quantity theory of money is not an adequate model of aggregate demand.

## 15-1a  Some Determinants of Velocity

Because it is abundantly clear that velocity fluctuates a lot, the equation of exchange is useful as a model of GDP determination only if we can explain and predict movements in velocity. That turns out to be a difficult task, however.

One reason is that banks and other financial institutions keep changing the nature of the transaction accounts available to customers and inventing other ways to make payments. Think, for example, of credit cards and PayPal. The consequence is that funds sometimes move quickly in and out of M1 or M2—which are the denominators of $V_1$ and $V_2$—making velocity hard to predict.

A second important determinant of velocity is the rate of interest. Why? Because the higher the rate of interest, the greater the *opportunity cost* of holding money. Therefore, as market interest rates rise, people want to hold smaller cash balances, which means that the existing stock of money circulates faster. Velocity rises.

> It is this factor that most directly undercuts the usefulness of the quantity theory of money as a guide for monetary policy. We have learned that expansionary monetary policy, which increases bank reserves and the money supply, also decreases the interest rate. But if interest rates fall, other things being equal, velocity (V) also falls. Thus, *when the Fed raises the money supply (M), the product M × V should increase by a smaller percentage than does M itself.*

We therefore conclude that:

> Velocity is not a constant. Among other things, it normally increases when interest rates rise.

## 15-1b  Monetarism: The Quantity Theory Modernized

For this and other reasons, most economists believe that the relationship between $M$ and nominal GDP is a loose one. For example, we cannot predict nominal GDP very well by predicting $V$.

But adherents to a school of thought called **monetarism** disagree. Although monetarists realize that velocity changes, they claim that such changes are fairly *predictable*—certainly in the long run and perhaps even in the short run. As a result, they claim, the best way to study economic activity is to start with the equation of exchange in growth-rate form:

**Monetarism** is a mode of analysis that uses the equation of exchange to organize and analyze macroeconomic data.

$$\%\Delta M + \%\Delta V = \%\Delta P + \%\Delta Y$$

From here, careful study of the determinants of money growth and of changes in velocity can be used to *predict* the growth rate of nominal GDP. Similarly, given an understanding of movements in $V$, *controlling* $M$ would give the Fed good control over nominal GDP. These ideas are the central tenets of monetarism.

The monetarist and Keynesian approaches are two competing theories of *aggregate demand*. Keynesians divide economic knowledge into four neat compartments marked $C$, $I$, $G$, and $(X - IM)$, and then add them all up to obtain aggregate demand. In Keynesian analysis, money affects the economy by first affecting interest rates. Monetarists, by contrast, organize their knowledge into two alternative boxes labeled $M$ and $V$, and then multiply the two to obtain aggregate demand. In the monetarist model, the role of money is not necessarily limited to working through interest rates.

The bit of arithmetic that multiplies $M$ and $V$ to get $P \times Y$ is neither more nor less profound than the one that adds up $C$, $I$, $G$, and $(X - IM)$ to get $Y$, and certainly both are

## Policy Debate

## Does Money Growth Always Cause Inflation?

Monetarists have long claimed that, in the famous words of the late Milton Friedman, "inflation is always and everywhere a monetary phenomenon." By this statement, Friedman meant that changes in the growth rate of the money supply (%$\Delta M$) are far and away the principal cause of changes in the inflation rate (%$\Delta P$)—in all places and at all times.

Few economists question the dominant role of rapid money growth in accounting for extremely high rates of inflation. For example, money was printed so fast during the German hyperinflation of the 1920s or the Zimbabwean hyperinflation of several years ago that the printing presses had a difficult time keeping up! But most economists question the words "always and everywhere" in Friedman's dictum. Aren't many cases of moderate inflation driven by factors other than the growth rate of the money supply?

The answer appears to be "yes." The accompanying charts use recent U.S. history as an illustration. In the scatter diagram on the left, each point records both the growth rate of the M2 money supply and the inflation rate (as measured by the Consumer Price Index) for a particular year between 1982 and 2014. There is no obvious relationship.

Monetarists often argue that this comparison is unfair because the effect of money supply growth on inflation operates with a *lag* of perhaps two years. So the right-hand scatter diagram compares inflation with money supply growth *two years later*. It tells essentially the same story. More sophisticated versions of scatter plots like these have led most economists to reject the monetarist claim that inflation and money supply growth are tightly linked.

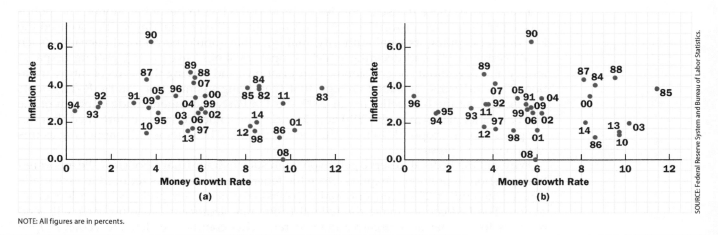

NOTE: All figures are in percents.

SOURCE: Federal Reserve System and Bureau of Labor Statistics.

---

correct. The real question is which framework is more *useful* in practice. That is, which approach works better as a model of aggregate demand?

There is no generally correct answer for all economies in all periods of time. But a glance back at Figure 1 will show you why most economists abandoned monetarism by the early 1990s. During the 1960s and 1970s, velocity (at least $V_2$) was fairly stable, which helped monetarism win many converts in the United States and around the world. Since then, however, velocity has behaved so erratically here and in many other countries that there are few monetarists left.

Nonetheless, as we will see later in this chapter, some faint echoes of the debate between Keynesians and monetarists can still be heard. For example, one objection to the Fed's highly expansionary monetary policies after 2008 was that they sowed the seeds of rapid money supply growth and hence of inflation. However, although few economists doubt that there is a strong *long-run* relationship between $M$ and $P$, most question whether this relationship is useful in the short run. (See the box "Does Money Growth Always Cause Inflation?")

## 15-2  DEBATE: SHOULD THE FED USE UNCONVENTIONAL MONETARY POLICIES?

Executing conventional monetary policy properly in real time is fraught with practical difficulties and is sometimes controversial. But *defining* conventional monetary policy is straightforward. In normal times, the Federal Reserve pushes the federal funds *down* when it wants to give the economy a boost and pushes it *up* when it wants to restrain the economy. It accomplishes this by either *buying* Treasury bills in the open market to create more bank reserves or *selling* T-bills to destroy reserves. In addition, the Fed sometimes lends money to banks, although the amounts involved are normally quite small. That's about it.

In principle, anything else the Fed does to influence the economy qualifies as "unconventional" monetary policy. In practice, we learned in the last chapter that the Fed's unconventional monetary policies during and after the financial crisis consisted mainly of three types of actions:

- Creating bank reserves by buying assets *other than* Treasury bills. The "other" category included both longer-term Treasury bonds and private-sector assets such as mortgage-backed securities. (More on this shortly.)
- Lending massive amounts to banks and even to some non-banks, such as investment houses and one giant insurance company.
- Participating in emergency "rescue" operations for troubled financial institutions (examples: Bear Stearns, AIG, Lehman Brothers, and many others).

Every one of these unusual policies embroiled the Fed in heated economic and political controversies—controversies that continue right to the present day. Critics accused the Fed of overstepping its legal authority, making what should be political decisions (such as allocating credit and deciding which companies should live or die), putting taxpayer money at risk without congressional appropriations, and sowing the seeds of future inflation. The criticisms resonated enough that then-Congressman Ron Paul's (R–TX) book, *End the Fed*, hit the best-seller list in 2009; the Tea Party movement made criticism of the Fed part of its platform in the 2010 and 2012 elections; and Congress entertained (but did not pass) several proposals to limit the Fed's authority. The latter is still happening as this edition goes to press.

Why did the Federal Reserve get involved in such extraordinary policies? We answered that question in previous chapters: Once the federal funds rate was reduced to essentially zero at the end of 2008, conventional expansionary monetary policy was no longer an option. The Fed cannot make the federal funds rate *negative* because no bank will lend reserves to another at a negative interest rate. This conundrum left the Federal Open Market Committee (FOMC) two broad choices. It could give up and hope for the best—including hoping that expansionary fiscal policy would take over the job of stimulating the economy. Or it could experiment with a variety of unconventional and mostly unprecedented policies that it would never even have considered in normal times. It chose the latter.

Here's one example, based on the distinctions among different interest rates that we made in Chapter 13. In 2009, the FOMC decided to purchase more than $1 trillion of the mortgage-backed securities (MBS) that played such a major role in the crisis. (See Chapter 14, especially "From the Housing Bubble to the Financial Crisis.") Their rationale for taking this unprecedented action was straightforward. The panic had destroyed the markets for MBS and other mortgage-related securities and derivatives—thereby crippling the mortgage market. Treasury interest rates had fallen, as investors shunned anything that looked even a little risky. But interest rate spreads on MBS over Treasuries had soared to extraordinary levels, so rates on MBS remained high.[1] Yet there were still hardly any buyers. So the Fed entered the market as what amounted to the "buyer of last resort." Its intent was clear: By purchasing a huge volume of MBS, the Fed intended to raise MBS prices and lower their yields, thereby shrinking the risk spreads over Treasuries. If it succeeded, interest rates on MBS would fall even if Treasury rates remained the same.

Did it work? It appears so. Rates on both MBS and home mortgages came down, risk premiums gradually returned to normal, and the Fed even turned a profit on its operations. Nonetheless, it is undeniable that the Fed took on more risk than it normally does. Under conventional monetary policy, the Fed buys only Treasury securities, which have

---

[1] If you need to review the concept of risk premiums in interest rates, turn back to Chapter 13, especially the box "Which Interest Rate?"

## The Fed Fights Recession

When things first started to deteriorate in the financial markets in the summer of 2007, the federal funds rate was sitting at 5.25 percent. Sensing trouble, the Federal Open Market Committee (FOMC) began to cut interest rates in September 2007. It moved slowly at first; by year-end, the funds rate was at 4.25 percent. Only in late January 2008 did the FOMC become alarmed about the potential macroeconomic fallout from the financial crisis and start cutting rates aggressively—dropping the funds rate from 4.25 percent to 2 percent in about three months. The Fed then sat with its 2 percent funds rate for more than five months, watching both financial developments and the deteriorating economy. Then the Lehman Brothers catastrophe happened in mid-September. A few weeks later, the Fed sprang into action again, cutting the funds rate from 2 percent to the 0–0.25 percent range on December 16, 2008. Shortly thereafter, it declared that the super-low federal funds rate would remain in effect "for an extended period." And indeed it has. At this writing, that period has extended more than six years.

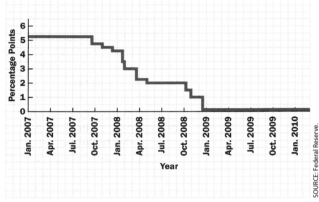

**Federal Funds Rate, 2007–2010**

SOURCE: Federal Reserve.

NOTE: The federal funds rate remained in the 0–0.25 percent range into 2015.

zero risk of default. With this particular type of unconventional monetary policy, it bought mortgage-backed securities, which can default.

Yet the Federal Reserve willingly took on this and other risks for several reasons. First, time was of the essence during the acute stages of the crisis, and Congress is not designed to move fast. The Fed took a number of extraordinary actions on very short notice and without congressional debate, including several via telephonic meetings on Sunday evenings.

Second, only the central bank can serve as lender of last resort, a power that requires the ability to "print money." Congress wisely took this power away from itself almost a century ago, and explicitly lodged it at the Fed. In one famous incident during the heat of the crisis, a congressional leader asked then-Chairman Ben Bernanke if he had the $80 billion they needed to fill a hole. Mr. Bernanke replied that he had $800 billion, if necessary! As things turned out, he had much more.

Third, as it became clear that the weak economy would require more and more stimulus, the huge federal budget deficit—which we will discuss further in the next chapter—became an increasingly serious constraint on fiscal policy. After all, either lowering taxes or raising spending increases the deficit. The Fed is under no such constraint.

To critics of the Fed's unconventional policies, however, none of these reasons were sufficient to justify its sweeping actions. By playing a pivotal role in decisions about which financial institutions would survive and which would fail, they argued, the Fed was both assuming authority that rightfully belongs to Congress and inserting itself into politics. By putting its own money at risk, they claimed, the Fed was tacitly appropriating taxpayer money—a power reserved to Congress by the Constitution. By printing so much money (actually, bank reserves), they worried, the Fed was opening the door to future inflation.

This debate between the Fed's critics and its supporters began in the heat of battle and is still going on today, even though the Fed's asset purchases came to a halt in October 2014. Critics now want to see the Fed's gigantic balance sheet shrink and interest rates rise from their super-low levels. As this edition went to press, the latter was expected soon.

The vehement criticisms that were raised against unconventional monetary policies have raised doubts about the Fed's willingness to engage in them again, should the need arise. Only time will tell. The debate goes on.

*"Daddy's not mad at you, dear— Daddy's mad at the Fed."*

From *The Wall Street Journal.* Reprinted with the permission of Cartoon Features Syndicate.

## 15-3  DEBATE: SHOULD POLICY MAKERS FIGHT ASSET PRICE BUBBLES?

The tech stock bubble burst violently in the year 2000, destroying trillions of dollars of stock market wealth in the process. (In 2014, some observers were worrying about whether another tech stock bubble was developing.) The house price bubble burst rather more gradually, starting in 2006. But it, too, destroyed trillions of dollars of wealth. More important, and unlike the bursting of the stock market bubble, the bursting of the house price bubble almost dragged the entire financial system down with it. These stunning events imparted new urgency to an old debate: Should the central bank, or any other branch of government, try to "let the air out of" asset price bubbles before they grow too large and burst on their own?

Given our recent bitter experience, it may seem like the answer must be a resounding *yes*. And a growing number of observers think so. But the Federal Reserve's traditional answer to this question has been *no*. Its two main reasons are straightforward.

First, identifying asset price bubbles *before* they burst is a tricky business—some would say an impossible business. Remember the definition of an asset price bubble from the previous chapter: an increase in the price of an asset or assets *that goes far beyond what can be justified by improving fundamentals*. As Shakespeare might have said, there's the rub. Once asset prices—whether for stocks, houses, gold, or anything else—collapse, everyone looks back at the crazy valuations at the peak and concludes that there was a bubble. It was "obvious." But such judgments are not so easily made before the fact. In particular, when the fundamentals are improving, it can be devilishly difficult to distinguish between the "bubbly" part of any price increase and the sensible part based on better fundamentals. Recent cases in point include Twitter, Instagram, and Alibaba stock—and, in an earlier day, shares in Amazon, Priceline, Yahoo!, and many others. The Fed has no particular expertise in making such judgments. Indeed, it is likely that no one else does, either!

Second, the Fed may not have any policy instruments that it can aim directly at an asset price bubble. For example, suppose the Fed had recognized that there was a tech-stock bubble in early 1998—well before the Internet craze really went wild. What could it have done? Raised interest rates? Well, maybe. But raising the federal funds rate, which reduces aggregate demand, is a rather blunt tool, not at all well-targeted at the stock market in general or at tech stocks in particular. Raising interest rates might have killed the economy before it burst the bubble.

If it is hard to know whether there is a bubble or not, and hard to know what to do about a bubble anyway, then a central bank that sets out to burst bubbles may do more harm than good.

Case closed? Not quite. The immense damage done when the house-price bubble burst has led the Fed and many others to rethink the issue—which it is still doing today. Isn't there some sensible position intermediate between the poles of pure *laissez faire* and active bubble bursting? Maybe there is.

History teaches us that the most harmful bubbles are those that are financed by heavy *borrowing* and extensive use of *leverage*.[2] For example, we mentioned in the last chapter that many of the worst subprime mortgages required almost no down payments, making leverage almost infinite. By contrast, relatively few tech stocks in the late 1990s (or in the 2010s) were purchased "on credit"; most buyers paid cash. This difference had two important implications when prices collapsed. First, owners of tech stocks with no loans to repay were better able to weather the storm in 2000–2001 than were heavily indebted homeowners in 2008–2009. Second, because the collapse of the tech-stock bubble in 2000 did not lead to massive defaults on loans, banks were not dragged into the mess. The contrast with the bursting of the house-price bubble could not be starker.

So one important way to mitigate the consequences of bubbles may be to keep a watchful eye on bank lending practices, especially when lending involves a lot of leverage, and to crack down on them when necessary. The Fed and others are supposed to do this under the new regulatory system created by the Dodd-Frank Act of 2010. Notice that the policy

---

[2] If you need to review the concept of leverage, turn back to Chapter 14, especially "Leverage, Profits, and Risk."

emphasis is on recognizing bad lending practices and excessive leverage—not on recognizing asset price bubbles in real time. The former is much easier to do than the latter. That said, how it will all work out in practice remains to be seen.

Finally, notice that the objective enunciated in the previous paragraph is *to mitigate the consequences* of bubbles, not *to prevent* bubbles. Most economists think preventing bubbles is impossible. The history of capitalism is replete with them. Where there are speculative assets—gold in the gold rush, land in the land rush, tech stocks in the Internet craze, bitcoins in 2014, and so on—people seem eager to speculate on them. Indeed, one of the first stocks ever issued led to the very first stock market bubble in England back in 1720: the South Sea bubble, which claimed Sir Isaac Newton, among its many victims.[3]

In fact, a number of economists, most prominently the late Hyman Minsky, have argued that bubbles are an inherent part of the cycle of financial capitalism—almost as if they were hard-wired in. When times are good, loan defaults are rare, and stock prices are rising, people tend to forget the past and become over-optimistic—ignoring, for example, possible losses on loans and the hazards that are inherent in high leverage. This cavalier attitude toward risk helps inflate the bubble.

When the bubble inevitably bursts, investors and banks are left holding the proverbial bag. In worst cases, the whole financial system can be threatened—as happened in the United States after 1929 and after 2008. After the crash, people become wary of risk again. Frightened may be a better word. So, for a while, the financial system operates more conservatively and with far greater safety. Leverage declines. But then, as nothing bad happens, as asset prices start rising again, as loan defaults become rare, and as memories of the bad times fade, the illusion of safety develops once again—and the whole cycle repeats.

For these and other reasons, most economists and financial market experts believe it is impossible to prevent price bubbles. But it *may be* possible to limit their size, and it definitely *is* possible to limit the damage they do when they burst by building sturdier financial structures.

## 15-4 DEBATE: SHOULD WE RELY ON FISCAL OR MONETARY POLICY?

The dramatic and multifaceted policy responses to the Great Recession by the Federal Reserve, the Congress, and both the Bush and Obama White Houses gave new impetus to an old debate: When there is a perceived need for macroeconomic management, should we rely on monetary policy, on fiscal policy, or on some combination of the two?

One key aspect of this debate, which came to the fore dramatically during the crisis, is which type of medicine—fiscal or monetary—works *faster*. Until now, we have ignored questions of timing and pretended that the authorities noticed the need for stabilization policy instantly, decided on a course of action right away, administered the appropriate medicine at once—and then the macroeconomy reacted immediately. In reality, each of these steps takes time.

First, delays in data collection mean that the most recent data describe the state of the economy one to three months ago. When things are changing fast, that's a problem. Second, one of the prices of democracy is that the government often takes a long time to decide what should be done, to muster the necessary political support, and to put its decisions into effect. Finally, our $17 trillion economy is a bit like a sleeping elephant that reacts sluggishly to moderate fiscal and monetary prods. As it turns out, these **lags in stabilization policy**, as they are called, play a pivotal role in the choice between fiscal and monetary policy. Here's why.

The main policy tool for manipulating consumer spending (C) is the personal income tax, and Chapter 8 documented why the fiscal policy planner can feel fairly confident that each $1 of tax reduction will lead to about 90 to 95 cents of additional spending *eventually*. But not all of this extra spending happens at once.

**Lags in stabilization policy** refer to delays between the time when the need for stabilization policy arises and the time when the policy has its actual effects on the economy.

---

[3] You can find an entertaining account of the South Sea bubble in Wikipedia.

First, consumers must learn about the tax change. Then they may need to be convinced that the change is permanent. Finally, there is simple force of habit: Households need time to adjust their spending habits when circumstances change. For all these reasons, consumers may increase their spending by only 30 to 50 cents for each \$1 of additional income within the first few months after a tax cut. Only gradually will they raise their spending by about 90 to 95 cents for each additional dollar of income.

Lags are much longer for investment ($I$), which provides the main vehicle by which monetary policy affects aggregate demand. Planning for capacity expansion in a large corporation is a long, drawn-out process. Ideas must be submitted and approved. Plans must be drawn up, funding acquired, and orders for machinery or contracts for new construction placed. And most of this activity occurs *before* any appreciable amount of money is spent. Economists have found that much of the response of investment to changes in either interest rates or tax provisions takes several *years* to develop.

The fact that $C$ responds more quickly than $I$ has important implications for the choice among alternative stabilization policies. The reason is that the most common varieties of fiscal policy either affect aggregate demand directly—because $G$ is a component of $C + I + G + (X - IM)$—or work through consumption with a relatively short lag, whereas monetary policy primarily affects investment. Therefore:

> Conventional types of fiscal policy actions, such as changes in *G* or in personal taxes, probably affect aggregate demand more promptly than do monetary policy actions.

Does that make fiscal policy the superior stabilization tool? Not necessarily, for the lags we have just described, which are beyond policy makers' control, are not the only ones that affect the timing of stabilization policy. Additional lags stem from the behavior of the policy makers themselves. We refer here to the delays that occur while policy makers study the state of the economy, contemplate which steps they should take, and put their decisions into effect.

Here monetary policy has a huge advantage. The Federal Open Market Committee (FOMC) meets eight times a year, and more often if necessary. (It met frequently during the crisis.) So monetary policy decisions can be (and were) made on short notice. Once the Fed decides on a course of action, it executes its plan immediately by either buying or selling Treasury securities in the open market.

In contrast, federal budgeting procedures normally operate on the annual budget cycle. Except in unusual cases like 2008 and 2009, major fiscal policy initiatives occur only at the time of the annual budget. In principle, tax laws can be changed at any time. However, the wheels of Congress normally grind slowly and are often gummed up by partisan politics. For these reasons, it may take months for Congress to change fiscal policy.

Or so it was thought for years. But Congress proved three times in the last 15 years that it can act quickly in a perceived emergency. First in 2001, then again in 2008, and then dramatically in 2009, both houses of Congress rapidly passed, and the president signed, fiscal stimulus bills that put checks into the hands of consumers when the economy was threatened by recession—even though, in the second case, the White House and Congress were controlled by different parties. This recent experience has many observers rethinking the old conventional wisdom, which held that:

> Policy lags are normally much shorter for monetary policy than for fiscal policy.

Could it be that this is no longer true?

So where does the combined effect of expenditure lags (which are longer for monetary policy) and policy lags (which are longer for fiscal policy) leave us? With nothing very conclusive, we are afraid. In practice, most students of stabilization policy concluded years ago that the unwieldy and often partisan nature of our political system made active use of fiscal policy for stabilization purposes quite difficult. Monetary policy, they claimed, was the only realistic game in town and therefore had to bear most of the burden of stabilization policy.

But recent events have questioned that conventional wisdom—for at least three reasons. One is the speedy fiscal responses just mentioned, which demonstrated that Congress can act quickly when it must. A second is that the massive recessionary gap that opened up in the Great Recession suggested that we needed *both* fiscal *and* monetary policy to push the economy out of the proverbial ditch. And the third was discussed in an earlier section: Once the federal funds rate reaches zero, monetary policy faces special problems and can probably use some help from fiscal policy.

## 15-5  DEBATE: THE SHAPE OF THE AGGREGATE SUPPLY CURVE

Another lively debate over stabilization policy revolves around the shape of the economy's aggregate supply curve. Many economists think of the aggregate supply curve as quite flat, as in Figure 2(a), so that large increases in output can be achieved with little inflation. Other economists envision the supply curve as quite steep, as shown in Figure 2(b), so that prices respond strongly to changes in output. The differences for public policy are substantial.

If the aggregate supply curve is flat, expansionary fiscal or monetary policies that raise the aggregate demand curve can buy large gains in real GDP at low cost in terms of inflation. In Figure 3(a), stimulation of demand pushes the aggregate demand curve outward

*Figure 2*

**Alternative Views of the Aggregate Supply Curve**

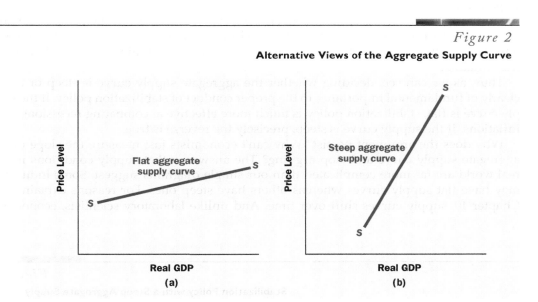

(a)

(b)

*Figure 3*

**Stabilization Policy with a Flat Aggregate Supply Curve**

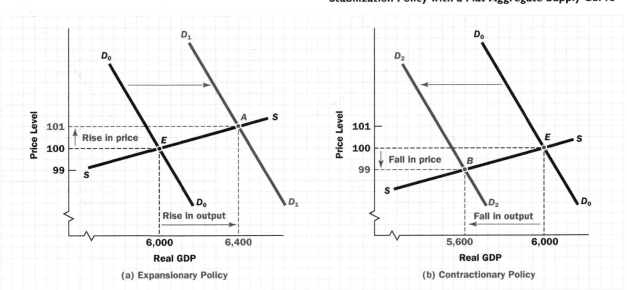

(a) Expansionary Policy

(b) Contractionary Policy

NOTE: Real GDP in billions of dollars per year.

from $D_0D_0$ to $D_1D_1$, thereby moving the economy's equilibrium from point $E$ to point $A$. The substantial rise in output ($400 billion in the diagram) is accompanied by only a pinch of inflation (1 percent). So the antirecession policy is quite successful.

Conversely, when the supply curve is flat, a restrictive stabilization policy is not a very effective way to bring inflation down. It serves mainly to reduce real output instead, as Figure 3(b) shows. Here a leftward shift of the aggregate demand curve from $D_0D_0$ to $D_2D_2$ moves equilibrium from point $E$ to point $B$, lowering real GDP by $400 billion but cutting the price level by merely 1 percent. Fighting inflation by contracting aggregate demand is obviously quite costly in this example.

Things are just the reverse if the aggregate supply curve is steep. In that case, expansionary fiscal or monetary policies will cause a good deal of inflation without boosting real GDP much. This situation is depicted in Figure 4(a), in which expansionary policies shift the aggregate demand curve outward from $D_0D_0$ to $D_1D_1$, thereby moving the economy's equilibrium from $E$ to $A$. Output rises by only $100 billion but prices shoot up 10 percent.

Similarly, contractionary policy is an effective way to bring down the price level without much sacrifice of output, as shown by the shift from $E$ to $B$ in Figure 4(b). Here it takes only a $100 billion loss of output (from $6,000 billion to $5,900 billion) to "buy" 10 percent less inflation.

Thus, as we can see, deciding whether the aggregate supply curve is steep or flat is clearly of fundamental importance to the proper conduct of stabilization policy. If the supply curve is flat, stabilization policy is much more effective at combating recessions than inflations. If the supply curve is steep, precisely the reverse is true.

Why does the argument persist? Why can't economists just measure the slope of the aggregate supply curve and stop arguing? The answer is that supply conditions in the real world are far more complicated than our simple diagrams suggest. Some industries may have flat supply curves whereas others have steep ones. For reasons explained in Chapter 10, supply curves shift over time. And unlike laboratory scientists, economists

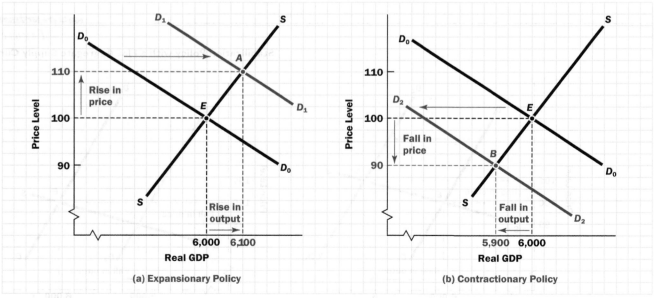

*Figure 4*

**Stabilization Policy with a Steep Aggregate Supply Curve**

(a) Expansionary Policy

(b) Contractionary Policy

NOTE: Real GDP in billions of dollars per year.

cannot perform controlled experiments that would reveal the shape of the aggregate supply curve directly. Instead, they use statistical inference to make educated guesses.

Although empirical research continues, economists' understanding of aggregate supply remains less settled than our understanding of aggregate demand. Nevertheless, many economists believe that the outline of a consensus view has emerged. This view holds that *the steepness of the aggregate supply schedule depends on the time frame.*

In the short run, the aggregate supply curve is quite flat, making Figure 3 the more relevant picture of reality. Over short periods, therefore, fluctuations in aggregate demand have large effects on output but only minor effects on prices. In the long run, however, the aggregate supply curve becomes quite steep, perhaps even vertical. In that case, Figure 4 is a better representation of reality, so that changes in demand affect mainly prices, not output.[4] The implication is that

> Any change in aggregate demand will have most of its effect on *output* in the short run but on *prices* in the long run.

## 15-6 DEBATE: SHOULD THE GOVERNMENT INTERVENE AT ALL?

We have yet to consider what may be the most fundamental and controversial debate of all—the issue posed at the beginning of the chapter. Is it likely that government policy can stabilize the economy successfully? Or are even well-intentioned efforts likely to do more harm than good?

This controversy has raged for decades. In part, the debate is political or even philosophical. Liberals tend to be more intervention-minded and hence more favorably disposed toward activist stabilization policies. Conservatives are more inclined to keep the government's hands off the economy and hence favor adhering to fixed rules. Such political differences are not surprising. But more than ideology propels the debate. We need to understand the economics.

Critics of stabilization policy point to the lags and uncertainties that surround the operation of both fiscal and monetary policies—lags and uncertainties that we have stressed repeatedly in this and earlier chapters. Will the Fed's actions have the desired effects on the money supply? What will these actions do to interest rates and spending? Can fiscal policy actions be taken promptly? How large is the expenditure multiplier? The list could go on and on.

These skeptics look at this formidable catalog of difficulties, add a dash of skepticism about our ability to forecast the future, and worry that stabilization policy may fail. They therefore advise the authorities to pursue passive policies rather than active ones—adhering to fixed rules that, although incapable of ironing out every bump and wiggle in the economy's growth path, will at least keep it roughly on track.

Advocates of active stabilization policies admit that perfection is unattainable. However, they are much more optimistic about the prospects for success, and they are much *less* optimistic about how smoothly the economy would grow in the absence of demand management. They therefore advocate discretionary increases in government spending (or decreases in taxes) and lower interest rates when the economy has a recessionary gap—and the reverse when the economy has an inflationary gap. Such policies, they believe, will help keep the economy closer to its full-employment growth path.

Each side can point to evidence that buttresses its own view.

Activists look back with pride at the tax cut of 1964 and the sustained period of economic growth that it ushered in. They also point to the tax cut of 1975 (which was enacted quickly, at just about the trough of a severe recession) and the even speedier fiscal stimulus

---

[4] The reasoning behind the view that the aggregate supply curve is flat in the short run but steep in the long run will be developed in Chapter 17.

packages enacted after 9/11, in February 2008, and then again in February 2009. Advocates of using discretionary monetary policy extol the Federal Reserve's switch to "easy money" in 1982; its expert steering of the economy between 1992 and 2000; and its quick responses to the threats to the economy after 9/11 and the financial panic in September 2008.

Advocates of rules remind us of the government's refusal to curb runaway demand during the 1966–1968 Vietnam buildup, its overexpansion of the economy in the 1972 election year, and the monetary overkill that helped bring on the sharp recession of 1981–1982. Some also argue that the Fed helped fuel the housing bubble by holding interest rates too low in 2003–2004.

In truth, the historical record of fiscal and monetary policy is far from glorious. The authorities have sometimes taken appropriate and timely actions to stabilize the economy, but at other times they clearly either took inappropriate steps or did nothing at all. The question of whether the government should adopt passive rules or attempt an activist stabilization policy therefore merits a closer look. As we shall see now, the *lags* in the effects of policy discussed earlier in this chapter play a pivotal role in the debate.

### 15-6a  Lags and the Rules-versus-Discretion Debate

Lags lead to a fundamental difficulty for stabilization policy—a difficulty so formidable that it has prompted some economists to conclude that attempts to stabilize economic activity are likely to do more harm than good. To see why, refer to Figure 5, which charts the behavior of both actual and potential GDP over the course of a business cycle in a hypothetical economy with no stabilization policy. At point A, the economy begins to slip into a recession and does not recover to full employment until point D. Then, between points D and E, it overshoots potential GDP and enters an inflationary boom.

The argument in favor of stabilization policy runs something like this: Policy makers recognize that the recession is a serious problem at point B, and they take appropriate actions promptly. These actions have their major effects around point C and therefore limit both the depth and the length of the recession.

But suppose the lags are really longer and less predictable than those just described. Suppose, for example, that actions do not come until point C and that stimulative policies do not have their major effects until after point D. Then the policy will be of little help during the recession and will actually do harm by overstimulating the economy during the ensuing boom. Thus:

**In the presence of long lags, attempts at stabilizing the economy may actually succeed in destabilizing it.**

For this reason, some economists argue that we are better off leaving the economy alone and relying on its natural self-corrective forces to cure recessions and inflations. Instead of embarking on periodic programs of monetary and fiscal stimulus or restraint, they advise policy makers to stick to fixed rules that ignore current economic events.

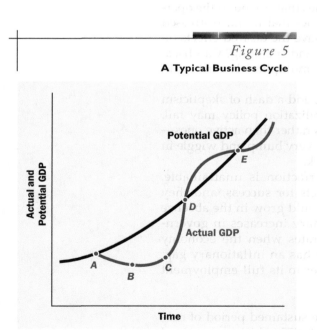

*Figure 5*

**A Typical Business Cycle**

## 15-7  DIMENSIONS OF THE RULES-VERSUS-DISCRETION DEBATE

Are the critics right? Should we give up on discretionary policy and put the economy on autopilot—relying on automatic stabilizers and the economy's natural self-correcting mechanisms? As usual, the answer depends on many factors.

## 15-7a  How Fast Does the Economy's Self-Correcting Mechanism Work?

In Chapter 10, we emphasized that the economy has a self-correcting mechanism. If that self-correcting mechanism is fast and efficient, recessions and inflations will disappear quickly by themselves, making the case for policy intervention weak. Indeed, if such problems typically last only a short time, long lags in discretionary stabilization policy might mean that the medicine has its major effects only after the disease has run its course. In terms of Figure 5, this is a case in which point *D* comes very close to point *A*. In fact, a distinct minority of economists used precisely this reasoning to argue against a fiscal stimulus after the 9/11 terrorist attacks and again after the financial panics in 2007 and 2008. But few made the argument once the 2007–2009 recession deepened.

Although extreme advocates of rules argue that this is indeed what happens, most economists agree that the economy's self-correcting mechanism is slow and not terribly reliable, even when supplemented by the automatic stabilizers. On this count, then, a point is scored for discretionary policy.

## 15-7b  How Long Are the Lags in Stabilization Policy?

We just explained why long and unpredictable lags in monetary and fiscal policy make it hard for stabilization policy to do much good. Short, reliable lags point in just the opposite direction. Thus advocates of fixed rules emphasize the length of lags, whereas proponents of discretion tend to discount them.

Who is right depends on the circumstances. Sometimes policy makers take prompt action, and the economy receives at least some stimulus from expansionary policy within a year after slipping into a recession. The tax reductions and sharp cuts in interest rates that followed both the 9/11 tragedy and the financial crisis of 2007–2009 are recent examples. Although far from perfect, the effects of such timely actions were certainly felt soon enough to do some good. However, as we have seen, very slow policy responses may actually prove destabilizing. Because history offers examples of each type, we can draw no general conclusion.

## 15-7c  How Accurate Are Economic Forecasts?

One way to compress the policy-making lag dramatically is to forecast economic events accurately. If we could see a recession coming a full year ahead of time (which we certainly *cannot* do), even a sluggish policy response would still be timely. In terms of Figure 5, this would be a case in which the recession is predicted well before point *A*.

Over the years, economists in universities, government agencies, and private businesses have developed a number of techniques to assist them in predicting what the economy will do. Unfortunately, none of these methods is terribly accurate. To give a rough idea of magnitudes, forecasts of either the inflation rate or the real GDP growth rate for the year ahead typically err by $\pm\frac{3}{4}$ to 1 percentage point. In a bad year for forecasters, errors of 2 or 3 percentage points occur.

Is this forecasting record good enough? That depends on how the forecasts are used. It is certainly not good enough to support so-called *fine-tuning*—that is, attempts to keep the economy within a hair's breadth of full employment. But it probably is good enough for policy makers interested in using discretionary stabilization policy to close persistent and sizable gaps between actual and potential GDP, such as those of the years 2008–2014. For example, when the large fiscal stimulus package was enacted in February 2009, just about everyone was convinced that we would still have a huge recessionary gap for years to come. And they were right, even though forecasts made at the time were not very accurate.

## 15-7d  The Size of Government

One bogus argument sometimes heard is that active fiscal policy must inevitably lead to a growing public sector. Because proponents of fixed rules tend to be opponents of big government as well, they view this growth as undesirable. Of course, others think that a larger public sector is just what society needs.

This argument, however, is completely beside the point because, as we pointed out in Chapter 11: *One's opinion about the proper size of government should have nothing to do with one's view on stabilization policy.* For example, President George W. Bush was as conservative as they come and, at least rhetorically, he was devoted to shrinking the size of the public sector.[5] But his tax-cutting initiatives in 2001–2003 constituted an extremely activist fiscal policy to spur economic growth, as did his stimulus program in 2008. Furthermore, much of stabilization policy is monetary policy, which neither increases nor decreases the size of government.

### 15-7e  Uncertainties Caused by Government Policy

Advocates of rules are on stronger ground when they argue that frequent changes in tax laws, government spending programs, or monetary conditions make it difficult for firms and consumers to formulate and carry out rational plans. They argue that the authorities can provide a more stable environment for the private sector by adhering to fixed rules so that businesses and consumers know what to expect.

No one disputes that a more stable environment is better for private planning, *other things equal.* However, supporters of discretionary policy emphasize that "other things" are not likely to be equal, and that stability in the economy is more important than stability in the government budget (or in Federal Reserve operations). The whole idea of stabilization policy is to *limit* gyrations in the pace of economic activity by *creating* timely gyrations in the government budget and/or in monetary policy. Which atmosphere is better for business, they ask: one in which fiscal and monetary rules keep things peaceful on Capitol Hill and at the Federal Reserve while recessions and inflations wrack the economy, or one in which government changes its policy abruptly on occasion but the economy grows more smoothly? They think the answer is self-evident. The question, of course, is whether stabilization policy can succeed in practice.

### 15-7f  A Political Business Cycle?

A final argument put forth by advocates of rules is political rather than economic. Fiscal policy decisions are made by elected politicians: the president and members of Congress. When elections are on the horizon (and for members of the House of Representatives, they *always* are), these politicians may be at least as concerned with keeping their jobs as with doing what is right for the economy. This situation leaves fiscal policy subject to "political manipulation"—lawmakers may take inappropriate actions to attain short-run political goals. A system of purely automatic stabilization, its proponents argue, would eliminate this peril.

It is certainly possible that politicians could deliberately *cause* economic instability to help their own reelection. Indeed, some observers of such "political business cycles" have claimed that several American presidents have taken full advantage of the opportunity. Furthermore, even without any insidious intent, politicians may take the wrong actions for perfectly honorable reasons. Decisions in the political arena are never clear-cut, and it certainly is easy to find examples of grievous errors in the history of U.S. fiscal policy.

Taken as a whole, then, the political argument against discretionary fiscal policy seems to have a great deal of merit. But what are we to do about it? It is unrealistic to believe that fiscal decisions could or should be made by a group of objective and nonpartisan technicians. Tax and budget policies require inherently *political* decisions that, in a democracy, should be made by elected officials.

This fact may seem worrisome in view of the possibilities for political chicanery, but it should not bother us any more (or any less) than similar maneuvering in other areas of policy making. After all, the same problem besets international relations, national defense, formulation and enforcement of the law, and so on. Politicians make all these decisions for us, subject only to sporadic accountability at elections. Is there any reason why fiscal decisions should be different?

---

[5] In fact, the size of the federal government expanded rapidly during his presidency, in part because of national security concerns, but also because of domestic spending.

## Between Rules and Discretion

In recent years, a number of economists and policy makers have sought a middle ground between saddling monetary policy makers with rigid rules and giving them complete discretion, as the Federal Reserve has in the United States.

One such approach is called "inflation targeting." As practiced in the United Kingdom, for example, inflation targeting starts when an elected official (the Chancellor of the Exchequer, who is roughly equivalent to the U.S. Secretary of the Treasury) chooses a numerical target for the inflation rate—currently, this target is 2 percent. The United Kingdom's central bank, the Bank of England, is then bound by law to try to reach this target. In that sense, the system functions somewhat like a *rule*. However, monetary policy makers are given complete *discretion* as to how they go about trying to achieve this goal. Neither the Chancellor nor Parliament interferes with day-to-day monetary policy decisions. The Federal Reserve's previous chairman, Ben Bernanke, was a big advocate of inflation targeting when he was a professor at Princeton University. And in 2012, the Fed officially adopted a 2 percent inflation target.

Another approach is called the "Taylor rule," after Professor John Taylor of Stanford University. Almost 25 years ago, Taylor noticed that the Fed's interest rate decisions during the chairmanship of Alan Greenspan could be described by a simple algebraic equation. This equation, now called the Taylor rule, starts with a 2 percent *real* interest rate, and then instructs the Fed to *lower* the interest rate in proportion to any

recessionary gap and to *raise* it in proportion to any excess of inflation above 2 percent (which is the Fed's inflation goal). A rule like this, Taylor argued, based on past research, might not be perfect, but it will generally produce good results.

No central bank uses the Taylor rule as a mechanical rule. But many central banks around the world, including the Fed, find the Taylor rule useful as a benchmark to guide their decision making—thus blending, once again, features of both rules and discretion.

*The Bank of England's Monetary Policy Committee.*

But monetary policy *is* different. Because Congress was concerned that elected officials focused on the short run would pursue inflationary monetary policies, it long ago gave decision-making authority over monetary policy to the unelected technocrats at the Federal Reserve. Politics influences monetary policy only very indirectly: The Fed reports to Congress, and the president has the power to appoint Federal Reserve governors whose views are to his liking. For the most part, however, the Fed is apolitical.

## A Nobel Prize for the Rules-versus-Discretion Debate

In 2004, economists Finn Kydland and Edward Prescott were awarded the Nobel Prize for a fascinating contribution to the rules-versus-discretion debate. They called attention to a general problem that they labeled "time inconsistency," and their analysis of this problem led them to conclude that the Fed should follow a rule.

A close-to-home example will illustrate the basic time inconsistency problem. Suppose your instructor announces in September that a final exam will be given in December. The main purpose of the exam is to ensure that students study and learn the course materials, and the exam itself creates work for the faculty and both work and stress for the students. So when December rolls around, it may seem "optimal" to call off the exam at the last moment. Of course, if that happened regularly, students would soon stop studying for exams. So actually giving the exam is the better long-run policy. One way to solve this time inconsistency problem is to adopt a simple *rule* stating that announced exams will always be given, rather than allowing individual faculty members to cancel exams at their *discretion*.

Kydland and Prescott argued that monetary policy makers face a similar time inconsistency problem. They may first announce a stern anti-inflation policy (analogous to giving an exam). But then, when the moment of truth (December) arrives, they may relent because they don't want to cause unemployment (all that work and stress). Kydland and Prescott's suggested solution: The Fed and other central banks should adopt *rules* that remove period-by-period *discretion*.

## Issue Revisited | *What Should Be Done?*

So, where do we come out on the question posed at the start of this chapter? On balance, is it better to pursue the best discretionary policy we can, knowing full well that we will never achieve perfection? Or is it wiser to rely on fixed rules and the automatic stabilizers?

In weighing the pros and cons, your basic view of the economy is crucial. Some economists believe that the economy, if left unmanaged, would generate a series of ups and downs that would be difficult to predict, but that it would correct each of them by itself in a relatively short time. They conclude that, because of long lags, poor forecasts, and human foibles, policy makers have only limited ability to anticipate whether the economy will need stimulus or restraint by the time their actions take effect. Consequently, they advocate fixed rules.

Other economists see the economy like a giant ship with a great deal of inertia. Under this view, if we observe a large inflationary or recessionary gap today, it will likely still be there a year or two from now because the self-correcting mechanism works slowly. In such a world, accurate forecasting is not imperative, even if policy lags are long. If we base policy on a forecast of a 5 percent gap between actual and potential GDP a year from now, and the gap turns out to be only 2 percent, we still will have done the right thing despite the terrible forecast. Holders of this view of the economy tend to support discretionary policy, especially during deep slumps like the recent one.

There is certainly no consensus on this issue, either among economists or politicians. After all, the question touches on political ideology as well as economics, and liberals often look to government to solve social problems, whereas conservatives consistently point out that many efforts of government fail despite the best intentions. A prudent view of the matter might be that

> The case for active discretionary policy is strong when the economy has a serious deficiency or excess of aggregate demand. However, advocates of fixed rules are right that it is unwise to try to iron out every little wiggle in the growth path of GDP.

One thing seems certain: The rules-versus-discretion debate is likely to go on for quite some time.

## Summary

1. **Velocity** ($V$) is the ratio of nominal GDP to the stock of money ($M$). It indicates how quickly money circulates.

2. One important determinant of velocity is the rate of interest ($r$). At higher interest rates, people find it less attractive to hold money because money pays zero or little interest. Thus, when $r$ rises, money circulates faster, and $V$ rises.

3. **Monetarism** is a type of analysis that focuses attention on velocity and the money supply. Although monetarists realize that $V$ is not constant, they believe that it is predictable enough to make it a useful tool for policy analysis and forecasting.

4. Because fiscal policy actions affect aggregate demand either directly through $G$ or indirectly through $C$, the expenditure lags between fiscal actions and their effects on aggregate demand are probably fairly short. By contrast, monetary policy operates mainly on investment, $I$, which responds slowly to changes in interest rates.

5. However, the policy-making lag normally is much longer for fiscal policy than for monetary policy. Hence, when the two lags are combined, it is not clear which type of policy acts more quickly.

6. If the Federal Reserve (or any other central bank) reduces short-term interest rates to virtually zero, and the economy still needs stimulus, it may want to turn to unconventional monetary policies, such as massive lending as the "lender of last resort" and large-scale purchases of atypical assets. However, critics argue that such operations take the Fed beyond its proper powers, may politicize it, and can unleash future inflation.

7. The Fed has traditionally shied away from bursting asset bubbles, or even trying to limit their growth. Recent experience, however, has led the Fed and other central banks to rethink that position—especially when bubbles are fed by excessive lending and high leverage.

8. When the aggregate supply curve is very flat, changes in aggregate demand will have large effects on the nation's real output but small effects on the price level. Under those circumstances, stabilization policy works well as an antirecession device, but it has little power to combat inflation.

9. When the aggregate supply curve is steep, changes in aggregate demand have small effects on real output but large effects on the price level. In such a case, stabilization policy can do much to fight inflation but is not a very effective way to cure unemployment.

10. The aggregate supply curve is likely to be relatively flat in the short run but relatively steep in the long run. Hence, stabilization policy affects mainly output in the short run but mainly prices in the long run.

11. When the lags in the operation of fiscal and monetary policy are long and unpredictable, attempts to stabilize economic activity may actually destabilize it.

12. Some economists believe that our imperfect knowledge of the channels through which stabilization policy works, the long lags involved, and the inaccuracy of forecasts make it unlikely that discretionary stabilization policy can succeed.

13. Other economists recognize these difficulties but do not believe they are quite as serious. They also place much less faith in the economy's ability to cure recessions and inflations on its own. They therefore think that discretionary policy is not only advisable, but essential.

14. Stabilizing the economy by fiscal policy need not imply a tendency toward "big government."

## Key Terms

equation of exchange   296

lags in stabilization policy   303

monetarism   298

quantity theory of money   297

velocity   296

## Test Yourself

1. How much money by the M1 definition (cash plus checking account balances) do you typically have at any particular moment? Divide this amount into your total income over the past 12 months to obtain your own personal velocity. Are you typical of the nation as a whole?

2. The following table provides data on nominal gross domestic product and the money supply (M1 definition) in recent selected years. Compute velocity for each year. Do you see any trend? How does it compare with the trend that prevailed from about 1996 to about 2006? (See Figure 1(a).)

| Year | End-of-Year Money Supply (M1) | Nominal GDP |
|------|-------------------------------|-------------|
| 2010 | $1,836 | $14,958 |
| 2011 | 2,160 | 15,534 |
| 2012 | 2,447 | 16,245 |
| 2013 | 2,648 | 16,798 |

3. Which of the following events would strengthen the argument for the use of discretionary policy, and which would strengthen the argument for rules?

   a. Structural changes make the economy's self-correcting mechanism work more quickly and reliably than before.

   b. New statistical methods are found that improve the accuracy of economic forecasts.

   c. A Republican Congress is elected when there is a Democratic president. Congress and the president differ sharply on what should be done about the national economy.

4. **(More difficult)** The money supply ($M$) is the sum of bank deposits ($D$) plus currency in the hands of the public (call that $C$). Suppose the required reserve ratio is 20 percent and the Fed provides $50 billion in bank reserves ($R = \$50$ billion).

   a. First assume that people hold no currency ($C = 0$). How large will the money supply ($M$) be? If the Fed increases bank reserves to $R = \$60$ billion, how large will $M$ be then?

   b. Next, assume that people hold 20 cents worth of currency for each dollar of bank deposits; that is, $C = 0.2D$. Define the *monetary base* ($B$) as the sum of bank reserves ($R$) plus currency: $B = R + C$. If the Fed now creates $50 billion worth of monetary base, how large will $M$ be? (*Hint:* You will need a little bit of algebra to figure this out. Remember that the $50 billion monetary base is divided between two purposes: bank reserves and currency.) Now, if the Fed increases the monetary base to $B = \$60$ billion, how large will $M$ be?

   c. What do you notice about the relationship between $M$ and $B$?

## Discussion Questions

1. Use the concept of opportunity cost to explain why velocity is higher at higher interest rates.

2. Given the behavior of velocity shown in Figure 1, would it make more sense for the Federal Reserve to formulate targets for M1 or M2?

3. Distinguish between the expenditure lag and the policy lag in stabilization policy. Does monetary or fiscal policy have the shorter expenditure lag? What about the policy lag?

4. Given all the pros and cons, do you think the Federal Reserve should try to prevent asset price bubbles from forming? If so, how would it do that?

5. Explain why their contrasting views on the shape of the aggregate supply curve lead some economists to argue much more strongly for stabilization policies to fight unemployment and other economists to argue much more strongly for stabilization policies to fight inflation.

6. Explain why lags make it possible that policy actions intended to stabilize the economy will actually destabilize it.

7. Many observers think that the Federal Reserve succeeded in using deft applications of monetary policy to "fine-tune" the U.S. economy into the full-employment zone in the 1990s without worsening inflation. Use the data on money supply, interest rates, real GDP, unemployment, and the price level given on the inside back cover of this book or in the Macroeconomic Data-at-a-Glance powered by FRED digital tool available in MindTap to evaluate this claim.

8. During the year 2008, U.S. economic performance deteriorated sharply. Can this decline be blamed on inferior monetary or fiscal policy? (You may want to ask your instructor about this question.)

9. In December 2008, the Fed reduced the federal funds rate to approximately zero. What should it have done then? Why? What did it actually do?

# BUDGET DEFICITS IN THE SHORT AND LONG RUN

*Blessed are the young, for they shall inherit the national debt.*

HERBERT HOOVER

Monetary policy and fiscal policy are typically thought of as tools for short-run economic *stabilization*—that is, as ways to combat either inflation or unemployment. Debates over the Federal Reserve's next interest-rate decision, or over this year's federal budget, often are dominated by short-run considerations such as: Does the economy need to be stimulated or restrained *right now?*

But the monetary and fiscal policy choices the government makes today also have profound effects on our economy's ability to produce goods and services *in the future.* We began Part 2 by emphasizing long-run growth, and especially the role of capital formation (see Chapters 6 and 7). But for most of Part 3, we have been preoccupied with the shorter-run issues of inflation, unemployment, and recession—partly because of the salience of the financial crisis of 2007–2009 and the lingering effects of the Great Recession (Chapter 14).

This chapter integrates the two perspectives by considering *both* the long-run *and* short-run implications of monetary and especially fiscal policy decisions. What difference does it make if we stimulate or restrain the economy with fiscal or monetary policy? Should we strive to balance the budget? What are the economic virtues and vices of large budget deficits, both now and in the future?

## CONTENTS

| Issue | *Is the Federal Government Budget Deficit Too Large?* |

The federal budget deficit soared during the Great Recession, partly because the weak economy reduced tax receipts, and partly because of the extraordinary fiscal stimulus program enacted in 2009 to fight the recession. The deficit, which was a mere $161 billion in fiscal year 2007, rose to $459 billion in fiscal 2008, and then to an amazing $1.413 *trillion* in fiscal 2009. As late as fiscal 2012, it was still over a trillion dollars.[1]

So it was not surprising that the federal budget deficit became both a huge economic issue and a major political hot potato starting in 2010. The Obama

---

[1] *Reminder:* The fiscal year of the U.S. government ends on September 30. Thus, fiscal year 2015 runs from October 1, 2014 to September 30, 2015.

administration's February 2010 budget proposal promised smaller deficits—but not yet. Many Republican (and some Democratic) critics argued then that we should not wait that long. The president responded by, among other things, creating a bipartisan commission to report back by December 2010. When their report came in, it was widely praised—and largely ignored.

In the meantime, dissatisfaction with the massive budget deficit became perhaps the nation's biggest political issue. It helped Republicans win control of the House of Representatives in the 2010 elections and, not surprisingly, congressional Republicans focused on spending cuts thereafter. Partisan battles over the deficit and taxes continued right through and after President Obama's reelection in 2012—finally ending (sort of!) with a big compromise budget bill in January 2013.

While these political battles were raging, other voices—from both economists and some politicians—warned against reducing the budget deficit too hastily while the economy was still so weak. Either raising taxes or cutting spending while the economy was struggling to lift itself off the canvas was dangerous, they argued. Doing so could send us back into recession.

Which side was right? Is it important to shrink the budget deficit quickly? Or should we be more patient when the economy is weak, delaying any tax hikes and expenditure cuts for later? And should we be worried about the current federal budget deficit (for fiscal year 2015), which is still over $400 billion? Putting politics aside, by the end of this chapter you will be in an excellent position to make up your own mind on these and related public policy questions.

## 16-1 SHOULD THE BUDGET ALWAYS BE BALANCED? THE SHORT RUN

Americans have long been attracted by the idea of balancing the government budget year after year—so much so that constitutional amendments to require a balanced budget have been proposed and debated many times. Let us begin our examination of the virtues and vices of balanced budgets by reviewing the basic principles of fiscal policy that we have learned so far (especially in Chapter 11).

These principles certainly do *not* imply that we should always maintain a balanced budget, much as that notion may appeal to our intuitive sense of prudence. Rather, they instruct fiscal policy makers to focus on *balancing aggregate supply and aggregate demand*. They therefore point to the desirability of budget *deficits* when private demand, $C + I + (X - IM)$, is too weak and of budget *surpluses* when private demand is too strong. The budget should be balanced, according to these principles, only when $C + I + G + (X - IM)$ under a balanced-budget policy approximately equals potential GDP. Such a situation may sometimes prevail, but it will not necessarily be the norm. It has certainly not been the case in recent years.

The reason why a balanced budget is not always advisable should be clear from our earlier discussion of stabilization policy. Consider the fiscal policy that the federal government would follow if its goal were to maintain a balanced budget every year, as state governments try to do. Suppose the budget was initially balanced, and then private spending sagged for some reason, as it did sharply in 2008. The multiplier would pull GDP down. Because personal and corporate tax receipts fall as GDP declines, the budget would automatically swing into the red—as it did then. If the government wanted to restore budget balance, it would then have to *cut spending* or *raise taxes*—exactly the opposite of the appropriate fiscal policy response to a recession, and exactly the opposite of what the federal government actually did at the time. Thus:

> Attempts to balance the budget during recessions—as was done, say, during the Great Depression—will prolong and deepen slumps.

This is precisely what many observers were worried might happen in the United States, the United Kingdom, and many other countries if fiscal stimulus was withdrawn too soon in 2010 and thereafter. So there were vigorous debates over this issue in many countries—debates which continue in some. Importantly, the arguments were over *when* budget deficits should be reduced, not *whether*. Everyone agreed that deficits needed to be smaller *eventually*.

The same problem arises in the other direction. Budget balancing also can lead to inappropriate fiscal policy under boom conditions. If rising tax receipts induce a budget-balancing government to spend more or to cut taxes, then fiscal policy will "boom the boom"—with unfortunate inflationary consequences.

## 16-2 THE IMPORTANCE OF THE POLICY MIX

Actually, the issue is even more complicated than we have indicated so far. As we know, fiscal policy is not the only way the government affects aggregate demand. It also influences aggregate demand through its *monetary policy*. For this simple reason,

> **The appropriate fiscal policy depends, among other things, on the current stance of monetary policy (and vice-versa). Although a balanced budget may be appropriate under one monetary policy, a deficit or a surplus may be appropriate under another.**

An example will illustrate the point. Suppose Congress and the president believe that the aggregate supply and demand curves will intersect approximately at full employment if the budget is balanced. Then a balanced budget would seem to be the appropriate fiscal policy. But now suppose monetary policy turns contractionary, pulling the aggregate demand curve inward to the left, as shown by the blue arrow in Figure 1, creating a recessionary gap. If the fiscal authorities wish to restore GDP to its original level, they must shift the aggregate demand curve back to its original position, $D_0 D_0$, as indicated by the maroon arrow. To do so, they must either raise spending or cut taxes, thereby opening up a budget deficit. Thus, because both monetary and fiscal policies affect aggregate demand, the tightening of *monetary* policy changes the appropriate *fiscal* policy from a balanced budget to a deficit.

By the same token, a given target for aggregate demand implies that any change in *fiscal* policy will alter the appropriate *monetary* policy. For example, we can reinterpret Figure 1 as indicating the effects of increasing the budget deficit by raising government spending or cutting taxes (the maroon arrow). Then, if the Fed wants real GDP to remain at $Y_1$, it must raise interest rates enough to restore the aggregate demand curve to $D_1 D_1$ (the blue arrow).

The upshot is that we should not expect a balanced budget to be the norm. How, then, can we tell whether any particular deficit is too large or too small? From the discussion so far, it would appear that the answer depends on the strength of private-sector aggregate demand and the stance of monetary policy, but those are not the only considerations. Another important one is the desired *composition* of GDP.

To see why, we need to understand that fiscal policy influences interest rates. Think about what happens to real output and the price level following, say, an increase in government spending. We learned in previous chapters that both real GDP $(Y)$ and the price level $(P)$ rise, so nominal GDP certainly rises. Chapter 13's analysis of the market for bank reserves also taught us that rising prices and output, by increasing the money volume of transactions, push the demand curve for bank reserves outward to the right—as depicted in Figure 2 (which basically repeats Figure 8 from Chapter 13). If there is no change in the supply of reserves, the rate of interest must rise. Thus, *expansionary fiscal policy normally raises interest rates*.

If the government uses its spending and taxing weapons in the opposite direction, the same process works in reverse. Falling output and (possibly) falling prices shift the demand

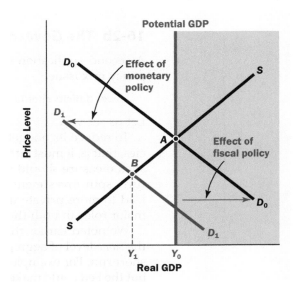

*Figure 1*

**The Interaction of Monetary and Fiscal Policy**

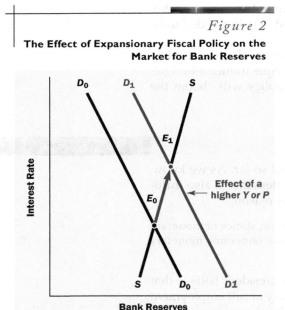

**Figure 2**

**The Effect of Expansionary Fiscal Policy on the Market for Bank Reserves**

curve for reserves inward to the left. With a fixed supply curve, equilibrium in the market for bank reserves leads to a lower interest rate. So we conclude that:

> Monetary policy is not the only type of policy that affects interest rates. Fiscal policy does, too. Specifically, increases in government spending or tax cuts normally push interest rates up, whereas restrictive fiscal policies normally pull interest rates down.

The apparently banal fact that changes in fiscal policy affect interest rates has several important consequences. Here are two:

## 16-2a The Multiplier Formula Revisited

Expansionary fiscal policy raises interest rates, which deters private investment spending. So when the government raises the $G$ component of $C + I + G + (X - IM)$, one side effect will probably be a reduction in the $I$ component. Consequently, total spending will rise by *less* than simple multiplier analysis might suggest. The fact that a surge in government demand ($G$) discourages some private demand ($I$) provides yet another reason why the oversimplified multiplier formula of earlier chapters, $1/(1 - \text{MPC})$, exaggerates the size of the multiplier:

> Because a rise in $G$ (or, for that matter, an autonomous rise in any component of total expenditure) pushes interest rates higher, and hence deters some investment spending, the increase in the sum $C + I + G + (X - IM)$ is smaller than the oversimplified multiplier formula predicts.

Combining this observation with our previous analysis of the multiplier, we now have accumulated the following list of

**REASONS WHY THE OVERSIMPLIFIED FORMULA OVERSTATES THE MULTIPLIER**

1. It ignores variable imports, which reduce the size of the multiplier.
2. It ignores price-level changes, which reduce the size of the multiplier.
3. It ignores the income tax, which reduces the size of the multiplier.
4. It ignores the rising interest rates that accompany any autonomous increase in spending, which also reduce the size of the multiplier.

With so many reasons, it is no wonder that the actual multiplier, which is estimated to be well under two for the U.S. economy, is so much less than the oversimplified formula suggests.

## 16-2b The Government Budget and Investment

A second application of the idea that fiscal policy affects interest rates is crucial to the policy mix issue.

> Lower deficits should lead to higher levels of private investment spending.

Let us see why.

To reduce its budget deficit, the government must engage in *contractionary* fiscal policies, that is, it must either reduce spending or raise taxes. But as we have just learned, any such measure should *reduce* real interest rates. These lower real interest rates should, in turn, spur investment spending. This simple insight—that lower budget deficits should lead to more private investment, and higher budget deficits should lead to less—plays major roles in both the analysis of this chapter and the public debate over the deficit.

We noted earlier that various *combinations* of fiscal and monetary policy can lead to the *same* level of aggregate demand, and hence to the *same* real GDP and price level in the short run. For example, the government could reduce aggregate demand by raising taxes, but the Fed could make up for it by cutting interest rates. Or the reverse could happen: The government could cut taxes while the Fed raises interest rates, leaving aggregate demand unchanged. The long-run consequences of these alternative mixes of monetary and fiscal policy may be quite different, however, because of their effects on interest rates.

In particular, both more expansionary fiscal policy (tax cuts or higher government spending) and tighter monetary policy should produce *higher* real interest rates and therefore *lower* investment. Thus, such a policy mix should shift the composition of total expenditure, $C + I + G + (X - IM)$, toward more G, more C (from tax cuts), and less I.[2] The expected result is less capital formation, and therefore slower growth of *potential* GDP. As we shall see shortly, it was precisely that policy mix—large tax cuts and tight money—that the U.S. government chose in the early 1980s and, to a lesser extent, in the years 2004–2006.

The opposite policy mix—tighter budgets and looser monetary policy—should produce the opposite results: lower real interest rates, more investment, and hence faster growth of potential GDP. And it is precisely that mix that the U.S. government managed to engineer with great success in the 1990s. Congress raised taxes and cut spending, which reduced aggregate demand, while the Federal Reserve kept interest rates low enough to restore the lost demand. The results were excellent. Lowering the budget deficit and then turning it into a surplus, economists believe, was an effective way to increase the investment share of GDP, which soared from 13 percent in 1992 to 19 percent in 2000. The general point is

> The composition of aggregate demand is a major determinant of the economy's long-run growth rate. If a larger fraction of GDP is devoted to investment, the nation's capital stock will grow faster and the aggregate supply schedule will shift more quickly to the right, accelerating growth.

International data likewise show a positive relationship between growth and the share of GDP invested. Figure 3 displays, for a set of 24 countries on four continents, both investment as a share of GDP and growth in per capita output over two decades (the 1970s and 1980s). Countries with higher investment rates clearly experienced higher growth, on average.

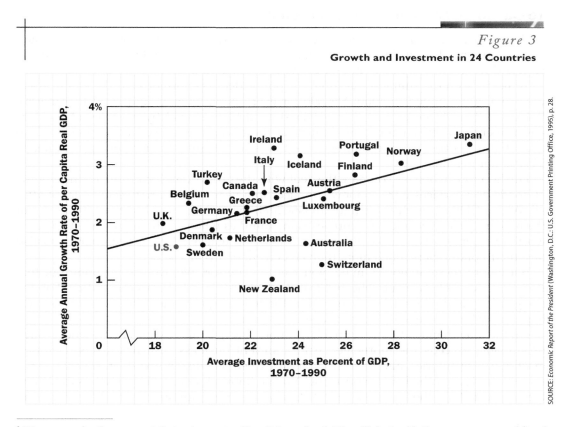

*Figure 3*

**Growth and Investment in 24 Countries**

SOURCE: *Economic Report of the President* (Washington, D.C.: U.S. Government Printing Office, 1995), p. 28.

---

[2] We assume for the moment that net exports, $X - IM$, are fixed. We will deal with the consequences of fiscal and monetary policy on exports and imports in Chapter 20.

So it appears that when we ask whether the budget should be in balance, in deficit, or in surplus, we have posed a good but complicated question. Before attempting to answer it, we need to get some facts straight.

## 16-3 DEFICITS AND DEBT: TERMINOLOGY AND FACTS

First, some critical terminology. People frequently confuse two terms that have different meanings: *budget deficits* and the *national debt*. We must learn to distinguish between the two.

The **budget deficit** is the amount by which the government's expenditures exceed its receipts during some specified period of time, usually a year. If, instead, receipts exceed expenditures, we have a **budget surplus**. For example, during fiscal year 2014, the federal government raised nearly $3 trillion in revenue and spent almost $3.58 trillion, resulting in a deficit of about $580 billion.

The **national debt**, also called the *public debt*, is the total value of the government's indebtedness at a moment in time. Thus, for example, the U.S. national debt at the end of fiscal year 2014 was nearly $18 trillion.

These two concepts—deficit and debt—are closely related because the government accumulates *debt* by running *deficits* or reduces its debt by running *surpluses*. The relationship between the debt and the deficit or surplus can be explained by a simple analogy. As you run water into a bathtub ("run a deficit"), the accumulated volume of water in the tub ("the debt") rises. Alternatively, if you let water out of the tub ("run a surplus"), the level of the water ("the debt") falls. Analogously, budget deficits raise the national debt, whereas budget surpluses lower it. However, getting rid of the deficit (shutting off the flow of water) does not eliminate the accumulated debt (drain the tub). It just stops the debt from growing.

> The **budget deficit** is the amount by which the government's expenditures exceed its receipts during a specified period of time, usually a year. If receipts exceed expenditures, it is called a **budget surplus** instead.
>
> The **national debt** is the federal government's total indebtedness at a moment in time. It is the result of previous budget deficits.

### 16-3a Some Facts about the National Debt

With this distinction in mind, let us now look at the size and nature of the accumulated public debt and then at the annual budget deficit. How large a public debt do we have? How did we get it? Who owes it? Is it growing or shrinking?

To begin with the simplest question, the public debt is enormous. At the end of fiscal year 2014, it amounted to about $56,000 for every man, woman, and child in America. But more than 40 percent of this outstanding debt was held by agencies of the U.S. government—in other words, one branch of the government owed it to another. If we deduct this portion, the net national debt was about $10.5 trillion, or approximately $33,000 per person.

Furthermore, when we compare the debt with the gross domestic product—the volume of goods and services our economy produces in a year—it does not seem so large after all. With a GDP of nearly $18 trillion in late 2014, the net debt was less than 60 percent of the nation's yearly income. By contrast, many families who own homes owe *several years'* worth of income to the banks that granted them mortgages. Many U.S. corporations also owe their bondholders much more than 60 percent of a year's sales.

But before these analogies make you feel too comfortable, we should point out that simple analogies between public and private debt are almost always misleading. For one thing, individuals do not live forever. But the federal government does—or at least we hope so—which increases its capacity to carry debt.

On the other hand, a family with a large mortgage debt also owns a home whose value presumably exceeds the mortgage.[3] And a solvent business firm has assets (factories, machinery, inventories, and so forth) that far exceed its outstanding debt in value. Is the same thing true of the U.S. government? No one knows for sure. How much is the White House worth? Or the national parks? And what about military bases, both here and

---

[3] This used to be true for the vast majority of American homeowners, but after the house-price bubble burst in 2006, many millions owed more on their mortgages than their houses were worth. Some still do.

abroad? Because these government assets are not sold on markets, no one really knows their true value. But many people suspect that the government's debt today exceeds the value of its assets.

Figure 4 charts the path of the *net* national debt from 1915 to 2014, expressing each year's net debt as a fraction of that year's nominal GDP. Looking at the debt *relative to GDP* is important for two reasons. First, we must remember that everything grows in a growing economy. Given that private debt has expanded greatly since 1915, it would be surprising indeed if the public debt had not grown as well. In fact, federal debt grew more slowly than did either private debt or GDP for most of the period since World War II. Two periods of time—the years from 1983 to 1994 and the years from 2003 to 2012—stand out as exceptions in Figure 4, with the debt-to-GDP ratio climbing sharply.

Second, the debt is measured in dollars and, as long as there is any inflation, the amount of purchasing power that each dollar represents declines each year. Dividing the debt by nominal GDP, as is done in Figure 4, adjusts for both real growth and inflation, and so puts the debt numbers in better perspective.

Figure 4 shows us how and when the U.S. government acquired all this debt. Notice the sharp increases in the ratio of debt to GDP during World War I, the Great Depression, and especially World War II. Thereafter, you see an unmistakable downward trend until the recession of 1974–1975. In 1945, the net national debt was the equivalent of nearly a year's worth of GDP. By 1974, this figure had been whittled down to just two months' worth.

Thus, until the 1980s, the U.S. government had acquired most of its debt either to finance wars or as the result of recessions. As we will see later, the *cause* of the debt is quite germane to the question of whether the debt is a burden. So it is important to remember that:

**Until about 1983, almost all of the U.S. national debt stemmed from financing wars or from the loss of tax revenues that accompany recessions.**

Then things changed. From about 1983 until about 1993, the national debt grew faster than nominal GDP, reversing the pattern that had prevailed since 1945. This spurt happened without wars and with only one recession. By 1993, the debt exceeded five months' GDP—nearly triple the ratio in 1974. This development alarmed many economists and public figures at the time.

*Figure 4*

**The U.S. National Debt Relative to GDP, 1915–2014**

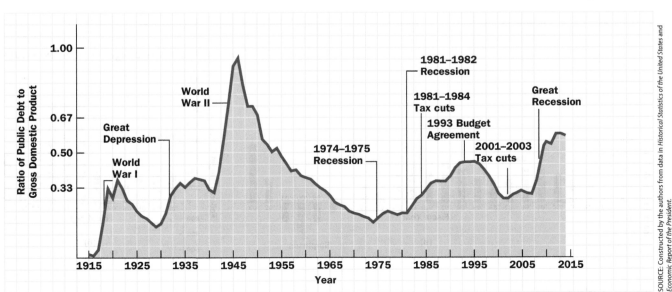

SOURCE: Constructed by the authors from data in *Historical Statistics of the United States* and *Economic Report of the President.*

At that point, however, the government took decisive actions to reduce the budget deficit. The ratio of debt to GDP then fell for nearly a decade, stopped only by President George W. Bush's large tax cuts in 2001. More recent events—especially the huge losses of tax revenue from the Great Recession and the dramatic fiscal policy efforts to fight it—pushed the debt-to-GDP ratio sharply higher again. By about 2010 it had regained, roughly, its value in the 1950s. But since then, policy changes (mostly spending cuts) have stopped the debt-to-GDP ratio from rising further.

## 16-4 INTERPRETING THE BUDGET DEFICIT OR SURPLUS

We have observed that the federal government ran large budget deficits from the early 1980s until the mid-1990s, and then again since the mid-2000s. Figure 5 displays the history. It is split into two panels, with very different scales because deficits measured in dollars have been far larger since 2003 than they were before. (Both panels include 2003.) Panel (a) shows that the federal budget deficit ballooned from just $79 billion in fiscal year 1981 to $208 billion (5.9 percent of GDP) by fiscal year 1983—setting a record at the time. The government managed to turn the budget to surplus during the fiscal years 1998 through 2001, but then large deficits reemerged after the Bush tax cuts. All that was dwarfed, however, by what happened starting in 2008. The federal budget deficits of fiscal years 2009–2012 were enormous, even mind-boggling, averaging almost 8.5 percent of GDP. What do these numbers mean? How should we interpret them?

### 16-4a The Structural Deficit or Surplus

First, it is important to understand that the same fiscal program can lead to a deficit or a surplus, depending on the state of the economy. Failure to appreciate this point has led many people to assume that a larger deficit always signifies a more expansionary fiscal policy—which it does not.

Think, for example, about what happens to the budget during a recession. As GDP falls, the government's major sources of tax revenue—income taxes, corporate taxes, and payroll taxes—all shrink because firms and people pay lower taxes when they earn less. Similarly, some types of government spending, notably transfer payments such as unemployment benefits, rise when GDP falls because more people are out of work. Recall that the deficit is the difference between government expenditures, which are either purchases or transfer payments, and tax receipts:

$$\text{Deficit} = G + \text{Transfers} - \text{Taxes} = G - (\text{Taxes} - \text{Transfers}) = G - T$$

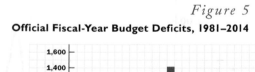

*Figure 5*

**Official Fiscal-Year Budget Deficits, 1981–2014**

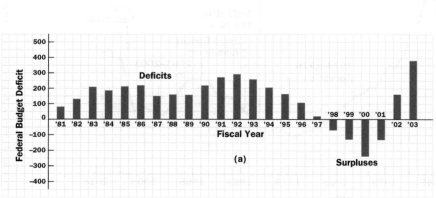

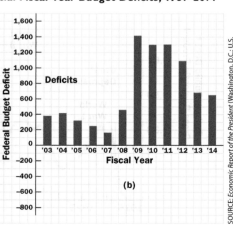

NOTE: Amounts are in billions of dollars.

SOURCE: *Economic Report of the President* (Washington, D.C.: U.S. Government Printing Office, 2015).

Because a falling GDP leads to higher transfer payments and lower tax receipts:

**The deficit rises in a recession and falls in a boom, even with no changes in fiscal policy.**

Figure 6 depicts this relationship between GDP and the budget deficit. The government's fiscal program is summarized by the maroon and blue lines. The horizontal maroon line labeled $G$ indicates that federal purchases of goods and services are approximately unaffected by GDP. The rising blue line labeled $T$ (for taxes minus transfers) indicates that taxes rise and transfer payments fall as GDP rises. Notice that the same fiscal policy (i.e., the same two lines) leads to a large deficit if GDP is $Y_1$, a balanced budget if GDP is $Y_2$, or a surplus if GDP is as high as $Y_3$. Clearly, the deficit itself is not a good measure of the government's fiscal policy.

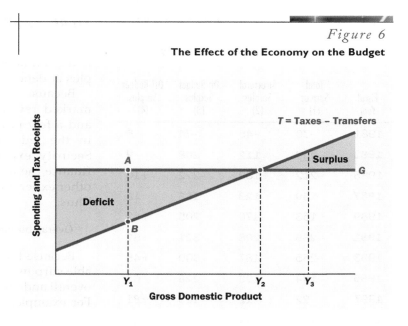

*Figure 6*

**The Effect of the Economy on the Budget**

To seek a better measure, economists pay more attention to what is called the **structural budget deficit or surplus**. This hypothetical measure replaces both the spending and taxes in the *actual* budget by estimates of how much the government *would be* spending and receiving, given current tax rates and expenditure rules, if the economy were operating at some fixed, high-employment level. For example, if the high-employment benchmark in Figure 6 was $Y_2$ and actual GDP was only $Y_1$, the structural deficit would be zero even though the actual deficit would be $AB$.

The **structural budget deficit or surplus** is the hypothetical deficit or surplus we *would have* under current fiscal policies if the economy were operating near full employment.

Because it is based on the spending and taxing the government *would be* doing at some fixed level of GDP, rather than on *actual* expenditures and receipts, the structural deficit does not depend on the state of the economy. It changes *only* when policy changes, *not* when GDP changes. For that reason, most economists view it as a better measure of the thrust of fiscal policy than the actual deficit.

This new concept helps us understand the changing nature of the large budget deficits of the 1980s, the stunning turn to surpluses in the late 1990s, and the amazing swing back to large deficits since 2008. The first two columns of data in Table 1 show both the actual surplus and the structural surplus every other year since 1981. (Most of the numbers are negative, indicating *deficits*.) Because of recessions in 1983 and 1991, the actual deficit was far larger than the structural deficit in those years. But the difference between the two was small in 1989 and 1997, when the economy was near full employment, and then changed sign (i.e., the structural surplus was *smaller* than the actual surplus) in 1999 and 2001.

Several interesting facts stand out when we compare the numbers in the first and second columns. First, even though the *official* deficit fell between fiscal 1983 and fiscal 1995, the *structural* deficit grew slightly—despite years of allegedly "tight" budgets. This trend toward larger structural deficits alarmed keen observers of the federal budget. Second, the $381 billion swing in the budget deficit from 1993 to 1999 (from a deficit of $255 billion to a *surplus* of $126 billion) far exceeded the change in the structural deficit, which fell by "only" $236 billion. This last number, which is still impressive, is a better indicator of how much fiscal policy changed during the period.

Third, the movement from a modest-sized structural *surplus* in 2001 to a large structural *deficit* in 2003, due mainly to the Bush tax cuts, was both rapid and huge. Then, while the Great Recession opened up a yawning gap between the actual and structural deficits ($350 billion in 2009), the structural deficit itself soared to more than $1 trillion as the government spent huge sums to fight the recession. Finally, between 2009 and 2013, both the actual and the structural deficit fell substantially.

## Table 1

### Alternative Budget Concepts, 1981–2013

| Fiscal Year | Total Surplus (1) | Structural Surplus (2) | On-Budget Surplus (3) | Off-Budget Surplus (4) |
|---|---|---|---|---|
| 1981 | −79 | −45 | −74 | −5 |
| 1983 | −208 | −112 | −208 | 0 |
| 1985 | −212 | −189 | −222 | +10 |
| 1987 | −150 | −129 | −168 | +18 |
| 1989 | −153 | −170 | −205 | +52 |
| 1991 | −269 | −208 | −321 | +52 |
| 1993 | −255 | −187 | −300 | +45 |
| 1995 | −164 | −123 | −226 | +62 |
| 1997 | −22 | −12 | −103 | +81 |
| 1999 | +126 | +49 | +2 | +124 |
| 2001 | +128 | +62 | −32 | +160 |
| 2003 | −378 | −301 | −538 | +160 |
| 2005 | −318 | −327 | −494 | +176 |
| 2007 | −161 | −182 | −342 | +181 |
| 2009 | −1,413 | −1,063 | −1,550 | +137 |
| 2011 | −1,300 | −891 | −1,367 | +67 |
| 2013 | −680 | −423 | −719 | +39 |

NOTE: Amounts are in billions of dollars.

SOURCE: Congressional Budget Office.

## 16-4b On-Budget versus Off-Budget Surpluses

When you read about the budget, you sometimes see references to the "off-budget" surplus or deficit and the "on-budget" surplus or deficit. What do those terms mean?

Because Social Security benefits are financed by an earmarked revenue source—the payroll tax—Social Security and a few minor items have traditionally been segregated in the federal fiscal accounts. Specifically, both Social Security expenditures and the payroll tax receipts that finance them are treated as off-budget items, whereas most other expenditures and receipts are classified as on-budget. Thus:

Overall budget deficit = Off-budget deficit + On-budget deficit

Because the Social Security System had been running sizable surpluses until very recently, the difference between the overall and on-budget deficits was substantial for many years. For example, in fiscal year 2007, the overall budget showed just a $161 billion deficit (column 1 of Table 1). But this was composed of a much-larger $342 billion on-budget *deficit* (column 3) less a $181 billion Social Security *surplus* (column 4). By 2013, you can see, the off-budget surplus had shrunk to just $39 billion, and it is now virtually gone.

Some people claim that such a discrepancy between on- and off-budget deficits means that the Social Security surplus has been hiding the "true" deficit. That's a matter of semantics. Nothing is hidden; the facts given in Table 1 are public and widely known. But you need to interpret them correctly. If you are interested in knowing how much the federal government must borrow each year, the *total* deficit (column 1) is the number you want.

## 16-4c Conclusion: What Happened to the Deficit?

Table 1 helps us understand the remarkable ups and downs of the federal budget deficit since the early 1980s. Column 1 shows the overall surplus (if positive) or deficit (if negative) every other year from 1981 to 2013, and column 2 shows the corresponding *structural* surplus. Finally, columns 3 and 4 break the overall surplus into its *on-budget* and *off-budget* components. The table tells the following story about the evolution of the budget deficit.

The large Reagan tax cuts in the early 1980s ballooned the budget deficit from $79 billion to $212 billion, and more than 100 percent of this deterioration was structural (see column 2). Late in the 1980s, the deficit started rising again—even though Social Security began to run small surpluses (see column 4). The overall deficit reached $269 billion in 1991, but then began to shrink. One reason was the burgeoning Social Security surplus, which increased by $115 billion between 1993 and 2001. The strong economy helped, too. Notice that the actual surplus rose much more than the structural surplus. But most of the deficit-reducing "work" was on-budget and structural, as tax increases and expenditure restraint during the Clinton years finally got the budget under control—briefly, as it turned out.

During the George W. Bush administration, a combination of large tax cuts, a burst of spending, and weaker economic growth pushed the deficit up to a new record high of $378 billion in fiscal year 2003. But both the actual and structural deficits receded sharply by 2007. The recession started late in 2007 and the rest, as they say, is history. The depressed economy plus the Obama administration's massive anti-recession measures teamed up to produce a colossal $1.4 trillion deficit in 2009, three-quarters of which was structural. Such large numbers had previously been unimaginable. But considerable progress in bringing the deficit down has been made since then. Lately, the federal budget deficit has been running around 3 percent of GDP, which is close to the historical average.

## 16-5  WHY IS THE NATIONAL DEBT CONSIDERED A BURDEN?

Now that we have gained some perspective on the facts, let us consider the charge that budget deficits place intolerable burdens on future generations. Perhaps the most frequently heard reason is that *future Americans will be burdened by heavy interest payments*, which will necessitate higher taxes. But think about who will receive those interest payments: mostly the future Americans who own the bonds. Thus, one group of future Americans will be making interest payments to another group of future Americans—which cannot be a burden on the nation as a whole.[4]

However, there *is* a future burden to the extent that U.S. debt is held by foreigners. The share of our net national debt owned by foreign individuals, businesses, and governments has been rising over the years and is now well above 50 percent. Paying interest on this portion of the debt will indeed burden future Americans in a very concrete way: For years to come, a portion of America's GDP will be sent abroad to pay interest on the debts we incurred in previous years. For this reason, many thoughtful observers are becoming concerned that the United States is borrowing too much from abroad.[5] Thus, we conclude that

> **If the national debt is owned by domestic citizens, future interest payments just transfer funds from one group of Americans to another. However, the portion of the national debt owned by foreigners does constitute a burden on the nation as a whole.**

Many people also worry that every nation has a limited capacity to borrow, just like every family and every business. If it exceeds this limit, it is in danger of being unable to pay its creditors and may go bankrupt—with calamitous consequences for everyone. For many countries, this concern is indeed valid and serious. For example, debt crises have done major damage to countries in Latin America, Asia, and Africa over the years. In this decade, even European countries such as Greece, Ireland, Portugal, and Spain have faced actual or potential debt crises that called the stability of the euro area into question. And, Argentina defaulted on some of its debt in 2014.

But the U.S. government need not worry about defaulting on its debt for one simple reason. *The American national debt is an obligation to pay U.S. dollars:* Each debt certificate obligates the Treasury to pay the holder so many U.S. dollars on a prescribed date. But think about where those dollars come from. The U.S. government—specifically the Federal Reserve—prints them up! So in the worst case, if the U.S. government had no better way to pay off its creditors, it could always print whatever money it needed to do so. In a word, *no nation need default on debts that call for repayment in its own currency.*[6]

However, printing the necessary money is not an option for other countries whose debts call for payment in U.S. dollars, as a number of Southeast Asian countries learned in 1997 and as Argentina learned in 2001 and again in 2014. Nor is it an option for individual members of the euro zone because the European Central Bank (ECB), not the government of any member country, controls the volume of euros. When Greece first ran into debt trouble in the spring of 2010, for example, printing euros was not an option.

---

[4] However, the future taxes that will have to be raised to pay the interest may reduce the efficiency of the economy.

[5] We will discuss the linkages between the federal budget deficit and foreign borrowing in greater detail in Chapter 20.

[6] However, Russia astounded the financial world in 1998 by *choosing* to default on its ruble-denominated debt.

It does not, of course, follow that acquiring more debt through budget deficits is necessarily a good idea for the United States. Sometimes, it is clearly a bad idea. Nonetheless:

> **There is a fundamental difference between nations that borrow in their own currency (such as the United States) and nations that borrow in some other currency (which is often the U.S. dollar). The former need never default on their debts; the latter might have to.**

The U.S. government does, however, have a limit on how much debt it can have outstanding at any point in time. Congress imposes a legal *ceiling* on the amount of debt the Treasury is allowed to issue, raising that limit from time to time as deficits push the national debt up closer to the ceiling. The debt limit *must* be raised periodically as long as the deficit is positive because *any* positive deficit makes the debt grow. If the debt ceiling is not raised when necessary, the United States could be thrown into technical default on its legal obligations. But sometimes a political volcano erupts when a vote to raise the national debt ceiling comes up. (See the box "Raising the National Debt Ceiling.")

## 16-6 BUDGET DEFICITS AND INFLATION

We now turn to the effects of deficits on macroeconomic outcomes. It often is said that deficit spending causes inflation. Let us consider that argument with the aid of the standard aggregate supply-and-demand diagram in Figure 7.

Initially, equilibrium is at point $A$, where demand curve $D_0D_0$ and supply curve $SS$ intersect. Output is $7,000 billion, and the price index is 100. In the diagram, the aggregate demand and supply curves intersect precisely at potential GDP, indicating

## Raising the National Debt Ceiling

As we have mentioned, Congress must raise the national debt ceiling from time to time. Otherwise, the U.S. Treasury would lose the legal authority to borrow money, and the government would virtually shut down. But because Americans don't like a rising national debt, this is a difficult vote for many members of Congress. Some simply refuse to vote for it—and normally that's a harmless gesture because the bill passes easily.

But now and then, when the White House and Congress are controlled by different parties, partisan warfare breaks out. One such example came in 1995, when Bill Clinton was president. Republican Speaker of the House Newt Gingrich (R–GA) actually precipitated a partial shutdown of the U.S. government when neither side "blinked" in negotiations to trim the deficit. The shutdown provoked a public uproar that damaged Republicans politically.

More recently, raising the national debt ceiling turned into a major and recurring political issue as House Republicans decided to protest what they saw as President Obama's profligate budget policies by refusing to raise the debt limit. In 2011, the House, led by Speaker John Boehner (R–OH), balked at raising the limit until, literally, *after* the last minute. The stalemate was finally broken by an agreement in early August, but the process was so messy that it led to the first-ever downgrade of the U.S. government's credit rating.

The bickering got worse in 2013, when there were several near-collisions with the debt ceiling, each one averted by a gimmick or a stopgap measure, until the continued political wrangling led to a shutdown of many U.S. government functions in October. The politics of the government shutdown once again proved to be terrible for the Republicans, who agreed to end it after about two weeks. But the debt ceiling issue wasn't "settled" until February 2014. The word "settled" is in quotes, however, because the issue will never truly be settled as long as we have a budget deficit and a ceiling on the national debt—which, by the laws of arithmetic, must grow each year.

that the economy is operating at full employment. Let us also assume that the budget is initially balanced.

Now suppose the government raises spending or cuts taxes enough to shift the aggregate demand schedule outward from $D_0D_0$ to $D_1D_1$. Equilibrium shifts from point A to point B, and the graph shows the price level rising from 100 to 106, or 6 percent. But that is not the end of the story, because point B represents an inflationary gap. We know from previous chapters that inflation will continue until the aggregate supply curve shifts far enough inward that it passes through point C, at which point the inflationary gap is gone. In this example, deficit spending will eventually raise the price level 12 percent.

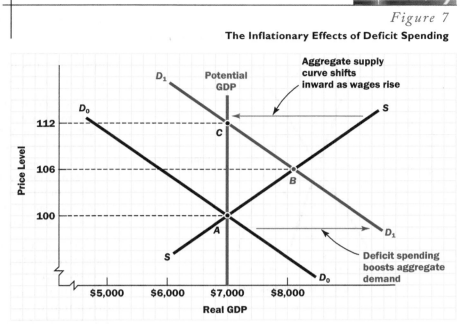

*Figure 7*

**The Inflationary Effects of Deficit Spending**

NOTE: Real GDP amounts are in billions of dollars.

Thus, the cries that budget deficits are inflationary have the ring of truth. How much truth they hold depends on several factors. One is the slope of the aggregate supply curve. Figure 7 clearly shows that a steep supply curve would lead to more inflation than a flat one. A second factor is the degree of resource utilization. Deficit spending is more inflationary in a fully-employed economy (such as that depicted in Figure 7) than in an economy with lots of slack.

Finally, we must remember that the Federal Reserve's monetary policy can always cancel out any potential inflationary effects of deficit spending by pulling the aggregate demand curve back to its original position. Once again, the *policy mix* is crucial.

## 16-6a The Monetization Issue

Will the Federal Reserve always neutralize the expansionary effect of a higher budget deficit? This question brings up another reason why some people worry about the inflationary consequences of deficits. They fear that the Federal Reserve may feel compelled to "monetize" part of the deficit by purchasing some of the newly issued government debt. Let us explain, first, why the Fed might make such purchases and, second, why these purchases are called **monetizing the deficit**.

Deficit spending, we have just noted, normally drives up both real GDP and the price level. As we emphasized earlier in this chapter, such an economic expansion would shift the demand curve for bank reserves outward to the right—as depicted by the movement from $D_0D_0$ to $D_1D_1$ in Figure 2. That diagram shows that, if the Federal Reserve took no action to shift the supply curve, interest rates would rise as equilibrium moves from point $E_0$ to point $E_1$.

Suppose now that the Fed does not want interest rates to rise. What can it do? To prevent the incipient rise in r, it would have to engage in *expansionary monetary policy* that creates new bank reserves, thereby shifting the supply curve for reserves outward to the right—as indicated in Figure 8. With the maroon supply curve $S_1S_1$, equilibrium would be at point C rather than at point B, leaving interest rates unchanged. Because the Federal Reserve usually pursues expansionary monetary policy by purchasing Treasury bills in the open market, deficit spending might therefore induce the Fed to buy more government debt.

The central bank is said to **monetize the deficit** when it purchases bonds issued by the government.

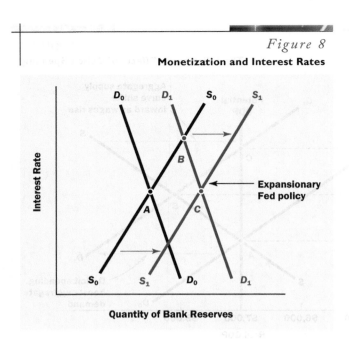

*Figure 8*

**Monetization and Interest Rates**

Interest Rate

$D_0$  $D_1$  $S_0$  $S_1$

B

A  C

← Expansionary Fed policy

$S_0$  $S_1$  $D_0$  $D_1$

**Quantity of Bank Reserves**

But why is this process called *monetizing* the deficit? The reason is simple. As we learned in Chapter 12, creating more bank reserves generally leads, via the multiple expansion process, to an increase in the money supply. By this indirect route, then, larger budget deficits may lead to a larger money supply. To summarize:

> If the Federal Reserve takes no countervailing actions, an expansionary fiscal policy that increases the budget deficit will raise real GDP and prices, thereby raising the demand for bank reserves and driving up interest rates (Figure 2). If the Fed does not want interest rates to rise, it can engage in expansionary open-market operations; that is, it can purchase more government debt. If the Fed does so, both bank reserves and the money supply will increase (Figure 8). In this case, we say that part of the deficit is *monetized*.

Monetized deficits are more inflationary than non-monetized deficits for the simple reason that expansionary monetary and fiscal policies *together* are more inflationary than expansionary fiscal policy *alone*. But is this a real worry? Does the Fed actually monetize any substantial portion of the deficit? Normally, it does not. The clearest evidence is the fact that the Fed managed to *reduce* inflation in the 1980s, and again in the early 2010s, even as the government ran huge budget deficits. But over the years, monetization of deficits *has* been a serious cause of inflation in many other countries, ranging from Latin America to Russia, Israel, Zimbabwe, and elsewhere.

## 16-7 DEBT, INTEREST RATES, AND CROWDING OUT

So far, we have looked for possible problems that the national debt might cause on the *demand* side of the economy, but the real worry comes on the *supply* side. In brief, large budget deficits discourage investment and thereby retard the growth of the nation's capital stock.

The mechanism is easy to understand by presuming (as is generally the case) that the Fed does not engage in any substantial monetization. In that case, as we have just seen, budget deficits tend to *raise* interest rates. We know from earlier chapters that the rate of interest ($r$) is a major determinant of investment spending ($I$). In particular, higher $r$ leads to less $I$. Lower investment today, in turn, means that the nation will have less capital tomorrow, so the size of *potential* GDP will be smaller. This, according to most economists, is the true sense in which a larger national debt may burden future generations—and, conversely, a smaller national debt may help them.

> A larger national debt can lead a nation to bequeath less capital to future generations. If they inherit less plant and equipment, these generations will be burdened by a smaller productive capacity—a lower potential GDP. By that mechanism, large deficits can retard economic growth. By the same logic, budget surpluses can stimulate capital formation and spur economic growth.

**Crowding out** occurs when deficit spending by the government forces private investment spending to contract.

Phrasing this point another way explains why it is often called the **crowding-out** effect. Consider what happens in financial markets when the government engages in deficit spending. If it spends more than it takes in, the government must borrow the rest. It does so by selling bonds, which compete with corporate bonds and other financial instruments for the available supply of funds. As some savers decide to buy government bonds, the funds remaining to invest in private bonds shrink. Thus, some private borrowers get "crowded out" of the financial markets as the government claims an increasing share of the economy's saving.

Some critics of deficit spending have taken this lesson to its illogical extreme by arguing that each \$1 of government spending crowds out exactly \$1 of private spending, leaving "expansionary" fiscal policy with no net effect on total demand. In their view, when $G$ rises, $I$ falls by an equal amount, leaving the total of $C + I + G + (X - IM)$ unchanged. Under normal circumstances, we would not expect this to occur. Why? First, moderate budget deficits push up interest rates only slightly. Second, private spending is only moderately sensitive to interest rates. Even at the higher interest rates that government deficits cause, most corporations will continue to borrow to finance their capital investments.

Furthermore, in times of economic slack, a counterforce arises that might be called the **crowding-in** effect. Deficit spending presumably quickens the pace of economic activity. That, at least, is its purpose. As the economy expands, businesses find it more profitable to add to their capacity in order to meet greater consumer demand. Because of this *induced investment,* as we called it in earlier chapters, an increase in $G$ may *increase* investment, rather than *decrease* it as the crowding-out hypothesis predicts.

**Crowding in** occurs when government spending, by raising real GDP, induces increases in private investment spending.

The strength of the crowding-in effect depends on how much additional real GDP is stimulated by government spending (i.e., on the size of the multiplier) and on how sensitive investment spending is to the improved business opportunities that accompany rapid growth. It is even conceivable that the crowding-in effect could dominate the crowding-out effect in the short run, so that $I$ rises, on balance, when $G$ rises.

But how can this be true in view of the crowding-out argument? Certainly, if the government borrows more *and the total volume of private saving is fixed,* then private industry must borrow less. That's just arithmetic. The fallacy in the strict crowding-out argument lies in supposing that the economy's flow of saving is really fixed. If government deficits succeed in raising output, we will have more income and therefore more saving. In that way, *both* government *and* industry can borrow more.

Which effect dominates—crowding out or crowding in? Crowding *out* stems from the increases in interest rates caused by deficits, whereas crowding *in* derives from the faster real economic growth that deficits typically produce. In the short run, the crowding-in effect—which results from the outward shift of the aggregate demand curve—is often the more powerful, especially when the economy is at less than full employment.

*"Would you mind explaining again how high interest rates and the national deficit affect my allowance?"*

From *The Wall Street Journal*—Permission, Cartoon Features Syndicate

In the long run, however, the supply side dominates because, as we have learned, the economy's self-correcting mechanism pushes actual GDP toward potential GDP. When the economy is approximately at potential, the crowding-out effect takes over: Higher interest rates lead to less investment, causing the capital stock and potential GDP to grow more slowly. Turned on its head, this is the basic long-run argument for reducing the budget deficit: Smaller budget deficits should raise investment and speed up the growth of potential GDP.

## 16-7a The Bottom Line

Let us summarize what we have learned so far about the crowding-out controversy.

- The basic argument of the crowding-out hypothesis is sound: *Unless the economy produces enough additional saving,* more government borrowing will force out some private borrowers, who are discouraged by the higher interest rates. This process will reduce investment spending and cancel out some of the expansionary effects of higher government spending.

- Crowding out is rarely strong enough to cancel out the *entire* expansionary thrust of government spending. Some net stimulus to the economy remains.

- If deficit spending induces substantial GDP growth, then the crowding-in effect will lead to more income *and* more saving—perhaps so much more that private industry can borrow *more* than it did previously, despite the increase in government borrowing.

- The crowding-out effect is likely to dominate in the long run or when the economy is operating near full employment. The crowding-in effect is likely to dominate in the short run, especially when the economy has a great deal of slack.

## 16-8 THE MAIN BURDEN OF THE NATIONAL DEBT: SLOWER GROWTH

This analysis of crowding out versus crowding in helps us understand whether or not the national debt imposes a burden on future generations:

> When government budget deficits take place in a high-employment economy, the crowding-out effect probably dominates. So deficits exact a toll by leaving a smaller capital stock, and hence lower potential GDP, to future generations. However, deficits in an economy with high unemployment may well lead to more investment rather than less. In this case, the crowding-in effect dominates and deficit spending increases growth. The new debt is therefore a blessing rather than a burden.

Which case applies to the U.S. national debt? To answer this question, let us go back to the historical facts and recall how we accumulated all that debt prior to the 1980s. The first cause was the financing of wars, especially World War II. Because this debt was contracted in a fully employed economy, it undoubtedly constituted a burden in the formal sense of the term. After all, the bombs, ships, and planes that it financed were used up in the war, not bequeathed as capital to future generations.

Yet today's Americans may not feel terribly burdened by the decisions of those in power in the 1940s, for consider the alternatives. We could have financed the entire war by taxation and thus placed the burden on consumption rather than on investment. But that choice would truly have been ruinous, and probably impossible, given the colossal wartime expenditures. Alternatively, we could have printed money, which would have unleashed an inflation that nobody wanted. Finally, the government could have spent much less money and perhaps not have won the war. Compared to those alternatives, Americans of subsequent generations probably have not felt burdened by the massive deficit spending undertaken in the 1940s.

A second major contributor to the national debt prior to 1983 was a series of recessions. But these are precisely the circumstances under which budget deficits might prove to be a blessing rather than a burden. So it was only in the 1980s that we began to have the type of deficits that are truly burdensome—deficits acquired in a fully employed, peacetime economy.

This sharp departure from historical norms is what made those budget deficits worrisome. The tax cuts of 1981–1984 blew a large hole in the government budget, and the recession of 1981–1982 ballooned the deficit even further. By the late 1980s, the U.S. economy had recovered to full employment, but a structural deficit of $100–$150 billion per year remained. This persistent deficit was something that had never happened before. Such large structural deficits posed a real threat of crowding out and constituted a serious potential burden on future generations.

After a brief interlude of budget surpluses in the late 1990s, large structural deficits reemerged in the early 2000s, caused by a combination of large tax cuts and rapid spending growth. By 2007, that deficit problem, too, seemed under control. But then came the Great Recession, and the government's strenuous efforts to contain it, and the budget ballooned to unheard-of heights. At the time if this writing, with budget deficits around 3 percent of GDP, the debt-to-GDP ratio has been successfully stabilized. But many economists and budget analysts remain worried about what the future might bring.

Let us now summarize our evaluation of the actual burden of the U.S. national debt:

- The national debt will not lead the nation into bankruptcy, but it does impose a burden on future generations to the extent that it is sold to foreigners or contracted in a fully employed, peacetime economy. In the latter case, it will reduce the nation's capital stock.

- Under some circumstances, budget deficits are appropriate for stabilization-policy purposes.

- Until the 1980s, the actual public debt of the U.S. government was mostly contracted as a result of wars and recessions—precisely the circumstances under which new debt does not constitute a burden. However, the large deficits of the 1980s and early 2000s were not mainly attributable to recessions and were therefore worrisome.

- The gigantic budget deficits of recent years are mostly attributable to the Great Recession and the fiscal actions designed to fight it. So they should not constitute a burden in the usual sense. However, it is important that the budget deficit shrink as the economy returns to full employment.

---

**Issue Revisited** | *Is the Budget Deficit Still Too Large?*

We are now in a position to address the issues posed at the beginning of this chapter: Is the federal budget deficit too large? Must it be reduced quickly? To tackle these questions, we need to understand how and why fiscal policy changed, and we need to distinguish between the short-run (demand side) and long-run (supply side) effects of budget deficits.

The deficit was actually fairly small, relative to the size of the economy, in fiscal year 2007—about 1.1 percent of GDP. (See Table 1.) Then the Great Recession struck, and the deficit soared to an amazing $1.4 billion (nearly 10 percent of GDP) by fiscal 2009. In dollar terms, that shattered all records. And as a share of GDP, it was the largest deficit this country had seen since World War II. How did this happen? Three main factors contributed.

One was the depth of the Great Recession, which was the worst since the 1930s. With GDP so far below potential, it was natural for the budget to swing toward larger deficits—for reasons emphasized in this chapter (see, especially, Figure 6). And it did. We saw in Table 1 that the cyclical component of the deficit rose from about –$20 billion in 2007 to $350 in 2009. Most of that increase in the deficit came from lower tax receipts.

The second major factor was the extraordinary spending and lending the U.S. government did to limit the financial collapse and assist the recovery. The largest and most prominent part of the government's comprehensive financial rescue was the $700 billion *Troubled Assets Relief Program* (TARP) that we discussed in Chapter 14. It was not the only part, though. The rescue operations were and remain highly controversial. But no one disputes the fact that they made the budget deficit larger for a while.[7]

Third came the $800 billion-plus fiscal stimulus package that Congress enacted in February 2009, just one month into the new Obama administration. The package consisted of tax cuts and increased government expenditures designed to boost aggregate demand and, thereby, to limit the severity of the recession and assist the recovery. The stimulus package was also controversial, but again, everyone recognizes that it raised the deficit substantially.

Congress and the president agreed on yet another large package of tax cuts in December 2010. Then, in an eleventh-hour agreement in early January 2013, they agreed to make the Bush tax cuts of 2002–2003 permanent for all but the richest Americans. Those were the fiscal policies. What were their effects?

In the short run, aggregate demand factors dominate economic performance, and the stimulus from both higher spending and tax cuts provided an expansionary force just when the economy needed one. Moving to much larger deficits probably cushioned the recession and sped up the recovery by boosting aggregate demand, as shown in Figure 9.

In the long run, however, output gravitates toward potential GDP, no matter what happens to aggregate demand. So

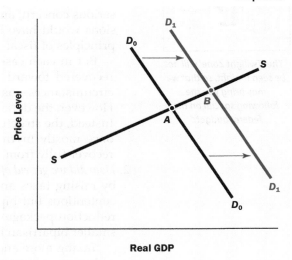

*Figure 9*

**The Short-Run Effect of Larger Deficits or Smaller Surpluses**

---

[7] Most of the government's money has already been returned, and more will be. Current estimates show very small net costs—perhaps even a net profit.

*Figure 10*

**The Long-Run Effect of Larger Deficits or Smaller Surpluses**

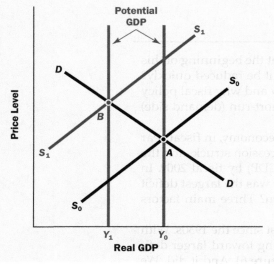

aggregate supply eventually rules the roost. And that is where the long-run costs of fiscal stimulus emerge. Larger budget deficits lead to higher real interest rates and hence to lower levels of private investment. That makes the nation's capital stock grow more slowly, thereby retarding the growth rate of potential GDP. This slower growth is depicted in Figure 10, which shows large budget deficits leading to a potential GDP of $Y_1$ instead of $Y_0$ in the future. With the same aggregate demand curve, *DD*, the result is lower real GDP.

So, on balance, were the large fiscal deficits of 2008–2013 appropriate? Most, but not all, economists would say yes. In those years, the economy clearly needed a lot of *short-run* stimulus. As the economy recovers, mammoth deficits may start to crowd out some investment spending, however. And that, in turn, would slow down the economy's potential growth in the *long run*. For that reason, thoughtful proponents of fiscal stimulus wanted to ensure that any new spending programs or tax cuts were temporary; and opponents of stimulus wanted to keep the package small.

But almost everyone agrees that the United States still has a long-run deficit problem that must be addressed. Very recently, the debt-to-GDP ratio has been stabilized; so the red flag is down. But as Social Security and Medicare expenses for the baby boom generation mount in the coming years, the debt-to-GDP ratio may start rising again. The story is not over.

## 16-9 THE ECONOMICS AND POLITICS OF THE U.S. BUDGET DEFICIT

Given what we have learned in this chapter about the theory and facts of budget deficits, we can now address some of the major issues that have been debated in the political arena for years.

From *The Wall Street Journal*—Permission, Cartoon Features Syndicate

*"The 'Twilight Zone' will not be seen tonight, so that we may bring you the following special on the federal budget."*

1. *Were the deficits of the 1980s, 1990s, and 2000s a problem?* In 1981–1982, 1990–1991, and again in 2001, the U.S. economy suffered through recessions. And after 2007, the economy grew very weak again. Under such circumstances, crowding out is not a serious concern, and actions to close the deficit during or right after these recessions would have threatened the subsequent recoveries. According to the basic principles of fiscal policy, large deficits were appropriate in each case.

   But in each case, crowding out became a more serious issue as the economy recovered toward full employment. Budget deficits should decline under such circumstances—as they did in the 1990s, again from 2004 to 2007, and since 2011. However, the deficit did not fall in the 1980s, nor in the period from 2002 to 2004. Instead, the structural deficit rose. Worries about the burden of the national debt, once mostly myths, became all too realistic then, as they may again once we recover fully from the Great Recession.

2. *How did we get rid of the deficit in the 1990s?* In part, we did it the old-fashioned way: by raising taxes and reducing spending in three not-so-easy steps. There was a contentious but bipartisan budget agreement in 1990, a highly partisan deficit-reduction package in 1993 (that passed without a single Republican vote), and a smaller bipartisan budget deal in 1997.

   Taxing more and spending less constitutes contractionary fiscal policy, which reduces aggregate demand. However, this effect did not hurt the U.S. economy in the 1990s because fiscal and monetary policies were well coordinated. If fiscal policy turns contractionary to reduce the deficit, monetary policy can turn expansionary to counteract the effects on aggregate demand. In this way, we can hope to shrink the deficit without shrinking the economy. As argued earlier in this chapter, such a change in the *policy mix* should also bring down interest rates, because both tighter budgets and easier money tend to have that effect. Indeed, that is just what happened in the 1990s. Interest rates fell, and the Fed made sure that aggregate demand was sufficient to keep the economy growing.

In addition, surprisingly rapid economic growth in the late 1990s generated much more tax revenue than anyone thought likely only a few years earlier. And the so-called off-budget surplus also increased. Both of these developments helped the federal budget turn rapidly from deficit into surplus.

3. *How did the surplus give way to such large deficits so rapidly in the 2000s?* As we have noted, the answer came in three parts under President George W. Bush: recession, tax cuts, and higher levels of spending, especially on national defense, homeland security, and Medicare. It is hardly a mystery that sharply rising expenditures and rapidly falling revenue pushed the budget from the black into the red. Then the budget situation got much worse under President Obama for reasons we have discussed: The economy deteriorated, and the government did what it could—at great expense—to stop the slide into recession.

4. *What are the future prospects for the federal budget deficit?* According to an old adage, one thing you should never try to predict is the future; it will certainly hold some surprises for us. One thing we know for sure is that more and more baby boomers, people born after 1946, will reach the magic age of 65—making them eligible for Medicare and, soon thereafter, for full Social Security benefits. This factor alone will push federal spending higher unless Congress enacts future tax increases or cuts promised benefits. On the other hand, medical care costs have risen far slower over the last five-to-seven years than previous predictions had projected—which is certainly good news for the long-run deficit. Will this moderation in health-care costs continue? Nobody really knows.

## Summary

1. Rigid adherence to budget balancing would make the economy less stable, by reducing aggregate demand (via tax increases and reductions in government spending) when private spending is low and by raising aggregate demand when private spending is high.

2. Because both monetary and fiscal policy influence aggregate demand, the appropriate **budget deficit** or **surplus** depends on monetary policy. Similarly, the appropriate monetary policy depends on budget policy.

3. The same level of aggregate demand can be generated by more than one **mix of fiscal and monetary policy**, but the composition of GDP will be different in each case. Larger budget deficits and tighter money tend to produce higher interest rates, a smaller share of investment in GDP, and slower growth. Smaller budget deficits and looser monetary policy lead to a larger investment share and faster growth.

4. One major reason for the large budget deficits of the early 1980s, early 1990s, and now is the fact that the economy operated well below full employment. In those years, the **structural deficit**, which uses estimates of what the government's receipts and outlays would be at full employment to correct for business-cycle fluctuations, was much smaller than the actual deficit.

5. The need to make future interest payments on the public debt is a burden only to the extent that the national debt is owned by foreigners.

6. The argument that a large **national debt** can bankrupt a country like the United States ignores the fact that our national debt consists entirely of obligations to pay U.S. dollars—a currency that the government can raise by increasing taxes or create by printing money.

7. Budget deficits can be inflationary because they expand aggregate demand. They are even more inflationary if they are **monetized**—that is, if the central bank buys some of the newly issued government debt in the open market.

8. Unless the deficit is substantially monetized, deficit spending forces interest rates higher and discourages private investment spending. This process is called the **crowding-out effect**. If a great deal of crowding out occurs, then deficits impose a serious burden on future generations by leaving them a smaller capital stock with which to work.

9. Higher government spending (G) may also produce a **crowding-in effect**. If expansionary fiscal policy succeeds in raising real output (Y), more investment will be induced by the higher Y.

10. Whether crowding out or crowding in dominates largely depends on the time horizon. In the short run, and especially when unemployment is high, crowding in is probably the stronger force, so higher $G$ does not cause lower investment. But, in the long run, the economy will be near full employment, and the proponents of the crowding-out hypothesis will be right: High government spending will mainly displace private investment.

11. Larger deficits may spur growth (via aggregate demand) in the short run but deter growth (via aggregate supply and potential GDP) in the long run.

12. Whether or not deficits create a burden depends on how and why the government incurred the deficits in the first place. If the government runs deficits to fight recessions, more investment may be crowded in by rising output than is crowded out by rising interest rates. Deficits contracted to carry on wars certainly impair the future capital stock, although they may not be considered a burden for noneconomic reasons. Because these two cases account for most of the debt the U.S. government contracted until the mid-1980s, that debt cannot reasonably be considered a serious burden. However, some of the deficits since 1984 are more worrisome on this score.

## Key Terms

budget deficit   320

budget surplus   320

crowding in   329

crowding out   328

monetizing the deficit   327

national debt   320

structural budget deficit or surplus   323

## Test Yourself

1. Explain the difference between the budget deficit and the national debt. If the deficit gets turned into a surplus, what happens to the debt?

2. Explain in words why the *structural* budget might show a surplus while the *actual* budget is in deficit. Illustrate your answer with a diagram like Figure 6.

3. If the Federal Reserve lowers interest rates, what will happen to the government budget deficit? (*Hint:* What will happen to tax receipts and interest expenses?) If the government wants to offset the effects of the Fed's actions on aggregate demand, what might it do? How will this action affect the deficit?

## Discussion Questions

1. Explain how the U.S. government managed to accumulate a debt of more than $18 trillion. To whom does it owe this debt? Is the debt a burden on future generations?

2. Comment on the following: "Deficit spending paves the road to ruin. If we keep it up, the whole nation will go bankrupt. Even if things do not go this far, what right have we to burden our children and grandchildren with these debts while we live high on the hog?"

3. Newspaper reports frequently suggest that the administration (regardless of who is president) wants the Fed

to lower interest rates. In view of your answer to Test Yourself Question 3, why do you think that might be the case?

4. Explain the difference between crowding out and crowding in. Given the current state of the economy, which effect would you expect to dominate today?

5. Given the current state of the economy, what sort of fiscal-monetary policy mix seems most appropriate to you now? (*Note:* There is no one correct answer to this question. It is a good question to discuss in class.)

*We must seek to reduce inflation at a lower cost in lost output and unemployment.*

JIMMY CARTER

Try putting yourself in the shoes of Federal Reserve Chair Janet Yellen as the Fed backs away from the hyper-expansionary monetary policies it has been pursuing since 2008. Critics are telling you that the Fed's current monetary policy stance will eventually push inflation up, so you'd better tighten up quickly. But you know that any tightening of monetary policy will slow the growth of aggregate demand. Two things you would like to know are how much your actions are likely to slow down real GDP growth, and hence limit the decline in unemployment, and how much they are likely to reduce inflation.

We first encountered the idea that monetary policy normally moves unemployment and inflation in opposite directions in the short run as part of our list of *Ideas for Beyond the Final Exam* in Chapter 1. Back then, we noted that there is a bothersome *trade-off between inflation and unemployment*: High-growth policies that reduce unemployment tend to raise inflation, and slow-growth policies that reduce inflation tend to raise unemployment. We subsequently observed, in Chapter 15, that the trade-off looks rather different in the short run than in the long run because the aggregate supply curve is fairly flat in the short run but quite steep (or vertical) in the long run. A statistical relationship called the *Phillips curve* seeks to summarize the quantitative dimensions of the trade-off between inflation and unemployment in both the short and long runs. This chapter is about the Phillips curve; that is, it is about one of the things that Janet Yellen is wondering about right now.

## CONTENTS

| Issue | *Is the Trade-Off between Inflation and Unemployment a Relic of the Past?* |
|---|---|

In the late 1990s, unemployment in the United States fell to extremely low levels—the lowest in 30 years. Yet, in stark contrast to prior experience, inflation did not rise. This pleasant conjunction of events set many people talking about a glorious "New Economy" in which there was no longer any trade-off between inflation and unemployment.

Then, in the early 2010s, inflation declined only slightly despite the massive unemployment—as high as 10 percent—brought on by the Great Recession. Once again, people started wondering whether the long-feared trade-off was just a memory now. Can the modern economy speed along without fear of rising inflation? Or slow down without bringing inflation down with it? These are questions the Federal Reserve has been wrestling with for decades, and they are the central questions for this chapter. Our answers, in brief, are: no, no, and no. We will devote most of this chapter to explaining why.

## 17-1  DEMAND-SIDE INFLATION VERSUS SUPPLY-SIDE INFLATION: A REVIEW

We begin by reviewing some of what we have learned about inflation in earlier chapters. One major cause of inflation, although certainly not the only one, is *rapid growth of aggregate demand*. We know that any autonomous increase in spending—whether initiated by consumers, investors, the government, or foreigners—has multiplier effects on aggregate demand. So each additional $1 of $C$ or $I$ or $G$ or $(X - IM)$ leads to more than $1 of additional demand. We also know that firms normally find it profitable to supply additional output only at higher prices; that is, the aggregate supply curve slopes upward. Hence, a stimulus to aggregate demand normally pulls up both real output and prices.

Figure 1, which is familiar from earlier chapters, reviews this conclusion. Initially, the economy is at point $A$, where the aggregate demand curve $D_0D_0$ intersects the aggregate supply curve $SS$. Then something happens to increase spending, and the aggregate demand curve shifts horizontally to $D_1D_1$. The new equilibrium is at point $B$, where both prices and output are higher than they were at $A$. Thus, the economy experiences both inflation and increased output. The slope of the aggregate supply curve measures the amount of inflation that accompanies any specified rise in output and therefore calibrates the trade-off between inflation and economic growth.

We also have learned in this book that inflation does not always originate from the demand side. Anything that retards the growth of aggregate supply—for example, an increase in the price of foreign oil—can shift the economy's aggregate supply curve inward. This sort of inflation is illustrated in Figure 2, where the aggregate supply curve

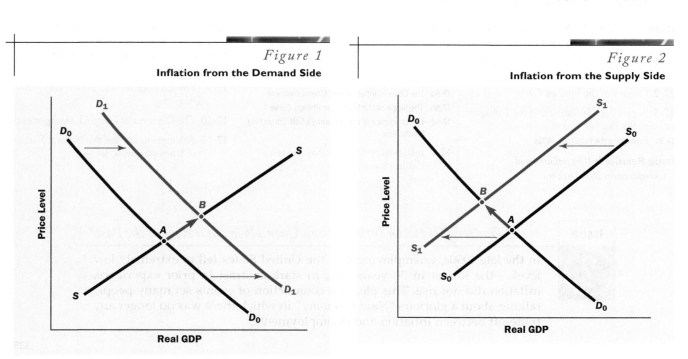

*Figure 1*

**Inflation from the Demand Side**

*Figure 2*

**Inflation from the Supply Side**

shifts inward from $S_0S_0$ to $S_1S_1$, and the economy's equilibrium consequently moves from point A to point B. Prices rise as output falls. We have *stagflation*.

Notice that although inflation can emanate from either the demand side or the supply side of the economy, a crucial difference arises between the two sources. **Demand-side inflation** is normally accompanied by rapid growth of real GDP (as in Figure 1), whereas **supply-side inflation** is normally accompanied by stagnant or even falling GDP (as in Figure 2). This distinction has major practical importance, as we will see in this chapter.

**Demand-side inflation** is a rise in the price level caused by rapid growth of aggregate demand.

**Supply-side inflation** is a rise in the price level caused by slow growth (or decline) of aggregate supply.

## 17-2  ORIGINS OF THE PHILLIPS CURVE

Let us begin by supposing that most economic fluctuations are driven by gyrations in *aggregate demand*, as our brief review of U.S. macroeconomic history in Chapter 5 suggested. In that case, we have just seen that GDP growth and inflation should rise and fall together. Is this what the data show?

We will see shortly, but first let us translate the prediction into a corresponding statement about the relationship between inflation and *unemployment*. Faster growth of real output naturally means faster growth in the number of jobs and, hence, lower unemployment. Conversely, slower growth of real output means slower growth in the number of jobs and, hence, higher unemployment. So we conclude that if business fluctuations emanate from the demand side, unemployment and inflation should move in opposite directions: Inflation should fall when unemployment rises and rise when unemployment falls.

Figure 3 illustrates the idea. In very round numbers, the unemployment rate in the United States in 2014 averaged 6.5 percent, and the Consumer Price Index was about 2 percent higher than in 2013. Point B in Figure 3 records these two (approximate) numbers. Had aggregate demand grown faster, inflation would have been higher and unemployment would have been lower. To create a concrete example, let us suppose that unemployment would have been 5 percent and inflation would have been 3 percent—as shown by point A in Figure 3. By contrast, had aggregate demand grown more slowly than it actually did, unemployment would have been higher and inflation lower. In Figure 3, we suppose that unemployment would have been 8 percent and inflation would have been just 1 percent (point C). This figure displays the principal empirical implication of our theoretical model:

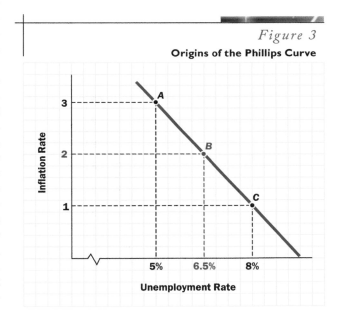

*Figure 3*

**Origins of the Phillips Curve**

If fluctuations in economic activity are caused primarily by variations in the rate at which the aggregate demand curve shifts outward from year to year, then the data should show an inverse relationship between unemployment and inflation.

Now we are ready to look at real data. Do we actually observe such an inverse relationship between inflation and unemployment? Nearly 60 years ago, the economist A. W. Phillips plotted data on unemployment and the rate of change of money *wages* (not prices) for several extended periods of British history on a series of scatter diagrams, one of which is reproduced as Figure 4. He then sketched in a curve that seemed to fit the data well. This type of curve, which we now call a **Phillips curve**, shows that wage inflation normally is high when unemployment is low and is low when unemployment is high. So far, so good. These data illustrate the short-run trade-off between inflation and unemployment, one of our *Ideas for Beyond the Final Exam*.

Phillips curves are more commonly constructed for price inflation, and Figure 5 shows such a Phillips-type diagram for the United States over the years 1954 to 1969. This curve also appears to fit the data well. As viewed through the eyes of our theory, these facts suggest that

A **Phillips curve** is a graph depicting the rate of unemployment on the horizontal axis and either the rate of inflation or the rate of change of money wages on the vertical axis. Phillips curves are normally downward sloping, indicating that higher inflation rates are associated with lower unemployment rates.

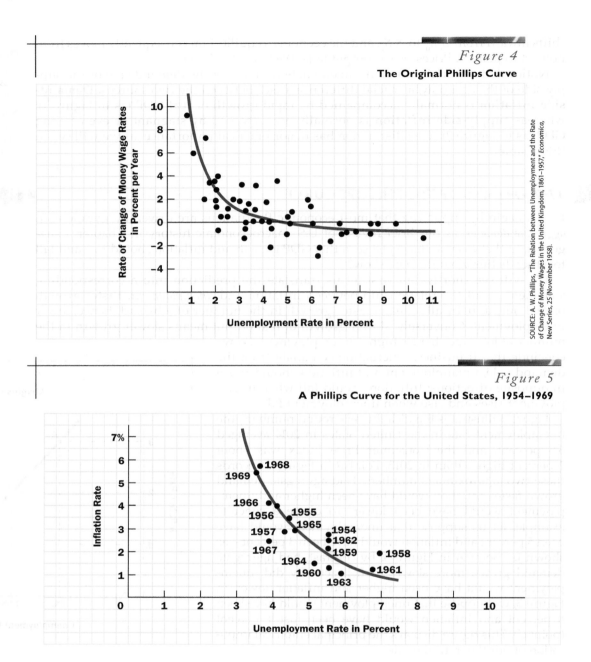

Figure 4*

**The Original Phillips Curve**

SOURCE: A. W. Phillips, "The Relation between Unemployment and the Rate of Change of Money Wages in the United Kingdom, 1861–1957," *Economica*, New Series, 25 (November 1958).

*Figure 5*

**A Phillips Curve for the United States, 1954–1969**

economic fluctuations in Great Britain between 1861 and 1913 and in the United States between 1954 and 1969 probably arose primarily from changes in the growth rate of aggregate demand. The simple model of demand-side inflation really does seem to describe what happened.

During the 1960s and early 1970s, many economists thought of the Phillips curve as a "menu" of choices available to policy makers. In this view, policy makers could opt for low unemployment and high inflation—as in 1969—or for high unemployment and low inflation—as in 1961. The Phillips curve was thought to measure the quantitative trade-off between inflation and unemployment. And for a number of years it seemed to work well.

Then something happened. The economy in the 1970s and early 1980s behaved far worse than the historical Phillips curve had led economists to expect. In particular, given the unemployment rates in each of those years, inflation was astonishingly high by past standards. This fact is shown clearly by Figure 6, which simply adds to Figure 5 the data points for 1970 to 1984. So something went badly wrong with the old view of the Phillips curve as a menu for policy choices. But what? There are two major answers to this question, and a full explanation contains elements of each.

## 17-3  SUPPLY-SIDE INFLATION AND THE COLLAPSE OF THE PHILLIPS CURVE

We begin with the simpler answer, which is that much of the inflation in the years from 1972 to 1982 did not emanate from the demand side at all. Instead, the 1970s and early 1980s were full of adverse "supply shocks"—events such as crop failures in 1972–1973 and oil price increases in 1973–1974 and again in 1979–1980. These events pushed the economy's aggregate supply curve inward to the left, as was shown in Figure 2. What kind of "Phillips curve" will be generated when economic fluctuations come from the supply side?

Figure 2 reminds us that output will decline (or at least grow more slowly) and prices will rise faster when the economy is hit by an adverse supply shock. Now, in a growing population with more people looking for jobs each year, a stagnant economy that does not generate enough new jobs will suffer a rise in unemployment. Thus inflation and unemployment will rise together:

> If fluctuations in economic activity emanate from the supply side, higher rates of inflation will be associated with higher rates of unemployment, and lower rates of inflation will be associated with lower rates of unemployment.

The major supply shocks of the 1970s stand out clearly in Figure 6. (Remember—these are real data, not textbook examples.) Food prices soared from 1972 to 1974, and again in 1978. Energy prices skyrocketed in 1973–1974, and again in 1979–1980. Clearly, the inflation and unemployment data generated by the U.S. economy in 1972–1974 and in 1978–1980 are consistent with our model of supply-side inflation. Most economists believe that supply shocks, not demand shocks, dominated the decade from 1972 to 1982.

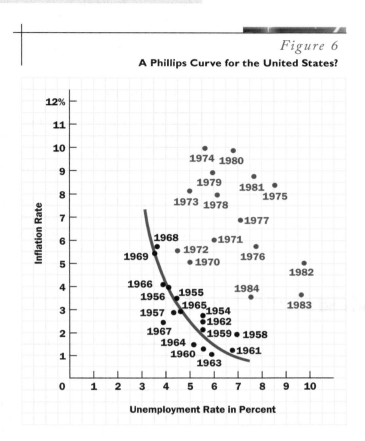

*Figure 6*

**A Phillips Curve for the United States?**

### 17-3a  Explaining the Fabulous 1990s

Now let's stand this analysis of supply shocks on its head. Suppose the economy experiences *favorable* supply shocks, rather than adverse ones, so the aggregate supply curve shifts *outward* at an unusually rapid rate. Any number of factors—such as a drop in oil prices, bountiful harvests, or exceptionally rapid technological advances—can have this effect.

Whatever the cause, Figure 7 (which duplicates Figure 14 of Chapter 10) depicts the consequences. The aggregate demand curve shifts outward as usual, but the aggregate supply curve shifts out more than it would in a "normal" year. So the economy's equilibrium winds up at point *B* rather than at point *C*, meaning that economic growth is *faster* (*B* is to the right of *C*) and inflation is *lower* (*B* is below *C*). Thus, inflation falls while rapid growth reduces unemployment.

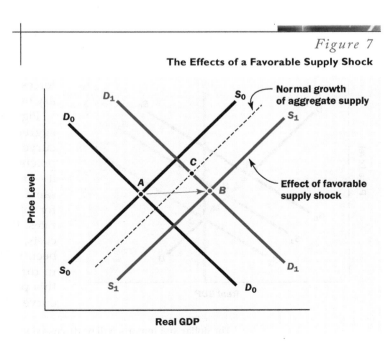

*Figure 7*

**The Effects of a Favorable Supply Shock**

Figure 7 more or less characterizes the experience of the U.S. economy from 1996 to 1998. Oil prices plummeted, lowering costs to American businesses and households. Stunning advances in technology made computer prices drop even more rapidly than usual. And the rising value of the U.S. dollar made imported goods cheaper to Americans.[1] Thus, we benefited from a series of favorable supply shocks, and the effects were as depicted in Figure 7. The U.S. economy grew rapidly, and inflation and unemployment fell together.

---

| Issue Revisited | *Why Inflation and Unemployment Both Declined* |

We now have the answer to the question posed at the start of this chapter. We do not need to add anything new or mysterious to explain the marvelous economic performance of the second half of the 1990s. According to the basic macroeconomic theory taught in this book, favorable supply shocks should produce rapid economic growth with falling inflation—which is just what happened. The U.S. economy did so well, in part, because we were so fortunate.

Incidentally, with the abundant supplies of oil and natural gas discovered and developed in the United States and Canada in recent years—and with more presumed to come—we may have a series of favorable oil shocks in our future.

---

## 17-4  WHAT THE PHILLIPS CURVE IS NOT

So one view of what went wrong with the Phillips curve is that adverse supply shocks dominated the 1970s and early 1980s. But there is another view, one that holds that policy makers misinterpreted the Phillips curve and tried to pick combinations of inflation and unemployment that were simply unsustainable.

Specifically, we have learned that the Phillips curve is a *statistical relationship* between inflation and unemployment that we expect to emerge *if business cycle fluctuations arise mainly from changes in the growth rate of aggregate demand.* But in the 1970s and 1980s, the curve was widely misinterpreted as depicting a number of *alternative equilibrium points* from which policy makers could choose.

To understand the flaw in this reasoning, let us quickly review an earlier lesson. We know from Chapter 10 that the economy has a **self-correcting mechanism** that will cure both inflations and recessions *eventually*, even if the government does nothing. That idea is important in this context because it tells us that many combinations of output and prices cannot be maintained indefinitely. Some will self-destruct. Specifically, if the economy finds itself far from the normal full-employment level of unemployment, forces will be set in motion that tend to erode the inflationary or recessionary gap.

Figure 8 depicts the case of a recessionary gap where aggregate supply curve $S_0S_0$ intersects aggregate demand curve $DD$ at point $A$. With equilibrium output well below potential GDP, the economy has unused industrial capacity and unsold output, so inflation will be tame. At the same time, the availability of unemployed workers eager for jobs limits the rate at which labor can push up wage rates. Because wages are the main component of business costs, when they decline (relative to what they would have been without a recession) so do costs. These lower costs, in turn, stimulate greater production. Figure 8 illustrates this process by an outward shift of the aggregate supply curve—from $S_0S_0$ to the blue curve $S_1S_1$.

The economy's **self-correcting mechanism** refers to the way money wages react to either a recessionary gap or an inflationary gap. Wage changes shift the aggregate supply curve and therefore change equilibrium GDP and the equilibrium price level.

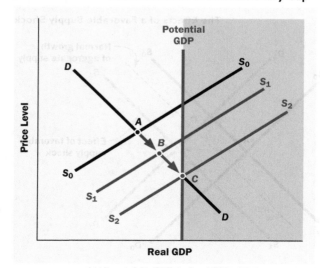

*Figure 8*

**The Elimination of a Recessionary Gap**

---

[1] The dollar and imports will be discussed in detail in Chapter 20.

As the figure shows, the outward shift of the aggregate supply curve brought on by the recession pushes equilibrium output up as the economy moves from point *A* to point *B*. Thus, the size of the recessionary gap begins to shrink. This process continues until the aggregate supply curve reaches the position indicated by the maroon curve $S_2S_2$ in Figure 8. Here wages have fallen enough to eliminate the recessionary gap, and the economy has reached a full-employment equilibrium at point *C*.[2]

We can relate this sequence of events to our discussion of the origins of the Phillips curve with the help of Figure 9, which is a hypothetical Phillips curve. Point *a* in Figure 9 corresponds to point *A* in Figure 8: It shows the initial recessionary gap with unemployment (assumed to be 8 percent) above full employment, which we assume to occur at 5 percent.

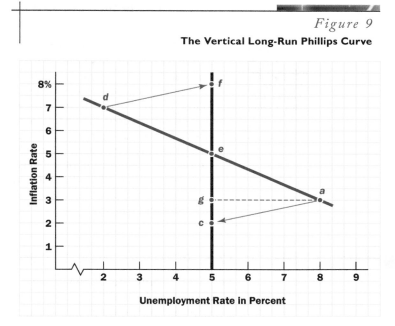

*Figure 9*

**The Vertical Long-Run Phillips Curve**

We have just seen that point *A* in Figure 8— and therefore also point *a* in Figure 9—is not sustainable. The economy tends to rid itself of the recessionary gap through the disinflation process just described. The adjustment path from *A* to *C* depicted in Figure 8 would appear on our Phillips curve diagram as a movement toward less inflation and less unemployment—something like the maroon arrow from point *a* to point *c* in Figure 9.

Similarly, points representing inflationary gaps—such as point *d* in Figure 9—are also not sustainable. They, too, are gradually eliminated by the self-correcting mechanism. Wages are forced up by the abnormally low unemployment, which in turn pushes prices higher. Higher prices deter investment spending by forcing up interest rates, and they deter consumer spending by lowering the purchasing power of consumer wealth. The inflationary process continues until the amount people want to buy is brought into line with the amount firms want to sell at normal full employment. During such an adjustment period, unemployment and inflation both rise—as indicated by the maroon arrow from point *d* to point *f* in Figure 9. Putting these two conclusions together, we see that

**On a Phillips curve diagram such as Figure 9, neither points corresponding to an inflationary gap (like point *d*) nor points corresponding to a recessionary gap (like point *a*) can be maintained indefinitely. Inflationary gaps lead to rising unemployment and rising inflation. Recessionary gaps lead to falling inflation and falling unemployment.**

All the points that are sustainable in the long run (such as *c*, *e*, and *f*), therefore, correspond to the *same* rate of unemployment, which is therefore called the **natural rate of unemployment**. The natural rate corresponds to what we have so far been calling the "full-employment" unemployment rate.

Thus, the Phillips curve connecting points *d*, *e*, and *a* is not a menu of policy choices at all. Although we can move from a point such as *e* to a point such as *d* by stimulating aggregate demand sufficiently, the economy will not be able to remain at *d*. We cannot keep unemployment at such a low level indefinitely. Instead, policy makers must choose from among points such as *c*, *e*, and *f*, all of which correspond to the same "natural" rate of unemployment. For obvious reasons, the line connecting these points is called the **vertical long-run Phillips curve**. It is this vertical Phillips curve,

The economy's self-correcting mechanism always tends to push the unemployment rate back toward a specific rate of unemployment that we call the **natural rate of unemployment**.

The **vertical long-run Phillips curve** shows the menu of inflation/unemployment choices available to society in the long run. It is a vertical straight line at the natural rate of unemployment.

---

[2] This simple analysis assumes that the aggregate demand curve does not move during the adjustment period. If it is shifting to the right, the recessionary gap will disappear even faster, but inflation will not slow down as much. (EXERCISE: Construct the diagram for this case by adding a shift of the aggregate demand curve to Figure 8.)

connecting points such as *e* and *f*, that represents the true long-run menu of policy choices. We thus conclude:

**Ideas for Beyond the Final Exam**

**THE TRADE-OFF BETWEEN INFLATION AND UNEMPLOYMENT** In the short run, it is possible to "ride up the Phillips curve" toward lower levels of unemployment by stimulating aggregate demand. (See, e.g., point *d* in Figure 9.) Conversely, by restricting the growth of demand, it is possible to "ride down the Phillips curve" toward lower rates of inflation (such as point *a* in Figure 9). Thus, there is a *short-run trade-off between unemployment and inflation.* Stimulating demand will improve the unemployment picture but worsen inflation; restricting demand will lower inflation but aggravate the unemployment problem.

*However, there is no such trade-off in the long run.* The economy's self-correcting mechanism ensures that unemployment will eventually return to the natural rate no matter what happens to aggregate demand. In the long run, faster growth of demand leads only to higher inflation, not to lower unemployment; and slower growth of demand leads only to lower inflation, not to higher unemployment.

## 17-5 FIGHTING UNEMPLOYMENT WITH FISCAL AND MONETARY POLICY

Now let us apply this analysis to a concrete policy problem—one that has troubled policy makers in the United States and in many other countries in recent years. Should the government use its ability to manage aggregate demand through fiscal and monetary policy to combat unemployment? And if so, how? To focus the discussion, we will deal with recent history.

When the Great Recession started in December 2007, the unemployment rate stood at 5 percent, pretty much in line with estimates of the natural rate of unemployment. We were at something like point *e* in Figure 9, though with much lower inflation (around 2.5 percent). But then the economy started to weaken, gradually at first, and the unemployment rate crept up—to about 6 percent by the summer of 2008. We were moving down the Phillips curve in the direction of point *a* in Figure 9. The recession got far worse in the last quarter of 2008 and the first quarter of 2009, with GDP contracting about 3.5 percent in just six months. Unemployment began to skyrocket—reaching 9 percent in April 2009 and topping out at 10 percent in October. Think of this as being something like point *a* in Figure 9, with a large recessionary gap.

Even if fiscal and monetary policy makers did nothing, the economy's self-correcting mechanism would have gradually eroded the recessionary gap. Both unemployment and inflation would have declined slowly as the economy moved along the maroon arrow from point *a* to point *c* in Figure 9. Eventually, as the diagram shows, the economy would have returned to its natural rate of unemployment (assumed here to be 5 percent) and inflation would have fallen—in the example, from 3 percent to 2 percent.

The eventual outcome is quite satisfactory: Both unemployment and inflation are lower at the end of the adjustment period (point *c*) than at the beginning (point *a*). But it may take an agonizingly long time to get there. And American policy makers since 2008 have not viewed patience as a virtue. Rather than keep hands off, the Federal Reserve started cutting interest rates aggressively in 2008. Fiscal policy reacted as well, with Congress passing a tax cut in 2008, large fiscal stimulus package in early 2009, and another, smaller one in December 2010.

According to the theory we have learned, such large doses of expansionary fiscal and monetary policy should push the economy up the short-run Phillips curve from a point like *a* toward a point like *e* in Figure 9. Compared to simply relying on the self-correcting mechanism, then, the strong policy responses presumably led to a faster recovery from the 2007–2009 recession—which was certainly the intent of the president, Congress, and the Fed. But Figure 9 points out that it probably will also leave us with a higher inflation rate in the end (5 percent in the figure, much lower in reality).

This example illustrates the range of choices open to policy makers. They can wait patiently while the economy's self-correcting mechanism pulls unemployment down to the natural rate—leading to a long-run equilibrium like point *c* in Figure 9. Or they can rush the process along with expansionary monetary and fiscal policy—and wind up with the same unemployment rate but higher inflation (point *e*). In what sense, then, do policy makers face a *trade-off* between inflation and unemployment? The answer, illustrated by this diagram, is

**The cost of reducing unemployment more rapidly by expansionary fiscal and monetary policies is a permanently higher inflation rate.**

## 17-6 WHAT SHOULD BE DONE?

Should the government pay the inflationary costs of fighting unemployment? When the transitory benefit (lower unemployment for a while) is balanced against the permanent cost (higher inflation), have we made a good bargain?

We have noted that the U.S. government opted for strong policy responses in 2008–2010. Thus, two forces were at work simultaneously: The self-correcting mechanism was pulling the economy toward point *c* in Figure 9, and expansionary monetary and fiscal policies were pushing it toward point *e*. The net result was an intermediate path—something like the dotted line leading to point *g* in Figure 9. As the economy started to return slowly to full employment in 2010 and after, growth resumed and inflation was relatively stable. That remains the case as this edition goes to press.

How do policy makers make decisions like this? Our analysis highlights three critical issues on which the answer depends.

### 17-6a The Costs of Inflation and Unemployment

In Chapter 6, we examined the social costs of inflation and unemployment. Many of the benefits of lower unemployment are readily measured in dollars and cents. Basically, we need only estimate how much higher real GDP is each year. However, the costs of the permanently higher inflation rate are more difficult to measure. So there is considerable controversy over the costs and benefits of using demand management to fight unemployment.

Economists and political leaders who believe that inflation is extremely costly may deem it unwise to accept the inflationary consequences of reducing unemployment faster. And indeed, a few dissenters in 2007–2010, when the Fed was doing everything it could think of to fight the recession, were worried about future inflation. Most U.S. policy makers apparently disagreed with that view, however—especially because inflation was already low and edging lower. They decided that fighting unemployment was the higher priority.

But things do not always work out that way. In the 1980s and 1990s, European authorities often avoided expansionary stabilization policies and allowed unemployment to remain high, rather than accept the risk of higher inflation. Even in the 2010s, with the ill effects of the Great Recession lingering on in the form of high unemployment, many European policy makers were loath to use expansionary policies. Partly for this reason, the inflation rate in the euro zone dropped perilously close to zero by 2014.

### 17-6b The Slope of the Short-Run Phillips Curve

The shape of the short-run Phillips curve is also critical. Look back at Figure 9, and imagine that the Phillips curve connecting points *a*, *e*, and *d* was much steeper. In that case, the inflationary costs of using expansionary policy to reduce unemployment would be more substantial. By contrast, if the short-run Phillips curve was much flatter than the one shown in Figure 9, unemployment could be reduced with less inflationary cost.

### 17-6c The Efficiency of the Economy's Self-Correcting Mechanism

We have emphasized that once a recessionary gap opens, the economy's natural self-correcting mechanism will eventually close it—even in the absence of any policy response. The obvious question is: How long must we wait? If the self-correcting mechanism—which works through reductions in wage inflation—is fast and reliable, high unemployment will not last very long. So the costs of waiting will be small. But if wage inflation responds only

# Inflation Targeting and the Phillips Curve

In Chapter 15, we mentioned *inflation targeting* as a new approach to monetary policy that has gained adherents in many countries. The Federal Reserve joined the ranks of inflation targeters in 2012, although, unlike most of its peer institutions, it also has an unemployment target. In practice, inflation targeting requires monetary policy makers to rely heavily on the Phillips curve. Why? Because a central bank with, say, a 2 percent inflation target is obligated to pursue a monetary policy that it believes will drive the inflation rate to 2 percent after, say, a year or two. But how does the central bank know which policy will accomplish this goal?

*Knowing* the proper policy with certainty is, of course, out of the question. But a central bank can use a model similar to the aggregate supply/demand model taught in this book to *estimate* how its policy choices will affect the unemployment rate, say, this year and next. Then it can use a Phillips curve to *estimate* how that unemployment path will affect inflation. In fact, that is more or less what inflation-targeting central banks from New Zealand to Norway now do.

JEWEL SAMAD/Getty Images

slowly to unemployment, the costs of waiting may be enormous—which is how things have looked to most U.S. policy makers in the years since 2008.

The efficacy of the self-correcting mechanism is also surrounded by controversy. Most economists believe that the weight of the evidence points to extremely sluggish wage behavior: Wage inflation appears to respond slowly to economic slack. In terms of Figure 9, this lag means that the economy will traverse the path from *a* to *c* at an agonizingly slow pace, so that a long period of weak economic activity will be necessary to bring down inflation.

But a significant minority opinion finds this assessment far too pessimistic. Economists in this group argue that the costs of reducing inflation are not nearly so severe and that the key to a successful anti-inflation policy is how it affects people's *expectations* of inflation. To understand this argument, we must first understand why expectations are relevant to the Phillips curve.

## 17-7 INFLATIONARY EXPECTATIONS AND THE PHILLIPS CURVE

Recall from Chapter 10 that the main reason the economy's aggregate supply curve slopes upward—that is, why output increases as the price level rises—is that businesses typically purchase labor and other inputs under long-term contracts that fix input costs in money terms. (The money wage rate is the clearest example.) As long as such contracts are in force, *real* wages fall as the prices of goods rise. Labor therefore becomes cheaper in real terms, which persuades businesses to expand employment and output. Buying low and selling high is, after all, the route to higher profits.

Table 1 illustrates this general idea in a concrete example. We suppose that workers and firms agree today that the money wage to be paid a year from now will be $10 per hour. The table then shows the real wage corresponding to each alternative inflation rate. For example, if inflation is 4 percent, the real wage a year from now (in today's purchasing power) will be $10.00/1.04 = $9.62. Clearly, the higher the inflation rate, the higher the price level at the end of the year and the lower the real wage.

Lower real wages provide an incentive for firms to increase output, as we have just noted. But lower real wages also impose losses

*Table 1*

**Money and Real Wages under Unexpected Inflation**

| Inflation Rate | Price Level One Year from Now | Wage per Hour One Year from Now | Real Wage per Hour One Year from Now |
|---|---|---|---|
| 0% | 100 | $10.00 | $10.00 |
| 2 | 102 | 10.00 | 9.80 |
| 4 | 104 | 10.00 | 9.62 |
| 6 | 106 | 10.00 | 9.43 |

NOTE: Each real wage figure is obtained by dividing the $10 nominal wage by the corresponding price level a year later and multiplying by 100. Thus, for example, when the inflation rate is 4 percent, the real wage at the end of the year is ($10.00/104) × 100 = $9.62.

of purchasing power on workers. Thus, workers are, in some sense, "cheated" by inflation if they sign a contract specifying a fixed money wage in an inflationary environment.

Many economists doubt that workers will sign such contracts *if they can see inflation coming*. Wouldn't it be wiser, these economists ask, to insist on being compensated for the coming inflation? After all, firms should be willing to offer higher money wages if they expect inflation, because they realize that higher money wages need not imply higher *real* wages.

Table 2 illustrates the mechanics of such a deal. For example, if people expect 4 percent inflation, the contract could stipulate that the wage rate be increased to $10.40 (which is 4 percent more than $10) at the end of the year. That would keep the real wage at $10 (because $10.40/1.04 = $10.00), the same as it would be under zero inflation. The other money wage figures in Table 2 are derived similarly.

If workers and firms behave this way, and if they forecast inflation accurately, then the real wage will remain unchanged as the price level rises. (Notice that, in Table 2, the expected future real wage is $10 per hour regardless of the expected inflation rate.) Prices and wages will go up together. So workers will not lose from inflation, and firms will not gain. Then there is no reason for firms to raise production when the price level rises. In a word, the aggregate supply curve becomes vertical. In general:

> If workers can see inflation coming, and if they receive compensation for it, inflation does not erode *real* wages. But if real wages do not fall, firms have no incentives to increase production. In such a case, the economy's aggregate supply curve will not slope upward but, rather, will be a vertical line at the level of output corresponding to potential GDP.

Such a curve is shown in Panel (a) of Figure 10. Because a vertical aggregate supply curve leads to a vertical Phillips curve, it follows that even the *short-run* Phillips curve would be vertical under these circumstances, as in Panel (b) of Figure 10.[3]

If this analysis is correct, it has profound implications for the costs and benefits of fighting inflation. To see this, refer once again to Figure 9, but now use the graph to depict the strategy of fighting inflation by causing a recession. Suppose we start at point *e*, with

*Table 2*

**Money and Real Wages under Expected Inflation**

| Expected Inflation Rate | Expected Price Level One Year from Now | Wage per Hour One Year from Now | Expected Real Wage per Hour One Year from Now |
|---|---|---|---|
| 0% | 100 | $10.00 | $10.00 |
| 2 | 102 | 10.20 | 10.00 |
| 4 | 104 | 10.40 | 10.00 |
| 6 | 106 | 10.60 | 10.00 |

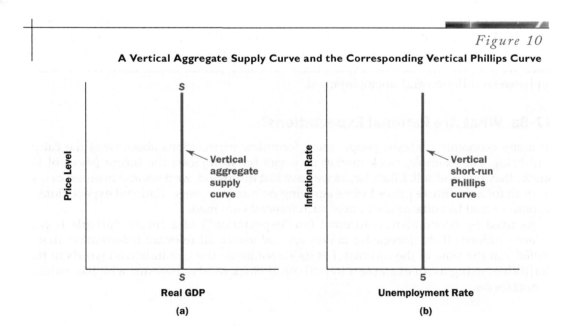

*Figure 10*

**A Vertical Aggregate Supply Curve and the Corresponding Vertical Phillips Curve**

(a)

(b)

---

[3] Test Yourself Question 1 at the end of the chapter asks you to demonstrate that a vertical aggregate supply curve leads to a vertical Phillips curve.

5 percent inflation. To move to point *c* (representing 2 percent inflation), the economy must take a long and unpleasant detour through point *a*. Specifically, contractionary policies must push the economy down the Phillips curve toward point *a* before the self-correcting mechanism takes over and moves the economy from *a* to *c*. In words, we must suffer through a recession to reduce inflation.

But what if even the *short-run* Phillips curve were *vertical* rather than downward sloping? In this case, the unpleasant recessionary detour would not be necessary. Instead, inflation could fall without unemployment rising. The economy could move vertically downward from point *e* to point *c*.

Does this optimistic analysis describe the real world? Can we really slay the inflationary dragon so painlessly? Not necessarily, for our discussion of expectations so far has made at least one unrealistic assumption: that businesses and workers can predict inflation accurately. Under this assumption, as Table 2 shows, real wages are unaffected by inflation—leaving the aggregate supply curve vertical, even in the short run.

But forecasts of inflation are often inaccurate. Suppose workers underestimate inflation. For example, suppose they expect 4 percent inflation but actually get 6 percent. Then real wages will decline by 2 percent. More generally, real wages will fall if workers underestimate inflation at all. The effects of inflation on real wages will be somewhere in between those shown in Tables 1 and 2.[4] So firms will retain some incentive to raise production as the price level rises, which means that the aggregate supply curve will retain some upward slope. We thus conclude that:

The short-run aggregate supply curve is *vertical* when inflation is predicted accurately but *upward sloping* when inflation is underestimated. Thus, only *unexpectedly* high inflation will raise output, because only unexpected inflation reduces real wages.[5] Similarly, only an *unexpected* decline in inflation will lead to a recession.

Because people often fail to anticipate changes in inflation correctly, this analysis seems to leave our earlier discussion of the Phillips curve almost intact for practical purposes. Indeed, most economists nowadays believe that the Phillips curve slopes downward in the short run but is vertical in the long run.

## 17-8  THE THEORY OF RATIONAL EXPECTATIONS

**Rational expectations** are forecasts that, although not necessarily correct, are the best that can be made given the available data. Rational expectations, therefore, cannot err systematically. If expectations are rational, forecasting errors are pure random numbers.

However, an influential minority of economists disagrees. This group, believers in the hypothesis of **rational expectations**, insists that the Phillips curve is vertical even in the short run. To understand their point of view, we must first explain rational expectations. Then we will see why rational expectations have such radical implications for the trade-off between inflation and unemployment.

### 17-8a  What Are Rational Expectations?

In many economic contexts, people must formulate expectations about what the future will bring. For example, stock market investors try to forecast the future prices of the stocks they buy and sell. Likewise, as we have just discussed, workers and businesses may want to forecast future prices before agreeing on a money wage. Rational expectations is a controversial hypothesis about how such forecasts are made.

As used by economists, a forecast (an "expectation") of a future variable is considered rational if the forecaster makes *optimal* use of all relevant information that is *available* at the time of the forecast. Let us elaborate on the two italicized words in this definition, using as an example a hypothetical stock market investor who has rational expectations.

---

[4] To make sure you understand why, construct a version of Table 2 based on the assumption that workers expect 4 percent inflation (and hence set next year's wage at $10.40 per hour), regardless of the actual rate of inflation. If you create this table correctly, it will show that higher inflation leads to lower real wages, as in Table 1.

[5] To see this point, compare Tables 1 and 2.

First, proponents of rational expectations recognize that *information is limited*. An investor interested in Google stock would like to know how much profit the company will make in the coming years. Armed with such information, she could predict the future price of Google stock more accurately. But that information is simply unavailable. The investor's forecast of the future price of Google shares is not "irrational" just because she cannot foresee the future. On the other hand, if Google stock normally goes down on Fridays and up on Mondays, she should be aware of this fact.

Next, we have the word *optimal*. As used by economists, it means using proper statistical inference to process all the relevant information that is available when a forecast is made. In brief, to have rational expectations, your forecasts do not have to be correct, but they cannot have systematic errors that you could avoid by applying better statistical methods. This requirement, although exacting, is not quite as outlandish as it may seem. A good billiards player makes expert use of the laws of physics even without understanding the theory. Similarly, an experienced stock market investor may make good use of information even without formal training in statistics.

## 17-8b Rational Expectations and the Trade-Off

Let us now see how some economists have used the hypothesis of rational expectations to deny that there is a trade-off between inflation and unemployment—even in the short run.

Although they recognize that inflation cannot always be predicted accurately, proponents of rational expectations insist that workers will not make *systematic* errors. Remember that our argument leading to a sloping short-run Phillips curve tacitly assumed that workers are slow to recognize changes. They thus *underestimate* inflation when it is rising and *overestimate* it when it is falling. Many observers see such systematic errors as a realistic description of human behavior. But advocates of rational expectations disagree, claiming that it is fundamentally illogical. Workers, they argue, will always make the best possible forecast of inflation, using all the latest data and the best available economic models. Such forecasts will sometimes be too high and sometimes too low, but they will not err systematically in one direction or the other. Consequently:

**If expectations are rational, the difference between the *actual* rate of inflation and the *expected* rate of inflation (the forecasting error) must be a pure random number, that is:**

**Inflation − Expected inflation = A random number**

Now recall that the argument in the previous section concluded that employment is affected by inflation only to the extent that inflation *differs* from what was expected. But under rational expectations, such differences are *random*. No *predictable* change in inflation can make the *expected* rate of inflation deviate from the *actual* rate of inflation. Hence, according to the rational expectations hypothesis, unemployment will always remain at the natural rate—except for random, and therefore totally unpredictable, gyrations due to forecasting errors. Thus:

**If expectations are rational, inflation can be reduced without a period of high unemployment because the short-run Phillips curve, like the long-run Phillips curve, will be vertical.**

According to the rational expectations view, the government's ability to manipulate aggregate demand gives it no ability to influence real output and unemployment because the aggregate supply curve is vertical even in the short run. (To see why, experiment by moving an aggregate demand curve when the aggregate supply curve is vertical, as in Figure 10(a).) The government's manipulations of aggregate demand are planned ahead and are therefore predictable, and any *predictable* change in aggregate demand will change the *expected* rate of inflation. It will therefore leave real wages unaffected.

The government can influence output only by making *unexpected* changes in aggregate demand. But unexpected changes are not easy to engineer if expectations are rational, because people understand what policy makers are up to. For example, if the authorities typically react to high inflation by reducing aggregate demand, people will soon come to anticipate this reaction. And *anticipated* reductions in aggregate demand do not cause *unexpected* changes in inflation.

### 17-8c An Evaluation

Believers in rational expectations are optimistic about reducing inflation without losing any output, even in the short run. Are they right?

As a piece of pure logic, the rational expectations argument is impeccable. But as is common in the world of economic policy, controversy arises over how well the theoretical idea applies in practice. Although the theory has attracted many adherents, the evidence to date leads most economists to reject the extreme rational expectations position in favor of the view that a trade-off between inflation and unemployment does exist in the short run. Here are some of the reasons.

**Old Contracts May Embody Outdated Expectations** Many contracts for labor and other raw materials cover such long periods of time that the expectations on which they were based, although perhaps rational at the time, may appear "irrational" from today's point of view. For example, consider three-year labor contracts drawn up in January 2008. Inflation had averaged 3.3 percent over the preceding three years. Perhaps it was rational then to expect inflation over the *next* three years to average 3.3 percent also, and contracts were written up accordingly. As things turned out, the Great Recession reduced inflation sharply—to an average of just 1.4 percent over the years 2008, 2009, and 2010. Contracts built on an assumption of 3.3 percent inflation therefore left real wages higher than intended, giving firms reason to reduce employment and therefore output—even though no one behaved irrationally.

**Expectations May Adjust Slowly** Many people believe that inflationary expectations do not adapt as quickly to changes in the economic environment as the rational expectations theory assumes. If, for example, the government embarks on an anti-inflation policy, workers may continue to expect high inflation for a while. Thus, they may continue to insist on rapid money wage increases. Then, if inflation actually slows down, real wages will rise faster than anyone expected, and unemployment will result. Such behavior may not be strictly rational, but it may be realistic.

**When Do Workers Receive Compensation for Inflation?** Some observers question whether wage agreements typically compensate workers for expected inflation *in advance*, as assumed by the rational expectations theory. More typically, they argue, wages catch up to actual inflation after the fact. If so, real wages will be eroded by inflation for a while, as in the conventional view.

**What the Facts Show** The facts have not been kind to the rational expectations hypothesis. The theory suggests that unemployment should hover around the natural rate most of the time, with random gyrations in one direction or the other. Yet this is far from what the data show. The theory also predicts that pre-announced (and thus expected) anti-inflation programs should be relatively painless. Yet, in practice, fighting inflation has proven very costly in virtually every country. Finally, many direct tests of the rationality of expectations have cast doubt on the hypothesis. For example, survey data on people's expectations rarely meet the exacting requirements of rationality.

All of these problems with rational expectations should not obscure a basic truth, however. In the long run, the rational expectations view should be more or less correct because people will not cling to incorrect expectations indefinitely. As Abraham Lincoln pointed out with characteristic wisdom, you cannot fool all the people all the time.

## 17-9 WHY ECONOMISTS (AND POLITICIANS) DISAGREE

This chapter has now taught us some of the reasons why economists disagree about the proper conduct of stabilization policy. It also helps us understand some of the related political debates.

Should the government take strong actions to prevent or reduce inflation? You will say *yes* if you believe that (1) inflation is more costly than unemployment, (2) the short-run

Phillips curve is steep, (3) expectations react quickly, and (4) the economy's self-correcting mechanism works smoothly and rapidly. These views on the economy tend to be held by believers in rational expectations.

You will say *no* if you believe that (1) unemployment is more costly than inflation, (2) the short-run Phillips curve is flat, (3) expectations react sluggishly, and (4) the self-correcting mechanism is slow and unreliable. These views are held by many Keynesian economists, so it is not surprising that they often oppose using recession to fight inflation.

The tables turn, however, when the question becomes whether to use demand management to bring a recession to a rapid end. The Keynesian view of the world—that unemployment is costly, that the short-run Phillips curve is flat, that expectations adjust slowly, and that the self-correcting mechanism is unreliable—leads to the conclusion that the benefits of fighting unemployment are high and the costs are low. Keynesians are therefore eager to fight recessions. The rational expectations positions on these four issues are precisely the reverse, and so are the policy conclusions.

## 17-10 THE DILEMMA OF DEMAND MANAGEMENT

We have seen that policy makers face an unavoidable trade-off. If they stimulate aggregate demand to reduce unemployment, they will aggravate inflation. If they restrict aggregate demand to fight inflation, they will cause higher unemployment.

But wait. Early in the chapter we learned that when inflation comes from the supply side, inflation and unemployment are *positively* correlated: They go up or down together. Does this mean that monetary and fiscal policy makers can escape the trade-off between inflation and unemployment? Unfortunately not.

> Shifts of the aggregate supply curve can cause inflation and unemployment to rise or fall together, and thus can destroy the statistical Phillips curve relationship. Nevertheless, anything that monetary and fiscal policy can do will make unemployment and inflation move in *opposite* directions because monetary and fiscal policies influence only the *aggregate demand* curve, not the *aggregate supply* curve.
>
> Thus, no matter what the source of inflation, and no matter what happens to the Phillips curve, the monetary and fiscal policy authorities still face a disagreeable trade-off between inflation and unemployment. Many policy makers have failed to understand this principle, which is one of the *Ideas* we hope you will remember well *Beyond the Final Exam.*

Ideas for Beyond the Final Exam

Naturally, the unpleasant nature of this trade-off has led both economists and public officials to search for a way out of the dilemma. We conclude this chapter by considering some of these ideas—none of which is a panacea.

## 17-11 ATTEMPTS TO REDUCE THE NATURAL RATE OF UNEMPLOYMENT

One highly desirable approach—if only we knew how to do it—would be to reduce the natural rate of unemployment. Then we could enjoy lower unemployment without higher inflation. The question is: How?

The most promising approaches have to do with education, training, and job placement. The data clearly show that more educated workers are unemployed less frequently than less educated ones are. Vocational training and retraining programs, if successful, help unemployed workers with obsolete skills acquire abilities that are currently in demand. By so doing, they both raise employment and help alleviate upward pressures on wages in jobs where qualified workers are in short supply. Government and private job placement and counseling services play a similar role. Such programs try to match workers to jobs better by funneling information from prospective employers to prospective employees.

These ideas sound sensible and promising, but two big problems arise in implementation. First, training and placement programs sometimes look better on paper than in practice. In some cases, people are trained for jobs that do not exist by the time they finish their training—if, indeed, the jobs ever existed.

Second, the high cost of these programs restricts the number of workers who can be accommodated, even in successful programs. For this reason, publicly supported job training is done on a very small scale in the United States—much less than in most European countries. Small expenditures can hardly be expected to make a large dent in the natural rate of unemployment.

Many observers believe the natural rate of unemployment may have risen in the United States in recent years, despite these attempts to reduce it. Why? One reason is that *work experience* has much in common with formal training—workers become more productive by learning on the job. With protracted long-term unemployment, the American workforce has been accumulating less experience on the job than it used to, which, according to many economists, has raised the natural rate of unemployment. (For some other possible reasons, see "Has the Natural Rate of Unemployment Gone Up?")

**Indexing**—which refers to provisions in a law or contract that automatically adjust monetary payments whenever a specific price index changes—presents a very different approach to the inflation-unemployment dilemma. Instead of trying to improve the terms of the trade-off, *indexing seeks to reduce the social costs of inflation.*

The most familiar example of indexing is an escalator clause in a wage agreement. Escalator clauses provide for automatic increases in money wages—without the need for new contract negotiations—whenever the price level rises by more than a specified amount. Such agreements thus act to protect workers partly from inflation, even if their expectations were way off. Nowadays, with inflation low and stable, relatively few workers are covered by escalator clauses. They were far more common when inflation was higher.

Interest payments on bonds or bank accounts can also be indexed, and the U.S. government began doing so with a fraction of its bonds in 1997. The most extensive indexing to be found in the United States today, however, appears in government transfer payments. Social Security benefits, for instance, are indexed so that retirees are not victimized by inflation.

**Indexing** refers to provisions in a law or a contract whereby monetary payments are automatically adjusted whenever a specified price index changes. Wage rates, pensions, interest payments on bonds, income taxes, and many other things can be indexed in this way, and have been. Sometimes such contractual provisions are called *escalator clauses.*

## Has the Natural Rate of Unemployment Gone Up?

Prior to the onset of the Great Recession at the end of 2007, most economists believed the natural rate of unemployment in the United States was approximately 5 percent. If unemployment fell below that critical rate, they said, inflation would start to rise. And if unemployment rose above 5 percent, inflation would start to fall. Experience since then is broadly consistent with that belief. Once we take out the influence of food and energy prices, U.S. inflation has mostly been declining since 2008 amid high unemployment.

But there is a problem. The unemployment rate was above 6 percent from August 2008 to August 2014, and was above 7 percent from December 2008 to December 2013. So the direction of inflation—down—is equally consistent with a natural rate of unemployment of 6 percent or 7 percent. Pessimists in 2014 claimed that certain jobs, and even certain industries, had disappeared from the United States *permanently*; they were never coming back. There was, according to this argument, a "mismatch" between the skills of the American labor force and the skills that the modern job market demanded. If true, such a mismatch would mean the natural rate of unemployment was higher. But is it true? Optimists noted that deep and long recessions always bring talk of a sharply higher natural rate—and yet, as the economy recovers, unemployment has always fallen. This will happen again, they argued, though it may take a long time.

At present, it is too early to tell who is right. The unemployment rate did not drop below 6.5 percent until April 2014, making it almost impossible to tell whether the natural rate of unemployment is closer to 5 percent or closer to 6 percent. Both numbers are well below recent experience. But since June 2014, the unemployment rate has hovered near 6 percent. If this keeps up, economists will be better positioned to estimate the natural rate of unemployment again. Sometimes you just have to wait for more data.

REX LARSEN/Grand Rapids Press/Landov

Some economists believe that the United States should follow the example of several foreign countries and adopt a more widespread indexing system. Why? Because, they argue, it would take most of the sting out of inflation. To see how, let us review some of the social costs of inflation that we enumerated in Chapter 6.

One important cost is the capricious redistribution of income caused by unexpected inflation. We saw that borrowers and lenders normally incorporate an *inflation premium* equal to the *expected rate of inflation* into the nominal interest rate. Then, if inflation turns out to be higher than expected, the borrower has to pay the lender only the agreed-on nominal interest rate, including the premium for *expected* inflation; he does not have to compensate the lender for the (higher) *actual* inflation. Thus, the borrower enjoys a windfall gain and the lender loses out. The opposite happens if inflation turns out to be lower than expected.

If interest rates on loans were indexed, none of this would occur. Borrowers and lenders would agree on a fixed *real* rate of interest, and the borrower would compensate the lender for whatever actual inflation occurred. No one would have to guess what the inflation rate would be.[6]

A second social cost mentioned in Chapter 6 stems from the fact that our tax system levies taxes on nominal interest and nominal capital gains. As we learned, this flaw in the tax system leads to extremely high effective tax rates in an inflationary environment. But indexing can cure this problem. We need only rewrite the tax code so that *real* interest payments and *real* capital gains are taxed.

In the face of all these benefits, why does our economy not employ more indexing? One obvious reason is that inflation has been low for many years now. Indexing received much more attention decades ago, when inflation was much higher. A second reason is that some economists fear that indexing will erode society's resistance to inflation. With the costs of inflation so markedly reduced, they ask, what will stop governments from inflating more and more? They fear that the answer is: nothing. Voters who stand to lose nothing from inflation are unlikely to pressure their legislators into stopping it. Opponents of indexing worry that a mild inflationary disease could turn into a ravaging epidemic in a highly indexed economy.

## Summary

1. Inflation can be caused either by rapid growth of aggregate demand or by sluggish growth of aggregate supply.

2. When fluctuations in economic activity emanate from the **demand side,** prices will rise rapidly when real output grows rapidly. Because rapid growth means more jobs, unemployment and inflation will be inversely related.

3. This inverse relationship between unemployment and inflation is called the **Phillips curve.** In the United States, data for the 1950s and 1960s display a clear Phillips curve relation, but data for the 1970s and 1980s do not.

4. The Phillips curve is not a menu of long-run policy choices for the economy, because the **self-correcting mechanism** guarantees that neither an inflationary gap nor a recessionary gap can last indefinitely.

5. Because of the self-correcting mechanism, the economy's true long-run choices lie along a **vertical long-run Phillips curve,** which shows that the so-called **natural rate of unemployment** is the only unemployment rate that can persist indefinitely.

6. In the short run, the economy can move up or down along its short-run Phillips curve. Temporary reductions in unemployment can be achieved at the cost of higher inflation, and temporary increases in unemployment can be used to fight inflation. This *short-run trade-off between inflation and unemployment* is one of our *Ideas for Beyond the Final Exam.*

7. Whether it is advisable to use unemployment to fight inflation depends on four principal factors: the relative social costs of inflation versus unemployment, the efficiency of the economy's self-correcting mechanism, the shape of the short-run Phillips curve, and the speed at which inflationary expectations are adjusted.

8. If workers expect inflation to occur, and if they demand (and receive) compensation for inflation, output will be independent of the price level. Both the aggregate supply curve and the short-run Phillips curve are vertical in this case.

9. Errors in predicting inflation will change real wages and therefore the quantity of output that firms wish

---

[6] For example, an indexed loan with a 2 percent real interest rate would require a 5 percent nominal interest payment if inflation were 3 percent, a 7 percent nominal interest payment if inflation were 5 percent, and so on.

to supply. Thus, unpredicted movements in the price level will lead to a normal, upward-sloping aggregate supply curve.

10. According to the **rational expectations** hypothesis, errors in predicting inflation are purely random. As a consequence, except for some random gyrations, the aggregate supply curve is vertical even in the short run.

11. Many economists reject the rational expectations view. Some deny that expectations are "rational" and believe instead that people tend, for example, to underpredict inflation when it is rising. Others point out that contracts signed years ago may embody expectations that do not seem "rational" in terms of what we know today.

12. When fluctuations in economic activity are caused by shifts of the aggregate supply curve, output will grow slowly (causing unemployment to rise) when inflation rises. Hence, the rates of unemployment and inflation will be positively correlated. Many observers feel that this sort of stagflation is why the Phillips curve collapsed in the 1970s. Similarly, a series of favorable supply shocks help explain the combination of low

inflation and strong economic growth we enjoyed in the late 1990s.

13. Even if inflation is initiated by supply-side problems, so that inflation and unemployment rise together, the monetary and fiscal authorities still face this trade-off: Anything they do to improve unemployment is likely to worsen inflation, and anything they do to reduce inflation is likely to aggravate unemployment. (This is part of one of our *Ideas for Beyond the Final Exam*.) The reason is that monetary and fiscal policies mainly influence the aggregate demand curve, not the aggregate supply curve.

14. Policies that improve the functioning of the labor market—including retraining programs and employment services—can, in principle, lower the natural rate of unemployment. To date, however, the U.S. government has enjoyed only modest success with these measures.

15. **Indexing** is another way to approach the trade-off problem. Instead of trying to improve the trade-off, it concentrates on reducing the social costs of inflation. Opponents of indexing worry, however, that the economy's resistance to inflation may be lowered by indexing.

## Key Terms

| | | |
|---|---|---|
| demand-side inflation   337 | Phillips curve   337 | supply-side inflation   337 |
| indexing   350 | rational expectations   346 | vertical long-run Phillips curve   341 |
| natural rate of unemployment   341 | self-correcting mechanism   340 | |

## Test Yourself

1. Show that if the economy's aggregate supply curve is vertical, fluctuations in the growth of aggregate demand produce only fluctuations in inflation with no effect on output.

2. Long-term government bonds now pay approximately 3 percent nominal interest. Would you prefer to trade

yours in for an indexed bond that paid a 1 percent real rate of interest? What if the real interest rate offered were zeroed? What if it were *negative* 1 percent? What do your answers to these questions reveal about your personal beliefs about future inflation?

## Discussion Questions

1. When inflation and unemployment fell together in the 1990s, some observers claimed that policy makers no longer faced a trade-off between inflation and unemployment. Were they correct?

2. "There is no sense in trying to shorten recessions through fiscal and monetary policy because the effects of these policies on the unemployment rate are sure to be temporary." Comment on both the truth of this statement and its relevance for policy formulation.

3. Why is it said that decisions on fiscal and monetary policy are, at least in part, political decisions that cannot be made on "objective" economic criteria?

4. What is a Phillips curve? Why did it seem to work so much better in the period from 1954 to 1969 than it did in the 1970s?

5. Explain why expectations of inflation affect the wages that result from labor-management bargaining.

6. What is meant by "rational" expectations? Why does the hypothesis of rational expectations have such stunning implications for economic policy? Would believers in rational expectations want to shorten a recession by expanding aggregate demand? Would they want to fight inflation by reducing aggregate demand? Relate this analysis to your answer to Test Yourself Question 1.

7. It is often said that the Federal Reserve Board typically cares more about inflation and less about unemployment than the administration. If this is true, why might presidents often worry about what the Fed might do to interest rates?

8. The year 2014 closed with the unemployment rate just below 6 percent, real GDP growing at roughly 2.5 percent, inflation below 2 percent, and the federal budget showing a deficit under 3 percent of GDP.

a. Give one or more arguments for engaging in expansionary monetary or fiscal policies under these circumstances.

b. Give one or more arguments for engaging in contractionary monetary or fiscal policies under these circumstances.

c. Which arguments do you find more persuasive? (This is a question you might want to discuss in class.)

# THE UNITED STATES IN THE WORLD ECONOMY

Globalization has become a buzzword. Some people extol its virtues and view it as something to be encouraged. Others deplore its real or imagined costs and seek to stop globalization in its tracks. For example, globalization is often viewed as a threat to the livelihoods of American workers.

We will examine several aspects of the globalization debate in Part 4. But love it or hate it, one thing is clear: The U.S. economy is thoroughly integrated into a broader world economy. What happens in the United States influences other countries, and events abroad reverberate back here. Trillions of dollars' worth of goods and services—American software, Chinese toys, Japanese cars—are traded across international borders each year. A vastly larger dollar volume of financial transactions—trade in stocks, bonds, and bank deposits, for example—takes place in the global economy at lightning speed. And lightning is the word, as the global financial panic in 2008–2009 made evident.

Although we have mentioned these subjects before, Part 4 brings international factors from the wings to center stage. Chapter 18 studies the factors that underlie *international trade*, and Chapter 19 takes up the determination of *exchange rates*—the prices at which the world's currencies are bought and sold. Then Chapter 20 integrates these international influences into our model of the macroeconomy.

If you want to understand why so many Americans are worried about losing jobs to international trade, why many thoughtful observers worry that the international monetary system needs an overhaul, or why the financial turmoil that began here spread around the globe so quickly, read these three chapters with care.

CHAPTERS

# INTERNATIONAL TRADE AND COMPARATIVE ADVANTAGE

# 18

*No nation was ever ruined by trade.*

BENJAMIN FRANKLIN

Economists emphasize international trade as the source of many of the benefits of *globalization*—a loosely defined term that indicates a closer knitting together of the world's national economies. Of course, countries have always been linked in various ways. The Vikings, after all, visited North America long before Christopher Columbus. In recent decades, however, dramatic improvements in transportation, telecommunications, and international relations have drawn the nations of the world ever closer together economically. This process of globalization is often portrayed as something new. But in fact, it is not—as the box "Is Globalization Something New?" points out. Still, it is changing the way the people of the world think and live.

Economic events in other countries affect the United States for both macroeconomic and microeconomic reasons. For example, we learned in Parts 2 and 3 that the level of net exports is an important determinant of a nation's output and employment. But we did not delve very deeply into the factors that determine a nation's exports and imports. Chapters 19 and 20 will take up these *macroeconomic* linkages in greater detail. First, however, this chapter studies some of the *microeconomic* linkages among nations: How are patterns and prices of world trade determined? How and why do governments often interfere with foreign trade? The central idea of this chapter is one we have encountered before (in Chapters 1 and 3): the *principle of comparative advantage*. We develop it fully here.

## CONTENTS

---

| Issue | *How Can Americans Compete with "Cheap Foreign Labor"?* |
|:---:|:---|

Americans (and the citizens of many other nations) often want their government to limit or prevent import competition. Why? One major reason is the common belief that imports take bread out of American workers' mouths. According to this view, "cheap foreign labor" steals jobs from Americans and pressures U.S. businesses to lower wages. For many years, attention focused on the phenomenon of manufacturing jobs moving abroad. More recently, there has been just as much concern over the "off-shoring" of a wide variety of service jobs—ranging from call center operators to lawyers. Such worries resonate politically, especially in an atmosphere of high unemployment. It is natural to look for scapegoats, and foreigners are a natural candidate.

Oddly enough, the facts appear to be inconsistent with the idea that trade kills jobs. For one thing, wages in most countries that export to the United States have risen dramatically in recent decades—much faster than wages here. Table 1 shows hourly compensation rates for production workers in manufacturing in nine countries on three continents, each expressed as a percentage of hourly compensation in the United States, in 1975 and 2012. Only workers in Mexico lost ground to American workers over this 37-year period. (Canadian workers exactly kept pace.) Labor in Europe gained substantially on their U.S. counterparts—rising in France, for example, from about three-quarters of the U.S. standard to 12 percent above. And the wage gains in Asia were nothing short of spectacular. Labor compensation in South Korea, for example, soared from just 5 percent of U.S. levels to more than half.[1] Yet while all this was going on, American imports of automobiles from Japan, electronics from Taiwan, and textiles from Korea expanded rapidly.

Ironically, then, the United States' dominant position in the international marketplace *deteriorated* as wage levels in Europe and Asia were rising closer to our own. Clearly, something other than exploiting cheap foreign labor must be driving international trade—in contrast to what the "commonsense" view of the matter suggests. In this chapter, we will learn precisely what is wrong with this commonsense view.

*Table 1*

**Labor Costs in Industrialized Countries as a Percentage of U.S. Labor Costs**

| | 1975 | 2012 |
|---|---|---|
| **Germany** | 83% | 128% |
| France | 76 | 112 |
| Canada | 103 | 103 |
| Japan | 48 | 99 |
| United Kingdom | 53 | 88 |
| Spain | 40 | 75 |
| South Korea | 5 | 58 |
| Taiwan | 6 | 27 |
| Mexico | 23 | 18 |

NOTE: Data are compensation estimates per hour, converted at exchange rates, and relate to production workers in the manufacturing sector.

SOURCE: U.S. Bureau of Labor Statistics.

## 18-1 WHY TRADE?

The earth's resources are distributed unequally across the planet. Although the United States produces its own coal and wheat, it depends almost *entirely* on the rest of the world for such basic items as rubber and coffee. Similarly, the Persian Gulf states have little arable land suitable for farming but sit atop huge pools of oil. Because of the seemingly whimsical distribution of the earth's resources, every nation must trade with others to acquire what it lacks.

Even if countries had all the resources they needed, other differences in natural endowments such as climate, terrain, and so on would lead them to engage in trade. Americans *could* grow their own bananas and coffee in hothouses, albeit with great difficulty. But these crops are grown much more efficiently in such places as Honduras and Brazil, where the climates are appropriate.

The skills of a nation's labor force also play a role. If New Zealand has a large group of efficient farmers and few workers with industrial experience, whereas the opposite is true in Japan, it makes sense for New Zealand to specialize in agriculture, let Japan concentrate on manufacturing, and then trade with one another.

Finally, a small country that tried to produce every product its citizens wanted to consume would end up with many industries that are simply too small to utilize modern mass-production techniques or to take advantage of other economies of large-scale operations. For example, some countries operate their own international airlines for reasons that can only be explained as expressions of national pride, not rational economic calculations.

[1] China would be an even more extreme example, but we lack Chinese data dating back to 1975.

# Is Globalization Something New?

Few people realize that the industrialized world was, in fact, highly globalized prior to World War I, before the ravages of two world wars and the Great Depression severed many international linkages. Furthermore, as the British magazine *The Economist* pointed out some years ago, globalization has not gone nearly as far as many people imagine.

Despite much loose talk about the "new" global economy, today's international economic integration is not unprecedented. The 50 years before the first world war saw large cross-border flows of goods, capital and people. That period of globalisation, like the present one, was driven by reductions in trade barriers and by sharp falls in transport costs, thanks to the development of railways and steamships. The present surge of globalisation is in a way a resumption of that previous trend....

Two forces have been driving [globalization]. The first is technology. With the costs of communication and computing falling rapidly, the natural barriers of time and space that separate national markets have been falling too. The cost of a three-minute telephone call between New York and London has fallen from $300 (in 1996 dollars) in 1930 to $1 today....

The second driving force has been liberalisation.... Almost all countries have lowered barriers to trade.... [T]he ratio of trade to output... has increased sharply in most countries since 1950. But by this measure Britain and France are only slightly more open to trade today than they were in 1913....

Product markets are still nowhere near as integrated across borders as they are within nations. Consider the example of trade between the United States and Canada, one of the least restricted trading borders in the world. On average, trade between a Canadian province and an American state is 20 times smaller than domestic trade between two Canadian provinces, after adjusting for distance and income levels.

The financial markets are not yet truly integrated either. Despite the newfound popularity of international investing, capital markets were by some measures more integrated at the start of this century than they are now.... [And] labour is less mobile than it was in the second half of the 19th century, when some 60m people left Europe for the New World.

SOURCE: "Schools Brief: One World?" *The Economist*, www.economist.com. © The Economist. © The Economist Newspaper Limited, London (October 18, 1997).

To summarize, the main reason why nations trade with one another is to exploit the many advantages of **specialization**, some of which were discussed in Chapter 3. International trade greatly enhances living standards for all parties involved because:

1. **Every country lacks some vital resources that it can get only by trading with others.**
2. **Each country's climate, labor force, and other endowments make it a relatively efficient producer of some goods and a relatively inefficient producer of others.**
3. **Specialization permits larger outputs via the advantages of large-scale production.**

> **Specialization** means that a country devotes its energies and resources to only a small proportion of the world's productive activities.

## 18-1a Mutual Gains from Trade

For centuries, many people have believed that one nation gains from trade only at the expense of another. After all, the mere act of trading doesn't produce anything new. So if one country gains from a swap, it is argued, the other country must necessarily lose. One consequence of this mistaken belief was and continues to be attitudes that call for each country to try to take advantage of its trading partners on the (fallacious) grounds that one nation's gain must be another's loss.

Yet, as Adam Smith emphasized, and as we learned back in Chapter 3, both parties must expect to gain something when they engage in *voluntary exchange*. Otherwise, why would they agree to trade?

How can mere exchange of goods leave both parties better off? The answer is that although trade does not increase the total output of goods, it does allow each party to acquire items better suited to its tastes. Suppose Levi has four cookies and nothing to drink, whereas Malcolm has two glasses of milk and nothing to eat. A trade of two of Levi's cookies for one of Malcolm's glasses of milk will not increase the total supply of either milk or cookies, but it almost certainly will make both boys better off.

By exactly the same logic, both the United States and Mexico must reap gains when Mexicans voluntarily ship tomatoes to the United States in return for American chemicals. In general, as we emphasized in Chapter 3:

Ideas for Beyond the Final Exam

**TRADE IS A WIN–WIN SITUATION** Both parties must expect to gain from any *voluntary exchange.* Trade brings about mutual gains by redistributing products so that both parties end up holding more preferred combinations of goods than they held before. This principle, which is one of our *Ideas for Beyond the Final Exam,* applies to nations just as it does to individuals.

## 18-2  INTERNATIONAL VERSUS INTRANATIONAL TRADE

The 50 states of the United States may be the most eloquent testimonial to the large gains that can be realized from specialization and free trade. Florida specializes in growing oranges, Michigan builds cars, California makes software, and New York specializes in finance. All of these states trade freely with one another and, as a result, enjoy great prosperity. Try to imagine how much lower your standard of living would be if you could consume only items produced in your home state.

The essential logic behind international trade is no different from that underlying trade among different states; the basic reasons for trade are equally applicable within a country or among countries. Why, then, do we study international trade as a special subject? There are at least three reasons.

### 18-2a  Political Factors in International Trade

First, domestic trade takes place under a single national government, whereas foreign trade always involves at least two governments. But a nation's government is normally much less concerned about the welfare of other countries' citizens than it is about its own. So, for example, the U.S. Constitution prohibits tariffs on trade among states, but it does not prohibit the United States from imposing tariffs on imports from abroad. One major issue in the economic analysis of international trade is the use and misuse of legal impediments to international trade.

### 18-2b  The Many Currencies Involved in International Trade

Second, all trade within the borders of the United States is carried out in U.S. dollars, whereas most trade across national borders involves at least two currencies. (The main exception is the countries that share the euro.) Rates of exchange among different currencies can and do change. In 1985, it took about 250 Japanese yen to buy a dollar; now it takes only about 120. Variability in exchange rates brings with it a host of complications and policy problems.

### 18-2c  Impediments to Mobility of Labor and Capital

Third, it is much easier for labor and capital to move about within a country than to move from one nation to another. If jobs are plentiful in California but scarce in Ohio, workers can move freely to follow the job opportunities. Of course, personal costs such as the financial burden of moving and the psychological burden of leaving friends and familiar surroundings may discourage mobility. But such relocations are not inhibited by immigration quotas, by laws restricting the employment of foreigners, or by the need to learn a new language.

There are also greater impediments to the transfer of capital across national boundaries than to its movement within a country. For example, many countries have rules limiting foreign ownership. Even the United States limits foreign ownership of broadcast outlets and airlines, and political furors regularly arise when a foreign company (lately, often Chinese) seeks to purchase a prominent U.S. company. In some countries, foreign investment is also subject to special political risks, such as the danger of outright expropriation or nationalization after a change in government.

Even if nothing as extreme as expropriation occurs, capital invested abroad faces significant risks from exchange rate variations. An investment valued at 250 million yen is worth $2.5 million to American investors when the dollar is worth 100 yen, but it is worth only $1 million when it takes 250 yen to buy a dollar.

## 18-3 THE LAW OF COMPARATIVE ADVANTAGE

The gains from international specialization and trade are clear and intuitive when one country is better at producing one item and its trading partner is better at producing another. For example, no one finds it surprising that Brazil sells coffee to the United States and the United States exports software to Brazil. We know that coffee can be produced using less labor and other inputs in Brazil than in the United States. Likewise, the United States can produce software at a lower resource cost than can Brazil.

In such a situation, we say that Brazil has an **absolute advantage** in coffee production, and the United States has an absolute advantage in software production. In such cases, it is obvious that both countries can gain by producing the item in which they have an absolute advantage and then trading with one another.

What is much less obvious, but equally true, is that these gains from international trade still exist *even if one country is more efficient than the other in producing everything.* This lesson, the principle of **comparative advantage**, is one we first encountered in Chapter 3. It is, in fact, one of the most important of our *Ideas for Beyond the Final Exam,* so we repeat it here for convenience.

> **THE SURPRISING PRINCIPLE OF COMPARATIVE ADVANTAGE** Even if one country is at an absolute *dis*advantage relative to another country in the production of every good, it still has a *comparative advantage* in making the good at which it is *least inefficient* (compared with the other country).
>
> The great classical economist David Ricardo (1772–1823) discovered one of the most important thoughts in all of economics more than 200 years ago: that two countries can still gain from trade even if one is more efficient than the other in *every* industry—that is, even if one has an absolute advantage in producing every commodity.
>
> In determining the most efficient patterns of production, it is *comparative* advantage, not *absolute* advantage, that matters. Thus a country can gain by importing a good even if that good can be produced more efficiently at home. Such imports make sense if they enable the country to specialize in producing goods at which it is *even more* efficient.

*One country is said to have an* **absolute advantage** *over another in the production of a particular good if it can produce that good using smaller quantities of resources than can the other country.*

*One country is said to have a* **comparative advantage** *over another in the production of a particular good relative to other goods if it produces that good less inefficiently as compared with the other country.*

## 18-4 THE ARITHMETIC OF COMPARATIVE ADVANTAGE

Let us see precisely how comparative advantage works using a hypothetical example first suggested in Chapter 3. Table 2 offers a rather exaggerated impression of the trading positions of the United States and Japan a few years ago. We imagine that labor is the only input used to produce computers and television sets in the two countries and that the United States has an absolute advantage in manufacturing both goods. In this example, one year's worth of labor can produce either 50 computers or 50 TV sets in the United States but only 10 computers or 40 televisions in Japan. So the United States is more efficient at producing each good. Nonetheless, as we will now show, it makes sense for the United States to specialize in producing computers and then trade with Japan to get the TV sets it wants.

To demonstrate this point, we begin by noting that the United States has a comparative advantage in producing *computers,* whereas Japan has a comparative advantage in producing *televisions.* Specifically, the numbers in Table 2 show that the United States can produce 50 televisions with one year's labor, whereas Japan can produce only 40, giving the United States a 25 percent efficiency edge over Japan. However, the United States is five times as efficient as Japan in producing computers: It can produce 50 per year of labor rather than 10.

*Table 2*

**Alternative Outputs from One Year of Labor Input**

|  | In the United States | In Japan |
|---|---|---|
| Computers | 50 | 10 |
| Televisions | 50 | 40 |

*Table 3*

**Example of the Gains from Trade**

|  | United States | Japan | Total |
|---|---|---|---|
| Computers | +25,000 | – 10,000 | +15,000 |
| Televisions | – 25,000 | +40,000 | +15,000 |

Because America's competitive edge is far greater in computers than in televisions, we say that the United States has a *comparative advantage* in computers.

From the Japanese perspective, these same numbers indicate that Japan is only *slightly less* efficient than the United States in TV production but *drastically less* efficient in computer production. So Japan's comparative advantage is in producing televisions. According to Ricardo's law of comparative advantage, then, the two countries can gain if the United States specializes in producing computers, Japan specializes in producing TVs, and the two countries trade.

Let's verify that this conclusion is true. Suppose Japan transfers 1,000 years of labor out of the computer industry and into TV manufacturing. According to the numbers in Table 2, its computer output will *fall* by 10,000 units and its TV output will *rise* by 40,000 units. This information is recorded in the middle column of Table 3. Suppose, at the same time, the United States transfers 500 years of labor out of television manufacturing (thereby losing 25,000 TVs) and into computer making (thereby gaining 25,000 computers). Table 3 shows us that these transfers of resources in the two countries increase the *world's* production of *both* outputs. Together, the two countries now make 15,000 additional TVs and 15,000 additional computers—a nice outcome.

Was there some sleight of hand here? How did *both* the United States *and* Japan gain *both* computers *and* TVs? The explanation is that the process we have just described involves more than just a swap of a fixed bundle of commodities, as in our earlier example of cookies and milk. It also involves *a change in production arrangements*. Some of Japan's inefficient computer production is taken over by more efficient American makers. And some of America's TV production is taken over by Japanese television companies, which are *less inefficient* at making TVs than Japanese computer manufacturers are at making computers. In this way, *world productivity is increased*. The underlying principle is both simple and fundamental:

> **When every country does what it can do best, all countries can benefit because more of every commodity can be produced without increasing the amounts of labor and other resources used.**

Where does the United States hold and lack comparative advantage? For answers, just look at what we export to the rest of the world and import from abroad. Among our big export powerhouses are the aerospace industry, agriculture, chemicals, high-tech services of all sorts, software, financial services (still!), entertainment, and higher education. We are, of course, huge importers of television sets, automobiles, clothing, toys, and much else.

## 18-4a The Graphics of Comparative Advantage

The gains from trade also can be illustrated graphically, and doing so helps us understand whether such gains are large or small.

The lines *US* and *JN* in Figure 1 are closely related to the production possibilities frontiers of the two countries, differing only in that they pretend that each country has the same amount of labor.[2] In this case, we assume that each has 1 million person-years of labor. For example, Table 2 tells us that for each 1 million years of labor, the United States can produce

*Figure 1*

**Production Possibilities Frontiers for Two Countries
(per million person-years of labor)**

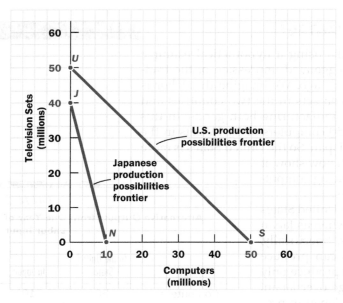

---

[2] To review the concept of the production possibilities frontier, see Chapter 3.

50 million TVs and no computers (point *U* in Figure 1), 50 million computers and no TVs (point *S*), or any combination in between (the line *US*). Parallel reasoning leads to line *JN* for Japan.

America's actual production possibilities frontier would be even higher, relative to Japan's, than shown in Figure 1 because the U.S. workforce is so much larger. But Figure 1 is more useful because it highlights the differences in *efficiency* (rather than in mere size), which is what determines both absolute and comparative advantage. Let's see how.

The fact that line *US* lies *above* line *JN* means that the United States can manufacture more televisions and more computers than Japan *even with the same amount of labor*. This difference reflects our assumption that the United States has an absolute advantage in both commodities.

America's *comparative* advantage in computer production and Japan's comparative advantage in TV production are shown in a different way: by the relative *slopes* of the two lines. Look back to Table 2, which shows that the United States can acquire a computer on its own by giving up one TV. Thus, the *opportunity cost* of acquiring a computer in the United States is giving up one television set. This opportunity cost is depicted graphically by the slope of the U.S. production possibilities frontier in Figure 1, which is $OU/OS = 50/50 = 1$.

Table 2 also tells us that the opportunity cost of a computer in Japan is four TVs. This relationship is depicted in Figure 1 by the slope of Japan's production possibilities frontier, which is $OJ/ON = 40/10 = 4$.

> A country's *absolute* advantage in production over another country is shown by its having a higher per capita production possibilities frontier. The difference in the *comparative* advantages between the two countries is shown by the difference in the slopes of their frontiers.

Because opportunity costs differ in the two countries, gains are possible if the two countries specialize and trade with one another. Specifically, it is cheaper, in terms of real resources forgone, for *either* country to acquire its computers in the United States. By a similar line of reasoning, the opportunity cost of TVs is higher in the United States than in Japan, so it makes sense for both countries to acquire their televisions in Japan.[3]

Notice that if the slopes of the two production possibilities frontiers, *JN* and *US*, were equal, then opportunity costs would be the same in each country. In that case, no potential gains would arise from trade. Gains from trade arise from *differences* across countries, not from similarities. This is an important point about which people are often confused. It is often argued that two very different countries, say, the United States and Mexico, cannot gain much by trading with one another while two rather similar countries, say, the United States and Canada can. The fact is just the opposite:

> Two very similar countries may gain little from trading with one another. Large gains from trade are most likely when countries are very different.

The pattern is apparent in U.S. trade statistics—with one big exception. Canada, while rather similar to the United States, is our biggest trading partner. But that is mainly because the two nations share a huge and very porous border. However, our next three biggest trading partners, in order, are China, Mexico, and Japan—three countries very different from the United States.

How nations divide the gains from trade depends on the prices that emerge from world trade—a complicated topic that we take up in the appendix to this chapter. But we already know enough to see that world trade must, in our example, leave a computer costing more than one TV and less than four. Why? Because if giving up a computer gained you less than one TV (its opportunity cost in the United States) on the world market, the United States would produce its own TVs rather than buying them from Japan. And if acquiring a computer cost more than four TVs (its opportunity cost in Japan), Japan would produce its own computers rather than buy them from the United States. So we conclude that, if both countries are to trade, the rate of exchange between TVs and computers must end up somewhere between 4:1 and 1:1. Generalizing:

---

[3] EXERCISE: Provide this line of reasoning.

If two countries voluntarily trade two goods with one another, the rate of exchange between the goods must fall in between the price ratios that would prevail in the two countries in the absence of trade.

To illustrate the gains from trade in our concrete example, let's assume that the world price ratio settles at 2:1—meaning that one computer costs as much as two televisions. How much, precisely, do the United States and Japan gain from world trade in this case?

Figure 2 helps us visualize the answers. The maroon production possibilities frontiers, *US* in Panel (b) and *JN* in Panel (a), are the same as in Figure 1. But the United States can do better than line *US*. Specifically, with a world price ratio of 2:1, the United States acquires two TVs for each computer it gives up, rather than just one (which is the opportunity cost of a computer in the United States). Hence, if the United States produces only computers—point *S* in Figure 2(b)—and buys its TVs from Japan, America's *consumption possibilities* will be as indicated by the blue line that emanates from point *S* with a slope of two—that is, each computer sold to Japan brings the United States two television sets. (The line ends at point *A* because 40 million TV sets is the most that Japan can produce.) Because trade allows the United States to choose a point on *AS* rather than on *US*, trade opens up consumption possibilities that were simply not available before (shaded gray in the diagram).

A similar story applies to Japan. If the Japanese produce only television sets—point *J* in Figure 2(a)—they can acquire a computer from the United States for every two TVs they give up as they move along the blue line *JP* (whose slope is two). This result is better than they can achieve on their own, because a sacrifice of two TVs in Japan yields only one-half of a computer. Hence, world trade enlarges Japan's consumption possibilities from *JN* to *JP*.

Figure 2 shows graphically that gains from trade arise to the extent that the world price ratio (2:1 in our example) differs from domestic opportunity costs (4:1 and 1:1 in our example). How the two countries share the gains from trade depends on the exact prices that emerge from world trade. As explained in the appendix, that in turn depends on relative supplies and demands in the two countries.

*Figure 2*

**The Gains from Trade**

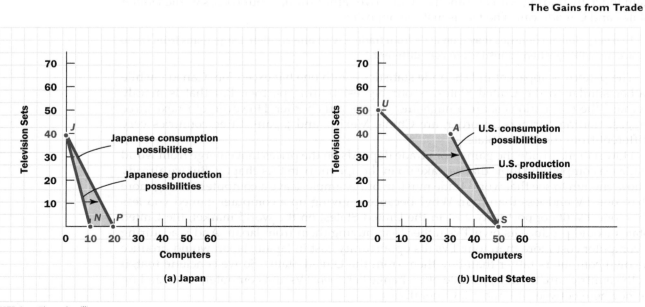

(a) Japan

(b) United States

NOTE: Quantities are in millions.

## 18-4b Must Specialization Be Complete?

In our simple numerical and graphical examples, international specialization is always *complete*—for example, the United States makes all the computers and Japan makes all the TV sets. But if you look at the real world, you find mostly *incomplete* specialization. For example, the United States is the world's biggest importer of automobiles, but we also manufacture lots of cars here. In fact, we even export some of them. This stark discrepancy between theory and fact might worry you. Is something wrong with the theory of comparative advantage?

Actually, there are many reasons why specialization is typically incomplete, despite the validity of the principle of comparative advantage. Two of them are simple enough to merit mentioning right here.

First, some countries are just too small to provide the world's entire output, even when they have a strong comparative advantage in the good in question. In our numerical example, Japan just might not have enough labor and other resources to produce the entire world output of televisions. If so, some TV sets would have to be produced in the United States.

Second, you may have noticed that in this chapter we have drawn all the production possibilities frontiers (PPFs) as *straight lines*, whereas in previous chapters they were always *curved*. The reason is purely pedagogical: Straight lines create simple examples that lend themselves to numerical solutions. But it is undoubtedly more realistic to assume that real-world PPFs are bowed outward, as in Chapter 3. That sort of technology leads to incomplete specialization, but it is a complication best left to more advanced courses.

---

| Issue Revisited | *Comparative Advantage Exposes the "Cheap Foreign Labor" Fallacy* |
|---|---|

The principle of comparative advantage takes us a long way toward understanding the fallacy in the "cheap foreign labor" argument described at the beginning of this chapter. Given the assumed productive efficiency of American labor, and the assumed inefficiency of Japanese labor, wages would be much higher in the United States.

Under these circumstances, one might expect American workers to be apprehensive about any agreement to permit open trade between the two countries: "How can we hope to meet the unfair competition of those underpaid Japanese workers?" Japanese laborers might also be concerned: "How can we hope to meet the competition of those Americans, who are so efficient in producing everything?"

The principle of comparative advantage shows us that both fears are unjustified. As we have just seen, when trade opens up between Japan and the United States, *workers in both countries will be able to earn higher real wages than before* because of the increased productivity that comes through specialization.

As Figure 2 shows, once trade opens up, Japanese workers should be able to acquire more TVs *and* more computers than they did before. As a consequence, their living standards should *rise*, even though they have been left vulnerable to competition from the super-efficient Americans. Workers in the United States should also end up with more TVs and more computers. So their living standards should also rise, even though they have been exposed to "unfair" competition from cheap Japanese labor.

These higher standards of living, of course, reflect the higher real wages earned when workers become more productive in both countries. The lesson to be learned here is elementary:

**Nothing helps raise living standards more than a greater abundance of goods.**

## 18-5 TARIFFS, QUOTAS, AND OTHER INTERFERENCES WITH TRADE

Despite the large mutual gains from international trade, nations often interfere with the free movement of goods and services across national borders. In fact, until the rise of the free-trade movement about 200 years ago (with Adam Smith and David Ricardo at its vanguard), it was taken for granted that one of the essential tasks of government was to impede trade, presumably in the national interest.

Then, as now, many people argued that the proper aim of government policy was to promote exports and discourage imports, for doing so would increase the amount of money foreigners had to send to the nation. According to this so-called **mercantilist** view, a nation's wealth consists of the amount of gold or other monies at its command.

**Mercantilism** is a doctrine that holds that exports are good for a country, whereas imports are harmful.

Obviously, governments can pursue such a policy only within certain limits. A country *must* import vital foodstuffs and critical raw materials that it cannot provide for itself. Moreover, mercantilists ignore a simple piece of arithmetic: It is mathematically impossible for *every* country to sell more than it buys, because one country's exports must be some other country's imports. If everyone competes in the mercantilist game by cutting imports to the bone, then exports must shrivel up, too. The result is that everyone will be deprived of the mutual gains from trade. Indeed, that is precisely what happens in a trade war.

After a disastrous experiment with protectionism in the 1930s, the United States moved away from mercantilist policies designed to impede imports and gradually assumed a leading role in promoting free trade. Over the past 80-plus years, U.S. tariffs and other trade barriers have come down dramatically.

In 1995, the United States led the world to complete the Uruguay Round of tariff reductions and, just before that, the country joined Canada and Mexico in the North American Free Trade Agreement (NAFTA). The latter caused a political firestorm in the United States in 1993 and 1994, with critic (and 1992 presidential candidate) Ross Perot colorfully predicting a "giant sucking sound" as American workers lost their jobs to competition from "cheap Mexican labor." (Does that argument sound familiar?) But it didn't happen; instead, America created a vast number of net new jobs in the years 1995–2000.

Still, large-scale trade agreements are uphill battles in most countries, where protectionist sentiment is often strong. Most of the world's trading nations have been formally engaged—at least in principle—in a seemingly endless round of trade talks under guidelines adopted in Doha, Qatar, in 2001. But at this writing, the Doha Round seems to be going nowhere. Perhaps closer to eventual success (but perhaps not), the U.S. government is currently engaged in negotiations toward a Trans-Pacific Partnership, which would be a free-trade agreement including eleven other countries in the Asia-Pacific region.

Modern governments use three main devices when seeking to control trade: tariffs, quotas, and export subsidies.

A **tariff** is a tax on imports.

A **tariff** is simply a tax on imports. An importer of cars, for example, may be charged $2,000 for each auto brought into the country. Such a tax will, of course, make automobiles more expensive and favor domestic models over imports. It will also raise revenue for the government. In fact, tariffs were a major source of tax revenue for the U.S. government during the eighteenth and nineteenth centuries—and also a major source of political controversy. Nowadays, the United States is a low-tariff country, with only a few notable exceptions. However, some other countries rely on heavy tariffs to protect their industries. Indeed, tariff rates of 100 percent or more are not unknown in some countries.

A **quota** specifies the maximum amount of a good that is permitted into the country from abroad per unit of time.

A **quota** is a legal limit on the amount of a good that may be imported. For example, the government might allow no more than 5 million foreign-made cars to be imported in a year. In some cases, governments ban the importation of certain goods outright—a quota of zero. The United States now imposes quotas on a smattering of goods, including textiles, meat, and sugar. Most imports, however, are not subject to quotas. By reducing supply, quotas naturally raise the prices of the goods subject to quotas. For example, sugar is vastly more expensive in the United States than it is elsewhere in the world.

An **export subsidy** is a payment by the government to exporters to permit them to reduce the selling prices of their goods so they can compete more effectively in foreign markets.

An **export subsidy** is a government payment to an exporter. By reducing the exporter's costs, such subsidies permit exporters to lower their selling prices and compete more effectively in world trade. Overt export subsidies are rare in the United States. But some foreign governments use them extensively to assist their domestic industries—a practice that provokes bitter complaints from American manufacturers about unfair competition. In one prominent example over many years, heavy government subsidies helped the European Airbus consortium take a sizable share of the world commercial aircraft market away from U.S. manufacturers like Boeing and McDonnell-Douglas.

## 18-5a Tariffs versus Quotas

Although both tariffs and quotas reduce international trade and increase domestic prices, there are some important differences between these two ways to restrict trade and protect domestic industries.

First, under a quota, profits from the higher price in the importing country usually go into the pockets of the foreign and domestic sellers of the products. Limitations on supply from abroad mean (a) that customers in the importing country must pay more for the product and (b) that suppliers, whether foreign or domestic, receive more for every unit they sell. For example, the right to sell sugar in the United States under the tight sugar quota has been extremely valuable for decades. Privileged foreign and domestic firms can—and often do—make a lot of money from quota rights.

By contrast, when trade is restricted by a tariff instead, some of the "profits" go as tax revenues to the government of the importing country. (Domestic producers still benefit, because they are exempt from the tariff.) In this respect, a tariff is certainly a better proposition than a quota for the country that enacts it.

Another important distinction between the two measures arises from their different implications for productive efficiency. Because a tariff handicaps all foreign suppliers equally, it still enables those foreign firms and nations that can supply the goods most cheaply to serve the domestic market—presumably because they are more efficient. A quota, by contrast, necessarily awards its import licenses more or less capriciously— perhaps in proportion to past sales or based on political favoritism. There is no reason to expect the most efficient suppliers to get the import permits. For example, the U.S. sugar quota was for years suspected of being a major source of corruption in the Caribbean.

## How Popular Is International Trade?

Since World War II, the world has mainly moved away from protectionism and toward freer trade. However, the people of the world—and especially Americans—are not entirely convinced that this trend is desirable. In what almost certainly was the most comprehensive polling ever conducted on the subject, the Pew Research Center in 2014 asked nearly 49,000 people in 44 countries a series of questions about international trade. The first (the two leftmost bars in the accompanying figure) was very general: "Are growing trade and business ties with other countries a good thing?" Majorities agreed that it is, though Americans were less enthusiastic than most. More pointed questions about the downsides of trade showed sharper U.S.–world divergences. For example, when people were asked whether trade destroys or creates jobs (the two middle bars in the figure), 50 percent of Americans thought trade destroyed jobs, but only 19 percent of people around the world thought so. And when people were asked about trade's effects on wages, 45 percent of Americans, but just 21 percent of people around the world, thought trade lowered wages. No wonder expansion of free trade is a tough sell in American politics.

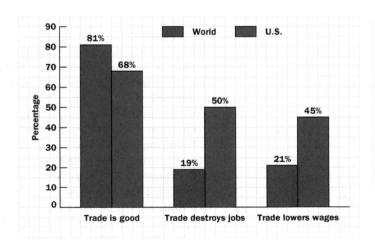

If a country must inhibit imports, two important reasons support a preference for tariffs over quotas:

1. Some of the revenues resulting from tariffs go to the government of the importing country rather than to foreign and domestic producers.
2. Unlike quotas, tariffs offer greater benefits to more efficient exporters.

## 18-6  WHY INHIBIT TRADE?

To state that tariffs provide a better way to inhibit international trade than quotas leaves open a far more basic question: Why limit trade in the first place? It was estimated some years back that the cost of trade restrictions in the form of higher prices to American consumers amounted to about 10 percent of imports. (That figure would be less today because of trade liberalizations.) Why should they be asked to pay these higher prices? A number of answers have been given. Let's examine each in turn.

### 18-6a  Gaining a Price Advantage for Domestic Firms

A tariff forces foreign exporters to sell more cheaply by restricting their market access. If the foreign firms do not cut their prices, they will be unable to sell their goods. So, in effect, a tariff amounts to government intervention to rig prices in favor of domestic producers.[4]

Not bad, you say. However, this technique works only as long as foreigners accept the tariff exploitation passively—which they rarely do. Often they retaliate by imposing tariffs or quotas of their own on imports from the country that began the tariff game. Such tit-for-tat behavior can easily lead to a trade war in which everyone loses through the resulting reductions in trade. Something like this, in fact, happened to the world economy in the 1930s, and it helped prolong the worldwide depression. Preventing such trade wars is one main reason why nations that belong to the World Trade Organization (WTO) pledge not to raise tariffs.

> Tariffs or quotas can benefit particular domestic industries in a country that is able to impose them without fear of retaliation. But when every country uses them, every country is likely to lose in the long run.

### 18-6b  Protecting Particular Industries

The second, and probably more frequent, reason why countries restrict trade is to protect particular favored industries from foreign competition. If foreigners can produce steel or shoes more cheaply, domestic businesses and unions in these industries are quick to demand protection. And their governments may be quite willing to grant it.

This is where the "cheap foreign labor" argument is most likely to be invoked. Protective tariffs and quotas are explicitly designed to rescue firms that are too inefficient to compete with foreign exporters in an open world market. But it is precisely this harsh competition that earns consumers the chief benefits of international specialization: better products at lower prices. So protection comes at a cost.

Thinking back to our numerical example of comparative advantage, we can well imagine indignant complaints from Japanese computer makers as the opening of trade with the United States leads to increased imports of American-made computers. At the same time, American TV manufacturers would probably express outrage over the flood of imported TVs from Japan. Yet it is Japanese specialization in televisions and U.S. specialization in computers that enables citizens of both countries to enjoy higher standards of living. If governments interfere with this process, consumers in both countries will lose.

---

[4] For more details on this, see the appendix to this chapter.

Industries threatened by foreign competition often argue that some form of protection against imports is needed to prevent job losses. For example, the U.S. steel industry has made exactly this argument time and time again since the 1960s. And the U.S. government has often delivered some trade protection in response. But basic macroeconomics teaches us that there are better ways to stimulate employment, such as raising aggregate demand.

A program that limits foreign competition will be more effective at preserving employment *in the particular protected industry*. However, such job gains typically come at a high cost to consumers and to the economy. Table 4 displays estimates made some years ago of the costs to American consumers of using tariffs and quotas to save jobs in selected industries. In every case, the costs far exceeded the annual wages of the workers in the protected industries—ranging as high as astounding $600,000 per job for the sugar quota.

*Table 4*

**Estimated Costs of Protectionism to Consumers**

| Industry | Cost per Job Saved |
| --- | --- |
| Apparel | $139,000 |
| Costume jewelry | 97,000 |
| Shipping | 415,000 |
| Sugar | 600,000 |
| Textiles | 202,000 |
| Women's footwear | 102,000 |

SOURCE: Gary C. Hufbauer and Kimberly Ann Elliott, *Measuring the Costs of Protectionism in the United States* (Washington, D.C.: Institute for International Economics, January 1994), Table 1.3, pp. 12–13.

Nevertheless, complaints over proposals to reduce tariffs or quotas may be justified unless something is done to ease the cost to individual workers of switching to the product lines that trade makes profitable.

**The argument for free trade between countries cannot be considered airtight if governments do not assist the citizens in each country who are harmed whenever patterns of production change drastically—as would happen, for example, if governments suddenly reduced tariff and quota barriers.**

In our example, owners of television factories in the United States and of computer factories in Japan may see large investments suddenly rendered unprofitable. Workers in those industries may see their special skills and training devalued in the marketplace. Displaced workers also pay heavy intangible costs—they may need to move to new locations and/or new industries, uprooting their families, losing old friends, and so on. Although the *majority* of citizens undoubtedly gain from free trade, that is no consolation to those who are its victims.

To mitigate these problems, the U.S. government follows two basic approaches. First, our trade laws offer temporary protection from sudden surges of imports, on the grounds that unexpected changes in trade patterns do not give businesses and workers enough time to adjust.

Second, the government has set up **trade adjustment assistance** programs to help workers and businesses that lose their jobs or their markets to imports. Firms may be eligible for technical assistance, government loans or loan guarantees, and permission to delay tax payments. Workers may qualify for retraining programs, longer periods of unemployment compensation, and funds to defray moving costs. Each form of assistance is designed to ease the burden on the victims of free trade so that the rest of us can enjoy its considerable benefits.

**Trade adjustment assistance** provides special unemployment benefits, loans, retraining programs, and other aid to workers and firms that are harmed by foreign competition.

## 18-6c National Defense and Other Noneconomic Considerations

A third rationale for trade protection is the need to maintain national defense. For example, even if the United States were not the most efficient producer of aircraft, it might still be rational to produce our own military aircraft so that no foreign government could ever cut off supplies of this strategic product.

The national defense argument is fine as far as it goes, but it poses a clear danger: Even industries with the most peripheral relationship to defense are likely to invoke this argument on their behalf. For example, for many years the U.S. watchmaking industry argued for protection on the grounds that its skilled workers would be invaluable in wartime!

Similarly, the United States has occasionally banned either exports to or imports from nations such as Cuba and Iran on political grounds. Such actions may have important economic effects, creating either bonanzas or disasters for particular American industries. But they are justified by politics, not by economics. Noneconomic reasons also explain quotas on importation of whaling products and on the furs of other endangered species.

## 18-6d The Infant-Industry Argument

The **infant-industry argument** for trade protection holds that new industries need to be protected from foreign competition until they develop and flourish.

Yet a fourth common rationale for protectionism is the so-called **infant-industry argument**, which has been prominent in the United States at least since Alexander Hamilton presented his landmark *Report on Manufactures* to Congress in 1791. Promising new industries often need breathing room to flourish and grow. If we expose these infants to the rigors of international competition too soon, the argument goes, they may never develop to the point where they can survive on their own in the international marketplace.

This argument, although valid in certain instances, is less defensible than it seems at first. Protecting an infant industry is justifiable only if the prospective future gains are sufficient to repay the upfront costs of protectionism. But if the industry is likely to be so profitable in the future, why doesn't private capital rush in to take advantage of the prospective net profits? After all, the annals of business are full of cases in which a new product or a new firm lost money at first but profited handsomely later on. In recent times, Apple, Google, Amazon, and Facebook all lost money in their early days.

The infant-industry argument for protection stands up to scrutiny only if private funds are unavailable for some reason, despite an industry's glowing profit prospects. Even then it may make more sense to provide a government loan rather than to provide trade protection.

In an advanced economy such as ours, with well-developed capital markets to fund new businesses (as opposed to the young United States in 1791), it is difficult to think of legitimate examples where the infant-industry argument applies. Even if such a case were found, we would have to be careful that the industry not remain in diapers forever. In too many cases, industries are awarded protection when young and, somehow, never mature to the point where protection can be withdrawn. We must be wary of infants that never grow up.

## 18-6e Strategic Trade Policy

A stronger argument for (temporary) protection has sometimes influenced trade policy in the United States and elsewhere. Proponents of this line of thinking agree that free trade for all is the best system. But they point out that we live in an imperfect world in which many nations refuse to play by the rules of the free-trade game. And they fear that a nation that pursues free trade in a protectionist world is likely to lose out. It therefore makes sense, they argue, to threaten to protect your markets unless other nations agree to open theirs.

The United States has followed this strategy in trade negotiations with several countries in recent decades. In one prominent case, the U.S. government threatened to impose high tariffs on several European luxury goods unless Europe opened its markets to imported bananas from the Americas. A few years later, the European Union turned the tables, threatening to increase tariffs on a variety of U.S. goods unless we changed a tax provision that amounted to an export subsidy. In each case, a dangerous trade war was narrowly averted when an agreement was struck at the eleventh hour.

The **strategic argument for protection** holds that a nation may sometimes have to threaten protectionism to induce other countries to drop their own protectionist measures.

The **strategic argument for protection** is a difficult one for economists to counter. Although it recognizes the superiority of free trade, it argues that *threatening* to turn protectionist is the best way to achieve free and open trade. (See the box "Can Protectionism Save Free Trade?") Such a strategy might work, but it clearly involves great risks. If threats that the United States will turn protectionist induce other countries to scrap their existing protectionist policies, then the gamble will have succeeded. But if the gamble fails, protectionism increases.

# Can Protectionism Save Free Trade?

In this classic column, former New York Times columnist, William Safire shook off his long-standing attachment to free trade and argued eloquently for retaliation against protectionist nations.

Free trade is economic motherhood. Protectionism is economic evil incarnate…. Never should government interfere in the efficiency of international competition.

Since childhood, these have been the tenets of my faith. If it meant that certain businesses in this country went belly-up, so be it…. If it meant that Americans would be thrown out of work by overseas companies paying coolie wages, that was tough….

The thing to keep in mind, I was taught, was the Big Picture and the Long Run. America, the great exporter, had far more to gain than to lose from free trade; attempts to protect inefficient industries here would ultimately cost more American jobs.

While playing with my David Ricardo doll and learning nursery rhymes about comparative advantage, I was listening to another laissez-fairy tale: Government's role in the world of business should be limited to keeping business honest and competitive. In God we antitrusted. Let businesses operate in the free marketplace.

Now American businesses are no longer competing with foreign companies. They are competing with foreign governments who help their local businesses. That means the world arena no longer offers a free marketplace; instead, most other governments are pushing a policy that can be called helpfulism.

Helpfulism works like this: A government like Japan decides to get behind its baseball-bat industry. It pumps in capital, knocks off marginal operators, finds subtle ways to discourage imports of Louisville Sluggers, and selects target areas for export blitzes. Pretty soon, the favored Japanese companies are driving foreign competitors batty.

How do we compete with helpfulism? One way is to complain that it is unfair; that draws a horselaugh. Another way is to demand a "Reagan Round" of trade negotiations under GATT, the Gentlemen's Agreement To Talk, which is equally laughable. Yet another way is to join the helpfuls by subsidizing our exports and permitting our companies to try monopolistic tricks abroad not permitted at home. But all that makes us feel guilty, with good reason.

The other way to deal with helpfulism is through—here comes the dreadful word—protection. Or, if you prefer a euphemism, retaliation. Or if that is still too severe, reciprocity. Whatever its name, it is a way of saying to the cutthroat cartelists we sweetly call our trading partners: "You have bent the rules out of shape. Change your practices to conform to the agreed-upon rules, or we will export a taste of your own medicine."

A little balance, then, from the free trade theorists. The demand for what the Pentagon used to call "protective reaction" is not demagoguery, not shortsighted, not self-defeating. On the contrary, the overseas pirates of protectionism and exemplars of helpfulism need to be taught the basic lesson in trade, which is: tit for tat.

SOURCE: William Safire, "Smoot-Hawley Lives," *The New York Times*, March 17, 1983. Copyright © 1983 by The New York Times Company. All rights reserved. Used by permission and protected by the Copyright Laws of the United States. The printing, copying, redistribution, or retransmission of the material without express written permission is prohibited.

David Burnett/Contact Press Images

## 18-7 CAN CHEAP IMPORTS HURT A COUNTRY?

One of the most curious—and illogical—features of the protectionist position is the fear of low import prices. Countries that subsidize their exports are often accused of **dumping**— of getting rid of their goods at unjustifiably low prices. Economists find this argument strange. As a nation of consumers, we should be indignant when foreigners charge us *high* prices, not *low* ones. That commonsense rule guides every consumer's daily life. Only from the topsy-turvy viewpoint of an industry seeking protection are low prices seen as counter to the public interest.

**Dumping** means selling goods in a foreign market at lower prices than those charged in the home market.

Ultimately, the best interests of any country are served when its imports are as cheap as possible. It would be ideal for the United States if the rest of the world were willing to provide us with goods at no charge. We could then live in luxury at the expense of other countries.

However, benefits to the United States as a whole do not necessarily accrue to every single American. If quotas on, say, sugar imports were dropped, American consumers and industries that purchase sugar would gain from lower prices. At the same time, however, owners of sugar fields and their employees would suffer serious losses in the form of lower profits, lower wages, and lost jobs—losses they would fight fiercely to prevent. For this reason, politics often leads to the adoption of protectionist measures that would likely be rejected on strictly economic criteria.

# Unfair Foreign Competition

Satire and ridicule are often more persuasive than logic and statistics. Exasperated by the spread of protectionism under the prevailing mercantilist philosophy, the French economist Frédéric Bastiat decided to take the protectionist argument to its illogical conclusion. The fictitious petition of the French candlemakers to the Chamber of Deputies, written in 1845 and excerpted here, has become a classic in the battle for free trade.

We are subject to the intolerable competition of a foreign rival, who enjoys, it would seem, such superior facilities for the production of light, that he is enabled to inundate our national market at so exceedingly reduced a price, that, the moment he makes his appearance, he draws off all custom for us; and thus an important branch of French industry, with all its innumerable ramifications, is suddenly reduced to a state of complete stagnation. This rival is no other than the sun.

Our petition is, that it would please your honorable body to pass a law whereby shall be directed the shutting up of all windows, dormers, skylights, shutters, curtains, in a word, all openings, holes, chinks, and fissures through which the light of the sun is used to penetrate our dwellings, to the prejudice of the profitable manufactures which we flatter ourselves we have been enabled to bestow upon the country.…

We foresee your objections, gentlemen; but there is not one that you can oppose to us…which is not equally opposed to your own practice and the principle which guides your policy.… Labor and nature concur in different proportions, according to country and climate, in every article of production.… If a Lisbon orange can be sold at half the price of a Parisian one, it is because a natural and gratuitous heat does for the one what the other only obtains from an artificial and consequently expensive one.…

Does it not argue the greatest inconsistency to check as you do the importation of coal, iron, cheese, and goods of foreign manufacture, merely because and even in proportion as their price approaches zero, while at the same time you freely admit, and without limitation, the light of the sun, whose price is during the whole day at zero?

Culver Pictures

SOURCE: Frédéric Bastiat, *Economic Sophisms* (New York: G. P. Putnam's Sons, 1922).

---

**Issue Resolved**    *Last Look at the "Cheap Foreign Labor" Argument*

The preceding discussion reveals the fundamental fallacy in the argument that the United States as a whole should fear cheap foreign labor. The average American worker's living standard must rise, not fall, if other countries willingly supply their products to us more cheaply. As long as the government's monetary and fiscal policies succeed in maintaining high levels of employment, we cannot possibly lose by getting world products at bargain prices. Some recent data are revealing in this respect. As late as 2007, with a financial crisis brewing and a massive trade deficit equal to 5.1 percent of GDP, the U.S. unemployment rate averaged only 4.6 percent. By contrast, by 2013, the trade deficit was down to just 2.6 percent of GDP, but unemployment averaged 7.4 percent.

We must add a few important qualifications, however. First, our macroeconomic policy may not always be effective—a possibility that was made all too obvious by the Great Recession. If workers displaced by foreign competition cannot find new jobs, they will indeed suffer from international trade. But high unemployment reflects a shortcoming of the government's monetary and fiscal policies, not of its international trade policies. That said, it is still a huge problem, which has made trade liberalization quite unpopular.

Second, we have noted that an abrupt stiffening of foreign competition can hurt U.S. workers by not allowing them adequate time to adapt to the new conditions. If change occurs fairly gradually, workers can be retrained and move into the industries that now require their services. Indeed, if the change is slow enough, normal attrition may suffice. But competition that inflicts its damage overnight is certain to impose real costs on the affected workers—costs that are no less painful for being temporary. That is why our trade laws make provisions for people and industries damaged by import surges.

In fact, the economic world is constantly changing. The recent emergence of China, India, and other third-world countries, for example, has created stiff new competition for workers in America and other rich nations—competition they never imagined when they signed up for jobs that may now be imperiled by international trade. The same is true of many workers in service jobs (ranging from call center operators to lawyers) who never dreamed that their jobs might be done electronically from thousands of miles away. It is not irrational, and it is certainly not protectionist, for countries like the United States to use trade adjustment assistance and other tools to cushion the blow for these workers.

But these are, after all, only qualifications to an overwhelming argument. They call for intelligent monetary and fiscal policies and for transitional assistance to unemployed workers, not for abandonment of free trade. In general, the nation as a whole need not fear competition from cheap foreign labor.

> In the long run, labor will be "cheap" only where it is not very productive. Wages will be high in countries with high labor productivity, and this high productivity will enable those countries to compete effectively in international trade despite their high wages. It is thus misleading to say that the United States held its own in the international marketplace until recently *despite* high wages. Rather, it is much more accurate to note that the higher wages of American workers were a result of higher worker productivity, which gave the United States a major competitive edge—an edge we still have in many industries, by the way.

Remember, where standards of living are concerned, it is *absolute* advantage, not *comparative* advantage, that counts. The country that is most efficient in producing every output can pay its workers more in every industry.

## Summary

1. Countries trade for many reasons. Two of the most important are that differences in their natural resources and other inputs create discrepancies in the efficiency with which they can produce different goods, and that specialization offers greater economies of large-scale production.

2. Voluntary trade will generally be advantageous to both parties in an exchange. This concept is one of our *Ideas for Beyond the Final Exam*.

3. International trade is more complicated than trade within a nation because of political factors, differing national currencies, and impediments to the movement of labor and capital across national borders.

4. Two countries will gain from trade with each other if each nation exports goods in which it has a **comparative advantage**. Even a country that is inefficient across the board will benefit by exporting the goods in whose production it is *least inefficient*. This concept is another of the *Ideas for Beyond the Final Exam*.

5. When countries specialize and trade, each can enjoy consumption possibilities that exceed its production possibilities.

6. The "cheap foreign labor" argument ignores the principle of comparative advantage, which shows that real wages (which determine living standards) can rise in both importing and exporting countries as a result of **specialization**.

7. **Tariffs** and **quotas** aim to protect a country's industries from foreign competition. Such protection may sometimes be advantageous to that country, but not if foreign countries adopt tariffs and quotas of their own in retaliation.

8. From the point of view of the country that imposes them, tariffs offer at least two advantages over quotas: Some of the gains go to the government rather than to foreign producers, and they provide greater incentive for efficient production.

9. When a nation eliminates protection in favor of free trade, some industries and their workers will lose out. Equity then demands that these people and firms be compensated in some way. The U.S. government offers protection from import surges and various forms of **trade adjustment assistance** to help those workers and industries adapt to the new conditions.

10. Several arguments for protectionism can, under the right circumstances, have validity. They include the national defense argument, the **infant-industry argument**, and the use of trade restrictions for strategic purposes. But each of these arguments is frequently abused.

11. **Dumping** will hurt certain domestic producers, but it benefits domestic consumers.

## Key Terms

| | | |
|---|---|---|
| absolute advantage   361 | infant-industry argument   370 | strategic argument for protection   370 |
| comparative advantage   361 | mercantilism   366 | tariff   366 |
| dumping   371 | quota   366 | trade adjustment assistance   369 |
| export subsidy   366 | specialization   359 | |

## Test Yourself

1. The following table describes the number of yards of cloth and barrels of wine that can be produced with a week's worth of labor in England and Portugal. Assume that no other inputs are needed.

| | In England | In Portugal |
|---|---|---|
| Cloth | 8 yards | 12 yards |
| Wine | 2 barrels | 6 barrels |

   a. If there is no trade, what is the price of wine in terms of cloth in England?

   b. If there is no trade, what is the price of wine in terms of cloth in Portugal?

   c. Suppose each country has 1 million weeks of labor available per year. Draw the production possibilities frontier for each country.

   d. Which country has an absolute advantage in the production of which good(s)? Which country has a comparative advantage in the production of which good(s)?

   e. If the countries start trading with each other, which country will specialize and export which good?

   f. What can be said about the price at which trade will take place?

2. Suppose that the United States and Mexico are the only two countries in the world and that labor is the only productive input. In the United States, a worker can produce 12 bushels of wheat or 2 barrels of oil in a day. In Mexico, a worker can produce 2 bushels of wheat or 4 barrels of oil per day.

   a. What will be the price ratio between the two commodities (i.e., the price of oil in terms of wheat) in each country if there is no trade?

   b. If free trade is allowed and there are no transportation costs, which commodity would the United States import? What about Mexico?

   c. In what range would the price ratio have to fall under free trade? Why?

   d. Picking one possible post-trade price ratio, show clearly how it is possible for both countries to benefit from free trade.

## Discussion Questions

1. You have a dozen shirts and your roommate has six pairs of shoes worth roughly the same amount of money. You decide to swap six shirts for three pairs of shoes. In financial terms, neither of you gains anything. Explain why you are nevertheless both likely to be better off.

2. In the eighteenth century, some writers argued that one person in a trade could be made better off only by gaining at the expense of the other. Explain the fallacy in this argument.

3. Country A has a cold climate with a short growing season, but a highly skilled labor force (think of Finland). What sorts of products do you think it is likely to produce? What are the characteristics of the countries with which you would expect it to trade?

4. After the removal of a quota on sugar, many U.S. sugar farms go bankrupt. Discuss the pros and cons of removing the quota in the short and long runs.

5. Country A has a mercantilist government that believes it is always best to export more than it imports. As a consequence, it exports more to Country B every year than it imports from Country B. After 100 years of this arrangement, both countries are destroyed in an earthquake. What were the advantages or disadvantages of the surplus to Country A? To Country B?

6. Under current trade law, the president of the United States must report periodically to Congress on countries engaging in unfair trade practices that inhibit U.S. exports. How would you define an "unfair" trade practice? Suppose Country X exports much more to the United States than it imports, year after year. Does that constitute evidence that Country X's trade practices are unfair? What would constitute such evidence?

7. Suppose the United States finds Country X guilty of unfair trade practices and penalizes it with import quotas. So U.S. imports from Country X fall. Suppose, further, that Country X does not alter its trade practices in any way. Is the United States better or worse off? What about Country X?

# Appendix *Supply, Demand, and Pricing in World Trade*

As noted in the text, price determination in a world market with free trade depends on supply and demand conditions in each of the countries participating in the market. This appendix works out some of the details in a two-country example.

When applied to international trade, the usual supply-demand model must deal with (at least) *two demand curves:* that of the exporting country and that of the importing country. In addition, it may also involve *two supply curves,* because the importing country may produce part of its own consumption. (Think, e.g., of automobiles in the United States, which come from both domestic and foreign producers.) Furthermore, equilibrium does *not* take place at the intersection point of *either* pair of supply-demand curves. Why? Because if the two countries trade at all, the exporting nation must supply more than it demands while the importing nation must demand more than it supplies.

All three of these complications are illustrated in Figure 3, which shows the supply and demand curves of a country that *exports* wheat in Panel (a) and of a country that *imports* wheat in Panel (b) For simplicity, we assume that these countries do not deal with anyone else. Where will the two-country wheat market reach equilibrium?

Under free trade, the equilibrium price must satisfy two requirements:

1. The quantity of wheat *exported* by one country must equal the quantity of wheat *imported* by the other country, for that is how *world* supply and demand balance.
2. The price of wheat must be the same in both countries.[5]

In Figure 3, these two conditions are met at a price of $2.50 per bushel. At that price, the distance *AB* between what the exporting country produces and what it consumes equals the distance *CD* between what the importing country consumes and what it produces. This means that the amount the exporting country wants to sell at $2.50 per bushel exactly equals the amount the importing country wants to buy at that price.

At any higher price, producers in both countries would want to sell more and consumers in both countries would want to buy less. For example, if the price rose to $3.25 per bushel, the exporter's quantity supplied would rise from *B* to *F*, and its quantity demanded would fall from *A* to *E*, as shown in Panel (a). As a result, more wheat would be available for export—*EF* rather than *AB*. For exactly the same reason, the price increase would cause higher production and lower sales in the importing country, leading to a reduction in imports from *CD* to *GH* in Panel (b).

But this means that the higher price, $3.25 per bushel, cannot be sustained in a free and competitive international market. With export supply *EF* far greater than import demand *GH*, there would be pressure on

*Figure 3*

**Supply-Demand Equilibrium in the International Wheat Trade**

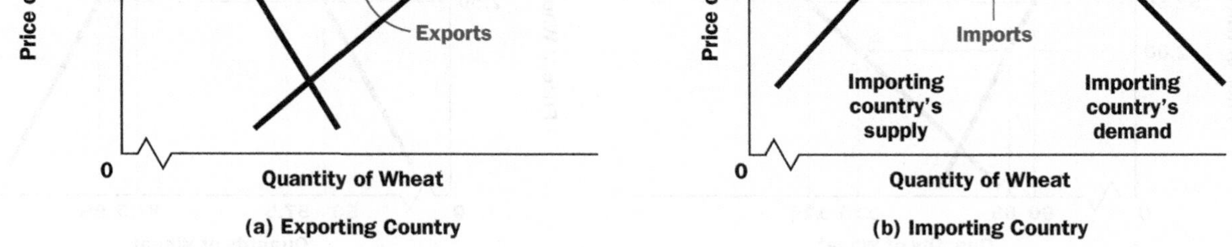

(a) Exporting Country

(b) Importing Country

---

[5] To keep things simple, we ignore such details as the costs of shipping wheat from one country to the other.

price to fall back toward the $2.50 equilibrium price. Similar reasoning shows that no price below $2.50 can be sustained. Thus:

> In international trade, the equilibrium price is the one that makes the exporting country want to sell exactly the amount that the importing country wants to buy. Equilibrium will thus occur at a price at which the horizontal distance AB in Figure 3(a) (the excess of the exporter's quantity supplied over its quantity demanded) is equal to the horizontal distance CD in Figure 3(b) (the excess of the importer's quantity demanded over its quantity supplied). At this price, the *world's* quantity demanded equals the *world's* quantity supplied.

## How Tariffs and Quotas Work

However, as noted in the text, nations do not always let markets operate freely. Sometimes they intervene with quotas that limit imports or with tariffs that make imports more expensive. Although both tariffs and quotas restrict supplies coming from abroad and drive up prices, they operate slightly differently. A tariff works by raising prices, which in turn reduces the quantity of imports demanded. The sequence associated with a quota is just the reverse—a restriction in supply forces prices to rise.

The supply and demand curves in Figure 4 illustrate how tariffs and quotas work. Just as in Figure 3, the equilibrium price of wheat under free trade is $2.50 per bushel (in both countries). At this price, the

exporting country produces 125 million bushels—point B in Panel (a)—and consumes 80 million (point A). So its exports are 45 million bushels—the distance AB. Similarly, the importing country consumes 95 million bushels—point D in Panel (b)—and produces only 50 million (point C), so its imports are also 45 million bushels—the distance CD.

Now suppose the government of the importing nation imposes a *quota* limiting imports to 30 million bushels. The free-trade equilibrium with imports of 45 million bushels is now illegal. Instead, the market must equilibrate at a point where both exports and imports are only 30 million bushels. As Figure 4 indicates, this requirement implies that there must be different prices in the two countries.

Imports in Panel (b) will be 30 million bushels—the distance QT—only when the price of wheat in the importing nation is $3.25 per bushel, because only at this price will quantity demanded exceed domestic quantity supplied by 30 million bushels. Similarly, exports in Panel (a) will be 30 million bushels—the distance RS—only when the price in the exporting country is $2.00 per bushel.

At this price, quantity supplied exceeds quantity demanded in the exporting country by 30 million bushels. Thus, the quota *raises* the price in the importing country to $3.25 and *lowers* the price in the exporting country to $2.00. In general:

> An import quota on a product normally reduces the volume of that product traded, raises the price in the importing country, and reduces the price in the exporting country.

*Figure 4*

**Quotas and Tariffs in International Trade**

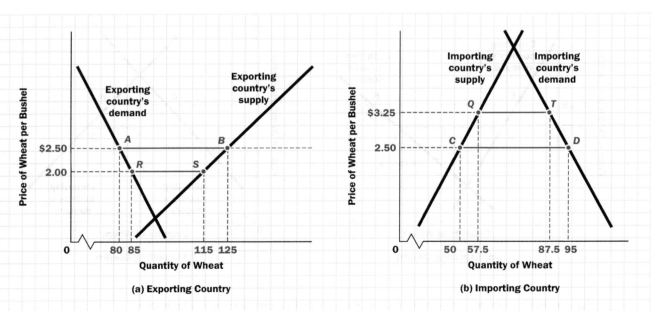

(a) Exporting Country

(b) Importing Country

NOTE: Quantities are in millions of bushels.

A tariff can accomplish exactly the same restriction of trade. In our example, a quota of 30 million bushels leads to a price that is $1.25 higher in the importing country than in the exporting country ($3.25 versus $2.00). Suppose that, instead of a quota, the importing nation were to impose a $1.25 per bushel *tariff*. International trade equilibrium would then have to satisfy the following two requirements:

1. The quantity of wheat *exported* by one country must equal the quantity of wheat *imported* by the other, just as before.
2. The price that consumers in the importing country pay for wheat must *exceed* the price that suppliers in the exporting country receive by the amount of the *tariff* (which is $1.25 in the example).

By consulting the graphs in Figure 4, you can see exactly where these two requirements are met. If the exporter produces at *S* and consumes at *R*, while the importer produces at *Q* and consumes at *T*, then exports and imports are equal (at 30 million bushels), and the two domestic prices differ by exactly $1.25. (They are $3.25 and $2.00.) But this is exactly the same equilibrium we found under the quota. What we have

just discovered is a general result of international trade theory:

> Any restriction of imports that is accomplished by a quota normally can also be accomplished by a tariff.

In this case, the tariff corresponding to an import quota of 30 million bushels is $1.25 per bushel.

We mentioned in the text that a tariff (or a quota) forces foreign producers to sell more cheaply. Figure 4 shows how this works. Suppose, as in Panel (b), that a $1.25 tariff on wheat raises the price in the importing country from $2.50 to $3.25 per bushel. This higher price drives down imports from an amount represented by the length of the blue line *CD* to the smaller amount represented by the maroon line *QT*. In the exporting country, this change means an equal reduction in exports, as illustrated by the change from *AB* to *RS* in Panel (a).

As a result, the price at which the exporting country can sell its wheat is driven down—from $2.50 to $2.00 in the example. Meanwhile, producers in the importing country, which are exempt from the tariff, can charge $3.25 per bushel. Thus, as noted in the text, a tariff (or a quota) can be thought of as a way to "rig" the domestic market in favor of domestic firms.

## Summary

1. The prices of goods traded between countries are determined by supply and demand, but one must consider explicitly the demand curve and the supply curve of *each* country involved. Thus, the equilibrium price must make the excess of quantity supplied over quantity demanded in the exporting country equal to the excess of quantity demanded over quantity supplied in the importing country.

2. When trade is restricted, the combinations of prices and quantities in the various countries that are achieved by a quota can also be achieved by a tariff.

3. Tariffs or quotas favor domestic producers over foreign producers.

## Test Yourself

1. The following table presents the demand and supply curves for laptop computers in Japan and the United States.

| Price per Computer | Quantity Demanded in United States | Quantity Supplied in United States | Quantity Demanded in Japan | Quantity Supplied in Japan |
|---|---|---|---|---|
| $ 200 | 90 | 30 | 50 | 50 |
| 400 | 80 | 35 | 40 | 55 |
| 600 | 70 | 40 | 30 | 60 |
| 800 | 60 | 45 | 20 | 65 |
| 1,000 | 50 | 50 | 10 | 70 |
| 1,200 | 40 | 55 | 0 | 75 |

NOTE: Quantity is in thousands.

a. Draw the demand and supply curves for the United States on one diagram and those for Japan on another one.
b. If the United States and Japan do not trade, what are the equilibrium price and quantity in the laptop market in the United States? In Japan?
c. Now suppose trade is opened up between the two countries. What will be the equilibrium price in the world market for laptops? What has happened to the price of laptops in the United States? In Japan?
d. Which country will export laptops? How many?
e. When trade opens, what happens to the quantity of laptop computers produced, and therefore employment, in the computer industry in the United States? In Japan? Who benefits and who loses initially from free trade?

# THE INTERNATIONAL MONETARY SYSTEM: ORDER OR DISORDER?

**19**

*Cecily, you will read your Political Economy in my absence. The chapter on the Fall of the Rupee you may omit. It is somewhat too sensational.*

MISS PRISM IN OSCAR WILDE'S *THE IMPORTANCE OF BEING EARNEST*

**M**iss Prism, the Victorian tutor, may have had a better point than she knew. In the summer of 1997, the Indonesian rupiah (not the Indian rupee) fell, and economic disaster quickly followed. The International Monetary Fund rushed to the rescue with billions of dollars and pages of advice. But its plan failed, and some say it may even have helped precipitate the bloody riots that led to the fall of the Indonesian government.

True to Miss Prism's instructions, this chapter does not concentrate on sensational political upheavals. Rather, it focuses on a seemingly mundane topic: how the market determines rates of exchange among different national currencies. Nevertheless, events in Southeast Asia in 1997–1998, in Brazil and Russia in 1998–1999, and in many other times and places have amply demonstrated that dramatic exchange rate movements can have severe human as well as financial consequences. Even in the United States, people have often worried about the consequences of a declining dollar. This chapter and the next will help you understand why.

## CONTENTS

| Puzzle | *Has the Value of the Dollar Really Sagged?* |

People often fret about the alleged decline of the U.S. dollar—either as a fearful prospect for the future, or as a description of our presumably dreadful recent past. We'll have to wait and see about the future. But as a description of the recent past, the dollar alarmists have it quite wrong. Since the end of 2007 (when the Great Recession started), the dollar has actually risen against more currencies than it has fallen. True, the Chinese yuan was worth about 16.3 cents in late 2014, versus only 13.7 cents in late 2007, and the Japanese yen was also up about 5 percent against the dollar. But the Canadian dollar had fallen from about 100 U.S. cents to about 89, the British pound had declined from more than $2.00 to about $1.57, and the Mexican peso had slipped from about 9.2 cents to about 7.4 cents. This is hardly the profile of a U.S. dollar in decline.

But that simple fact doesn't mean all has been well in the United States. We did, for example, experience our worst recession since the 1930s during this period. Nor does it mean that Canada, Mexico, and the United Kingdom, for example, all fared worse than we did, while China and Japan fared better. In fact, the behavior of a country's exchange rate is a poor indicator of the health of its economy. But to understand why, we must first understand what determines exchange rates, which is one main task of this chapter.

## 19-1 WHAT ARE EXCHANGE RATES?

We noted in the previous chapter that international trade is more complicated than domestic trade. There are no national borders to be crossed when, say, California lettuce is shipped to Massachusetts. The consumer in Boston pays with *dollars*, just the currency that the farmer in Modesto wants. If that same farmer ships lettuce to Japan, however, consumers there will have only Japanese yen with which to pay, rather than the dollars the farmer in California wants. Thus, for international trade to take place, there must be some way to convert one currency into another. The rates at which such conversions are made are called **exchange rates**.

The **exchange rate** states the price, in terms of one currency, at which another currency can be bought.

There is an exchange rate between every pair of currencies. For example, one British pound is currently the equivalent of about $1.60. The exchange rate between the pound and the dollar, then, may be expressed as roughly "$1.60 to the pound" (meaning that it costs $1.60 to buy a pound) or about "62.5 pence to the dollar" (meaning that it costs 62.5 percent of a British pound to buy a dollar).

Exchange rates vis-à-vis the United States dollar have changed dramatically over time. In a nutshell, the dollar soared in the period from mid-1980 to early 1985, fell relative to most major currencies from early 1985 until early 1988, and then fluctuated with no clear trend until the spring of 1995. From then until early 2002, the dollar was mostly on the rise. Then, from February 2002 through December 2004, the dollar reversed course and fell steadily. From then until 2007, the dollar was relatively stable, until late 2007 when, as already noted, it started rising again. By 2014, news stories were being written about the muscular U.S. dollar. This chapter seeks to explain such currency movements.

A nation's currency is said to **appreciate** when exchange rates change so that a unit of its currency can buy more units of foreign currency.

Under our present system, currency rates change frequently. When other currencies become more expensive in terms of dollars, we say that they have **appreciated** relative to the dollar. Alternatively, we can look at this same event as the dollar buying less foreign currency, meaning that the dollar has **depreciated** relative to another currency.

**What is a depreciation to one country must be an appreciation to the other.**

A nation's currency is said to **depreciate** when exchange rates change so that a unit of its currency can buy fewer units of foreign currency.

For example, if the cost of a British pound *rises* from $1.50 to $2, the cost of a U.S. dollar in terms of pounds simultaneously *falls* from 67 pence to 50 pence. The United Kingdom has experienced a currency *appreciation* while the United States has experienced a currency *depreciation*. In fact, the two mean the same thing. These two ways of viewing the exchange rate are reciprocals of one another, that is, $1/1.5 = 0.67$ and $1/2.0 = 0.50$. And of course, when a number goes up, its reciprocal goes down.

When many currencies are changing in value at the same time, the dollar may be appreciating with respect to one currency but depreciating with respect to another. Table 1 offers a selection of exchange rates prevailing in July 1980, February 1985, June 1995, April 2002, April 2008, and December 2014, showing how many dollars or cents it cost at each of those times to buy each unit of foreign currency. Between February 1985 and April 2002, the dollar *depreciated* sharply relative to the Japanese yen and most European currencies. For example, the British pound rose from $1.10 to $1.44. During that same period, however, the dollar *appreciated* dramatically relative to the Mexican peso; it bought about 0.2 pesos in 1985 but more than 9 in 2002.[1] Since April 2002, the dollar has

---

[1] In fact, the dollar bought about 200 pesos in February 1985, but that is because the old peso was replaced by a new peso in January 1993, which moved the decimal point three places.

*Table 1*

**Exchange Rates with the U.S. Dollar**

| Country | Currency | Symbol | Cost in Dollars | | | | | |
|---------|----------|--------|-----------|---------------|-----------|------------|------------|---------------|
| | | | July 1980 | February 1985 | June 1995 | April 2002 | April 2008 | December 2014 |
| Australia | dollar | $ | $1.16 | $0.74 | $0.72 | $0.53 | $0.93 | $0.85 |
| Canada | dollar | $ | 0.87 | 0.74 | 0.73 | 0.63 | 0.99 | 0.88 |
| France | franc | FF | 0.25 | 0.10 | 0.20 | * | * | * |
| Germany | mark | DM | 0.57 | 0.30 | 0.71 | * | * | * |
| Italy | lira | L | 0.0012 | 0.00049 | 0.0061 | * | * | * |
| Japan | yen | ¥ | 0.0045 | 0.0038 | 0.0118 | 0.0076 | 0.0096 | 0.0085 |
| Mexico | new peso | $ | 44.0† | 5.0† | 0.16 | 0.11 | 0.09 | 0.07 |
| Sweden | krona | Kr | 0.24 | 0.11 | 0.14 | 0.10 | 0.17 | 0.13 |
| Switzerland | franc | S.Fr. | 0.62 | 0.36 | 0.86 | 0.60 | 0.98 | 1.04 |
| United Kingdom | pound | £ | 2.37 | 1.10 | 1.59 | 1.44 | 1.99 | 1.57 |
| — | euro | € | — | — | — | 0.88 | 1.58 | 1.25 |

NOTE: Exchange rates are in U.S. dollars per unit of foreign currency.
\* These exchange rates were locked together at the start of the euro in January 1999.
† On January 1, 1993, the peso was redefined so that 1,000 old pesos were equal to 1 new peso. Hence, the numbers 44 and 5 listed for July 1980 and February 1985 were actually 0.044 and 0.005 on the old basis.

SOURCE: International Financial Statistics and *The Wall Street Journal.*

*de*preciated against most currencies. But as you can see in Table 1, it has *ap*preciated against most currencies since April 2008.

Although the terms *appreciation* and *depreciation* are used to describe movements of exchange rates in free markets, a different set of terms is employed to describe decreases and increases in currency values that are set by governments. When an officially set exchange rate is altered so that a unit of a nation's currency buys fewer units of foreign currency, we say there has been a **devaluation** of that currency. When the exchange rate is altered so that the currency buys more units of foreign currency, we say there has been an upward **revaluation**. We will return to devaluations and revaluations shortly, but first let's look at how the free market determines exchange rates.

A **devaluation** is a reduction in the official value of a currency.

A **revaluation** is an increase in the official value of a currency.

## 19-2 EXCHANGE RATE DETERMINATION IN A FREE MARKET

In 1999, eleven European countries adopted a new common currency, the euro. Why does a euro now cost about $1.30 and not $1.20 or $1.40? In a world of **floating exchange rates**, with no government interferences, the answer would be straightforward. Exchange rates would be determined by the forces of supply and demand, just like the prices of apples, computers, and haircuts.

In a leap of abstraction, imagine that the dollar and the euro are the only currencies on earth, so the market need determine only one exchange rate. Figure 1 depicts the determination of this exchange rate at the point (denoted *E* in the figure) where demand curve *DD* crosses supply curve *SS*. At this price ($1.30 per euro), the number of euros demanded is equal to the number of euros supplied.

**Floating exchange rates** are rates determined in free markets by the law of supply and demand.

In a free market, exchange rates are determined by supply and demand. At a rate below the equilibrium level, the number of euros demanded would exceed the number supplied, and the price of a euro would be bid up. At a rate above the equilibrium level, quantity supplied would exceed quantity demanded, and the price of a euro would fall. Only at the equilibrium exchange rate is there no tendency for the rate to change.

*Figure 1*

**Determination of Exchange Rates in a Free Market**

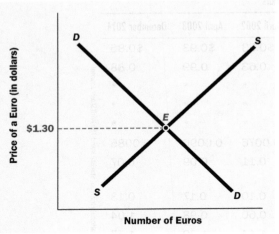

As usual, supply and demand determine price. However, in this case, we must ask where the supply and demand come from. Why does anyone demand a euro? The answer comes in three parts:

1. *International trade in goods and services.* This factor was the subject of the previous chapter. If Jane Doe, an American, wants to buy a new BMW, she will first have to buy euros with which to pay the car dealer in Bavaria.[2] Thus, Jane's demand for a European car leads to a demand for European currency. In general, *demand for a country's exports leads to demand for its currency.*[3]
2. *Purchases of physical assets such as factories and machinery overseas.* If IBM wants to buy a small Irish computer manufacturer, the owners will no doubt want to receive euros. So IBM will first have to acquire euros. In general, *direct foreign investment leads to demand for a country's currency.*
3. *International trade in financial instruments such as stocks and bonds.* If American investors want to purchase French stocks, they will first have to acquire the euros that the sellers will insist on for payment. In this way, demand for European financial assets leads to demand for European currency. Thus, *demand for a country's financial assets leads to demand for its currency.* In fact, nowadays the volume of international trade in financial assets among the major countries of the world is so large that it swamps the other two sources of demand.

Now, where does the supply come from? To answer this question, just turn all of these transactions around. Europeans who want to buy U.S. goods and services, make direct investments in the United States, or purchase U.S. financial assets will have to offer their euros for sale in the foreign-exchange market (which is mainly run through banks) to acquire the needed dollars. To summarize:

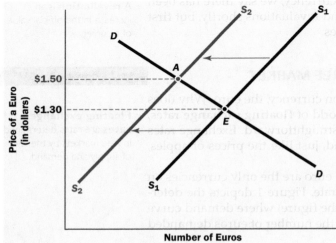

*Figure 2*

**The Effect of Declining Demand for U.S. Assets on the Exchange Rate**

The *demand* for a country's currency is derived from the demands of foreigners for its export goods and services and for its assets—including financial assets, such as stocks and bonds, and real assets, such as factories and machinery. The *supply* of a country's currency arises from its imports, and from foreign investment by its own citizens.

To illustrate the usefulness of even this simple supply-and-demand analysis, think about how the exchange rate between the dollar and the euro should change if Europeans become worried about the safety of U.S. assets. As European investors reduce their desires to buy U.S. assets, they will supply fewer euros for sale (in order to buy the necessary dollars). In terms of the supply-and-demand diagram in Figure 2, that decreased sale of euros will shift the supply curve inward from the black line $S_1S_1$ to the blue line $S_2S_2$. Equilibrium would shift from point $E$ to point $A$, and the exchange rate would rise from $1.30 per euro to $1.50 per euro. Thus, the decreased

---

[2] Actually, she will not do so because banks generally handle foreign-exchange transactions for consumers. An American bank probably will buy the euros for her. Even so, the effect is exactly the same as if Jane had done it herself.

[3] See Discussion Question 2 at the end of this chapter.

supply of euros by European citizens would cause the euro to *appreciate* relative to the dollar.

**Exercise** Test your understanding of the supply-and-demand analysis of exchange rates by showing why each of the following events would lead to a depreciation of the euro (an appreciation of the dollar) in a free market:

1. American investors become worried about prospects for profit on the German stock market.
2. A boom in France leads to more French purchases of American goods.
3. Interest rates on government bonds rise in the United States but are stable in Italy. (*Hint:* Which country's citizens will be attracted to invest by high interest rates in the other country?)

To say that supply and demand determine exchange rates in a free market is at once to say everything and to say nothing. If we are to understand the reasons why some currencies appreciate whereas others depreciate, we must look into the factors that move the supply and demand curves. Economists believe that the principal determinants of exchange rate movements differ significantly in the short, medium, and long runs. In the next three sections, we turn to the analysis of exchange rate movements over these three "runs," beginning with the short run.

### 19-2a Interest Rates and Exchange Rates: The Short Run

Most experts in international finance agree that interest rates and financial flows are the major determinants of exchange rates—certainly in the short run, and probably in the medium run as well. Specifically, one variable that often seems to call the tune in the short run is *interest rate differentials*. A multitrillion-dollar pool of so-called *hot money*—owned by banks, investment funds, multinational corporations, and wealthy individuals of all nations—travels rapidly around the globe in search of the highest interest rates.

As an example, suppose British government bonds pay a 3 percent rate of interest when yields on equally safe American government securities rise to 5 percent. British investors will be attracted by the higher interest rates in the United States and will offer pounds for sale in order to buy dollars, planning to use those dollars to buy American securities. At the same time, American investors will find it more attractive to keep their money at home, so fewer pounds will be demanded by Americans.

When the demand schedule for pounds shifts inward and the supply curve shifts outward, the effect on price is predictable: The pound will depreciate, as Figure 3 shows. In the figure, the supply curve of pounds shifts outward from $S_1S_1$ to $S_2S_2$ when British investors seek to sell pounds in order to purchase more U.S. securities. At the same time, American investors wish to buy fewer pounds because they no longer desire to invest as much in British securities. Thus, the demand curve shifts inward from $D_1D_1$ to $D_2D_2$. The result, in our example, is a depreciation of the pound from $1.75 to $1.50. In general:

> Other things equal, countries that offer investors higher rates of return attract more capital than countries that offer lower rates. Thus, a rise in interest rates is expected to lead to an appreciation of the currency, and a drop in interest rates is expected to lead to a depreciation.

It is useful to think of interest rate differentials as standing in for the relative returns on all sorts

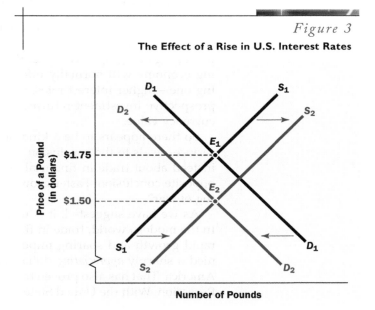

*Figure 3*

The Effect of a Rise in U.S. Interest Rates

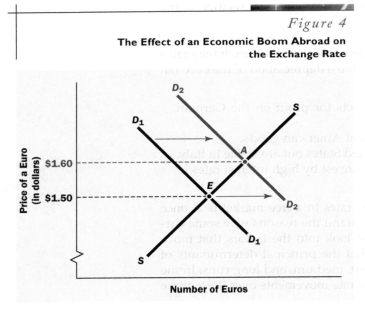

*Figure 4*

**The Effect of an Economic Boom Abroad on the Exchange Rate**

of financial assets in the two countries. In the late 1990s and the early part of this decade, prospective returns on American assets rose well above comparable returns in most other countries—especially those in Europe and Japan. In consequence, foreign capital was attracted here, American capital stayed at home, and the dollar soared—to levels that proved unsustainable. Similarly, if a nation suffers from capital flight, as Iceland and several of the Baltic states did in 2008–2009, it must offer extremely high interest rates to attract foreign capital. Conversely, when foreign capital "flew" to the safe haven of the United States during and after the financial crisis, the dollar rose.

## 19-2b  Economic Activity and Exchange Rates: The Medium Run

The medium run is where the theory of exchange rate determination is most unsettled. Economists once reasoned as follows: Because consumer spending increases when income rises and decreases when income falls, the same thing is likely to happen to spending on imported goods. So *a country's imports will rise quickly when its economy booms and rise only slowly when its economy stagnates.*

For the reasons illustrated in Figure 4, then, a boom in the United States should shift the *demand* curve for euros *outward* as Americans seek to acquire more euros to buy more European goods. And that, in turn, should lead to an appreciation of the euro (depreciation of the dollar). In the figure, the euro rises in value from $1.50 to $1.60.

However, if Europe was booming at the same time, Europeans would buy more American exports, which would shift the *supply* curve of euros outward (not shown in the diagram) as Europeans offered to sell more euros to get the dollars they wanted. On balance, the value of the dollar might rise or fall. It appears that what matters is whether exports are growing faster than imports.

A country that grows faster than the rest of the world should find its imports growing faster than its exports. Thus, its demand curve for foreign currency should shift outward more rapidly than its supply curve. *Other things equal,* that will make its currency depreciate.

This reasoning is sound—so far as it goes. And it leads to the conclusion that a "strong economy" might produce a "weak currency." But the three most important words in the preceding paragraph are "other things equal." Usually, they are not. Specifically, a booming economy will normally offer more attractive prospects to investors than a stagnating one—higher interest rates, rising stock market values, and so on. This difference in prospective investment returns, as we noted earlier, should attract capital and boost its currency value.

So there appears to be a kind of tug of war. Thinking only about trade in goods and services leads to the conclusion that faster growth should *weaken* the currency. Thinking instead about trade in financial assets (such as stocks and bonds) leads to precisely the opposite conclusion: Faster growth should *strengthen* the currency. Which side wins this tug of war?

As we have suggested, it is usually no contest—at least among the major currencies. In the modern world, trade in financial assets is by far the dominant factor. For example, rapid growth and soaring imports in the United States during the late 1990s accompanied a sharply *appreciating* dollar as investors from all over the world brought funds to America. That has also proven true, though far less dramatically, since the end of the Great Recession. With the United States, for the most part, growing faster than Europe, superior investment opportunities here have attracted capital from Europe, causing the dollar to appreciate relative to many European currencies. We conclude that

Stronger economic performance often leads to currency *appreciation* because it improves prospects for investing in the country.

## 19-2c The Purchasing-Power Parity Theory: The Long Run

We come at last to the long run, where an apparently simple principle ought to govern exchange rates. As long as goods can move freely across national borders, exchange rates should eventually adjust so that the same product costs the same amount of money, whether measured in dollars in the United States, euros in Germany, or yen in Japan—except for differences in transportation costs and the like. This simple statement forms the basis of the major theory of exchange rate determination in the long run:

The *purchasing-power parity theory of exchange rate determination* holds that the exchange rate between any two national currencies adjusts to reflect differences in the price levels in the two countries.

An example will illustrate the basic truth in this theory and also suggest some of its limitations. Suppose German and American steel are identical and that these two nations are the only producers of steel for the world market. Suppose further that steel is the only tradable good that either country produces.

*Question:* If American steel costs $300 per ton and German steel costs 200 euros per ton, what must be the exchange rate between the dollar and the euro?

*Answer:* Because 200 euros and $300 each buy a ton of steel, the two sums of money must be of equal value. Hence, each euro must be worth $1.50. At any higher price for a euro, such as $1.60, steel would cost $320 per ton in Germany (200 euros at $1.60 each) but only $300 per ton in the United States. In that case, all foreign customers would shop for their steel in the United States—which would increase the demand for dollars and decrease the demand for euros. Similarly, any exchange rate below $1.50 per euro would send all the steel business to Germany, driving the value of the euro up toward its purchasing-power parity level.

Exercise   Show why, in the previous example, an exchange rate of $1.40 per euro is too low to lead to an equilibrium in the international steel market.

The purchasing-power parity theory is used to make long-run predictions about the effects of inflation on exchange rates. To continue our example, suppose that steel (and other) prices in the United States rise while prices in Germany remain constant. The purchasing-power parity theory predicts that the euro will appreciate relative to the dollar. It also predicts the amount of the appreciation. After the U.S. inflation, suppose that the price of American steel is $330 per ton, whereas German steel still costs 200 euros per ton. For these two prices to be equivalent, 200 euros must be worth $330, or one euro must be worth $1.65. The euro, therefore, must rise from $1.50 to $1.65.

According to the purchasing-power parity theory, differences in domestic inflation rates are a major cause of exchange rate movements. If one country has higher inflation than another, its exchange rate should depreciate.

For many years, this theory seemed to work tolerably well. Although precise numerical predictions based on purchasing-power parity calculations were never very accurate (see "Purchasing-Power Parity and the Big Mac"), nations with higher inflation did at least experience depreciating currencies. But in the 1980s and 1990s, even this rule broke down. For example, although the U.S. inflation rate was consistently higher than both Germany's and Japan's, the dollar nonetheless rose sharply relative to both the German mark and the Japanese yen from 1980 to 1985. The same thing happened again between 1995 and 2002. Clearly, the theory is missing something. What?

# Purchasing-Power Parity and the Big Mac

Since 1986, *The Economist* magazine has been using a well-known international commodity—the Big Mac—to assess the purchasing-power parity theory of exchange rates, or as the magazine once put it, "to make exchange-rate theory more digestible."

Here's how it works. In theory, the local price of a Big Mac, when translated into U.S. dollars by the exchange rate, should be the same everywhere in the world—after all, it's the same product. But the following numbers show that the theory does not work terribly well.

For example, although a Big Mac cost an average of $4.62 in the United States in January 2014, it sold for about 16.6 yuan in China. Using the official exchange rate of 6.05 yuan to the dollar, that amounted to just $2.74. Thus, according to the hamburger parity theory, the yuan was grossly undervalued.

By how much? The price in China was just 59 percent of the price in the United States ($2.74/$4.62 = 0.593). So the yuan was 41 percent below its Big Mac parity—and therefore should appreciate. The other numbers in the table have similar interpretations.

True Big Mac aficionados may find these data helpful when planning international travel, but can deviations from Big Mac parity predict exchange rate movements? Surprisingly, they can.

Years ago, when the Big Mac index was still pretty young, economist Robert Cumby studied Big Mac prices and exchange rates in 14 countries over a 10-year period. He found that deviations from hamburger parity were transitory. Their "half-life" was just a year, meaning that 50 percent of the deviation tended to disappear within a year. Thus, the undervalued currencies in the accompanying table would be predicted to appreciate during 2014, whereas the overvalued currencies would be expected to depreciate.

### Deviations from Big Mac Purchasing-Power Parity, January 2014

| Country | Big Mac Prices (converted to dollars) | Percent Over (+) or Under (−) Valuation against Dollar |
|---|---|---|
| **United States** | **$4.62** | — |
| Norway | 7.80 | +69% |
| Brazil | 5.25 | +13% |
| Canada | 5.01 | + 8% |
| Euro area | 4.96 | + 7% |
| Great Britain | 4.63 | — |
| Japan | 2.97 | − 36% |
| China | 2.74 | − 41% |
| Russia | 2.62 | − 43% |
| South Africa | 2.16 | − 53% |

SOURCES: "Grease-Proof Taper: Our Bun-Loving Guide to Currencies," *The Economist*, www.economist.com. © The Economist Newspaper Limited, London (January 25, 2014); and Robert Cumby, "Forecasting Exchange Rates and Relative Prices with the Hamburger Standard: Is What You Want What You Get with McParity?" Georgetown University, May 1997.

Many things, but perhaps the principal failing of the purchasing-power parity theory is, once again, that it focuses too much on trade in goods and services. Financial assets such as stocks and bonds are also traded actively across national borders—and in vastly greater dollar volumes than goods and services. In fact, the *daily* volume of foreign-exchange transactions is astounding—in excess of $5 trillion, which is far more than an entire *month's* worth of world trade in goods and services. The vast majority of these transactions are financial. If investors decide that, say, U.S. assets are a better bet than Japanese assets, the dollar will rise, even if our inflation rate is well above Japan's. For this and other reasons,

**Most economists believe that other factors are much more important than relative price levels for exchange rate determination in the short run. But in the long run, purchasing-power parity plays an important role.**

## 19-2d  Market Determination of Exchange Rates: Summary

You have probably noticed a theme here: International trade in financial assets certainly dominates short-run exchange rate changes, may dominate medium-run changes, and also influences long-run changes. We can summarize this discussion of exchange rate determination in free markets as follows:

1. We expect to find *appreciating* currencies in countries that offer investors *higher rates of return* because these countries will attract capital from all over the world.

2. To some extent, these are the countries that are growing faster than average because strong growth tends to produce attractive investment prospects. However, such fast-growing countries will also be importing relatively more than other countries, which tends to pull their currencies down.

3. Currency values generally will appreciate in countries with lower inflation rates than the rest of the world's, because buyers in foreign countries will demand their goods and thus drive up their currencies.

Reversing each of these arguments, we expect to find *depreciating* currencies in countries with relatively high inflation rates, low interest rates, and poor growth prospects.

## 19-3  WHEN GOVERNMENTS FIX EXCHANGE RATES: THE BALANCE OF PAYMENTS

Many exchange rates today are truly floating, determined by the forces of supply and demand without government interference. Others are not. Furthermore, some people claim that exchange rate fluctuations are so troublesome that the world would be better off with fixed exchange rates. For these reasons, we turn next to a system of **fixed exchange rates**, or rates that are set by governments.

Naturally, under such a system the exchange rate, being fixed, is not closely watched. Instead, international financial specialists focus on a country's *balance of payments*—a term we must now define—to gauge movements in the supply of and demand for a currency.

To understand what the balance of payments is, look at Figure 5, which depicts a situation that might represent, say, Argentina in the winter of 2001–2002—an *overvalued* currency. Although the supply and demand curves for pesos indicate an equilibrium exchange rate of $0.50 to the peso (point *E*), the Argentine government is holding the rate at $1. Notice that, at $1 per peso, more people supply pesos than demand them. In the example, suppliers offer to sell 8 billion pesos per year, but purchasers want to buy only 4 billion. This gap between the 8 billion pesos that some people wish to sell and the 4 billion pesos that others wish to buy is what we mean by Argentina's **balance of payments deficit**—4 billion pesos (or $4 billion) per year in this hypothetical case. It appears as the horizontal distance between points *A* and *B* in Figure 5.

How can governments flout market forces in this way? Because sales and purchases on any market must be equal, the excess of quantity supplied over quantity demanded—or 4 billion pesos per year in this example—must be bought by the Argentine government. To purchase these pesos, it must give up some of the foreign currency it holds as reserves. Thus, the Central Bank of Argentina would be losing about $4 billion in reserves per year as the cost of keeping the peso at $1.

Naturally, this situation cannot persist forever, as the reserves eventually will run out. And this is the fatal flaw of a fixed exchange rate system. Once

**Fixed exchange rates** are rates set by government decisions and maintained by government actions.

The **balance of payments deficit** is the amount by which the quantity supplied of a country's currency (per year) exceeds the quantity demanded. Balance of payments deficits arise whenever the exchange rate is pegged at an artificially high level.

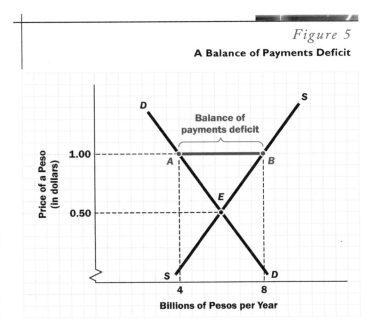

*Figure 5*

**A Balance of Payments Deficit**

Figure 6

**A Balance of Payments Surplus**

Price of a Yuan (in dollars)

$0.20

0.16

D    S
E
A         B
Balance of payments surplus
S         D

600    1,000

**Billions of Yuan per Year**

The **balance of payments surplus** is the amount by which the quantity demanded of a country's currency (per year) exceeds the quantity supplied. Balance of payments surpluses arise whenever the exchange rate is pegged at an artificially low level.

The **current account** balance includes international purchases and sales of goods and services, cross-border interest and dividend payments, and cross-border gifts to and from both private individuals and governments. It is approximately the same as net exports.

The **capital account** balance includes purchases and sales of financial assets to and from citizens and companies of other countries.

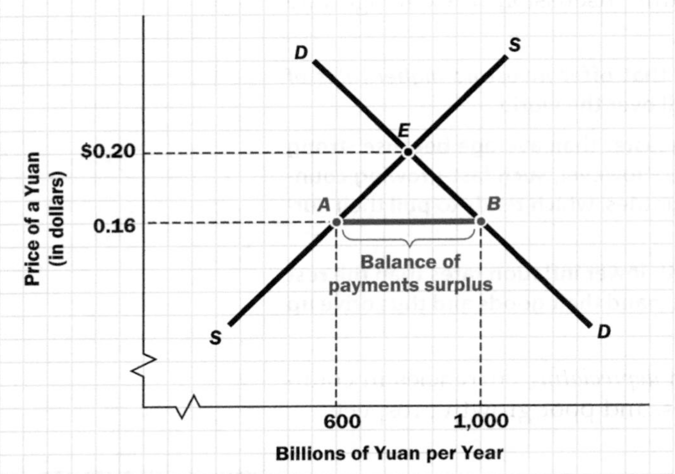

speculators become convinced that the exchange rate can be held for only a short while longer, they will sell the currency in massive amounts rather than hold on to money whose value they expect to fall. That is precisely what began to happen to Argentina in 2001. Lacking sufficient reserves, the Argentine government succumbed to market forces and let the peso float in early 2002. It promptly depreciated.

For an example of the reverse case, a severely undervalued currency, we can look at contemporary China. Figure 6 depicts demand and supply curves for Chinese yuan that intersect at an equilibrium price of 20 cents per yuan (point *E* in the diagram). Yet, in the example, we suppose that the Chinese authorities are holding the rate at 16 cents. At this rate, the quantity of yuan demanded (1,000 billion) greatly exceeds the quantity supplied (600 billion). The difference is China's **balance of payments surplus**, shown by the horizontal distance *AB*.

China can keep the rate at 16 cents only by selling all the additional yuan that foreigners want to buy—400 billion yuan per year in this example. In return, the country must buy the equivalent amount of U.S. dollars ($64 billion). All of this activity serves to increase China's reserves of U.S. dollars. But notice one important difference between this case and the overvalued peso:

> The accumulation of reserves does not force a central bank to revalue in the way that sufficiently large losses of reserves can force a devaluation.

Thus China has been keeping its currency undervalued and accumulating huge dollar reserves for years—to the irritation of many other countries, including the United States.

This asymmetry is a clear weakness in a fixed exchange rate system. In principle, an exchange rate disequilibrium can be cured either by a *devaluation* by the country with a balance of payments deficit or by an upward *revaluation* by the country with a balance of payments surplus. In practice, though, only deficit countries are forced to act.

Why do surplus countries refuse to revalue? One reason is often a stubborn refusal to recognize some basic economic realities. They tend to view the disequilibrium as a problem only for the deficit countries and, therefore, believe that the deficit countries should take the corrective steps. This view, of course, makes no sense in a worldwide system of fixed exchange rates. Some currencies are overvalued *because* some other currencies are undervalued. In fact, the two statements mean the same thing.

The other reason why surplus countries resist upward revaluations is that such actions would make their products more expensive to foreigners and thus cut into their export sales. This, in fact, is the main reason why China has been maintaining an undervalued currency for years despite the protestations of many other nations. China's leaders believe that vibrant export industries are the key to job growth, development—and tranquility at home.

The balance of payments comes in two main parts. The **current account** totes up exports and imports of goods and services, cross-border payments of interest and dividends, and cross-border gifts. It is close, both conceptually and numerically, to what we have called *net exports* (*X* − *IM*) in previous chapters. The United States has been running extremely large current account deficits for many years.

The current account represents only one part of our balance of payments, however, for it leaves out all purchases and sales of assets. Purchases of U.S. assets by foreigners bring foreign currency to the United States, and purchases of foreign assets cost us foreign currency. Netting the capital flows in each direction gives us our surplus or deficit on **capital account**. In recent years, this part of our balance of payments has registered persistently large *surpluses* as foreigners have acquired massive amounts of U.S. assets.

In what sense, then, does the overall balance of payments balance? There are two possibilities. If the exchange rate is *floating*, all *private* transactions—current account plus capital account—must add up to zero because dollars purchased equals dollars sold. But if, instead, the exchange rate is *fixed,* as shown in Figures 5 and 6, the two accounts need not balance one another. Government purchases or sales of foreign currency make up the surplus or deficit in the overall balance of payments.

## 19-4 A BIT OF HISTORY: THE GOLD STANDARD AND THE BRETTON WOODS SYSTEM

It is difficult to find examples of strictly fixed exchange rates in the historical record. About the only time exchange rates were truly fixed was under the old gold standard, at least when it was practiced in its ideal form.[4]

### 19-4a The Classical Gold Standard

Under the **gold standard**, governments maintained fixed exchange rates by an automatic equilibrating mechanism that went something like this: All currencies were defined in terms of gold; indeed, some were actually made of gold. When a nation ran a balance of payments *deficit,* it had to *sell gold* to finance the deficit. Because the domestic money supply was based on gold, losing gold to foreigners meant that the money supply fell *automatically,* thus raising interest rates. Those higher interest rates attracted foreign capital. At the same time, this restrictive "monetary policy" pulled down output and prices, which discouraged imports and encouraged exports. The balance of payments problem quickly rectified itself.

The **gold standard** is a way to fix exchange rates by defining each participating currency in terms of gold and allowing holders of each participating currency to convert that currency into gold.

This automatic adjustment process meant, however, that under the gold standard no nation had control of its domestic monetary policy. An analogous problem arises in any system of fixed exchange rates, regardless of whether it makes use of gold:

> Under fixed exchange rates, monetary policy must be dedicated to pegging the exchange rate. It cannot, therefore, be used to manage aggregate demand.

The gold standard posed one other serious difficulty: The world's commerce was at the mercy of gold discoveries. Major gold finds would mean higher prices and booming economic conditions, through the standard monetary-policy mechanisms that we studied in earlier chapters. But when the supply of gold failed to keep pace with growth of the world economy, prices had to fall in the long run and employment had to fall in the short run.

### 19-4b The Bretton Woods System

The gold standard collapsed for good amid the financial chaos of the Great Depression of the 1930s and World War II. Without it, the world struggled through a serious breakdown in international trade.

As the war drew to a close, representatives of the industrial nations, including John Maynard Keynes of Great Britain, met at a hotel in Bretton Woods, New Hampshire, to devise a stable monetary environment that would enable world trade to resume. Because the United States held the lion's share of the world's reserves at the time, these officials naturally turned to the dollar as the basis for the new international economic order.

The Bretton Woods agreements reestablished fixed exchange rates based on the free convertibility of the U.S. dollar into gold. The United States agreed to buy or sell gold to maintain the $35 per ounce price that President Franklin Roosevelt had established in 1933. The other signatory nations, which had almost no gold in any case, agreed to buy and sell *dollars* to maintain their exchange rates vis-à-vis the dollar at agreed-upon levels.

Under the **Bretton Woods system** of fixed exchange rates, the price of the U.S. dollar was fixed in terms of gold and the prices of all other currencies were fixed in terms of dollars.

The **Bretton Woods system** succeeded in refixing exchange rates and restoring world trade—two notable achievements. But, eventually, it displayed the flaws of any fixed

---

[4] As a matter of fact, although the gold standard lasted (on and off) for hundreds of years, it was rarely practiced in its ideal form. Except for a brief period of fixed exchange rates in the late nineteenth and early twentieth centuries, governments periodically adjusted exchange rates even under the gold standard.

exchange rate system. Changes in exchange rates were permitted only as a last resort—which, in practice, came to mean that the country had a chronic *deficit* in the balance of payments of sizable proportions. Such nations were allowed to *devalue* their currencies relative to the dollar. So the system was not really one of fixed exchange rates but, rather, one in which rates were "fixed until further notice." Because devaluations came only after a long run of balance of payments deficits had depleted the country's reserves, these devaluations often could be clearly foreseen and normally had to be large. Speculators therefore saw glowing opportunities for profit and would "attack" weak currencies with waves of selling.

A second problem arose from the asymmetry mentioned earlier: Deficit nations could be forced to devalue, whereas surplus nations could resist upward revaluations. Because the value of the U.S. dollar was fixed in terms of gold, the United States was the one nation in the world that had no way to devalue its currency. The only way the dollar could fall was if the surplus nations would revalue their currencies upward. They did not adjust frequently enough, though, so the United States developed an overvalued currency and chronic balance of payments deficits.

The overvalued dollar finally destroyed the Bretton Woods system in 1971, when President Richard Nixon unilaterally ended the game by announcing that the United States would no longer buy or sell gold at $35 per ounce.

## 19-5 ADJUSTMENT MECHANISMS UNDER FIXED EXCHANGE RATES

Under the Bretton Woods system, devaluation was viewed as a last resort, to be used only after other methods of adjusting to payments imbalances had failed. What were these other methods?

We encountered most of them in our earlier discussion of exchange rate determination in free markets. Any factor that *increases the demand* for, say, Argentine pesos or that *reduces the supply* will push the value of the peso upward—if it is free to adjust. But if the exchange rate is pegged, the balance of payments deficit will shrink instead. (Try this for yourself using Figure 5.)

Recalling our earlier discussion of the factors that underlie the demand and supply curves, we see that one way a nation can shrink its balance of payments deficit is to *reduce its aggregate demand,* thereby discouraging imports and cutting down its demand for foreign currency. Another is to *lower its rate of inflation,* thereby encouraging exports and discouraging imports. Finally, it can *raise its interest rates* to attract more foreign capital.

In other words, deficit nations are expected to follow restrictive monetary and fiscal policies *voluntarily,* just as they would have done *automatically* under the classical gold standard. However, just as under the gold standard, this medicine is often unpalatable.

A surplus nation could, of course, take the opposite measures: pursuing *expansionary* monetary and fiscal policies to increase economic growth and *lower* interest rates. By increasing the supply of the country's currency and reducing the demand for it, such actions would reduce that nation's balance of payments surplus. But surplus countries often do not relish the inflation that accompanies expansionary policies, and so, once again, they leave the burden of adjustment to the deficit nations. The general point about fixed exchange rates is that

> Under a system of fixed exchange rates, a country's government loses some control over its domestic economy. Sometimes balance of payments considerations may force it to contract its economy in order to cut down its demand for foreign currency, even though domestic needs call for expansion. At other times, the domestic economy may need to be reined in, but balance of payments considerations suggest expansion.

That was certainly the case in Argentina in 2002, when interest rates soared in order to attract foreign capital and the government pursued contractionary fiscal policies to curb the country's appetite for imports. Both actions contributed to a long and deep recession. Argentina took the bitter medicine needed to defend its fixed exchange rate for quite a while. However, high unemployment eventually led to riots in the streets, toppled the government, and persuaded the Argentine authorities to abandon the fixed exchange rate with the U.S. dollar.

The situation in Greece starting in 2010 was even starker. Its exchange rate was truly fixed because it had abolished the drachma when it joined the euro in 2001. But the value of the euro was too high for Greece's troubled economy, just as in the Argentine example in Figure 5. Unfortunately for Greece, it had no option to devalue, as Argentina eventually did. Furthermore, as a member of the euro zone, Greece had no monetary policy of its own; a single monetary policy for all member countries was (and is) made by the European Central Bank (ECB). So the only way for Greece to defend itself against what amounted to a run on Greek assets was for the government to accept a sharp *fiscal* contraction, raising taxes and cutting government spending. Such policies, as we know, reduce aggregate demand and worsen a recession. At this writing, Greece has suffered a decline in GDP comparable to what the United States experienced during the Great Depression of the 1930s!

## 19-6  WHY TRY TO FIX EXCHANGE RATES?

In view of these and other problems with fixed exchange rates, why did the international financial community work so hard to maintain them for so many years? And why do some nations, such as China and the euro zone, still fix their exchange rates today? The answer is that floating exchange rates also pose problems.

Chief among these worries is the possibility that freely floating rates might prove to be highly variable rates, thereby adding an unwanted element of risk to foreign trade. For example, if the exchange rate is $1.30 to the euro, then a Parisian dress priced at 500 euros will cost $650. Should the euro appreciate to $1.50, that same dress would cost $750. An American department store thinking of buying the dress may need to place its order far in advance and will want to know the cost *in dollars*. It may be worried about the possibility that the value of the euro will rise, making the dress cost more than $650. And such worries might inhibit trade.

*"Then it's agreed. Until the dollar firms up, we let the clamshell float."*

There are two responses to this concern. First, freely floating rates might prove to be fairly stable in practice. Prices of most ordinary goods and services, for example, are determined by supply and demand in free markets and do not fluctuate unduly. Unfortunately, experience since 1973 has dashed this hope. Exchange rates have proved to be extremely volatile, which is why some observers now favor a return to greater fixity in exchange rates.

A second possibility is that speculators might relieve business firms of exchange rate risks—for a fee, of course. Consider the department store example. If each euro costs $1.30 today, the U.S. department store manager can assure herself of paying exactly $650 for the dress several months from now by arranging for a speculator to deliver 500 euros to her at $1.30 per euro on the day she needs them. If the euro appreciates in the interim, the speculator, not the department store, will take the financial beating. Of course, if the euro depreciates, the speculator will pocket the profits. Thus, speculators play an important role in a system of floating exchange rates.

The widespread fears that speculative activity in free markets will lead to wild gyrations in prices, although occasionally valid, are often unfounded. The reason is simple.

> To make profits, international currency speculators must, on average, *buy* currencies when their values are low (thus helping to support weak currencies by boosting demand) and *sell* currencies when their values are high (thus holding down the price by adding to supply). This means that successful speculators must come into the market more often as *buyers* when demand for a currency is weak (or when supply is strong) and as *sellers* when demand is strong (or supply is scant). In doing so, they help limit price fluctuations. Looked at the other way around, speculators will *destabilize* prices only if they systematically lose money.[5]

Notice the stark—and ironic—contrast to the system of fixed exchange rates in which speculation often leads to wild "runs" on currencies that are on the verge of devaluation—as happened in Mexico in 1995, several Southeast Asian countries in 1997–1998, Brazil in

[5] See Test Yourself Question 4 at the end of the chapter.

1999, and Argentina in 2001. Speculative activity, which may well be *destabilizing* under fixed rates, is more likely to be *stabilizing* under floating rates.[6]

We do not mean to imply that speculation makes floating rates trouble-free. At the very least, speculators will demand a fee for their services—a fee that adds to the costs of trading across national borders. In addition, speculators will not assume *all* exchange rate risks. For example, few contracts on foreign currencies last more than, say, a year or two. Thus, a business cannot easily protect itself from exchange rate changes over periods of many years. Finally, speculative markets can and do get carried away from time to time, moving currency rates in ways that are difficult to understand, that frustrate the intentions of governments, and that devastate some people—as happened in Mexico in 1995 and in Southeast Asia in 1997.

Despite all of these problems, international trade has flourished under floating exchange rates. So perhaps exchange rate risk is not as burdensome as some people think.

## 19-7  THE CURRENT "NONSYSTEM"

The international financial system today is an eclectic blend of fixed and floating exchange rates, with no grand organizing principle. Indeed, it is so diverse that it is often called a "nonsystem."

Some countries still peg their currencies in the old Bretton Woods manner. The most prominent example is China, which for years has limited the appreciation of its currency (the yuan) by selling as many yuan as necessary, accepting U.S. dollars in trade. Over the years, China's purchases have accumulated to about $4 *trillion* in foreign currency reserves.

The nations of the euro zone, of course, have locked their exchange rates vis-a-vis one another by adopting a common currency (the euro). A few small countries, such as Panama and Ecuador, have taken the more extreme step of actually adopting the U.S. dollar for use as domestic currency. A few other nations tie their currencies to a hypothetical "basket" of several foreign currencies, rather than to just one.

More nations, however, let their exchange rates float, although not always freely. Such floating rates change slightly on a day-to-day basis, and market forces determine the basic trends, up or down. But governments do not hesitate to intervene to moderate exchange movements whenever they feel such actions are appropriate. Typically, interventions are aimed at ironing out what are deemed to be transitory fluctuations, but sometimes central banks oppose basic exchange rate trends. For example, the Federal Reserve and other central banks sold dollars aggressively in 1985 to push the dollar *down* and then bought dollars in 1994 and 1995 to push the dollar *up*. As we will discuss in the next chapter, the Japanese also acquired well over a trillion dollars trying to prevent the yen from floating up too much. The terms **dirty float** or **managed float** have been coined to describe this mongrel system.

Under a **"dirty"** or **"managed" float**, the government intervenes from time to time to influence the value of its currency.

### 19-7a  The Role of the IMF

The **International Monetary Fund (IMF)**, which was established at Bretton Woods in 1944, examines the economies of all its member nations on a regular basis. When a country runs into serious financial difficulties, it may turn to the IMF for financial assistance. The IMF typically provides loans, but with many strings attached. For example, if the country has a large current account deficit—as is normally the case when countries come to it for aid—the IMF will typically insist on contractionary fiscal and monetary policies to curb the country's appetite for imports. Often, this mandate spells recession.

During the 1990s, the IMF found itself at the epicenter of a series of very visible economic crises: in Mexico in 1995, in Southeast Asia in 1997, in Russia in 1998, and in Argentina in 2001. Although each case was different, they shared some common elements.

---

[6] After their respective currency crises in 1995 and 1999, both Mexico and Brazil floated their currencies. Each weathered the subsequent international financial storms rather nicely. But Argentina, with its fixed exchange rate, struggled.

Most of these crises were precipitated by the collapse of a fixed exchange rate that previously had been pegged to the U.S. dollar. In each case, the currency plummeted, with ruinous consequences. Questions were raised about the country's ability to pay its bills. In each case, the IMF arrived on the scene with lots of money and lots of advice, determined to stave off default. In the end, each country suffered through a severe recession—or worse. Both Russia and Argentina defaulted on their debts.

The IMF's increased visibility naturally brought it increased criticism. Some critics complained that the IMF set excessively strict conditions on its client states, requiring them, for example, to cut their government budgets and raise interest rates during recessions—which made bad economic situations even worse.

Other critics worried that the IMF was serving as a bill collector for banks and other financial institutions from the United States and other rich countries. Because the banks loaned money irresponsibly, these critics argued, they deserved to lose some of it. By bailing them out of their losses, the IMF simply encouraged more reckless behavior in the future.

Numerous suggestions for reform were offered, but few were adopted. Then the debate over the IMF went quiet for several years, for a very simple reason: The world economy improved, and most of the nations that formerly needed IMF help no longer required it. The prominence of the IMF faded remarkably but, it turned out, only temporarily. When the Great Recession went global in late 2008, a long list of mostly poorer countries clamored for IMF assistance. Then in 2010, the list of applicants grew to include a European country (Greece) for the first time in decades. As it strived—unsuccessfully, as it turned out—to marshal the resources necessary to stave off a default by the Greek government, the European Union turned to the IMF for assistance in both financing the rescue operation and monitoring Greece's austerity program.

## 19-7b  The Volatile Dollar

As mentioned earlier, floating exchange rates have proven to be volatile exchange rates. No currency illustrates this point better than the U.S. dollar (see Figure 7). As Table 1 showed, in July 1980 a U.S. dollar bought less than 2 German marks, about 4 French francs, and about 830 Italian lire. Then it started rising like a rocket (see Figure 7). By the time it peaked in February 1985, the mighty dollar could buy more than 3 German marks, about 10 French francs, and more than 2,000 Italian lire. Such major currency changes affect world trade dramatically.

The rising dollar was a blessing to Americans who traveled abroad or who bought foreign goods—because foreign prices, when translated to dollars by the exchange rate, looked cheap to Americans.[7] But the arithmetic worked just the other way around for

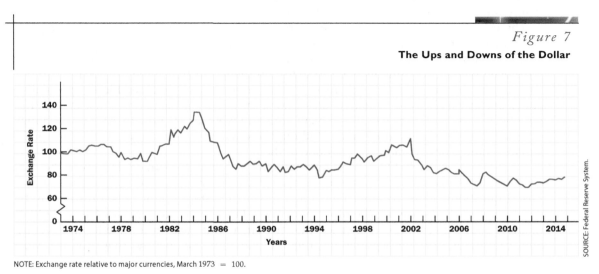

*Figure 7*

**The Ups and Downs of the Dollar**

NOTE: Exchange rate relative to major currencies, March 1973 = 100.

SOURCE: Federal Reserve System.

[7] EXERCISE: How much does a 100-euro hotel room in Paris cost in dollars when the euro is worth $1.25? $1? 80 cents?

U.S. firms seeking to sell their goods abroad; foreign buyers found everything American very expensive.[8] It was no surprise, therefore, that as the dollar climbed our exports fell, our imports rose, and many of our leading manufacturing industries were decimated by foreign competition. An expensive currency, Americans came to learn, is a mixed blessing.

From early 1985 until early 1988, the value of the dollar fell even faster than it had risen. The cheaper dollar curbed American appetites for imports and alleviated the plight of our export industries, many of which boomed. However, rising prices for imported goods and foreign vacations were a source of consternation to many American consumers.

Over the following seven years, the overall value of the dollar did not change very much—although there was a small downward drift. Then, in the spring of 1995, the dollar began another sizable ascent that lasted until early 2002. After that, as we noted earlier in this chapter, the dollar fell for about two years and then was pretty stable until 2007–2008, when it tumbled briefly but sharply before rising again. Lately, the dollar has been rising again. All in all, the behavior of the dollar has been anything but boring. Fortunes have been made and lost speculating on what it will do next.

## 19-7c The Birth and Adolescence of the Euro

As noted earlier, floating exchange rates are no panacea. One particular problem confronted the members of the European Union (EU). As part of their long-range goal to create a unified market like that of the United States, they perceived a need to establish a single currency for all member countries—a monetary union.

The process of convergence to a single currency took place in steps, more or less as prescribed by the Treaty of Maastricht (1992), over a period of years. Member nations encountered a number of obstacles along the way. But to the surprise of many skeptics, all such obstacles were overcome, and the euro became a reality on schedule. Electronic and checking transactions in 11 EU nations were denominated in euros rather than in national currencies in 1999, euro coins and paper money were introduced successfully in 2002, and the number of participating countries has since risen in stages to 18, with more on line to get in. All of these transformations went remarkably smoothly.

That said, the euro did not spring into life as a fully grown adult. In its earlier years, there were plenty of doubters, and even now a few doubters remain. The new European currency made its debut at $1.18 in January 1999, but promptly fell to a low point of $0.83 in October 2000—a stunning 30 percent decline in less than two years. After that, however, the euro climbed in value relative to the dollar for years, reaching a high of $1.60 in 2008, before falling again. At this printing, the euro is worth about $1.25.

The establishment of the euro was a great economic experiment that marked a giant step beyond merely fixing exchange rates. A government can end a fixed exchange rate regime at any time. And, as we have seen, speculators sometimes break fixed exchange rates even when governments want to maintain them. But the single European currency was created by an international treaty and is more or less invulnerable to speculative attack because it *abolished* exchange rates among the participating nations. Just as there has long been no exchange rate between New York and New Jersey, now there is no exchange rate between Germany and France. Although monetary unions may create other problems, exchange rate instability is not one of them.

Or at least that is what European governments hoped and assumed. However, the debt crisis of 2010–2011 that began in Greece and spread to Ireland, Portugal, and elsewhere raised questions about whether (and how) the euro system might fail—presumably by one or more nations leaving the monetary union. (The prime suspect was Greece.) Other member countries steadfastly insisted that any such "exit" was unthinkable, and eventually, after many difficult negotiations, they put lots of money behind that promise. Most

---

[8] EXERCISE: How much does a $55 American camera cost a German consumer when the euro is worth $1.20? $1? 80 cents?

## Puzzle Resolved | *Why the Dollar Rose, Then Fell, Then Rose*

What we have learned in this chapter helps us understand what brought the dollar down between 2002 and 2004, and then again in 2007 and 2008. The story actually begins well before that.

During the Great Boom of the late 1990s, the United States was *the* place to invest. Funds poured in from all over the world to purchase American stocks, American bonds, and even American companies—especially in the information technology field. Yahoo! was indeed a fitting name for the age. As we have learned in this chapter, the rising demand for U.S. assets bid up the price of U.S. currency (see Figure 7 again).

But the soaring dollar sowed the seeds of its own destruction. Two of its major effects were (a) to make U.S. goods and services look much more expen-

© The New Yorker Collection, 2002 Mick Stevens from cartoonbank.com. All rights reserved.

*"His mood is pegged to the dollar"*

sive to potential buyers abroad and (b) to make foreign goods look much cheaper to Americans. So our imports grew much faster than our exports. In brief, we developed a huge *current account deficit* (which is roughly exports *minus* imports) to match our large *capital account surplus.*

The Internet bubble, of course, started to burst in 2000, pulling the stock market down with it. Then the September 11, 2001, terrorist attacks raised further doubts about the strength of the U.S. economy. For these and other reasons, foreign investors apparently began to question the wisdom of holding so many American assets. With the U.S. current account still deeply in the red, and the foreign demand for U.S. capital sagging, there was only one way for the (freely floating) dollar to go: down. And so it did.

At first, the financial crisis continued this trend, and the dollar sank to new lows in 2008. The crisis was, after all, made in America. Then something surprising happened: The dollar actually rose sharply from July 2008 until March 2009. Why? We have learned the reason in this chapter: When the financial crisis reached its most acute stages, investors all over the world sought the safety of U.S. assets, especially U.S. Treasury debt. Since 2010, the dollar has had a few ups and downs (lately, up), with little trend in either direction.

---

dramatically, Mario Draghi, the president of the ECB, pledged in July 2012 that the central bank would do "whatever it takes" to preserve the euro. After that, speculation about the euro's demise pretty much ended, even though the debt problems of Greece and other countries persisted.

## Summary

1. **Exchange rates** state the value of one currency in terms of other currencies and thus translate one country's prices into the currencies of other nations. Exchange rates therefore influence patterns of world trade.

2. If governments do not interfere by buying or selling their currencies, exchange rates will be determined in free markets by the usual laws of supply and demand. Such a system is said to be based on **floating exchange rates.**

3. Demand for a nation's currency is derived from foreigners' desires to purchase that country's goods and

services or to invest in its assets. Under floating rates, anything that increases the demand for a nation's currency will cause its exchange rate to **appreciate.**

4. Supply of a nation's currency is derived from the desire of that country's citizens to purchase foreign goods and services or to invest in foreign assets. Under floating rates, anything that increases the supply of a nation's currency will cause its exchange rate to **depreciate.**

5. Purchasing-power parity plays a major role in long-run exchange rate movements. The **purchasing-power parity theory** states that relative price levels in any

two countries determine the exchange rate between their currencies. Therefore, countries with relatively low inflation rates normally will have appreciating currencies.

6. Over shorter periods, however, purchasing-power parity has little influence over exchange rate movements. The pace of economic activity and, especially, the level of interest rates exert greater influences.

7. Capital movements are typically the dominant factor in determining exchange rates in the short and medium runs. A nation that offers international investors higher interest rates, or better prospective returns on investments, will typically see its currency appreciate.

8. An exchange rate can be fixed at a nonequilibrium level if the government is willing and able to mop up any excess of quantity supplied over quantity demanded or provide any excess of quantity demanded over quantity supplied. In the first case, the country is said to be suffering from a **balance of payments deficit** because of its overvalued currency. In the second case, an undervalued currency has given it a **balance of payments surplus.**

9. The gold standard was a system of **fixed exchange rates** in which the value of every nation's currency was fixed in terms of gold. This system created problems because nations could not control their own money supplies and because the world could not control the total supply of gold.

10. After World War II, the gold standard was replaced by the **Bretton Woods system,** in which exchange rates

were fixed in terms of U.S. dollars and the dollar was in turn tied to gold. This system broke down in 1971, when the dollar became chronically overvalued.

11. Since 1971, the world has moved toward a system of relatively free exchange rates, but with plenty of exceptions. We now have a thoroughly mixed system of **"dirty"** or **"managed" floating,** which continues to evolve and adapt.

12. Floating rates are not without their problems. For example, importers and exporters justifiably worry about fluctuations in exchange rates.

13. Under **floating exchange rates,** investors who speculate on international currency values provide a valuable service by assuming the risks of those who do not wish to speculate. Normally, speculators stabilize rather than destabilize exchange rates, because that is how they make profits.

14. The value of the U.S. dollar has been volatile. It rose dramatically from 1980 to 1985, making our imports cheaper and our exports more expensive. From 1985 to 1988, the dollar tumbled, which had precisely the reverse effects. Then the dollar climbed again between 1995 and 2002, leading once again to a large trade imbalance. From 2002 to 2004, and then again in 2007–2008, the dollar fell further. But it has since recovered.

15. The European Union has established a single currency, the euro, for most of its member nations. In recent years, the euro has been volatile, owing to actual or potential debt problems in several countries.

## Key Terms

appreciate   380
balance of payments deficit   387
balance of payments surplus   388
Bretton Woods system   389
capital account   388

current account   388
depreciate   380
devaluation   381
dirty or managed float   392
exchange rate   380

fixed exchange rates   387
floating exchange rates   381
gold standard   389
revaluation   381

## Test Yourself

1. Use supply and demand diagrams to analyze the effect of the following actions on the exchange rate between the dollar and the yen:

   a. Japan opens its domestic markets to more foreign competition.
   b. Investors come to believe that values on the Tokyo stock market will fall.
   c. The Federal Reserve cuts interest rates in the United States.
   d. The U.S. government, to help settle the problems of the Middle East, gives huge amounts of foreign aid to Israel and her Arab neighbors.

   e. The United States has a recession while Japan booms.
   f. Inflation in the United States exceeds that in Japan.

2. For each of the following transactions, indicate how it would affect the U.S. balance of payments if exchange rates were fixed:

   a. You spent the summer traveling in Europe.
   b. Your uncle in Canada sent you $20 as a birthday present.
   c. You bought a new Honda, made in Japan.
   d. You bought a new Honda, made in Ohio.
   e. You sold some stock you own on the Tokyo Stock Exchange.

3. Suppose each of the transactions listed in Test Yourself Question 2 was done by many Americans. Indicate how each would affect the international value of the dollar if exchange rates were floating.

4. We learned in this chapter that successful speculators buy a currency when demand is weak and sell it when demand is strong. Use supply and demand diagrams for two different periods (one with weak demand, the other with strong demand) to show why this activity will limit price fluctuations.

## Discussion Questions

1. What items do you own or routinely consume that are produced abroad? From what countries do these items come? Suppose Americans decided to buy fewer of these things. How would that affect the exchange rates between the dollar and these currencies?

2. If the dollar appreciates relative to the euro, will the German camera you have wanted become more or less expensive? What effect do you imagine this change will have on American demand for German cameras? Does the American demand curve for euros, therefore, slope upward or downward? Explain.

3. During the first half of the 1980s, inflation in (West) Germany was consistently lower than that in the United States. What, then, does the purchasing-power parity theory predict should have happened to the exchange rate between the mark and the dollar between 1980 and 1985? (Look at Table 1 to see what actually happened.)

4. How are the problems of a country faced with a balance of payments deficit similar to those posed by a government regulation that holds the price of milk above the equilibrium level? (*Hint:* Think of each in terms of a supply-demand diagram.)

5. Under the old gold standard, what do you think happened to world prices when a huge gold strike occurred in California in 1849? What do you think happened when the world went without any important new gold strikes for 20 years or so?

6. Explain why the members of the Bretton Woods conference in 1944 wanted to establish a system of fixed exchange rates. What flaw led to the ultimate breakdown of the system in 1971?

7. Suppose you want to reserve a hotel room in London for the coming summer but are worried that the value of the pound may rise between now and then, making the room too expensive for your budget. Explain how a speculator could relieve you of this worry. (Don't actually try it—speculators deal only in very large sums!)

8. In 2011 and 2012, market forces raised the international value of the Japanese yen. Why do you think the government of Japan was unhappy about this currency appreciation? (*Hint:* Japan was trying to recover from both a recession and a disastrous earthquake/tsunami at the time.) If they wanted to stop the yen's appreciation, what actions might the Bank of Japan (Japan's central bank) have taken? Ask your instructor what the Bank of Japan subsequently did in 2013 and 2014.

# EXCHANGE RATES AND THE MACROECONOMY

**20**

*No man is an island, entire of itself.*

JOHN DONNE

One prominent aspect of globalization is that economic events that originate in one country reverberate quickly around the globe, sometimes at lightning speed. A stunning example arose in 2007, after the housing boom ended in the United States. A number of so-called subprime mortgages (meaning mortgages granted to people with questionable credit) started to go bad. As the trickle of defaults turned into a flood, it triggered a worldwide financial crisis when several financial businesses in—of all places—France and Germany ran into serious trouble. Why there? It turned out that these institutions, thousands of miles away, had invested heavily in U.S. subprime mortgages. It is indeed a small world.

This was just one example of a general phenomenon. Economic events that originate in the U.S. reverberate around the globe, and fluctuations in foreign growth, inflation, and interest rates affect the U.S. economy. Anyone who ignores these international linkages cannot hope to understand how the modern world economy works.

The macroeconomic model we developed in earlier chapters did a bit of that, but not enough because it ignored such crucial influences as exchange rates (which were assumed to be fixed) and international financial movements (which were ignored). The previous chapter showed how major macroeconomic variables such as gross domestic product (GDP), prices, and interest rates affect exchange rates. In this chapter, we complete the circle by studying how changes in the exchange rate affect the domestic economy.

Then we bring international capital flows into the picture and learn how monetary and fiscal policy work in an **open economy**. In particular, we build a model suitable for a *large open economy* with *substantial capital flows* and a *floating exchange rate*—in short, a model meant to resemble the contemporary United States, which is indeed not "an island, entire of itself."

An **open economy** is one that trades with other nations in goods and services, and perhaps also trades in financial assets.

## CONTENTS

**Issue** | *Is a Rising Currency Value a Blessing?*

Central bankers do not normally "talk down" their currencies. Rather, they often take pride in a high or rising currency value. It almost seems to be in their DNA. If their policies seem likely to depreciate their currencies, they almost deny it. Yet in 2013 and 2014, both Mario Draghi,

©Robert Hoetink/Shutterstock.com

the president of the European Central Bank (ECB), and Haruhiko Kuroda, the governor of the Bank of Japan, took policy actions that were clearly designed to weaken the euro and the yen, respectively. And they didn't hide either their intent or their belief that the euro and the yen were too expensive. (Janet Yellen, chair of the Federal Reserve, made no such anti-dollar statements.)

Why were Messrs, Draghi and Kuroda concerned about the high values of the euro and the yen? And what actions did they take to bring their currencies down? We will examine these questions as the chapter progresses.

## 20-1  INTERNATIONAL TRADE, EXCHANGE RATES, AND AGGREGATE DEMAND

We know from earlier chapters that a country's net exports, $X - IM$, are one component of its aggregate demand, $C + I + G + (X - IM)$. It follows that an autonomous increase in exports or decrease in imports has a multiplier effect on the economy, just like an increase in consumption, investment, or government purchases.[1] Figure 1 depicts this conclusion on an aggregate demand-and-supply diagram. A rise in net exports shifts the aggregate demand curve outward to the right, pushing equilibrium from point A to point B. Both GDP and the price level rise.

What forces might make net exports increase? One factor mentioned in Chapter 8 was a rise in *foreign incomes*. If foreign economies boom, their citizens are likely to spend more on a wide variety of products, some of which will be American exports. Thus, Figure 1 can be used to illustrate the effect on the U.S. economy of more rapid growth in foreign countries. By like reasoning, a recession abroad would reduce U.S. exports and shift the U.S. aggregate demand curve inward. Thus, as we learned in Chapter 9:

The **exchange rate** states the price, in terms of one currency, at which another currency can be bought.

**Booms or recessions in one country tend to be transmitted to other countries through international trade in goods and services.**

This phenomenon was illustrated painfully in 2009, when the worldwide recession led to a collapse of exports in virtually every country, thereby magnifying the reduction in global aggregate demand.

A second important determinant of net exports was mentioned in Chapter 8, but not discussed in depth there: the relative prices of foreign and domestic goods. The idea is a straightforward application of the law of demand. Namely, if the prices of the goods of Country X rise, people everywhere will tend to buy fewer of them—and therefore more of the goods of Country Y. As we will see next, this simple idea holds the key to understanding how **exchange rates** affect international trade.

### 20-1a  Relative Prices, Exports, and Imports

First assume—just for this short section—that exchange rates are *fixed*. Think about what happens if the prices of American goods fall while, say, Japanese prices are constant. With U.S. products now less expensive *relative to Japanese products,* both Japanese and American consumers will buy

*Figure 1*
**The Effects of Higher Net Exports**

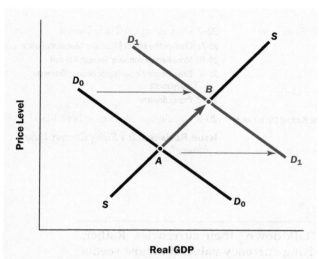

---

[1] The Chapter 9 appendix showed that international trade lowers the numerical value of the multiplier. Autonomous changes in $C, I, G,$ and $(X - IM)$ all have the same multiplier.

more American goods and fewer Japanese goods. That means America's exports will rise and its imports will fall, thus adding to aggregate demand in the United States (and subtracting from aggregate demand in Japan). Conversely, a rise in American prices (relative to Japanese prices) will *decrease* U.S. net exports and aggregate demand. Thus:

A *fall* in the relative prices of a country's exports tends to *increase* that country's net exports and, thereby, to raise its real GDP. Analogously, a *rise* in the relative prices of a country's exports will *decrease* that country's net exports and GDP.

Precisely the same logic applies to changes in Japanese prices. If Japanese prices rise, Americans will export more to and import less from Japan. So $X - IM$ in the United States will rise, boosting GDP here. Figure 1 applies to this case without change. By similar reasoning, falling Japanese prices decrease U.S. net exports and depress our economy. Thus:

Price increases for foreign products raise a country's net exports and hence its GDP. Price decreases for foreign products have the opposite effects.

*Table 1*

**Exchange Rates and Home Currency Prices**

| Exchange Rate | ¥30,000 Japanese TV Set | | $1,000 U.S. Home Computer | |
|---|---|---|---|---|
| | Price in Japan | Price in the United States | Price in the United States | Price in Japan |
| $1 = 120 yen | ¥30,000 | $250 | $1,000 | ¥120,000 |
| 1 = 100 yen | 30,000 | 300 | 1,000 | 100,000 |

## 20-1b The Effects of Changes in Exchange Rates

From here, it is simple to figure out how changes in exchange rates affect a country's net exports, because *currency appreciations or depreciations change international relative prices.*

Recall that the basic role of an exchange rate is to convert one country's prices into another country's currency. Table 1 uses two examples of U.S.–Japanese trade to remind us of this role. Suppose the dollar depreciates from 120 yen to 100 yen. From the American consumer's viewpoint, a television set that costs ¥30,000 in Japan goes up in price from $250 (i.e., 30,000/120) to $300 (i.e., 30,000/100). To Americans, it is as if Japanese manufacturers raised TV prices by 20 percent. Naturally, Americans will react by purchasing fewer Japanese products, so American imports decline.

Now consider the implications for Japanese consumers interested in buying American personal computers that cost $1,000. When the dollar falls from 120 yen to 100 yen, they see the price of these computers falling from ¥120,000 to ¥100,000. To them, it is as if American producers had offered a one-sixth markdown. Under such circumstances, we expect U.S. sales to the Japanese to rise, so U.S. exports should increase. Putting these two findings together, we conclude that

A currency **depreciation** should *raise* net exports and therefore *increase* aggregate demand. Conversely, a currency **appreciation** should *reduce* net exports and therefore *decrease* aggregate demand.

The aggregate supply-and-demand diagram in Figure 2 illustrates this conclusion. If the currency depreciates, net exports rise and the aggregate demand curve shifts outward from $D_0D_0$ to the maroon line $D_1D_1$. Both prices and output rise as the economy's equilibrium moves from $E_0$ to $E_1$. If the currency appreciates instead, everything operates in reverse: Net exports fall, the aggregate demand curve shifts inward to the blue line $D_2D_2$, and both prices and output decline.

This simple analysis helps us understand why the U.S. trade deficit grew so enormously in the late 1990s

A nation's currency is said to **depreciate** when exchange rates change so that a unit of its currency can buy fewer units of foreign currency.

A nation's currency is said to **appreciate** when exchange rates change so that a unit of its currency can buy more units of foreign currency.

*Figure 2*

**The Effects of Exchange Rate Changes on Aggregate Demand**

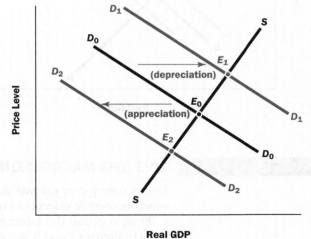

and early 2000s and then fell. We learned in the previous chapter that the international value of the dollar began to climb in 1995. According to the reasoning we have just completed, within a few years such an appreciation of the dollar should have boosted U.S. imports and damaged U.S. exports. That is precisely what happened. In constant dollars, American imports soared by more than 40 percent between 1997 and 2002, whereas American exports rose by only 7 percent. The result was that a $155 billion real net export deficit in 1997 turned into a monumental $585 billion deficit by 2002. Subsequently, the dollar's *decline* helped push the trade deficit down from a record $786 billion in 2006 to "only" $392 billion in 2009. (Changes since 2009 have been small.)

## 20-2 AGGREGATE SUPPLY IN AN OPEN ECONOMY

So far we have concluded that a currency depreciation increases aggregate demand and that a currency appreciation decreases it. To complete our model of macroeconomics in an open economy, we must turn to the implications of international trade for *aggregate supply*.

Part of the story is familiar. We know from previous chapters that the United States, like all economies, purchases some of its productive inputs from abroad. Over the years, oil has been the most prominent example by far, though that is changing rapidly now as the United States moves toward energy independence. But we also rely on foreign suppliers for metals such as titanium, raw agricultural products such as coffee beans, and thousands of other items used by American industry. When the dollar depreciates, all of these imported inputs cost more in U.S. dollars—just as if foreign prices had risen.

The consequence is clear: With imported inputs more expensive, American firms will be forced to charge higher prices at any given level of output. Graphically, this means that *the aggregate supply curve will shift upward* (or inward to the left).

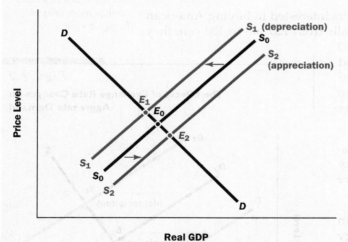

*Figure 3*

**The Effects of Exchange Rate Changes on Aggregate Supply**

When the dollar *depreciates*, the prices of imported inputs rise. The U.S. aggregate supply curve therefore shifts *inward*, pushing up the prices of American-made goods and services. By exactly analogous reasoning, an *appreciation* of the dollar makes imported inputs cheaper and shifts the U.S. aggregate supply curve *outward*, thus pushing American prices down. (See Figure 3.)

Beyond this, a depreciating dollar has additional inflationary effects that do not even show up on a standard aggregate demand-and-supply diagram, because the price level depicted on the vertical axis normally is *the price of gross domestic product*. Most obviously, prices of imported goods are included in U.S. price indexes like the Consumer Price Index (CPI) even though they are not made here. So when the dollar prices of Japanese cars, French wine, and Swiss watches increase, the CPI goes up *even if no American prices rise*. For this and other reasons, the inflationary impact of a dollar depreciation on *consumer* prices is greater than that indicated by Figure 3.

## 20-3 THE MACROECONOMIC EFFECTS OF EXCHANGE RATES

Let us now put aggregate demand and aggregate supply together and think through the macroeconomic effects of changes in exchange rates.

First, suppose the international value of the dollar falls. Referring back to the maroon lines in Figures 2 and 3, we see that this depreciation will shift the aggregate demand curve *outward* and the aggregate supply curve *inward*. The result, as Figure 4 shows, is that the

U.S. price level certainly rises. But whether real GDP rises or falls depends on whether the supply or demand shift is the dominant influence. The evidence strongly suggests that aggregate *demand* shifts are usually larger, so we expect GDP to rise. Hence:

A currency depreciation is inflationary and probably also expansionary.

The intuitive explanation for this result is clear. When the dollar falls, foreign goods become more expensive to Americans; that effect is directly inflationary. At the same time, aggregate demand in the United States is stimulated by rising net exports. As long as the expansion of demand outweighs the adverse shift of the aggregate supply curve brought on by currency depreciation, real GDP should rise. But wait. By this reasoning, shouldn't the massive depreciations of several Southeast Asian currencies in 1997 and 1998 have given these economies tremendous boosts? In fact, however, the so-called Asian Tigers suffered horrific slumps—as did Mexico when the peso tumbled in 1995. Why? The answer is that our simple analysis of aggregate supply and demand omits a detail that, although unimportant for the United States, is critical in many developing nations.

Countries that borrow in foreign currency see their debt burdens increase whenever their currency values decline. For example, an Indonesian business that borrowed $1,000 in July 1997, when $1 was worth 2,500 rupiah, thought it owed 2.5 million rupiah. When the dollar suddenly became worth 10,000 rupiah, the company's debt skyrocketed to 10 million rupiah. Many businesses found themselves unable to cope with their crushing debt burdens and went bankrupt. So although currency depreciation is expansionary in the United States, it was sharply contractionary in Indonesia.

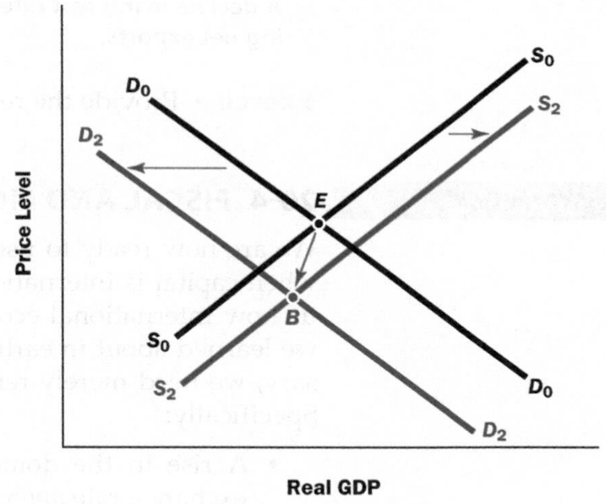

Returning to rich countries such as the United States, let's now reverse direction and look at what happens when the currency *appreciates*. In this case, net exports *fall*, so the aggregate demand curve shifts *inward*. At the same time, imported inputs become cheaper, so the aggregate supply curve shifts *outward*. Both of these shifts are shown in Figure 5. Once again, as the diagram shows, we can be sure of the movement of the price level: It falls. Output also falls if the demand shift is larger than the supply shift, as is likely. Thus:

A currency appreciation is disinflationary and probably also contractionary.

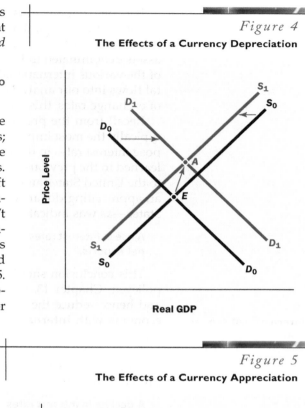

*Figure 4*

**The Effects of a Currency Depreciation**

*Figure 5*

**The Effects of a Currency Appreciation**

This analysis explains why many economists and financial experts cringed several times during the previous decade when the yen appreciated relative to the dollar. Japan was trying to emerge from a long period of deflation and mediocre growth. The last thing it needed, they argued, was a decrease in aggregate demand. Similar reasoning applies to China today. The Chinese authorities do not want to let an appreciating yuan slow down Chinese growth.

## 20-3a Interest Rates and International Capital Flows

One important piece of our international economic puzzle is still missing. We have analyzed international trade in goods and services in some detail, but we have so far ignored international movements of *capital*.

For some nations, this omission is inconsequential because they rarely borrow or lend on international capital markets. Things are quite different for the United States, however, because the vast majority of international financial flows involve either buying or selling assets denominated in U.S. dollars. In addition, we cannot hope to understand the origins of the various international financial crises of recent decades without incorporating capital flows into our analysis. Fortunately, given what we have just learned about the effects of exchange rates, this omission is easily rectified.

Recall from the previous chapter that interest rate differentials and capital flows are typically the most important determinants of exchange rate movements. Specifically, suppose interest rates in the United States rise while foreign interest rates are unchanged. We learned in the previous chapter that this change in relative interest rates will attract capital to the United States and cause the dollar to appreciate. This chapter has just taught us that an appreciating dollar will, in turn, reduce net exports, prices, and output in the United States—as was indicated in Figure 5. Thus:

> **A rise in interest rates tends to contract the economy by appreciating the currency and reducing net exports.**

This conclusion should have a familiar ring. Remember, when we studied monetary policy in Chapter 13, we observed that higher interest rates deter investment spending and hence reduce the $I$ component of $C + I + G + (X - IM)$. Now, in studying an open economy with **international capital flows**, we see that higher interest rates also reduce the $X - IM$ component. Thus, *international capital flows strengthen the negative effects of higher interest rates on aggregate demand.*

> **International capital flows** are purchases and sales of financial assets across national borders.

If interest rates fall in the United States, or rise abroad, everything we have just said is turned in the opposite direction. The conclusion is

> **A decline in interest rates tends to expand the economy by depreciating the currency and raising net exports.**

**Exercise**  Provide the reasoning behind this conclusion.

## 20-4  FISCAL AND MONETARY POLICIES IN AN OPEN ECONOMY

We are now ready to use our model to analyze how fiscal and monetary policies work when capital is internationally mobile and the exchange rate floats. Doing so will teach us how international economic relations modify the effects of stabilization policies that we learned about in earlier chapters. Fortunately, no new theoretical apparatus is necessary; we need merely remember what we have learned in the chapter up to this point. Specifically:

- A rise in the domestic interest rate leads to capital *inflows*, which make the exchange rate *appreciate*. A currency appreciation *reduces* aggregate demand and *raises* aggregate supply (see Figure 5).
- A fall in the domestic interest rate leads to capital *outflows*, which make the exchange rate *depreciate*. A currency depreciation *raises* aggregate demand and *reduces* aggregate supply (see Figure 4).

### 20-4a  Fiscal Policy Revisited

Keeping these two points in mind, suppose the government cuts taxes or raises spending. Aggregate demand increases, which pushes up both real GDP and the price level in the usual manner. This effect is shown as the shift from $D_0D_0$ to the maroon line $D_1D_1$ in Figure 6. In a **closed economy**, that is the whole story. But in an *open economy* with international capital flows, we must add in macroeconomic effects that work through the interest rate and the exchange rate. We do this by answering two questions.

> A **closed economy** is one that does not trade with other nations in either goods or assets.

First, what will happen to the exchange rate? We know from earlier chapters that a fiscal expansion pushes up interest rates. At higher interest rates, American securities become more attractive to foreign investors, who go to the foreign-exchange markets to buy dollars with which to purchase them. This buying pressure drives up the value of the dollar. Thus, at least for a rich country that can easily sell its bonds on the world market:

A fiscal expansion normally makes the exchange rate appreciate.

Second, what are the effects of a higher dollar? We know that when the dollar rises in value, American goods become more expensive abroad and foreign goods become cheaper here. So exports fall and imports rise, driving down the $X - IM$ component of aggregate demand. The fiscal expansion thus winds up increasing both America's *capital account surplus* (by attracting foreign capital) and its *current account deficit* (by reducing net exports). In fact, the two must rise by equal amounts because, under floating exchange rates, it is always true that[2]

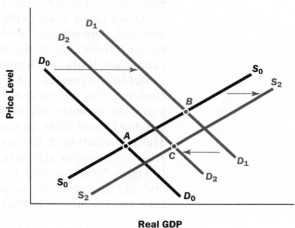

*Figure 6*

**A Fiscal Expansion in an Open Economy**

Current account surplus + Capital account surplus = 0

Because a fiscal expansion leads to a trade deficit in this way, many economists believe that the large U.S. trade deficits of the 1980s were a side effect of the large tax cuts made early in the decade—and that the tax cuts of 2001–2003 once again pushed the trade deficit up. We will return to that issue shortly.

For now, note that the induced rise in the dollar will shift the aggregate supply curve *outward* and the aggregate demand curve *inward*, as we saw in Figure 5. Figure 6 adds these two shifts (in blue lines) to the effect of the original fiscal expansion (in maroon). The final equilibrium in an open economy is point C, whereas in a closed economy it would be point B. By comparing points B and C, we can see how international linkages change the picture of fiscal policy that we painted earlier in the book.

Two main differences arise. First, a higher exchange rate makes imports cheaper and thereby offsets part of the inflationary effect of a fiscal expansion. Second, a higher exchange rate reduces the expansionary effect on real GDP by reducing $X - IM$. Here we have a new kind of "crowding out," different from the one we studied in Chapter 16. There we learned that an increase in G will crowd out some *private investment* spending by raising interest rates. Here, an increase in G, by raising both interest rates and the exchange rate, crowds out *net exports*. But the effect is the same: The fiscal multiplier is reduced. Thus, we conclude that

International capital flows reduce the power of fiscal policy.

Table 2, which shows actual U.S. data, suggests that this new international variety of crowding out was much more important than the traditional type of crowding out during the huge fiscal expansion of the 1980s. Between 1981 and 1986, the share of investment in GDP barely changed despite the rise in the shares of both consumer spending and government purchases. Only the share of net exports, $X - IM$, fell—from zero to –2.5 percent.

American economists thus learned an important lesson. In 1981, many economists worried that large government budget deficits would crowd out private investment. By the end of the decade, most were more concerned that deficits were crowding out net exports and producing a massive trade deficit.

*Table 2*

**Percentage Shares of Real GDP in the United States, 1981 and 1986**

| Year | C | I | G | X – IM |
|---|---|---|---|---|
| 1981 | 61.0% | 14.4% | 24.5% | 0.0% |
| 1986 | 62.8 | 14.5 | 25.1 | –2.5 |
| Change | +1.8 | +0.1 | +0.6 | –2.5 |

NOTE: Totals do not add up to 100 percent because of rounding and deflation.

---

[2] If you need review, turn back to Chapter 19's discussion of the balance of payments.

## 20-4b  Monetary Policy Revisited

Now let us consider how *monetary policy* works in an open economy with floating exchange rates and international capital mobility. To remain consistent with the history of the United States in the 1980s, we consider a *tightening,* rather than a loosening, of monetary policy.

As we know from earlier chapters, contractionary monetary policy *reduces* aggregate demand, which lowers both real GDP and prices. This situation is shown in Figure 7 by the shift from $D_0D_0$ to the maroon line $D_1D_1$, and it looks like the exact opposite of a fiscal expansion. Without international capital flows, that would be the end of the story.

But in the presence of internationally mobile capital, we must also think through the consequences for interest rates and exchange rates. As we know from previous chapters, a monetary contraction *raises* interest rates. Hence, tighter money attracts foreign capital into the United States in search of higher rates of return. The exchange rate therefore *rises.* The appreciating dollar encourages imports and discourages exports; so $X - IM$ falls. America therefore winds up with an inflow of capital and an increase in its trade deficit. In Figure 7, the two effects of the exchange rate appreciation appear in the blue lines $S_2S_2$ and $D_2D_2$: Aggregate supply shifts *outward* and aggregate demand shifts *inward.* This time, as you can see in the figure:

**International capital flows increase the power of monetary policy.**

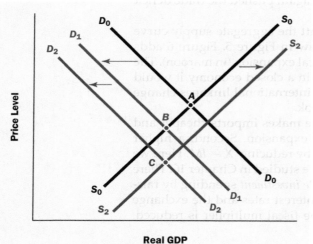

*Figure 7*

**A Monetary Contraction in an Open Economy**

**Real GDP**

In a closed economy, higher interest rates *reduce invest-ment* spending, $I$. In an open economy, these same higher interest rates also appreciate the currency and reduce *net exports,* $X - IM$. Thus, the effect of monetary policy is enhanced.

It may seem puzzling that capital flows *strengthen* monetary policy but *weaken* fiscal policy. The explanation of these contrasting results lies in their effects on interest rates. The main international repercussion of either a fiscal *expansion* or a monetary *contraction* is to raise interest rates and the exchange rate, thereby crowding out net exports. That means that the initial effects of a fiscal expansion on aggregate demand are *weakened,* whereas the initial effects of a monetary contraction are *strengthened.*

These ideas were well-understood by both Mario Draghi of the European Central Bank and Haruhiko Kuroda of the Bank of Japan in 2013–2014. Managing monetary policy for large, open economies that needed more aggregate demand, they turned several policy dials in expansionary directions, knowing full well that such actions gain some of their power from depreciating the euro and the yen.

## 20-5  INTERNATIONAL ASPECTS OF DEFICIT REDUCTION

We have now completed our theoretical analysis of the macroeconomics of open econo-mies. Let us put the theory to work by applying it to the events of the 1990s, when fiscal policy was tightened and monetary policy was eased. Should reducing the budget deficit (or raising the surplus) strengthen or weaken the dollar?

As discussed in Chapter 16, the U.S. government transformed its mammoth budget deficit into a notable surplus during the 1990s by raising taxes and cutting expenditures. Column (1) of Table 3 reviews the predicted effects of a fiscal contraction: It should lower real interest rates, make the dollar depreciate, reduce real GDP, and be less disinflationary than normal because of the falling dollar. This information is recorded by entering + signs for increases and – signs for decreases.

Eliminating the budget deficit reduced aggregate demand. But the Federal Reserve restored the missing demand by lowering interest rates so that the economy would not suffer a slump. According to the analysis in this chapter, such a monetary expansion should lower real interest rates, make the dollar depreciate, raise real GDP, and be a bit more inflationary than usual because of the falling dollar. These effects are recorded in column (2) of Table 3.

Column (3) puts the two pieces together. We conclude that a policy mix of fiscal *contraction* and monetary *expansion* should reduce interest rates strongly, push down the value of the dollar, and strongly stimulate our foreign trade. The net effects on output and inflation are uncertain, however: The balance depends on whether the fiscal contraction overwhelms the monetary expansion, or vice versa.

*Table 3*

**Expected Effects of Policy**

| | (1) | (2) | (3) |
|---|---|---|---|
| Variable | Fiscal Contraction | Monetary Expansion | Combination |
| Real interest rate | − | − | − |
| Exchange rate | − | − | − |
| Net exports | + | + | + |
| Real GDP | − | + | ? |
| Inflation | − | + | ? |

What actually happened? First, interest rates did fall, just as predicted. The rate on 10-year U.S. government bonds dropped from almost 7 percent in late 1992 to just over 4.5 percent in December 1998; by 1998 American households were enjoying the lowest home mortgage rates since the 1960s. (Those rates have been even lower lately.) Second, the U.S. economy expanded rapidly between 1992 and 1998; apparently, the monetary stimulus overwhelmed the fiscal contraction. Third, inflation fell despite such rapid growth. As we explained in Chapter 10, one major reason was a series of favorable supply shocks that pushed inflation down.

What about the exchange rate and international trade? Here the theory did less well. The dollar generally declined from 1993 to 1995, as the theory predicts. But then it turned around and rose sharply from 1995 to 1998, just when the budget deficit was turning into a surplus. America's trade performance was even more puzzling. According to the theory, a lower budget deficit should have led to a lower exchange rate, and therefore to a smaller **trade deficit**. But, in fact, America's real net exports sagged from just −$42 billion in 1992 to −$275 billion in 1998. What went wrong?

A country's **trade deficit** is the excess of its imports over its exports. If, instead, exports exceed imports, the country has a **trade surplus**.

## 20-5a The Loose Link between the Budget Deficit and the Trade Deficit

To answer this question, let's explore the connection between the budget deficit and the trade deficit in more detail. To do so, we need one simple piece of arithmetic.

Begin with the familiar equilibrium condition for GDP in an open economy:

$$Y = C + I + G + (X - IM)$$

Because GDP can either be spent, saved, or taxed away,[3]

$$Y = C + S + T$$

Equating these two expressions for $Y$ gives

$$C + I + G + (X - IM) = C + S + T$$

Finally, subtracting $C$ from both sides and bringing the $I$ and $G$ terms over to the right–hand side leads to an accounting relationship between the trade deficit and the budget deficit:

$$X - IM = (S - I) - (G - T)$$

Notice that this equation is a matter of *accounting*, not economics. It must hold in *all* countries at *all* times, and it has nothing to do with any particular economic theory.

---

[3] If you do not see why, recall that GDP equals disposable income (*DI*) plus taxes (*T*), $Y = DI + T$, and that disposable income can either be consumed or saved, $DI = C + S$. These two definitions together imply that $Y = C + S + T$.

In words, it says that a trade deficit—a *negative* value of $X - IM$—can arise from one of two sources: a government budget deficit ($G$ larger than $T$) or an excess of investment over saving ($I$ larger than $S$).

Now let's apply this accounting relationship to actual U.S. events in the 1990s. As we know, the government deficit, $G - T$, fell precipitously. Other things equal, that should have *reduced* the trade deficit. But other things were *not* equal. The equation reminds us that the balance between saving and investment matters, too. As shares of GDP, business investment boomed while household saving declined from 1992 to 1998. So $(S - I)$ moved sharply in the negative direction. And that change, as our equation shows, should *raise* the trade deficit (reduce net exports).

In brief, taken by itself, deficit reduction would have increased net exports. In reality, sharp changes in private economic behavior—specifically, less saving and more investment—overwhelmed the government's actions and made net exports fall instead. The link from the budget deficit to the trade deficit can be a loose one.

## 20-6  SHOULD WE WORRY ABOUT THE TRADE DEFICIT?

The preceding explanation suggests that the large U.S. trade deficits over the past 20 years or so are a symptom of a deeper trouble: The nation as a whole—including both the government and the private sector—has been consuming more than it has been producing for years. The United States has therefore been forced to borrow the difference from foreigners. The trade deficit is just the mirror image of the required capital inflows.

Those who worry about trade deficits point out that these capital inflows create debts on which interest and principal payments must be made in the future. In this view, we Americans have been mortgaging our futures to finance higher consumer spending.

But another, quite different, interpretation of the trade deficit is possible. Suppose foreign investors come to see the United States as an especially attractive place to invest their funds. Then capital will flow here, not because Americans need to *borrow* it, but because foreigners are eager to *lend* it. The desire of foreigners to acquire American assets should push the value of the dollar up, which should in turn push America's net exports down. In that case, the trade deficit would still be the mirror image of the capital inflows, but it would signify America's economic *strength*, not its weakness.

Each view has elements of truth, but the second raises a critical question: How long can it go on? As long as the United States continues to run large trade deficits, foreigners will have to continue to accumulate large amounts of U.S. assets—one way or another. As we noted in the previous chapter, starting in 2002, private investors abroad concluded—for a time—that they had acquired about all the American assets they wanted.

Those decisions would have marked the day of reckoning for the United States but for two important facts. First, the governments of Japan and China decided to buy hundreds of billions of dollars of U.S. Treasury securities (selling equivalent amounts of their own currencies) rather than let the yen and the yuan appreciate. These large *government* capital inflows allowed the United States to continue to run mammoth trade deficits for a few more years. Second, in 2008–2009, the financial crisis brought lots of worried investors to our shores, eager to buy U.S. dollar assets, especially Treasury securities. That "flight to safety" held up the value of the dollar then—and it still does.

## 20-7  ON CURING THE TRADE DEFICIT

How can we reduce our foreign trade deficit and ease our addiction to foreign borrowing? There are four basic ways.

### 20-7a  Change the Mix of Fiscal and Monetary Policy

The fundamental equation

$$X - IM = (S - I) - (G - T)$$

suggests that a *decrease in the budget deficit* (i.e., shrinking $(G - T)$) is one good way to reduce the trade deficit. According to the analysis in this chapter, a reduction in $G$ or an increase in $T$ would lead to lower real interest rates in the United States, a depreciating dollar, and, eventually, a smaller trade deficit.

When the government curtails its spending or raises taxes, aggregate demand falls. If we do not want the shrinking budget deficit to slow economic growth, we must compensate for it by providing monetary stimulus. Like contractionary fiscal policy, expansionary monetary policy lowers interest rates, depreciates the dollar, and should therefore help reduce the trade deficit. So the policy recommendation actually amounts to tightening *fiscal* policy and loosening *monetary* policy.

Since about 2011, this is roughly what the U.S. government has done. The federal budget deficit shrank from about $1.3 trillion in fiscal year 2011 to "only" about $480 billion in fiscal 2014, while the Federal Reserve increased its super-expansionary monetary policy, mainly through quantitative easing. As might be expected, our trade deficit fell, but only slightly. What else might work?

## 20-7b More Rapid Economic Growth Abroad

One factor behind the growing U.S. trade deficit is that the economies of many foreign nations—the customers for our exports—grew more slowly than the U.S. economy for years. The U.S. government has frequently argued that if foreign economies would grow faster, they would buy more American goods, thereby raising U.S. exports and reducing our trade deficit. So we have regularly urged our major trading partners to stimulate their economies and to open their markets more to American goods—and still do. But these exhortations have had only modest success. When the U.S. economy slowed down in 2007–2009, our trade deficit did recede a bit. But no one thinks slower U.S. growth is a very good remedy.

## 20-7c Raise Domestic Saving or Reduce Domestic Investment

Our fundamental equation calls attention to two other routes to a smaller trade deficit: More saving or less investment.

The U.S. personal saving rate (saving as a share of disposable income) hit postwar lows during the years before the financial crisis. The 3 percent average saving rate of the years 2005–2007 was the lowest since the Great Depression of the 1930s. If Americans would simply save more, we would need to borrow less from abroad. This solution, too, would lead to a cheaper dollar and a smaller trade deficit.

The trouble is that no one has yet found a reliable way to get Americans to save more—except via extreme losses of wealth such as those experienced in the crisis and the recession. Over the years, the U.S. government has tried a wide variety of tax incentives for saving, and more are suggested every year. But little evidence suggests that any of them has worked. Instead, large increases in both stock market wealth and housing wealth in the early 2000s convinced Americans that it was prudent to save *even less* than they used to. Only the massive wealth destruction brought on by the financial crisis persuaded Americans to save more: The saving rate averaged almost 6 percent in the years 2009–2011. But now most of that lost wealth has been rebuilt, and the saving rate has crept down again. Americans don't like to save!

If the other cures for our trade deficit fail to work, the deficit may cure itself in a particularly unpleasant way: by reducing U.S. domestic investment. The 2007–2009 recession accomplished this in a very rude way, reducing the share of investment in real GDP from 17.7 percent in 2007 to 13 percent in 2009. (It also curbed our appetite for imports.) But these side effects of recession are only temporary, and the longer-run problem remains: If our trade deficit persists, we will have to borrow more and more from foreigners who, at some point, will start demanding higher interest rates. At best, higher interest rates will lead to lower investment in the United States. At worst, interest rates will skyrocket, and we will experience a severe recession.

"But we're not just talking about buying a car—we're talking about confronting this country's trade deficit with Japan."

### 20-7d Protectionism

We have saved the worst remedy for last. One seemingly obvious way to cure our trade deficit is to limit imports by imposing stiff tariffs, quotas, and other protectionist devices. We discussed protectionism, and the reasons why almost all economists oppose it, in Chapter 18. Despite the economic arguments against it, protectionism has an undeniable political allure. It seems, superficially, to "save American jobs," and it conveniently shifts the blame for our trade problems onto foreigners.

In addition to depriving us and other countries of the benefits of comparative advantage, protectionism might not even succeed in reducing our trade deficit, however. One reason is that other nations may retaliate. If we erect trade barriers to reduce our imports, *IM* will fall. But if foreign countries erect corresponding barriers to our exports, *X* will fall, too. On balance, our *net* exports, *X − IM*, may or may not improve. But world trade will surely suffer. This game may have no winners, only losers.

Even if other nations do not retaliate, tariffs and quotas may not improve the U.S. trade deficit much. Why? If they succeed in reducing American spending on imports, tariffs and quotas will thereby reduce the supply of dollars on the world market—which will push the value of the dollar up. A rising dollar, of course, would hurt U.S. exports and encourage more imports. The fundamental equation

$$X - IM = (S - I) - (G - T)$$

reminds us that protectionism can raise $(X - IM)$ only if it raises the budget surplus, raises saving, or reduces investment.[4]

## 20-8  CONCLUSION: NO NATION IS AN ISLAND

When the poet John Donne wrote that "no man is an island," he was not referring to economic globalization. In the modern world, no nation is isolated from economic developments elsewhere on the globe. Instead, we live in a world economy in which the fates of nations are intertwined. The major trading countries are linked by exports and imports, by capital flows, and by exchange rates. What happens to national income, prices, and interest rates in one country affects other nations. No events make this point clearer than the international financial crises that erupt from time to time.

As we noted in the previous chapter, one root cause of almost all of the crises of the 1990s was countries' decisions to fix their exchange rates to the U.S. dollar. Unfortunately for nations such as Thailand, South Korea, and Indonesia, the dollar rose spectacularly from 1995 to 1997. With their exchange rates tied to the dollar, the Thai baht, the Korean won, and the Indonesian rupiah automatically appreciated relative to most other currencies—making their exports more costly. Soon these one-time export powerhouses found themselves in an unaccustomed position: running large trade deficits.

Then the crisis hit, and all three of these countries watched their currencies tumble in value. The sharp depreciations restored their international competitiveness, but they also impoverished many of their citizens. Naturally, the shrinking Asian economies curbed their appetites for American goods, so our exports to the region fell—which contributed to further deterioration in the U.S. trade deficit.

---

[4] Here tariffs, which raise revenue for the government, have a clear advantage over quotas, which do not.

Thus, a primarily American development (the rise of the dollar) harmed the Asian economies, and then a primarily Asian development (deep recessions in the Asian Tigers) hurt the U.S. economy.

Similarly, the financial crisis of 2007–2009 started here in America, beginning with subprime mortgages but then spreading. For about the first year, it was (mostly) a U.S. phenomenon. But after the collapse of Lehman Brothers in September 2008, the financial crisis deepened and—more to the point of this chapter—spread throughout the world, devastating economic growth almost everywhere. The nations of the world are indeed linked economically.

| Issue Revisited | *Is a Rising Currency Value a Blessing?* |

Recall the question with which we began this chapter: Why did the central banks of both the euro zone and Japan want to depreciate their currencies in 2013 and 2014? We now see the answer. Remember, *a falling currency will boost exports and growth*, and both the ECB and the Bank of Japan were pulling out all the stops to get their economies growing faster. In addition, Japan was trying to get rid of a stubborn deflation—that is, persistently *negative* inflation rates—that had plagued the nation for years, while Europe was trying to avoid the dread deflation disease. This chapter has taught us that *currency depreciation raises inflation*. So it all made good sense—from their perspectives.

But note that their trading partners might have felt differently. To the extent that European and Japanese monetary policies succeeded in depreciating the euro and the yen, they would automatically make the dollar and other currencies appreciate—which would be expected to slow down export growth in the United States and elsewhere. A cheaper euro and a cheaper yen mean a dearer dollar. There is no getting around it: For better or for worse, we all live in one world.

## Summary

1. The nations of the world are linked together economically because national income, prices, and interest rates in one country affect those in other countries. They are thus **open economies.**

2. Because one country's imports are another country's exports, rapid (or sluggish) economic growth in one country contributes to rapid (or sluggish) growth in other countries.

3. A country's net exports depend on whether its prices are high or low relative to those of other countries. Because exchange rates translate one country's prices into the currencies of other countries, the exchange rate is a key determinant of net exports.

4. If the currency depreciates, net exports rise and aggregate demand increases, thereby raising both real GDP and the price level. A depreciating currency also reduces aggregate supply by making imported inputs more costly.

5. If the currency appreciates, net exports fall and aggregate demand, real GDP, and the price level all decrease. An appreciating currency also increases aggregate supply by making imported inputs cheaper.

6. **International capital flows** respond strongly to rates of return on investments in different countries. For example, higher domestic interest rates lead to currency appreciations, and lower interest rates lead to depreciations.

7. Contractionary monetary policies raise interest rates and therefore make the currency appreciate. Both the higher interest rates and the stronger currency reduce aggregate demand. Hence, international capital flows make monetary policy more powerful than it would be in a closed economy.

8. Expansionary fiscal policies also raise interest rates and make the currency appreciate. In this case, the international repercussions cancel out part of the demand–expanding effects of the policies. Hence, international capital flows make fiscal policy less powerful than it would be in a closed economy.

9. Because eliminating the budget deficit in the 1990s combined tighter fiscal policy with looser monetary policy, it lowered interest rates. That should have pushed the dollar down and led to a smaller **trade deficit** in the United States. However, changes in private economic behavior—specifically, lower saving and higher investment—offset the presumed international effects of deficit reduction, and the trade deficit kept growing.

10. Budget deficits and trade deficits are linked by the fundamental equation $(X - IM) = (S - I) - (G - T)$.

11. It follows from this equation that the U.S. trade deficit must be cured by some combination of lower budget deficits, higher savings, and lower investment.

12. Protectionist policies might not cure the U.S. trade deficit because (a) they will make the dollar appreciate and (b) they may provoke foreign retaliation.

## Key Terms

| | | |
|---|---|---|
| appreciation   401 | exchange rate   400 | trade deficit or surplus   407 |
| closed economy   404 | international capital flows   404 | $X - IM = (S - I) - (G - T)$   410 |
| depreciation   401 | open economy   399 | |

## Test Yourself

1. Use an aggregate supply-demand diagram to analyze the effects of a currency appreciation.

2. Explain why $X - IM = (S - I) - (G - T)$. Now multiply both sides of this equation by –1 to get

$$IM - X = (I - S) + (G - T)$$

and remember that the trade deficit, $IM - X$, is the amount we have to borrow from foreigners to get

$$\text{Borrowing from foreigners} = (I - S) + (G - T)$$

Explain the common sense behind this version of the fundamental equation.

3. **(More difficult)** Suppose consumption and investment are described by the following:

$$C = 150 + 0.75DI$$
$$I = 300 + 0.2Y - 50r$$

Here $DI$ is disposable income, $Y$ is GDP, and $r$, the interest rate, is measured in percentage points. (E.g., a 5 percent interest rate is $r = 5$.) Exports and imports are as follows:

$$X = 300$$
$$IM = 250 + 0.2Y$$

Government purchases are $G = 800$, and taxes are 20 percent of income. The price level is fixed and the central bank uses its monetary policy to peg the interest rate at $r = 8$.

a. Find equilibrium GDP, the budget deficit or surplus, and the trade deficit or surplus.

b. Suppose the currency appreciates and, as a result, exports and imports change to

$$X = 250$$
$$IM = 0.2Y$$

Now find equilibrium GDP, the budget deficit or surplus, and the trade deficit or surplus.

## Discussion Questions

1. For years, the U.S. government has been trying to get Japan and the European Union to expand their economies faster. Explain how more rapid growth in Japan would affect the U.S. economy.

2. If inflation is lower in Germany than in Italy, and the exchange rate between the two countries is fixed (as it is, because of the monetary union), what is likely to happen to the balance of trade between the two countries?

3. Explain why a currency depreciation leads to an improvement in a country's trade balance.

4. Explain why American fiscal policy is less powerful and American monetary policy is more powerful than indicated in the closed-economy model described earlier in this book.

5. Given what you now know, do you think it was a good idea for the United States to adopt a policy mix of tight money and large government budget deficits in the early 1980s? Why or why not? What were the benefits and costs of reversing that policy mix in the 1990s?

6. In 2001, 2002, and 2003, Congress passed the series of tax cuts that President Bush had requested. What effect did this policy likely have on the U.S. trade deficit? Why?

7. In 2010 and 2011, the international value of the dollar fell. This development was viewed with alarm in Japan. Why?

Answers to odd-numbered Discussion Questions are available at www.cengagebrain.com. At the CengageBrain.com home page, search for the ISBN of your text (from the back cover of your book) using the search box at the top of the page. This will take you to the product page where these resources can be found.

## Chapter 1: What Is Economics?

### Answers to Appendix Questions

1.

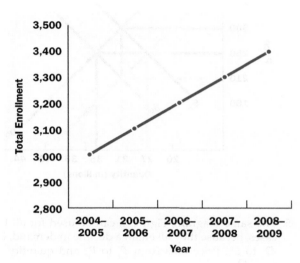

Slope is 100 interpreted as 100 new students each academic year.

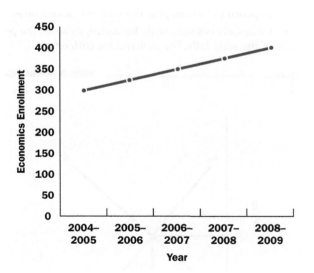

Slope is 25 interpreted as 25 new economics students each academic year.

3.

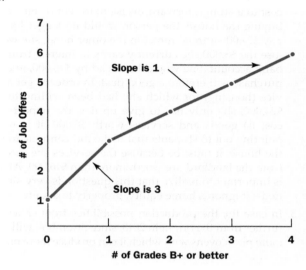

A marginal increase in the number of job offers is relatively larger with the first good grade compared to additional good grades.

5. A => 30 hours labor and 40 yards cloth = 20 units of output.

B => 40 hours labor and 28 yards cloth = 20 units of output.

Common: 20 units of output; Difference: Amount of labor and cloth charge—more labor, less cloth.

## Chapter 2: The Economy: Myth and Reality

1. The United States is the country with the largest economy in the world. The relatively large population in the United States is a contributing factor, but productivity of workers and accumulated wealth are significant reasons why the U.S. economy is so large.

3. There are several possible answers to this question—the question is designed to get students to think about these differences before using models. One straightforward answer is that the factors of production in Connecticut produce output that is worth more than what is produced in New Mexico. This could be because labor is more productive in Connecticut because of a better educated workforce. Another answer is that the cost of living is higher in Connecticut than it is in New Mexico.

5. Although there are many small businesses in the U.S. economy, the value of what they produce is relatively small. For example, a local grocer cannot produce the

same amount as a large national grocery store. It would take several small grocers to match the production of a large store. So, though a large retailer like Walmart is considered to be one business, its production exceeds that of a smaller business.

# Chapter 3: The Fundamental Economic Problem: Scarcity and Choice

1. This question asks the students to apply opportunity cost to a straightforward decision: to rent or buy. After buying the house, the person would no longer have to pay $24,000 annual rent. On the other hand, she would lose the $8,000 she currently earns in interest from her bank account. She would be ahead by $16,000, and the purchase is therefore a good deal. In order to get a service (housing) for which she had been willing to pay $24,000, she only has to give up (i.e., the opportunity cost is) goods and services worth $8,000. It is worth pointing out to students that if she did continue to rent the house, it must be because the services she receives from the landlord are worth more than $16,000. Also, it is important to realize that this question is very simplified—it ignores home equity, property taxes, etc.

3. In case (b), the production possibilities frontier will be further from the origin in 2018, since Stromboli will have more pizza ovens with which it can produce more pizzas.

# Chapter 4: Supply and Demand: An Initial Look

1. a. The demand curve for a medicine that means life or death for a patient will be vertical. One would not expect a decline in quantity demanded as the price rises, if that decline meant that the patient would die.

   b. The demand curve for french fries in a food court with many other stands will be fairly flat, perhaps even horizontal. If the firm raises its price at all, many if not most of its customers will just move to a different stand. Thus a small change in price results in a large change in the amount of fries bought.

3. The answers to all three parts are shown in Figure 2.

   a. Initially, the equilibrium price is $250, and the equilibrium quantity is 35 million bicycles, as shown by the intersection of $D_0$ and $S_0$.

   b. If demand falls by 8 million bikes per year, the new demand curve is $D_1$. The price falls to $210, and the quantity falls to 31 million, as shown by the intersection of $D_1$ and $S_0$. Although demand falls by 8 million at each price, the quantity exchanged falls by only 4 million because the price fall has induced a movement out along the new demand curve, as well as a movement back along the old supply curve.

   c. If supply falls by 8 million bikes per year, the new supply curve is $S_1$. The price rises to $300, and the quantity falls to 31 million, as shown by the intersection of $D_0$ and $S_1$. Although supply falls by 8 million at each price, the quantity exchanged falls by only

4 million because the price increase has induced a movement out along the new supply curve, as well as a movement back along the old demand curve.

   d. If demand and supply each fall by 8 million bikes per year, the equilibrium price is $250, and the equilibrium quantity is 27 million bicycles, as shown by the intersection of $D_1$ and $S_1$.

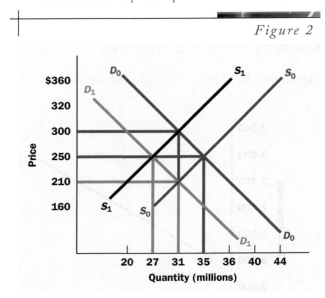

*Figure 2*

5. The same diagram, Figure 4, can be used for all three cases, because they all entail a decline in demand, from $D_0$ to $D_1$. Price falls from $P_0$ to $P_1$, and quantity falls from $Q_0$ to $Q_1$.

   a. In a drought, people have less need for umbrellas, so demand falls.

   b. Popcorn is a complement for movie tickets, so when popcorn prices rise, the demand for tickets falls.

   c. Coca-Cola is a substitute for coffee, so when the price of the soda falls, the demand for coffee falls.

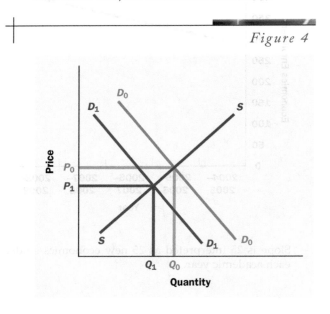

*Figure 4*

7. a. With a 50-cent tax per pound of beef, Table 2 in the text must be adjusted:

| Price Paid by Consumers (dollars per pound) | Price Received by Farmers (dollars per pound) | Quantity Supplied (pounds per year) |
|---|---|---|
| 8.00 | 7.50 | 90 |
| 7.90 | 7.40 | 80 |
| 7.80 | 7.30 | 70 |
| 7.70 | 7.20 | 60 |
| 7.60 | 7.10 | 50 |
| 7.50 | 7.00 | 40 |
| 7.40 | 6.90 | 30 |

b. Using the new Table 4-2, Figure 6 shows that the new supply curve, $S_1$, lies above the original curve, $S_0$, by a distance of 50 cents at each output. The new equilibrium price is approximately $7.53, and the new equilibrium quantity is approximately 43 pounds.

*Figure 6*

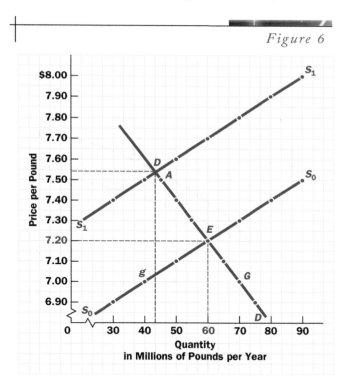

c. Yes, beef consumption falls by approximately 17 pounds.

d. The equilibrium price rises by approximately 23 cents, which is less than the tax.

e. Both consumers and producers will be paying the tax. Consumers pay a greater portion because demand was more inelastic, meaning that the quantity demanded did not change as much as the price changed. Producers pay a smaller portion because supply was somewhat more elastic, meaning that the quantity supplied changed a bit more as price changed.

## Chapter 5: An Introduction to Macroeconomics

1. Microeconomist: a. and d.; Macroeconomist: b. and c.
3. a. Raises GDP by $50,000.
   b. Raises GDP by $10,000.
   c. GDP does not rise, because there is no market transaction.
   d. GDP rises by $500,000, the value of the newly constructed house.
   e. GDP does not rise, because nothing new was produced.
   f. Raises GDP by $25,000.
   g. GDP actually falls by $100. The casino is selling "gambling services" to you, which are measured by how much you lose. Winning $100 therefore reduces sales of gambling services.
   h. GDP does not rise. Because nothing new is produced, capital gains and losses do not count in GDP.
   i. GDP does not change because you did not produce a good or service.
   j. Raises GDP by $100.

## Chapter 6: The Goals of Macroeconomic Policy

1. After 25 years Country A's economy has grown by 109% because $(1.03)^{25} = 2.09$. After 25 years Country B's economy has grown by 167% because $(1.04)^{25} = 2.67$. If we index both countries' GDP to be 100 at the start of the 25-year period, by the end of the period, Country A's GDP would be 209 and Country B's would be 267. Therefore, Country B's economy would be roughly 28% larger than that of Country A because $(267 - 209)/(209) = .28$.

   The gap between the GDPs of the two countries is *larger than* 25% due to the *compounding* of a 1% higher growth rate for 25 years.

3. If actual GDP grew faster than potential GDP from 2010 to 2013, unemployment should have decreased. Similarly, from 2006 to 2010, unemployment should have increased because actual GDP was growing slower than potential GDP. Unemployment did, in fact, fall between 2010 and 2013 and increase between 2006 and 2010.

5. a. 12 percent; b. 8 percent; c. 4 percent; d. −3 percent

**Answers to Appendix Questions**

1.

| | 1970 | 1980 | 1990 | 2000 | 2010 |
|---|---|---|---|---|---|
| Dow Jones Industrial Average (DJIA) | 753 | 891 | 2,679 | 10,735 | 10,663 |
| CPI | 38.8 | 82.4 | 130.7 | 172.2 | 218.1 |
| Deflated DJIA | 1,941 | 1,081 | 2,050 | 6,234 | 4,889 |

The deflated DJIA is found by dividing the DJIA by the CPI of the same year, and then multiplying by the base year CPI, which is 100. Stock prices do not rise every decade. They declined notably during the decades between 1970 and 1980 and between 2000 and 2010 but rose between 1980 and 2000. Stocks were most valuable in 2000.

3.

|  | 2010 | 2011 | 2012 |
|---|---|---|---|
| Nominal GDP | 14,958 | 15,534 | 16,245 |
| Real GDP | 14,779 | 15,052 | 15,471 |
| GDP Deflator | 101.2 | 103.2 | 105.0 |

5.

|  | 1970 | 1980 | 1990 | 2000 | 2010 |
|---|---|---|---|---|---|
| Money wages | $3.40 | $6.85 | $10.20 | $14.02 | $19.07 |
| CPI | 38.8 | 82.4 | 130.7 | 172.2 | 218.1 |
| Real wages | $8.76 | $8.31 | $7.80 | $8.14 | $8.74 |

|  | 1970–1980 | 1980–1990 | 1990–2000 | 2000–2010 |
|---|---|---|---|---|
| Growth, money wages | 101.5% | 48.9% | 37.5% | 36.0% |
| Growth, real wages | −5.1% | −6.1% | 4.4% | 7.4% |

Money wages grew fastest in the decade 1970–1980, but real wages grew fastest in 2000–2010. In fact, real wages declined from 1970 to 1990.

## Chapter 7: Economic Growth: Theory and Policy

1. The productivity growth for each country is shown in the fourth column:

| | 2004 Output per Hour | 2014 Output per Hour | Productivity Growth 2004–2014 |
|---|---|---|---|
| Country A | $40.00 | $48.00 | 20% |
| Country B | 25.00 | 35.00 | 40% |
| Country C | 2.00 | 3.00 | 50% |
| Country D | 0.50 | 0.60 | 20% |

Productivity growth was highest for Country C, which had a very low initial level of productivity. But note that the productivity growth for Country D lagged far behind Countries B and C despite Country D's lower starting point. As mentioned in the text, not all countries (such as Country D here) are able to participate in the convergence process. However, Countries B and C did close some of the gap on Country A.

3. The prices of items b, d, and e would be expected to rise rapidly over time, as each of these are personally provided services for which productivity improvements are difficult or impossible. By contrast, items a and c are not personally provided. In fact, productivity in these two electronically delivered services has increased dramatically over time, pushing down their prices.

5. Draw a graph similar to Figure 1 in the text. Higher levels of capital increase labor productivity, resulting in higher levels of output produced with the same quantity of labor. For example, in Figure 1 increasing the amount of capital from $K_1$ to $K_2$ increases the output from $Y_a$ to $Y_b$. Labor productivity increases when the capital stock is larger because workers can use the additional capital to produce more goods and services. For example, imagine loading and unloading a semitrailer truck by hand versus using a forklift. One forklift operator can load and unload the truck in far less time than can be done by hand.

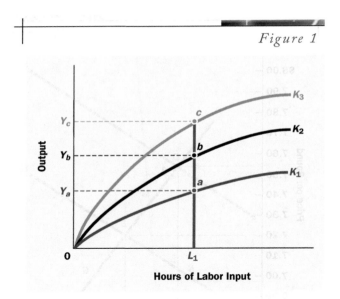

*Figure 1*

## Chapter 8: Aggregate Demand and the Powerful Consumer

1. Consumption (largest), government spending, investment, net exports (smallest—actually negative in the United States).

3. Line $C_0$ is the consumption function. The marginal propensity to consume can be calculated from the data for any pair of years. For example, for the period 2013–2014:

$$\text{MPC} = [C_{(2014)} - C_{(2013)}]/[Y_{(2014)} - Y_{(2013)}]$$
$$= (2,160 - 1,920)/(2,700 - 2,400)$$
$$= 240/300$$
$$= 0.8$$

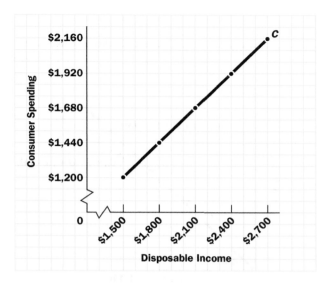

## Answers to Appendix Review Questions

1. a. Included: GDP rises by $25,000.

   b. Not included, because it was produced in another country. Actually, it is *included* as part of C, but then *deducted* as part of *IM*, which enters *negatively* in $C + I + G + (X - IM)$.

   c. Not included, since it was not produced this year.

   d. Included: GDP rises by $500 million (in investment, $I$).

   e. Not included; it's a government transfer payment.

   f. Included, as investment in inventory: GDP rises by $15 million.

   g. Included, as consumption (legal services): GDP rises by $10,000.

   h. Not included: previously produced.

3. GDP as the Sum of Final Demands (all figures in millions)

| | Source | | | | |
|---|---|---|---|---|---|
| | Specific Motors | Super Duper | Government | Rest of World | Total |
| C | 4.8 | 14.0 | | 1.0 | 19.8 |
| I | 0.8 | | | | 0.8 |
| G | 0.3 | | 0.8 | | 1.1 |
| X | 0.9 | | | | 0.9 |
| −IM | | | | −1.0 | −1.0 |
| Y | | | | | 21.6 |

GDP as the Sum of Incomes (all figures in millions)

| | Source | | | | |
|---|---|---|---|---|---|
| | Specific Motors | Super Duper | Farmers | Government | Total |
| Wages | 3.8 | 4.5 | | 0.8 | 9.1 |
| + Interest | 0.1 | 0.2 | 0.7 | | 1.0 |
| + Rent | 0.2 | 1.0 | 2.0 | | 3.2 |
| + Profits | 1.6 | 0.9 | 4.3 | | 6.8 |
| = Nat. Income | | | | | 20.1 |
| + Ind. Bus.Tax | 0.5 | 0.2 | | | 0.7 |
| = NNP | | | | | 20.8 |
| + Depreciation | 0.6 | 0.2 | | | 0.8 |
| = GDP | | | | | 21.6 |

Personal income = National income + Transfer payments
$$= 20.1 + 1.2 = 21.3$$
Disposable income = Personal income − Taxes
$$= 21.3 + 1.33 = 19.97$$

(since taxes are 10% of wages + interest + rent, which total 13.3)

Note: Profits were computed as follows:

| | Specific Motors | Super Duper | Farmers |
|---|---|---|---|
| Revenues | 6.8 | 14.0 | 7.0 |
| − Wages | −3.8 | −4.5 | |
| − Interest | −0.1 | −0.2 | −0.7 |
| − Rent | −0.2 | −1.0 | −2.0 |
| − Intermediate Goods | | −7.0 | |
| − Depreciation | −0.6 | −0.6 | −0.2 |
| − Ind. Tax | −0.5 | −0.2 | |
| = Profits | −1.6 | 0.9 | 4.3 |

## Chapter 9: Demand-Side Equilibrium: Unemployment or Inflation?

1.

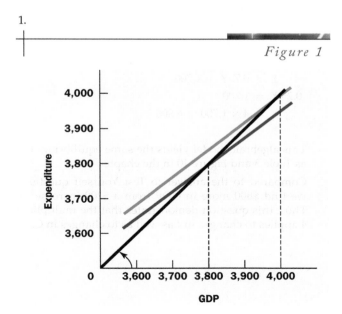

*Figure 1*

The original equilibrium GDP is at $Y = 3,800$, where spending equals output. This is shown by the intersection of the lower of the two expenditure lines in Figure 1 with the 45° line. The MPC calculated from the data is 0.90, so the multiplier is 10. If investment spending rises by \$20 (to \$260), the equilibrium GDP will increase by $\$20 \times 10 = \$200$, which is represented by a vertical shift (by \$20) to the upper expenditure function in the diagram.

3.

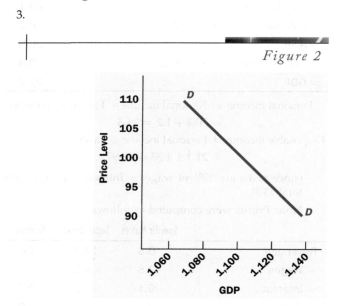

*Figure 2*

At lower prices, the real value of money and other assets that are denominated in money terms is higher. Since wealth influences consumption, at lower prices consumption is higher.

5.  $Y = C + I + G + (X - IM)$
    $C = 300 + 0.75DI$
    $C = 300 + 0.75(Y - 1,200)$
    $C = 300 + 0.75Y - 900$
    $C = -600 + 0.75Y$
    $Y = -600 + 0.75Y + 1,100 + 1,300 - 100$
    $Y = 0.75Y + 1,700$
    $0.25Y = 1,700$
    $Y = 4 \times 1,700 = 6,800$

This algebraic model yields the same equilibrium GDP as Table 3 and Figure 10 in the chapter.

Compared to the answer to Test Yourself question 4, we find \$800 more in GDP from a \$200 increase in $I$. Thus, this question demonstrates that the multiplier of 4 applies to changes in $I$ as well as to changes in $C$.

7.

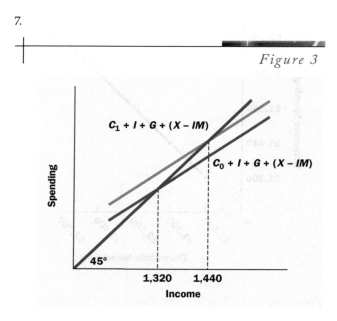

*Figure 3*

| Income | Before Shift | | After Shift | |
|--------|-------------|-------------|-------------|-------------|
|        | Consumption | Expenditure | Consumption | Expenditure |
| 1,080  | 880   | 1,160 | 920   | 1,200 |
| 1,140  | 920   | 1,200 | 960   | 1,240 |
| 1,200  | 960   | 1,240 | 1,000 | 1,280 |
| 1,260  | 1,000 | 1,280 | 1,040 | 1,320 |
| 1,320  | 1,040 | 1,320 | 1,080 | 1,360 |
| 1,380  | 1,080 | 1,360 | 1,120 | 1,400 |
| 1,440  | 1,120 | 1,400 | 1,160 | 1,440 |
| 1,500  | 1,160 | 1,440 | 1,200 | 1,480 |
| 1,560  | 1,200 | 1,480 | 1,240 | 1,520 |

The graph indicates that equilibrium GDP rises from 1,320 to 1,440, or by 120. The oversimplified multiplier formula can be used in this case. The marginal propensity to consume can be calculated between any two income levels. The numbers in the table show that each \$60 of additional income leads to \$40 more in consumer spending, so the MPC is $40/60 = 2/3$, and the multiplier is $1/[1 - (2/3)] = 3$. So a shift in consumption of 40 should raise equilibrium GDP by 120, which it does.

## Answers to Appendix A Questions

1.  $Y = C + I + G + (X - IM)$
    $C = 150 + 0.75(Y - 400)$
    $C = 150 + 0.75Y - 300$
    $C = -150 + 0.75Y$
    $Y = -150 + 0.75Y + 300 + 400 - 50$
    $Y = 0.75Y + 500$
    $0.25Y = 500$
    $Y = 4 \times 500 = 2,000$

3. Saving is equal to disposable income minus consumption.

In question 1: $S = (Y - T) - C$

$$S = (2{,}000 - 400) - [-150 + 0.75\,(2{,}000)]$$
$$S = 1{,}600 - (-150 + 1{,}500)$$
$$S = 1{,}600 - 1{,}350$$
$$S = 250$$

$S$ is not equal to $I$.

In question 2: $S = (Y - T) - C$

$$S = (1{,}400 - 400) - [50 + 0.5\,(1{,}400)]$$
$$S = 1{,}000 - (50 + 700)$$
$$S = 1{,}000 - 750$$
$$S = 250$$

In question 2, $S$ is equal to $I$. The difference is that $X$ and $IM$ are equal in question 2 but unequal in question 1.

5. a. $Y = C + I + G + (X - IM)$

$$C = 100 + 0.8\,(Y - 500)$$
$$C = 100 + 0.8Y - 400$$
$$C = -300 + 0.8Y$$
$$Y = -300 + 0.8Y + 700 + 500 + 0$$
$$Y = 0.8Y + 900$$
$$0.2Y = 900$$
$$Y = 5 \times 900 = 4{,}500$$

b. $S = (Y - T) - C$

$$S = (4{,}500 - 500) - [-300 + 0.8\,(4{,}500)]$$
$$S = 4{,}000 - 3{,}300 = 700,$$ which is equal to investment, so $S = I$.

c. Now $X - IM = 100$, so the last four lines of 5(a) are replaced by

$$Y = -300 + 0.8Y + 700 + 500 + 100$$
$$Y = 0.8Y + 1{,}000$$
$$0.2Y = 1{,}000$$
$$Y = (1/0.2) \times 1{,}000$$
$$Y = 5 \times 1{,}000 = 5{,}000$$
$$S = (Y - T) - C$$
$$S = (5{,}000 - 500) - [-300 + 0.8(5{,}000)]$$
$$S = 4{,}500 - 3{,}700 = 800$$

Now, $S$ is not equal to $I$.

## Answers to Appendix B Questions

1.

| GDP | Exports | Imports | Net Exports |
|---|---|---|---|
| 2,500 | 400 | 250 | 150 |
| 3,000 | 400 | 300 | 100 |
| 3,500 | 400 | 350 | 50 |
| 4,000 | 400 | 400 | 0 |
| 4,500 | 400 | 450 | 250 |
| 5,000 | 400 | 500 | 2,100 |

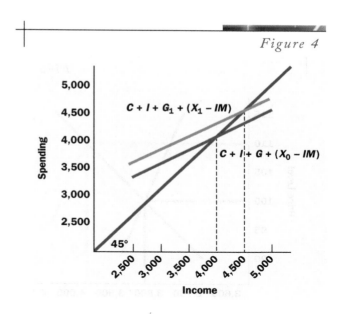

*Figure 4*

3. In Figure 4, the intersection of the upper expenditure line with the 45° line shows an equilibrium GDP of 4,500. (The lower expenditure line shows the solution to Test Yourself question 2, with a GDP of 4,000.) Exports have risen by 250, and GDP has risen by 500, so the multiplier is 2.

## Chapter 10: Bringing in the Supply Side: Unemployment *and* Inflation?

1.

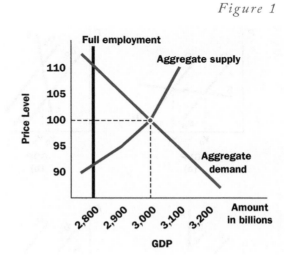

*Figure 1*

Equilibrium real output is $3,000 billion, while the price level is 100. Since full employment is at $2,800 billion, there is an inflationary gap of $200 billion.

3.

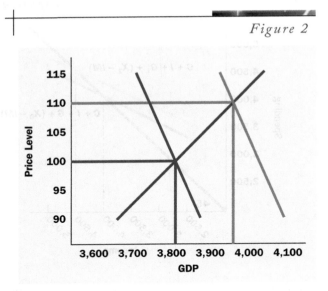

*Figure 2*

a. In Chapter 26, Test Yourself question 2, the marginal propensity to consume was 0.9, and the (oversimplified) multiplier was therefore 10. The table in this question confirms that when investment rises by 20, from 240 to 260, aggregate demand rises by 200 at any given price level. For example, at a price level of 105, aggregate demand rises from 3,770 to 3,970.

b. Initial equilibrium: $P = 100$, $Y = 3,800$. Eventual equilibrium: $P = 110$, $Y = 3,940$. The multiplier, taking account of price increases, is $140/20 = 7$, which is less than 10.

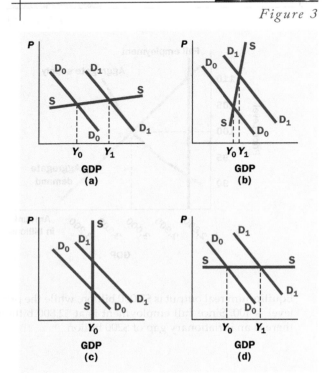

*Figure 3*

# Chapter 11: Managing Aggregate Demand: Fiscal Policy

1.

| GDP | Taxes | Disposable Income | Consumption | Total Expenditure |
|---|---|---|---|---|
| 1,360 | 400 | 960 | 720 | 1,450 |
| 1,480 | 400 | 1,080 | 810 | 1,540 |
| 1,600 | 400 | 1,200 | 900 | 1,630 |
| 1,720 | 400 | 1,320 | 990 | 1,720 |
| 1,840 | 400 | 1,440 | 1,080 | 1,810 |

*Figure 1*

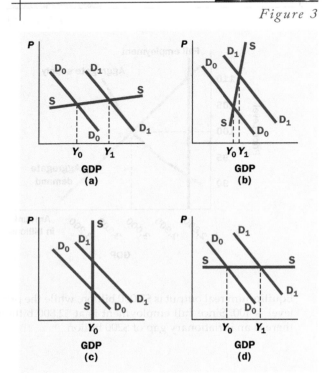

Equilibrium GDP is 1,720 (see diagram). The marginal propensity to consume is 0.75 and the multiplier is 4. If government purchases fall by 60, and the price level is unchanged, GDP would fall by $4 \times 60 = 240$, that is, to 1,480.

3. At each level of GDP, $G$ rises by 120, while $C$ falls by three quarters of 120, or 90. Therefore, there is a net increase in expenditures of 30, as follows:

| GDP | Taxes | Disposable Income | Consumption | Total Expenditure |
|---|---|---|---|---|
| 1,360 | 520 | 840 | 630 | 1,480 |
| 1,480 | 520 | 960 | 720 | 1,570 |
| 1,600 | 520 | 1,080 | 810 | 1,660 |
| 1,720 | 520 | 1,200 | 900 | 1,750 |
| 1,840 | 520 | 1,320 | 990 | 1,840 |

Equilibrium GDP is now 1,840, which is 120 more than in Test Yourself question 1.

5. The answer to Test Yourself question 2 is 1,720. So you want to increase GDP by 120 (raising it to 1,840). Because the marginal propensity to consume is 0.75, and the marginal tax rate is 1/3, the multiplier is 2.

Therefore, you must take some action that will have the initial effect of raising expenditure by 60. You may raise government spending on GDP by 60, or you may lower taxes or raise transfer payments by 80 (since 3⁄4 of 80 is 60).

## Answers to Appendix A Questions

1. a. variable tax (as GDP rises, people drive more); b. variable tax; c. fixed tax; d. variable tax

3. The higher fixed tax reduces consumer spending, but the lower income-tax rate increases consumer spending. The question is: Which effect is larger? The answer is found by seeing which tax change is larger, since $C$ depends on $DI = Y - T$. At a GDP of $Y = 10,000$ billion, a two percentage point cut in the income-tax rate reduces tax receipts by \$200 billion, which is larger than the \$100 billion fixed-tax increase. So $C$, and hence equilibrium GDP on the demand side, rises.

## Answer to Appendix B Questions

1.
$$Y = C + I + G + (X - IM)$$
$$C = 120 + 0.8DI$$
$$DI = Y - T$$
$$DI = Y - (200 + 0.25Y)$$
$$DI = 0.75Y - 200$$
$$C = 120 + 0.8(0.75Y - 200)$$
$$C = 120 + 0.6Y - 160$$
$$C = 0.6Y - 40$$
$$Y = 0.6Y - 40 + 320 + 480 - 80$$
$$Y = 0.6Y + 680$$
$$0.4Y = 680$$
$$Y = (1/0.4) \times 680$$
$$Y = 2.5 \times 680 = 1,700$$

Equilibrium GDP is 1,700.

There are three different ways to find the multipliers, any one of which is correct.

For government purchases:

i. Note from the preceding equations that equilibrium GDP is 2.5 times all autonomous spending. Since $G$ is autonomous spending, the multiplier for $G$ is 2.5.

ii. Raise $G$ from 480 to 481. Working through the algebra previously shown, this comes to $0.4Y = 681$, which implies that $Y = 1,702.5$. So the increase in $G$ of 1 has raised $Y$ by 2.5, and the multiplier is 2.5.

iii. From the formula in the appendix, the multiplier is

$$1/[1 - b(1 - t)] = 1/[1 - 0.8(1 - 0.25)]$$
$$= 1/[1 - 0.8(0.75)] = 1/(1 - 0.6)$$
$$= 1/0.4 = 2.5$$

For fixed taxes:

i. Note that a rise in fixed taxes decreases GDP (so the sign of the multiplier is negative) and that

it increases spending in the first round by the marginal propensity to consume times the tax reduction. So the tax multiplier is the multiplier previously found, multiplied by (minus) the MPC, or $2.5 \times (-0.8) = -2$.

ii. Raise fixed taxes in the model from 200 to 201.

Working through the algebra, this comes to $0.4Y = 679.2$, or $Y = 1,698$. So an increase in taxes of 1 has reduced GDP by 2, and the multiplier is $-2$.

iii. From the formula in the appendix, the tax multiplier is

$$-b/[1 - b(1 - t)] = -0.8/[1 - 0.8(1 - 0.25)]$$
$$= -0.8/[1 - 0.8(0.75)] = -0.8/(1 - 0.6)$$
$$= -0.8/0.4 = -2$$

To raise GDP by 100, the government can (a) raise $G$ by 40, and the multiplier of 2.5 will do the rest, or (b) lower taxes or raise transfer payments by 50, and the multiplier of $-2$ will do the rest.

3. a.   $Y = C + I + G + (X - IM)$
$$C = 0.9(Y - T)$$
$$C = 0.9[Y - (1/3)Y]$$
$$C = 0.9[(2/3)Y]$$
$$C = 0.6Y$$
$$Y = 0.6Y + 100 + 540 - 40$$
$$Y = 0.6Y + 600$$
$$0.4Y = 600$$
$$Y = (1/0.4) \times 600$$
$$Y = 2.5 \times 600 = 1,500$$
$$\text{Budget deficit} = G - T$$
$$= 540 - [(1/3) \times 1,500]$$
$$= 540 - 500$$
$$= 40$$

b. Since the budget deficit in part a is 40, the government would reduce its purchases by 40, to 500.

Repeating the steps above, but now with $G = 500$:
$$Y = 0.6Y + 100 + 500 - 40$$
$$Y = 0.6Y + 560$$
$$0.4Y = 560$$
$$Y = (1/0.4) \times 560$$
$$Y = 2.5 \times 560 = 1,400$$
$$\text{Budget deficit} = G - T$$
$$= 500 - [(1/3) \times 1,400]$$
$$= 500 - 466 \, 2/3$$
$$= 33 \, 1/3$$

GDP falls by 100 to 1,400. That drop reduces tax receipts, which are one-third of GDP, by 33 1⁄3 (to 466 2/3). So in the new equilibrium, the deficit has fallen by only 6 2/3 (to 33 1⁄3), not by the full 40 in lower spending. Although $G$ fell by the amount of the deficit, this in turn caused $Y$ to fall, which in turn lowered taxes, and the deficit persisted.

## Chapter 12: Money and the Banking System

1. Under those conditions, the money multiplier is 1/.10, or 10, so an infusion of $12 million into reserves will support an increase in money of $120 million.

3.

| (a) | | (b) | | (c) | |
|---|---|---|---|---|---|
| **Assets** | **Liabilities** | **Assets** | **Liabilities** | **Assets** | **Liabilities** |
| Reserves  −100 | Deposits  −100 | Reserves  +100 | Deposits  +100 | **Hometown Bank** | |
| | | | | Reserves      −500 | Deposits      −500 |
| | | | | **Big City Bank** | |
| | | | | Reserves      +500 | Deposits      +500 |
| | | | | **All Banks** | |
| | | | | Reserves no change | Deposits no change |

## Chapter 13: Monetary Policy: Conventional and Unconventional

1. In each case, there is $60 billion in the form of cash in circulation, and the rest of the money supply is held in bank deposits, backed by $60 billion in reserves. The total money supply is calculated:

| Reverse Ratio | Money Multiplier | Total Deposits | Money Supply |
|---|---|---|---|
| 10% | 10 | 600 | 660 |
| 12.5% | 8 | 480 | 540 |
| 162/3% | 6 | 360 | 420 |

The M1 money supply always exceeds total deposits by the $60 billion in cash outside banks.

3. Note: All figures are in billions of dollars.

| Bill Gates | | Bank of America | | Federal Reserve | |
|---|---|---|---|---|---|
| **Assets** | **Liabilities** | **Assets** | **Liabilities** | **Assets** | **Liabilities** |
| Deposits at B of A  +5 | no change | Reserves  +5 | Deposits  +5 | Bonds  +5 | Bank |
| Bonds        −5 | | | | | Reserves  +5 |

The Fed simply creates the $5 billion (in the form of bank reserves) to buy the bonds. In the long run, it makes no difference whether the Fed buys the bonds from a bank or from an individual. In this case, Bank of America's $5 billion in new reserves are offset by $5 billion in new deposits, so that not all of the new reserves are excess reserves, whereas if the Fed had bought the bonds from Bank of America directly, there would have been no change in deposits, and all the new reserves would have been excess. In the long run, however, the new reserves of $5 billion will support the same increase in deposits. Why? Because in this case, the original transaction between the Fed and Bill Gates already creates $5 billion in new deposits.

5. a. A $5 billion increase in the bank reserves lowers interest rates by 2.5 percentage points.

  b. A reduction in interest rates of 2.5 percentage points stimulates $75 billion of new investment spending.

  c. Aggregate demand rises by $150 billion.

  d. The aggregate supply curve is horizontal, and GDP rises by $150 billion.

7. If banks held onto all $5 billion in excess reserves, there would be no impact on the economy and GDP. The additional excess reserves would not drive down interest rates, not create additional investment, and so on.

## Chapter 14: The Financial Crisis and the Great Recession

1. With a 4 percent expected default rate, the interest rate should be 7 percent (4% + 3%). If the expected default rate rises to 8 percent, the interest rate should rise to 11 percent (8% + 3%). (Note: These suggested answers assume, for example, 4 percent and 8 percent default probabilities with 100 percent loss, or 8 percent and 16 percent default probabilities with 50 percent loss, and so on. Thus, other correct answers are possible.)

3. Deposits are liabilities because, if converted into cash, the bank will have to pay out the cash.

## Chapter 15: The Debate over Monetary and Fiscal Policy

1. Based on recent data, the velocity of money in the United States, for M1, is about 9.5–10. Students will probably calculate a much higher velocity for themselves.

3. a. If the self-correcting mechanism is faster and more reliable, there is less need for discretionary policy, and the case for rules is strengthened.

   b. If economic forecasts are improved, there is a better chance that the correct stabilization policy will be identified, and so the case for discretionary policy is strengthened.

   c. If the branches of government are in conflict over economic policy, the chances of a sensible policy being enacted are reduced, and the policy lag is likely to be lengthened, so the case for rules is strengthened.

## Chapter 16: Budget Deficits in the Short and Long Run

1. The budget deficit is an annual-flow concept. It is the excess of government expenditures over government revenues in a given year. The national debt is an accumulated stock of debt. It is increased each year by the deficit or reduced by the surplus. If the deficit becomes a surplus, the debt will fall (although the accumulated debt may still be very large).

3. Expansionary monetary policy will raise GDP, and this will raise tax receipts. The lower interest rates will also decrease the government's interest payments. Both changes will reduce the government's budget deficit. If the government tries to counteract the Fed's positive effect on aggregate demand, it will institute a more contractionary fiscal policy by decreasing government spending or raising taxes, or both. The deficit will shrink still more.

## Chapter 17: The Trade-Off between Inflation and Unemployment

1. Figure 1 shows that when the aggregate supply curve is vertical, shifting aggregate demand curves change only the price level, not output.

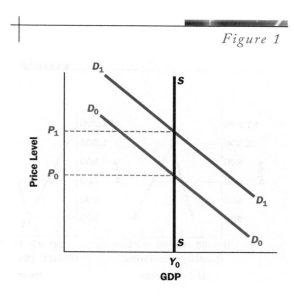

*Figure 1*

## Chapter 18: International Trade and Comparative Advantage

1. a. In the absence of trade, one barrel of wine costs four yards of cloth in England.

   b. In the absence of trade, one barrel of wine costs two yards of cloth in Portugal.

   c.

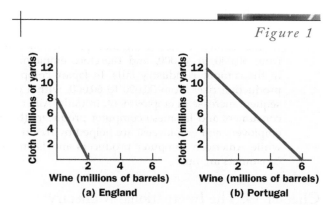

*Figure 1*

   d. Portugal has the absolute advantage in the production of both goods, and the comparative advantage in wine. England has the comparative advantage in cloth.

   e. When trade opens, England will specialize in cloth and export it to Portugal, which in turn will specialize in wine and export it to England.

   f. In the international market, the price of a barrel of wine will wind up somewhere between four yards and two yards of cloth, perhaps three. Stated another way, the price of one yard of cloth will be between ½ gallon of wine and ¼ gallon of wine.

## Answers to Appendix Questions

1. a.

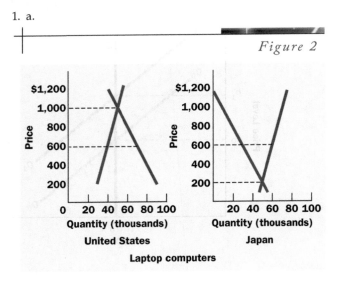

*Figure 2*

b. If there is no trade, in the United States the equilibrium price is $1,000 and the equilibrium quantity is 50,000 units. In Japan, the price is $200 and the quantity is 50,000.

c. The new world price will be $600 because, at that price, world quantity demanded is 100,000 units (70,000 plus 30,000) and world quantity supplied is also 100,000 units (40,000 plus 60,000). The price of computers has fallen in the United States and risen in Japan. (Note: To arrive at the answer graphically, construct world demand and supply curves. The equilibrium will be found at a world price of $600.)

d. Japan will export 30,000 computers.

e. In the United States, computer production falls from 50,000 to 40,000, and therefore employment in the computer industry falls. In Japan, computer production rises from 50,000 to 60,000, with a consequent increase in employment. Initially, American consumers and Japanese computer producers (both employers and employees) are helped by free trade, while American computer producers and Japanese consumers are hurt.

## Chapter 19: The International Monetary System: Order or Disorder?

1. One can use supply and demand curves for either the yen or the dollar. If one chooses the market for dollars, then the exchange rate measured on the vertical axis is the price of a dollar in yen:

a. Japanese imports increase and U.S. exports increase. So the demand for dollars rises, and the dollar therefore appreciates.

b. Because Japanese stocks are less attractive, there is less capital outflow from the United States to Japan to buy stocks. The supply of dollars decreases, and the dollar therefore appreciates.

c. With lower interest rates, American financial assets become less attractive. So capital flows out of the United States (or less flows in). This increases the supply of dollars, leading to a depreciation of the dollar.

d. The increase in foreign aid increases the supply of dollars and leads to a depreciation of the dollar.

e. Because the Japanese economy booms and the U.S. economy is in a recession, Japanese imports increase while U.S. imports fall. Japanese demand for dollars therefore increases, while U.S. supply of dollars decreases. So the dollar appreciates.

f. At any given exchange rate, higher U.S. inflation causes an increase in imports and a decrease in exports. This leads to consequent increases in the supply of dollars and decreases in the demand for dollars. Therefore, the dollar depreciates.

3. Items (a) and (c) would lead to a depreciation of the dollar. Items (b) and (e) would lead to an appreciation. Item (d) would have no effect on the value of the dollar because it is purely a domestic transaction.

## Chapter 20: Exchange Rates and the Macroeconomy

1. In Figure 1, the economy begins at A, with price $P_0$ and output $Y_0$, resulting from aggregate demand $D_0$ and aggregate supply $S_0$. The currency appreciation leads to a decrease in exports and therefore a decrease in aggregate demand to $D_1$. Because imported inputs become less expensive, it also leads to an increase in aggregate supply to $S_1$. The price level will definitely fall, to $P_1$ in the diagram. Whether output falls or rises depends on the relative strength of the aggregate demand and aggregate supply effects, but since the aggregate demand shift is probably greater, output is likely to decrease, as shown in the diagram, to $Y_1$.

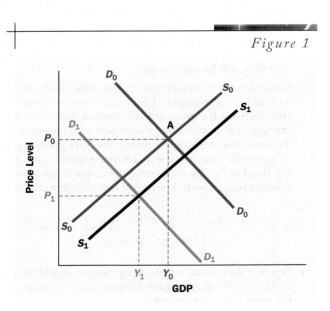

*Figure 1*

3. a.

$$Y = C + I + G + (X - IM)$$
$$C = 150 + 0.75\,DI$$
$$C = 150 + 0.75(0.8)Y$$
$$C = 150 + 0.6Y$$
$$I = 300 + 0.2Y - 50(r)$$
$$I = 300 + 0.2Y - 50(8)$$
$$I = 0.2Y - 100$$
$$(X - IM) = 300 - (250 + 0.2Y)$$
$$(X - IM) = 50 - 0.2Y$$
$$Y = 150 + 0.6Y + 0.2Y - 100 + 800 + 50 - 0.2Y$$
$$Y = 900 + 0.6Y$$
$$.4Y = 900$$
$$Y = 2.5(900)$$
$$Y = 2,250$$
$$G - T = 800 - 0.2(2,250)$$
$$G - T = 800 - 450$$
$$G - T = 350$$
$$X - IM = 50 - 0.2(2,250)$$
$$X - IM = 50 - 450$$
$$X - IM = -400$$

b.

$$Y = C + I + G + (X - IM)$$
$$C = 150 + 0.75\,DI$$
$$C = 150 + 0.75(0.8)Y$$
$$C = 150 + 0.6Y$$
$$I = 300 + 0.2Y - 50(r)$$
$$I = 300 + 0.2Y - 50(8)$$
$$I = 0.2Y - 100$$
$$(X - IM) = 250 - (0.2Y)$$
$$(X - IM) = 250 - 0.2Y$$
$$Y = 150 + 0.6Y + 0.2Y - 100 + 800 + 250 - 0.2Y$$
$$Y = 1,100 + .6Y$$
$$.4Y = 1,100$$
$$Y = 2.5(1,100)$$
$$Y = 2,750$$
$$G - T = 800 - 0.2(2,750)$$
$$G - T = 800 - 55$$
$$G - T = 250$$
$$X - IM = 250 - 0.2(2,750)$$
$$X - IM = 250 - 550$$
$$X - IM = -300$$

# GLOSSARY

**45° line** Rays through the origin with a slope of 1 are called 45° lines because they form an angle of 45° with the horizontal axis. A 45° line marks off points where the variables measured on each axis have equal values. (p. 18)

**45° line diagram** An income-expenditure diagram, or 45° line diagram, plots total real expenditure (on the vertical axis) against real income (on the horizontal axis). The 45° line marks off points where income and expenditure are equal. (p. 174)

**Absolute advantage** One country is said to have an absolute advantage over another in the production of a particular good if it can produce that good using smaller quantities of resources than can the other country. (p. 361)

**Abstraction** Abstraction means ignoring many details so as to focus on the most important elements of a problem. (p. 9)

**Aggregate demand** Aggregate demand is the total amount that all consumers, business firms, government agencies, and foreigners spend on final goods and services. (p. 148)

**Aggregate demand curve** The aggregate demand curve shows the quantity of domestic product that is demanded at each possible value of the price level. (p. 84)

**Aggregate supply curve** The aggregate supply curve shows, for each possible price level, the quantity of goods and services that all the nation's businesses are willing to produce during a specified period of time, holding all other determinants of aggregate quantity supplied constant. (p. 194)

**Aggregation** Aggregation means combining many individual markets into one overall market. (p. 82)

**Allocate its scarce resources** Allocation of scarce resources refers to society's decisions on how to divide its scarce input resources among the different outputs produced in the economy and among the different firms or other organizations that produce those outputs. (p. 47)

**Appreciate** A nation's currency is said to appreciate when exchange rates change so that a unit of its currency can buy more units of foreign currency. (p. 401)

**Asset** An asset of an individual or business firm is an item of value that the individual or firm owns. (p. 247)

**Automatic stabilizer** An automatic stabilizer is a feature of the economy that reduces its sensitivity to shocks, such as sharp increases or decreases in spending. (p. 218)

**Autonomous increase in consumption** An autonomous increase in consumption is an increase in consumer spending without any increase in consumer incomes. It is represented on a graph as a shift of the entire consumption function. (p. 183)

**Balance of payments deficit** The balance of payments deficit is the amount by which the quantity supplied of a country's currency (per year) exceeds the quantity demanded. Balance of payments deficits arise whenever the exchange rate is pegged at an artificially high level. (p. 387)

**Balance of payments surplus** The balance of payments surplus is the amount by which the quantity demanded of a country's currency (per year) exceeds the quantity supplied. Balance of payments surpluses arise whenever the exchange rate is pegged at an artificially low level. (p. 388)

**Balance sheet** A balance sheet is an accounting statement listing the values of all assets on the left side and the values of all liabilities and *net worth* on the right side. (p. 247)

**Barter** Barter is a system of exchange in which people directly trade one good for another, without using money as an intermediate step. (p. 236)

**Bretton Woods system** Under the Bretton Woods system of fixed exchange rates, the price of the U.S. dollar was fixed in terms of gold and the prices of all other currencies were fixed in terms of dollars. (p. 389)

**Bubble** A bubble is an increase in the price of an asset or assets that goes far beyond what can be justified by improving *fundamentals*, such as dividends and earnings for shares of stock or incomes and interest rates for houses. (p. 280)

**Budget deficit** The budget deficit is the amount by which the government's expenditures exceed its receipts during a specified period of time, usually a year. (p. 320)

**Budget surplus** If receipts exceed expenditures, it is called a budget surplus instead. (p. 320)

**Capital** A nation's capital is its available supply of plant, equipment, and software. It is the result of past decisions to make *investments* in these items. (p. 132)

**Capital account** The capital account balance includes purchases and sales of financial assets to and from citizens and companies of other countries. (p. 388)

**Capital formation** Capital formation is synonymous with investment. It refers to the process of building up the capital stock. (p. 133)

**Capital gain** A capital gain is the difference between the price at which an asset is sold and the price at which it was bought. (p. 117)

**Central bank** A central bank is a bank for banks. The United States' central bank is the *Federal Reserve System*. (p. 260)

**Central bank independence** Central bank independence refers to the central bank's ability to make decisions without political interference. (p. 261)

**Closed economy** A closed economy is one that does not trade with other nations in either goods or assets. (p. 404)

**Collateral** Collateral is the asset or assets that a borrower pledges in order to guarantee repayment of a loan. If the borrower fails to pay, the collateral becomes the property of the lender. (p. 284)

**Commodity money** Commodity money is an object in use as a medium of exchange that also has a substantial value in alternative (nonmonetary) uses. (p. 238)

**Comparative advantage** One country is said to have a comparative advantage over another in the production of a particular good relative to other goods if it produces that good less inefficiently as compared with the other country. (p. 361)

**Consumer expenditure** Consumer expenditure (C) is the total amount spent by consumers on newly produced goods and services (excluding purchases of new homes, which are considered investment goods). (p. 148)

**Consumer Price Index (CPI)** The Consumer Price Index (CPI) is measured by pricing the items on a list representative of a typical urban household budget. (p. 123)

**Consumption function** The consumption function shows the relationship between total consumer expenditures and total disposable income in the economy, holding all other determinants of consumer spending constant. (p. 154)

**Convergence hypothesis** The convergence hypothesis holds that nations with low levels of productivity tend to have high productivity growth rates, so that international productivity differences shrink over time. (p. 131)

**Coordination failure** A coordination failure occurs when party A would like to change his behavior if party B would change his, and vice versa, and yet the two changes do not take place because the decisions of A and B are not coordinated. (p. 179)

**Correlated** Two variables are said to be correlated if they tend to go up or down together. Correlation need not imply causation. (p. 12)

**Crowding in** Crowding in occurs when government spending, by raising real GDP, induces increases in private investment spending. (p. 329)

**Crowding out** Crowding out occurs when deficit spending by the government forces private investment spending to contract. (p. 328)

**Current account** The current account balance includes international purchases and sales of goods and services, cross-border interest and dividend payments, and cross-border gifts to and from both private individuals and governments. It is approximately the same as net exports. (p. 388)

**Cyclical unemployment** Cyclical unemployment is the portion of unemployment that is attributable to a decline in the economy's total production. Cyclical unemployment rises during recessions and falls as prosperity is restored. (p. 111)

**Deflating** Deflating is the process of finding the real value of some monetary magnitude by dividing by some appropriate price index. (p. 124)

**Deflation** Deflation refers to a sustained decrease in the general price level. (p. 90)

**Demand curve** A demand curve is a graphical depiction of a demand schedule. It shows how the quantity demanded of some product will change as the price of that product changes during a specified period of time, holding all other determinants of quantity demanded constant. (p. 58)

**Demand schedule** A demand schedule is a table showing how the quantity demanded of some product during a specified period of time changes as the price of that product changes, holding all other determinants of quantity demanded constant. (p. 57)

**Demand-side inflation** Demand-side inflation is a rise in the price level caused by rapid growth of aggregate demand. (p. 337)

**Deposit creation** Deposit creation refers to the process by which a fractional reserve banking system turns $1 of bank reserves into several dollars of bank deposits. (p. 248)

**Deposit insurance** Deposit insurance is a system that guarantees that depositors will not lose money even if their bank goes bankrupt. (p. 245)

**Depreciate** A nation's currency is said to depreciate when exchange rates change so that a unit of its currency can buy fewer units of foreign currency. (p. 401)

**Depreciation** Depreciation is the value of the portion of the nation's capital equipment that is used up within the year. It tells us how much output is needed just to maintain the economy's capital stock. (p. 165)

**Devaluation** A devaluation is a reduction in the official value of a currency. (p. 381)

**Development assistance** Development assistance ("foreign aid") refers to outright grants and low-interest loans to poor countries from both rich countries and multinational institutions like the World Bank. The purpose is to spur economic development. (p. 141)

**Discount rate** The discount rate is the interest rate the Fed charges on loans that it makes to banks. (p. 270)

**Discouraged worker** A discouraged worker is an unemployed person who gives up looking for work and is therefore no longer counted as part of the labor force. (p. 110)

**Disposable income** Disposable income (*DI*) is the sum of the incomes of all individuals in the economy after all taxes have been deducted and all transfer payments have been added. (p. 149)

**Division of labor** Division of labor means breaking up a task into a number of smaller, more *specialized* tasks so that each worker can become more adept at a particular job. (p. 48)

**Dumping** Dumping means selling goods in a foreign market at lower prices than those charged in the home market. (p. 371)

**Economic model** An economic model is a simplified, small-scale version of an aspect of the economy. Economic models are often expressed in equations, by graphs, or in words. (p. 12)

**Efficiently** A set of outputs is said to be produced efficiently if, given current technological knowledge, there is no way one can produce larger amounts of any output without using larger input amounts or giving up some quantity of another output. (p. 46)

**Equation of exchange** The equation of exchange states that the money value of GDP transactions must be equal to the product of the average stock of money times velocity. That is: $M \times V = P \times Y$. (p. 296)

**Equilibrium** An equilibrium is a situation in which there are no inherent forces that produce change. Changes away from an equilibrium position will occur only as a result of "outside events" that disturb the status quo. (p. 65)

**Excess reserves** Excess reserves are any reserves held in excess of the legal minimum. (p. 248)

**Exchange rate** The exchange rate states the price, in terms of one currency, at which another currency can be bought. (p. 380)

**Expenditure schedule** An expenditure schedule shows the relationship between national income (GDP) and total spending. (p. 172)

**Export subsidy** An export subsidy is a payment by the government to exporters to permit them to reduce the selling prices of their goods so they can compete more effectively in foreign markets. (p. 366)

**Factors of production** Inputs or factors of production are the labor, machinery, buildings, and natural resources used to make outputs. (p. 22)

**Federal funds rate** The federal funds rate is the interest rates that banks pay and receive when they borrow reserves from one another. (p. 261)

**Fiat money** Fiat money is money that is decreed as such by the government. It is of little value as a commodity, but it maintains its value as a medium of exchange because people have faith that the issuer will stand behind the pieces of printed paper and limit their production. (p. 238)

**Final goods and services** Final goods and services are those that are purchased by their ultimate users. (p. 86)

**Fiscal policy** The government's fiscal policy is its plan for spending and taxation. It can be used to steer aggregate demand in the desired direction. (p. 93)

**Fixed exchange rates** Fixed exchange rates are rates set by government decisions and maintained by government actions. (p. 387)

**Fixed taxes** Fixed taxes are taxes that do not vary with the level of GDP. (p. 228)

**Floating exchange rates** Floating exchange rates are rates determined in free markets by the law of supply and demand. (p. 381)

**Foreclosure** Foreclosure is the legal process through which a mortgage lender obtains control of the property after the mortgage goes into default. (p. 284)

**Foreign direct investment** Foreign direct investment is the purchase or construction of real business assets—such as factories, offices, and machinery—in a foreign country. (p. 141)

**Fractional reserve banking** Fractional reserve banking is a system under which bankers keep as reserves only a fraction of the funds they hold on deposit. (p. 242)

**Frictional unemployment** Frictional unemployment is unemployment that is due to normal turnover in the labor market. It includes people who are temporarily between jobs because they are moving or changing occupations, or are unemployed for similar reasons. (p. 110)

**Full employment** Full employment is a situation in which everyone who is willing and able to work can find a job. At full employment, the measured unemployment rate is still positive. (p. 111)

**GDP deflator** The price index used to deflate nominal GDP is called the GDP deflator. It is a broad measure of economy-wide inflation that includes the prices of all goods and services in the economy. (p. 124)

**Gold standard** The gold standard is a way to fix exchange rates by defining each participating currency in terms of gold and allowing holders of each participating currency to convert that currency into gold. (p. 389)

**Government purchases** Government purchases (*G*) refer to the goods (such as airplanes and paper clips) and services (such as school teaching and police protection) purchased by all levels of government. (p. 149)

**Gross domestic product (GDP)** Gross domestic product (GDP) is the sum of the money values of all final goods and services produced during a specified period of time, usually one year. (p. 85)

**Gross national product (GNP)** Gross national product (GNP) is a measure of all final production, making no adjustment for the fact that some capital is used up each year and thus needs to be replaced. (p. 165)

**Gross private domestic investment (I)** Gross private domestic investment (I) includes business investment in plant, equipment, software, and other intellectual property products; residential construction (new houses); and inventory investment. (p. 163)

**Growth policy** Growth policy refers to government policies intended to make the economy grow faster in the long run. (p. 102)

**Human capital** Human capital is the amount of skill embodied in the workforce. It is most commonly measured by the amount of education and training. (p. 130)

**Income-expenditure diagram** An income-expenditure diagram (or 45° line diagram), plots total real expenditure (on the vertical axis) against real income (on the horizontal axis). The 45° line marks off points where income and expenditure are equal. (p. 174)

**Index number** An index number expresses the cost of a market basket of goods relative to its cost in some "base" period, which is simply the year used as a basis of comparison. (p. 122)

**Index number problem** When relative prices are changing, there is no such thing as a "perfect price index" that is correct for every consumer. Any statistical index will understate the increase in the cost of living for some families and overstate it for others. At best, the index can represent the situation of an "average" family. (p. 123)

**Indexing** Indexing refers to provisions in a law or a contract whereby monetary payments are automatically adjusted whenever a specified price index changes. Wage rates, pensions, interest payments on bonds, income taxes, and many other things can be indexed in this way, and have been. Sometimes such contractual provisions are called escalator clauses. (p. 350)

**Induced increase in consumption** An induced increase in consumption is an increase in consumer spending that stems from an increase in consumer incomes. It is represented on a graph as a movement along a fixed consumption function. (p. 183)

**Induced investment** Induced investment is the part of investment spending that rises when GDP rises and falls when GDP falls. (p. 173)

**Infant-industry argument** The infant-industry argument for trade protection holds that new industries need to be protected from foreign competition until they develop and flourish. (p. 370)

**Inflationary gap** The inflationary gap is the amount by which equilibrium real GDP exceeds the full-employment level of GDP. (p. 199)

**Inputs** Inputs or factors of production are the labor, machinery, buildings, and natural resources used to make outputs. (p. 22)

**Insolvent** A company is insolvent when the value of its liabilities exceeds the value of its assets, that is, when its net worth is negative. (p. 282)

**Interest rate spread** An interest rate spread is the difference between an interest rate on a risky asset and the corresponding interest rate on a risk-free Treasury security. (p. 280)

**Intermediate good** An intermediate good is a good purchased for resale or for use in producing another good. (p. 86)

**International capital flows** International capital flows are purchases and sales of financial assets across national borders. (p. 404)

**International Monetary Fund (IMF)** The International Monetary Fund (IMF), which was established at Bretton Woods in 1944, examines the economies of all its member nations on a regular basis. (p. 392)

**Invention** Invention is the act of discovering new products or new ways of making products. (p. 136)

**Investment spending** Investment spending (I) is the sum of the expenditures of business firms on new plant, equipment, software and households on new homes. Financial "investments" are not included and neither are resales of existing physical assets. (p. 149)

**Invisible hand** Invisible hand is a phrase used by Adam Smith to describe how, by pursuing their own self-interests, people in a market system are "led by an invisible hand" to promote the well-being of the community. (p. 56)

**Labor force** The labor force is the number of people holding or seeking jobs. (p. 104)

**Labor productivity** Labor productivity is the amount of output a worker turns out in an hour (or a week, or a year) of labor. If output is measured by GDP, it is GDP per hour of work. (p. 103)

**Lags in stabilization policy** Lags in stabilization policy refer to delays between the time when the need for stabilization policy arises and the time when the policy has its actual effects on the economy. (p. 303)

**Law of supply and demand** The law of supply and demand states that in a free market the forces of supply and demand generally push the price toward the level at which quantity supplied and quantity demanded are equal. (p. 66)

**Leverage** When an asset is bought with leverage, the buyer uses borrowed money to supplement his or her own funds. Leverage is typically measured by the ratio of assets to equity. For example, if the buyer commits $100,000 of his or her own funds and borrows $900,000 to purchase a $1 million asset, we say that leverage is 10-to-1 ($1 million divided by $100,000). (p. 280)

**Liability** A liability of an individual or business firm is an item of value that the individual or firm owes. Many liabilities are known as *debts*. (p. 247)

**Liquidity** An asset's liquidity refers to the ease with which it can be converted into cash. (p. 241)

**M1** The narrowly defined money supply, usually abbreviated M1, is the sum of all coins and paper money in circulation, plus certain checkable deposit balances at banks and savings institutions. (p. 241)

**M2** The broadly defined money supply, usually abbreviated M2, is the sum of all coins and paper money in circulation, plus all types of checking account balances, plus most forms of savings account balances, plus shares in money market mutual funds. (p. 241)

**Managed float** Under a "dirty" or "managed" float, the government intervenes from time to time to influence the value of its currency. (p. 392)

**Marginal propensity to consume (MPC)** The marginal propensity to consume (MPC) is the ratio of the change in consumption relative to the change in disposable income that produces the change in consumption. On a graph, it appears as the slope of the consumption function. (p. 154)

**Market system** A market system is a form of economic organization in which resource allocation decisions are left to individual producers and consumers acting in their own best interests without central direction. (p. 50)

**Medium of exchange** The medium of exchange is the object or objects used to buy and sell other items such as goods and services. (p. 238)

**Mercantilism** Mercantilism is a doctrine that holds that exports are good for a country, whereas imports are harmful. (p. 366)

**Mixed economy** A mixed economy is one with some public influence over the workings of free markets. There may also be some public ownership mixed in with private property. (p. 36)

**Monetarism** Monetarism is a mode of analysis that uses the equation of exchange to organize and analyze macroeconomic data. (p. 298)

**Monetary policy** Monetary policy refers to actions taken by the Federal Reserve to influence aggregate demand, mainly by changing interest rates. (p. 94)

**Monetize the deficit** The central bank is said to monetize the deficit when it purchases bonds issued by the government. (p. 327)

**Money** Money is the standard object used in exchanging goods and services. In short, money is the medium of exchange. (p. 238)

**Money multiplier** The money multiplier is the ratio of newly created bank deposits to new reserves. (p. 252)

**Money-fixed asset** A money-fixed asset is an asset whose value is a fixed number of dollars. (p. 156)

**Mortgage** A home mortgage is a particular type of loan used to buy a house. The house normally serves as the collateral for the mortgage. (p. 280)

**Multinational corporations** Multinational corporations are corporations, generally large ones, that do business in many countries. Most, but not all, of these corporations have their headquarters in developed countries. (p. 141)

**Multiplier** The multiplier is the ratio of the change in equilibrium GDP ($Y$) divided by the original change in spending that causes the change in GDP. (p. 179)

**National debt** The national debt is the federal government's total indebtedness at a moment in time. It is the result of previous budget deficits. (p. 320)

**National income** National income is the sum of the incomes that all individuals in the economy earn in the forms of wages, interest, rents, and profits. It excludes government transfer payments and is calculated before any deductions are taken for income taxes. (p. 149)

**National income accounting** The system of measurement devised for collecting and expressing macroeconomic data is called national income accounting. (p. 162)

**Natural rate of unemployment** The economy's self-correcting mechanism always tends to push the unemployment rate back toward a specific rate of unemployment that we call the natural rate of unemployment. (p. 341)

**Near moneys** Near moneys are liquid assets that are close substitutes for money. (p. 241)

**Net exports** Net exports, or ($X - IM$), is the difference between exports ($X$) and imports ($IM$). It indicates the difference between what we sell to foreigners and what we buy from them. (p. 149)

**Net national product (NNP)** Net national product (NNP) is a measure of production. NNP is conceptually identical to national income. However, in practice, national income accountants estimate income and production independently; and so the two measures are never precisely equal. (p. 164)

**Net worth** Net worth is the value of all assets minus the value of all liabilities. (p. 248)

**Nominal GDP** Nominal GDP is calculated by valuing all outputs at current prices. (p. 86)

**Nominal rate of interest** The nominal rate of interest is the percentage by which the money the borrower pays back exceeds the money that was borrowed, making no adjustment for any decline in the purchasing power of this money that results from inflation. (p. 117)

**On-the-job training** On-the-job training refers to skills that workers acquire while at work, rather than in school or in formal vocational training programs. (p. 136)

**Open economy** An open economy is one that trades with other nations in goods and services, and perhaps also trades in financial assets. (p. 399)

**Open-market operations** Open-market operations refer to the Fed's purchases or sales of government securities, normally Treasury bills, through transactions in the open market. (p. 261)

**Opportunity cost** The opportunity cost of a decision is the value of the next best alternative that must be given up because of that decision (e.g., working instead of going to school). (p. 4)

**Optimal decision** An optimal decision is one that best serves the objectives of the decision maker, whatever those objectives may be. It is selected by explicit or implicit comparison with the possible alternative choices. The term *optimal* does not mean that we, the observers or analysts, approve or disapprove of the objective itself. (p. 42)

**Origin (of a graph)** The "0" point in the lower-left corner of a graph where the axes meet is called the origin. Both variables are equal to zero at the origin. (p. 15)

**Outputs** The **outputs** of a firm or an economy are the goods and services it produces. (p. 42)

**Personal saving rate** The personal saving rate is the ratio of consumer saving to disposable income. (p. 156)

**Phillips curve** A Phillips curve is a graph depicting the rate of unemployment on the horizontal axis and either the rate of inflation or the rate of change of money wages on the vertical axis. Phillips curves are normally downward sloping, indicating that higher inflation rates are associated with lower unemployment rates. (p. 337)

**Potential GDP** Potential GDP is the real GDP that the economy would produce if its labor and other resources were fully employed. (p. 104)

**Price ceiling** A price ceiling is a maximum that the price charged for a commodity cannot legally exceed. (p. 71)

**Price floors** A price floor is a legal minimum below which the price charged for a commodity is not permitted to fall. (p. 73)

**Price index** A price index expresses the cost of a market basket of goods relative to its cost in some "base" period, which is simply the year used as a basis of comparison. (p. 122)

**Principle of increasing costs** The principle of increasing costs states that as the production of a good expands, the opportunity cost of producing another unit generally increases. (p. 44)

**Production function** The economy's production function shows the volume of output that can be produced from given inputs (such as labor and capital), given the available technology. (p. 104)

**Production indifference map** A production indifference map is a graph whose axes show the quantities of two inputs that are used to produce some output. A curve in the graph corresponds to some given quantity of that output, and the different points on that curve show the different quantities of the two inputs that are just enough to produce the given output. (p. 19)

**Productivity** Productivity is the amount of output produced by a unit of input. (p. 196)

**Property rights** Property rights are laws and/or conventions that assign owners the rights to use their property as they see fit (within the law)—for example, to sell the property or to reap the benefits (such as rents or dividends) while they own it. (p. 134)

**Purchasing power** The purchasing power of a given sum of money is the volume of goods and services that it will buy. (p. 113)

**Purchasing-power parity theory of exchange rate determination** The *purchasing-power parity theory of exchange rate determination* holds that the exchange rate between any two national currencies adjusts to reflect differences in the price levels in the two countries. (p. 385)

**Quantitative easing** Quantitative easing refers to open-market purchases of assets other than Treasury bills. (p. 271)

**Quantity demanded** The quantity demanded is the number of units of a good that consumers are willing and can afford to buy over a specified period of time. (p. 57)

**Quantity supplied** The quantity supplied is the number of units that sellers want to sell over a specified period of time. (p. 61)

**Quantity theory of money** The quantity theory of money assumes that velocity is (approximately) constant. In that case, nominal GDP is proportional to the money stock. (p. 297)

**Quota** A quota specifies the maximum amount of a good that is permitted into the country from abroad per unit of time. (p. 366)

**Rational expectations** Rational expectations are forecasts that, although not necessarily correct, are the best that can be made given the available data. Rational expectations, therefore, cannot err systematically. If expectations are rational, forecasting errors are pure random numbers. (p. 346)

**Ray through the origin, or a ray** Lines whose $Y$-intercept is zero have so many special uses in economics and other disciplines that they have been given a special name: a ray through the origin, or a ray. (p. 17)

**Real GDP** Real GDP is calculated by valuing outputs of different years at common prices. Therefore, real GDP is a far better measure than nominal GDP of changes in total production. (p. 86)

**Real GDP per capita** Real GDP per capita is the ratio of real GDP divided by population. (p. 89)

**Real rate of interest** The real rate of interest is the percentage increase in purchasing power that the borrower pays to the lender for the privilege of borrowing. It indicates the increased ability to purchase goods and services that the lender earns. (p. 117)

**Real wage rate** The real wage rate is the wage rate adjusted for inflation. Specifically, it is the nominal wage divided by the price index. The real wage thus indicates the volume of goods and services that the nominal wages will buy. (p. 113)

**Recapitalization** A bank is said to be recapitalized when some investor, private or government, provides new equity capital in return for partial ownership. (p. 290)

**Recession** A recession is a period of time during which the total output of the economy declines. (p. 85)

**Recessionary gap** The recessionary gap is the amount by which the equilibrium level of real GDP falls short of potential GDP. (p. 199)

**Relative price** An item's **relative price** is its price in terms of some other item rather than in terms of dollars. (p. 115)

**Required reserves** Required reserves are the minimum amount of reserves (in cash or the equivalent) required by law. Normally, required reserves are proportional to the volume of deposits. (p. 245)

**Resources** Resources are the instruments provided by nature or by people that are used to create goods and services. Natural resources include minerals, soil, water, and air. Labor is a scarce resource, partly because of time limitations (the day has only 24 hours) and partly because the number of skilled workers is limited. Factories and machines are resources made by people. These three types of resources are often referred to as land, labor, and capital. They are also called inputs or factors of production. (p. 40)

**Revaluation** A revaluation is an increase in the official value of a currency. (p. 381)

**Risk of default** The risk of default on any loan or security is the risk that the borrower may not pay in full or on time. (p. 267)

**Risk premium** Market interest rates generally include a risk premium (or "spread" over Treasuries) to compensate the lender for the probability of loss if the borrower fails to repay the loan in full or on time. (p. 267)

**Run on a bank** A run on a bank occurs when many depositors withdraw cash from their accounts all at once. (p. 236)

**Scatter diagram** A scatter diagram is a graph showing the relationship between two variables (such as consumer spending and disposable income). Each year is represented by a point in the diagram, and the coordinates of each year's point show the values of the two variables in that year. (p. 152)

**Securitization** Loans are securitized—that is, transformed into marketable securities—when they are packaged together into a bond-like instrument that can be sold to investors, potentially all over the world. (p. 284)

**Self-correcting mechanism** The economy's self-correcting mechanism refers to the way money wages react to either a recessionary gap or an inflationary gap. Wage changes shift the aggregate supply curve and therefore change equilibrium GDP and the equilibrium price level. (p. 203)

**Shift in a demand curve** A shift in a demand curve occurs when any relevant variable other than price changes. If consumers want to buy more at any and all given prices than they wanted previously, the demand curve shifts to the right (or outward). If they desire less at any given price, the demand curve shifts to the left (or inward). (p. 58)

**Shortage** A shortage is an excess of quantity demanded over quantity supplied. When there is a shortage, buyers cannot purchase the quantities they desire at the current price. (p. 65)

**Slope of a curved line** The slope of a curved line at a particular point is defined as the slope of the straight line that is tangent to the curve at that point. (p. 16)

**Slope of a straight line** The slope of a straight line is the ratio of the vertical change to the corresponding horizontal change as we move to the right along the line between two points on that line, or, as it is often said, the ratio of the "rise" over the "run." (p. 15)

**Specialization** Specialization means that a country devotes its energies and resources to only a small proportion of the world's productive activities. (p. 359)

**Spread** Market interest rates generally include a risk premium (or "spread" over Treasuries) to compensate the lender for the probability of loss if the borrower fails to repay the loan in full or on time. (p. 267)

**Stabilization policy** Stabilization policy is the name given to government programs designed to prevent or shorten recessions and to counteract inflation (i.e., to stabilize prices). (p. 96)

**Stagflation** Stagflation is inflation that occurs while the economy is growing slowly ("stagnating") or in a recession. (p. 93)

**Store of value** A store of value is an item used to store wealth from one point in time to another. (p. 238)

**Strategic argument for protection** The strategic argument for protection holds that a nation may sometimes have to threaten protectionism to induce other countries to drop their own protectionist measures. (p. 370)

**Structural budget deficit or surplus** The structural budget deficit or surplus is the hypothetical deficit or surplus we would have under current fiscal policies if the economy were operating near full employment. (p. 323)

**Structural unemployment** Structural unemployment refers to workers who have lost their jobs because they have been displaced by automation, because their skills are no longer in demand, or because of similar reasons. (p. 111)

**Subprime mortgage** A mortgage is classified as subprime if the borrower fails to meet the traditional credit standards of "prime" borrowers. (p. 280)

**Supply curve** A supply curve is a graphical depiction of a supply schedule. It shows how the quantity supplied of a product will change as the price of that product changes during a specified period of time, holding all other determinants of quantity supplied constant. (p. 61)

**Supply schedule** A supply schedule is a table showing how the quantity supplied of some product changes as the price of that product changes during a specified period of time, holding all other determinants of quantity supplied constant. (p. 61)

**Supply-demand diagrams** A supply-demand diagram graphs the supply and demand curves together. It also determines the equilibrium price and quantity. (p. 64)

**Supply-side inflation** Supply-side inflation is a rise in the price level caused by slow growth (or decline) of aggregate supply. (p. 337)

**Surplus** A surplus is an excess of quantity supplied over quantity demanded. When there is a surplus, sellers cannot sell the quantities they

desire to supply at the current price. (p. 65)

**Systemic risk** Systemic risk refers to risks to the entire system of banks or financial institutions. It arises because these institutions, especially the largest ones, are interlinked in many ways. (p. 246)

**Systemically important ("too big to fail")** A systemically important (or "too big to fail") financial institution is one that, by virtue of its size or interconnectedness, can threaten the entire system if it runs into trouble. (p. 247)

**Tangent to the curve** A tangent to the curve is a straight line that touches, but does not cut, the curve at a particular point. (p. 16)

**Tariff** A tariff is a tax on imports. (p. 366)

**Theory** A theory is a deliberate simplification of relationships used to explain how those relationships work. (p. 11)

**Trade adjustment assistance** Trade adjustment assistance provides special unemployment benefits, loans, retraining programs, and other aid to workers and firms that are harmed by foreign competition. (p. 369)

**Trade deficit** A country's trade deficit is the excess of its imports over its exports. If, instead, exports exceed imports, the country has a trade surplus. (p. 407)

**Transfer payments** Transfer payments are sums of money that the government gives certain individuals as outright grants rather than as payments for services rendered to employers. Some common examples are Social Security and unemployment benefits. (p. 151)

**Troubled Assets Relief Program (TARP)** The Troubled Assets Relief Program (TARP) enabled the U.S. Treasury to purchase assets and equity from banks and other financial

institutions as a means of strengthening the financial sector. (p. 289)

**Unconventional monetary policy** Unconventional monetary policy is a generic term referring to unusual forms (or volumes) of central bank lending and to unusual types of open-market operations. (p. 270)

**Unemployment insurance** Unemployment insurance is a government program that replaces some of the wages lost by eligible workers who lose their jobs. (p. 112)

**Unemployment rate** The unemployment rate is the number of unemployed people, expressed as a percentage of the labor force. (p. 107)

**Unit of account** The unit of account is the standard unit for quoting prices. (p. 238)

**Value added** The value added by a firm is its revenue from selling a product minus the amount paid for goods and services purchased from other firms. (p. 166)

**Variable taxes** Variable taxes are taxes that vary with the level of GDP. (p. 228)

**Velocity** Velocity indicates the number of times per year that an "average dollar" is spent on goods and services. It is the ratio of nominal gross domestic product (GDP) to the number of dollars in the money stock. That is: Velocity = Nominal GDP/Money stock. (p. 296)

**Vertical long-run Phillips curve** The vertical long-run Phillips curve shows the menu of inflation/unemployment choices available to society in the long run. It is a vertical straight line at the natural rate of unemployment. (p. 341)

**Y-intercept** The Y-intercept of a line or a curve is the point at which it touches the vertical axis (the Y-axis). The X-intercept is defined similarly. (p. 17)

# INDEX

# SELECTED U.S. MACROECONOMIC

| Year | (1) Gross Domestic Product | (2) Personal Consumption Expenditure | (3) Gross Private Domestic Investment | (4) Government Purchases | (5) Net Exports | (6) Gross Domestic Product | (7) Personal Consumption Expenditure | (8) Gross Private Domestic Investment | (9) Government Purchases | (10) Net Exports | (11) Real GDP per Capita (in chained 2009 dollars) |
|------|------|------|------|------|------|------|------|------|------|------|------|
| | (in billions of dollars) | | | | | (in billions of chained 2009 dollars)[a] | | | | | |
| 1929 | 104.6 | 77.4 | 17.2 | 9.6 | 0.4 | 1,056.6 | 781 | 123.6 | 165.7 | -12.2 | 8,677 |
| 1933 | 57.2 | 45.9 | 2.3 | 8.9 | 0.1 | 778.3 | 637.6 | 27.3 | 178 | -12.6 | 6,198 |
| 1939 | 93.5 | 67.2 | 10.2 | 15.2 | 0.8 | 1,163.6 | 860.1 | 105.6 | 268.3 | -6.5 | 8,891 |
| 1945 | 228.2 | 120.0 | 12.4 | 96.6 | -0.8 | 2,217.8 | 1061.5 | 93.9 | 1604.5 | -32.6 | 15,849 |
| 1950 | 300.2 | 192.2 | 56.5 | 50.7 | 0.7 | 2,184.0 | 1360.5 | 293.7 | 569.6 | -12.1 | 14,343 |
| 1955 | 426.2 | 258.7 | 73.8 | 93.3 | 0.5 | 2,739.0 | 1637.3 | 337.7 | 901 | -18.8 | 16,507 |
| 1960 | 543.3 | 331.6 | 86.5 | 121 | 4.2 | 3,108.7 | 1891 | 359.7 | 1007 | -17.7 | 17,207 |
| 1965 | 743.7 | 443.6 | 129.6 | 164.9 | 5.6 | 3,976.7 | 2376 | 529.6 | 1224.2 | -25.9 | 20,467 |
| 1970 | 1,075.9 | 647.7 | 170.1 | 254.2 | 4 | 4,722.0 | 2903 | 585.2 | 1457.7 | -66.6 | 23,029 |
| 1975 | 1,688.9 | 1032.8 | 257.3 | 382.9 | 16 | 5,385.4 | 3405.1 | 623.5 | 1483.8 | -8.7 | 24,936 |
| 1976 | 1,877.6 | 1150.2 | 323.2 | 405.8 | -1.6 | 5,675.4 | 3595 | 742.5 | 1491.6 | -50.2 | 26,029 |
| 1977 | 2,086.0 | 1276.7 | 396.6 | 435.8 | -23.1 | 5,937.0 | 3746.5 | 848.4 | 1509.2 | -78.9 | 26,957 |
| 1978 | 2,356.6 | 1426.2 | 478.4 | 477.4 | -25.4 | 6,267.2 | 3911.2 | 946.6 | 1553.7 | -80.5 | 28,157 |
| 1979 | 2,632.1 | 1589.5 | 539.7 | 525.5 | -22.5 | 6,466.2 | 4004.1 | 979.8 | 1582.6 | -56.4 | 28,731 |
| 1980 | 2,862.5 | 1754.6 | 530.1 | 590.8 | -13.1 | 6,450.4 | 3991.5 | 881.2 | 1612.5 | 6.5 | 28,388 |
| 1981 | 3,211.0 | 1937.5 | 631.2 | 654.7 | -12.5 | 6,617.7 | 4050.8 | 958.7 | 1628 | 1.3 | 28,839 |
| 1982 | 3,345.0 | 2073.9 | 581 | 710 | -20 | 6,491.3 | 4108.4 | 833.7 | 1658 | -23 | 28,021 |
| 1983 | 3,638.1 | 2286.5 | 637.5 | 765.7 | -51.6 | 6,792.0 | 4342.6 | 911.5 | 1721.6 | -79.2 | 29,052 |
| 1984 | 4,040.7 | 2498.2 | 820.1 | 825.2 | -102.7 | 7,285.0 | 4571.6 | 1160.3 | 1783.2 | -154 | 30,892 |
| 1985 | 4,346.7 | 2722.7 | 829.6 | 908.4 | -114 | 7,593.8 | 4811.9 | 1159.5 | 1904 | -175.6 | 31,917 |
| 1986 | 4,590.2 | 2898.4 | 849.1 | 974.5 | -131.9 | 7,860.5 | 5014 | 1161.3 | 2007.7 | -193.9 | 32,734 |
| 1987 | 4,870.2 | 3092.1 | 892.2 | 1030.8 | -144.8 | 8,132.6 | 5183.6 | 1194.4 | 2066.9 | -184.9 | 33,566 |
| 1988 | 5,252.6 | 3346.9 | 937 | 1078.2 | -109.4 | 8,474.5 | 5400.5 | 1223.8 | 2094.8 | -136 | 34,661 |
| 1989 | 5,657.7 | 3592.8 | 999.7 | 1151.9 | -86.7 | 8,786.4 | 5558.1 | 1273.4 | 2155.1 | -103.9 | 35,598 |
| 1990 | 5,979.6 | 3825.6 | 993.5 | 1238.4 | -77.9 | 8,955.0 | 5672.6 | 1240.6 | 2224.3 | -76.5 | 35,875 |
| 1991 | 6,174.0 | 3960.2 | 944.3 | 1298.2 | -28.6 | 8,948.4 | 5685.6 | 1158.8 | 2250.9 | -32.8 | 35,372 |
| 1992 | 6,539.3 | 4215.7 | 1013 | 1345.4 | -34.7 | 9,266.6 | 5896.5 | 1243.7 | 2262.1 | -35.7 | 36,126 |
| 1993 | 6,878.7 | 4471.0 | 1106.8 | 1366.1 | -65.2 | 9,521.0 | 6101.4 | 1343.1 | 2243.3 | -78.2 | 36,631 |
| 1994 | 7,308.8 | 4741.0 | 1256.5 | 1403.7 | -92.5 | 9,905.4 | 6338 | 1502.3 | 2245.5 | -111 | 37,645 |
| 1995 | 7,664.1 | 4984.2 | 1317.5 | 1452.2 | -89.8 | 10,174.8 | 6527.6 | 1550.8 | 2257.5 | -101 | 38,211 |
| 1996 | 8,100.2 | 5268.1 | 1432.1 | 1496.4 | -96.4 | 10,561.0 | 6755.6 | 1686.7 | 2279.2 | -114.6 | 39,203 |
| 1997 | 8,608.5 | 5560.7 | 1595.6 | 1554.2 | -102 | 11,034.9 | 7009.9 | 1879 | 2322 | -145.3 | 40,473 |
| 1998 | 9,089.2 | 5903.0 | 1735.3 | 1613.5 | -162.7 | 11,525.9 | 7384.7 | 2058.3 | 2370.5 | -265.5 | 41,783 |
| 1999 | 9,660.6 | 6307.0 | 1884.2 | 1726 | -256.6 | 12,065.9 | 7775.9 | 2231.4 | 2451.7 | -377.1 | 43,241 |
| 2000 | 10,284.8 | 6792.4 | 2033.8 | 1834.4 | -375.8 | 12,559.7 | 8170.7 | 2375.5 | 2498.2 | -477.8 | 44,513 |
| 2001 | 10,621.8 | 7103.1 | 1928.6 | 1958.8 | -368.7 | 12,682.2 | 8382.6 | 2231.4 | 2592.4 | -502.1 | 44,504 |
| 2002 | 10,977.5 | 7384.1 | 1925 | 2094.9 | -426.5 | 12,908.8 | 8598.8 | 2218.2 | 2705.8 | -584.3 | 44,880 |
| 2003 | 11,510.7 | 7765.5 | 2027.9 | 2220.8 | -503.7 | 13,271.1 | 8867.6 | 2308.7 | 2764.3 | -641.9 | 45,745 |
| 2004 | 12,274.9 | 8260.0 | 2276.7 | 2357.4 | -619.2 | 13,773.5 | 9208.2 | 2511.3 | 2808.2 | -734.8 | 47,039 |
| 2005 | 13,093.7 | 8794.1 | 2527.1 | 2493.7 | -721.2 | 14,234.2 | 9531.8 | 2672.6 | 2826.2 | -782.3 | 48,167 |
| 2006 | 13,855.9 | 9304.0 | 2680.6 | 2642.2 | -770.9 | 14,613.8 | 9821.7 | 2730 | 2869.3 | -794.3 | 48,977 |
| 2007 | 14,477.6 | 9750.5 | 2643.7 | 2801.9 | -718.5 | 14,873.7 | 10041.6 | 2644.1 | 2914.4 | -712.6 | 49,377 |
| 2008 | 14,718.6 | 10013.6 | 2424.8 | 3003.2 | -723.1 | 14,830.4 | 10007.2 | 2396 | 2994.8 | -557.8 | 48,770 |
| 2009 | 14,418.7 | 9847.0 | 1878.1 | 3089.1 | -395.4 | 14,418.7 | 9847 | 1878.1 | 3089.1 | -395.4 | 47,002 |
| 2010 | 14,964.4 | 10202.2 | 2100.8 | 3174 | -512.7 | 14,783.8 | 10036.3 | 2120.4 | 3091.4 | -458.8 | 47,798 |
| 2011 | 15,517.9 | 10689.3 | 2239.9 | 3168.7 | -580 | 15,020.6 | 10263.5 | 2230.4 | 2997.4 | -459.4 | 48,205 |
| 2012 | 16,163.2 | 11083.1 | 2479.2 | 3169.2 | -568.3 | 15,369.2 | 10449.7 | 2435.9 | 2953.9 | -452.5 | 48,962 |
| 2013 | 16,768.1 | 11484.3 | 2648 | 3143.9 | -508.2 | 15,710.3 | 10699.7 | 2556.2 | 2894.5 | -420.4 | 49,700 |